JAGANNĀTHAM

Recent Archaeology and Contemporary Approaches

(A Special Volume in Honour of Professor J.N. Pal)

Prof. J. N. Pal

Advisory Board

JAGANNĀTHAM

Recent Archaeology and Contemporary Approaches

(A Special Volume in Honour of Professor J.N. Pal)

Editors

Brijesh Rawat
Surabhi Srivastava
Sachin Kumar Tiwary

Publisher

Pathak Publisher & Distributors
New Delhi (India)

First Published 2023

Published by:
Pathak Publisher & Distributors
in colloboration with
Research India Press
E-6/34, Sangam Vihar,
New Delhi-110062

Printed in India.

Composing & Layout :-
Harsh Computer Point
(Khubru Road, Gandhi Nagar, Sonipat, Haryana)
Mob. 9466702560, bpanghal@gmail.com

Contents

Foreword

It gives me immense pleasure that an edited book is being published in the honor of Professor J.N. Pal by some brilliant scholars of Archaeology and History .

Professor J.N. Pal needs no introduction in the field of Ancient History and Archaeology not only at national level but across the world. An ingenious scholar, explorer and excavator on field and simultaneously his personal virtues like honesty, humility, dedication and passion for self study make him the most venerated academician. I shall not be exaggerating in pronouncing him the most luminous star on the horizon of Indian archaeology. I greatly admire his contribution to this field.

Professor J.N. Pal having the University of Allahabad as his alma mater also studied at the School of Archaeology, Archaeological Survey of India, New Delhi. He began his academic journey as a curator of the departmental Museum of the Department of Ancient History, Culture and Archaeology at the University of Allahabad, Prayagraj and went on to accomplish the higher scholarly positions of Lecturer, Reader, Professor and Head of the department.

His scholarly excellence embraces various distinct Explorations, Excavations, Documentations, Book publications, Research papers, Paper presentations and endless deliverance of special lectures. His distinguished research papers are published by internationally acclaimed journal Science proving that Professor Pal's intellect knows no boundaries.

This book comprises only thirty significantly enriched academic research papers by accomplished authors from different genres of archaeology and history. This volume will be a milestone for the students and the research scholars in their academic pursuit. I wish Professor J.N. Pal a very long, healthy, prosperous and harmonious life.

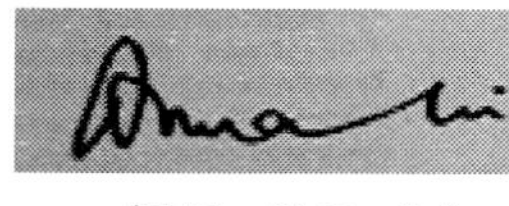

(DR. B.R. Mani)
Director General, National Museum, New Delhi
Former Additional Director General, Archaeological Survey of India, New Delhi

Editorial

Professor J.N. Pal has spent more than 40 years teaching at Allahabad University in Prayagraj. He is a distinguished field archaeologist, Pre and Proto- historian, Paleo- anthropologist, Paleo-zoologist, Museuologist, and art critic. He studied from the Archaeological Survey of India's Institute of Archaeology. He served as the curator of the Kaushambi Museum (Professor G.R. Sharma Memorial Museum) at the University of Allahabad's Department of Ancient History , Culture and Archaeology from 1974 to 1977. More than 21 research researchers for Ph-D. studies have been under his supervision. He led more than 16 excavations projects nationwide project including Koldihwa (1974), Mahagara (1975,1976), Mahadaha (1978,1979), Damdama (1982-1985), Sihawal-1(1980), Baghor (1980 and 1982), Merhauli (1984), Maihar (1985 to 1988), Jhusi (1995, 1988, 1999, 2002, 2003), Amilkoni (1988) and Tokwa. He research the Mesolithic sites in 1993 with Ms. Diane E. Hawkkey of the Anthropology Department at Arizona University in Tempe, Arizona and 1986, 1991 and 2003 with Professor John R. Lukacs of the University of Oregon in Eugene, Oregon , both in the United States. He frequently travels to European and Asian Nations for International Seminars and Conferences and is a member of many National and International organizations in the subject . He is the author of more than 16 books and more than 150 research publications. He is a skilled editor, administrator and excavator. In National and International Seminars and Conferences, he has delivered more than 140 research papers.

An edited book on *JAGANNĀTHAM : Recent Archaeology and Contemporary Approaches* is an effort to present, updated recent works in the field of archaeology. This book is an essential source for students and professionals in the current field of archeology and culture. This book includes different research articles ranging from Rural Archaeology, Environmental Archaeology, Settlement Archaeology, Archaeology of Indus Valley, Tool typology and Technology, Prehistory, Rock Art, Art and Architecture, Buddhist and Jaina Art, Numismatics, Tribal Culture Heritage and Management. It will be a valuable source for students, researchers and scholars of Archaeology in global context. The book has 03 reminiscences and Thirty research papers. In this book only 03 research papers and 01 reminiscences written in Hindi. The publication of an edited book in honor of a reputed Archaeologist Professor J.N. Pal is an important milestone in the field of archaeology. Such a book can provide a valuable overview of the Archaeologist's work, and Serves as a valuable resource for other Archaeologists. Furthermore, it can help to ensure that the Archaeologist's legacy is always remembered and respected.

The research articles have been classified under different segments based on their themes. Each segment provides an overview of different fields of archaeology highlighting its various sub disciplines and approaches. A comprehensive rainbow of Archaeology, Pre and Proto history, Rock art, Art, Iconography, Architecture, Epigraphy, Numismatics and Culture is presented in the present book . Several eminent Archaeologists like K. Paddayya, V.H. Sonavane, R.K. Mohanti, Ajit Kumar, K. Krishnan, Y.S. Farswan, Mohammad Najrul Bari, Martin Williams etc. have contributed their research articles to make this edition invaluable.

The editors are indebted to all the contributors for their support and Dr. B.R. Mani for writing the foreword and to Research India press, New Delhi for bearing the responsibility of publishing this book.

Brijesh Rawat
Surabhi Srivastava
Sachin Kumar Tiwary

A Biographical Sketch

Professor Jagannath Pal (J.N. Pal) was born on 2nd March 1950 in village called Tina, post- Sagra Sunderpur, district Pratapgarh of Uttar Pradesh to Late Mrs. Rajni Pal and Shri Bhagwati Deen Pal. Though both the parents were unlettered and his father could only write his own name yet Professor Pal's grandfather and his elder brother received formal education and worked as government servants (Postman) in Karachi (during pre partitioned era, now in Pakistan) under British rule. Professor Pal's father was sent to school but he could not make any progress but later with each passing year his father realized the importance of education and tried his level best to get his four sons educated. Unfortunately, Professor Pal's elder brother along with two younger brothers too could not make much progress in school . In a conversation with Professor Pal he recollected that he got enrolled in a school at the age of six when his father dragged him out of a group of boys engaged in grazing cattle. One *munshiji* (teacher) admitted him and by the orders of the school administration his *agele* (wrist bands) and *kathula* (pendant) with *tabeez* (totem) were removed and he formally joined the school . Thus, the education of this child began who later became one of the most renowned scholar of his field. Professor Pal's better half Mrs. Suman Pal though academically not much well versed but her sharp intelligence and worldly Knowledge has contributed immensely in the brought up of her children . Professor Pal is blessed with three children, two daughters and one son. His eldest daughter Abha Pal holds her post graduation degree in Ancient History and after attaining her D. Phil from the University of Allahabad, she is currently teaching at Navyuga Girls Degree College, Lucknow. His son Sunit Pal, a computer engineer by profession is working in Sunnyvale, California, U.S.A. While the youngest daughter Swabha Pal completed her education at Film and Television Institute , Pune and is currently employed as a Film editor in Mumbai. Professor Pal though coming from a very humble background and despite all odds succeeded in fulfilling his father's dream of having an educated family.

Professor J.N. Pal is a renowned field Archaeologist, a distinguished Pre and Proto historian, Paleo-anthropologist, Paleo-zoologist, Museologist and art critic, who has served more than four decades at Allahabad University, Prayagraj. An alumnus of Institute of Archaeology, Archaeological Survey of India. He has been the Curator of Kausambi Museum (Professor G.R. Sharma, Memorial Museum), Department of Ancient History, Culture and Archaeology, University of Allahabad 1974-1977. He has supervised more than 25 research scholars for Ph-D work. He has discovered a large number of archaeological sites in Uttar Pradesh during his explorations and has directed more than 16 excavation projects in the country, some are Koldihwa (1974), Mahagara (1975,1976), Pachoh (1976), Mahadaha (1978,1979), Damdama (1982 to 1985), Sihawal-1(1980), Baghor (1980 and1982), Merhauli (1984), Maihar (1985 to 1988), Jhusi (1995,1998,1999, 2002, 2003), Amilkoni (1998), Tokwa (2000, 2002-03), Baidha (2001-02), Hetapatti (2004-05) and many more. He jointly studied the Mesolithic sites with Ms. Diane E. Hawkey of Department of Anthropology, Arizona State University, Tempe, Arizona, U.S.A. in 1993 and the Mesolithic human skeletons from Mahadaha and Damdama with Professor John R. Lukacs of University of Oregon, Eugene, U.S.A. in 1986, 1991, 2003.

He is a member of various distinguished National and International Organizations of this field and has widely travelled to European and Asian countries in International Seminars and Conferences. He has more than 15 books and more than 150 research papers published to his credit. He is an able administrator, excavator and editor. He has presented more than 140 research papers in various National and International Seminars and Conferences.

Surabhi Srivastava
Sachin Kumar Tiwary

Select Publications

Name: Professor Jagannath Pal

Home Address: 61D/3D/4, Gayatri Nagar, Allahabad 211 004, U. P., India. Telephone 0532-2544586, Mobile 9415636643; e-mail: jnpal@hotmail.com

Date of Birth: 2nd March, 1950

Positions Held: Re-appointed Professor, Department of Ancient History, Culture and Archaeology, Allahabad State University, Allahabad, from July 2016 to February 2020.

Professor and Head, Department of Ancient History, Culture and Archaeology, University of Allahabad since 7th June 2010 to 6th June 2012.

Professor (11-12-2003 to till now), Reader (21-11-1986 to 10-12-2003), Lecturer (5-12-1977 to 20-11-1986) and Curator (5-10-1974 to 4-12-1977) in the Department of Ancient History, Culture and Archaeology, University of Allahabad.

Field of Specialization: Prehistoric, Protohistoric and Historical Archaeology.

Education: D. Phil. 1983, University of Allahabad, Thesis Title: Archaeology of Southern Uttar Pradesh.

P G Diploma in Archaeology, 1973 School of Archaeology, Archaeological Survey of India, New Delhi. Subject: Archaeology and allied Subjects, passed in First Division.

M. A. 1972 University of Allahabad, Subject: Ancient History, Culture and Archaeology, passed in First Division.

B. A. 1970 University of Allahabad, Subject: Ancient History, Culture and Archaeology; Sanskrit; Philosophy, passed in First Division.

Intermediate 1968 U. P. Education Board, Subject: Math, Hindi, English, Sanskrit, passed in First Division.

High School 1966 U. P. Education Board, Subject: Math, Hindi, English, Sanskrit, Geography, passed in First Division.

Teaching Experience: Teaching since 1977 Archaeology to Postgraduate classes and Indian and world History, Culture and Art to Graduate classes.

Participated in the UGC Summer Institute in New Archaeology in the Department of Archaeology, Deccan College, Pune (16th June – 12th July 1986).

Research Guidance to Research Scholars for the D. Phil. Degree

1. Vijay Prakash Varma, *Archaeology of Faizabad District*, Degree Awarded in 1993
2. Surendra Pratap Singh, *Society and Culture as Reflected in Naishadhiya Charitam*, Degree Awarded in 1995.
3. Anil Kumar Dubey, *A Study of the Settlement Pattern in the Middle Gangetic Plain with Special Reference to Jaunpur District*, Degree Awarded in 1997.
4. Prahlad Baranwal, *Ethno-Archaeological Investigations in the Middle Gangetic Plain*, Degree Awarded in 1999.
5. Ram Singh, *Archaeological Investigations in the Sai River Basin and Lake Sites in Jaunpur District*, Degree awarded in 2003.
6. Lakshman Prasad, *Art and Archaeology of Kushinagar District*, Thesis submitted in December 2002, Degree awarded in 2003.
7. Mahanth Yadav, *Archaeology of the Lower Ghaghara Valley*, Degree awarded in 2004.
8. Sarita Kumari, *A Study of Manufacturing Technique and Use of the Stone and Bone Implements of the Mesolithic Culture of the Vindhyas and Ganga Plain*, Degree awarded in 2005.
9. Meera Pal, *A Study of Resource Material of the Mesolithic Culture of the Gangetic Plain*, Degree awarded in 2005.
10. Ramakant, *Neolithic Technology and Settlement Pattern in the Vindhyas*, Degree awarded in 2006.
11. Subas Chandra Pal, *Navin Anushandhanon ke Alok Mein Madhya Ganga Ghati ki Kala ka Udbhav evam Vikas*, Degree awarded in 2010.
12. Pushp Lata Bharti, *Social and Economic Conditions of the Middle Ganga Valley during the 6th Century B.C. to Second Century B.C.*, Degree awarded in 2013.

13. Amar Bahadur, *Fatehpur Janpad ke Vishesh Sandarbha Men Nichale Doab Ka Puratattva,* Degree awarded in 2013.
14. Vinod Yadav, *A Study of Upper Palaeolithic Culture in North Central India,* Degree awarded in 2014.
15. Dinkar Kumar, *Azamgaeh Janpad Ke Vishesh Sandarbh Men Ghaghara Nadi Ghati Ka Puratattvik Anveshan,* Degree awarded in 2014.
16. Prabhat Kumar Goswami, *Palaeo-environment of the Middle Gangetic Plain, Prehistory and Protohistory with Special reference to Sant Kabir Nagar District,* persuing since 6-7-2009, Degree awarded in 2018.
17. Rajnish Soni, *Origin and Development of Ceramic Industries of the Middle Ganga Valley with special Reference to Jhusi,* persuing since 11-11-2010, Degree awarded in 2018.
18. Radha Swami Maurya, *Social Life as Reflected in the Art of Bundelkhand,* Degree awarded in 2018.
19. Drupad Kumar, *Uttar Bharat Mein Krishakon ki Samajik Evam Arthik Sthiti Ka Addhyayan.* Degree awarded in 2018.
20. Kiran Pal, *Vindhya Evam Gangeya Kshetra Men Krishi tatha Pashu Palan ka Udbhav Evam Vikash.* Degree awarded in 2018
21. Abhisek Singh, *Madhya Ganga Ke Maidan Mein Baudh Purasthalon Ka Aitihasik aur Puratattvik Addhyayan (Chhathi Shatabdi Esa Purva se Chaturth Shatabdi Esvi Tak).* Degree awarded in 2018.
22. Shiv Shankar, Madhya Ganga Ghati Men Samajik-Dharmik Parivartan (Chhati Shatabdi Eisha Purva Se Pratham Shatabddi Ishvi Tak), persuing at Department of Ancient History, Culture and Archaeology, Nehru Gram Bharti Deemed University, Kotwa Jamunipur, Dubawal, Allahabad since 29-8-2015. Thesis awarded in 2020.

Supervisor for a Small Study and Research Grant

Supervised a Small Study and Research Grant Project entitled *Ethno-Archaeological Interpretation of Rock Art from Kaimur District of Bihar* of Nehru Trust for the Indian Collections at the Victoria and Albert Museum, New Delhi for the year 2013-14, Candidate Dr. Schin Kumar Tiwary.

Membership in Professional Organizations

Archaeological Society of India (Lifetime Member)

Indian Society for Prehistoric and Quaternary Studies (Lifetime Member)

Rock Art Society of India (Lifetime Member)

Indian History and Culture Society (Lifetime Member)

Indo-Pacific Prehistoric Association (Lifetime Member)

Indian Academy of Social Sciences (Lifetime Member)

World Archaeological Congress

U.P. History Congress (Life Member)

National Research Institute of Human Culture, Varanasi (Life Member)

Executive Committee of Indian Society for Prehistoric and Quaternary Studies

Secretary (Prehistory), Indian Archaeological Society 2013-15

Joint Editor: Monograph Series of Indian Archaeological Society

Principal Editor: ICON: Journal of Archaeology and Culture

Co-Director: U.G.C. National Seminar on Farming Culture of India, April 19-20, 2003.

Co-ordinator: Refresher Course

Local Secretary: National Seminar on Fifty Years of Indian Archaeology: Retrospect and Prospects, Department of Ancient History, Culture and Archeology, University of Allahabad, November 14-16, 1998.

Member Central Advisory Board of Archaeology: Nominated as member of Central Advisory Board of Archaeology, Archaeological Survey of India, Ministry of Culture, Government of India by President of India vide Resolution No. F.9/2/2008-EE(CABA) dated 17-2-2014 and published in Gazette of India on 8th March 2014 for a period of four years.

Organized the Symposium 'New Archaeological Discoveries in Asia and the Pacific' in World Archaeological Congress-3, New Delhi, December 4-11, 1994

Worked on the Project 'Bio-archaeology of the Mesolithic North India' and was awarded the International Collaborative Research Grant by Wenner-Gren Foundation

Co-director in the Joint International Project on Bio-archaeology of Mesolithic North India provided the opportunity to do Microwear analysis of microliths at the Department of Anthropology, University of Oregon, Eugene, U. S. A. in April-June 1995. The research program in 'Use-wear Analysis of Microliths from Experimental and Archaeological Contexts' was conducted at the University of Oregon during the period of 12 April through 20 June 1995.

Delivered several **Guest Lectures** in a graduate seminar entitled 'Bio-archaeology' in the

Department of Anthropology, University of Oregon, Eugene, U. S. A. during the period of 12 April to 20 June 1995.

Collaborator to Research Project of American Institute of Indian Studies' Prehistoric People of the Ganga Valley: Health Status and Genetic Affinities' with Prof. John R. Lukacs of Department of Anthropology, University of Oregon, Eugene, February 1992.

Director International Collaborative Project on Archaeo-Geological investigation in the Middle Son Valley with Dr. M. Petraglia and his team of Oxford University, Field season 2007-08 and 2008-09.

Archaeological Field Work Experience

Participated in the archaeological excavation and exploration expeditions in the Vindhyas and the Ganga valley conducted by Department of Ancient History, Culture and Archaeology, University of Allahabad since 1974. Main excavated sites are:

1. Koldihwa 1974: (Neolithic to Early Iron Age site in Belan Valley)
2. Mahagara 1975,1976: (Neolithic site in the Belan Valley)
3. Pachoh 1976: (Neolithic site in the Belan Valley)
4. Mahadaha 1978,1979: (Mesolithic site in the Ganga Valley)
5. Damdama 1982 to 1985: (Mesolithic site in the Ganga Valley)
6. Sihawal-I 1980: (Acheulian site in the Son Valley)
7. Baghor-I 1980 and 1982: (Upper Palaeolithic site in the Son Valley)
8. Baghor-IV 1983: (Late Upper Palaeolithic site in the Son Valley)
9. Merhauli 1984: (Mesolithic site in the Son Valley)
10. Maihar 1985 to 1988: (Acheulian site in the Lilji Valley,Satna District, M. P.)
11. Jhusi 1995, 1998, 1999, 2002, 2003: (Neolithic to Early Medieval Period)
12. Amilkoni 1998: (N.B.P.W. to Kusan Period site District Rewa (M.P., Tons Valley)
13. Tokwa (2000, 2002-03: (Neolithic to Early Historical Period, on the Confluence of the Adwa and Belan Valley)
14. Baidha 2001-02: (Acheulian to Mesolithic site in the Adwa Valley)
15. Hetapatti 2004-05 (Neolithic to early historic site in the mid Ganga valley)

16. Hetapatti 2005-06 (Neolithic to early historic site in the mid Ganga valley)
17. Explorations and Exploratory digging/section scrapping of the Palaeolithic sites in the middle Son valley 2007-08
18. Explorations and Exploratory digging/section scrapping of the Palaeolithic sites in the middle Son valley 2008-09
19. Excavation Neolithic to Early Historical Site Hetapatti 2010-11.

Presidential Addreses

1. **Sectional President,** Ancient History, **U.P. History Congress, 2009**: Beginnings of Agriculture in the Middle Ganga Plain, Sectional Presidential Address, Ancient Section, U.P. History Congress, XXth Session, October 3-4, 2009, Department of Humanities and Social Sciences, VBS Purvanchal University, Jaunpur, U.P.
2. **President, Indian Society for Prehistoric and Quaternary Studies, 2013**: Prehistory of the Middle Son Valley, Presidential Address delivered during the Annual Conference ISPQS, December 14-16, 2013, Banaras Hinddu University, Varanasi.

Visiting Fellow in the Department of Ancient Indian History, Culture and Archaeology, A. P. S. University, Rewa for two sessions- May 1992 and January 1989

Participated in the **Summer Institute** in New Archaeology sponsored by the University Grants Commission and organized by the Department of Archaeology, Deccan College, Pune, June 16 to July 12, 1986

Experience of Anthropological Study

Studied the Mesolithic human skeletons from Sarai Nahar Rai and Mahadaha with Prof. K. A. R. Kennedy of Cornell University, Ithaca, U. S. A. in 1980.

Studied the dental/skeletal remains from Mesolithic sites with Ms. Diane E. Hawkey of Department of Anthropology, Arizona State University, Tempe, Arizona, U. S. A. in 1993.

Studied the Mesolithic human skeletons from Mahadaha and Damdama with Prof. John R. Lukacs of University of Oregon, Eugene, U. S. A. in 1986, 1991, 2003.

Experience of Archaeo-zoological Study

Studied and analyzed the animal bone remains from Damdama with Dr. P. K. Thomas of Deccan College, Pune, in 1989 and 1991.

Studied and analyzed the animal bone remains from Mahadaha and Jhusi with Dr. P. P. Joglekar of Deccan College, Pune, in 1999 and 2001.

Experience of Palaeobotanical Study

Collected the samples of archaeobotanical remains and samples for phytolith from Mesolithic and Neolithic sites of the Belan Valleys for the identification of grains with Dr. Dorian Q. fuller of Institute of Archaeology, London in 2002 and with Emma Harvey of the same Institute in September 2003

Collected and anlysed archaeo-botanical remains from the excavations at Tokwa (Mirzapur District) and Jhusi (Allahabad District) with Dr. K.S. Saraswat and A.K. Pokharia of Birbal Shahni Institute of Palaeobotany, Lucknow in March to June 2003.

Experience of Archaeo-geological Study

Studied the geological deposits of the Pleistocene and Holocene periods of the Belan, Son and the Ganga with Prof. Martin Williams and Keith Royce of Department of Earth Sciences of Macqurie University, School of Earth Sciences and Quaternary Research Unit, Macquarie University, North Ryde, New South Wales, Australia.

Administrative Experience

Curator of Kausambi Museum (Professor G.R. Sharma, Memorial Museum), Department of Ancient History, Culture and Archaeology, University of Allahabad 1974-1977.

Member of the Teachers Support Fund Committee, University of Allahabad.

Member of the Board of Trusty, Student Union, University of Allahabad.1997-98.

Member of Executive Council of Allahabad University from 14-6-2001 to 13-6-2002.

Member Scheduled Caste/Scheduled Tribe Standing Committee, University of Allahabad (vide letter No. 377 dated 2-2-1994 under the UGC D.O. No.F.2-1/88 (SCT) dated 26-3-1988).

Co-ordinator of National Service Scheme 1985-1986.

Member Academic Council, Uttar Pradesh Rajarshi Tandan Open University, Allahabad

Lectures as Resource Person for Refresher Course to University and College Teachers

Special Guest of Valedictory Function, Refresher Course on New Dimensions in the Study of History, Culture and Archaeology (Sept. 6 to Sept. 26, 2014), Department of Ancient History, Archaeology and Culture, DDU University, Gorakhpur on September 26, 2014.

Two lectures: (i) Archaeology of the Mid Ganga valley and (ii) Archaeology of the Vindhyas, Refresher course in history at the UGC-Academic Staff College, BHU, Varanasi on 20-8-2010 and 21-8-2010.

Three lectures: (i) Archaeological Data of Middle Palaeolithic Culture of India, (ii) Archaeological Data of Mesolithic Culture of India and (iii) Archaeological Data of Neolithic Culture of India, Refresher Course on 'Analysis and Interpretation of the Archaeological Data Relating to Cultures, Society and religions of India', sponsored by UGC at the Department of Ancient History, Culture and Archaeology, University of Allahabad, September 20, 2001 to October 10, 2001.

Prehistoric Society: a Reconstruction, Refresher Course on 'Social Content of Indian Culture and the Question of its Relevance', sponsored by UGC at the Department of Ancient History, Culture and Archaeology, University of Allahabad, September 13, 2000.

Controversies of Indian Prehistory, Refresher Course on Major Currents and Controversies of Indian History and Culture, sponsored by UGC at the Department of Ancient History, Culture and Archaeology, University of Allahabad, 19 March, 1998.

Controversy of Second Urbanization in India, Refresher Course on Major Currents and Controversies of Indian History and Culture, sponsored by UGC at the Department of Ancient History, Culture and Archaeology, University of Allahabad, 22 March, 1998.

Palaeolithic Cultures and Art in the Vindhyas, Refresher Course on History and Art sponsored by UGC at Jiwaji University, Gwalior, 27 January 1997.

Upper Palaeolithic Culture and Art in the Vindhyas, Refresher Course on History and Art sponsored by UGC at Jiwaji University, Gwalior, 27 January, 1997.

Mesolithic Culture and Art in the Vindhyas. Refresher Course on History and Art sponsored by UGC at Jiwaji University, Gwalior, 28 January, 1997.

Mesolithic Culture and Art in the Gangetic Plain, Refresher Course on History and Art sponsored by UGC at Jiwaji University, Gwalior, 28 January, 1997.

Evolution and Growth of Incipient Socio-economic Formation in the Mesolithic Age and Socio-economic Formation and Technology in the Neolithic Age, Seventh Refresher Course in History, University of Allahabad, 27-7-96 and 30-7-96.

First Colonization of the Gangetic Plain, and Prehistoric Faunal Remains from the Ganga Valley, Refresher Course in 'Gangetic Valley in Indian History with Special Reference to Ancient

India, University of Allahabad, 31-8-93 and 14-9-93.

Expansion of Prehistoric Population in the Gangetic Plain, Academic Staff College, Aligarh Muslim University, Aligarh, 25-7-1989.

PUBLICATIONS

Published Books

1. ICON: *Journal of Archaeology and Culture*, ISSN: 2347-7032, Volume I, 2014 **Principal Editor**.
2. ICON: *Journal of Archaeology and Culture*, ISSN: 2347-7032, Volume II, 2015 **Principal Editor**
3. 2016. *Holocene Foragers of North India: The Bioarchaeology of Mesolithic Damdama*, in co-authorship of John R. Lukacs, with contributions by M.C. Gupta, V.D. Misra, Greg C. Nelson and G. Robbins Schug, BAR International Series 2783, Oxford, United Kingdom.
4. 2012, *Quaternary International*, Volume 251 (Special Issue of Toba Volcanic Super-irruption of 74,000 Years Ago) in co-guest editorship of Michael D. Petraglia and Ravi Korisettar.
5. 2009, *Excavations at Jhusi (Pratishthanpur): A Fresh Light on the Archaeological Profile of the Middle Ganga Plain (Archaeology and Zooarchaeology)*, in co-authorship of V.D. Misra, M.C. Gupta and P.P. Joglekar, Indian Archaeological Society, New Delhi.
6. 2003, *Mesolithic Damdama: Dental Histology and Age Estimation,* in co-authorship of Gwendolyn M. Robbins, V.D. Misra and M.C. Gupta.
7. 2003, *Mesolithic Mahadaha: The Faunal Remains,* in co-authorship of P.P. Joglekar, V.D. Misra and M.C. Gupta, Department of Ancient History, Culture and Archaeology, University of Allahabad.
8. 2002, *Mesolithic India,* in co-editorship of V.D. Misra, Department of Ancient History, Culture and Archaeology, University of Allahabad.
9. 2002, *Allahabad: Aspects of Historical and Cultural profile,* in co-editorship of O.P. Srivastava, Anamika Roy, M.C. Gupta, Department of Ancient History, Culture and Archaeology, University of Allahabad.
10. 2000, *Social History and Social Theory,* in co-editorship of V.D. Misra, University of Allahabad, Department of Ancient History, Culture and Archaeology, University of Allahabad.
11. 2000, *Peeping Through the Past: Prof. G.R. Sharma Memorial Volume,* in co-editorship S.C. Bhattacharaya, V.D. Misra and J.N. Pandey, Department of Ancient History, Culture and Archaeology, University of Allahabad.

12. 1997, *Indian Prehistory: 1980* in co-editorship of V. D. Misra, Department of Ancient History, Culture and Archaeology, University of Allahabad.

13. 1993. John R. Lukacs and J.N. Pal Mesolithic Subsistence in North India: Inferences from Dental Attributes, *Current Anthropolgy* Volume 14, Number 5, December 1993, pp. 745-765.

14. 1992, *Human Skeletal Remains from Mahadaha: A Gangetic Mesolithic Site* in co-authorship with Kenneth A. R. Kennedy, John R. Lukacs, Robert F. Paster, Thomas S. Johnston, Nancy C. Lovell, Brian E. Hemphill and Christopher B. Burrow, South Asia Occasional Papers and Theses No. 11, South Asia Program Cornell University, Ithaca.

15. 1986, *Archaeology of Southern Uttar Pradesh: Ceramic Industries of Northern Vindhyas*, Swabha Prakashan, Allahabad.

16. 1980, *Excavations at Mahadaha* in co-authorship with G. R. Sharma and V. D. Misra, Department of Ancient History, Culture and Archaeology, University of Allahabad.

17. 1980, *Beginnings of Agriculture* in co-authorship with G. R. Sharma, V. D. Misra, D. Mandal and B. B. Misra, Department of Ancient History, Culture and Archaeology, University of Allahabad.

Research Papers Published

1. 2021. Middle Palaeolithic Culture, in *Prehistoric foundations of Bharata,* Part I, (Ed. A. Sundara), The Mythic Society, Bengaluru.

2. 2021. Mesolithic Culture, in *Prehistoric foundations of Bharata,* Part I, (Ed. A. Sundara), The Mythic Society, Bengaluru.

3. 2020. Chris Clarkson, Clair Harris, Bo Li, Christina M. Neudorf, Richard G. Roberts, Christine Lane, Kasih Norman, Jagannath Pal, Sacha Jones, Ceri Shipton, Jinn Koshy, M.C. Gupta, D.P. Mishra, A.K. Dubey, Nocole Boivin & Michael Petraglia. Human occupation of northern India spans the Toba super-eruption ~74,000 years ago, *Nature Communication.*

4. 2018. The First Colonizers of the Gangetic Plain: Prelude to the Beginnings of Agriculture, *Purva,* Vol. 2, No. 1.

5. 2017. Palaeoenvironment and Prehistory of the Middle Son valley, North-Central India, in *Prehistoric Research in the Indian Subcontinent: A Reappraisal and New Directions,* (Eds. K. Paddayy and Bishnupriya Basak), Primus Books, Delhi.

6. 2017. Rock Art in Uttar Pradesh and Adjoining Area of the Vindhyas, in *Rock Art in India: In Felicitation of Prof. V.H. Sonawane,* Volume II, (Eds. Sadasiba Pradhan, Dibishada B. Grnayak),

B.R. Publishing Corporation, Delhi.

7. 2017. Neolithic in the Middle Ganga Plain and Neighbouring Vindhyas: One of the Early Centres of Domestication of Plants and Animals, *Puratattva* 47.

8. 2016. Mesolithic Foragers of the Ganga Plain and Adjoining Hilly Region of the Vindhyas, in *A Companion to South Asia in the Past,* (Eds. Gwen Robbins Schug and Subhas R. Walimbe, Wiley Blackwell, West Sussex.

9. 2016. Burial Practices of the First Colonizers of the Gangetic Plain: Prelude to the Beginnings of Agriculture in the Ganga Plain and Vindhyas, *Puratattva* 46.

10. 2014. Prehistory of the Middle Son Valley, *Man and Environmenti* XXXIX (2).

11. 2014. Ceri Shipton, S. Mishra, K. Paddayya, Sushama G. Deo, J.N. Pal,

N. Roseboom,C. Gaillard, M.C. Gupta and Y. Hou Empirical Differences between the Earlier and Later Acheulian in India in Recent Advances in Acheulian Culture Studies (Ed. K. Paddayya), ISPQS, Pune.

12. 2014. Microlithic Industries and the Issue of the Mesolithic, in *Prehistoric Roots (History of Ancient India, Volume I)* (Eds. Dilip K. Chakrabarti and Makkhan Lal), Vivekanand International Foundation and Aryan Books International, New Delhi.

13. 2014. Baghor I, in *Prehistoric Roots (History of Ancient India, Volume I)* (Eds. Dilip K. Chakrabarti and Makkhan Lal), pp. 372-38

14. 1. Vivekanand International Foundation and Aryan Books International, New Delhi.

15. 2014. Madhya Pradesh and Adjoining Uttar Pradesh: Palaeolithic Culture of the Belan and Son valleys, in co-authorship of R.K. varma and V.D. Misra, in *Prehistoric Roots (History of Ancient India, Volume I)* (Eds. Dilip K. Chakrabarti and Makkhan Lal), Vivekanand International Foundation and Aryan Books International, New Delhi.

16. 2014. Jhusi (Pratishthanpur), in *The Texts, Political History and Administration till 200 BC (History of Ancient India, Volume III)* (Eds. Dilip K. Chakrabarti and Makkhan Lal), Vivekanand International Foundation and Aryan Books International, New Delhi.

17. 2014. Kausambi, in *The Texts, Political History and Administration till 200 BC (History of Ancient India, Volume III)* (Eds. Dilip K. Chakrabarti and Makkhan Lal),

18. Vivekanand International Foundation and Aryan Books International, New Delhi.

19. 2014. First Farmers of the Vindhyas, ICON: Journal of Archaeology and Culture, 1.

20. 2013. New Researches in the Prehistoric Archaeology of the Vindhyas, *Puratattva* 43.

21. 2013. Beginning of Agriculture: Northern Vindhyas and the Middle Gangetic Plain, in *Prehistory of India* (Ed. M.K. Dhavalikar), A Comprehensive History of India, Vol. 1, Part I, Comprehensive History of India Society and Manohar Publishers & Distributors, New Delhi.

22. 2012. Society and Economy in the Middle Ganga Plain during the time of Buddha, *Sanskriti Sandhana* XXV (2).

23. 2012. Book Review, *Ecology and Archaeology of Kosal Region* of Pushp Lata Singh, *Man and Environment* XXXVII(2).

24. 2012. Beginning of Agriculture and Domestication in the Upper Vindhyas, *Purakala* 22.

25. 2012. Petraglia, M.D., Ravi Korisettar, J.N. Pal, The Toba Volcanic super-irruption of 74, 000 years ago: Climate change, environments and evolving humans, guest editorial, *Quaternary International,* 251.

26. 2012. Petraglia, M.D., Peter Ditchfield, Sacha Jones, Ravi Korisettar, J.N. Pal, The Toba Volcanic super-irruption, environmental change, and hominid occupation history in India over the last 140, 000 years, *Quaternary International* 251.

27. 2012. Lewis, Laura., Peter Ditchfield, J.N. Pal, Michael Petraglia, Grain size distributionanalysis of sediments containing Younger Toba tephra from Ghoghara, Middle Son valley, India, *Quaternary International* 251.

28. 2012. Haslam, M., Clair Harris, Cris Clarkson, J.N. Pal, Ceri Shipton, Alison Crouwther, Jinu Koshy, Janardhana Bora, Peter Ditchfield, Harindra Prasad Ram, Kathryn Price, A.K. Dubey, M. Petraglia, Dhaba: An initial report on an Acheulean, Middle Palaeolithic and microlithic locality in the middle Son Valley, north-central India. *Quaternary International* 258.

29. 2011. Haslam, M., Roberts, R.G., Shipton, C., Pal, J.N., Fenwick, J., Ditchfield, P., Bovin, N., Dubey, A.K., Gupta, M.C., Petraglia, M., Late Acheulian Hominins at the Marine Isotope Stage 6/5e transition in north-central India. *Quaternary Research* 75.

30. 2011. Parallels in Prehistoric Cultures of Iran and India, in *Cultural Parallels: India and Iran,* (Atul Kumar Sinha, Abhay Kumar Singh Eds.), Anamika Publishers and Distributors (P) Ltd, New Delhi.

31. 2011.Kausambi: A Great Centre of Buddhist Art, in *Kausambi Ka Swarnim Itihas Evam Vartaman* (Ed. S.K. Pandey), Meera Publications, Allahabad.

32. 2009. Beginnings of agriculture in the Middle Ganga Plain, Presidential Address, Ancient History Section, U.P. History Congress, XXth Session, October 3-4, 2009, Department of Humanities and

Social Sciences, VBS Purvanchal University, Jaunpur (U.P.).

33. 2009. The Neolithic Culture in the Northern Vindhyas and the Middle Gangetic Plain, in *Status of Prehistoric Studies in the Twenty-First Century in India* (Ranjana Ray and Vidula Jayaswal Eds.). BAR International Series, Oxford.

34. 2009. Recent Researches in the Archaeology of the Ganga Plain and the Vindhyas, in *Recent Research Trends in South Asian Archaeology (Proceedings of the Professor H.D. Sankalia Birth Centenary Seminar (10-12 December 2007)* (K. Paddayya, P.P. Joglekar, Kishor K. Basa, Reshma Sawant Eds.). Deccan College Post-Graduate and Research Institute, Pune.

35. 2009. The Palaeolithic of the Middle Son Valley. North-Central India: Changes in Hominin Lithic Technology and Behaviour during the Upper Pleistocene, in co-authorship of Sacha C. Jones, *Journal of Anthropological Archaeology* Volume 28, Issue 3 (September).

36. 2009. Anil Kumar Pokharia, B. Sekar, Jagannath Pal, Alka Srivastava. Possible Evidence of Pre-Columbian Transoceanic Voyages Based on Conventional LSc and AMS C-14 Dating of Associated Charcoal and Carbonized Seed of Custard Apple (Annona Squamosa L.), *Radiocarbon,* Vol. 51, Nr. 3.

37. 2008. Recent Excavations at Tokwa: Fresh Light on the Early Farming Culture of the Vindhyas, *History of Science, Philosophy and Culture in Indian Civilization* (general ed. D.P. Chattopadhyaya) Volume V Part I, *History of Agriculture in India (upto c. 1200 AD)* (eds. Lallanji Gopal and V.C. Srivastava), Concept Publishing Company, New Delhi.

38. 2008. Joglekar, P.P., J.N. Pal, V.D. Misra and M.C. Gupta. Faunal Remain recovered from the Neolithic Phase at Jhusi, District Allahabad, Uttar Pradesh. *Puratattva* 38.

39. 2008. Gupta, M.C., J.N. Pal and V.D. Misra 2008. Beginnings of Agriculture in the Middle Ganga Plain with Special Reference to Recent Excavations at Jhusi, *History of Science, Philosophy and Culture in Indian Civilization* (general ed. D.P. Chattopadhyaya) Volume V Part I, *History of Agriculture in India (upto c. 1200 AD)* (eds. Lallanji Gopal and V.C. Srivastava), pp. 87-99, Cocept Publishing Company, New Delhi.

40. 2007-08. The Early Farming Culture of the Middle Ganga Plain with Special Reference to the Excavations at Jhusi and Hetapatti. *Pragdhara,* No. 18.

41. 2007.Liquid scintillation counting and AMS C-14 radiocarbon dating of associated charcoals and carbonized seed of *Annona squamosa* L. to analyse its antiquity in India, in co-authorship of B. Sekar, Anil K. Pokharia, G.V. Ravi Prasad, R.K. Chowdhury, G. Rajagopalan, *Currecnt Science* 93 (10) 25 November 2007.

42. 2007. Review article on Gurudakshina: Facets of Indian Archaeology (Part I), in *Eastern Anthropologist* 60(2).

43. 2007. Review of Ethnoarchaeological Research in the Ganga Basin and Future Directions, in *Anthropology for Archaeology: Proceedings of the Professor Irawai Karve Birth Centenary Seminar* Eds. S.R. Waalimbe, P.P. Joglekar, Kishor K. Basa. Deccan College Post-Graduate and Research Institute, Pune.

44. 2006, Human Response to Holocene Climatic Conditions in the Gangetic Plain, *Udayan: Prof. U.P. Arora Felicitation Volume*, Anamika Prakashan, New Delhi.

45. 2006, River Response to Quaternary Climatic Fluctuations: Evidence from the Son and Belan Valleys, North-central India, in co-authorship of Martin J. Williams, M. Jayaswal and A.K. Singhvi, *Quaternary Science Reviews* 25.

46. 2006, Excavations at Jhusi: Preliminary Observations, in co-authorship of V.D. Misra and M.C. Gupta, *Art Archaeology and Cultural History of India: Prof. U.N. Roy Felicitation Volume* (Ed C.P. Sinha), B.R. Publishing House, New Delhi.

47. Pal, J.N. and M.C. Gupta 2005. Excavations at Hetapatti (Allahabad District): Some Preliminary Observations *Journal of Interdisciplinary Studies in History and Archaeology,* 2 (2) (Winter 2005).

48. Pal, J.N. 2005. A History of the Development of Human Cultures in the Tons Valley, in K.K. Chakravarty, G.L. Badam (Eds.) *River Valley Cultures of* India, Indira Gandhi Rashtiya Manav Sangrahalaya, Bhopal and Aryan Books International, New Delhi.

49. 2005, The Middle Son Valley and the Toba Supervolcanic Eruption of 74 kyr BP: Youngest Toba Tuff Deposits and Palaeolithic Association, in co-authorship of Sacha C. Jones, *Journal of Interdisciplinary Studies in History and Archaeology,* Volume 2, Number 1 (Summer 2005).

50. 2005, Palaeolithic Art Activities and their Stratigraphic Context in the Vindhyas, *Purakala,* Volume 14-15.

51. 2005, Early Agriculture of the Neolithic Vindhyas (North-central India), in co-authorship of E.L. Harvey, D. Fuller, M.C. Gupta, *South Asian Archaeology* (Ed. Ute Franke-Vogt and Hans-Joachim Weishaar), Deutsches Archaologisches Institut, Aachen.

52. 2004, Infra Red Stimulated Luminescence Ages for Prehistoric cultures in the Son and Belan Valleys, North Central India, in co-authorship of M.A.J. Williams, M.Jayaswal and A.K. Singhvi, *Journal of Interdisciplinary Studies in History and Archaeology,* Volume 1, Number 2 (Winter 2004).

53. 2004, Significance of Recent Excavations at Tokwa in the Vindhya and Jhusi in the Gangetic Plain, in co-authorship of M.C. Gupta, *Journal of Interdisciplinary Studies in History and Archaeology,* Volume

1, Number 1 (Summer 2004).

54. 2003, Skeletal Variation among Mesolithic People of the Ganga Plain: New Evidence of habitual Activity and Adaptation to Climate, Asian perspectives, University of Hawaii.

55. 2002-2003, Archaeological Investigations at Baidha and neighbouring Area in the Adwa Valley in Mirzapur District, Uttar Pradesh (with M.C. Gupta) *Pragdhara* No. 13.

56. 2002-2003, Further Excavations at Jhusi: Evidence of Neolithic Culture (with V.D. Misra and M.C. Gupta), *Pragdhara,* No. 13.

57. 2002. Subsistence Activities among the Mesolithic People of North India as Revealed by Microwear Studies of Microliths, in *Mesolithic India* (V.D. Misra and J.N. Pal Eds.), Allahabad: Department of Ancient History, Culture and Archaeology, University of Allahabad.

58. 2002. Faunal Remains from Damdama: Evidence for the Mesolithic Food Economy of the Gangetic Plain, in co-authorship with P. K. Thomas, P. P. Joglekar, V. D. Misra and J. N. Pandey, in *Mesolithic India* (V.D. Misra and J.N. Pal Eds.), Allahabad: Department of Ancient History, Culture and Archaeology, University of Allahabad.

59. 2002. The Mesolithic Phase in the Ganga Valley, *Recent Studies in Indian Archaeology,* Indian Council of Historical Research, New Delhi, Monograph Series VI.

60. 2002. Mesolithic Gangetic Plain, in *Mesolithic India* (V.D. Misra and J.N. Pal Eds.), Allahabad: Department of Ancient History, Culture and Archaeology, University of Allahabad.

61. 2002, Jhusi: Archaeological and Historical Implications as Revealed from the Excavations at Ancient Pratishthanpur (with V.D. Misra and M.C. Gupta), in *Allahabad: Aspects of Historical and Cultural profile,* (O.P. Srivastava, Anamika Roy, M.C. Gupta Eds). Department of Ancient History, Culture and Archaeology, University of Allahabad.

62. 2001-2002 Excavation at Amilkoni, Rewa District, Madhya Pradesh and Exploration around Amilkoni, *Pragdhara* No. 12.

63. 2001, Neolithic Culture of the Northern Vindhyas with special reference to Tokwa (with V.D. Misra and M.C. Gupta), *Bharti,* Bulletin of the Department of Ancient Indian History, Culture and Archaeology, B.H.U. Varanasi 25 (I and II) 1998-99.

64. 2001, Origin and Developmental Process of Human Cultures in the Vindhyas: Its Role in the Growth of Civilization in the Ganga Valley, in Eds. V. Yasuda, and V. Shinde *Monsoon and Civilization*, Pune.

65. 2001, Excavation at Jhusi: Archaeological and Historical Implication (with V.D. Misra and

M.C. Gupta), *Contemporary Historiography – Methodology and Trends* (ed. Dr. Sita Ram Dubey), Pratibha Prakashan, Delhi.

66. 2000-2001, Excavation at Tokwa: A Neolithic-Chalcolithic Settlement (with V.D. Misra and M.C. Gupta), *Pragdhara*, No. 11.

67. 2000, Mesolithic and Neolithic Societies of the Vindhyas and the Middle Gangetic Plain, in V.D. Misra and J.N. Pal (Eds.) *Social History and Social Theory.* University of Allahabad.

68. 2000, Exploration at Tokwa: A Neolithic Chalcolithic Settlement on the Confluence of the Belan and Adwa Rivers, in collaboration with V.D. Misra, B.B. Misra and M.C. Gupta, in S.C. Bhattacharaya, V.D. Misra, J.N. Pandey, J.N. Pal (Eds.) *Peeping through the Past: Prof. G.R. Sharma Memorial Volume,.*

69. 1999-2000, Further Excavations at Jhusi (1998-99), (with V.D. Misra and M.C. Gupta), *Pragdhara* No. 10.

70. 1999, Jhusi Men Puratattvik Utkhanan: Kya Kahate Hain Ye Avaseeya Jamav ? *Maya,* 15 July.

71. 1999, Excavation at Amilkoni, Dist. Rewa, Madhya Pradesh, in collaboration with V.D. Misra, D.K. Shukla, M.C. Gupta, *Citi Vithika,* (Journal of Art, History, Culture and Literature) Vol. 4, Nos. 1-2, 1998-99 (ed.) G.C. Pande.

72. 1998-99 Further Excavation At Jhusi, District Allahabad, Uttar Pradesh –1998 (With V.D. Misra and M.C. Gupta), *Pragdhara* No. 9.

73. 1998 Agricultural and Non-agricultural Economy of the Early Farming Culture of the Vindhyas, Central India, in *Facets of Indian Culture* (Gustav Roth Felicitation Volume, Bihar Puravid Parishad, Patna, pp. 1-4.

74. 1998 Economy of the Early Farming Cultures of the Vindhyas - Central India with Special Reference to Baghelkhand, in *Reconstructing History* (Essays in Honour of Prof. V. C. Srivastava), Volume I (Eds. V. D. Misra, R. N. Singh, Jeewan Rai and R. N. Misra), Tara Book Agency, Varanasi.

75. 1997-98 Preliminary Report on the Explorations around Sharda Vihar (near Kerwa Dam) in the Vicinity of Bhopal, Madhya Pradesh, (With V.D. Misra, P. Sinha and M.C. Gupta) *Pragdhara* No. 8.

76. 1997-98 Historiography of Prehistoric Cultures and Art in North India, *Citi-Vithika,* (Journal of Art, History, Culture and Literature), Vol. 3, Nos. 1-2.

77. 1997 The Neolithic Cultures of the Northern Vindhyas and the Middle Gangetic Plain, in *Art Archaeology and Culture of Eastern India: Dr. B.S. Verma Felicitation Volume* (C.P. Sinha Ed.),

Bihar Puravid Parishad, Patna.

78. 1997 Environmental Change and Human Adaptation in the Quaternary Period in the Vindhyas, Central India, in *Him-Kanti: Archaeology, Art and History, Prof. K. P. Nautiyal Felicitation Volume* (B. M. Khanduri and Vinod Nautiyal Eds.), Book India Publishing Co. Delhi.

79. 1997 Ceramic Industries of the Mesolithic Period of the Vindhyas, in *Indian Prehistory: 1980* (V. D. Misra and J. N. Pal Eds.), Department of Ancient History, Culture and Archaeology, University of Allahabad, Allahabad.

80. 1997 The Upper Palaeolithic Culture of the Vindhyan Region, in co-authorship with R. K. Varma, in *Indian Prehistory: 1980* (V. D. Misra and J. N. Pal Eds.), Department of Ancient History, Culture and Archaeology, University of Allahabad, Allahabad.

81. 1996-97 Microwear Studies of Microliths of the Mesolithic North India: Preliminary Report on Methods and Results, *Pragdhara* 7.

82. 1996-97 Recent Explorations in the Adwa Valley in the Districts of Mirzapur (U. P.) and Sidhi and Rewa (M. P.) in co-authorship with V. D. Misra and B. B. Misra, *Pragdhara* 7.

83. 1996 Lithic Use Wear Analysis and Subsistence Activities among the Mesolithic People of North India, in *Bioarchaeology of Mesolithic India: an Integrated Approach*, eds. Gennadii E. Afanas'ev, Serge Cleuziou, John R. Lukacs, Maurizio Tosi, Colloquium XXXIII, *The Prehistory of Asia and Ocenia*, International Union of Prehistoric and Protohistoric Sciences, Forli, Italy.

84. 1996 Chronology and Diet in Mesolithic North India: a Preliminary Report of New AMS C-14 Dates, ä-13C Isotope Values, and their Significance, in co-authorship with J. R. Lukacs and V. D. Misra, in *Bioarchaeology of Mesolithic India: an Integrated Approach*, eds. Gennadii E. Afanas'ev, Serge Cleuziou, John R. Lukacs, Maurizio Tosi, Colloquium XXXIII, *The Prehistory of Asia and Ocenia*, International Union of Prehistoric and Protohistoric Sciences, Forli, Italy.

85. 1996 Faunal Evidence for the Mesolithic Food Economy of the Gangetic Plain with Special Reference to Damdama, in co-authorship with P. K. Thomas, P. P. Joglekar, V. D. Misra and J. N. Pandey, in *Bioarchaeology of Mesolithic India: an Integrated Approach*, eds. Gennadii E. Afanas'ev, Serge Cleuziou, John R. Lukacs, Maurizio Tosi, Colloquium XXXIII, *The Prehistory of Asia and Ocenia*, International Union of Prehistoric and Protohistoric Sciences, Forli, Italy.

86. 1995-96 A preliminary Report on the Excavations at Jhusi 1995, in co-authorship with V. D. Misra, B. B. Misra and J. N. Pandey, *Pragdhara* 6.

87. 1995 A Preliminary Report of the Faunal Remains from Damdama, in co-authorship with P. K. Thomas, P. P. Joglekar, V. D. Misra and J. N. Pandey, *Man and Environment* XX (1).

88. 1995 Chhathin Shatabdi Ishapurva Ke Pahale Madhya Ganga Ka Maidan, *Hindi Kalam*, Volume 3 (*Itias Ka Itihas* Part 2): 81-86.

89. 1994-95 Chalcolithic Vindhyas, *Pragdhara* 5.

90. 1994 Mesolithic Settlements in the Ganga Plain, North India, *Man and Environment* XIX (1).

91. 1994 The Neolithic Vindhyas, in *Art and Archaeology of the Vindhyan Region and Aryans- A Myth or Reality* (ed. R. K. Varma), Department of Ancient Indian History, Culture and Archaeology, A. P. S. University, Rewa, M. P.

92. 1994 Some Masterpieces of Kausambi School of Art of Gupta Period, in *Indian Art and Culture* (Ed. G. C. Pande), Raka Prakashan, Allahabad.

93. 1993 Mesolithic Subsistence in North India: Inferences from Dental Attributes, in co-authorship with John R. Lukacs, *Current Anthropology* 34(5).

94. 1992-93 Palaeolithic Maihar, Satna District Madhya Pradesh: a Preliminary Report of Excavations, in co-authorship with J. N. Pandey, *Pragdhara* 3.

95. 1992 Mesolithic Human Burials in the Ganga Plain, North India, *Man and Environment* XVII(2).

96. 1992 Dental Anthropology of the Mesolithic Hunter-Gatherers: a Preliminary Report on the Mahadaha and Sarai Nahar Rai Dentition, in co-authorship with John R. Lukacs *Man and Environment* XVII (2).

97. 1992 Human Burial Practices at Mesolithic Damdama, in *Archaeological Perspective of Uttar Pradesh and Future Prospects*, Part I Ed. Rakesh Tewari), State Archaeological Organization, Uttar Pradesh, Lucknow.

98. 1992 Kalanjar Kshetra ki Pragaitihasik Prishthbhumi, in *Kalanjar: a Historical and Cultural Profile* (Ed. B. N. Roy), Pt. J. L. Nehru College, Banda.

99. 1992 Burial Practices and Archaeological Recovery, in *Human Skeletal Remains from Mahadaha: A Gangetic Mesolithic Site*, K. A. R. Kennedy, J. R. Lukacs, R. F. Paster, T. L. Johnston, N. C. Lovell, J. N. Pal, B. E. Hemphill and C. B. Burrow, South Asia Occasional Papers and Theses No. 13, South Asia Program, Cornell University, Ithaca.

100. 1991 Hunter-Gatherers of the Early Holocene Period of the Middle Gangetic Plain, in *Krishna Deo Felicitation Volume* (ed. C. P. Sinha), Ramanand Vidya Bhawan, Delhi.

101. 1990 The Neolithic Cultures of the Northern Vindhyas and the Middle Gangetic Plain, *Journal of Ancient Indian History*, 1987-88 XVII(1-2).

102. 1990 Chalcolithic Cultures of Southern Uttar Pradesh: Interrelationship of the Vindhyan Plateau

and the Gangetic Plain, in *Adaptation and Other Essays* (Eds. N. C. Ghosh and S. Chakrabarti), Vishwa Bharti, Shantiniketan.

103. 1990 The Early Farming Cultures of the Northern Vindhyas, *Bulletin of the Deccan College Postgraduate and Research Institute* (H. D. Sankalia Memorial Volume) 49.

104. 1990. Mesolithic Hunter-Gatherers of the Ganga Valley: Inferences for Social and Economic Life, *Archaeology and Art(Krishna Deva Felicitation Volume)* Part I, Chief Editor Dr. Chita Ranjan Prasad Sinha, Ramanand Vidya Bhawan, Delhi.

105. 1989 A Preliminary Study of Pleistocene Fossils from the Middle Son Valley, Madhya Pradesh, in co-authorship with G. L. Badam, V. D. Misra and J. N. Pandey, *Man and Environment* XIII: 41-47.

106. 1989 Kya Ram Pragaitihasik Hain? in *Sri Ram in Art and Archaeology* (ed. B. P. Sinha), The Bihar Puravid Parishad, Patna, pp. .

107. 1989 Further Excavations at Damdama-1987, in *Dimensions in Indian Archaeology* (Eds. S. K. Pandey and K. S. Ramchandran), New Delhi.

108. 1988. The Antecedents of the Village and Folk Culture in the Gangetic Plain, *Rural Life and Folk Culture in Ancient India,* Editor U.N. Roy, Department of Ancient History, Culture and Archaeology, University of Allahabad.

109. 1988 Mesolithic Double Burials from Recent Excavations at Damdama, *Man and Environment* XII.

110. 1988 Acheulian Occupation at Maihar, in co-authorship with J. N. Pandey, *Man and Environment* XII.

111. 1987 Neolithic Cord Impressed Ware of the Vindhyas, *Man and Environment* XI.

112. 1987 Microlithic Industry at Damdama, *Puratattva* 16(1985-86).

113. 1987 Madhya Ganga Ghati ki Pashan Kalin Sanskritiyan: Ek Sarvekshan, in *History and Culture,* B. P. Sinha Felicitation Volume, (Ed. Bhagwant Sahai), Ramanand Vidya Bhawan, Delhi.

114. 1986 Environmental and Archaeological Records of the Upper Palaeolithic Population in the Northern Vindhyas, in *Pleistocene Perspective,* Volume I, Allen and Unvin, England.

115. 1986 Mesolithic Hunter-Gatherers in the Ganga Valley: Inferences for Social and Economic Life, *Souvenir, Silver Jubilee Celebrations,* Department of Anthropology, Andhra University, Waltair.

116. 1985-86 Microlithic Industry from Damdama, *Puratattva* 16.

117. 1985 Some New Light on the Mesolithic Burial Practices of the Ganga Valley: Evidence from Mahadaha, Pratapgarh, Uttar Pradesh, *Man and Environment* IX.

118. 1985 An Assessment of the Epipalaeolithic Culture of Pratapgarh District, Uttar Pradesh, *A National Journal of Social Sciences*. .

119. 1985 A Preliminary Report on the Excavations at Damdama (1982-84), in co-authorship with R. K. Varma, V. D. Misra and J. N. Pandey, *Man and Environment* IX.

120. 1984 Epipalaeolithic Sites in Pratapgarh District, *Man and Environment* VIII.

121. 1984 Pragaitihasik Allahabad: Madhya Pashanik aur Navpashanik Sanskritiyan, *Bhartiya Itihas Sankalan Samiti Patrika* 2 .

122. 1984. Ram Katha Kshetra Ki Pragaitihasik Prishthabhumi, *Uttar Pradesh* August 1984, Suchana aur Jansampark Vibag Ka Prakashan , Year 13, Vol. 3. .

123. 1984 Pragaitihasik Allahabad: Puratattvik Khoj, *Uttar Pradesh*, Prayag Volume, Year 12, Feb., Lucknow 9.

124. 1983 Upper Palaeolithic Culture of the Middle Son Valley, *Puratattva* 12.

125. 1983 An Upper Palaeolithic Shrine in India, in co-authorship with J. M. Kenoyer, J. D. Clark and G. R. Sharma, *Antiquity* LVII

126. 1983 Bases of the Neolithic Culture of the Middle Ganga Valley, *Journal of the G. N. Jha Kendriya Sanskrit Vidyapeeth*, Pt. Baldeo Upadhyay Felicitation Volume XXXVII (1-4).

127. 1983 An Upper Palaeolithic Surface Collection from Rampur, in co-authorship with V. D. Misra, D. Mandal and P. Sinha, in *Palaeo-Environment and Prehistory in the Middle Son Valley* (Eds. G. R. Sharma and J. D. Clark), Abinash Prakashan, Allahabad.

128. 1983 Preliminary Report on Excavations at the Late Palaeolithic Site at Baghor I Locality, in co-authorship with J. Mark Kenoyer, D. Mandal and V. D. Misra, in *Palaeo-Environment and Prehistory in the Middle Son Valley* (Eds. G. R. Sharma and J. D. Clark), Abinash Prakashan, Allahabad, .

129. 1983 Report on the Excavation and Analysis of an Upper Acheulian Assemblage from Sihawal II, in co-authorship with J. Mark Kenoyer, in *Palaeo-Environment and Prehistory in the Middle Son Valley* (Eds. G. R. Sharma and J. D. Clark), Abinash Prakashan, Allahabad.

130. 1982 Dakshini Uttar Pradesh me Pragaitihask Sanskritiyon ka Itihas, *Manav* 10(3-4).

131. 1981 Prehistoric Survey of Southern Uttar Pradesh, *Bulletin of Museums and Archaeology* 27-28.

132. 1980-81. Upper Palaeolithic Culture of te Mid-Son Valley, *Puratattva,* 12.

133. 1980-81. Some Aspects of Mesolithic and Neolithic Societies of the Vindhyas and the Ganga Valley, *Journal of the Bihar Puravid Parishad,* Vol. IV &V.

134. 1981 Pratapgarh me Puratattvik Anveshan, *Uttar Pradesh,* Special Volume on Archaeology: 105-109.

135. 1980 Pratapgarh Janpad Men Puratattvik Anveshan, *Manav* 2-3.

136. 1977 Bhartiya Nava Pashanik Sanskritiyan, in *Bhartiya Pragaitihasik Sanskritiyan* (R. K. Varma), pp. 272-282, Paramjyoti Prakashan Allahabad.

Books Reviewed

1. Review of the book *Archaeology of Southern Uttar Pradesh: Ceramic Industries of Northern Vindhyas* in *Man and Environment* XI: 127-128, by Dilip K. Chakrabarti, 1987.
2. Review of the book *Archaeology of Southern Uttar Pradesh: Ceramic Industries of Northern Vindhyas* in *The Eastern Anthropologist* 40(1): 80-81, by P. K. Tewari, 1987.
3. Review of the book *Archaeology of Southern Uttar Pradesh: Ceramic Industries of Northern Vindhyas* in *L' Anthropology* by D. P. Agrawal.
4. Review of the book *Human Skeletal Remains from Mahadaha: A Gangetic Mesolithic Site* in *American Journal of Human Biology* 6(1): 100-101 by M. V. Iscan, Department of Anthropology, Florida Atlantic University, Boca Raton, Florida, 1994.

Papers Presented in the Conferences and Seminars

1. Jhusi (Pratishthanpur): A Site Presenting Complete Cultural Sequence of the Ganga Valley. International Conference on Significance of the Ganga River Civilization: Its Global Spread and Impact. Organized by Draupadi Dream Trust at Indira Gandhi National Centre for Arts, 5 and 6 December 2018.
2. Chief Guest in the Valedictory Session of the National Seminar, Cultural Heritage of Eastern Uttar Pradesh, Department of Ancient History, Archaeology and Culture, D.D.U. Gorakhpur University, 21-22 March 2018.
3. Chaired a Session one day National Seminar, Archaeology of Eastern Western Coast, Allahabad Museum 20 February 2018.

4. Stone Age Cultures of the Vindhyan Region, Prof. J.S. Negi Memorial Lecture, Ewing Christian College, Allahabad, 12 February 2018.

5. Chronology and Bio-archaeology of the Neolithic Culture of the Vindhyas and the Middle Ganga Plain, Joint Annual Conference of IAS, ISPQS & HCS, Banaras Hindu University, Varanasi, 4-6 November 2017.

6. Chaired Session D of 50th Annnual Conference of Indian Archaeological Society held at BHU Varanasi on 5th November 2017.

7. Chaired Session II of the National Seminar on Indian Civilization (2000-500 B.C., organized by Vivekanand International Foundation New Delhi in Association with Archaeological Survey of India, 17-18 June 2015.

8. Allahabad: A Heritage City of India, National Seminar on Rejuvenation of Culturally Significant Cities, organized by Sagar (Organisation for Art, Culture and Archaeology) at India International Centre, New Delhi on 22nd May 2015.

9. Special lecture: Archaeology of the Middle Ganga Valley and Ancient Indian Literature, National Seminar on Recent Field Researches in Indian Archaeology and Literature, Department of Ancient Indian History, Culture and Archaeology, Banaras Hindu University, Varanasi, 24 to 26 April, 2015.

10. Participated in the Meeting of Eminent Scholars to discuss thoroughly the scheme and to finalize the content of 11 Volumes of ambitious project of the Mythic Society (Daly Memorial Hall) Banglore for writing Indian History and Culture, 18-19 April 2015.

11. The Need for Buddhist Thoughts, Special Guest at National Seminar on Buddhist View and Socio-Cultural Legacy of India, organized by Balram Shodh Sansthan, Allahabad at Citizen Girls College, Naini, Allahabad, 22 February, 2015.

12. Chief Guest in the National Seminar on Global Challenges and Development of Higher Education, Shrimati Indira Gandhi Government Post-graduate Degree College, Lalganj, Mirzapur (U.P.), 26 and 27 February 2015

13. Inferring Climatic variations during Holocene from a Neolithic Site in Middle ganga Plain, in co-authorship of D.K. Chauhan, Deepika Tripathi and Manish Tewari, National Conference on Quaternary Climate Change: New Approaches and Emerging Challenges, organized by Birbal Sahni Institute of Palaeobotany, Lucknow with support from Department of Science and Technology, New Delhi; Ministry of Earth Sciences, Govt. of India, New Delhi; Oil India Limited, Noida U.P., December 15-16, 2014

14. Need to teach to general public the correct approach to history, National Seminar on Swarnim Bharat Ke Punarnirman Me Itihas Ki Prasangikata, Mahatma Gandhi Chitrakoot Gramodaya University, Chitrakoot, Satna M.P., 8 December 2014. (Special Guest)

15. First Colonizers of the Ganga Plain, Silver Jubilee Session U.P. History Congress, Veer Bahadur Singh Purvanchal University, Jaunpur (U.P.), 15-16 November 2014.

16. Prelude to Urbanization in the Central Ganga Valley, National Seminar on City and City Culture from earliest Times to Modern period, National Institute of Human Culture, Varanasi, 7-8 November 2014.

17. Burial Practices of the Mesolithic People of the Ganga Valley and Vindhyas, Seminar of Archaeological Society of India on 'Transition from Hunting-gathering to Domestication, Deccan College, Pune, 6-9 October 2014.

18. Alexander Cunningham and Archaeology of Central Ganga Plain, International Seminar on Sir Alexander Cunningham and the Art Heritage of India, February 20, 21 and 22, 2014, organized by Department of History of Art, Banaras Hindu University Varanasi in collaboration with Archaeological Survey of India.

19. Evidence of Neolithic Technology in the Ganga Plain, National Seminar on Science and Technology in Ancient India and their Relevance in Modern Times, 15th-16th February 2014, organized by Department of Ancient Indian History and Archaeology, University of Lucknow, Lucknow-07.

20. Archaeology of Kausambi; The Capital City of Vats Mahajanapada, National Seminar on Archaeology of Ancient and Medieval Capital Cities of India, organized by Allahabad Museum, Allahabad, 5-6 February, 2014.

21. Alexander Cunningham and Archaeology in Allahabad and Neighbouring Area, in a Colloquiuam on 'Indian Archaeology and Sir Alexander Cunningham: Yesterday, Today and Tomorrow', 23 January 2014, organized by Allahabad Museum in remembrance of Cunningham's 200th Birth Century.

22. Cultural and Archaeological Heritage of Allahabad District, National Seminar sponsored by ICHR, Sarveshwari P.G. Degree College, Dhanuha, Chaka, Naini Allahabad, December 21-22, 2013.

23. Prehistory of the Middle Son Valley, Presidential Address, 41 Annual Conference ISPQS, December 14-16, 2013, Banaras Hinddu University, Varanasi.

24. Archaeology and Culture of Bundelkhand, National Seminar, sponsored by University Grants Commission, Department of History, Culture and Archaeology, J.R. handicapped University, Chitrakoot (U.P.), December 7-8, 2013.

25. Excavations at Hetapatti, Allahabad, Uttar Pradesh, Seminar on Recent Excavations in Eastern India, organized by Directorate of Archaeology, Bihar and Bihar Puravid Parishad, Patna, November 11-12, 2013, Patna Museum, Patna.

26. Participated in the Interactive Workshop: Site Museums of ASI and Museums of National Importance, organized in collaboration with Allahabad Museum and Central Region of Archaeological Survey of India, Bhopal on 5th and 6th October, 2012.

27. Mesolithic and Neolithic Pottery, Refresher Course-cum Short Term Training Programme on Ceramics, Institute of Archaeology, Archaeological Survey of India, Lal Qila, New Delhi, (21st – 26th August 2012), 21-8-2012.

28. Monsoon and Archaeology of the Middle Ganga Plain with Special Reference to Recent Excavations, Monsoon Based Cultural and Vocational Programme under Ullas, Allahabad Museum, Allahabad, July 10, 2012.

29. Society and Culture during the time of Buddha in Middle Ganga Plain, National Seminar on Socio-Economic Changes in India: A Historical and Cultural Perspective (Vedic to Modern Times), organized under the auspices of the National Research Institute of Human Culture, Varanasi, May 11-13, 2012.

30. Archaeological Background of Buddhism in the Middle Ganga Plain, Seven-days Workshop on Bharat Men Sanskritik Samakalan Mein baudha dharm Ki Bhumika, Centre of Excellence, Department of History, Mahatma Gandhi Kashi Vidyapeeth, Varanasi, 20-27 February 2012.

31. Art Activity during the Early Farming Culture in the Vindhyas, The 16th Congress of the Rock Art Society of India, jointly organized by Archaeological Survey of India, Lucknow Circle and Department of Ancient Indian History and Archaeology, University of Lucknow, U.P., 27th to 29th November 2011.

32. Origin of the Neolithic Culture in the Ganga Valley, jointly with M.C. Gupta, 39th Annual Conference of Indian Society for Prehistoric and Quaternary Studies, Department of Archaeology, University of Kerala, Thiruvanantapuram, 11 to 13 November, 2011.\

33. Origin of the Chalcolithic Culture of the middle Ganga plain and the Vindhyas, jointly with M.C. Gupta, 45th Annual Conference of Indian Archaeological Society, Department of Archaeology, University of Kerala, Thiruvanantapuram, 11 to 13 November, 2011.

34. Some Aspects of Parallel Development of Prehistoric Cultures of Iran and India, International Conference on 'India and Iran: Our Cultural Legacy of the Past', organized by Poona College of Arts, Science & Commerce, Pune, March 3-5, 2011.

35. Significance of Context in Archaeology: A case Study in the Vindhyas, National Seminar on Interpretation of Historical Evidence and the Reconstruction of Past in History, Department of Ancient History and culture, MJP Rohilkhand University, Bareilly, 24-25 February 2011.

36. Prelude to Buddhism in the middle ganga Plain, National Seminar on Relevance of Buddhism in the Contemporary Aspects, sponsored by UGC and organized by Buddist Study Centre, Pratap Bahadur Post Graduate College, Pratapgarh City, Pratapgarh, U.P., November 13 and 14, 2010.

37. The Significance of Excavations at Jhusi, National Seminar on Archaeological and Historical Prospects in Allahabad Region, Nehru Gram Bharti University, Kotwa-Jamunipur, Allahabad, May 29, 2011.

38. The Archaeological Record of the Middle Son Valley, Conference 'The Toba Super-Eruption: A Critical Moment in Human Evolution' held at University of Oxford, February 20-21, 2010.

39. Status and Future Prospect of Prehistory in the Vindhyas, National Seminar on 'Uttar Pradesh Ka Puratattva: Naye Ayam' Uttar Pradesh State Archaeology Department, Lucknow, 10-11 February 2010.

40. Buddhist Art at Kausambi, International Seminar on Buddhist Heritage, Gujarat, organized by the Maharaja Sayajirao University of Baroda and Government of Gujarata during 15-17 January 2010.

41. Prof. B.P. Sinha Memorial Lecture on 3rd May 2009 in the premises of the Patna Museum on the invitation of Bihar Puravid Parishad, Patna.

42. Beginnings of Agriculture in the Middle Ganga Plain, Sectional Presidential Address, Ancient Section, U.P. History Congress, XXth Session, October 3-4, 2009, Department of Humanities and Social Sciences, VBS Purvanchal University, Jaunpur, U.P.

43. Review of Literature, Workshop on Research Methodology in Social Sciences. Organized by U.P. Rajarshi Tandan Open University at hotel Milan Palace, 24 May 2009.

44. A Revisit to the Prehistory of the Middle Son Valley, in co-authorship of M.C. Gupta, ISPQS XXXVI Annual Conference at Bhubaneshwar, 29-31 December 2008.

45. Faunal Remains from Neolithic Chalcolithic Phases at Tokwa, Mirzapur district Uttar Pradesh, in co-authorship of P.P. Joglekar, V.D. Misra and J.N. Pal, ISPQS XXXVI Annual Conference at Bhubaneshwar, 29-31 December 2008.

46. Neolithic Culture of Allahabad Region, in co-authorship of V.D. Misra and J.N. Pal, Annual Conference of Indian Archaeological Society Bhubaneshwar, 29-31 December 2008.

47. Excavations at Jhusi, Seminar on Art and Archaeology of Allahabad Region, organized by the Department of Ancient History, Culture, Archaeoogy and Museology, Ewing Cristian College, Allahabad, 30th April 2008.

48. The Cultural Sequence of the Ganga Plain: Evidence from the Excavations at Jhusi, National Seminar on Environments of Ancient India: Archaeological and Literary Critique and workshop on Metals and Technology of Early Indian Coins, Banaras Hindu University, Varanasi 8-10 March 2008.

49. Participated in the Symposia Applications of Science and Technology for the study of the Past, organized by Center of Advanced Study, Department of Ancient History, Culture and Archaeology, university of Allahabad, 17th February 2008.

50. South-East Asia and India: Contact in Prehistoric Periods, jointly with Prof. R.K. Varma, International seminar on India and South-East Asia: Shared Cultural Heritage, held at Allahabad Museum, Allahabad on 11 to 13 January 2008.

51. Participated in the Seminar on History of Indian Science and Technology organized by Infinity Foundation and Deccan College at Deccan College Pune on 13-16 December 2007.

52. Participated and presented personal remenescences and a full paper on Recent Researches in the archaeology of the Ganga Valley and the Vindhyas in the Prof. H.D. Sankalia Birth Centenary Seminar organized by Deccan Colleg, Pune from 10 to 12 December 2007.

53. Chronology of the Neolithic Culture of the Vindhyas and the middle Ganga Valley, jointly with Prof. V.D. Misra and M.C. Gupta, Annual Conference of Indian Society for Prehistoric and Quaternary Studies, Directorate of Culture and Archaeology, Raipur, Chhatishgarh. 2 to 4 december 2007.

54. Chronology of the Chalcolithic Culture of the Middle Ganga Valley and the Vindhyas, jointly with Prof. V.D. Misra and M.C. Gupta, Annual Conference of Indian Society for Prehistoric and Quaternary Studies, Directorate of Culture and Archaeology, Raipur, Chhatishgarh. 2 to 4 December 2007.

55. A two day Workshop on Land Scape, Demography and Subsistence in Prehistoric India: Exploratory Workshop on the Middle Ganges and the Vindhyas, at Leverhulme Centre for Human Evolutionary Studies, University of Cambridge and Ancient India and Iran Trust, 2-3 June 2007.

56. Jhusi Utkhanan Ke Pariprekshya men Madhya ganga Ghati men Sanskritik Anukram, National Seminar on The Process of Socio-Economic Change in Ancient India, Hiralal Ramnivas Postgraduate College, Khalilabad Sant Kabirnagar, 22 and 23 February 2007.

57. Excavations at Jhusi: Cultural Sequence of the Ganga Valley, 1st International Conference of South Asian Archaeology, Department of History, University of Mumbai, 16-18 December 2006.

58. Neolithic Culture of Eastern Uttar Pradesh in the Light of Excavations at Hetapatti, jointly with Dr. M.C. Gupta, Annual Conference of IAS, ISPQS and IHCS, Gwalior, 02-05 December 2006.

59. Neolithic ceramic Industry at Jhusi jointly with Dr. M.C. Gupta, Annual Conference of IAS, ISPQS and IHCS, Gwalior, 02-05 December 2006.

60. Early Farming Culture of the Middle Gangetic Plain with Special Reference to New Evidences from Excavations at Jhusi and Hetapatti (Allahabad District, Uttar Pradesh), International Seminar on First farmers in Global Perspective 18-20 january, 2006, Lucknow.

61. National seminar on the Upper Palaeolithic Cultures of India, Allahabad Museum, 7-9 April 2006

62. Excavations at Hetapatti: A Neolithic site on the Ganga, and A Sequence of Seven Cultures at Jhusi on the Confluence of the Ganga and Yamuna, National Seminar on the Ganges Civilization: the Shifting Paradigm Valley, BHU Varanasi 10-12 February 2006

63. Review of the Ethnoarchaeological Research in the Gangetic Basin, and Future Directions, International Seminar on the Contribution of Prof. Iravati Karve, December 2005, Pune

64. Excavations at Hetapatti (Allahabad) jointly with Dr. M.C. Gupta, Annual Conference of IAS, ISPQS and IHCS, Benglore December 2005.

65. Chronology of the Neolithic Culture of Vindhyas, jointly with Prof. V.D. Misra and M.C. Gupta, Annual Conference of IAS, ISPQS and IHCS, December 2005, Banglore.

66. Parallels in Prehistoric Cultures of Iran and India, International Seminar on parallels in the cultures of India and Iran, Allahabad Museum November 2005

67. Jhusi: a Key Site for the Cultural Sequence of the Middle Gangetic Plain, Paper presented in the National Seminar on the Archaeology of the Ganga Plain held during the Annual Conference of IAS, ISPQS and IHCS, Lucknow, 28 December 2004 to 31 December 2004.

68. Neolithic Phase at Jhusi, Paper presented in the Annual Conference of IAS, ISPQS and IHCS, 28 December 2004 to 31 December 2004.

69. Chalcolithic Phase at Jhusi, in co-authorship of V.D. Misra and M.C. Gupta, Paper presented in the Annual Conference of IAS, ISPQS and IHCS, 28 December 2004 to 31 December 2004.

70. Neolithic Culture at Tokwa, in co-authorship of M.C. Gupta, Paper presented in the Annual Conference of IAS, ISPQS and IHCS, 28 December 2004 to 31 December 2004.

71. Palaeolithic Art Activities in the Vindhyas, Paper presented in the Symposium B: Early Indian Petroglyphs and pre-Upper Palaeolithic Art of the World in the RASI – 2004 International Rock Art Congress nominated as the 10th Congress of the International Federation of Rock Art Organisations (IFRAO) held at Agra, 28 November to 02 December 2004.

72. Mesolithic Art in the Vindhyas and the Gangetic Plain, Paper presented in the Symposium D: Rock Art: New Discoveries in the RASI – 2004 International Rock Art Congress nominated as the 10th Congress of the International Federation of Rock Art Organisations (IFRAO) held at Agra, 28 November to 02 December 2004.

73. Stone Age in the Gangetic Plain, paper presented in the Fifteenth Session of Uttar Pradesh History Congress, Aligarh, U.P. 2-3 October 2004.

74. The Neolithic Culture of the Gangetic Plain with special reference to Jhusi, Paper presented in the Annual conference of IAS and ISPQS held at Department of Anthropology, Sri Venkateswara University, Tirupati, Andhra Pradesh, December 19-22, 2003.

75. Further Excavations at Tokwa: A Neolithic-Chalcolithic Site on the Confluence of the Belan and Adwa, Paper presented in the Annual Conference of IAS and ISPQS held at Department of Anthropology, Sri Venkateswara University, Tirupati, Andhra Pradesh, December 19-22, 2003.

76. The Prehistory of the Ramkatha Region, Paper presented in the National Seminar on Ramayan Tradition in historical Perspective, held on 4-5 November, 2003, organized by DSA Department of History, Ancient Indian History, Culture and Archaeology, HNB Garhwal university, Srinagar (Garhwal – 246174, Uttaranchal.

77. Neolithic Culture of the Belan Valley, Paper presented in the Seminar on The middle Ganga Plains through the Ages: Understanding Cultures through Archaeology, held on October 18 and 19, 2003, under the auspice of Gyan Pravah, Centre for Cultural Studies, Varanasi.

78. Early Farming Culture of the Vindhyas and the Ganga Plain: New Evidence from the Excavations at Tokwa, Paper presented in the UGC National Seminar on 'Farming Culture of India held in the Department of ancient History, Culture and Archaeology, University of Allahabad on April 19-20, 2003.

79. Jhusi in Literature and Archaeology, Paper presented in the National seminar on 'Archaeology and History: interrelationship' held in Allahabad Museum on February 26-28, 2003.

80. History of Allahabad as revealed by the excavations at Jhusi, Paper presented in the workshop on 'Local History of Allahabad' organized by Manav Vikas Sangrahalaya of the Govind Ballabh Pant Social Science Institute on January 11, 2003.

81. Excavations at Baidha: the Mesolithic Site on the Adwa in Mirzapur District, Paper presented in the Annual conference of IAS and ISPQS held at State Institute of Archaeology, Art History, Conservation and Museology, Hill Palace, Tripunithura, Ernakulam, Kerla, December 19-22, 2002.

82. The Cultural Sequence of the Middle Gangetic Plain as revealed by the Excavations at Jhusi, Paper presented in the Annual conference of IAS and ISPQS held at State Institute of Archaeology, Art History, Conservation and Museology, Hill Palace, Tripunithura, Hill Palace Ernakulam, Kerla, December 19-22, 2002.

83. The Cultural Relationship between Uttaranchal and the Gangetic Plain, paper presented in the National Seminar on Uttarnchal Kala, Sthapatya, Sanskriti aur Puratattva held at History Department, Government Postgraduate College, Kotdwar, Garhwal, Uttaranchal on 30-31 October 2002.

84. Archaeological Studies in the Vindhyas and Ganga Valley: An Multidisciplinary approach, Paper presented in the UGC National Seminar on 'Advances in History and Archaeology and the Question of Paradigm Shift' held in the Department of Ancient History, Culture and Archaeology, university of Allahabad on February 26-28, 2002.

85. Neolithic Culture of the Vindhyas with Special Reference to Tokwa, Paper Presented in the Joint Annual Conference of IAS and ISPQS at the Maharaja Sayaji University of Baroda, November 22-24, 2001.

86. Chalcolithic Culture of the Gangetic Plain with special Reference to Jhusi, Paper Presented in the Joint Annual Conference of IAS and ISPQS at the Maharaja Sayaji University of Baroda, November 22-24, 2001.

87. Mesolithic and Neolithic Pottery of the Vindhyas: Technological and Typological Study, Paper Presented in the Joint Annual Conference of IAS and ISPQS at the Maharaja Sayaji University of Baroda, November 22-24, 2001.

88. Origin and Developmental Process of Human Cultures in the Vindhyas: its Role in the Growth of Civilization in the Ganga Valley, 2nd International Workshop of the ALDP (Asian lake Drilling Programme) on Monsoon and Civilization, Pune, India, January 15-19, 2001.

89. Excavation at Tokwa (2000), Mirzapur, Joint annual conference of IAS and ISPQS, New Delhi, 2000.

90. Stone Age Sites in the Alakhananda Valley, National Seminar on Himalayan Glory-II, Allahabad Museum, Allahabad, December 12-14, 2000.

91. Stone Age Settlements in the Ganga Valley, National Seminar on Early Settlements in the Indo-Gangetic Basin: their Cultural and Archaeological Significance, Department of Ancient Indian history, Culture and Archaeology, D. A-V. College, Kanpur, January 29 and 30, 2000.

92. Recent Excavation at Jhusi, Joint Annual Conference of IAS and ISPQS, Deccan college, Pune, December 27-30, 1999.

93. Archaeological Sites in North India: Significance of their Tourist Approach, National Seminar on Pilgrimage Tourism, Department of History of Art, Tourism and Travel Management, Faculty of Arts, B.H.U., Varanasi, December 17-19, 1999.

94. Early Pottery of the Middle Gangetic Plain with Special Reference to Jhusi, National Seminar on Pottery in Ancient India, Bihar Puravid Parishad, Patna, March 5-6, 1999.

95. Middle Palaeolithic Culture of India: Retrospect and Prospects, National Seminar on Fifty Years of Indian Archaeology: Retrospect and Prospects, Department of Ancient History, Culture and Archeology, University of Allahabad, November 14-16, 1998.

96. Recent Excavation at Jhusi-1998, District Allahabad (Uttar Pradesh), Joint Annual Conferences of ISPQS and IAS, Department of Ancient History, Culture and Archeology, University of Allahabad, November 14-16, 1998.

97. Recent Excavations at Amilkoni, District Rewa, (Madhya Pradesh), Joint Annual Conferences of ISPQS and IAS, Department of Ancient History, Culture and Archeology, University of Allahabad, November 14-16, 1998.

98. Explorations in the Mid-Ganga Valley, Uttar Pradesh, Joint Annual Conferences of ISPQS and IAS, Department of Ancient History, Culture and Archeology, University of Allahabad, November 14-16, 1998.

99. Explorations in the Tons Valley, Joint Annual Conferences of ISPQS and IAS, Department of Ancient History, Culture and Archeology, University of Allahabad, November 14-16, 1998.

100. Development of Human Cultures in the Tons Valley, National Seminar on River Valley Cultures, Indira Gandhi Rashtriya Manav Sangrahalaya, Shamla Hills, Bhopal, September 21-24, 1998.

101. Interrelation of Cultures: Models for the Study of the Indian Archaeology, National Seminar on Models in History (Sponcered by ICHR, New Delhi), Department of Ancient Indian History, Culture and Archaeology, Banaras Hindu University, Varanasi, August 27-29, 1998.

102. Vindhya Kshetra ki Madhya Pashan Yugin Sanskriti, Vidvat Parishad Conference, Akhil Bhartiya Itihas Sanklan Yojana, Allahabad, 18-19 July 1998.

103. Prehistoric Background of Baghelkhand, National Seminar on Bhartiya Puratattva me Baghelkhand ki Bhumika, State Government Archaeological Museum, Rewa, 21 March, 1998.

104. The Problems of Indian Society: Socio-economic and Historical Perspective, Seminar on Indian Social Reality, Allahabad Museum, Allahabad, March 4-5, 1998.

105. Puratattvik Sangrhalayon ka Rashtra Nirman me Yogdan, National Perspective, Seminar on Indian Social Reality, March 4-5, 1998, Seminar on the Role of Museums in Cultural Education, Creativity and National Building, Allahabad Museum, Allahabad, 19Allahabad Museum, Allahabad.-21 December 1997.

106. Recent Explorations of Palaeolithic Sites at Kerwa Dam near Bhopal, Annual Conference of IAS and ISPQS at Department of Ancient Indian History, Culture and Archaeology, H. N. B. University, Srinagar (Garhwal), 16-18 October 1997.

107. 50 Years of Research of Mesolithic Culture in Uttar Pradesh, Seminar on 50 Years of Independence and Archaeology in U. P., U. P. State Archaeology Department, Lucknow, 25-26 September, 1997.

108. Historiography of Prehistoric Art and Culture of North India, National Seminar on Historiography of Indian Art and Culture with special reference to 50 years of independence, 16-18 August 1997, Allahabad Museum, Allahabad.

109. Prehistoric Art Motifs, National Seminar on Motifs in Indian Art, Allahabad Museum, Allahabad, 19-20 March 1997.

110. Centers of Buddhist Art and Architecture in the Middle Ganga Plain with Special reference to Kausambi, National Seminar on Buddhist Art and Architecture, 29-31 January 1997.

111. Nature and Process of Urbanization in the Middle Gangetic Plain: the Cradle of Buddha's activity, National Seminar on the Date of Buddha, Allahabad Museum, Allahabad, 12-13 April, 1996.

112. Significance of Prehistoric Researches in Allahabad District, All India Seminar on the Cultural Heritage of Allahabad, Department of Ancient History and Medieval History, Ewing Christian College, Allahabad, 28 March, 1996.

113. Bioarchaeological Studies of Northern Indian Mesolithic Culture with Special Reference to Damdama, and Micro-wear Studies of Microliths from North Indian Mesolithic Sites and Subsistence in the Mesolithic North India, National Seminar on Mesolithic in India, Department of Ancient History, Culture and Archaeology, University of Allahabad, 22-24 March, 1996.

114. Physical Anthropological Studies in the Department of Ancient History, Culture and Archaeology, University of Allahabad, National Seminar on the Allahabad School of History, Department of Ancient History, Culture and Archaeology, University of Allahabad and Group of History of Indian Sciences, Philosophy and Culture, Allahabad, 18-20 February, 1995.

115. Prehistoric Background of the Vindhyas with Special Reference to Baghelkhand, National Seminar on Regional Historiography of Baghelkhand, T. R. S. College, Rewa, 1995.

116. First Colonization of the Gangetic Plain in the Early Holocene, Paper presented in Theme 6: The Neogene and the Quaternary, Sub-theme 6C: Colonization, World Archaeological Congress-3, New Delhi, 4-11 December, 1994.

117. Environmental Change and Human Adaptation during the Quaternary Period in the Vindhyas Paper presented in Theme 6: The Neogene and the Quaternary, Sub-theme 6A: Environment and Chronology, World Archaeological Congress-3, New Delhi, 4-11 December, 1994.

118. Primary Context Sites of Palaeolithic Cultures of the Vindhyas: New Methods and Approaches, Workshop on Research Methods and Sources, Department of Ancient Indian History, Culture and Archaeology, Banaras Hindu University, Varanasi, 19 March, 1993.

119. Some Master Pieces of Kausambi School of Art of Gupta Period, National Seminar on Art and Culture of Madhya Desh, Allahabad Museum, Allahabad, 22-24 March, 1993.

120. Typology of Microlithic Industry: a Comparison of the Vindhyas and the Gangetic Plain, Annual Conference of IAS and ISPQS, Department of Ancient History and Culture, Rohilkhand University, Bareilly, 4-6 December, 1993.

121. The Subsistence Pattern in the Early Holocene in the Vindhyas and the Gangetic Plain, Annual Conference of IAS and ISPQS, Department of Studies in Ancient Indian History and Epigraphy, Karnatak University, Dharwad, 6-8 November, 1992.

122. Stone Age in the Gangetic Plain, an illustrated lecture delivered at State Museum Jhansi, 22 October, 1992.

123. Prehistoric Art in the Vindhyas, Annual Conference of IAS and ISPQS, State Archaeology and Museum, Madhya Pradesh, Bhopal, 16-18 December, 1991.

124. Neolithic Vindhyas, Symposium: Aryans- a Myth or Reality and Seminar: Art and Archaeology in the Vindhyan Region, Department of Ancient Indian History, Culture and Archaeology, A. P. S. University, Rewa, 6-8 December, 1991.

125. Exploitation of Plants in Prehistoric Vindhyas, International Conference during Celebration of Birth Centenary of Prof. Birbal Sahni, Department of Botany, University of Allahabad, 13-16

November, 1991.

126. Cultural Contact between Bundelkhand and Gangetic Plain, National Seminar on Bundelkhand, Pt. J. L. Nehru College, Banda, February 1991.

127. Environmental Change and Human Response during the Terminal Pleistocene Period in the Northern Vindhyas, International Seminar on Environmental Change and Human Response, Deccan College, Pune, December 1990.

128. Human Burial Practices at Mesolithic Damdama, Seminar on Archaeological Activities and Future Prospects in U. P., State Archaeology, Lucknow, 13-15 October, 1990.

129. Transformations of the Acheulian Culture in the Northern Vindhyas, Annual Conference of IAS and ISPQS, Nagarjuna University, Nagarjuna Nagar, Guntur, Andhra Pradesh, 22-24 December, 1989.

130. Palaeolithic Cultures of Bundelkhand, National Seminar on History, Culture and Archaeology of Bundelkhand Region, Pt. J. L.Nehru College, Banda, 5-6 December, 1989.

131. The Neolithic Culture of the Northern vindhyas and the Middle Gangetic Plain, Seminar on Archaeology of Eastern India, Bihar Puravid Parishad, Patna, 15-16 February, 1989.

132. Comments on the Papers of Participants in the Seminar on New Archaeology and India, Indian Council of Historical Research, New Delhi, 15-17 October, 1988.

133. Chalcolithic Cultures of Southern Uttar Pradesh, Annual Conference of IAS and ISPQS, Vishva Bharti, Santiniketan, 1-5 December, 1988.

134. Neolithic Cultures of Bundelkhand, National Seminar on History, Culture and Archaeology of Bundelkhand Region, Pt. J. L. Nehru College, Banda, 11-12 March, 1988.

135. Excavations at Damdama, Annual Conference of IAS and ISPQS, Dr. H. S. Gaur University, Sagar, 27-29 December, 1987.

136. Kya Ram Pragaitihasik Hain? Seminar on Ram in Art Archaeology and Literature, Bihar Puravid Parishad, Patna, 2-3 March,1987.

137. Neolithic Culture of the Vindhyas, and Archaeological and Environmental Records of the Upper Palaeolithic Culture of the Northern Vindhyas, World Archaeological Congress-1, Southampton and London, 1-7 September, 1986.

138. Mesolithic Hunter-Gatherers in the Ganga Valley, National Seminar on Anthropological Perspective of Man and Environment, Andhra University, Waltair, 1986.

139. Cord Impressed Ware: Manufacturing Technique of Neolithic Ceramic Industry, Annual

Conference of IAS and ISPQS, Guwahati, Assam, 1986.

140. Pragaitihasik Allahabad: Madhya Pashanik aur Nava Pashanik Sanskritiyan, Seminar on Regional History of Allahabad, Allahabad, 24-25 July, 1984.

141. Some New Light on the Mesolithic Burial Practices of the Ganga Valley: Evidence from Mahadaha, Pratapgarh, Uttar Pradesh, Annual Conference of IAS and ISPQS, Deccan College, Pune, 1983.

142. Ram Katha Kshetra ki Pragaitihasik Prishthabhumi, Seminar on Ram, Faizabad, 1983.

143. Some Aspects of Society of Mesolithic Culture of the Ganga Valley, in co-authorship with Prof. R. K. Varma, Seminar on Social Reality and Perception, Department of Ancient History, Culture and Archaeology, University of Allahabad, 1983.

144. Upper Palaeolithic Culture of the Middle Son Valley, Annual Conference of IAS and ISPQS, National Museum, New Delhi, 1982.

145. Some Aspects of the Mesolithic and Neolithic Societies of the Vindhyas and the Ganga Valley, Seminar on Social History and Social Theory, Department of Ancient History, Culture and Archaeology, University of Allahabad, 1982.

146. Chalcolithic Cultures of the Vindhyas and the Ganga Valley, in Co-authorship with Prof. G. R. Sharma and B. B. Misra, Indo-Soviet Joint Seminar on Copper Bronze Age Cultures of India and Central Asia: Contacts and Migrations, Department of Ancient History, Culture and Archaeology, University of Allahabad, 16-19 February, 1982.

147. Cultures Giving Base to the Neolithic Culture of the Middle Ganga Valley: Stone Age Cultures of the Ganga Valley, Annual Conference of IAS and ISPQS, Department of Anthropology, Andhra University, Waltair, 1981.

148. Upper Palaeolithic Culture of the Vindhyan Region, in co-authorship with R. K. Varma, Annual Conference of IAS and ISPQS, Department of Ancient History, Culture and Archaeology, University of Allahabad, 29th November to 3 December, 1980.

149. Mesolithic Ceramic Industries of the Vindhyas, Annual Conference of IAS and ISPQS, Department of Ancient History, Culture and Archaeology, University of Allahabad, 29th November to 3rd December, 1980.

About the Book

Madhya Pradesh ke Shailchitra Kala, Brijesh Rawat and Jagpal Singh, Research India Press, New Delhi, 2013.

PURA-PRALEKH, Ishwar Sharan Vishwakarma and Brijesh Rawat, Research India Press, New Delhi, 2022.

Bundelkhand ke Sanskriti evam Puratattva (PUROWAAK), Mustariya Ashok Kumar, B.R. Publishing Corporation, New Delhi, 2022

Other Activities

General Secretary, Mahatma Phule Foundation.

General Secretary, Akhil Bhartiya Kuruvanshi- Kuruba, Dhangar, Gadaria, Bharwad, Rabari-Mahasabha.

Writing Research Papers and popular articles in journals and magazines concerning social, cultural and economic problems of modern India.

Brijesh Rawat

List of Contributors

Abhayan G.S, Department of Archaeology, University of Kerala

Abhishek Roy, UGC Junior Research Fellow, Department of Archaeology and Ancient History, The Maharaja Sayajirao University of Baroda, Vadodara, Mobile no. 8851825777, E-mail: abhishekmsu2019@gmail.com

Abir Kumar Gorai, Curator and Consultant Maulana Azad Museum, Kolkata, E-mail: abirkumargorai@gmail.com, Mob: 9831699208

Ajit Kumar, Department of Archaeology, University of Kerala, Thiruvananthapuram, Kerala

Alexandra Figueiredo, Polytechnic Institute of Tomar, Geosciences Centre of Coimbra University; E-mail: alexfiga@ipt.pt

Ankush Dahat, Department of Archaeology, Nagpur University, Nagpur, Maharashtra.

Aswani O.K, Department of Archaeology, University of Kerala, Kariavattom Campus, Thiruvananthapuram, Kerala- 695581. E-mail: aswaniok@gmail.com

Bhanu Prakash Sharma, H. No. 9. Savita Sadan, Darpan Apartments, Near Rail Nagar, Priya Lakshmi Mill Road, Vadodara, Gujarat - 390 003 (Email: bhanu1927@gmail.com)

Brijesh Rawat, Department of History, Dr Shakuntala Misra National Rehabilitation University, Mohaan Road, Lucknow, 226017; E-mail: rawat.brijesh11gmail.com

Cláudio Monteiro, CAA Portugal ONG; E-mail: claudio.monteiro.cr@gmail.com

Deepak Kumar, Assistant Professor, Department of History, The Bhopal School of Social Sciences, Bhopal.

Fernando Augusto Coimbra, PhD, Polytechnic Institute of Tomar Geosciences Centre University of Coimbra, E-mail: coimbra.rockart@yahoo.com

Fernando Coimbra, Polytechnic Institute of Tomar, Geosciences Centre of Coimbra University; E-mail: coimbra.rockart@yahoo.com

Ishani Sinha, Department of A.I.H.C and Archaeology Deccan College Post Graduate and Research Institute, Pune. E-mail: sinhaishani3@gmail.com

J.P. Upadhyaya, Associate Professor, Department of AIHC, Ewing Christian College, Allahabad

Jagdish Parshad, Assistant Director, Haryana Academy of History and Culture, Kurukshetra, Haryana.

Jagpal Singh, Adjunct Faculty, Department of Archaeology, The University of Hebrew, Jerusalem, Israel.

K. Krishnan, Department of Archaeology and Ancient History, Faculty of Arts,The Maharaja Sayajirao University of Baroda, Vadodara, Gujarat- 390 002 (E-mail: Krishnan.msu@gmail.com)

K. Paddayya, Emeritus Professor and Former Director, Deccan College (Deemed University) Pune 411006. E-mail: k.paddayya@gmail.com

K.C. Srivastava, Independent Author, 645A/165 Janaki Vihar Colony, Prabhat Chouraha, Madion Gaon Road, Lucknow, E-mail: kcsrivastava1944@gmail.com

Martin Williams, Earth Sciences, School of Physical Sciences, University of Adelaide, Adelaide, SA 5005, Australia, E-mail: martin.williams@adelaide.edu.au

मृदुला खुराना, भूगोल विभाग, कलिंगा विश्वविद्यालय, न्यू रायसेन, झारखंड

Mohammad Nazrul Bari, Department of History School of Social and Behavioral Sciences Central University of Karnataka, Aland Road, Kadganchi, Gulbarga, Karnataka, India, 585367, Mob. 9481173687, E-mail: mail2drbari@gmail.com/albari31@rediffmail.com

R.K. Mohanty, Professor, Department of AIHC and Archaeology. Deccan College, Pune.

Rajesh S. V., Department of Archaeology, University of Kerala, Kariavattom Campus, Thiruvananthapuram, Kerala - 695 581 (Email: rajeshkeraliyan@ yahoo.co.in, abhayangs@gmail.com)

Ranjana Ray, Professor Emeritus, Formerly of Department of Anthropology, Calcutta University, Res: 49/53, Prince Gulam Md. Shah Road, Kolkata 700033 E-Mail: prof.ranjana.ray@gmail.com

Renu Shukla, Professor, Department of AIHC and Archaeology, Kanya Gurukul, Dehradun Campus, Gurukul Kangri Vishwavidyalaya, Dehradun, INDIA

Sadasiba Pradhan, Professor, Department of AIHC & Archaeology, Utkal University, Utkal, Odisa.

Schin Kumar Tiwary, Department of AIHC and Archaeology, BHU, Varanasi.

Shashi Bala Srivastava, Professor, M.M.M. PG College, Deoria, U.P., 645A/165 Janaki Vihar Colony, Prabhat Chouraha, Madion Gaon Road, Lucknow, E-mail: kcsrivastava1944@gmail.com

Shubha Majumder, Superintending Archaeologist Archaeological Survey of India. E-mail: shubha.archaeology@gmail.com

Soumyajit Das, Senior Research Fellow (UGC), Department of Anthropology, University of Calcutta, 35, Ballygunge Circular Road, Kolkata - 700019. Mob. 9432530420, E-mail: withluvbittu@gmail.com

सुनील कुमार झा, उपनिदेशक, बिहार संग्रहालय, पटना, बिहार, मो.– 9955713206, E-mail: suniljhaasi@gmail.com

Surabhi Srivastava, Assistant Professor, Department of History, Dr. Shakuntala Misra National Rehabilitation University, Lucknow, 226017

V.H. Sonawane, Retired Professor of Archaeology, Department of Archaeology and Ancient History, The Maharaja Sayajirao University of Baroda, Vadodara 390002, Gujarat.

विनोद यादव, असिस्टेंट प्रोफेसर, प्राचीन इतिहास, संस्कृति एवं पुरातत्व विभाग, राजकीय महाविद्यालय मंगरौरा, प्रतापगढ़, उत्तर प्रदेश

Vibha Rathod, Department of History, The Bhopal School of Social, Bhopal.

Vinuraj B, Assistant Archaeologist, Archaeological Survey of India, Thrissur- 680012. E-mail: vinuraj777@gmail.com

Vishwanath Verma, Professer & Head, Department of Ancient History Harish Chandra P. G. College, Varanasi- 01

Yogambar Singh Farswan, Professor, Environmental Archaeology Department of History and Archaeology, H.N. Bahuguna Garhwal University (A Central University) Srinagar (Garhwal) Uttarakhand-246174 India. E-mail: farswanys@gmail.com; farswanys@yahoo.co.in

List of Illustrations

गुरुवे नमः

विश्वनाथ वर्मा

प्रसिद्ध पुरातत्वविद्, पुरातत्व एवं परम्परा के श्रेष्ठ संवाहक आचार्य प्रवर प्रो. जगन्नाथ पाल जी के चरणों में सादर समर्पित। गंगा-यमुना एवं अदृश्य सरस्वती के पवित्र जल से सिंचित अनादि काल से भारतीय जन मानस के आस्था एवं विश्वास का केन्द्र प्रयागराज (इलाहाबाद) में विलक्षण प्रतिभा सम्पन्न प्रो. पाल जी ने इण्टरमीडियट तक की शिक्षा प्रतापगढ़ जनपद के ग्रामीण परिवेश से प्राप्त करने के बाद उच्च शिक्षा हेतु भारत के ख्याति प्राप्त इलाहाबाद विश्वविद्यालय, इलाहाबाद में 1969 ई. में स्नातक शिक्षा हेतु प्रवेश लिया एवं श्रेष्ठ गुरूजनों के सानिध्य एवं स्वयं के परिश्रम से 1970 ई. में स्नातक उपाधि अर्जित करने के बाद सन् 1972 ई. में स्नातकोत्तर उपाधि प्राप्त किया। आपको यहाँ के श्रेष्ठ विद्वान् आचार्यों के साथ अध्ययन का पूर्ण अवसर प्राप्त हुआ।

प्रो. पाल ने स्नातकोत्तर उपाधि के बाद भारतीय पुरातत्व के सम्वर्धन में महत्वपूर्ण भूमिका का निर्वाह किया। सन् 1983 ई. में प्रो. राधाकान्त वर्मा के कुशल निर्देशन में डी. फिल. की उपाधि इलाहाबाद विश्वविद्यालय, इलाहाबाद से प्राप्त किया। पुरातत्व के प्रति आप का अगाध स्नेह इसी से स्पष्ट हो जाता है कि आपने अपने विद्यार्थी जीवन में ही इलाहाबाद विश्वविद्यालय के पुरातत्व विभाग द्वारा अत्याधिक महत्वपूर्ण कोलडिहवा नामक पुरातात्विक महत्व के पुरास्थल के उत्खनन में स्व. प्रो. गोवर्धन राय शर्मा के नेतृत्व में कार्य किया एवं प्राप्त सामग्रियों के सूक्ष्म सर्वेक्षण के आधार पर तिथि निर्धारण और उसके महत्वपूर्ण अवशेषों के महत्व के निर्धारण में महत्वपूर्ण भूमिका का निर्वाह किया। इस नवपाषाणिक काल के महत्वपूर्ण पुरास्थल से हमें सबसे प्राचीनतम् खेती के साक्ष्य मिले हैं। प्राचीन इतिहास, संस्कृति एवं पुरातत्व विभाग द्वारा उत्खनित महत्वपूर्ण पुरास्थलों में कोलडिहवा, महगरा, महदहा, दमदमा, सरायनाहरराय, सिंहावल, बघोर, मैहर, झूँसी आदि अनेक पुरास्थलों का उत्खनन आपके कुशल निर्देशन में किया गया। जहाँ से अत्याधिक महत्वपूर्ण सामग्रियों को प्राप्त कर भारतीय पुरातत्व को शिखर पर पहुँचाने में आपको महती भूमिका रही है। मात्र भारत ही नहीं, अपितु विदेशों में आपके द्वारा उत्खनन कार्य को सम्पादित कराने में महत्वपूर्ण सुझाव दिया गया। साथ ही, आपके कुशल मार्ग निर्देशन में लगभग 22 शोधार्थियों ने डी.फिल. की उपाधि प्राप्त किया।

प्रो. पाल के शताधिक शोध पत्र राष्ट्रीय एवं अन्तर्राष्ट्रीय मान्य शोध पत्रिकाओं में प्रकाशित हो चुके हैं। आप द्वारा अब तक 15 से अधिक प्रकाशित पुस्तकें राष्ट्रीय एवं अन्तर्राष्ट्रीय स्तर पर प्रसिद्धि प्राप्त हैं। पुरातत्व के विविध पक्षों यथा- प्रागैतिहास एवं पुरा-इतिहास के उपकरणों, ताम्र एवं कांस्य कालीन उपकरणों पर आयोजित आयोजनों में आपने अपने महत्वपूर्ण व्याख्यान प्रस्तुत किया और साथ ही साथ, अनेकानेक शैक्षिक समितियों ने आपको सम्मानित पदों पर आमंत्रित अध्येता के रूप में नामित किया। आप 7 जून, 2010 से 6 जून, 2012 तक अध्यक्ष, प्राचीन इतिहास, संस्कृति एवं पुरातत्व विभाग, इलाहाबाद विश्वविद्यालय, इलाहाबाद, के पद पर कार्यरत रहे।

प्रो. पाल पूर्णतः सादगी के प्रतिमूर्ति अपने विद्यार्थियों के लिए सदैव चिन्तित रहे हैं और आज भी अपने विद्यार्थियों के उज्जवल भविष्य के लिए तत्पर रहते हैं। आपके आशीर्वाद से अनेकानेक विश्वविद्यालयों एवं महाविद्यालयों में आपके शिष्यों एवं विद्यार्थियों को कार्य करने का अवसर प्राप्त हुआ है। गुरू-शिष्य परम्परा का एक उहाहरण मैं स्वयं हूँ। आपके मार्गदर्शन एवं कुशल निर्देन में अनेक विद्यार्थी प्रशासनिक एवं महत्वपूर्ण पदों पर कार्यरत हैं, जो आपके श्रेष्ठ व्यक्तित्व का सबसे महत्वपूर्ण पक्ष है। आपकी धर्मपत्नी श्रीमती सुमन पाल तो गुरूमाता की साक्षात् प्रतिमूर्ति हैं, विद्यार्थियों को हमेशा ' बेटा ' कहकर उनके द्वारा किया गया सम्बोधन माता-पुत्र के सहज सम्बन्ध को प्रतिबिम्बित करता है।

वैसे तो, प्रो. पाल सर का आशीर्वाद तो मुझे बराबर मिलता रहा है और रहेगा भी। एक संस्मरण जो मैं कभी नहीं भूल सकता, वह यह है, कि जब आप अपनी पहली विदेश यात्रा पर जा रहे थे। हम जैसे कुछ शिष्यों ने आपके मना करने के बाद भी आपको इलाहाबाद स्टेशन पर बिदा करने के लिए पहुँच गये। उस समय आपने सबसे पहले यही पूछा कि प्लेटफार्म टिकट लिया है या नहीं। हम लोगों ने कहा कि लिया है। उस समय स्टेशन पर हम सभी के पूज्य स्व. प्रो. विद्याधर मिश्र, डा. बी. बी. मिश्र, डा. मानिक चन्द्र गुप्ता एवं अन्य सहयोगीगण भी उपस्थित थे। उस समय जो भावुकतापूर्ण क्षण था, वह मैं कभी नहीं भूल सकता।

प्रो. पाल सर के सम्बन्ध में एक बात और कहना चाहता हूँ कि जो आज तक मुझे विस्मित करती रही, वह यह कि, प्रो. पाल को किसी भी स्थिति में मैंने क्रोधित, विचलित अथवा असंयमित होते हुए नहीं देखा है। यदि आप उनसे मिलने जाइये तो सबसे पहले पूछते हैं कि कैसे हैं? कब आये? इत्यादि। इसके बाद बहुत कम बोलना और धीरे से बोलना आपकी असली पहचान है। मानो धैर्य, संयम आदि को बनाये रखने के लिए अनमोल ऊर्जा को प्रो. पाल सर ने लगा दिया। महाकवि भारवि का यह कथन मुझे प्रो. पाल सर के लिए उचित ही लगता है कि, 'युधिष्ठिर! उसे पराजित करना आसान नहीं जिसका मुँह कभी क्रोध में भी टेढ़ा न हुआ हो, संयम की पराकाष्ठा, इस प्रकार का व्यक्तित्व निश्चय ही अनाक्रान्त होता है।'

सर्वथा माँ भारती के चरणों में अध्ययनरत् श्रद्धेय प्रो. जगन्नाथ पाल संस्कृति एवं पुरातत्व के सम्वर्धन में संलग्न हैं। आप उदारता की प्रतिमूर्ति, कर्त्तव्यनिष्ठ, कार्यसंस्कृति के प्रबल समर्थक, ईमानदारी और सादगी को जीवन का परमलक्ष्य मानने वाले हैं। आपके आशीर्वाद से मुझे जीवनपथ प्राप्त हुआ है, ऐसे श्रेष्ठ व्यक्तित्व, मनीषी प्रो. पाल सर का सर्वथा वन्दन एवं अभिनन्दन करता हूँ। सामान्य गुरूवरेण्य के अभिनन्दनीय व्यक्तित्व एवं बहुआयामी अवदानों के प्रति नतसिर भाव से, संकल्पित मन से आपके सम्मानार्थ यह संस्मरण आपके चरणों में सादर समर्पित है और आपके स्वस्थ जीवन की कामना के साथ बारम्बार प्रणाम करता हूँ।

Prof. J.N. Pal: I know

J.P. Upadhyaya

Admired for enhancing knowledge in the field of archaeology, Prof. JN Pal was born on March 2, 1950 in a village Tina, located between Lalganj and SagraSundarpur on Pratapgarh-Raibareli road in Pratapgarh district, India. He is an archaeologist with a remarkable history of working on major projects.

Prof. Pal has a brilliant academic records and expertise in the field of Ancient History, Culture and Archaeology at University of Allahabad. Prof. Pal has been a tenured professor. In 1974, he joined the Department of Ancient History, Culture and Archaeology, University of Allahabad as a curator, and ensuingly became professor in 2003; as Head of the Department(2010-2012). He was appointed as senior professor at Allahabad State University(2016-2020).

His knowledge, competence and dedication have garnered numerous research works in the field of archaeological exploration and excavation in the Vindhyas and Ganges Valley conducted by University of Allahabad since 1974. He meticulously guides students, teachers and researchers in respect to their research works to present their results in an appealing, articulate and professional manner. Whether it is penning journal publications, writing articles or presenting his research at academic conferences across the globe. Drawing on more than 42 years of academic experience, makes him a global phenomenon for his brilliant works. Having authored 15 books and one hundred twenty five research papers, he is dedicated to encouraging holistic learning, which iscentered on Archaeology.

Prof. Pal exemplifies the academic world in the field archaeology. He has participated in the archaeological excavation and exploration expeditions in the Vindhayas and Ganga valley conducted by the Department of Ancient history, Culture and Archaeology, University of Allahabad since 1974. Some of the sites excavated by him and his team are: Koldihwa, Mahagara, Panchoh, Mahadaha, Damdama, Sihawal-1, BaghorI and Baghor IV, Medhauli, Maihar, Jhusi, Amilkoni, Tokwa, Baidha, Hetapatti, etc. The results, brought about these excavations has shed new light on the past societies in trans-Vindhayan and Ganga valley.

He serves as the member of Archaeological Society of India, Indian Society for Prehistoric and Quaternary Studies, Rock Art Society of India, Indian History and Culture Society, Indo-Pacific, Prehistoric Association, Indian Academy of Social Sciences, World Archaeological Congress and National Research Institute of Human Culture. He has also catered as joint editor of Monograph Series of Indian Archeological Society, Principal editor ICON, Journal of Archaeology and Culture, Co-Director UGC National Seminar on Farming Cultures of India(2003). He formerly served as Co-ordinator of Refresher Course, and local Secretary, National Seminar on Fifty Years of Indian Archaeology : Retrospect and Prospects, Department of Ancient History, Culture and Archaeology, University of Allahabad(1998). In 2014, he was nominated as a member of Cultural Advisory Board of Archaeology, Archaeological Survey of India, Ministry of Culture, Government of India by President of India for a period of four years.

In 1994, a Symposium "New Archaeological Discourses in Asia and Pacific" was organized by Prof. Pal in world archaeological Congress-3, New Delhi. He also served the project "Bio-archaeology of Mesolithic North India" and was awarded 'The International Collaborate Research Grant' by Wenner-Gren Foundation.

An ardent love of learning, intense zeal, high seriousness of purpose - all these combined with a broad culture and high scholarship are some of the features that distinguished Prof. Pal as an erudite personality. He excelled in his position in the archaeological field as well as in social activities. He is generous and very down to the earth. I wish he always shine like star and quench the thirst of knowledge seekers with his wisdom and knowledge, and always walk on the path of glory.

An Academic Journey

Yogambar Singh Farswan

Hon'ble Professor Jagannath Pal is well-known figure in Indian Archaeology, who is familiar in archaeology family as Dr. J.N. Pal. Professor Jagannath Pal was borne on 2nd March 1950 in a marginal and normal farmer's family in a village, Tina in Pratapgarh district of Uttar Pradesh, which is located 30 km east of district headquarter Pratapgarh on the way to Pratapgarh-Raibareli road. He has acquired his Primary Education in a Primary Pathshala near his village and Junior Education from Junior High School, Sagra Sundarpur, at a distance of one mile east of his village.

Though Professor Pal has faced so many problems to get their education but his hard work, patience and keenness made him a meritorious student, as he has passed his High School and Intermediate examination in First Division from Uttar Pradesh Education Board in 1966 and 1968 respectively. Not only has this he also passed his Graduate and Post Graduate examination in First Division in 1970 and 1972 respectively from University of Allahabad. He has also achieved the Post Graduate Diploma in Archaeology, in 1973 from School of Archaeology, Archaeological Survey of India, New Delhi again with First Division.

It is very interesting to share that Professor Pal opted special combination of subjects at High School and Intermediate level, which was three literatures (English, Hindi & Sanskrit) with Mathematics. Meanwhile, he has passed his Graduation with significant subject's combination of Ancient History, Culture and Archaeology; Sanskrit and Philosophy.

After getting Master's degree in Ancient Indian History, Culture and archaeology and Post Graduate Diploma in Archaeology, Professor Pal joined as a Curator in Kausambi Museum (Professor G.R. Sharma, Memorial Museum), Department of Ancient History, Culture and Archaeology, University of Allahabad and served there from October, 1974 to November, 1977. In December 1977 he has achieved the higher goal of his life and appointed as a Lecturer in the same department of the same University and in-between this time, he has got the highest Degree of his life (D.Phil.) in 1983 from University of Allahabad and title of his research was "Archaeology of Southern Uttar Pradesh".

Professor Pal provided his invaluable services of teaching and research from December 1977 to October 2002 as a kecturer; November 1986 to November 2003 as a Reader and December 2003 to February 2020 as a Professor in the department of Ancient History, Culture and Archaeology of Allahabad University, along with a number of administrative responsibilities such as, Head of the department, Coordinator, Refresher Course; Co-Director, UGC National Seminar; Joint Editor, Monograph Series of Indian Archaeological Society; Principal Editor, ICON: Journal of Archaeology and Culture; Supervisor for a Small Study and Research Grants; Local Secretary, National Seminar on Fifty Years of Indian Archaeology; Member of the Teachers Support Fund Committee; Member of the Board of Trusty, Student Union; Member of Executive Council; Member Scheduled Caste/ Scheduled Tribe Standing Committee; Co-ordinator of National Service Scheme; Member Academic Council; etc.

The main fields of specializations of Professor Pal are Prehistoric, Protohistoric and Historical Archaeology and during span of his academic life he has guided 22 Research Scholars for the Doctor of Philosophy (D.Phil.) Degree, who has made their contribution in strengthening the aforesaid fields of Indian Archaeology.

Based on his research work under the Project 'Bio-archaeology of the Mesolithic North India; Professor Pal was awarded the International Collaborative Research Grant by Wenner-Gren Foundation, USA and got the opportunity of Co-director in the above Joint International Project. Under this project he has visited at the Department of Anthropology, University of Oregon, Eugene, U. S. A. for Microwear analysis of microliths and spent there from April-June, 1995 and also delivered several Guest Lectures in a graduate seminars on Bio-archaeology.

Professor Pal has also gained the opportunity of Collaborator in an advanced Research Project of American Institute of Indian Studies' Prehistoric People of the Ganga Valley: Health Status and Genetic Affinities' with Prof. John R. Lukacs of Department of Anthropology, University of Oregon, Eugene, February 1992. His another achievement was Director, International Collaborative Project on Archaeo-Geological investigation in the Middle Son Valley with Dr. M. Petraglia and his team of Oxford University, during Field season 2007-08 and 2008-09.

Though Professor Pal is an archaeologist but he has also considered scientific analyses of Archaeo-zoological, Archaeo-botanical and geo-archaeological samples for their studies and collected these samples from different sites i.e. Damdama, Mahadaha, Tokwa; Mesolithic and Neolithic sites of the Belan Valleys; Pleistocene and Holocene periods of the Belan, Son and the Ganga valleys and all these analyses were carried out with Dr. Dorian Q. Fuller of Institute of Archaeology, London in 2002 and with Emma Harvey of the same Institute in September 2003; Prof. Martin Williams and Keith Royce of Department of Earth Sciences of Macqurie University, School of Earth Sciences and Quaternary Research Unit, Macquarie University, North Ryde, New South Wales, Australia; and with Prof. John

R. Lukacs of University of Oregon, Eugene, U. S. A. in 1986, 1991, 2003 respectively.

Professor Pal Participated in a number of archaeological excavations, explorations and expeditions in the Vindhyas and the Ganga valley, conducted by the Department of Ancient History, Culture and Archaeology, University of Allahabad since 1974 and excavated more than 20 important archaeological sites belonging to Paleolithic, Acheulian, Mesolithic, Neolithic, NBPW and Kushana culture from Belan, Ganga, Son, Lilji and Adwa valley of U.P. and M.P. Based on the systematic analyses of archaeological remains recovered from excavations and explorations he has published more than 15 Books and around 120 research papers in various International and National refried and reviewed Research Journals. So I can say that these are the biggest Academic Achievements of his life.

At the same time he has also reviewed some books such as, Archaeology of Southern Uttar Pradesh: Ceramic Industries of Northern Vindhyas in Man and Environment & the Eastern Anthropologies; and Human Skeletal Remains from Mahadaha: A Gangetic Mesolithic Site in American Journal of Human Biology. He has participated and presented his invaluable Research work in around 150 International and National conferences and seminars.

Professor Pal is having an active Life membership of more than 10 International and National academic societies of Archaeology, History and Culture. Keeping in view of the academic and Research work done by Professor Pal, various Government agencies involved him in their institutional boards and were nominated as member of Central Advisory Board of Archaeology, Archaeological Survey of India Ministry of Culture Govt. of India on 8th March 2014 for a period of four years.

Professor Pal has also achieved the Honours of Sectional President and President in U.P. History Congress and Indian Society for Prehistoric and Quaternary Studies respectively in 2009 and 2013.

Professor Pal has also achieved the experience of Visiting Fellow in the Department of Ancient Indian History, Culture and Archaeology, A. P. S. University, Rewa for two sessions- May 1992 and January 1989. He has delivered more than 25 Lectures as a Resource Person for Refresher Course to University and College Teachers in different Institutes.

Fortunately I first met to respected Professor Jagannath Pal sir in 1991 at State Archaeology and Museum, Madhya Pradesh, Bhopal during Annual Conference of IAS and ISPQS. In this conference I still remember that he has presented his paper on Prehistoric Art in the Vindhyas and I and my friends were very much impressed with his ideal behavior, supportive nature and knowledge of the subect. As we now he is very simple and ideal person in his life, especially with his soft spoken language, helpful nature and promoting behavior to youngsters. After having aforesaid significant academic achievements no everyone can be like Professor Pal. After 1991, I was regularly in touch with Professor Pal sir in various conferences in 1992, 1993, 1997, 1998, 1999, 2000, 2001, 2002, and 2003 at Karnatak University, Dharwad; H.N.B. University; University of Allahabad; Deccan college, Pune; New Delhi; University of Baroda; Tripunithura, Ernakulam, Kerla; HNB Garhwal University and Rohilkhand University, Bareilly respectively.

However, I have the deep interaction with Professor Pal sir during the conference of 1997 and 2003 as I was the part of the organizers in both these conferences and then I found the gravity and ideality of Professor Pal sir. In 1998 Professor Pal sir was the part of organizer of IAS conference and I again have seen his nature of tackling the various problems and issues. I have learned a lot of things from his friendly behavior and proud less nature as well the way of achieving the required knowledge of subject. Therefore, I salute such archaeologist and pray to God for Good health and long life Professor Jagannath Pal sir.

1

Rural Archaeology: A Case Study from Pamulapadu Village in Guntur District, Coastal Andhra Pradesh

K. Paddayya

Introduction

The lower or deltaic part of the Krishna basin, represented by the Krishna and Guntur districts of Andhra Pradesh located respectively on the left and right banks of the river, is one of the richest agricultural zones in the country (see map in Fig. 1). Its archaeological record is equally rich and includes famous sites such as Nagarjunakonda, Amaravati, Bhattiprolu and Jaggayyapeta. Colonel Colin Mackenzie's visit to Amaravati in 1797 marks the beginning of discovery of regular, mound-bearing ancient sites in South Asia (Paddayya 2005; Howes 2010). The area earmarked for developing new Amaravati as the capital of Andhra Pradesh forms part of the triangular tract between old Amaravati town, Guntur and Vijayawada. The tract on the right bank of the Krishna from Nagarjunakonda to Amaravati and further downstream up to its confluence in the Bay of Bengal has preserved elaborate evidence of continuous human occupation from the distant Stone Age to the medieval period.

As part of the Nagarjunakonda rescue excavations in the 1950s conducted by the Archaeological Survey of India (Subrahmanyam 1975), various localities yielding rich stone tool assemblages of the Palaeolithic and Mesolithic cultures were found in and around the valley, now turned into a huge water reservoir for irrigation by raising a dam across the Krishna (Soundara Rajan 1958). The valley has also preserved elaborate evidence of the Neolithic culture including human burials representing the beginnings of agropastoral way of life in the area (Sarkar and Misra 1972). The Yelleswaram excavations on the opposite (left) bank of the Krishna has brought to light rich evidence of the succeeding Iron Age in the form of stone circles and other megalithic tomb types (Khan 1963). This pattern of continuous prehistoric occupation is equally true of the area around the downstream site of Amaravati. In the course of excavations conducted here in the 1960s by the Archaeological Survey of India, an assemblage of Palaeolithic implements was recovered from surface around the adjacent site of Dharanikota (Sarkar and Nainar 2007:6). Neolithic celts were also picked up from surface

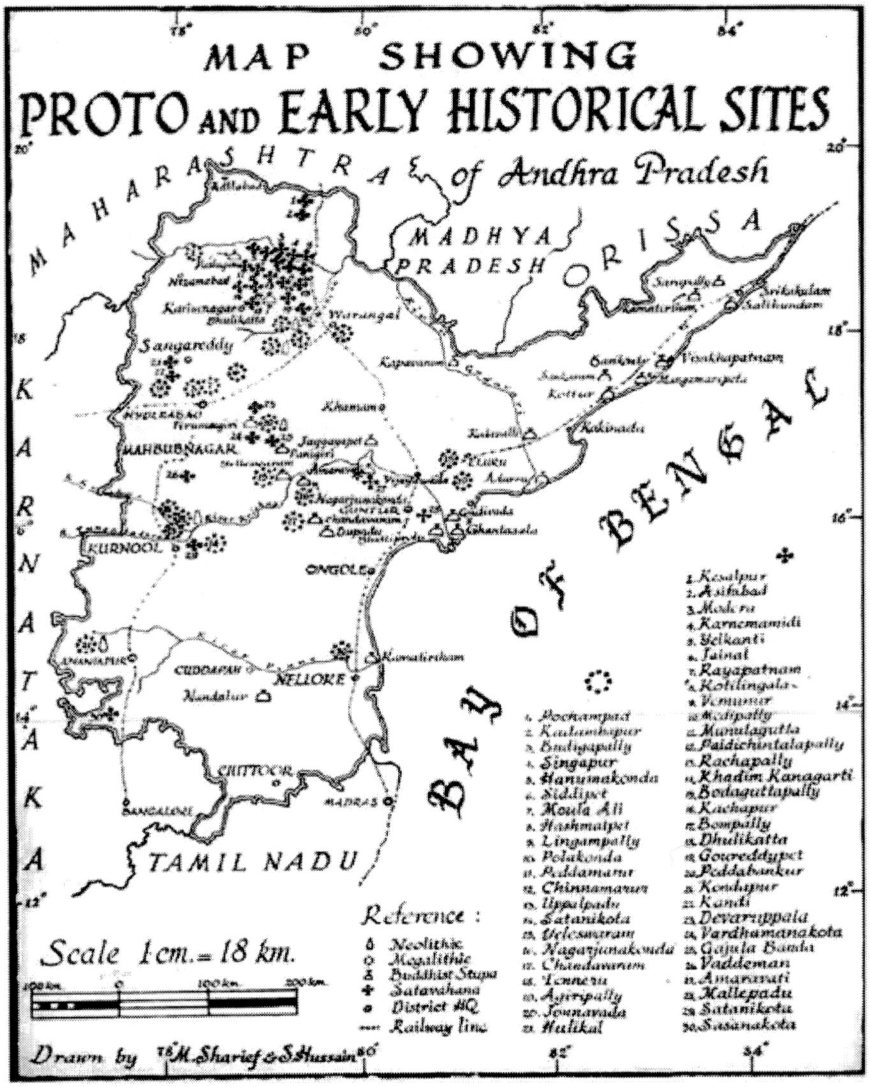

Fig. 1 : Map showing major archaeological sites of undivided Andhra Pradesh (after V.V. Krishna Sastry 1983). Asterik near Amaravati marks the location of Pamulapadu village.

from the Amaravati site area. In fact David Raju's (1990) intensive survey of the Guntur district from the Palnad zone to the coastal tract brought to light a number of Neolithic sites belonging to the later phase (1500 to 1000 B.C.) of the South Indian Neolithic Culture. In the Amaravati excavations megalithic cultural remains were recovered from levels underlying the Mahastupa and other stupas. Stone circles were found at the nearby sites of Lam, Motadaka and Nemalikallu (Sarkar and Nainar 2007: 6). Unfortunately, due to agricultural expansion of recent times these megalithic monuments have suffered large scale destruction. All these studies prove that the right bank of the Krishna from Nagarjunakonda up to the Bay of Bengal coast witnessed unbroken occupation during the prehistoric period.

Coming to the historical period, the fragmentary Asokan edict found in Amaravati excavations proves that already by the 3rd century B.C. the Mauryan influence from Magadha penetrated into the lower Krishna basin. Buddhism also began to take firm root during this period. The excavations at Vaddamanu yielded coins of a line of kings called the Sadas who ruled in the area before the Satavahanas (Sastry et al. 1990; Sarma 1992). The rule of later Satavahanas with Dhanyakataka (modern Dharanikota) as their capital marks the true beginning of the historical period. Then followed the Ikshvakus, Pallavas, Vishnukundins and Vengi Chalukyas. In the early part of the medieval period, the area was ruled by the imperial Cholas of Tanjore and then came up the Reddi kingdom of Kondavidu. The hold of the Cholas over the region in the 11th and 12th centuries was of a remote or indirect kind. Actually the Guntur area was divided among four or five local chiefdoms - the Velanati Cholas of Chandol, Kotas of Dharanikota, Durjayas of Nadendla, Haihayas of Palnad and Yadavas of Addanki. In the regime of Srikrishnadevaraya the area was freed from the Reddis of Kondavidu and made a part of the Vijayanagara empire (for details about this historical perspective, see Hanumantha Rao 2012). For some time covering the 18th century and early part of the following century, the Amaravati region was part of the Zamindari of Vasireddy Naidus. Towards the close of the 18th century Raja Venkadri Naidu shifted his capital from Chintapalli across the river to Amaravati village and developed it into a small town and as an important Saivite pilgrimage centre. Mackenzie's discovery of the Mahastupa at Amaravati in 1797 took place in the context of these town developmental activities.

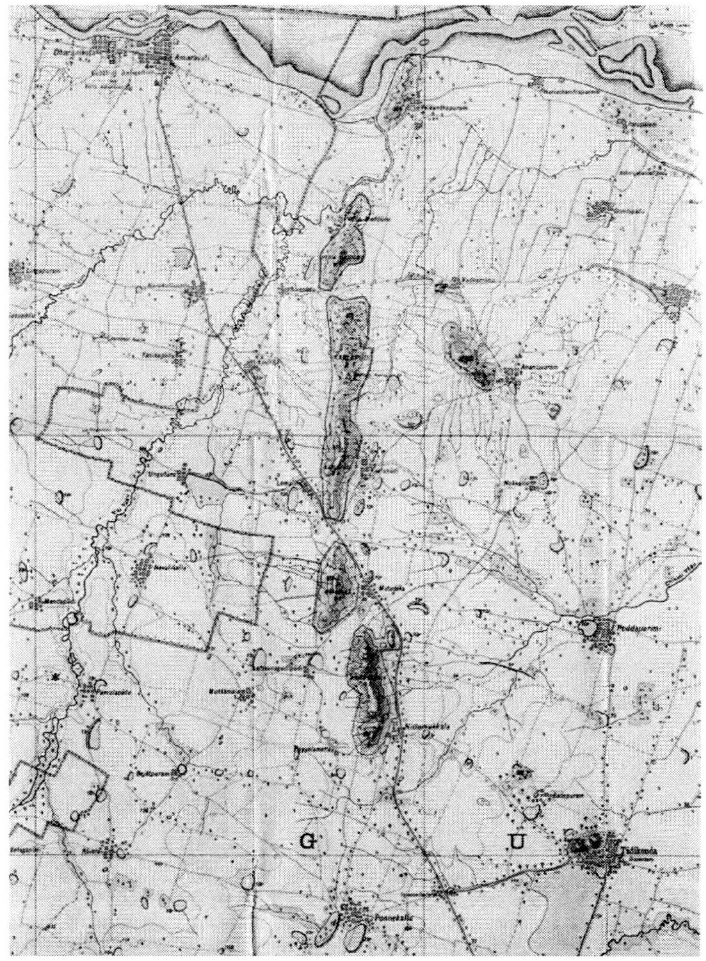

Fig. 2 : Map showing the location of Pamulapadu on the Kondaviti Vagu in relation to Amaravati. Asterik marks the ancient habitation site (after one inch-one mile toposheets 65 D/6 and 7 of Survey of India, 1931).

Briefly noted, the religious history of the region commenced in the later part of 3rd century B.C. Amaravati and Bhattiprolu rose as important seats of Buddhism, as facilitated by the monks sent by Asoka from the Magadha region. This new faith was welcomed by local people who were given to primitive animistic beliefs. Thanks to the benevolent support extended by the Satavahana and Ikshvaku dynasties, the Guntur area emerged as a major Buddhist zone and attracted visitors and pilgrims from far and wide including Sri Lanka and other neighbouring countries. While they patronized Buddhism, both Satavahana and Ikshvaku rulers professed Vedic religion and even performed Asvamedha and Rajasuya sacrifices. Thus Buddhism and Brahmanical religion flourished together in the region for more than a millennium. The Mahachaitya at Amaravati and other Buddhist places in the area continued to flourish till the 14th century. Difficulties arose in the early medieval period when a militant wave of Hinduism cropped up in the area. This is particularly true of the rise of radical Saivite sects like the Kalamukhas. It resulted in the usurpation of Buddhist centres by the Saivite sects. Even Amaravati and Nagarjunakonda were not spared. During the rule of Raja Venkadri Naidu Amaravati and Peddakakani emerged as major Saivite centres. Clashes arose between Saivite and Vaishnavite groups and these were resolved with the evolution of the concept of Harihara. It was against this background that Raja Venkadri Naidu gave patronage to Mangalagiri as a Vaishnavite centre and built the iconic Lakshmi-Narasimha temple with a tall, seven-storeyed gopuram or entrance tower.

Considering that the Nagarjunakonda-Amaravati corridor along the Krishna was intensively occupied right from the Stone Age times and that this human occupation was not only continuous but got intensified in the historical period, it is but natural that the area has preserved a rich archaeological record. Almost every village in the area has some antiquarian remains or the other - be they flaked or polished stone tools, stone circles or other tomb types, stupa or temple remains, ceramics, epigraphical records, coins, animal bones, etc. This paper documents the antiquarian remains from the village of Pamulapadu lying 12 km south of the famous Amaravati site.

Antiquarian Remains from Pamulapadu

Pamulapadu is part of Tadikonda Mandalam in the Mangalagiri Taluk of Guntur District (Fig. 2). It is located 22 km northwest of Guntur town and 10 km to the west of Tadikonda. It is close to the right bank of a minor stream called Kondaviti Vagu which rises in the Kondavidu hills and joins the Krishna at Vaikunthapuram after a northerly course of about 30 km. Pamulapadu is a small village of about 3000 people. It is essentially an agricultural settlement with a limited number of domestic animals comprising both cattle and sheep. Till the early part of post-Independence period jowar and bajra and tur were the major food crops with chillies and tobacco as the subsidiary ones. Now the area is covered by the Nagarjunasagar irrigation project and chillies and cotton have emerged as the principal crops. Pamulapadu has two localities of antiquarian interest: a) an ancient habitation site close the village and b) Siva or Mallikarjuna temple within the village.

Habitation Site

The habitation site, locally called patimattichenu in Telugu language (meaning farmland with ancient habitation deposit), lies to the west of the village and about a kilometre away from the left bank of Kondaviti Vagu. It is adjacent to the right side of the road leading to the neighbouring village of Mandepudi (Fig. 3). The ancient site is farmland now and the main part covers an area of about one hectare. The deposit has a thickness of about one metre. The elderly people in the village say that originally a mound-like formation existed at the spot which has been flattened due to ploughing and soil-quarrying activities over the last 100 to 150 years. Traces of thin habitation debris are also noted in the farmland around the main locality; this extension covers an area of two hectares and is spread on both sides of the road to Mandepudi.

The main habitation area is strewn with a fairly thick density of antiquities comprising pottery, stone tools such as hammerstones and rubberstones, and animal bones. Since the area has been used as farmland for a long period of time, the antiquities occur in a fragmented condition. Some of the villagers claim to have noticed gold coins on the site. In 2016 I made a sample collection which includes both thick and thin varieties of red ware belonging to the early historical period (Fig. 4). Cattle and sheep/goat are represented in the faunal remains (Fig. 5). The lithic collection also includes a much used polished axe of dolerite (Fig. 6). Its presence in the collection is important from two points of view. First, there are no hills around the village, much less any dolerite dykes. So it is certain that this artifact was introduced from outside. The nearest known group of granite hills with dolerite dykes is found between the villages of Nidumukkala and Karlapudi, lying 6 to 10 km to the east. It is possible that the dolerite artifact found at Pamulapadu was part of an assemblage of finished tools obtained from a production centre in these hills. Secondly, the presence of this artifact in the collection suggests the possibility that the site witnessed a regular Neolithic phase. This is not surprising because David Raju's survey has brought to light many Neolithic sites in the surrounding area. Ponnekallu, Nidumukkala and Amaravati lie within a radius of 8 to 15 km. This is probably also true of the Iron Age. No megalithic remains are seen now but the elderly people do recall the former existence of arrangements of large stone blocks at some spots around the village, which probably formed part stone circles and other grave types. The existence of Neolithic and Iron Age levels at the site needs to be ascertained through a vertical excavation in the main habitation area.

Siva Temple and Old Telugu Inscriptions

The second locality of antiquarian interest concerns the Mallikarjuna or Siva temple which has an antiquity 800 years. This temple forms part of a small complex of three shrines located in the western part of the present village, about 100 m away from the right bank of Kondaviti Vagu. The other shrines are dedicated to the deities Venugopalaswamy and Hanuman. Both belong to the modern period and were constructed about 200 years ago. The Venugopalaswamy temple has a four-storeyed gopuram marking its entrance. The old Siva temple was a simple flat-roofed structure and was constructed with large undressed granite blocks and slabs probably quarried from the low hill at Mukkamala, lying about 5 km to the east. This was a simple, squarish structure and was raised with traditional lime mortar as the cementing medium. A stone Sivalinga was the object of worship and the temple walls were plain without any sculptural representations. Due to rain water leakage from the roof this old shrine was demolished in 2016 and in its place a modern temple with a three-storeyed gopuram was constructed by the villagers. Hence no further details are available about the size and architectural features of the old Siva temple.

The focus of our interest is the stone pillar installed before the old shrine and the six inscriptions engraved on it in Old Telugu script. These inscriptions were first noticed by Robert Sewell in 1882 (Sewell 1882: 76) and later recorded fully by Epigraphy Branch of the Archaeological Survey of India and noted in its Annual Report for 1917. These are published in full in Volume 10 of South Indian Inscriptions (Texts) - Some Telugu Inscriptions from Andhra Pradesh (Ramaiah Pantulu 1986: Nos. 98, 180-183, 185, pp. 45, 91-3). The stone pillar is of dark-coloured dolerite and measures 60 inches

(1.52 m) in height. It is square-bodied with each side measuring 15 inches (38 cm) across. Like the dolerite axe mentioned above, the original block of this pillar was brought from some other place and the flat sides were shaped well and then polished to receive the engraved letters on all four sides. In the published report of the ASI the pillar is called Nandi-Naga pillar, because a small Nandi or bull-figure (about 10 cm in height) is carved on top of the pillar from parent rock itself and one of the flat sides has in the upper part a low relief figure of multi-hooded serpent with curled up body (Figs. 7 and 8).

The inscriptions in Old Telugu script cover all four sides of the stone pillar and all except No. 98 are dated Saka era 1094 (1172 A.D.) (Figs.9 to 10). Thus the old Mallikarjuna temple and with it the present Pamulapadu village can be said to have an antiquity of more than 800 years. All these inscriptions are donative in nature and record individual gifts of land and sheep for temple maintenance and keeping a perpetual lamp in it. Inscription No. 98 (No. 119 of Annual Report 1917) records a gift made to the temple by Velanadu Choda king Rajendra Choda and some others of a piece of land located in the Kondapadumatti locality on the northern side of the village. Inscription No. 180 (No. 120 of Annual Report 1917) records that one Kondana, grandson of Kondaparaddi of Pamulapadu, gave away in the name of his father Bhimaraddi and mother 55 sheep to Prola, son of Kotyaboya, for maintaining a perpetual lamp in the temple. Inscription No. 181 (No. 121 of Annual Report 1917) mentions that one Bolliraddi gifted 55 sheep to Prola, sone of Manyaboya, for keeping a perpetual lamp. Inscription No. 182 (No. 122 of Annual Report 1917) says that one Kommana also gave away in memory of his parents 55 sheep to Vema, son of Manuboya, for keeping a perpectual lamp. Inscription No. 183 (No. 123 of Annual Report 1917) mentions that one Vemi Nayaka donated in the name of his father Yerramaraddi 55 sheep to Gade, son of Somaboya, on the occasion of northern solstice for keeping a perpetual lamp in the temple. Inscription No. 185 (No. 124 of Annual Report 1917) states that one Kommana gave away in the names of his grandfather Suraparaddi and father Getiraddi 55 sheep to Mare, son of Kotyaboya, for purposes of keeping a perpetual lamp in the temple.

The scope of these epigraphical records is admittedly local and confined to village level religious activity, but these do at the same time give us some glimpses of the socio-religious conditions prevailing in the area in the early medieval period (11th and 12th centuries A.D.) marking the rule of the Telugu or Velanadu Choda kings. First, the erection of this temple dedicated to Mallikarjuna or Siva indicates the declining hold of Buddhism in the area and the revival of Hindu faith. Under the banner of the militant Kalamukhas Saivism began to emerge in a definite way in the area. The construction of Saiva temples at Mandapadu, Siripuran, Kakani, Amaravati and many other places in the surrounding area proves that the revival of Hindu faith assumed the form of a widespread movement. Simultaneously, under the patronage of the Haihayas of Palnad, Vaishnavism was also being revived, sometimes leading to clashes between the two Hindu sects. The concept of Harihara finally bridged the conflict between the two sects.

Secondly, Pamulapadu inscriptions give us some clues about the emerging structure of the society in the area. As the suffix suggests, Vemi Nayaka was probably a person of eminence who was endowed with some authority and provided leadership to the whole village settlement. The other donors too - Kondana, Bolliraddi and Kommana - would have been persons of some importance and they probably represented the dominant pastoral and agricultural classes in the village. It is significant that the Velanadu Choda chief Rajendra Chola himself was one of the donors and gifted land for the temple.

Thirdly, it is interesting to note that in five cases donations of sheep were given to members of the Boya community which was obviously an important component of the village society. Boyas, or Bedars as they are called in Karnataka, were originally a major hunting-gathering community spread over large parts of Andhra Pradesh and Karnataka. In the medieval period they emerged as a series of localized ruling principalities or Samsthanas which closely allied themselves with the Viayanagara emperors in military affairs. Pamulapadu inscriptions clearly show that certain Boya individuals were entrusted with temple worship and other priestly activities. This is yet another instance of the well-known practice noticed in the country of the absorption of non-Hindu, indigenous groups into the mainstream Hindu society with its origins in upper India. In this connection we may remind ourselves that even till today it is a Golla (representing the cowherd community) who daily both opens and closes the main door of Lord Venkateswara temple at Tirupati.

Lastly, land donations for temple worship were common in the country in the historical period and sometimes whole villages were granted to the Brahmins as Agraharas. The striking thing about Pamulapadu inscriptions concerns donations of sheep for temple maintenance. This is a clear indication that in the beginning part of the second millennium pastoralism was a dominant component of village economy and occupied a higher place in relation to agricultural practices. With increasing colonization of forest tracts and developments in tillage techniques and equipment, agriculture slowly gained ascendancy in the subsequent centuries. As mentioned earlier, the village economy at present is overwhelmingly agricultural with an emphasis on commercial crops like cotton and chillies. Gone are the vast tracts of pasture around the village and morning sights of herds of cattle and flocks of sheep/goats being led out from the village for grazing.

Conclusion

I would like to conclude by reiterating my opening statement that the lower part of the Krishna basin is tremendously rich in archaeological sites ranging in age from the Stone Age to the medieval period. It is true that major sites like Amaravati, Nagarjunakonda, Bhattiprolu and Jaggayyapeta have been subjected to detailed field investigations. But the archaeological record of the area is much more comprehensive and finds expression in some form or other at almost every village in the area. This is in fact true of most parts of the country. The village of Pamulapadu is just one example. Unfortunately, no systematic village-to-village survey of the type done by Julia Shaw (2007) in the Sanchi area of Madhya Pradesh has been undertaken in the Nagarjunakonda-Amaravati tract so far.

Considering that the area close to ancient Amaravati has now been selected for development as the capital for the recently bifurcated state of Andhra Pradesh and also in view of the increasing number of developmental activities taking place on the landscape, it is necessary to initiate planned intensive surveys and fully document the antiquarian remains before these suffer total destruction (Paddayya 2018).

Acknowledgements

My nephews Shri Katragadda Peddakoteswara Rao and Shri Katragadda Chinnakoteswara Rao have helped me in procuring photographs of the ancient habitation site, temples and inscriptions at Pamulapadu and in the collection of antiquities from the ancient site. My daughters Katragadda Janaki and Vijayalakshmi prepared photographs of the Nandi-Naga pillar. My cousin sister Smt. Vattikonda Venkataramamna has helped in sorting out the antiquities from the ancient site. Shri N.S.R. Anjaneyulu, Sarpanch, and elderly persons of the village have provided helpful information about the ancient site and temples. I am also glad to acknowledge the help rendered by by Dr. E. Sivanagi Reddy, formerly of the A.P. Government Department of Archaeology and Museums, in locating the published source of Pamulapadu inscriptions. Dr. Satish Naik, Deccan College, Pune, kindly organized the illustrations printed here and also assisted me in the finalization of the text.

References

David Raju, B, 1990, The Settlement and Subsistence Pattern of the Neolithic Culture of the Lower Krishna Valley, *Man and Environment 15 (2).*

Hanumantha Rao, B.S.L., 2012, *Guntur through Ages, Guntur: Tripura Sundari.*

Howes, Jennifer, 2010, *Illustrating India: The Early Colonial Investigations of Colin Mackenzie,* New Delhi: Oxford University Press.

Krishna Sastry, V.V., 1983, *The Pre and Early Historical Cultures of Andhra Pradesh,* Hyderabad: Government of Andhra Pradesh.

Paddayya, K, 2005, Colonel Colin Mackenzie and the Discovery of the Amaravati Site, *Deccan Studies 3(1).*

Paddayya, K, 2018, Issues in Archaeological Heritage Management in Andhra Pradesh: Polavaram Project and Capital Region Development, A Special Paper published by Department of Archaeology and Museums, Government of Andhra Pradesh, Vijayawada.

Ramayya Pantulu, J., 1986, *South Indian Inscriptions (Texts), Volume X - Some Telugu Inscriptions from Andhra Pradesh,* Mysore: Epigraphy Branch, Archaeological Survey of India, First published in 1948 by Manager of Publications, New Delhi, and printed at Ananda Press, Madras.

Sarkar, H. and B.N. Misra, 1972, *Nagarjunakonda.* New Delhi: Archaeological Survey of India.

Sarkar, H. and S.P. Nayanar, 2007, *Amaravati,* New Delhi: Archaeological Survey of India.

Shaw, Julia. 2007, *Buddhist Landscapes in Central India: Sanchi Hill and Archaeology of Religious and Social Changes, c. Third Century B.C. to Fifth Century A.D.,* London: The British Association for South Asian Studies.

Sastri, T.V.G. et al. 1990, *Vaddamanu Excavations (1981-1983),* Hyderabad: Birla Institute of Archaeological Studies.

Sewell, R., 1882, *Lists of Antiquarian Remains of the Presidency of Madras, Volume 1,* Madras: Archaeological Survey of India.

Sarma, I.K., 1992, *Vaddamanu Excavations,* Hyderabad: Government of Andhra Pradesh.

Soundara Rajan, K.V., 1958, Studies in the Stones Age of Nagarjunakonda and its Neighbourhood, *Ancient India 14.*

Subrahmanyam, B. and E. Sivanagi Reddy, 2012, *Buddhist Archaeology in Andhra Pradesh,* Hyderabad: Department of Archaeology and Museums, Government of Andhra Pradesh.

Subrahmanyam, R., 1975, *Nagarjunakonda I - (1954-1960),* New Delhi: Archaeological Survey of India.

Waheed Khan, A., 1963, *A Monograph on Yelleswaram Excavations,* Hyderabad: Government of Andhra Pradesh.

2

Importance of Advanced Scientific and Environmental Archaeological Analyses in Archaeology : A Review

Yogambar Singh Farswan

Introduction and review of literature

The title of my research paper is "Importance of Scientific and Environmental Archaeological Analyses in Archaeology: A Review", but I realized that before going to the main theme of the paper it is prime important to describe the concept, definition as well as meaning of environmental Archaeology, and how environmental archaeology can be useful in understanding or reconstructing the history of ancient settlement or occupants?. Therefore, the first question of the general peoples or a lay man will be what is environmental archaeology? For the better understanding, it is also necessary to know the basics or elements of environmental archaeology. A number of investigations have already proved that these elements have positive correlations with environmental science. So such type of correlations has also clarified that this field of archaeology (Environmental Archaeology) has been emerged as the basic fundamentals of Environmental Sciences, and at this point it is also important to know the comprehensive meaning of environmental science. Bintliff et al. (1988) reported that the usual emphasis in environmental archaeological research was towards reconstruction of palaeoenvironments with former diets and economies also being proposed from the study of seeds, bones and pollen. According to their studies the results of environmental research were often presented in separate chapters, or worse still in appendices to excavation reports. They have also realised that the environmental analysis was perceived as being separate from the principal archaeological objectives in excavations. But with the development of advanced scientific techniques and their application ultimately bounded archaeologists to carry environmental archaeological study along with the main principle of archaeology and a number of archaeologists carried out meaningful researches worldwide in this regard.

It is described that Environmental Science is the science that explores environmental evolution law in the global scope, reveals the relationship between human activities and natural ecology, and explores the effects of environmental changes on human survival, and researches the technical measures and management measures for the comprehensive prevention and control of regional environmental pollution (Ye Yincan *et al.* 2017). In general sense it is also defined as, the study of the effects of natural and unnatural processes, and interactions of the physical components of the planet on the environment; however, in broad way Environmental Science is defined as the interdisciplinary field which focused on ecology, geology, meteorology, biology, chemistry, engineering, and physics, to study environmental problems and human impacts on the environment. Under environmental science we study about the different activities takes place in the universe at present scenario.

Meanwhile, it is also evident that environmental science is a quantitative discipline with both applied and theoretical aspects and has been influential in informing the policies of governments around the world. Environmental science is considered separate from environmental studies, which emphasizes the human relationship with the environment and the social and political dimensions thereof. For example, whereas a researcher in environmental studies might focus on the economic and political dimensions of international climate-change protocols, an environmental scientist would seek to understand climate, change by quantifying its effects with models and evaluating means of mitigation. Though the study of the environment is as old as any human endeavour, the modern field of environmental science developed from the growing public awareness and concern about environmental problems in the 1960s and 70s. The published books such as, Rachel Carson's *Silent Spring* (1962) and Paul R. Ehrlich's *"The Population Bomb (1968)"*, together with nuclear proliferation and growing concerns over the anthropogenic release of toxins and chemicals, raised awareness about the need to study the effects of human actions on the environment.

In the summary of articles Archaeology in the 1960s; O'Connor (2019) described that, the environment was seen as having a "passive" interaction with humans. With the inclusion of Darwinism and ecological principles, however, this paradigm began to shift. Prominent theories and principles of the time (oasis theory, catastrophism, and *longue duree*) emphasized this philosophy. Catastrophism, for instance, discussed how catastrophes like natural disaster could be the determining factor in a society's survival (Evans 2003). The environment could have social, political, and economic impacts on human communities. It became more important for researchers to look at the direct influence the environment could have on a society. This gave rise to middle range theory and the major questions asked by environmental archaeology in the 20th and 21st centuries. Research has since led environmental archaeology to two major conclusions: humanity originated in Africa and agriculture originated in south-west Asia. Another important shift in thinking is within the field centred on the notion of cost-affectivity. Before, archaeologists thought that humans usually acted to maximize their use of resources, but have since come to believe that this is not the case. Subsequent theories/principles include sociality and agency and the focus on relationships between archaeological sites (Evans 2003), Government research audits and the 'commercialisation' of environmental archaeology (Elizabeth 2019) have also shaped the sub-discipline in more recent times (Howard 2019).

The emerging field of environmental science took on the task of quantifying the effects of disasters such as the 1979, three Mile Island accident or the impact of atmospheric sulphur dioxide and other emissions on acid rain. Environmental scientists analyze a wide variety of environmental problems and potential solutions, including alternative energy systems, pollution control, and natural resource management, and may be employed by government, industry, Universities, or non-profit organizations.

Karl W. Butzer (1934-2016) has been the notable pioneer of Environmental Archaeology, who was a German borne American Geographer, ecologist and archaeologist. He regularly offered a course on Pleistocene environments including Geoarchaeology at the University of Wisconsin, USA (1960-1966) and he taught courses like, physical geography, geomorphology and environmental archaeology at the University of Chicago (1966-1984). He has made a strong case for ecological approach to archaeology (1982) and discussed varying ecological relationships at different spatial and temporal scales (Bintliff, 1988). Bintliff (1988) edited a book *"Conceptual Issues in Environmental Archaeology"* in this book various aspects of environmental archaeology has been explained through more than 22 research papers. In this book articles are categorized in three main sections which includes; *1. Conceptual Issues at the site and Microregion Scale, 2.From Micro to Macro Region and 3. Conceptual Issues Associated with Environmental and Population Change.*

However, Louis Leakey also contributed to a vast amount of research in this field. Leakey and his wife Mary Leakey are most known for their work in on human origins in Africa. Louis Binford developed the middle range theory. Under this theory, researchers study the relationship between humans and the environment, which can be depicted in models. Eric Higgs researched the development of agriculture in Asia and the method of "site catchment analysis", which looks at the exploitation of land based on the land's potential (Evans 2003).

Keeping in view of the studies carried out in the field of environmental sciences, archaeologists also applied its reliability in reconstructing the history of ancient settlement. To know the reliability of this field. it is also important to be familiar about the actual meaning/definition of this branch of archaeology, therefore various researchers and scientists defined it in different ways.

Shackley (1981) described a detailed approach of this field through the book *"Environmental Archaeology"*, in this book he has provided an excellent account of *Sediments & Soils; Microorganisms; Ferns & Mosses; Pollen Analysis; Wood & Charcoal; Seeds Fruits & Nuts; Molluscs & Insects; Parasites & Animal Bones; Fish Remains & Marine Mammals; and Birds. He has defined this branch that "Environmental archaeology is an integral part of archaeological science with Archaeologists acting as co-ordinators for the products of a large number of different disciplines".*

Albarella 2001; Bintliff et al. 1988; Branch et al. 2005; Butzer 1971, 1982; Dimbleby 1965, Evans 1978, 2003; Evans and O'Connor 2001; Luff and Rowley-Conwy 1994; O'Connor 1998; Shackley, 1981; Wilkinson and Stevens, 2003 have reported that *"Environmental archaeology is an eclectic field directed toward understanding the ecology of human communities".*

According to Elizabeth J. Reitz, Lee A. Newsom, Sylvia J. Scudder, and C. Margaret Scarry (1998) *"Environmental researchers apply information and techniques from the earth and biological sciences to study relationships among peoples and their environments using organic and inorganic evidence from archaeological sites".*

It is also mentioned in the broacher of Florida History Museum (2017) that the primary focus of the Environmental Archaeology Program is research into the ancient relationship between people and their environments, including all aspects of that relationship, from the biotic to the abiotic, and from the physical to the symbolic. They are basically carrying out research work seeking to reconstruct ancient environments associated with archaeological sites and the use of plants, animals, and landscapes by the people who once inhabited these sites and main aim of their study is to see the impact of people on the world around them during ancient time and defined it as, *"Environmental archaeology is the interdisciplinary study of past human interactions with the natural world - a world that encompasses plants, animals, and landscapes".*

It has been reported by O'Connor (2019) that environmental archaeology is a sub-field of archaeology which emerged in 1970s and this field represents an archaeological-palaeoecological approach to studying the palaeoenvironment through the methods of human palaeoecology. Reconstructing past environments and past peoples' relationships and interactions with the landscapes they inhabited provides archaeologists with insights into the origin and evolution of anthropogenic environments, and prehistoric adaptations and economic practices (Wilkinson 2003 & Branch 2014). Based on these assumptions environmental archaeology was defined as *"The science of reconstructing the relationships between past societies and the environments they lived in".*

After going through all the relevant aspects of archaeology as well as studies carried so far in the field of environmental archaeology by different archaeologists/scientists, it is evident that this discipline of archaeology is basically deals with the interaction of ancient human to their environment, for their survival, therefore, in normal sense the environmental archaeology is defined as; *"the study of relationship in between ancient human and their existed environment is termed as environmental archaeology, and for studying such study various elements of environmental archaeology play their significant role".* Therefore, these elements must be considered in the investigation of environmental archaeology.

It is clarified through the history obtained from the Environmental archaeology programme of Florida Museum (2017) that environmental archaeology has emerged as a distinct discipline in the course of the last fifty years, however, at present it is grown rapidly in significance and established a major component of the excavation projects. Evans (1981) in his book *"Introduction to Environmental Archaeology"* described that the objective of the environmental archaeology not to merely learn about the changes in the palaeoenvironment, but to find out how people of the past adapt to the surrounding natural environment, how they obtained various resources from the natural environment and how they altered the natural environment.

The literarily data on various aspects of environmental archaeology includes the studies carried out by, Rapp (1930), Evans (1978), Birks and Birks (1980), Evans (1981), Butzer (1982), Keeley (1984), Griffen (1988: 115-108), Paine (1988: 1648-1654), Lawton and Warren (1988: 242-245), Thomas (1989: 55-73), Boyd (1990: 63-79), Vincent (1990), Evans (1991), Kiister (1991: 17-26), Harris and Thomas (1991), Jones (1992: 133-142), Bell (1992: 21-35), Bell and Boardman (1992), Colinvaux (1993), O'Connor (1993: 155-162), Goudie (1993: 1-168), Foster and Smout (1994), Lyman (1995: 369-424), Preece (1995), Reitz et al. (1996), Simmons (1997), Brown (1997), O'Connor (1998: 1-106) Grayson (2001), Wilkinson, (2003), Evans (2003), Van Der Veen (2007: 968-990), Butzer (2012), Branch (2014), Natural History Museum Florida (2017), Ye Yincan *et al.* (2017), O'Connor (2019), Pearson (2019), Howard (2019), Richer *et al.* (2019) etc.

Not only this various studies on phosphate, major & trace element analysis, estimation of isotopic ratios of carbon, nitrogen, oxygen, strontium etc. in archaeological soil and bones has also been carried out by different researchers in various parts of world including India, some of these are; Ambrose (1987: 87-107), Ambrose et.al (1989: 407-422), Antoine et al. (1988: 101-106), Aufderheide (1989: 237-260), Badam (1991: 22-41), Bintliff *et al.* (1990: 159-172), Borgognini (1989: 283-320), Brown (1973), Burton and Price (1990), Burton and Price (1991), Byrne and Paris (1987), Chisholm et al. (1982: 1131-1132), Conway (1983: 117-128), Currey (1984), Davies et. al (1988: 391-398), Deotare (1990: 61-62), Dietz (1957: 405-409), Ezzo (1991), Ezzo (1994: 1-34), Farswan and Nautiyal (1997a: 251-258), Farswan and Nautiyal (1997b: 227-239), Farswan *et al.* (2001: 223-232), Farswan and Price (2002: 1130), Farswan (2002:1130; 2003: 1117-1120; 2007: 53-68; 2008: 1310-1321; 2012a: 305-309; 2013a: 104-115), Farswan and Jaibir (2005: 492-499), Farswan and Jaibir (2009: 156-164), Farswan and Pharswan (2009: 25-43; 2013: 1279-1286; 2015: 75-81; 2019: 20-27), Farswan and Singh (2012: 305-309), Farswan *et al.* (2014: 129-134; 2015: 115-122), Singh and Farswan (2014: 196-206), Farswan and Singh (2015: 15-22), Francalacci (1989: 109-124), Gilbert (1985: 339-385), Gilbert *et al.* (1994: 173-185), Hare (1980: 208-210), Hegde and Pande (1972: 30-35), Heidenreich and Navratil (1973: 25-32), Heidenreich and Konard (1973: 33-62); Heidenreich *et al.* (1971: 179-237), Iyer (1971: 107), Iyer *et al.* (1973: 406-418), Joshi et al. (1978: 72-73), Joshi and Deotare (1982: 195-202), Katzenberg and Schwarcz (1984: 177), Khanduri *et al.* (1998-99: 13-28), Klepinger (1990: 513-517), Konard *et al.* (1983: 13-28), Lambert and Weydert-Homeyer (1993: 279-294), Lavy (1980: 113-123), Morgan and Schoeninger (1989: 276), Nautiyal *et al.* (1993: 115-127), Nautiyal *et al.* (1992: 41-50, 1995: 139-140), Parker and Toots (1980: 197-207), Parsons *et al.* (1962: 491-496), Pate (1994: 161-209), Pharswan and Farswan (2011: 43-48; 2012: 121-126), Price *et al.* (1985 a: 419-447; 1985b: 419-442), Provan (1971: 47-50), Proudfoot (1976: 93-113), Robinson (1963: 385-416), Rottlander (1976: 83-88), Runia (1987a: 234), Schoeninger (198: 137-91; 1989: 78-99), Schoeninger *et al.* (1983: 1381-1383), Schutkowski and Herrmann (1999: 675-685), Schwarcz *et al.* (1985: 187-206), Sealy and Van Der Merwe (1986: 135-150), Sillen and Kavanaugh (1982), Sillen (1988: 49-60), Singh and Farswan (2015: 131-139), Tieszen *et al.* (1979: 337-350), Toots and Voorheis (1965: 854-855), Van Der Merwe (1989: 105-125; 1991: 247-

264), Walker and De Niro (1986: 51-61), Woods (1984: 67-77) etc.

These studies revealed that we can get meaningful information from any archaeological site in relation to the cultures inhabited at that site during ancient periods (i.e. palaeo environment, palaeodiet, palaeo-climatic conditions, fauna, flora, developmental processes, process of domestication of plants and animals, development of technology etc.). Though, a number of studies on morphological analysis of faunal remains recovered from various archaeological site of India has already been carried out by various workers and some latest work among are done by Abhayan (2016); Deshpande et al. (2005-2006: 248-253), Driesch (1976), Haraniya *et al.* (2016: 482-502), Joglekar (2000-2001), Joglekar (2007-2008: 309-321), Joglekar *et al.* (2008: 51-59), Joglekar (2010-2012: 227-277), Joglekar (2015), Joglekar et.al (2009-2010: 43-69), Joglekar *et al.* (2010-2011: 35-44), Joglekar *et al.* (1994: 17-20), Pawankar and Thomas (2001: 109-126), Prummel and Frisch (1986: 567-577), Schmid (1972), Singh and Singh (2004),Tripathi and Upadhyay (2006-2007: 121-129), Singh *et al.* (2013: 32-54), Mishra *et al.* (1999), Joglekar *et al.* (2017: 102-118).

An advanced study has also carried out by Harney *et al.* (2019: 1-10) on ancient DNA in skeletons of Roopkund Lake, Uttarakhand and revealed from Mediterranean migrants in India. It is also clarified that a lot of studies on archaeological faunal remains and soils has been done by Farswan & Pharswan; and Farswan *et al.*, during last two decades; a brief results of some of them are described in next pages. But a lot of studies have to be carried out yet in the context of Indian Archaeology, especially in different sub disciplines of environmental archaeology. Therefore, keeping view of the same I am presenting this paper for the circulation of researchers as well as students of history, archaeology and anthropology as well, so that much-more studies in this branch may be carried out by various researchers.

Scope of Environmental and Scientific Archaeology

For considering any type of study under the discipline Environmental archaeology, it is also necessary that we should have a general knowledge of various subfields as well as elements of this branch, and these are described below. In detail:-

Subfields of Environmental archaeology

Traditionally Environmental archaeology is divided into three main subfields such as:-

1. Zooarchaeology (Archaeozoology)
2. Archaeobotany (Palaeobotany)
3. Geoarchaeology

Zooarchaeology (Archaeozoology)

This branch is also known as Archaeozoology or Palaeo-zoology or palaeontoarchaeology or osteoarchaeology. Under this branch, generally we study the faunal or animal remains, both vertebrate and invertebrate, recovered from various archaeological sites. However, the main techniques in analyses of faunal remains are morphological analysis and based on this analysis we can describe about various animal species inhabited by ancient peoples during different cultural periods of past occupation. Meanwhile, morphological analysis also revealed a quantitative number of different animal species in various cultural phases, as well as information about the number of domestic and wild species of animals. After morphological analysis, Chemical analysis and estimation of isotopic ratios are also carried out in faunal and human remains of different cultural periods. These analyses are helpful in providing the information about palaeodiet and palaeoclimatic conditions of the site. These studies also helpful in providing information for understanding the past life system, human diets, changed landscapes, management of animals, impact of human exploitation on other animal populations, and other interactions between animals and humans. Animal remains can provide evidence of predation by humans (or vice versa) or domestication. Despite revealing the specific relationships between animals and humans, discovery of animal bones, hides, or DNA in a certain area can describe the location's past landscape or climate.

Archaeobotany (Palaeobotany)

This branch is also known as palaeobotany and under this branch we generally study or interpret the plant or floral remains that are preserved at archaeological sites including macro remains such as wood, seeds, nuts, etc. Because these are fragile, they are only preserved in special conditions (desiccated, charred, frozen, waterlogged, or preserved as impressions in baked clay or daub). Archaeobotanists also study micro remains such as pollen, phytoliths, and spores, often found in the soils, as residues in pottery vessels, or in the sediments of stable water bodies around archaeological sites. By determining the uses of plants in historical contexts, researchers can reconstruct the diets of past humans, as well as determine their subsistence strategies and plant economy. Analysis of specimen like wood charcoal, for example, can reveal the source of fuel or construction for a society. Archaeobotanists also often study seed and fruit remains, along with pollen and starch. Plants can be preserved in a variety of ways, but the most common are carbonization, water logging, mineralization, and desiccation. A field within Archaeobotany is ethno-botany, which looks more specifically at the relationship between plants and humans, and the cultural impacts plants have had and continue to have on human societies.

Geoarchaeology

Geoarchaeology is the study of landscape and of geological processes or we can say that the study of geological processes and their relationship to the archaeological record. It looks at environments within the human timeline to determine how past societies may have influenced or been influenced by the environment. Sediment and soil are often studied because this is where the majority of artifacts are found, but also because natural processes and human behaviour can alter the soil and reveal its history. Apart from visual observation, computer programming and satellite imaging are often employed to reconstruct past landscapes or architecture

Some of the other related important fields are:-

Landscape archaeology

Landscape archaeology is the study of the ways in which people in the past constructed and used the environment around them. Landscape archaeology is inherently multidisciplinary in its approach to the study of culture, and is used by pre-historical, classic, and historic archaeologists. The key feature that distinguishes landscape archaeology from other archaeological approaches to sites is that there is an explicit emphasis on the sites' relationships between material culture, human alteration of land/cultural modifications to landscape, and the natural environment. The study of landscape archaeology (also sometimes referred to as the archaeology of the cultural landscape) has evolved to include how landscapes were used to create and reinforce social inequality and to announce one's social status to the community at large.

Analysis of landscapes

Many methods used to analyze archaeological sites are relevant to the analysis of landscapes. The archaeology of landscapes incorporates multiple research methods into its analysis in order to ensure that multiple sources of information are gathered; allowing for a sound interpretation of the site in question. These methods are -

1. Viewshed Analysis.	2. Archaeological Geophysics or Geophysical Survey.
3. Geographic Information Systems (GIS).	4. Global Positioning System (GPS)
5. Ground Penetrating Radar (GPR).	6. Remote Sensing
7. Electrical resistance meters	8. Lidar (Light Radar)
9. Electromagnetic (EM) conductivity	10. Magnetometers
11. Metal Detectors	13. Total station
13. Archaeological Excavation	14. Soil sampling
15. Pollen or Floral analyses	16. Faunal analysis
17. Data collection	18. Data processing and imaging
19. Archival Data Analysis	20. Data processing and imaging
21. Climatology	22. Archival data (including maps and census data)

Viewshed Analysis

Viewshed Analysis has aided in the archaeologists ability to study behavioural relationships between humans, their landscape, and material culture, in order to study migration, settlement patterns, and agency. Viewshed analysis also provides means with which archaeologists can recreate through an ability to recreate the line of sights possible from one point on a landscape and to situate a person within a defined landscape.

Archaeological Geophysics or Geophysical Survey

In archaeology, geophysical survey is ground-based physical sensing techniques used for archaeological imaging or mapping. Remote sensing and marine surveys are also used in archaeology, but are generally considered separate disciplines. Other terms, such as "geophysical prospection" and "archaeological geophysics" are generally synonymous. Geophysical methods used in archaeology are largely adapted from those used in mineral exploration, engineering, and geology. Archaeological mapping presents unique challenges, however, which have spurred a separate development of methods and equipment. Most commonly applied to archaeology are magnetometers, electrical resistance meters, ground penetrating radar (GPR) and electromagnetic (EM) conductivity meters. These methods can resolve many types of archaeological features, are capable of high sample density surveys of very large areas, and of operating under a wide range of conditions. Other established and emerging technologies are also helpful in archaeological applications.

Geographic Information Systems (GIS)

Geographic Information Systems, commonly referred to as GIS, provides a way in which archaeologists can visually represent archaeological data, and can be done in two ways: data visualization and representative visualization.

Global Positioning System (GPS)

The Global Positioning System (GPS), originally known as NAVSTAR GPS, is a satellite-based radio navigation system owned by the United States Government and operated by the United States Space Force. It is one of the global navigation satellite systems (GNSS) that provides geolocation and time information to a GPS receiver anywhere on or near the Earth where there is an unobstructed line of sight to four or more GPS satellites. Obstacles such as mountains and buildings block the relatively weak GPS signals.

Ground-Penetrating Radar (GPR)

This is perhaps the best known of these methods (although it is not the most widely applied in archaeology). The concept of radar is familiar to most people. In this instance, the radar signal, an electromagnetic pulse, is directed into the ground. Subsurface objects and stratigraphy (layering) will cause reflections that are picked up by a receiver. The travel time of the reflected signal indicates the depth. Data may be plotted as profiles, or as plan view maps isolating specific depths. GPR can be a powerful tool in favourable conditions (uniform sandy soils are ideal). It is unique both in its ability to detect some spatially small objects at relatively great depths and in its ability to distinguish the depth of anomaly sources.

Remote Sensing

Remote sensing is the acquisition of information about an object or phenomenon without making physical contact with the object and thus in contrast to on-site observation, especially the Earth. Remote sensing is used in numerous fields, including geography, land surveying and most Earth science disciplines (for example, hydrology, ecology, meteorology, oceanography, glaciology, geology); it also has military, intelligence, commercial, economic, planning, and humanitarian applications. In current usage, the term "remote sensing" generally refers to the use of satellite or aircraft-based sensor technologies to detect and classify objects on Earth. It includes the surface and the atmosphere and oceans, based on propagated signals (e.g. electromagnetic radiation). It may be split into "active" remote sensing (when a signal is emitted by a satellite or aircraft to the object and its reflection detected by the sensor) and "passive" remote sensing (when the reflection of sunlight is detected by the sensor).

Electrical Resistance Meters

It can be thought of as similar to the Ohmmeters used to test electrical circuits. In most systems, metal probes are inserted into the ground to obtain a reading of the local electrical resistance. A variety of probe configurations are used, most having four probes, often mounted on a rigid frame. Capacitive coupled systems that do not require direct physical contact with the soil have also been developed. Archaeological features can be mapped when they are of higher or lower resistivity than their surroundings. A stone foundation might impede the flow of electricity, while the organic deposits within a maiden might conduct electricity more easily than surrounding soils.

Lidar (Light Radar)

It is an optical remote sensing technology that can measure the distance to a target by illuminating the target with light, often using pulses from a laser. Lidar has many applications in the field of archaeology including aiding in the planning of field campaigns, mapping features beneath forest canopy, and providing an overview of broad, continuous features that may be indistinguishable on the ground. Lidar can also provide archaeologists with the ability to create high-resolution digital elevation models (DEMs) of archaeological sites that can reveal micro-topography that are otherwise hidden by vegetation. Lidar-derived products can be easily integrated into a Geographic Information System (GIS) for analysis and interpretation.

Electromagnetic (EM) Conductivity

This instrument has a response that is comparable to that of resistance meters (conductivity is the inverse of resistance). Underground archaeological features are detected by creating a magnetic field underground by applying an electric current that has a known frequency and magnitude through a sending coil. The currents spur a secondary current in underground conductors that is picked up by a receiving coil. Changes in the underground conductivity can indicate buried features. Some EM conductivity instruments are also capable of measuring magnetic susceptibility, a property that is becoming increasingly important in archaeological studies.

Magnetometers

It is used in geophysical survey and may use a single sensor to measure the total magnetic field strength, or may use two (sometimes more) spatially separated sensors to measure the gradient of the magnetic field (the difference between the sensors). In most archaeological applications the latter (gradiometer) configuration is preferred because it provides better resolution of small, near-surface phenomena. Magnetometers may also use a variety of different sensor types. Every kind of material has unique magnetic properties, even those that we do not think of as being "magnetic." Different materials below the ground can cause local disturbances in the Earth's magnetic field that are detectable with sensitive magnetometers. Magnetometers react very strongly to iron and steel, brick, burned soil, and many types of rock, and archaeological features composed of these materials are very detectable.

Metal Detectors

It is used for electromagnetic induction to detect metal. Although other types of instruments (notably magnetometers and electromagnetic conductivity meters) have some sensitivity to metal, specialized metal detectors are much more effective. Common hand-held metal detectors are widely used by archaeologists. Although not as commonly used in archaeology, sophisticated metal detectors are available having much greater sensitivity than hand-held models. These instruments are capable of data logging and sophisticated target discrimination. They can be mounted on wheeled carts for survey data collection.

Total Station

A total station (TS) or total station theodolite (TST) is an electronic/optical instrument used for surveying and building construction. It is an electronic transit theodolite integrated with electronic distance measurement (EDM) to measure both vertical and horizontal angles and the slope distance from the instrument to a particular point, and an on-board computer to collect data and perform triangulation calculations.

Archaeological Excavation

We know that site excavation has the potential to uncover building methods, such as the findings of postholes (which can mark the previous existence of fence lines or other site boundaries), timber, stones, and/or brick that marks the existence of man-made structures. Archaeological features often leave earthworks, signs of some type of modification to the natural environment that often appear as crop marks, soil marks, or even as plough marks in fields that, if historical, can indicate cultivation methods of the past, or, particularly if more recent, can lift archaeological material to the surface and, therefore, ruin the stratigraphy layering of materials from youngest to oldest. Features can be discovered by archaeologists both through excavation and through field survey or exploration.

Soil Sampling

Soil sampling is an important task in archaeological study and spatially under Archaeometry i.e. chemical analysis of archaeological remains. Soil samples from archaeological habitational sites are generally collected on the basis of grid techniques at different depths of excavation, which is to be set up at initial stage of excavation. In other type of sites samples are collected randomly along with the reference samples from the external periphery of the site.

Pollen or Floral analysis

Pollen analysis has allowed archaeologists to analyze vegetation selectively cultivated by area residents, the "native vegetation" of a particular area, and allow archaeologists to map out land use over time (which can be ascertained from weeds). But collecting a suitable sample is not all that easy. Failure to collect a suitable sample can be due in part to not sampling from areas where suitable pollen samples can be gathered (e.g. lakes and bogs, sites that were sufficiently exposed to air-borne pollen, sites that had both a long exposure to air and are deeply buried into the ground), or because pollen is vulnerable to destruction by the oxidation process or soil microbes such as bacteria and fungi, it negatively impacts an archaeologist's ability to collect a suitable pollen sample. The pollen and seed samples are collected by floating methods. Based on the pollen and seed analysis we can say that how much type of plant species were used by ancient people. Floral analysis will also be significantly useful in the reconstruction of agricultural history.

Faunal Analysis

Faunal analysis is based on morphological analysis of animal and human remains. In this analysis bones are analyzed up to the species level morphologically, to know the presence of various animal species or minimum number of identified species (MNISP) present in different cultural phases of past occupation and also to estimate the minimum number of individual (MNI) used by a particular group of past occupants. For the purpose of morphological analysis, stage microscope, research microscope, magnifying glasses and calipers are some important instruments, which are used under the valuable guidance of zoo-archaeologist. Faunal analysis also helps us in reconstructing the food habit, cultural contacts, activity areas, and process of domestication, pathological disease in ancient animal and human population and environment of the past occupation.

The aforesaid information such as, Pollen, soil, faunal, and floral analysis allows the archaeologist to understand the natural vegetation of an area, vegetation that was actively grown by area settlers, and the animal life that also lived in the area. An understanding of the plant and animal life specific to an area can lead to, for example, an analysis of the types of food available to members of the community, an understanding of the actual diet typical for a subset of a population, and site and skeletal dating. If landscape reconstruction and preservation, in particular, is a goal of an archaeological research project, pollen and soil analysis can aide in landscape archaeology to accurately interpret and reconstruct landscapes of the past.

Data Collection

It is broadly similar regardless of the particular sensing instrument. Survey usually involves walking with the instrument along closely spaced parallel traverses, taking readings at regular intervals. In most cases, the area to be surveyed is staked into a series of square or rectangular survey "grids" (terminology can vary). With the corners of the grids as known reference points, the instrument operator uses tapes or marked ropes as a guide when collecting data. In this way, positioning error can be kept to within a few centimetres for high-resolution mapping.

Survey systems with integrated global positioning systems (GPS) have been developed, but under field conditions, currently available systems lack sufficient precision for high-resolution archaeological mapping. Geophysical instruments (notably metal detectors) may also used for less formally "scanning" areas of interest.

Data Processing and Imaging

To convert raw numeric data into interpretable maps, data processing usually involves the removal of statistical outliers and noise, and interpolation of data points. Statistical filters may be designed to enhance features of interest (based on size, strength, orientation, or other criteria), or suppress obscuring modern or natural phenomena. Inverse modelling of archaeological features from observed data is becoming increasingly important. Processed data are typically rendered as images, as contour maps, or in false relief. When geophysical data are rendered graphically, the interpreter can more intuitively recognize cultural and natural patterns and visualize the physical phenomena causing the detected anomalies.

Climatology

Climatology means "place, zone"; or climate science is the scientific study of climate, scientifically defined as weather conditions averaged over a period of time. This modern field of study is regarded as a branch of the atmospheric sciences and a subfield of physical geography, which is one of the Earth sciences. Climatology now includes aspects of oceanography and biogeochemistry. The main methods employed by climatologists are the analysis of observations and modelling the physical laws that determine the climate. The main topics of research are the study of climate variability, mechanisms of climate changes and modern climate change.

Archival Data including Maps and Census Data)

Archival Data is used by any archaeologists that have any written texts available to them and is used in a multiple number of ways, depending on the research project and objective of the research and the data available in the archives. Archives are often employed to confirm archaeological findings, to understand the construction of a site, settlement patterns.

Bioarchaeology

The term bioarchaeology was first coined by British archaeologist Grahame Clark in 1972 as a reference to Zooarchaeology, or the study of animal bones from archaeological sites. Redefined in 1977 by Jane Buikstra, bioarchaeology in the United States now refers to the scientific study of human remains from archaeological sites, a discipline known in other countries as osteoarchaeology or palaeoosteology. In England and other European countries, the term 'bioarchaeology' is borrowed to cover all biological remains from sites.

Bioarchaeology was largely born from the practices of New Archaeology, which developed in the United States in the 1970s, as a reaction to a mainly cultural-historical approach to understanding the past. Proponents of New Archaeology advocated using processual methods to test hypotheses about the interaction between culture and biology, or a biocultural approach. Some archaeologists advocate a more holistic approach to bioarchaeology that incorporates critical theory and is more relevant to modern descent populations. It is now possible, human remains from archaeological sites are analyzed to determine sex, age, and health.

Paleodemography

Bioarchaeologists sometimes create life tables, a type of cohort analysis, to understand the demographic characteristics (such as risk of death or sex ratio) of a given age cohort within a population. Age and sex are crucial variables in the construction of a life table, although this information is often not available to bioarchaeologists. Therefore, it is often necessary to estimate the age and sex of individuals based on specific morphological characteristics of the skeleton.

Age estimation

The estimation of age in bioarchaeology and osteology actually refers to an approximation of skeletal or biological age-at-death. The primary assumption in age estimation is that an individual's skeletal age is closely associated with their chronological age. Age estimation can be based on patterns of growth and development or degenerative changes in the skeleton. Many methods tracking these types of changes have been developed using a variety of skeletal series. For instance, in children age is typically estimated by assessing their dental development, ossification and fusion of specific skeletal elements, or long bone length. In adults, degenerative changes to the pubic symphysis, the auricular surface of the ileum, the sternal end of the 4th rib, and dental attrition are commonly used to estimate skeletal age.

Sex Determination

Differences in male and female skeletal anatomy are used by bioarchaeologists to determine the biological sex of human skeletons. Humans are sexually dimorphic, although overlap in body shape and sexual characteristics is possible. Not all skeletons can be assigned a sex, and some may be wrongly identified as male or female. Sexing skeletons is based on the observation that biological males and biological females differ most in the skull and pelvis; bioarchaeologists focus on these parts of the body when determining sex, although other body parts can also be used. The female pelvis is generally broader than the male pelvis, and the angle between the two inferior pubic rami (the sub-pubic angle) is wider and more U-shaped, while the sub-pubic angle of the male are more V-shaped and less than 90 degrees. Phenice details numerous visual differences between the male and female pelvis. Pelvic and cranial features are considered to be more reliable indicators of biological sex.

Non-Specific Indicators

(A) Dental Non-Specific Stress Indicators Analysis

Enamel Hypoplasia

Enamel hypoplasia refers to transverse furrows or pits that form in the enamel surface of teeth when the normal process of tooth growth stops, resulting in a deficit of enamel. Enamel hypoplasias generally form due to disease and/or poor nutrition. By examining the spacing of perikymata grooves (horizontal growth lines), the duration of the stressor can be estimated, and although Mays argues that the width of the hypoplasia bears only an indirect relationship to the duration of the stressor. Studies of dental enamel hypoplasia are used to study child health. Unlike bone, teeth are not remodelled, so they can provide a more reliable indicator of past health events as long as the enamel remains intact. Dental hypoplasias provide an indicator of health status during the time in childhood when the enamel of the tooth crown is being formed. So it is now a day's used by archaeologists.

(B) Skeletal Non-Specific Stress Indicators Analysis

There are so many indicators found in the animal and human remains which are non-specific those are:-

1. Porotic Hyperostosis/Cribra Orbitalia

It was long assumed that iron deficiency anaemia has marked effects on the flat bones of the cranium of infants and young children. That as the body attempts to compensate for low iron levels by increasing red blood cell production in the young, sieve-like lesions develop in the cranial vaults (termed porotic hyperostosis) and/or the orbits (termed cribra orbitalia). This bone is spongy and soft. It is however; highly unlikely that iron deficiency anaemia is a cause of either porotic hyperostosis or cribra orbitalia. These are more likely the result of vascular activity in these areas and are unlikely to be pathological. The development of cribra orbitalia and porotic hyperostosis could also be attributed to other causes besides an iron deficiency in the diet, such as nutrients lost to intestinal parasites. However, dietary deficiencies are the most probable cause. Anaemia incidence may be a result of inequalities within society, and/or indicative of different work patterns and activities among different groups within society. Higher rates of cribra orbitalia among females may indicate lesser health status, or greater survival of young females with cribra orbitalia into adulthood.

2. Harris Hines

Harris lines form before adulthood, when bone growth is temporarily halted or slowed down due to some sort of stress (either disease or malnutrition). During this time, bone mineralization continues, but growth does not, nor does so at much reduced levels. If and when the stressor is overcome, bone growth will resume, resulting in a line of increased mineral density that will be visible in a radiograph. If there is not recovery from the stressor, no line will be formed.

3. Hair

The stress hormone cortisol is deposited in hair as it grows. This has been used successfully to detect fluctuating levels of stress in the later lifespan of mummies.

4. Mechanical Stress and Activity Indicators Analysis

Examining the effects that activities and workload has upon the skeleton allows the archaeologist to examine who was doing what kinds of labour, and how activities were structured within society. The division of labour within the household may be divided according to gender and age, or be based on other hierarchical social structures. Human remains can allow archaeologists to uncover patterns in the division of labour.

Living bones are subject to Wolff's law, which states that bones are physically affected and remodelled by physical activity or inactivity. Increases in mechanical stress tend to produce bones that are thicker and stronger. Disruptions in homeostasis caused by nutritional deficiency or disease or profound inactivity/disuse/disability can lead to bone loss. While the acquisition of bipedal locomotion and body mass appear to determine the size and shape of children's bones, activity during the adolescent growth period seems to exert a greater influence on the size and shape of adult bones than exercise later in life.

Markers of occupational stress, which include morphological changes to the skeleton and dentition as well as joint changes at specific locations have also been widely used to infer specific (rather than general) activities. Such markers are often based on single cases described in clinical literature in the late nineteenth century. One such marker has been found to be a reliable indicator of lifestyle: the external auditory exostosis also called surfer's ear, which is a small bony protuberance in the ear canal which occurs in those working in proximity to cold water.

5. Injury and Workload

Fractures to bones during or after excavation will appear relatively fresh, with broken surfaces appearing white and unweathered. Distinguishing between fractures around the time of death and post-depositional fractures in bone is difficult, as both types of fractures will show signs of weathering. Unless evidence of bone healing or other factors are present, researchers may choose to regard all weathered fractures as post-depositional.

Evidence of perimortal fractures (or fractures inflicted on a fresh corpse) can be distinguished in unhealed metal blade injuries to the bones. Living or freshly dead bones are somewhat resilient, so metal blade injuries to bone will generate a linear cut with relatively clean edges rather than irregular shattering.[6] Archaeologists have tried using the microscopic parallel scratch marks on cut bones in order to estimate the trajectory of the blade that caused the injury.

(C) Diet and Dental Health Analysis

1. Caries

Dental caries, commonly referred to as cavities or tooth decay, are caused by localized destruction of tooth enamel, as a result of acids produced by bacteria feeding upon and fermenting carbohydrates in the mouth. Subsistence based upon agriculture is strongly associated with a higher rate of caries than subsistence based upon foraging, because of the higher levels of carbohydrates in diets based upon agriculture. For example, bioarchaeologists have used caries in skeletons to correlate a diet of rice and agriculture with the disease. Females may be more vulnerable to caries compared to men, due to lower saliva flow than males, the positive correlation of estrogens with increased caries rates, and because of physiological changes associated with pregnancy, such as suppression of the immune system and a possible concomitant decrease in antimicrobial activity in the oral cavity.

2. Stable Isotope Analysis

Stable isotope analysis of carbon and nitrogen in human bone collagen allows bioarchaeologists to carry out dietary reconstruction and to make nutritional inferences. These chemical signatures reflect long-term dietary patterns, rather than a single meal or feast. Stable isotope analysis monitors the ratio of carbon 13 to carbon 12 (13C/12C), which is expressed as parts per mil (per thousand) using delta notation (?13C). The ratio of carbon isotopes varies according to the types of plants consumed with different photosynthesis pathways. The three photosynthesis pathways are C3 carbon fixation, C4 carbon fixation and Crassulacean acid metabolism. C4 plants are mainly grasses from tropical and subtropical regions, and are adapted to higher levels of radiation than C3 plants. Corn, millet and sugar cane are some well-known C4 domesticates, while all trees and shrubs use the C3 pathway. C3 plants are more common and numerous than C4 plants. Both types of plants occur in tropical areas, but only C3 plants occur naturally in colder areas. 12C and 13C occur in a ratio of approximately 98.9 to 1.1.

Isotope ratios in food, especially plant food, are directly and predictably reflected in bone chemistry, allowing researchers to partially reconstruct recent diet using stable isotopes as tracers. Nitrogen isotopes (14N and 15N) have been used to estimate the relative contributions of legumes verses nonlegumes, as well as terrestrial versus marine resources to the diet.

Stable isotope analysis of strontium and oxygen can also be carried out. The amounts of these isotopes vary in different geological locations. Because bone is a dynamic tissue that is remodelled over time, and because different parts of the skeleton are laid down at particular times over the course of a human life, stable isotope analysis can be used to investigate population movements in the past and indicate where people lived at various points of their lives. By the estimation of the aforesaid isotopes in the organic materials from archaeological sites we may be able to reconstruct the diet and dietary substances as well as climatic information of past settlement.

3. Archaeological Uses of DNA

DNA analysis of past populations is used by archaeology to genetically determine the sex of individuals, determine genetic relatedness, understand marriage patterns, and investigate prehistoric population movements.

(D) Bioarchaeological Treatments of Equality and Inequality Analysis

Aspects of the relationship between the physical body and socio-cultural conditions and practices can be recognized through the study of human remains. This is most often emphasized in a "biocultural bioarchaeology" model. It has often been the case that bioarchaeology has been regarded as a positivist, science-based discipline, while theories of the living body in the social sciences have been viewed as constructivist in nature. Archaeologists has argued that scientific or forensic treatments of human remains from archaeological sites construct a view of the past that is neither cultural nor historic, and has suggested that a biocultural version of bioarchaeology will be able to construct a more meaningful and nuanced history that is more relevant to modern populations, especially descent populations.

(E) Archaeological Ethics

There are ethical issues with bioarchaeology that revolve around treatment and respect for the dead. So to study the faunal remains and collecting the animal and faunal remains we should have a proper permission as well proper ways of chemical analysis without discouraging the feelings of peoples of the society.

For the benefit of students as well as researchers and being an environmental archaeologist some of the reliable information of above techniques or methods are being mentioned in this paper which are parts of the studies of various researchers mentioned in review of literature as well as contents of Encyclopaedia Wikipedia.

Meanwhile, I would also like to add that for conducting environmental archaeological invention there are some other archaeological techniques or methods which are equally important along with the above subfields.

1. Dendrochronology

It is an absolute dating method, which exploits the relationship between the earth's climate and the growth rate of trees. In American southwest initially it was used a chronological tool as a means of reconstructing palaeoclimate. It is a simple method of dating. In living trees, the number of rings from bark to the pith can be calculated to give an accurate age of the tree. But in archaeological wood samples, only patterns of ring remain intact and each of them represents a calendar year of growth, but of unknown age. The patterns of present and ancient sample are compared to achieve a cross match. By counting the number of rings from a tree ring of unknown age back to the cross match series of ancient sample, an absolute date of a site is determined. Sections of the tree are cut through woodcutter, which are examined in calibrated ocular.

2. Radiocarbon Dating

It is most widely used absolute dating method in archaeology. Materials used in this method are bone, charcoal, lithic etc. and the instrument used is Accelerator Mass Spectrometer (AMS), Carbon Accelerator. It can date the samples of organic materials ranging in age to 60,000 years B.P., which is based on the half-life of 14C of carbon (i.e. 5,569 years).

3. Thermo-Luminescence (TL) Dating

In this absolute dating method ceramics, lithic and metal objects can be used for dating, which can be date the ceramic material back to 2, 00,000 years with an accuracy of 10 percent. It is particularly useful in authentication of pottery. In this technique ceramic samples are heated above the 750-degree Celsius for emitting the light, and through the emitted light the date of the site is calculated.

4. Potassium Argon Dating

This method of dating is also just like to the radiocarbon dating which is based on the analysis of radioactive element of potassium (K). This is an important method for dating the oldest archaeological sites. The upper limit of this method is 30 billion years, because its half-life is 13 billion years. The radioactive of potassium is K40, which is degraded in to Calcium-40 and Argon-40.

5. Electron Spin Resonance (ESR)

It is an instrumental technique, which can dates archaeological specimens by assessing the amount of radiation damaged from soil radioactivity and cosmic rays. Which has accumulated at the time of object making? Soil is generally suitable sample for this technique.

6. Amino Acid Racemization

In this method the instrument used is gas chromatograph and materials used are bones. With help of Amino Acid Racemization we can date the samples of 5000 to 1, 00,000 years B. P., as the half-life of aspartic acid, the amino acid used in AAR dating of bone, is about 15,000 years at 20 degree Celsius.

7. Microstructure Analysis

(A) General Microscopy:

The hand lens and optical microscope are used laboratories to assist in visual examination of artifacts in archaeological.

(i) Metallography: Metallography is a form of microscopy, which employs light reflected from the polished and etched surface of a sample fragment of a metal object. The metal is made up of many molecules, or development of small grains. The size and shape of these individual grains are studied by using the Metallography, which gives information about the thermo-mechanical history of the object.

(ii) Petrography: It refers to the microscopic examination of non-metallic substances to identify their mineral constituents, which is done with the aid of polarizing and analyzer optical microscope. Actually each mineral has a unique set of optical properties. By using polarizing and analyzer optical microscopy it is therefore, possible to identify what mineral or crystal phases are present? It is also useful in identifying the source of the used clay in ceramic making.

(iii) Scanning Electron Microscopy (SEM): Scanning Electron Microscopy (SEM) is particularly useful in the detailed examination of surface texture, and it has been applied to ceramics, metal, stone artifacts as well as organic materials such as wood and bone. In SEM a small artifact is placed in an evacuated column then is bombarded with a beam of electrons, and secondary electron emitted by the sample are then collected and amplified by the instrument. In this process the entire surface must be scanned in order to produce a complete image. Resulting picture is displayed on a cathode ray tube, which can be photographed.

(B) Phase Analysis (X-Ray Diffraction, XRD):

XRD is used to identify minerals and other crystalline phases found in archaeological samples. It is especially useful in study of ceramics. This technique is a valuable tool on provenience studies of pottery, because some time the XRD results can associate raw minerals with the finished products. It has also been used to study the mineral phases in bone, stone and metal artifacts. Power camera or a diffractometer is usually used in XRD analysis.

8. Microstructure Analysis

(A) Spectroscopy and Spectrophotometry:

Instruments utilized in this method are Spectrophotometer and Flame Photometer. It is useful for estimating the concentration level of different elements in various types of archaeological objects.

(C) X-Ray Fluorescence (XRF):

This is also a method for analyzing the clay profile in which X-Ray fluorescent Spectrometer is used as an instrument. This method is significantly useful in tracing out the elemental composition in pottery and ceramics.

(D) Neutron Activation Analysis (NAA):

This method is used for the estimation of elemental composition in the metal and lithic objects. The instrument used is Neutron activation analyzer.

(E) Mass Spectrophotometry (MS):

Due to the use of mass spectrophotometer this method is known as mass spectrometry that is used in radiocarbon dating as well as estimation of isotopic ratios of different elements such as Carbon, Nitrogen, Strontium, Oxygen etc. in various types of organic materials.

(F) Atomic Absorption Spectrophotometry (AAS) and Inductively Coupled Plasma Emission Spectrophotometry (ICPES):

Both of these techniques are helpful in estimating the concentration level of different major and minor elements in archaeological faunal remains, soils, ceramics etc.

Due to deficiency of time it is impossible to talk about the detailed methodology of every technique. Therefore, I would like to describe about the importance of elemental analysis in archaeology as I am working on this discipline since last few years.

9. Trace Element Analysis in Archaeological Soil and Faunal Remains: Reflections on Habitational intensity and Palaeodietary Behaviour

Based on the trace element analysis in faunal remains and archaeological soils we can not only get the information about the palaeodiet, palaeoclimate but also can locate various activity areas of ancient occupation.

Case Studies on Trace element and Isotopic Ratios of Carbon and Nitrogen carried by the Author on various Archaeological and Modern Samples.

We have carried out a number of studies on trace element analysis and isotopic ratios of carbon, nitrogen in archaeological faunal remains and soils from various archaeological sites of mid-Central Garhwal Himalayas, excavated by the department of history and archaeology, HNB Garhwal University, Srinagar Garhwal Uttarakhand. Besides analysis of archaeological soils and faunal remains, studies on the analysis of modern soils and bone remains are also conducted accordingly. Summary of some of our investigations are described below :-

1. Reconstruction of Palaeodiet and Environmental Condition of Ancient Population of Mid-Central Garhwal Himalayas through the Estimation of Trace Elements and Isotopic Ratios of Carbon & Nitrogen

This investigation was based on the analysis of human and faunal remains recovered from different archaeological sites of Mid-central Garhwal Himalayas dated to c. 1000 B.C. to 1000 A.D. i.e. from Malari, Purola, Ranihat, Thapli, Banderkhet and Mordhwaj, Roopkund (16500 feet above from main sea level). For this purpose, the long and compact part of the limb bones of various animal species and human was collected from these archaeological sites during the excavation, which was carried out by the department of History and Archaeology, H.N.B. Garhwal University during the last 10 years.

The collected faunal remains or bone samples were cleaned and pretreated in the laboratory through different established techniques, digested chemically and finally trace elements were analysed through Atomic Absorption and Inductively coupled Plasma Emission Spectrophotometer, while isotopic ratios of carbon were estimated through Atomic Mass Spectrophotometer.

The results obtained from trace elemts and isotopic ratios indicated that all the animal species recovered from different archaeological sites of Mid-Central Garhwal Himalya belonged to terrestrial herbivore group and majority of these animals were domesticated. The estimated values of carbon isotope also indicated about the intake of C4 plants by the majority of these animals. Though the analytical values from the faunal remains of few animals are indicating a rich intake of C3 diet. Besides this, analysis of human remains from Roopkund Lake(16500, feet from main sea level, dated to 9th century A.D.) indicated a rich amount of omnivorous food in their diet with the consumption of C4 plants and some meat consuming pleoples were also noticed.

Estimated results of isotopic ratios of carbon and trace element analysis of faunal remains recovered from different archaeological sites of Mid-Central Garhwal Himalaya and adjoining areas also clearly indicated that the cattle and goats used by ancient occupants of this region, belong to the domestic herbivore group, whereas the pig belong to domestic omnivore group. The isotopic ratios estimated from the same faunal remains also indicated that the ancient people of this region had good knowledge of agriculture, as the domestic animals were nourished by such type of food. The significant animal species mainly used by these peoples were Cattle (cow, bull, ox, buffalo), sheep, goat, pig, ass, fowl, deer and fishes.

It has also been confirmed that majority of these animals were used for their food purpose, as the majority of faunal remains were having a number of cut marks. Besides this, the ancient people of Mid-Central Himalaya had also used some of the wild animals (deer and rabbit) and aquatic animals (fishes) for their food purpose, because deep cut marks were also found on these faunal remains. At the same time, it is interesting to note that more than 80 % of these animals were from young group, which also revealed that the ancient people of this region had a good knowledge of the nutritional value of meat. Therefore, they had sloughed young animals for their food purpose (Farswan & Nautiyal 1997: 25-258; Farswan & Price 2002: 1130; Farswan & Singh 2007: 53-68 and Farswan & Pharswan 2009: 25-43).

2. Investigation of Phosphorus Enrichment in the Burials of Kumaun, mid-Central Himalaya, India

In this study we have conducted soil analysis of archaeological soil samples collected from the megalithic burial sites of Sanana and Baseri, Ram Ganga valley, Almora district of Uttarakhand, to see the phosphate enrichment. It is also well-known that phosphate analysis is basically used an archaeological techniques to see the activity areas in the ancient or past occupational site, and it is usually the percentage of anthropogenic (organic) phosphate. The enrichment of anthropogenic (organic) phosphate means phosphate generated by human occupation through different activities.

But it is well known that in burial sites no any habitation activities is conducted, so we cannot see any enrichment of the anthropogenic (organic) phosphate, but our results obtained from elemental analysis of archaeological soils from Sanana and Basera clearly revealed that in both these burial sites enrichment of inorganic phosphate is noticed in place of organic phosphate (Farswan & Nautiyal 1997: 25-258).

3. Comparative Study of Occupational Intensity in modern Settlement of Alaknanda and nandakini Valley of Chamoli, Uttarakhand, India

These studies were carried out in the modern settlement of Nandakini and Alaknanda valley, district Chamoli (Uttarakhand), India. The goal of these studies was mainly to reconstruct the intensity of occupation in different locations of modern settlements through elemental analysis of anthropogenic soil. For this purpose, more than 500 soil samples were collected from different villages of the Nandakini and Alaknanda Valley. Trace element analysis was conducted using the inductively coupled plasma emission spectrometer (ICP).

The chemical analysis revealed that anthropogenic soils from hearth and cooking areas (HCAs), refuse deposition areas (RDAs), cow dung deposition areas (CDAs) and toilet areas (TLAs) are capable for holding rich compositions of calcium (Ca), magnesium (Mg), sodium (Na), potassium (K) and phosphorus (P), while anthropogenic soils from sleeping areas (SLAs), agricultural areas (AGAs) and barren land areas (BLAs) show a lower concentration of these elements, indicating that these soils are less capable for holding access composition of the said elements. These both investigation provided valuable information about the trace element analysis which is significantly useful in identifying activity-rich areas and non-activity areas in the past settlement (Pharswan and Farswan 2012: 121-126; Farswan 2013).

4. Effects of Buried Environment on the Bones of a Modern Ox (Boss indicus): Study of Isotopic Analysis &Trace Element Analysis

These two analytical studies were carried out mainly to see the effects of buried environment on the trace element profile and isotopic ratios carbon and nitrogen of an old Ox (Bos indicus) which was buried in April 2006 by the local villagers of Chauras after the death. Bone samples of Ox were recovered after excavation of the buried area of Chauras in the month of May 2010. This village is located in the right bank of river Alaknanda in Tehri district of Uttarakhand. The collected bone samples were cleaned and pretreated as per authentic scientific methods, later on examined morphologically to see the pre and post mortem changes, ash of the bones were made which were followed the chemical digestion. The final solutions obtained from different samples were passed through Inductively Coupled Plasma Emission Spectrometer (ICP) for estimating the concentration of trace elements i.e. Ca, Ba, Sr, Mg, P and Zn.

Results obtained from the study of trace element profile in various bone samples indicated that buried environmental conditions of Chauras have not affected the original profile of the elements in the bones of Ox which has also been confirmed by the hydrogen ion concentration (pH) estimated in different levels of buried ground and ratio of Ca/P as well. However, the morphological examination of bones indicated that a number of cavities were evolved in left femur. Meanwhile, it is interesting to note that the trace element profile of left femur of ox has been changed adversely as compared to reference samples. Therefore, it is believed that the adverse changes in the concentration of trace elements occurred due to the cavities evolved in the femur bone during the life span of Ox and these cavities may be developed due to some bone disease which could be the ultimate cause of death of Ox.

The estimated values of isotopic ratios of carbon and nitrogen from the bones of ox also revealed that the environmental preservative condition of Chauras have not affected the original condition of bone of ox, because ratios of these both element were similar to reference samples except in case of left femur. These studies clearly revealed that such type of scientific analysis is significant for reconstructing the environmental conditions and their effects (Farswan & Singh 2012: 305-309 & Farswan 2012: 1279-1288).

5. Study of Preservation Status and Dietary Reconstruction in the Human Remains recovered from Roopkund Lake, through Chemical Analysis

This study was carried out in the bone remains collected from Roopkund Lake in district Chamoli Garhwal, Uttarakhand which is located at 5029 meters from main sea level in between Nanda Ghunghti and Trishuli peak. This historical site belongs to 9th century A.D. The bone remains after preteatment and digestion were followed through established scientific methods, i.e. chemical analysis, for the estimation of concentration of different elements such as, calcium, strontium, barium, magnesium and zinc. The isotopic ratios of Carbon and Nitrogen were also estimated in the same samples of bone. Both these analyses were carried out through Inductively Coupled Plasma Spectroscopy (ICP) and Atomic Absorption Spectrophotometer (AAS).

Results obtained from the estimation of isotopic ratios of Carbon, Nitrogen and trace element analysis of faunal remains recovered from Roopkund Lake, Central Garhwal Himalaya revealed that the faunal remains of peoples buries around 9th century are well preserved till the date. It is also evident from the trace elements and isotopic ratios that these peoples belonged to omnivore group with rich C4 and meat consuming group as it is noticed in their diet. This information's clearly indicated that there were two groups of peoples which were buried at Roopkund.

6. Effects of Buried Environment on Trace Element Profile and Isotopic Ratios of Carbon of Bones from Experimental Himalayan Domestic Goat *(Capra jharal)*

This study was conducted in the bone remains of experimental goats, as they were fed by various types of induced diet sometimes eight years back. It was aimed to establish a base-line data of different elements in the bone remains of Himalayan domestic goats *(Capra jharal)* relation to different buried levels of depth.

Trace elements were analyses from those faunal remains through inductively coupled Plasma Emission (ICPE) Spectrophotometer. The results obtained are significant and it is observed that the preservation status play an important role in altering the concentration level of trace elements, and it is seen that the alteration is directly proportional to the buried level. Meanwhile it was also noticed that the lowest level i.e. 1.80 meter of depth was found suitable for the preservation of skeletal remains, as the value of pH and concentration of different trace elements analyses in the bone remains of goat buried at this level were unchanged up to eight years (Farswan *et.al* 2015: 115-122).

7. Effects of Buried Environment on the Morphology and Trace Element Profile of Faunal Remains: An Experimental Study

This study was carried out mainly to know the effects of buried environment on morphology as well as elemental profile of the faunal remains. For this purpose we have collected 50 modern bone samples of goat, sheep and ox from different locations of the Garhwal region and these samples were buried in the ground in various places, at different levels of depth with the measurement of pH at different buried levels. After four years all the buried bone samples were recovered; pretreated sequentially in the laboratory, examined morphologically and processed for getting the ash of each sample. Trace elements were estimated through spectrometry methods in Laboratory for archaeological chemistry, Wisconsin University, Madison, USA.

The morphological examination revealed that the bones buried in highly acidic and alkaline soil and at the level of 50 cm to 75 cm were proceeding towards the disintegration as they were recovered in bad condition, while other faunal remains which were buried in normal acidic and alkaline soil and beyond the level of 100 cm recovered in well preserved condition. However, elemental analysis also revealed that no any major changes in trace element profile has been observed among the faunal remains recovered in good conditions but in morphologically disintegrated faunal remains a significant change in the concentration level of different elements have been noticed. It clearly showed that both these factors are positively responsible for disintegration of archaeological remains (Farswan & Pharswan 2019: 20-27).

8. Utility of Trace element Analysis in Reconstructing the Intensity of Occupation in an Ancient Harappan Archaeological Site Dholavira

Trace element analysis was carried out in the soil samples from an important archaeological site Dholavira, to see the intensity of occupation in different cultural phases of occupation. It is evident from the archaeological remains recovered from Dholavira excavation that there were seven cultural phases in the settlement; it was excavated by Archaeological Survey of India, under the Directorship of Dr. R.S. Bisht. The results obtained from trace element analysis of soils from different cultural phases revealed that a gradual increase in these elements was observed up to fifth phase which was the peak/mature phase of the occupation. However, after fifth phase a gradual decrease in the values of trace elements were observed up to seventh phase which was the late cultural phase of the habitation. (Farswan *et al.* 2001: 223-239). Our results were positively relative to the chronological sequence established by ASI.

The archaeological studies mentioned above significantly revealed that such type of study i.e. various aspects environmental archaeology is a major part of the archaeology for reconstructing a real history of past occupation. Therefore, for establishing the base-line data, chemical analyses and isotopic ratios of modern human and animal bone from various species, various categories of food stuffs of these of animals, will be helpful to assess the relative utilization of food from different ecosystems, climatic zones, discrete geochemical environments, tropic levels and different photosynthetic categories of Indian biosphere, i.e. marine VS terrestrial, arid land VS humid, local catchments with sediments of different geological age, primary producers VS herbivore VS carnivore and C3 VS C4 VS CAM (Crassulacean Acid Metabolism) categories of photosynthetic plants (Farswan 2007 35-68).

At the end of this article I have to state that a lot of scope is there in Indian archaeological context to analyse various archaeological faunal remains chemically (Elemental analysis, estimation of isotopic ratios of calcium, nitrogen, oxygen, strontium et), for getting fruitful information about various prehistoric and historic ancient cultures, as a lot of sites has already been excavated by various Universities and archaeologists, but the faunal remains are still not analysed chemically at the large scale.

Acknowledgements

I am sincerely thankful to the authors mentioned in the review of literature and references to encourage me for adopting this valuable branch of archaeology, as a part of my investigation. Thankful are also due to the Encyclopaedia Wikipedia, as some the information we have got from this unique site.

My deep gratitude is due to my life partner Smt. Suman Rani Farswan, Principal, Government Girls Higher Secondary School, Lwali, Pauri, Garhwal, Uttarakhand, for her incredible support for the preparation of this article during COVID-19 lockdown.

References

Ambrose, S.A.,1987, Chemical and Isotopic Techniques of Reconstruction in Eastern North America, Emergent Horticultural Economics of the Eastern Woodlands, W. F. Keegan (ed.), Carbondale: *Center for Archaeological Investigations, Occasional Paper No.7.*

Ambrose, S. H. and M.J. De Niro,1989, Climate and Habit Reconstruction using Stable Carbon and Nitrogen Isotope Ratios of Collagen in Prehistoric Herbivore Teeth from Kenya, *Quaternary Research 31.*

Antoine, S.E., A.M. Pollard, P.Q. Dresser & A.W.R. Whittle,1988, Bone Chemistry and Dietary Reconstruction in Prehistoric Britain: Examples from Orkney, Scotland, *Proceeding of the 26th International Archaeometry Symposium.*

Aufderheide, A. C.,1989, Chemical Analysis of Skeleton, *Reconstruction of Life from the Skeleton* Iscan, M.Y. and K.A.R. Kennedy (eds.), New York.

Abhayan, G.S., 2016, Preparation and Application of Fish Bone Identification Keys for arappan Sites in Gujarat with Special Reference to Bagasra, Kanmer and Shikarpur, Ph.D. Thesis, Pune: Deccan College .

Badam, G. L.,1991, Faunal Remains from Thapli, *Emergence of Early Culture in mid-Central Garhwal Himalaya,* K.P. Nautiyal and B.M. Khanduri (eds.), 22-41. Museum of Himalayan Archaeology and Ethnography, Srinagar: HNB Garhwal University, Garhwal.

Bell, M. G.,1992, The prehistory of soil erosion, Bell, M. G. and J. Boardman (eds.), Past and Present Soil Erosion, *Archaeological and Geographical Perspectives (Oxbow Monograph 22),* Oxford: Oxbow Books.

Bell, M. G. and J. Boardman, 1992, Past and Present Soil Erosion, *Archaeological and Geographical Perspectives,Oxbow Monograph 22,* Oxford: Oxbow Books.

Bintliff, J. L., B.E. Davies, C.F. Gaffney and A.T. Waters, 1990, Trace metal accumulation in soil on and around ancient settlement in Greece, *Man's role in shaping of the eastern mediterranean landscape,* S. Bottom, G. Entjes-Nieborg and W. Van Zeist (eds), Rotterdam: Balkema.

Birks, H. J. B. and H.H. Birks,1980, *Quaternary Palaeoecology,* London: Edward Arnold .

Borgognini Tarli, S.M., 1989, Reconstruction of Mesolithic Diet using Dental Microwear and Trace element analysis: The Case of Grotto Dell Uzzo (Sicily), People and Change in Culture I, Hershkovitz (ed.), *Bar International series 508 (I),* Oxford.

Boyd, W. E., 1990, Towards a conceptual framework for environmental archaeology: environmental archaeology as a key to past environments, *Circaea 7.*

Ranch, Nick, 2014, *Environmental Archaeology: Theoretical and Practical Approaches,* London: Routledge.

Brown, A. B.,1973, *Bone Strontium Content as a Dietary Indicator in Human Skeletal Population,* Ph. D. Dissertation, University of Michigan.

Brown, A. G., 1997, *Alluival Geoarchaeology. Floodplain Archaeology and Environmental Change, CUP Manual in Archaeology,* Cambridge: Cambridge University Press.

Burton, J.H., and T.D. Price, 1990, The Ratio of Barium to Strontium as a Palaeodietary Indicator of Consumption of Marine Resources, *Journal of Archaeological Science 17.*

Burton, J. H and T.D.Price,1991, Palaeodietary Applications of Barium values in Bone, *Proceedings of the 27th International Symposium on Archaeometry,* Hiedelberg,1990, E. Pernicka and G. A. Wagner (eds).

Butzer, K. W.,1982, *Archaeology as Human Ecology, Method and Theory for a Contextual Approach,* Cambridge: Cambridge University Press.

Butzer, Karl W, 2012, Collapse, environment, and society, *PNAS, 109 (10).*

Byrne, K. B. and D.C Paris,1987, Reconstruction of the Diet of the Middle Woodland Amerindian Population at Abbot Farm by Bone Trace-element Analysis, *American Journal of Physical Anthropology 74.*

Chisholm, B. S., D.E. Nelson and H. Schwarcz,1982, Stable Carbon Isotopes as a measure of Marine versus Terrestrial Protein in Ancient Diets, *Science 216.*

Conway, J.S.,1983, An investigation of soil phosphorus distribution within occupational deposits from a Roman British hut group, *Journal of Archaeological Science 10.*

Currey, J.,1984, *The Mechanical Adaptations of Bones,* Princeton University, Princeton.

Davies, B. E., J.L. Bintliff, C.F. Gaffney and A.T. Waters 1988, Trace metal residues in soil as markers of ancient site occupancy in Greece, *Trace substances in environmental health XXII,* D. D. Hemp hill (ed.) Columbia: A symposium, MO.

Deotare, B. C., 1990, Chemical study of anthropic soils from Chalcolithic Tuljapur Garhi, *Man and Environment, XV (2).*

Deshpande-Mukherjee, A., P.K. Thomas, Purushottam Singh and A.K. Singh, 2005- 2006, Faunal Remains from Agiabir, Dt. Mirzapur, Uttar Pradesh, *Puratattva 36 .*

Dietz, E. F.,1957, Phosphorus accumulation in soil of an Indian habitation site, *American Antiquity, 22(4).*

Driesch Von Den, A., 1976, *A Guide to the Measurement of Animal Bones from Archaeological Sites,* Cambridge Massachusetts: Harvard University Press.

Evans, J. G.,1978, *Introduction to Environmental Archaeology,* London: Paul Elek.

Evans, J. G.,1981, *An introduction to environmental archaeology,* Granada: London.

Evans, J. G.,1991,An approach to the interpretation of dry ground, and set-ground molluscan taxocenes from central southern England, D.R. Harris and K.D. Thomas (eds.), *Modelling Ecological Change,* London: University College

London.

Evans, J.G., 2003, *Environmental archaeology and the social order,* London: Routledge.

Ezzo, J.A.,1991, Dietary change at Grasshopper Pueblo, Arizona: The evidence from Bone Chemistry Analysis, Ph.D. Dissertation, University of Wisconsin, Madison.

Ezzo, J. A.,1994, Putting the "Chemistry" Back into Archaeological Bone Chemistry Analysis: Modeling Potential Palaeodietary Indicators, *Journal of Anthropological Archaeology, 13.*

Farswan, Y.S. and Vinod Nautiyal,1997a, Investigation of Phosphorus Enrichment in the Burials of Kumaun, mid-Central Himalaya, India, *Journal of Archaeological Science, 24(3).*

Farswan, Y.S. and Vinod Nautiyal,1997b, Trace Element Analysis of Archaeo-faunal Remains of Garhwal Himalaya through I. C. P. Spectroscopy, B. M. Khanduri and V. Nautiyal (eds.) *HIM-KANTI (Prof. K.P. Nautiyal Felicitation Volume),* New Delhi: Book India Publishing Company.

Farswan, Y.S., T.D. Price and R.S. Bisht, 2001,Utility of Trace element Analysis in Reconstructing the Intensity of Occupation in Ancient Archaeological Site, *Indian Journal of Environment and Ecoplanning, 5(2).*

Farswan, Y.S. and T.D. Price, 2002, Reconstruction of Palaeodiet through Trace Element Analysis of Archaeological Faunal Remains, *Indian Journal of Environment and Ecoplanning, 6(2).*

Farswan, Y.S., 2002, Importance and Utility of Trace Element Analysis in Archaeological Study: Reflections on Palaeodietary Reconstruction, *Summary Published in the Proceedings of Indian History Congress, 62nd Session,* Bhopal.

Farswan, Y.S., 2003, Chemical Analysis of Anthropogenic Soils from the modern settlements of Garhwal Himalaya, *Proceedings of Indian History Congress, 63rd Session,* Amritsar.

Farswan, Y.S. and Jaibir Singh, 2005, Reconstruction of Occupational Intensity through Elemental Analysis of Anthropogenic Soils from the Modern Settlement of Garhwal Himalaya, *Journal of the Meerut University History Alumni, Vol. V.*

Farswan, Y.S. and Jaibir Singh, 2006, Application of Scientific Analysis in Reconstructions of Past history: With Special Reference to Inhabitants of Mid-Central Garhwal Himalayan, *Proceedings of National Seminar, Resource Appraisal, technology Application and Environmental Challenges in Central Himalaya,* M.S.S. Rawat (ed.), Vol. II .

Farswan, Y.S., 2007, Reconstruction of Palaeodiet and Environmental Condition of Ancient Population of Mid-Central Garhwal Himalayas through the Estimation of Trace Elements and Isotopic Ratios of Carbon in the Human and Animal Remains, *International Journal of Essential Sciences, Vol. 1(1).*

Farswan, Y.S., 2008, Reconstruction of Base-Line Data of Intensity of Occupation in Modern settlements of Garhwal Himalaya through elemental analysis of soil, *Proceedings of Indian History Congress, 68rd Session, Delhi.*

Farswan Y.S. and Jaibir Singh, 2009, Trace Element Analysis in Archaeological Soils from Garhwal Himalaya: To Reconstruct the Intensity of Occupation, *Research Journal of Social and Life Sciences, Vol.7 (4).*

Farswan, Y.S. and J.S. Pharswan,2009, Elemental Analysis and Estimation of Isotopic Ratios of Carbon in

Archaeological Faunal Remains from Mid-Central Garhwal Himalaya: A note for Palaeodietary and Palaeoenvironmental Reconstruction, *Proceedings of First Uttaranchal History and Culture Association, Vol-I, 2007.*

Farswan, Y.S., 2012a, Effects of Buried Environment on the Bones of a Modern Ox (Boss indicus)-II: Study of Isotopic Analysis, *Research Journal of Social and Life Sciences, Vol-XIII (II).*

Farswan, Y.S. and J. Singh, 2012, Effects of Buried Environment on the Bones of a Modern Ox (Boss Indicus)-I: Study of Trace Element Analysis, *Research Journal of Arts, Management and Social sciences, VII-I (4).*

Farswan, Y.S.,2012b, Study of Preservation Status and Dietary Reconstruction in the Human Remains recovered from Roopkund Lake, through Chemical Analysis, *Proceedings of Indian History Congress, 72nd Session.*

Farswan, Y.S. and J.S. Pharswan, 2013, Reconstruction of Intensity of Occupation through Trace element analysis of Archaeological soils from Garhwal Himalaya Uttarakhand, Himalayee Itihaas ke Vividh Aayaam, *Proceedings of Uttarakhand Itihaas Avam Sanskriti Parishad.*

Farswan, Y.S., 2013, Comparative Study of Occupational Intensity in modern Settlement of Alaknanda and nandakini Valley of Chamoli, Uttarakhand, India, *Proceedings of Indian History Congress, 73nd Session.*

Farswan, Y.S. J.S. Pharswan and H.S. Rawat 2014, Effects of Buried Environment on the Morphology and Trace Element Profile of Faunal Remains: An Experimental Study, *Asian Man (The): An International Journal, Vol. 8(2).*

Farswan, Y.S., H. Singh and J.S. Pharswan, 2015, Effects of Buried Environment on Trace Element Profile of Bones from Experimental Himalayan Domestic Goat, Capra Jharal, *Periodic Research, Vol-IV, ISSUE-II.*

Farswan, Y.S. and Jaibir Singh, 2015, Study of Preservation Status and Dietary Reconstruction in the Human Remains Recovered from Roopkund Lake through Chemical Analysis of Faunal Remains, *Journal of Chemistry and Chemical Engineering, USA, Vol.9.*

Farswan, Y.S. and J.S. Pharswan, 2015, Effects Of Induced Feeding on Trace Element Profile and Isotopic Ratios of Carbon in Himalayan Domestic Goat, Capra jharal, *The Mirror (An Annual Journal of History), Vol.2.*

Farswan, Y.S. and J.S. Pharswan, 2019, Effects of Buried Environment on the Morphology and Trace Element Profile of Faunal Remains: An Experimental Study, *Annals of Archaeology, Volume 2, Issue 2.*

Florida Museum of Natural History, 2017, "What is Environmental Archaeology?", *Broacher University of Florida.*

Foster, S. and T.C. Smout, 1994, *The History of Soils and Field Systems*, Edinburgh: Scottish Cultural Press.

Francalacci, P.,1989, Dietary Reconstruction at Arene Candide Cave (Linguria, Italy) by means of Trace Element Analysis, *Journal of Archaeological Science,16.*

Gilbert, R. I., 1985, Stress, Paleonutrition, and Trace Elements, *The Analysis of Prehistoric Diets*, R.I.Gilbert and J. H. Mielke (eds.), Orlando: Academic Press.

Gilbert, C., J. Sealy and A. Sillen,1994, An Investigation of Barium, Calcium and Strontium as Palaeodietary Indicators in the Southwestern Cape, South Africa, *Journal of Archaeological Science, 21.*

Goudie, A., 1993, *The Human Impact on the Natural Environment* (4th edition), Oxford: Blackwell.

Grayson, Donald K., 2001,The Archaeological Record of Human Impacts on Animal Populations, *Journal of World Prehistory, 15 (1).*

Griffen, K.,1988, Plant remains, Schia, E. (ed.), *Derkeologiske Utgravninger i Gamlebyen,* Oslo,S. Oslo: Alvheim and Eide.

Haraniya, Krutika, P.P. Joglekar and Pankaj Goyal, 2016, Osteological Keys for ifferentiating among Hind Limb Bones of Bos indicus, Bubalus bubalis and Boselaphus tragocamelus, Heritage 4:

Hillson, S., 1992, *Mammal Bones and Teeth,* London: Institute of Archaeology.

Hare, P.E.,1980, Organic Geochemistry of Bone, its Relation to the Survival of Bone in the Natural Environment, *Fossils in the Making,* A.K. Behrensmeyer and A.P. Hill (eds.), Chicago: University of Chicago.

Harney, E., A. Nayak, N. Patterson, P. Joglekar, V.T. Mushrif, S. Mallick, N. Rohland, J. Sedig, N. Adamski, R. Bernardos, N. Broomandkhoshbacht, B.J. Culleton, M. Ferry, T.K. Harper, M. Miche, J.Oppenheimer, K. Stewardson, Z., Harashawaradhana, Bartwal, M.S. Kumar, K. Diyundi, S.C. Roberts, P. Boivin, D.J. Kennett, K. Thangaraj, D. Reich & N. Rai,2019, Ancient DNA from the Skeletons of Roopkund Lake reveals Mediterranean migrants in India, *Nature Communication.*

Harris, D. R. and K.D. Thomas, 1991, *Modelling Ecological Change,* London: University College London.

Hegde, K. T. M. and S.N. Pande, 1972, Chemical analysis of mitathal copper objects, *Studies in Museology, VII.*

Heidenreich, C. E. and S. Navratil, 1973, Soil analysis at the Robitaille site, I- Determining the parameter of the village, *Ontario Archaeology, 20.*

Heidenreich, C. E. and V.A. Konard, 1973, Soil analysis at the Robitaille Site, Part-II: A Method Useful in Determining the Location of Longhouse Patterns, *Ontario Archaeology, 21.*

Heidenreich, C. E., A.R. Hill, D.M. Lap and S. Navatril, 1971, Soil and environmental analysis at the Robitaille Site, W. M. Harley and C. E. Heidenreich (eds), *Palaeoecology and Ontario prehistory,* Toronto: University of Toronto research report No. 2.

Howard, Andy J., 2019, Environmental Archaeology, Progress and Challenges, *Internet Archaeology (53),* doi:10.11141/ ia.53.1.

Iyer, R. K., 1971, Criteria for the Correlation of Trace Element Concentrations in Archaeological Specimens, Bombay: *BARC I.*

Iyer, R. K.,N.J. Rao, K.R. Krishnamoorthy, S.M. Das and S. Paramasivan,1973, Study of trace element distribution in Indian potsherds by neutron-activation analysis, D. P. Agrawal and A. Ghosh (eds), *Radiocarbon and Indian Archaeology.*

Joglekar, P.P.,2000-2001,Applications of Mathematics and Statistics in Archaeo-zoological Research at Deccan College, *Bulletin of the Deccan College Post-graduate and Research Institute 60-61.*

Joglekar, P.P., 2007-2008, A Fresh Appraisal of the Animal-based Subsistence and Domestic Animals in the Ganga Valley, *Pragdhara 18.*

Joglekar, P.P., V.D. Misra, J.N. Pal and M.C. Gupta, 2008, Faunal Remains from Neolithic Chalcolithic Phases at Tokwa, Mirzapur District, Uttar Pradesh, *Man and Environment XXXIII (2).*

Joglekar, P.P., 2010-2012, Animal Remains from Raja Nal-ka-Tila, District Sonbhadra, Uttar Pradesh, *Pragdhara, 21-22.*

Joglekar, P.P., 2015, Humans and Animals. Archaeozoological Approach, Pune: *Gayatri Sahitya.*

Joglekar, P.P., Vibha Tripathi and Prabhakar Upadhyay, 2009-2010, Faunal Diversity at Agiabir, District Mirzapur, a Multi-culture Site in Uttar Pradesh, *Pragdhara 20.*

Joglekar, P.P., P. Singh and Ashok Kumar Singh, 2010-2011, Animal Remains from Pre-NBPW Period at Agiabir, District Mirzapur, Uttar Pradesh, *Bulletin of the Deccan College Research Institute 70-71.*

Joglekar P.P., P.K. Thomas, Y. Matsushima and S.J. Pawankar, 1994, Osteological Differences between the Forelimb Bones of Ox (Bos indicus), Buffalo (Bubalus bubalis) and Nilgai (Boselaphus tragocamelus), *Journal of Bombay Veterinary College, 5 (1-2).*

Joglekar, P.P., C.V. Sharada, and V.S. Shinde, 2017, Animal Remains from the Mature Harappan Contexts at Farmana, Rohtak District, Haryana, India, *Puratattva 47.*

Jones, G. E. M., 1992, Weed Phytosociology and crop husbandry: identifying a contrast between ancient and modern practice, *Review of Palaeobotany and Palynology 73.*

Joshi, R. V., G.G. Mujumdar and B.C. Deotare,1978, Phosphate analysis and archaeology: A Note, *Man and Environment, II.*

Joshi, R. V. and B.C. Deotare,1982, Phosphate analysis of some archaeological site in Madhya Pradesh, *Indian Archaeology,* R. K. Sharma (ed.).

Katzenberg, M. A. and H.P. Schwarcz,1984, Dietary change in Southern Ontario Prehistory: Evidence from Strontium and Stable Isotopes of Carbon and Nitrogen, *American Journal of Physical Anthropology 63.*

Keeley, H. C. M.,1984, *Environmental Archaeology,* A Regional Review (Occasional Paper 6), London: Department of Ancient Monuments and Historic Buildings.

Kiister, H., 1991, Phytosociology, and Archaeobotany, D.R. Harris and K.D.Thomas (eds.), *Modelling Ecological Change,* London: University College London.

Khanduri, B.M., K.P. Nautiyal, V. Nautiyal, R.C. Bhatt, P.M. Saklani and Y.S. Farswan,1998-99, Excavation of Burial Complexes in Ramganga Valley, Kumaon Himalaya, *Puratattva 29.*

Klepinger, L. L.,1984, Nutritional Assessment from Bone, *Annual Review in Anthropology 13.*

Klepinger, L. L., 1990, Magnesium ingestion and Bone Magnesium Concentration in Palaeodietary Reconstruction: Cautionary Evidence from an Animal Model, *Journal of Archaeological Science 17.*

Konard, V. A. Robson, Bonnichsen and Vickie Clay, 1983, Soil Chemical Identification of ten thousand years of Prehistoric activity areas at the Munsungun Lake Thoroughfare, Maine, *Journal of Archaeological Science,10.*

Lambert, J. B. and J.M. Weydert-Homeyer, 1993, The Fundamental Relationship Between Ancient Diet and the Inorganic Constituents of Bone as Derived from Feeding Experiments, *Archaeometry 35(2).*

Lavy, Rachel,1980, Sources of soluble calcium and magnesium and their effects on sodium adsorption ratios of solutions in two soils of Israel, *Geoderma, 23.*

Lawton, J. H. and P.H. Warren, 1988, Static and dynamic explanations for patterns in food webs, *Trends in Ecology and Evolution 3.*

Lyman, R. L.,1995, Determining when rare (zoo-) Archaeological phenomena are truly absent, *Journal of Archaeological Method and Theory, 2.*

Morgan, M.E. and M.J. Schoeninger, 1989, Zinc and Strontium as Dietary Indicator in a Modern Tropical Community, *American Journal of Physical Anthropology 78.*

Nautiyal, K. P., B.M Khanduri, V. Nautiyal and Y.S. Farswan,1993, Excavation at Purola: An Important PGW-cum Vedic Ritual Site, *Spectrum of Indian Culture,* S.B. Deo Felicitation Volume.

Nautiyal, Vinod, Y.S. Farswan and A.K. Uniyal, 1995, Stable Carbon Isotope Analysis of Archaeological Bone from Garhwal Himalaya, *Science and Culture 61,(7-9).*

Nautiyal, Vinod, Y.S. Farswan and J.S. Rawat 1992, Phosphorus analysis of soil from archaeological sites in the mid-Central Himalaya and Ganga-Yamuna doab, *Man and Environment, XVII (1).*

O'Connor, T. P., 1993, Birds and the Scavenger Niche, *Archaeofauna 2.*

O'Connor, T.P., 1998, Environmental Archaeology: A Matter of Definition, *Environmental Archaeology, 2:1.*

O'Connor, T., 2019, Pinned Down in the Trenches? Revisiting environmental archaeology, *Internet Archaeology 53, doi:10.11141/ia.53.5.*

O. Colinvaux, P., 1993, *Ecology 2,* Chichester: Wiley .

Paine, R. T., 1988, Food Webs: Road maps of interaction, or grist for theoretical development? *Ecology 69.*

Parker, R. B. and H. Toots, 1980, Trace Elements in Bones as Palaeobiological indicator, A. K. Behrensmeyer and A. P. Hill (eds.), *Fossils in the Making,* Chicago: University of Chicago .

Parsons, R. B.,W.H. Shallots and F.F. Reicken,1962, Soil of Indian Mounds in North-East Iowa as Benchmarks for Studies of Soil Genesis, *Soil Sci. Am., Proc.*

Pate, F. D., 1994, Bone Chemistry and Palaeodiet, *Journal of Archaeological Method and Theory 1(2).*

Pawankar, S.J. and P.K. Thomas, 2001, Osteological Differences between Blackbuck (Antilope cervicapra), Goat (Capra hircus) and Sheep (Ovis aries), *Man and Environment 26(1).*

Pearson, Elizabeth, 2019, Commercial Environmental Archaeology: are we back in the dark ages or is environmental Archaeology a potential agent of change, *Internet Archaeology (53), doi:10.11141/ia.53.4.*

Pharswan, J.S. and Y.S. Farswan, 2011, Role and Utility of Trace Elements in Palaeodietary Reconstruction, *New York Science Journal, 4(11).*

Pharswan, J.S. and Y.S. Farswan,2012, Study of Occupational Intensity in Modern Settlement of Nandakini Valley, District-Chamoli, Uttarakhand, India, *Asian Man (The): An International Journal, Vol. 6(2).*

Preece, R. J. (ed.), 1995, *Island Britain: A Quaternary perspective (Special Publication 96),* London: Geological Society.

Price, T. D., M.J. Schoeninger and G.S. Armelagos, 1985a, Bone Chemistry and Past Behaviour: An Overview, *Journal of Human Evolution 14.*

Price, T. D., M.J. Schoeninger and G.J. Armelagos, 1985b, Bone Chemistry and the Reconstruction of Diet: Strontium Discrimination in White-tail Deer, *Journal of Archaeological Science 12.*

Provan, D.M.J., 1971, Soil phosphate analysis as a tool in Archaeology, *Norwegian Archaeological Review 4.*

Proudfoot, N., 1976, The analysis and interpretation of soil phosphorus in archaeological contents, D. A. Davidson & M.A. Shackley (eds), *Geoarchaeology,* London: Duck worth.

Prummel, W. and H.J. Frisch, 1986, A Guide for the Distinction of Species, Sex and Body Side in Bones of Sheep and Goat, *Journal of Archaeological Science 13.*

Rapp, George Robert,1930, Geoarchaeology: The earth-science approach to archaeological interpretation, *Hill, Christopher L.* 1959, New Haven.

Reitz, E. J., L.A. Newsom and S.J.Scudder,1996, *Case Studies in Environmental Archaeology (Interdisciplinary Contributions to Archaeology),* New York: Plenum Press.

Richer, Suzi, D. Stump, R. Marchant, 2019, Archaeology has No Relevance, *Internet Archaeology (53), doi:10.11141/ ia.53.2.*

Robinson, J. T., 1963, Adaptive Radiation in the Australopithecines and the Origin of Man, F. Howell and F. Bouriere (eds), *American Ecology and Human Evolution,* Aldine Publication Co.

Rottlander, R.C., 1976, Variation in the Chemical Composition of Bone as Indicator of Climatic Change, *Journal of Archaeological Science 3.*

Runia, L. T., 1987a, The Chemical Analysis of Prehistoric Bones: A Palaeodietary and Eco-archaeological Study of Bronze Age West-Friesland, *Bar International Series, 363.*

Schoeninger, M. J.,1981, The Agricultural "Revolution" : Its Effect on Human Diet in Prehistoric Israel, *Paleorient 7.*

Schoeninger, M. J., 1989, Reconstructing Prehistoric Human Diet, *Homo 39.*

Schoeninger, M. J., M.J. De Niro and H. Tauber, 1983, Stable Isotope Ratios of Bone Collagen Reflect Marine and Terrestrial Components of Prehistoric Human Diet, *Science 220.*

Schmid, E., 1972, *Atlas of Animal Bones*, Amsterdam: Elsevier.

Schutkowski, H. and B.Herrmann,1999, Diet, Status and Decomposition at Weingarten: Trace Element and Isotope

Analyses on Early Mediaeval Skeletal Material, *Journal of Archaeological Science 26.*

Schwarcz, H. P., J. Melbye and M.A. Katzenberg, 1985, Stable Isotopes in Human Skeletons of Southern Ontario: Reconstructing Palaeodiet, *Journal of Archaeological Science 12.*

Sealy, J. C. and Van Der Merwe, 1986, Isotopic Assessment of Holocene Human Diets in the South Western Cape, South Africa, *Current Anthropology 27.*

Sheila Mishra, M. Jain, S.K. Tandon, A.K. Singhvi, P.P. Joglekar, S.S. Bhatt,A.A. Kshirsagar, S. Naik, and A.M. Deshpande, 1999, Prehistoric Cultures and Late Quaternary Environments in the Luni Basin around Balotra, *Man and Environment XXIV (I).*

Sillen, A. and M. Kavanaugh, 1982, Strontium and Palaeodietary Research: A Review, *Year Book of Physical Anthropology 25.*

Sillen, A.,1988, Elemental and Isotopic analysis of Mammalian Fauna from Southern Africa and their Implications for Palaeodietary Research, *American Journal of Physical Anthropology 76.*

Simmons, I. G., 1997, *Humanity and Environment, A Cultural Ecology*, Harlow: Addison Wesley Longman.

Singh, Hitendra and Y.S. Farswan, 2014, Uttarakhand Himalaya Ke Parwatiya Kshetron Me Paramparagat Krishi Padhyati Ka Ek Adhyayan, *Research Journal of Social and Life Sciences, Vol.-XVI-I.*

Singh, Hitendra and Y.S. Farswan, 2015, Uttarakhand Himalaya Ke Uchcha Shikhariya Kshetron ke Krishi Samudayon Dwara Krishi Utpadakta Hetu Kiye Jane wale Dharmik Anushthano Ka Etihasik Adhyayan, *Research Journal of Arts, Management and Social Sciences, Vol. XII-I.*

Singh, P. and A.K. Singh, 2004, *Archaeology of Middle Ganga Plain - New Perspectives (Excavations at Agiabir)*, Shimla and New Delhi: Indian Institute of Advanced Study and Aryan Books International.

Singh, R.N., C.A. Petrie, P.P. Joglekar, S. Neogi, C. Lancelotti, A.K. Pandey and A. Pathak, 2013, Recent Excavations at Alamgirpur, Meerut District: A Preliminary Report, *Man and Environment, XXXVIII(1).*

Thomas, K. D., 1989, Hierarchical approaches to the evolution of complex Agricultural systems, A. Milles, D. Williams, and N. Gardner,(eds.), The Beginnings of Agriculture, *BAR International Series 496,* Oxford: British Archaeological Reports.

Tieszen, L. L., M.M. Senyimba, S.K. Imbamba and J.H. Truoghton, 1979, The Distribution of C3 and C4 Grasses and Carbon Isotope Discrimination along an Altitudinal and Moisture Gradient in Kenya, *Oecologia 37.*

Toots, H., and M.R. Voorheis, 1965, Strontium in Fossil Bones and the Reconstruction of Food Chains, *Science 149.*

Tripathi, Vibha and Prabhakar Upadhyay, 2006- 2007, Further Excavations at Agiabir (2005- 2006), *Puratattva 37.*

Tripathi,Vibha and Prabhakar Upadhyay, 2008- 2009, Excavations at Agiabir (2006-2007), *Puratattva 39.*

Van Der Merwe, N. J.,1989, Natural variation in ^{13}C Concentration and its Effect on Environmental Reconstruction using $^{13}C/^{12}C$ Ratios in Animal Bones, T.D. Price (ed.), *The Chemistry of Prehistoric Human Bone,* Cambridge: Cambridge University Press.

Van Der Merwe, N. J.,1991, Light Stable Isotopes and the Reconstruction of Prehistoric Diets, *Proceedings of the British Academy 77.*

Vincent, P.,1990, *The Biogeography of the British Isles,* London: Routledge.

Van Der Veen, Marijke, 2007, Formation processes of desiccated and carbonized plant remains-the identification of routine practice, *Journal of Archaeological Science, 34 (6).*

Walker, P. W., and M.J. De Niro,1986, Stable Carbon and Nitrogen Isotope Ratios in Bone Collagen as Indices of Prehistoric Dietary Dependence on Marine and Terrestrial Resources in Southern California, *American Journal of Physical Anthropology 71.*

Wilkinson, Keith, 2003, *Environmental Archaeology: Approaches, Techniques & Applications,* Stroud: Tempus.

Woods, W. I., 1984, Soil Chemical Investigation in Illinois Archaeology: Two Example Studies, J. Lambert (ed.), *Archaeological Chemistry-III.*

Ye Yincan et. al., 2017, *Marine Geo-Hazards in China,* Elsevier.

3

Settlement Archaeology of Rupen River, Mehsana District, North Gujarat (from 3rd Century BCE to 12th Century CE)

Abhishek Roy

Introduction

Present study is focuses on Rupen valley which is surrounded by Banaskantha and Patan from the North, Sabarkantha and Aravalli from the North East and Surendranagar and Ahmedabad from the southern side (District Gazetteer, Mehsana 1979: 1). According to legend, from ancient times whole North Gujarat is known as Anarta after the son of Saryata and Sukanya, a former very ancient Aryan tribe mentioned in the Rigveda. This name is also known from Mahabharata and Puranas (Sankalia 1949). Present study is focusing on the River Rupen, which was originated from Western side of the Taranga Hill of Aravalli range of Mehsana District. In previous years few scholars have conducted the extensive exploration in the context of Chalcolithic settlements (Sonawane & Ajithprasad 1994). Relatively little attention has been paid to later periods i.e. early historic and early medieval etc. in this scenario author try to focusing on these periods which are given above in Rupen Valley of Mehsana District.

Study area

The Rupen Valley is located in the north-west part of the state. Its main tributaries are the Pushpavati and Khari draining nearly 24.6 percent of the total catchment area (Aggarwal et al. 2019). Its rises at an elevation of about 300metre, and is about 150 km long flows into the saline marshes of little Rann. The plains area is semi-arid with mean annual rainfall of about 600 mm (Gibling &Tandon 1997). Present study region is mainly covered with thicker alluvium formation and windblown sands mostly coming from the southwest of the same state. Its flows through Kheralu, Visnagar, Mehsana, Chanasama taluka then disappear in the little Rann of Kutch. This river is ephemeral in nature and flow only during the monsoon period (Gazetteer Mehsana District 1979: 8). The main tributary of river Rupen is Pushmavati which is originates from Malekpur of Kheralu taluka of the district and several sub tributaries are also passes from several taluka such as; Siddhpur, Chanasma etc. another tributary is Khari, originates from Tandav village at Siddhpur taluka. The river Rupen has two main tributaries and as many as 12 sub-tributaries. Lastly these rivers are shallow and fed by rain water only.

For the present study author focusing on Rupen Valley and took only 12 sites which have enough potential and three sites are recently explored by the author which is also undertaken to reconstruct the settlement pattern of Rupen valley (Fig.1).

Previous Researches

Present study area has been studied sporadically by many scholars. There are mostly exploratory and few excavations have been conducted in the context of early historic and early medieval periods. From last two decades this area is extensively explored by M.S. University of Baroda reported more than hundred regional chalcolithic sites are present. With the finding out of the original platform of the Sun temple Modhera, Archaeological Survey of India western circle was conducted the excavation around the temple complex from 1965-66 and 1966 to 67 (IAR 1965-66:18 & 1966-67:8). In 1955 with the understanding ceramic chronology of the site, department of Archaeology and Ancient History, the M.S. University of Baroda took trench at Vadnagar, revealed a continuous sequence of three cultural periods from early historic to medieval (Subbarao & Mehta 1955). The recent excavation of the same site was carried out by the Directorate of Archaeology, Govt. of Gujarat under the supervision of the Y.S. Rawat has provided ample amount of archaeological evidences from this site and highlight the significance of Buddhism in Gujarat also an achievement of this excavation (Rawat 2012). Another exploration was undertaken by Orton Pinto in 2005 to understand the distribution of the red polished ware and to trace the trading network of the inland sites of Gujarat. But she explored only one site from North Gujarat region (Pinto-Orton 2013: 210). James Burgess and H. Cousens were the first scholars to study the architectural monuments of North Gujarat region, and studied very precisely with various approach and published the report in 1903 (Burgess & Cousens 1903)

Objective and methods

The aim of this paper is to study the distribution pattern of archaeological sites ranging from early historic to Medieval period in Rupen valley. An attempt is also made to understand the size of the sites, the origin and development of the sites in this region. Author also try to highlight the locational criteria of the settlements, it helps to understand the context and content of the sites. In this paper author are selected few earlier excavated sites and few recent re-explored or explored sites to reconstruct the settlement pattern of this river valley. In this scenario author took interest to explore and revisited the archaeological sites. Published excavation reports and article were also taken for study to understand the settlement pattern of this valley. Archaeological sites are also plotted and analyze with the help of GIS software and statistical tools.

Distribution of Archaeological Sites

Taranga (23^{0}58′N 72^{0}48′E) is located twenty kilometres northeast of Vadnagar. It's an isolated hill of the Aravalli range of the Kheralu taluka of Mehsana district. According to Y.S. Rawat that This hill is spread over an area of about 11km in perimeter and contain highest peak locally known as *Mallinath* peak or *Sidhhasila* which approximately 446m of above MSL. The earliest finding of the Taranga is belonging to the Buddhist pantheon. One marble of Buddhist deity *Tara* and few other sculptures of the *Avalokiteswara Padmapani* were found in 1938. Another one small panel depicting four *Dhayani* Buddha was found from the Jogida Hill. The influence of tantric elements is reflecting from these images. According to Y.S Rawat that Taranga hill revealed the presence of ancient fortification settlement with artificial cave; the total area consists of two settlements, first a hill fort which is located on the south eastern side of the peak of Taranga hill, and the second is an open area settlement in western side of the same fringe. A close investigation shows that fort wall has revealed with two distinct structural phase lower portion of the wall is made up of stone blocks but in few places the upper portion of the fort wall is constructed with the large burnt bricks. The sizes of the bricks are 49cm X 29cm X 8cm and 42cm X 26cm X 7cm respectively. Another significant discovery of Taranga site is an ancient dam, which signifies the important of ancient irrigation system of this area. Beside the right bank of the ephemeral river a small tank is also discovered which is belongs to early historic period. Ancient dam is also damaged due to modern anthropogenic activity. These walls are measured about 110m and 80m respectively. Large granites boulder are scattered over the bed rock of the ancient dam. The site has also yielded varieties of potsherds which may be dated to *Kshatrapa* to pre-*kshatrapa* period. The ceramic assemblage comprises red, grey, black and red and fine polished black and/or grey wares. The main shapes are saucer-cum-cup type lids, convex sided bowls, carinated *handi* (a wide mouth pot used for cooking), medium sized jars and a vase with a narrow elongated neck and with a featureless rim and a corrugated exterior, etc. some pot sherds are decorated with appliqué manner. Red polished ware of *Kshatrapa* period is totally absent from this site. Terracotta roof tiles are also found from this site. On the right bank of the rivulet appears to be an altered base of a small stupa because two large sized terracotta images of the Buddha in *padmasana* have been recovered from its top surface (Rawat 2012).

Vadnagar (23° 47′ N; 72° 39′ E), is located in the north eastern part of the district Mehsana on the bank of the river Rupen. from ancient times Vadnagar is known by several names such as, *Anandapur, Anartapura, Chamatkarpur, Vridhhanagar, Skandpura* and *Nagaraka* etc. around in 640 CE Chinese traveller Xuan Xang who is also visited this place and mentioned it in his own itinerary si-yu-ki as (o-nan- to- pu-lo = *Anandpur*). He mentions that there were more than 1000 monks of sammatiya schools in 10 monasteries at Vadnagar. The earlier excavation was conducted by Rao and Mehta of the Maharaja Sayajirao University of Baroda in 1953, with the aim of understanding the ceramic sequence of the site (Subbarao et. al 1955). The excavations also shows the existence of conch shell industry, manufacturing different varieties of bead, bangles etc. other important artefacts which were discovered from this site such as; terracotta sealings, red polished pot sherds, one lead coin etc. the excavation revealed three cultural periods from early historic to medieval.

But recent excavation was conducted under the supervision of Y.S. Rawat of Directorate of archaeology; government of Gujarat revealed the ample evidences of developed township and most important centre of Buddhist Pantheon in this region and played an important trading centre of North Gujarat (Anarta) region. The excavator has identified five periods of continuous occupation at the site; Period I: the formative stage of the settlement; Period II: the first fortified settlement (3rd century BCE to 1st century BCE); Period III: a re-planned town with a burnt brick fortification (1st century BCE to 11th century CE); Period IV: modification of internal planning (12th century to 17th century CE); Period V: period of present town planning (11th century up to the present day) (Fig. 2). Excavation has revealed different architectural evidences such as; secular and religious structure which is made of large and medium burnt bricks.

Excavations have been so far carried out at seven locations, three within and four outside the fortified town. The excavation outside the town was only small trial trenches, which provided information concerning the expansion of the town during different periods of its history. However, the following three locations within the fortified area have provided more fruitful results for the reconstruction of the complete cultural sequence of the site. From Ghaskhol Darwaza area Excavation revealed that a Buddhist complex, with monasteries and stupas, was established at this location around the 1st century CE, and that occupation continued until the 7th century CE. A stepped square tank made of reused bricks, built around the 12th century CE possibly to store water for the repair work of the fort wall, seems to be the only later major construction. Period I has yielded different types of potsherds, Punch marked coin, copper rings bone points, cowrie shells etc were found. From period II consists of post-holes at regular intervals on top of the walls and super structures, burnt bricks in header and stretcher with mud mortar. Evidences gathered were hearth and fire activities. Ceramics included Red Ware, Black and Red Ware, Grey Ware, and Micaceous Red Ware with antiquities like punched marked coins, and an ivory button seal engraved with *Brahmi* characters. In Period III the settlement was re-structured and the burnt brick fortification was seen for the first time. The streets had rows of houses on both sides. Large number of terracotta figurines, animal figurines pendant shape like human head; bangles etc were found during from the excavation of this site. Amphorae and torpedo shreds were found from the excavation (Rawat 2012).

Virta (23^{0}42′ N; 72^{0}18′ E) is also a small village consisted of small shrine of *neelkantheswar mahadeva* temple which is located half a mile west by north of Gorad. This shrine is very similar to that of Gorad, but it has addition of *mandapa*. The pillars was not richly decorated and well finished. More or less same figures are also located like that of Gorad temple (Burgess &Cousens 1903). The temple faces west. During the exploration author collected some brick bats and potsherds from near the pond area. The mound is high in nature, approximately 6 feet in high. The area of the mound is around 8 hectres in size and it stands on 75.5 MSL. A mound covers thorny and scrubby trees and herbs are partly covering that area (Fig. 3).

Kanoda (23°36′N, 72°15′E) is a small village on the Rupen river about four miles to the south west of Dhinoj. South side of this village one pretty little temple is present. The *mandapa* is left, but the shrine has all but disappeared, only foundation parts now remaining. Its door frame is fallen within it, lays in pieces- the two jambs and the lintel. *Shikhara* is erected in recent time by temple trust and temple is fully coloured by paint. The style of pillars is much like the others already described; we have the *chaitya window* on the basement of the screen wall. The domical roof of the hall has been decorated in the usual way but instead of a central pendant ornament, it has flat lotus (Burgess &Cousens 1903).

Gorad (23°41′ N; 72°18′ E) is located near the bank of the river Pushpavati. This temple is dedicated to Shiva locally it is known as *someshwar Mahadev* temple. It's a small temple facing east and a newly built porch. A part of the temple is partly below the present ground level. The *mandovara* consisting of the usual course of mouldings with beautiful sculpture of the lord *Shiva* in dancing mode and slaying the demon *Andhakasur* (Burgess & Cousens 1903). There is also a seated sculpture of goddess *maheswarimatrika* in one of the niches. The spire over the sanctum is partly ruined. A flat ceiling is decorated with floral motifs. Few sculptures are scattered in outside of this temple complex, these sculptures are the part of the temple and its depicted different deities. Outside the temple complex, quite a few amounts of tiny potsherds of grey ware, red ware were also found from the surface level of this site. Due to the modernization of this present locality the site is heavily disturbed by anthropogenic activity.

Palasar (23°41′N;72°16′E) is newly discovered site situated two km west of Virta Village, near the right bank of the Pushpavati River in Chanasma taluka, district Mehsana. This is a habitation site. The site is surrounded by agricultural field. The mound is flat in nature. This mound is stands at 76.6 MSL. Total area of the mound is around nine hectare. The whole mound is covered with vegetation. Few area of this mound is partly destroyed by modern anthropogenic activity. The artefacts mainly ceramics were found from the surface exploration on the mound, basically ceramics are red ware, grey ware, red slipped ware and are similar to the Modhera village. In the northern side of the mound the structure is exposed due to erosional activity. Ancient structure are consists of several courses made up of burnt brick. In this section several potsherds were also visible.

Dhinoj (23°39′25"N; 72°16′44"E) is located near the left bank of the Pushpavati River; it's one of the main tributary of river Rupen. It is a temple cum habitational site of the early medieval period. The old temple is square in plan and dedicated to goddess *vagheswari.* This Temple has a sanctum with an open *mandapa* and a porch. It seems to have been restored more than once. The basement of the *mandapa* and *vedika* is heavily decorated with various floral motifs in vertical manner and the broken compartments containing figures of deities (Burgess & Cousens 1903).The tiny vase and foliage pillars are very beautifully depicted. The usual elaborate ceiling has an elegant little lotus pendant in the centre. The doorway of the sanctum is heavily decorated with figures of goddess on the jamb and architrave. The porch is covered by geometrical designs. Around Dhinoj village remains of building, tanks and step well of early medieval sites are present (Burgess & Cousens 1903).

Sun Temple Modhera (23^{0}35′00"N; 72^{0}07′59"E) is situated on the left bank of the River Pushmavati; the main tributary of River Rupen. The sun temple Modhera was constructed by Bhima I of Solanki dynasties. The sun temple is a beautiful specimen of ancient Indian temple architecture and first attention was paid by Colonel Monier Williams nearly 200 years ago. The temple has lost its curvilinear *shikhara* and the *sabhamandapa* and porches. The principle deity (Sun God) is missing from *garbhagriha*. However, the sculptures curved on the exterior as well as interior wall of the circumambulatory path and *gudhamandapa* largely represent the solar deity. The temple itself determined into two separate structure connected by narrow passage consisting of an open pillared hall and an enclosed rectangular building in two compartments. The latter comprise an enclosed wall and *garbhagriha*. In front of the *Sabhamandapa Surya kunda* is situated, rectangular in shape is surrounded by curvilinear steps on all sides. On the flat platform, miniature temples are erected to dedicated different deities (Burgess & Cousens 1903).

Modhera Village: Village Modhera (23^{0}34.9200′N, 72^{0}8.4630′E) is situated within the Chanasma taluka of the Mehsana district of North Gujarat. It is located about 623 meter eastern side of the temple complex and structural mound is highly in nature. It stands at 58 to 59 metre above MSL (Mean Sea Level). The total area of this site is approximately 21 hectres. Presently ancient mound is heavily disturbed by modern anthropogenic activity. But in some places ancient structures were exposed. The brick size is 40 x 27 x 7 cm. The ceramics were found during the exploration consists of pots, *handis* and vessels etc. The pots are in Red Ware with medium necked with an out turned with a grooved rim, few are round rim with grooved, well fired in nature, section is medium, little amount of micaceous material sprinkled on the upper surface of the pottery. Red Slipped Ware was also found during the survey (Fig. 4). Few pots are black in colour with constricted neck having projecting rim, well fired and section is medium. The vessels or conical bowls are in Red Ware, conical in shaped with a straight rim, and flat base is predominant. Section is medium, well fired in nature. Earlier Red Polished ware was also reported from Modhera by Orton (Pinto-Orton 2013: 210). At the time of exploration few broken architectural and sculptural pieces are also discovered from the various places of this mound. Broken piece of multi-foliated *torana*, which is 37 inches in length and 17 inches in breadth, was discovered from the western zone of this village mound (Fig. 5).

Navgaji Mazar: Navgaji Mazar (23^{0}34.8210′N; 72^{0}7.8636′E) is a newly reported archaeological site which is located 700 metre south west corner of the Sun temple Modhera. This site is very close to the left bank of river Pushpavati. The total area of this site is five to six hectres and it is high in nature. Ample amount of ancient brick bats are scattered over this mound surface, but currently this mound is serving as modern burial ground. Complete bricks are also documented during field survey; the exact size of brick is 16.5 X 11 X 3.5 inches. Near to this mound ancient wall was vandalised by public works department of state government Gujarat. It is also documented by authors is 2.40 metre thick wall with four to five courses.

Hirimba no Timbo ($23^{0}34.64'$N; $72^{0}8.21'$E) is newly reported habitation site which is located near 1km south eastern side of the sun temple Modhera and it is more close to the Modhera Village site. The site is not too high in nature more or less plane and it's surrounded by an agricultural land. Total area of the site is three hectres. In Northern side of this mound ancient brick structure is exposed from the section which was vandalised by villagers. From the upper surface of the mound bears ample amount of potsherds and brickbats. In few places brickbats and several ceramic assemblages such as; red ware, grey ware, red slipped ware were also visible on the surface this mound.

Umta ($23^{0}46'$ N; $72^{0}33'$E) An excavation of the mound at village Umta, known as Rajgadhi mound in Visnagar taluk of the district, was carried out under the direction of B.S. Makwana, of the Department of Archaeology of the Government of Gujarat, assisted by H.S. Shah and O.P. Ajwalia. An area of 8 x 8 m and 5 x 10 m on the western side of the mound was taken up for excavation. he excavation revealed the structural remains of a temple, made of stone and marble, a few brick walls, and bastion made of bricks (IAR 1988-89).

Conclusion

In this paper author try to highlighted the emergence and locational criteria of archaeological settlements from early historic to early medieval periods. The spatial distribution of these archaeological sites indicates that river Rupen and its tributaries played a significant role to form the culture milieu of these periods. Interestingly all the sites are situated on the alluvium zone of the study area except Taranga, which is denudational origin. The alluvial soil is very much useful for agricultural purpose and probably from early historic times this area are very incentive for the inhabitant to reoccupy the sites again in early medieval and medieval times with the knowledge of refined technology.

The settlement pattern of this river basin is quite significant. After the chalcolithic period present study zone is very ill studied, only three early historic sites are excavated as well as exploration work is also very less in manner. Author has taken only 12 sites, few of them are re-explored and four sites are newly discovered during exploration. All the sites are distributed in linear pattern except three sites of Modhera and its surroundings are in clustered manner. Palasar is situating on the right bank of the Rupen River, Taranga is the only site is located on the origin of the Rupen River. Rest of the sites are located on the left bank of the same river. Most of the sites are multicultural and five of them belong to early historic period. However the habitation site varies from small to big in size (Figure IX). From early historic period this river basin played an important role to flourish the cultural landscape. The ecological zones and many other factors such as trading mechanism, political organization, warfare, religion and subsistence pattern affected the settlement pattern, distribution and their size in different ways (Trigger 1968). The habitational deposits are varies from site to site. In between all 12 sites, two of them are below five hectare, there are six settlements belong to category five to ten hectare, one settlement is belong to eleven to thirty hectare in size, another only one settlement is 60 hectare in size. Two settlements are unknown in term of its size. Statistical data showing that highest number of sites are between 5 to 10 hectare and all these sites are situating near the bank of the river.

The proximity of the perennial source of water is an important factor of the settlement location. According to Possehl (1980:85) "an obvious advantage to a riverine location is reliable supply of water to human and animal consumption as well as for domestic uses and irrigation". River Rupen is sluggish in nature during the dry season it became dry, then localised people were used the ground water and water of the modern artificial canals made all over in Gujarat. Panini mentions that the villages depended for their water supply on well (Kupa) to which were attached nipanas or water trough from which the cattle would drink (Agarwal 1953: 141).

In this paper author conducted exploration along with the river valley and takes the help some previous report and excavation materials. The cultural remains in the form of ceramic assemblages, antiquities and other cultural materials from these explored sites and compared with the published material of the Vadnagar excavation by Directorate of Archaeology Gujarat which was obtained from the proper strata. Red Polished potsherds, red slipped, red ware and stamped and incised ware represent the early historic Vadnagar and its adjoining areas along the river valley. The Present survey has drawn the attention towards showing various types of potsherds with different shapes and sizes. Earlier Red Polished ware was also reported from Modhera by Orton (Pinto-Orton 2013: 210). The present survey has brought to notice one stamped potsherd (floral design) from surface collection. Some architectural part of the temples, few habitational ruins and ceramic assemblage indicate that during early medieval times this region was also well flourished. Excavated structures and cultural materials of Vadnagar are also signify that from early historic to early medieval times these sites act as an important urban centre to develop the cultural landscape and trade network of North Gujarat. However it could be said that, all the archaeological sites in this region are more or less contemporary with the excavated site of Vadnagar. The present research paper is a mere stepping stone for further researches in this direction.

References

Agarwal, V.S., 1953, *India as known to Panini*, Lucknow: Lucknow University.

Aggarwal, A, P.K. Srivastava, A. Tiwari, R.S. Chatterjee & D.K. Gupta, 2019, ArcSwat based Geospatial modelling of Rainfall-runoff processes in Rupen basin, Mehsana district, Gujarat in *Disaster Advances vol.12* (10).

Burgess, James, and Henry Cousens, 1903, The Architectural Antiquites of Northern Gujarat, more especially of the districts included in the Baroda state, *Archaeological survey of Western India, New Imperial Series*, Archaeological Survey of India.

Gazetteer Mehsana District, 1979, Ahmedabad: Government of Gujarat.

Gibling, M.R. & S.K. Tandon., 1997, Erosinal marks on consolidated banks and slump blocks in the Rupen River, north-west India, *Sedimentology 44.*

Indian Archaeological Review, 1965-66, Archaeological Survey of India, New Delhi, 1973.

Indian Archaeological Review, 1966-67, Archaeological Survey of India, New Delhi, 1973.

Indian Archaeological Review, 1988-89, Archaeological Survey of India, New Delhi, 1973.

Pinto, O.N., 2013, Red Polished Ware in Gujarat: Surface collections from inland sites, *Connections and Complexity: New Approaches to the Archaeology of South Asia, edited by S.A. Abraham, P. Gullapalli, T.P. Raczek and U.Z. Rizvi,* Left coast Press.

Possehl, G. L., 1980, *Indus Civilization in Saurastra,* New Delhi: B.R. Publishing Corporation.

Rawat,Y.S., 2012, Recently Found Ancient Monastry and other Buddhist Remains at Vadnagar and Taranga In North Gujarat, India, *Bujang Valley and Early Civilization of South East Asia,* Stephen Ming, Soon Chia and Barbara Watson (ed) Andaya: KualaLumpur.

Sankalia, H.D., 1949, *Studies in the Historical & Cultural Geography and Ethnography of Gujarat,* Poona: Deccan College Postgraduate and Research Institute.

Sonawane, V.H. and P. Ajithprasad, 1994, Harappa Culture and Gujarat, *Man & Environment 19.*

Subbarao, B. and R.N. Mehta, 1955, Excavation at Vadnagar, *Journal of the Maharaja Sayajirao University of Baroda* 4.1.

Trigger, B. G., 1968, The Determinants of Settlement Patterns, *Settlement Archaeology,* Chang, K.C. (eds) Palo Alto: National Press.

4

Lothal and Its Neighbourhood: An Archaeological Survey

Rajesh S. V., Bhanu Prakash Sharma, K. Krishnan and Abhayan G. S.

Introduction

Though the existence of regional Chalcolithic cultures/traditionsin Gujarat was identified during 1950s, problem-oriented studies on this topic were initiated by the end of 1980s. Subsequent explorations in different regions of Gujarat and reanalysis of ceramics from previously excavated sites resulted in the identification of a number of regional Chalcolithic cultures/ceramic traditions in its different parts. Micaceous Red Ware, primarily reported from Bhal region (Rao 1963: 1-263, 1965: 30-37; Mehta et al. 1980; Mehta and Sonawane 1985), also attained importance in Indus archaeology in this period due to the comprehensive typo-technological and spatiotemporal analyses done by Herman and Krishnan (1994: 225-243). Subsequent to this, a few explorations (Dimri 1999; Krishnan and Dimri 2005) to understand the spatial distribution of this pottery and excavation at Vejalka II to understand its temporal distribution and relative abundance (Krishnan Personal Communication) were conducted.

In tune with the previous studies, with an aim to identify the distribution of Classical Harappan and other regional Chalcolithic cultures in a definable geographical subregionand to understand the intensity of sites, systematic archaeological explorations were carried out by the researchers around Classical Harappan settlement Lothal which is the earliest dated Micaceous Red Ware yielding site. It was assumed that this exploration would further contribute to the understanding of Micaceous Red Ware within the Chalcolithic context of Gujarat.

Study Area

The study area consists of 47 villages of Dhandhuka taluka, 56 villages of Dholka taluka and 2 villages of Bavla taluka in Ahmedabad district; 17 villages of Limbdi taluka in Surendranagar district, 8 villages of Khambhat taluka and 15 villages of Tarapur taluka in Anand district. It comes under

Bhal plains which receives discharge from Sabarmati, Bhogava, Sukha Bhadar and Lilka rivers. This area falls under semi-arid zone with a mean annual rainfall of 600 mm. The geology and drainage pattern of this region are extensively studied by various researchers (Rao 1979; Merh 1995; Dimri 1999; Khadkikar *et al.* 2004: 896-903). The land is fertile and supports both rabi and kharif crops. The land serves as habitat for both wild and domesticated animals.

Previous Studies

Previous researchers have carried out a variety of archaeological researches in this region. These have brought to light evidence of human activity in this area during the Prehistoric (Momin 1979; Rao 1963; Sankalia 1941, 1946; Subbarao 1958), Chalcolithic (Ajithprasad 2002: 129-158, 2011: 11-40; Bhan 1989: 219-142, 1992: 173-192, 2004: 243-273, 2018: 43-62; Bhattacharyya 1991: 53-57; Bindra 2003; Carter 2001: 183-201; Cork 2005: 411-423; Dikshit 1950: 3-55; Dimri 1994, 1998-99: 27-44, 1999, 2005: 377-386; Frenez 2014: 263-278; Frenez and Tosi 2005: 65-103, 2010; Ghosh and Lal 1963: 161-175; Ghurye 1939: 3-12; Gogte 2000: 7-14; Herman 1995: 187-198, 1997: 77-112; Herman and Krishnan 1994: 225-243; Hoffman and Miller 2009: 237-264; IAR 1953-54, 1954-55, 1955-56, 1956-57, 1957-58, 1958-59, 1959-60, 1995-96; Ilahi 2018, 2019; Ilahi *et al.* 2019: 257-269; Jam 2010; Jamison 2017; Joshi and Parpola 1987; Kenoyer and Miller 1999: 107-151; Khadkikar *et al.* 2004: 896-903; Khatri 1982; Krishnan 1982, 1986, 1992: 125-132, 2002: 377-385; Krishnan and Dimri 2005; Krishnan and Hegde 1988: 27-56; Krishnan and Rao 1994: 113-117; Kumar 1996; Lal 1963: 33-137; Law 2008; Leshnik 1972; Majumdar 1994; Mate 1985: 75-84; Mehta *et al.* 1980; Mirchandani 1980; Misra 1965: 44-52; Momin 1974: 57-63, 1976a: 54-56, 1976b: 51-54, 1979, 1984: 231-234; Panjwani 1981, 1989: 83-86; Possehl 1976; Possehl and Kennedy 1979: 592-593; Rajesh 2011; Rao 1956: 82-99, 1962: 14-30, 1963: 1-207, 1965: 30-37, 1973, 1979, 1985; Sonawane 1991: 225-232, 2000: 137-146, 2002: 159-172, 2005: 326-331; Sonawane and Ajithprasad 1994; Sonawane and Mehta 1985: 38-44; Subbarao 1958; Vats 1935: 34-38, 1937: 34-38; Vyas 1998), Early Historic (Rao 1963: 1963; Margabandhu 1981: 99-112; Mehta 1968) and Medieval Periods (Bhan 2006: 90-95; Insoll *et al.* 2004: 1161-1173; Hawkes 2019: 169-183; Kumar 2016, 2017; Kumar *et al.* 2019: 443-462; Mehta 1968, 1978-79). Besides, ethno-archaeological work (Bhan 2018: 43-62; Insoll *et al.* 2004; Kenoyer *et al.* 1991: 44-63, 1994: 281-306) carried out in this area is also significant for understanding the cultural processes in Chalcolithic and subsequent periods. This exploration was aimed at understanding the site intensity, intra-site and inter-site interactions within this area and also to examine the signatures of various regional Chalcolithic cultures/traditions in the area.

Exploration

Prior to field survey, in addition to literature review, the geo-morphological and archaeological potentials of the area were studied with the help of topographic sheets of 1:250000 and 1:50000 scale, satellite images, Google earth images and SRTM maps. Field walking was restricted at times to avoid trespassing through private land or land under cultivation. Nevertheless, an area falling under a 25 km radius circle with Lothal as the centre was surveyed. The sites reported earlier were also revisited. The geo-coordinates of the archaeological sites and rough estimate of the shape and size of the mound were recognized using Garmin Terex Vista handheld GPS. During the survey it was noticed that due to continuous use of the land for agricultural purposes sites have undergone either partial or complete destruction. The details of each site were recorded on a site recording sheet. Sampling, though random, was done with great care; however, difficulties were encountered in categorizing them in multicultural sites.

During the course of exploration, 19 sites (Figs. 1 and 2, Table 1) were identified and the artefacts from these newly explored and revisited sites were divided into representative cultures/traditions namely Classical Harappan/SorathHarappan (13), Late SorathHarappan (11), Micaceous Red Ware (8), Lustrous Red Ware (2) Early Historic (1) and Late Medieval (14). As the scope of this article is limited to Chalcolithic period, only cultural remains from 13 sites of the Urban Harappan (Classical Harappan, Sorath Harappan, Micaceous Red Ware and Black and Red Ware) and Post Urban Harappan (Micaceous Red Ware, Late Sorath Harappan, Lustrous Red Ware and Black and Red Ware) periods are discussed in detail.

Pottery from the study area (Figs. 3 – 13, Table 2) were categorized into different wares based on their colour, surface features, form, texture and probable manufacturing techniques. Its colour (Red, Buff, Grey and Black and Red) was determined by identifying its equivalents in the Munsell Soil Colour Chart (1954). Determination of its texture was done by comparing feel of its cross-section with the feel of different grades of sand paper (Grades 36, 50, 60, 80, 100 and 120) along with other parameters such as slip-body relationship and visible features of firing. It was found that the feel of coarse ceramics was equivalent to that of -36, 36, 50; fine wares to 100, 120 and 120+ and the medium ones to 60 and 80. Based on its typotechnological features, ceramics were classified as Urban Harappan, Post Urban Harappan, Early Historic and Medieval types.

Apart from ceramics, other major artefacts recovered from the study area include terracotta objects (perforated pottery discs/spindle whorls, ear stud/spindle whorl, imperforated pottery discs, triangular cakes, pinched cakes, hubbed wheel, balls and polisher/skin rubber), stone objects (lithic debitage of crypto crystalline silica, sandstone muller and grinding stone), shell objects (bead, bangle and debitage) and unidentified copper objects. Numerous animal bone fragments belonging to typical domestic species (cattle and sheep/goat), and antler of wild species (blue bull), many with mineralencrustation similar to that commonly observed in excavated faunal assemblages in the region, were collected from the disturbed surface of sites.

Relative Abundance of Micaceous Red Ware

Though the exact quantity of this ware in excavated sites in Bhal region is not clear, it is not a dominant ware in any of the sites. At Lothal (Rao 1979, 1985), and Rangpur (Rao 1963: 1-207), though the real quantity of the same is not mentioned in the excavation reports, they seem to be present in good quantity. The relative abundance of Micaceous Red Ware in the sites under study also showed that it is not the dominant ware in any of the sites (Fig. 14). Among the explored/ revisited sited Kotadiya showed its maximum presence followed by Koth.

Chronology

The relative chronology andcultural periods of the sites was established through comparative analysis of the ceramics from explored sites with various excavated sites in Gujarat and recalibrated radiocarbon dates from Lothal(Possehl 1994: 1-122; Reimer *et al.* 2009: 1-150) (Fig. 15). The ceramics from the survey region are comparable to the same from Lothal (A and B), Surkotada (IA, IB and IC), Rojdi (A, B and C), Rangpur (IIA, IIB, IIC and III), Kuntasi (II and II), Dholavira (IV-VII), Kanmer (I-III), Kanewal (A and B), Bagasra (I-IV), Shikarpur (I-III) Jaidak (IIA and IIB), Vagad (IA, IB and IC) and Nageswar (IA and IB). Thus, the explored sites are roughly datable to Urban Harappan (c. 2600 – 1900 BC) and Post Urban Harappan Phases (c. 1900 – 1300 BC) (Fig. 16, Table 3).

All the Chalcolithic sites in the explored area revealed Sorath/Urban Harappan artefacts. At the sites, except Vadgam II and Jalampar, Urban Harappan artefacts were found associated with Post Urban Harappan/Late Sorath Harappan cultural relics. Except at Balgamada, Rojka, Vadgam II, Panasina and Jalampar, Sorath Harappan ceramics were found associated with Micaceous Red Ware. At Rangpur and Kotadiya, Sorath Harappan ceramics were found along with Lustrous Red Ware. Lothal, Vadgam II and Panasina showed the presence of Black and Red Ware along with the Sorath Harappan ceramics. Based on the available c14 dates and relative chronology suggested for similar kind of artefacts yielding sites from other parts of Gujarat, all the explored Urban Harappan/Sorath Harappan artefacts can be roughly dated in between c. 2600-1900 BC and Late Sorath Harappan can be dated in between c. 1900-1600 BC(Fig. 16, Table 3).

The Micaceous Red Ware sites in the explored area are Padana, Kharad I, Kharad II, Kotadiya Lothal, Koth, Vadgam I and Rangpur. None of the sites showed its independent existence and they were found associated with Sorath Harappan and Late Sorath Harappan artefacts. Based on the available c14 dates and relative chronology suggested for Micaceous Red Ware yielding sites in Gujarat, this ceramic tradition can be roughly dated between c. 2600-1600 BC (Fig. 16, Table 3).

Lustrous Red Ware was only reported from Kotadiya and Rangpur and in both the sites it was found along with Sorath Harappan and Late Sorath Harappan artefacts and Micaceous Red Ware. Based on the available c14 dates and relative chronology suggested for Lustrous Red Ware yielding sites in Gujarat, ceramics of this local tradition can be roughly dated in between c. 1900-1300 BC(Fig. 16, Table 3).

Discussion and Conclusion

Almost all the sites, except the protected area of the site Lothal, are highly disturbed due to agricultural activities, soil removal and construction works. The use of tractors and JCB for land levelling and agricultural works, manual clearance of the sites by removing the ceramics and bone pieces also aggravate the loss of rich cultural heritage/cultural relics. The role of natural agencies like water cannot be ruled out as well. The size of the sites (calculated based on the concentration of artefacts) varies from 0.4 ha to 20.25 ha and the maximum deposit of the sites differs from 1 m to 6.5 m. Many a times, the distribution of the artefacts does not represent the exact size of the settlements as the modern land levelling techniques cause the spread of artefacts of a site into nearby areas/fields.

It was observed that the distribution of Chalcolithic sites was along the water bodies on fertile black cotton soil. None of the sites other than Lothal and Rangpur showed the presence of structures. Various ceramic types like Red Ware, Buff Ware, Gray Ware, Black and Red Ware, Micaceous Red Ware and Lustrous Red Ware and vitrified pot sherds collected from the study area, their manufacturing technique and decorative patterns clearly indicate the technological knowhow and aesthetic sense of the Classical Harappans and regional Chalcolithic people.

The availability of shell bangles, beads and shell debitage from the study area point towards the use of shell bangles and beads as ornaments, procurement of finished products or raw materials from different places or small scale shell bangle and bead production sites in the study area (Lothal is an exception). Perforated pottery discs and spindle whorls/ear studs (?) are indicators of possible spinning activities carried out at the area. If the spinning activity was in vogue, it indirectly throws light on the probabilities of cotton cultivation or goat/sheep domestication in the area. Grinding stones and pestle stones collected from various sites probably indicate food grain processing. The hubbed wheel from the site Rangpur is an example of terracotta toys used by the Chalcolithic community for childcare (Elke 2006). It also indirectly indicates the existence of wheeled vehicles like bullock cart. The availability of copper though in small amount from Panasina reveals the knowledge of metal processing techniques or procurement of finished objects from sites such as Lothal and Rangpur. Animal bones recovered from the sites might be the wastes of meat consumption. Results of the study clearly show that systematic surveys can produce authentic information regarding the distribution of sites and its nature. Similarly,excavations at selected sites are highly recommended for better understanding the complex characteristics of the cultural periods under discussion.

Acknowledgements

We would like to thank the Maharaja Sayajirao University of Baroda and the University of Kerala for all research facilities. We also express our heartfelt thanks to the villagers of survey region for their cooperation and help during the field work. The view sex pressed in this paper and all errors, both factual and interpretation are solel your own.

Table 1: Explored Sites in the Study Area

Sl. No.	Site	Village	Taluka and District	Co-ordinates	Site Size and Deposit	Condition of the Site	Cultural Affiliation*	References
1	Govind Parekh no Khetar	Balgamada	Dhandhuka, Ahmedabad	22° 17' 00.3" N, 71° 58' 35.9" E	400x400=16 ha 2m	disturbed due to road construction and agricultural activities	SH, LSH, LM	Dimri 1999
2	Rojasar/ Jasabhai Bachubhai no Khetar (Timbo)	Rojka	Dhandhuka, Ahmedabad	22° 20' 83.4" N, 72° 02' 18.0" E	100x100=1 ha 1m	Disturbed due to Agricultural activity	SH, LSH, EH, LM	Dimri 1999
3	Kediya Timbo	Padana	Dhandhuka, Ahmedabad	22° 20' 10.8" N, 71° 56' 53.2" E	300x150=4.5 ha 2.5m	Some portions disturbed due to agricultural activity	SH, LSH, MRW, LM	IAR 1995-1996: 7
4	Kharad I (Devabhai Kimbha no Timbo)	Kharad	Dhandhuka, Ahmedabad	22° 19' 10.4" N, 72° 00' 50.4" E	150x150 = 2.25 ha 1m	Disturbed due to Agricultural activity	SH, LSH, MRW, LM	IAR 1995-1996: 9
5	Kharad II (Jagdish Singh Dadubhai no Khetar)	Kharad	Dhandhuka, Ahmedabad	22° 19' 16.7" N, 71° 59' 29.7" E	450x450=20.25 ha 2m	Almost undisturbed	SH, LSH, MRW	IAR 1995-96: 9; Dimri 1999
6	Kotadiya (Kumar Pal Singh Baldev Singh no Khetar)	Kotadiya	Dhandhuka, Ahmedabad	22° 20' 05.6" N, 71° 59' 51.7" E	400x400=16 ha 1.5m	Disturbed due to Agricultural activity and construction of a small lane	SH, LSH, MRW, LRW, LM	IAR 1995-96: 9; Dimri 1999
7	Lothal	Saragwala	Dholka, Ahmedabad	22° 31' 37.2" N, 72° 14' 92.1" E	285x230= 6.55 ha 6.5m	Excavated, Protected by ASI	CH, SH, LSH, MRW, BRW	Rao 1956: 82-89; 1962: 14-30; 1965: 30-37; 1973; 1979; 1985
8	Manubhai no Khetar	Koth	Dholka, Ahmedabad	22° 37' 60.3" N, 72° 17' 83.3" E	100x100=1 ha 1m	Disturbed due to Agricultural activity, land levelling and soil removal	SH, LSH, MRW, LM	Rao 1963: 181 and 206, Rao 1979: 699
9	Vadgam I (Chandubhai Akhubhai no Timbo)	Vadgam	Khambhat, Anand	22° 20' 51.6" N, 72° 24' 79.2" E	400x400= 16 ha 1m	Disturbed due to Agricultural activity	SH, LSH, MRW	IAR 1964-65: 10-11, IAR 1972-73: 10; IAR 1974-75: 13
10	Vadgam II (Jamba Mohabat Singh no Khetar)	Vadgam	Khambhat, Anand	22° 29' 90.2" N, 72° 25' 94.0" E	150x150 = 2.25 ha 1m	Disturbed due to Agricultural activity	SH, BRW, LM	Rajesh 2011

11	Pampadia Hanumanji no Tekaro	Panasina	Limbdi, Surendranagar	22° 30' 74.0" N, 71° 58' 02.6" E	150x100=1.5 ha 1.5m	Disturbed due to agricultural activities, land leveling, soil removal and temple construction	SH, LSH, BRW, LM	Rao 1963: 185
12	Rangpur	Rangpur	Limbdi, Surendranagar	22° 24' 10.7" N, 71° 55' 69.8" E	300x200=6ha 6.5m	Excavated, disturbed due to the construction of houses, road, waste dumping, soil removal, agricultural activities and river action	SH, LSH, MRW, LRW	Vats 1935: 34-38; Ghurye 1939: 3-12; Dikshit 1950: 3-55; Rao 1963: 1-207
13	Talavadi	Jalampar	Limbdi, Surendranagar	22° 35' 34.4" N, 72° 03' 85.2" E	80x50= .4ha 1m	Disturbed due to pond construction and land levelling	SH	Rajesh 2011
14	Ramalpar	Rupgadh	Dholka	22° 38' 59.3" N, 72° 20' 10.4" E	100x100=1ha 2m	Disturbed due to agricultural activities	LM	Rajesh 2011
15	Taliya	Kadipur	Dholka, Ahmedabad	22° 39' 06.8" N, 72° 23' 63.8" E	150x150=2.25ha 1m	Disturbed due to agricultural activities	LM	Rajesh 2011
16	Sarodi Mata no Timbo	Dugari	Tarapur, Anand	22° 33' 04.7" N, 72° 28' 27.4" E	200x150=3ha 1m	Disturbed due to agricultural activities	LM	Rajesh 2011
17	Vankar no Khetar	Pasegam	Tarapur, Anand	22° 32' 28.9" N, 72° 27' 18.8" E	125x100=1.25ha 1m	Disturbed due to agricultural activities	LM	Rajesh 2011
18	Dangro	MotaTharadiya	Limbdi, Surendranagar	22° 32' 07.2" N, 71° 56' 97.8" E	100x100=1ha 1m	Disturbed due to agricultural activities	LM	Rajesh 2011
19	Devpura	Devpura	Limbdi, Surendranagar	22° 32' 89.1" N, 72° 04' 32.5" E	200x150=3 ha 1.5m	Disturbed due to agricultural activities	LM	Rajesh 2011

* CH: Classical Harappan, SH: Sorath Harappan, LSH: Late Sorath Harappan, MRW: Micaceous Red Ware, LRW: Lustrous Red Ware, BRW: Black and Red Ware, EH: Early Historic, LM: Late Medieval

Table 2: Features of the Classical Harappan and Regional Chalcolithic Pottery from the Study Area

Site Name	Village	Cultural Period	Ware	Texture in Order	Rim Diameter	Vessel Part	Shape	Core Condition	Decoration	Other Features	Similarity in Shape
Govind Parekh no Khetar	Balgamada	SH, LSH, LM	Red, Buff	Fine, Medium	10 – 44 cm	Rim, Base, Body	Pot, basin, bowl, Dish, dish on stand, Jar	Deoxidized, Oxidized	Geometric and Nongeometric	Regular Striation, Finger Marks	Rangpur, Rojdi, Surkotada, Lothal, Kuntasi, Bagasra, Shikarpur, Jaidak, Vagad, Kanewal
Jasabhai Bachubhai no Khetar (Timbo)	Rojka	SH, LSH, EH, LM	Red	Coarse, Medium, Fine	13 – 41 cm	Rim, Base, Body, Stem	Pot, basin, bowl, lamp, dish on stand, Jar	Oxidized, Deoxidized	Geometric and Nongeometric	Regular Striation	Rangpur, Rojdi, Surkotada, Kuntasi, Bagasra, Shikarpur, Jaidak, Vagad, Kanewal
KediyaTimbo	Padana	SH, LSH, MRW, LM	Red, Buff, Micaceous Red	Fine, Medium, Coarse	8 – 39 cm	Rim, Base, Body	Pot, Basin, Bowl, Stud Handle Bowl, Dish, Dish on Stand, Lid, Jar	Oxidized, Deoxidized	Geometric	Regular Striation, Finger Marks	Rangpur, Rojdi, Surkotada, Kuntasi, Bagasra, Shikarpur, Jaidak, Vagad, Kanewal
Kharad I	Kharad	SH, LSH, MRW, LM	Red, Buff, Micaceous Red	Fine, Medium, Coarse	7 – 45 cm	Rim, Base, Body, Stem	Pot, Basin, Bowl, Dish, Dish on Stand, Perforated Jar, Jar	Oxidized, Deoxidized	Geometric and Nature	Regular Striation, Finger Mark, Beating Paddling	Rangpur, Rojdi, Surkotada, Lothal, Kuntasi, Bagasra, Shikarpur, Jaidak, Vagad, Kanewal
Kharad II	Kharad	SH, LSH, MRW	Red, Micaceous Red, Buff, Black and Red	Coarse, Medium, Fine	10 – 43 cm	Rim, Base, Body, Stem, Stud Handle	Pot, Basin, Bowl, Stud Handle Bowl, Dish, Dish on Stand, Lamp, Perforated Jar, Jar	Oxidized, Deoxidized	Geometric, Nongeometric and Nature	Regular Striation, Finger Mark, Beating Paddling	Rangpur, Rojdi, Surkotada, Lothal, Kuntasi, Bagasra, Shikarpur, Jaidak, Vagad, Kanewal
Kotadiya	Kotadiya	SH, LSH, MRW, LRW, LM	Red, Micaceous Red, Buff, Lustrous Red	Fine, Medium, Coarse	7 – 43 cm	Rim, Base, Body, Neck and SHoulder, Stem, Stud Handle	Pot, Basin, Bowl, Stud Handle Bowl, Dish, Dish on Stand, Lid, Perforated Jar, Jar	Oxidized, Deoxidized	Geometric, Nongeometric and Nature	Regular Striation, Finger Mark, Beating Paddling	Rangpur, Rojdi, Surkotada, Lothal, Kuntasi, Bagasra, Shikarpur, Jaidak, Vagad, Kanewal
Lothal	Saragwala	CH, SH, LSH, MRW, BRW	Red, Micaceous Red, Buff, Black and Red, Gray	Coarse, Medium, Fine	6 – 41 cm	Rim, Base, Neck and Shoulder, Body	Pot, Basin, Bowl, Perforated Jar, Dish, Dish on Stand, Lid, Jar	Oxidized, Deoxidized	Geometric, Nongeometric and Nature	Regular Striation, Finger Mark, Beating Paddling, Graffiti	Rangpur, Rojdi, Surkotada, Kuntasi, Bagasra, Shikarpur, Jaidak, Vagad, Dholavira, Nageshwar, Kanmer

Contd...

Manubhai no Khetar	Koth	SH, LSH, MRW, LM	Red, Micaceous Red	Coarse, Medium, Fine	21 – 41 cm	Rim, Neck and Shoulder, Body	Pot, basin, lid, dish, dish on stand, Jar	Oxidized, Deoxidized	Geometric	Regular Striation, Scraping	Rangpur, Rojdi, Surkotada, Kuntasi, Bagasra, Shikarpur, Jaidak, Vagad,
Vadgam I	Vadgam	SH, LSH, MRW	Red, Micaceous Red, Gray	Coarse, Fine	8 – 43 cm	Rim, Base, Neck and Shoulder, Body, Stem	Pot, Basin, Bowl, Dish, Dish on Stand, Jar	Deoxidized, Oxidized	Geometric, Nongeometric and Nature	Regular Striation, Finger Mark, Beating Paddling	Rangpur, Rojdi, Surkotada, Kuntasi, Bagasra, Shikarpur, Jaidak, Vagad, Lothal
Vadgam II	Vadgam	SH, BRW, LM	Red, Black and Red	Coarse, Medium, Fine	12 – 48 cm	Rim, Base, Shoulder, Body	pot, basin, bowl, lid, dish, Jar	Deoxidized, Oxidized	Geometric and Nongeometric	Regular Striation, Finger Mark, Beating Paddling	Rangpur, Rojdi, Surkotada, Kuntasi, Bagasra, Shikarpur, Jaidak, Vagad, Lothal
PampadiaHanumanji no Tekaro	Panasina	SH, LSH, BRW, LM	Red, Buff, Black and Red	Coarse, Medium, Fine	8 – 56 cm	Rim, base, body, stud handle	Pot, basin, bowl stud handle bowl, dish, dish on stand, perforated jar, Jar	Deoxidized, Oxidized	Geometric and Nongeometric	Regular Striation	Rangpur, Rojdi, Surkotada, Kuntasi, Bagasra, Shikarpur, Jaidak, Vagad, Lothal, Kanewal
Rangpur	Rangpur	SH, LSH, MRW, LRW	Red, Lustrous Red, Micaceous Red	Coarse, Medium, Fine	6 – 55 cm	Rim, base, Shoulder, body, Stem	Pot, Basin, Bowl, Dish, Dish on Stand, Jar	Oxidized, Deoxidized	Geometric, Nongeometric and Nature	Regular Striation	Rojdi, Surkotada, Kuntasi, Bagasra, Shikarpur, Jaidak, Vagad, Lothal, Dholavira, Nageshwar, Kanmer, Kanewal
Talavadi	Jalampar	SH	Red	Coarse, Medium, Fine	14 – 38 cm	Rim, Base, Shoulder, Body, Stud Handle	Pot, Dish, Stud Handle Bowl, Dish on Stand	Deoxidized, Oxidized	Geometric and Nature	Regular Striation, Finger Mark, Beating Paddling	Rangpur, Rojdi, Surkotada, Kuntasi, Bagasra, Shikarpur, Jaidak, Vagad, Lothal

Table 3: Recalibrated Radiocarbon Dates from Lothal

Sl. No.	Sample No.	Site	Radiocarbon Age	One Sigma Range (Calib Rev 6.1.0)	Two Sigma Range (Calib Rev 6.1.0)	References
1	TF - 136	Lothal	3915±130	[cal BC 2575: cal BC 2202] 1.	[cal BC 2708: cal BC 2032] 0.946952	Possehl 1994, Reimer et al. 2009
2	TF - 22	Lothal	3845±110	[cal BC 2467: cal BC 2195] 0.922607	[cal BC 2580: cal BC 1972] 0.999055	Possehl 1994, Reimer et al. 2009
3	TF - 27	Lothal	3840±110	[cal BC 2466: cal BC 2194] 0.909813	[cal BC 2578: cal BC 1973] 0.999654	Possehl 1994, Reimer et al. 2009
4	TF - 26	Lothal	3830±120	[cal BC 2467: cal BC 2137] 1.	[cal BC 2582: cal BC 1932] 0.996707	Possehl 1994, Reimer et al. 2009
5	TF - 29	Lothal	3740±110	[cal BC 2299: cal BC 2009] 0.926593	[cal BC 2472: cal BC 1881] 1.	Possehl 1994, Reimer et al. 2009
6	TF - 133	Lothal	3740±110	[cal BC 2299: cal BC 2009] 0.926593	[cal BC 2472: cal BC 1881] 1.	Possehl 1994, Reimer et al. 2009
7	TF - 23	Lothal	3705±105	[cal BC 2210: cal BC 1947] 0.910617	[cal BC 2460: cal BC 1877] 0.987367	Possehl 1994, Reimer et al. 2009
8	TF - 19	Lothal	3650±130	[cal BC 2205: cal BC 1877] 0.938502	[cal BC 2351: cal BC 1730] 0.951812	Possehl 1994, Reimer et al. 2009
9	TF - 135	Lothal	3405±125	[cal BC 1832: cal BC 1605] 0.763775	[cal BC 1985: cal BC 1434] 0.981009	Possehl 1994, Reimer et al. 2009

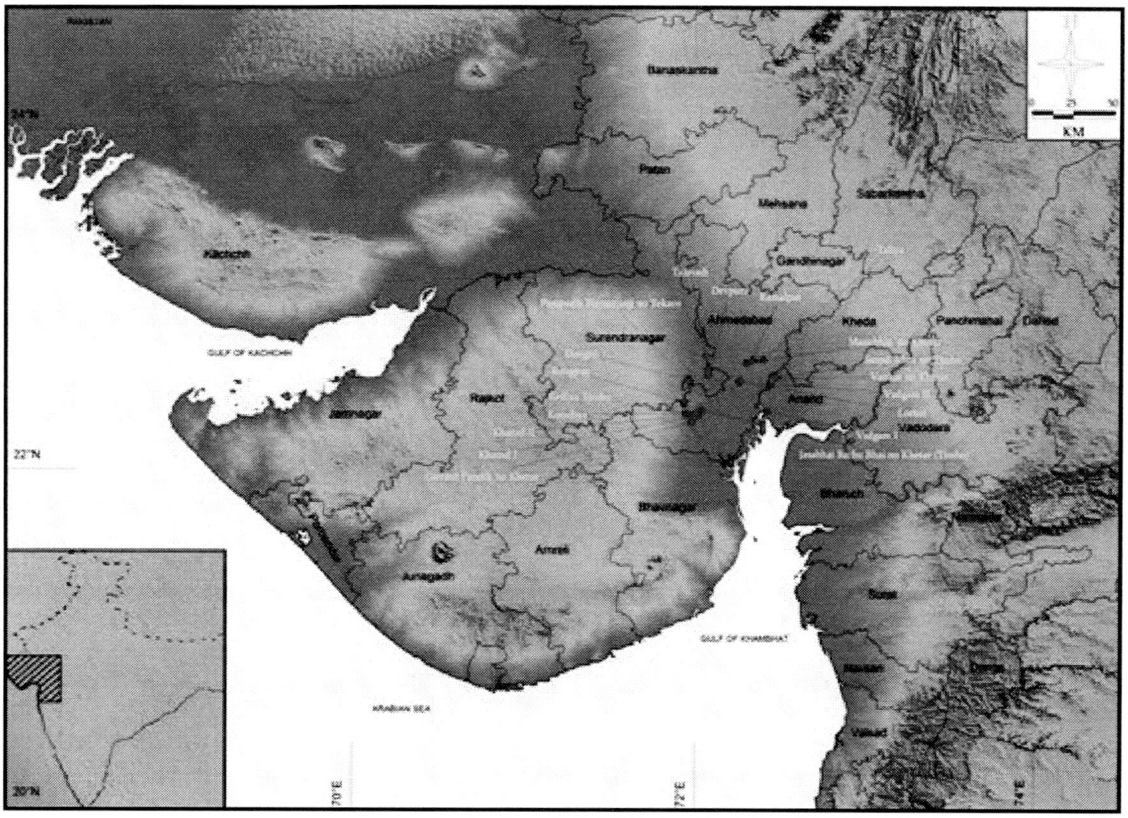

Fig. 1: Location Map of Explored Sites in the Study Area

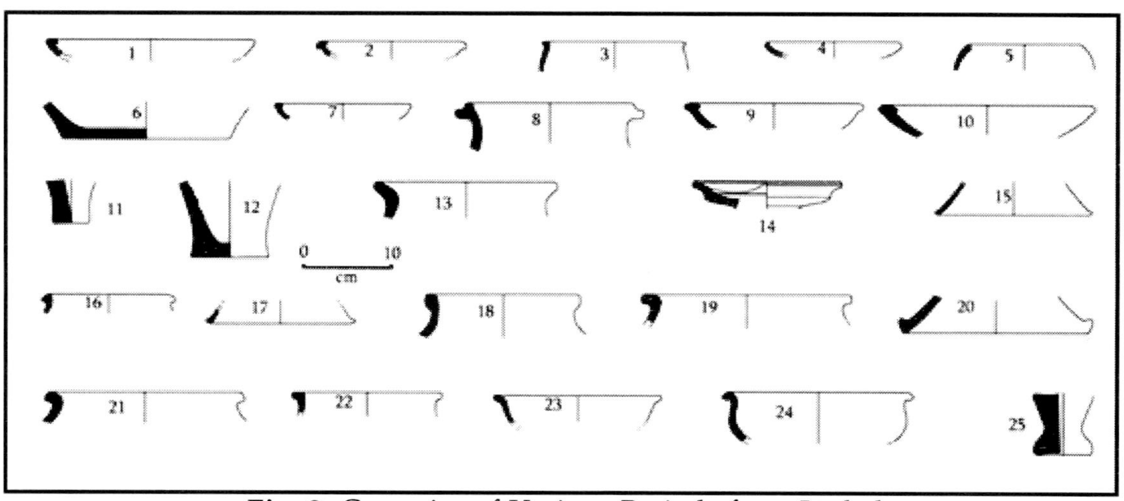

Fig. 2: Ceramics of Various Periods from Lothal

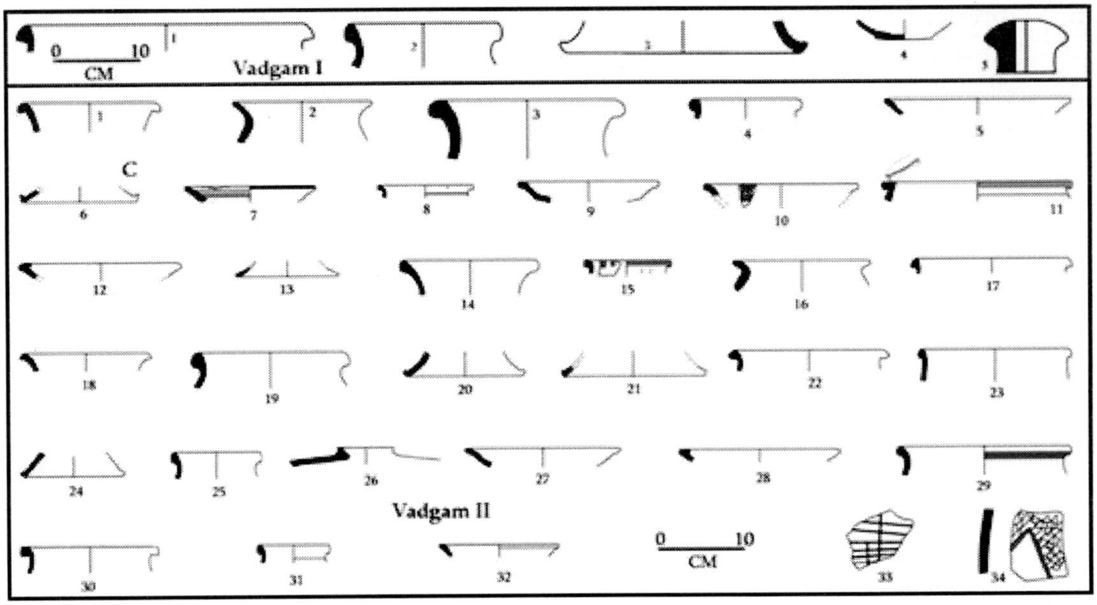

Fig. 3: Ceramics of Various Periods from Vadgam I and II

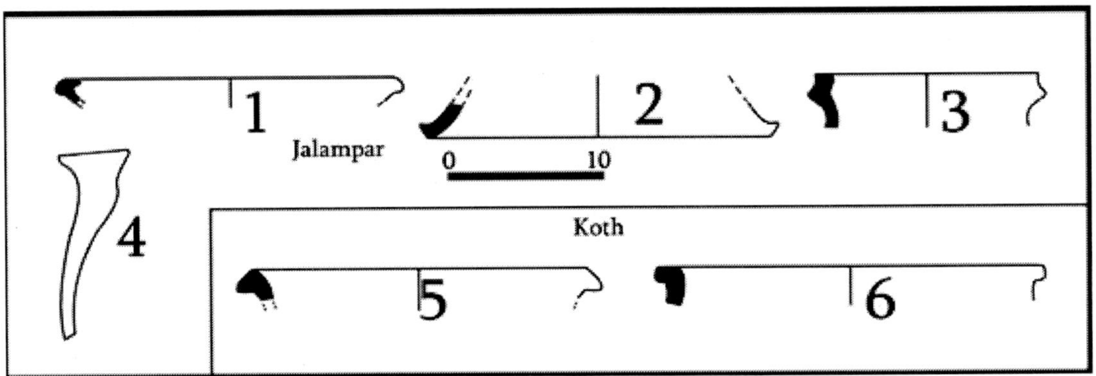

Fig. 4: Ceramics of Various Periods from JalamparTalavadi and Koth

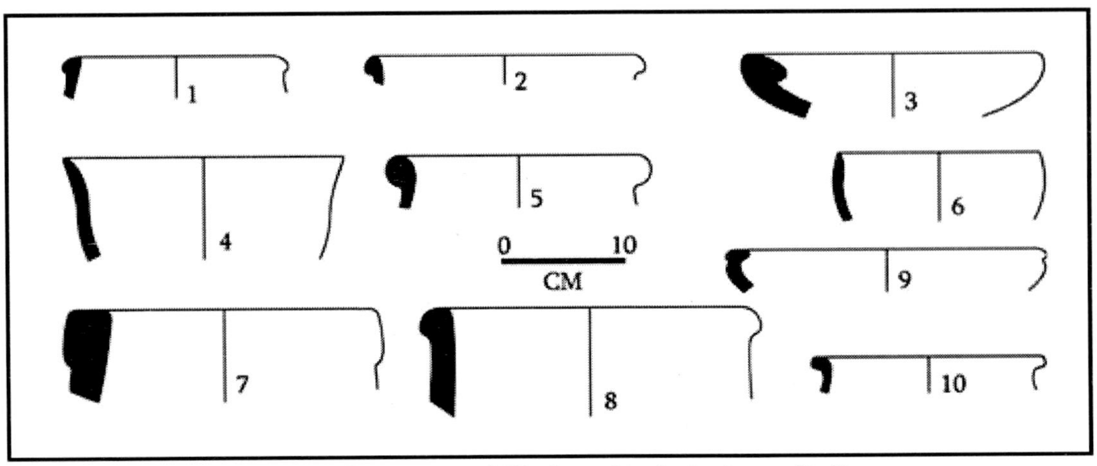

Fig. 5: Ceramics of Various Periods from Rojka

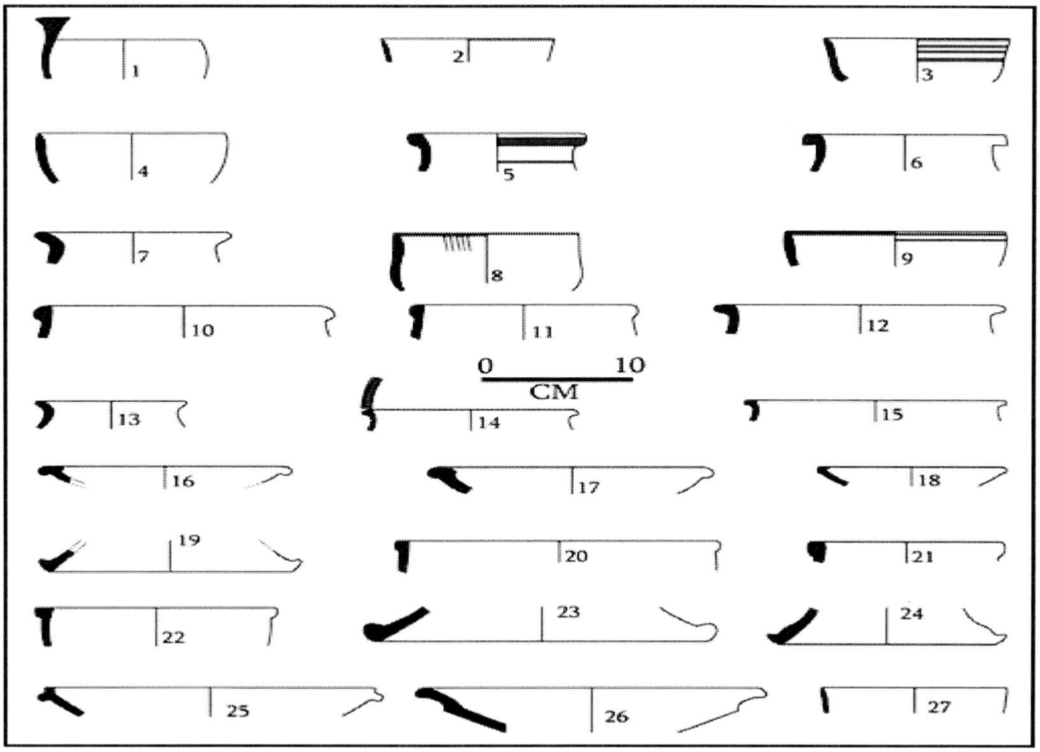

Fig. 6: Ceramics of Various Periods from Panasina

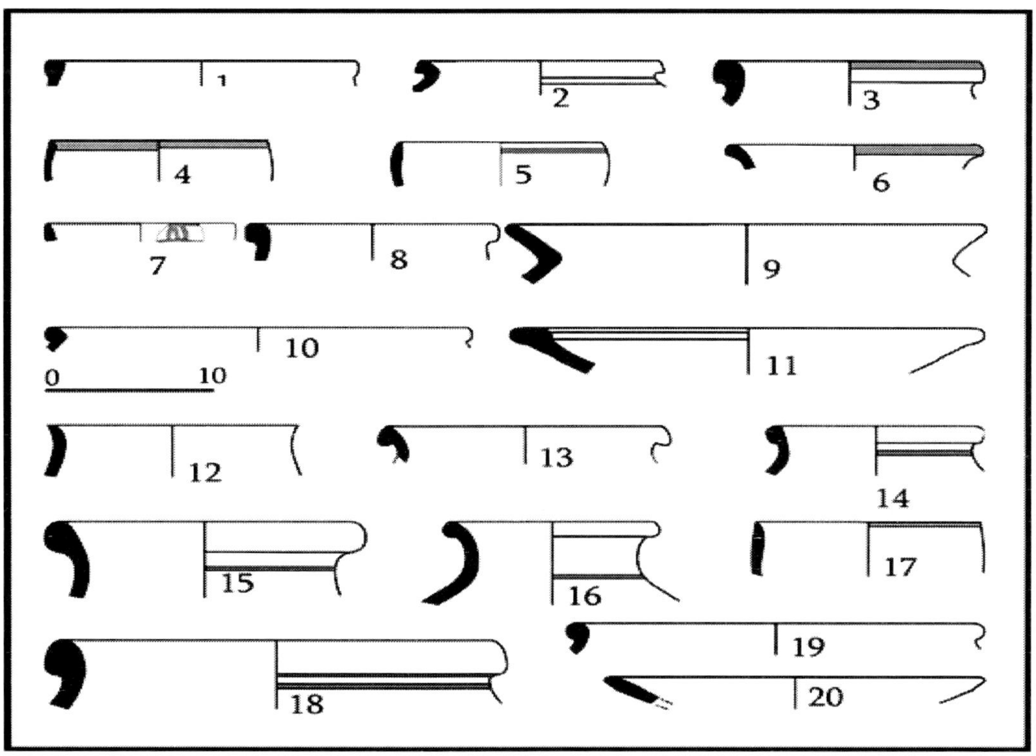

Fig. 7: Ceramics of Various Periods from Padana

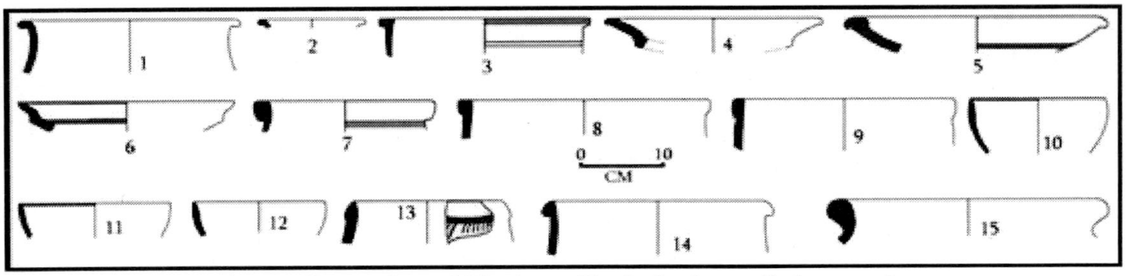

Fig. 8: Ceramics of Various Periods from Balgamada

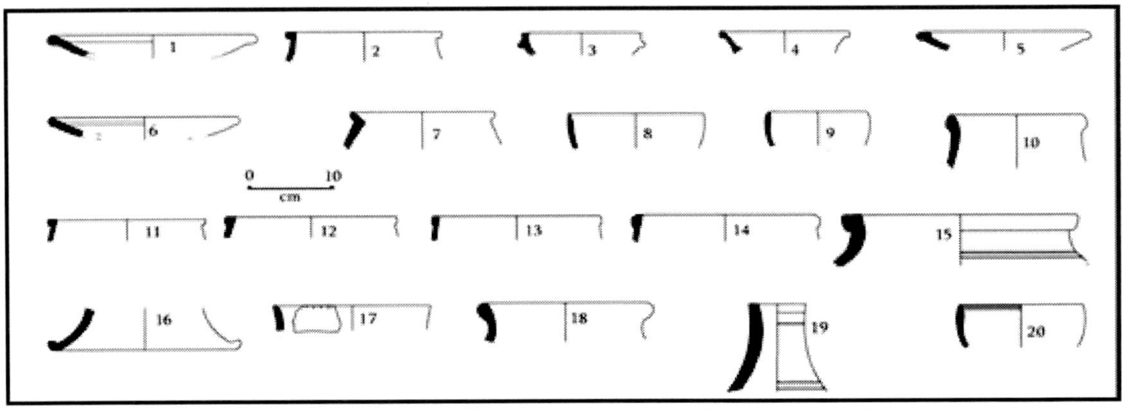

Fig. 9: Ceramics of Various periods from Kharad I

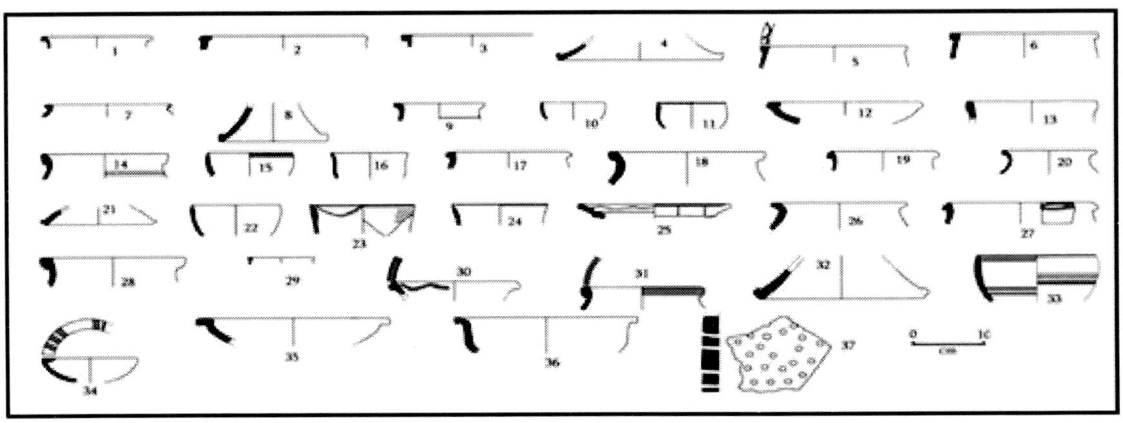

Fig. 10: Ceramics of Various periods from Kharad II

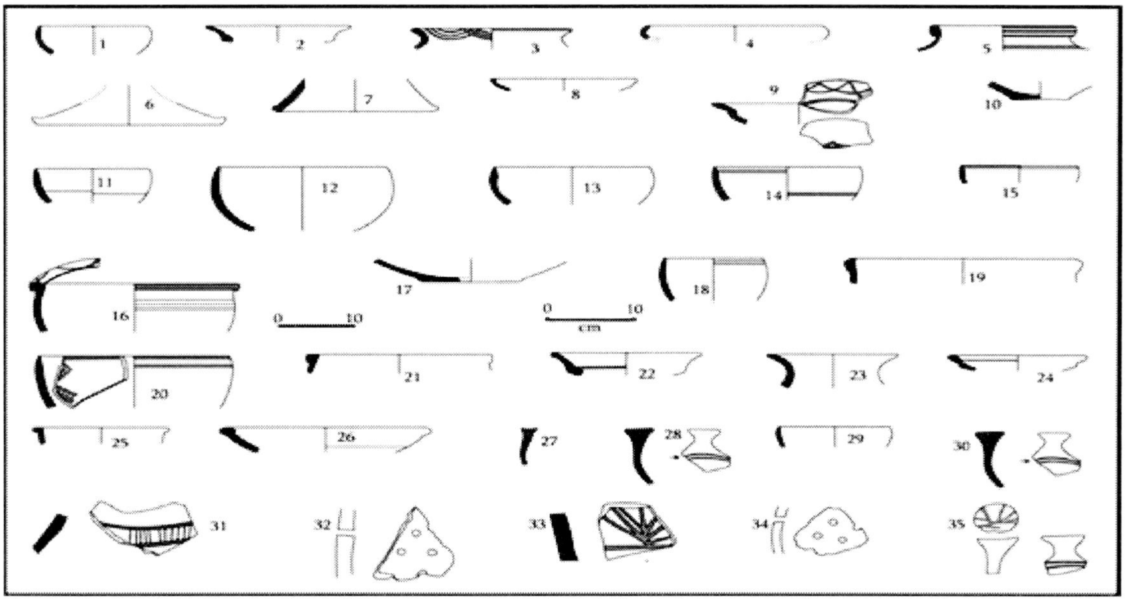

Fig. 11: Ceramics of Various periods from Kotadiya

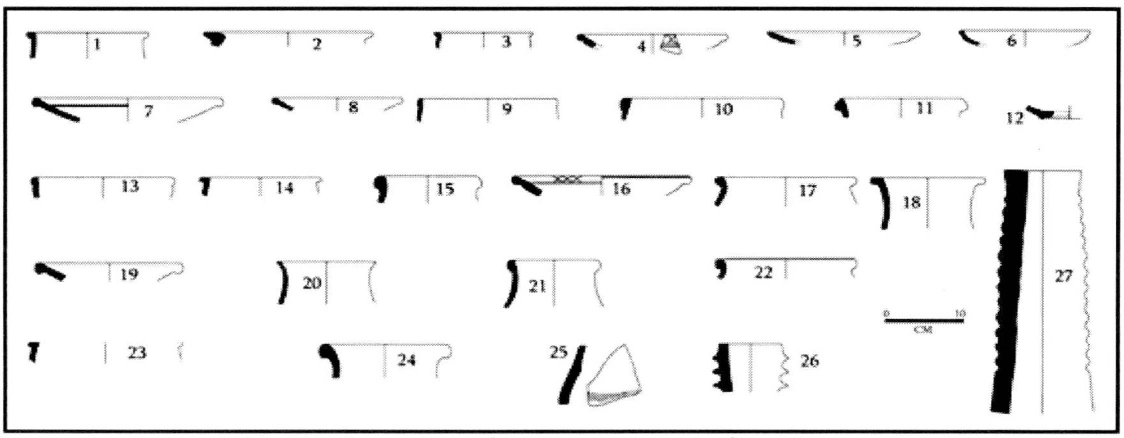

Fig. 12: Ceramics of Various periods from Rangpur

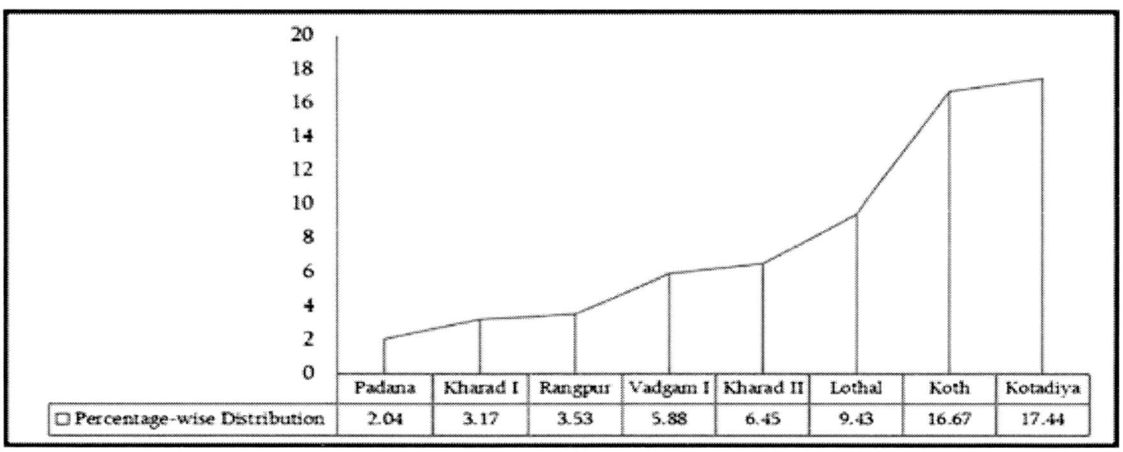

	Padana	Kharad I	Rangpur	Vadgam I	Kharad II	Lothal	Koth	Kotadiya
□ Percentage-wise Distribution	2.04	3.17	3.53	5.88	6.45	9.43	16.67	17.44

Fig. 13: Distribution of Micaceous Red Ware in Various Sites

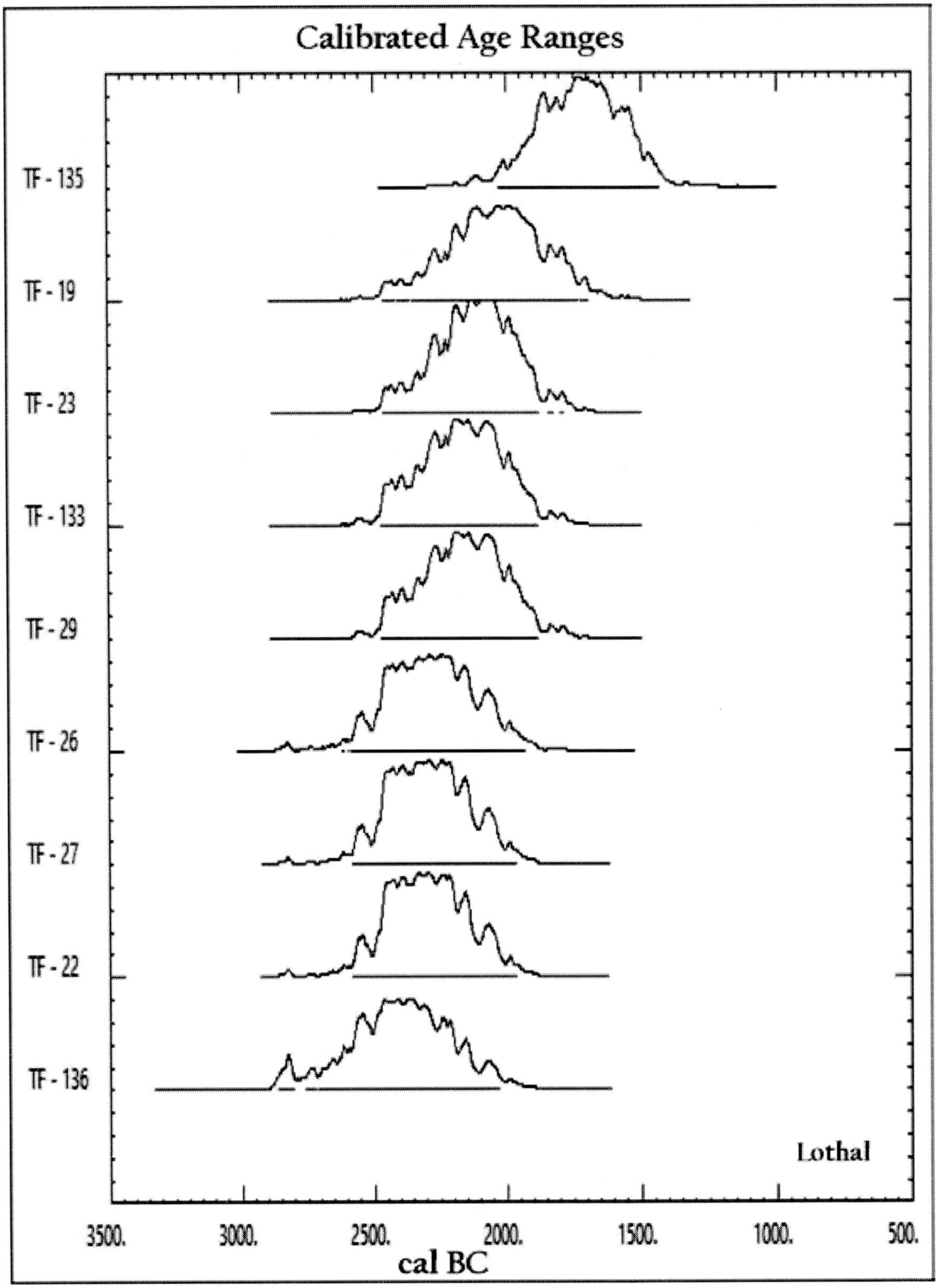

Fig. 14: Probability plot of recalibrated radiocarbon dates from Lothal
(Possehl 1994,Reimer et al. 2009)

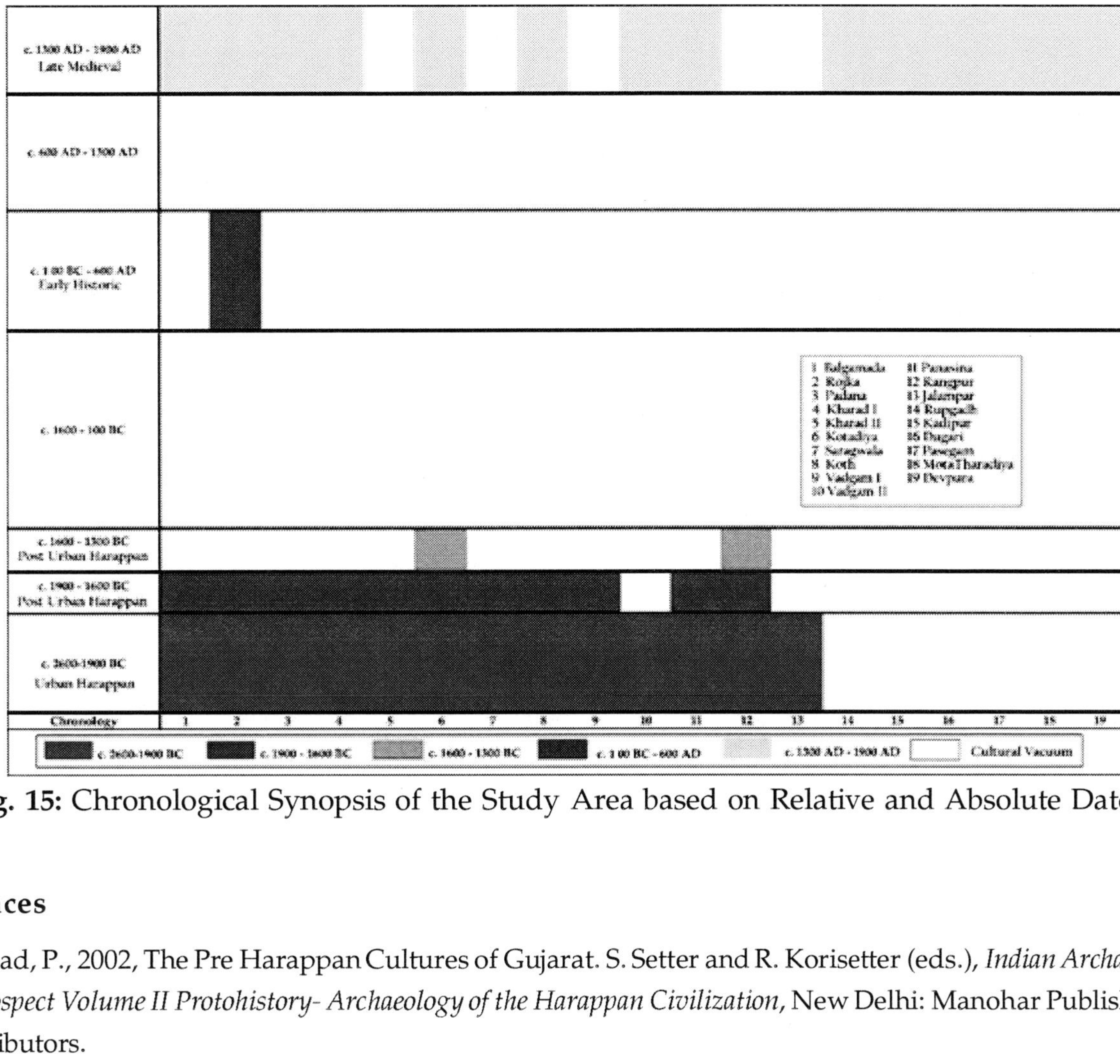

Fig. 15: Chronological Synopsis of the Study Area based on Relative and Absolute Dates

References

Ajithprasad, P., 2002, The Pre Harappan Cultures of Gujarat. S. Setter and R. Korisetter (eds.), *Indian Archaeology in Retrospect Volume II Protohistory- Archaeology of the Harappan Civilization*, New Delhi: Manohar Publishers and distributors.

Ajithprasad, P., 2011, Chalcolithic Cultural Patterns and the Early Harappan Interaction in Gujarat, T. Osada and M. Witzel (eds.), *Harvard Oriental Series, Opera Minerva Vol. 7, Cultural Relations Between the Indus and the Iranian Plateau During the Third Millennium BCE*, Indus Project, Research Institute for Humanities and Nature, June 7-8, 2008, Cambridge: Department of South Asian Studies, Harvard University.

Bhan, K. K., 1989, Late Harappan Settlements of Western India with Specific Reference to Gujarat, J. M. Kenoyer (ed.), *Old Problems and New perspectives in the Archaeology of South Asia*, Madison: Wisconsin Archaeological Reports.

Bhan, K. K., 1992, Late Harappan Gujarat, *The Eastern Anthropologist 45 (1-2).*

Bhan, K. K., 2004, Monsoon Behaviour and the Late Harappan Subsistence Pattern in Gujarat, Western India, Y. Yasuda and V. S. Shinde (eds.), *Monsoon and Civilization*, New Delhi: Lestre Press, Roli Books.

Bhan, K. K., 2006, Towards the understanding of medieval glazed pottery manufacture from Lashkarshah, Khambhat and Gujarat, *Man and Environment XXXI (2).*

Bhan, K. K., 2018, Some Important Aspects of Technology and Craft Production in the Indus Civilization with Specific Reference to Gujarat, *Walking with the Unicorn, Social Organization and Material Culture in Ancient South Asia. Jonathan Mark Kenoyer Felicitation Volume,*D. Frenez, G. Jamison, R. Law, M. Vidale and R. H. Meadow(eds.), Oxford: Archaeopress.

Bhattacharyya, R., 1991, Rangpur Seal-Probable Egyptian Connection of the Harappan Civilization, *Man and Environment XV (1).*

Bindra, S.C., 2003, Lothal: A Harappan Port Town Revisited, *Puratattva 33*

Carter, R. A., 2001, Saar and Its External Relations: New Evidence for Interaction Between Bahrain and Gujarat During the Early Second Millennium BC. *Arabian Archaeology and Epigraphy 12.*

Cork, E., 2005, Peaceful Harappans? Reviewing the Evidence for the Absence of Warfare in the Indus Civilisation of North-West India and Pakistan (c. 2500-1900 BC), *Antiquity 79.*

Dikshit, M. G., 1950, Excavations at Rangpur: 1947, *Bulletin of the Deccan College Post-Graduate and Research Institute XI (1).*

Dimri, K., 1994, *Ceramic Variability at Vagad with Special Emphasis to Micaceous Red Ware – A Petrographic Approach,* (Unpublished M. A. Dissertation), Department of Archaeology and Ancient History, Vadodara: The Maharaja Sayajirao University of Baroda .

Dimri, K., 1998-1999, Assessing the Distribution of Harappan Culture in North- Eastern Saurashtra: A Preliminary Report, *Pragdhara 9.*

Dimri, K., 1999, *Chalcolithic Settlements in Bhogava and Sukha Bhadar Valley,* (Unpublished Ph.D. Thesis), Department of Archaeology and Ancient History, Vadodara: The Maharaja Sayajirao University of Baroda .

Dimri, K., 2005, Mature Harappan Transitional Phase Settlements in Central Saurashtra Region, G. Patel and B. Shelat (eds.), *Rasik Bharati- Prof. R. C. Parikh Commemoration Volume,* Gandhinagar: Sanskrit Sahitya Academy.

Frenez, D., 2014, The Lothal Revisitation Project, A Fine Thread Connecting Ancient India to Contemporary Ravenna (Via Oman), Cerasetti (ed.), *My Life is Like the Summer Rose, Maurizio Tosi e l' Archeologia come modo di vivera (Papers in honour of Maurizio Tosi for his 70th Birthday),* Oxford: Bar International Series 2690.

Frenez, D. and M. Tosi, 2005, Lothal Sealings: Records from an Indus Civilization Towards the Eastern End of the Maritime Trade Networks Across the Arabian Sea. M. Pema (ed.), *Studi in Onore di Enrica Fiandra,* Contributi di Archeologia Egea e Vicinorientale: Naples .

Frenez, D. and M. Tosi, 2010, The "Lothal Revisitation Project", A Multidisciplinary Research Program Designed to Reconsider the Southeasternmost Hub of the Indus Civilization on the Arabian Sea. *Bhuj Round Table, International Conference on Gujarat Harappans and Chalcolithic Cultures.* Research Institute for Humanity and Nature, Kyoto, Gujarat State Department of Archaeology, Gandhinagar and Institute of Rajastha Studies, JRN Rajasthan Vidyapeeth, Udaipur, Bhuj.

Ghosh, S.S and K. Lal, 1963, Plant Remains from Rangpur and Other Explorations in Gujarat, *Ancient India 18-19.*

Ghurye, G. S., 1939, Two Old Sites in Kathiawar, *Journal of the University of Bombay VIII (1).*

Gogte, V. D., 2000, Indo-Arabian Maritime Contacts During the Bronze Age: Scientific Study of Pottery from Ras al-Junayz (Oman), *Admatu 2.*

Hawkes, J. D., 2019, The Elephant in the Room: Archaeology and the Early Medieval Period in India, E. Myrdal (ed.), *South Asian Archaeology and Art 2014*, New Delhi: Dev Publishers.

Herman, C. F., 1995, The Rangpur Sequence of "Harappan" Gujarat (India): A Reassessment. R. Allchin and B. Allchin (eds.), *South Asian Archaeology 1995*, Vol I. Science Publishers, Inc. USA and Oxford and IBH Publishing Co. Pvt. Ltd., New Delhi- Calcutta.

Herman, C. F., 1997, "Harappan" Gujarat: The Archaeology – Chronology Connection, *Paeorient 22 (2).*

Herman, C.F. and K. Krishnan, 1994, Micaceous Red Ware: A Gujarat Proto- Historic Cultural Complex or just Ceramic? A. Parpola and P. Koskikallio (eds.). *South Asian Archaeology 1993*, Vol I, Helsinki: Annales Academic Scientiarum Fennicae Series B, Vol 271.

Hoffman, B. C. and H. Miller, 2009, Production and Consumption of Copper-base Metals in the Indus Civilization, *Journal of World Prehistory 22* .

IAR, 1953-54, Ghosh, A. (ed.), 1954, Indian Archaeology 1953-54 – A Review, New Delhi: Archaeological Survey of India.

IAR 1954-55, Ghosh, A, (ed.), 1955, *Indian Archaeology 1954-55 – A Review,* New Delhi: Archaeological Survey of India.

IAR 1955-56, Ghosh, A., (ed.), 1956, *Indian Archaeology 1955-56 – A Review,* New Delhi: Archaeological Survey of India.

IAR 1955-56, Ghosh, A, (ed.), 1956, *Indian Archaeology 1955-56 – A Review*, New Delhi: Archaeological Survey of India.

IAR 1956-57, Ghosh, A, (ed.), 1957, *Indian Archaeology 1956-57 – A Review*, New Delhi: Archaeological Survey of India.

IAR 1957-58, Ghosh, A, (ed.), 1958, *Indian Archaeology 1957-58 – A Review*, New Delhi: Archaeological Survey of India.

IAR 1958-59, Ghosh, A., (ed.), 1959, *Indian Archaeology 1958-59 – A Review,* New Delhi: Archaeological Survey of India.

IAR 1959-60, Ghosh, A., (ed.), 1960, *Indian Archaeology 1959-60 – A Review,* New Delhi: Archaeological Survey of India.

IAR 1995-96, Menon, K. G. (ed.), 2002, *Indian Archaeology 1995-96 – A Review*, New Delhi: Archaeological Survey of India.

Ilahi, E. R., 2018, *Indus Script and Graffiti from Harappan Sites in Gujarat*, Unpublished M.A. Dissertation, Department of Archaeology, University of Kerala, Thiruvananthapuram.

Ilahi, E. R., 2019, *Shell and Shell Objects from Indus Age in Gujarat: A Cumulative Study*, Unpublished M.Phil. Dissertation, Department of Archaeology, University of Kerala, Thiruvananthapuram.

Ilahi, E. R., S. V. Rajesh and G. S. Abhayan, 2019, Indus Graffiti from Gujarat, Rajesh S. V., G. S. Abhayan, P. Nayar and E. R. Ilahi (eds.), *Human and Heritage: An Archaeological Spectrum of Asiatic Countries (Felicitation to Professor Ajit Kumar)*, 2019, I, New Delhi: New Bharatiya Book Corporation.

Insoll, T., D. A. Polya, K. Bhan, D. Irving and K. Jarvis, 2004, Towards an Understanding of the Carnelian Bead Trade from Western India to sub-Saharan Africa: The Application of UV-LA-ICP-MS to Carnelian from Gujarat, India, and West Africa, *Journal of Archaeological Science 31.*

Jam, S., 2010, *Fortification of Excavated Harappan Sites in Gujarat*, Unpublished M. A. Dissertation, Department of Archaeology and Ancient History, The Maharaja Sayajirao University of Baroda, Vadodara.

Jamison, G. M., 2017, *The Organization of Indus Unicorn Seal Production A Diachronic Comparative Study of Style, Skill and Socio political Organization*, Unpublished Ph.D. Thesis, Department of Anthropology, Madison: University of Wisconsin.

Joshi, J. P. and Parpola, 1987, *Corpus of Indus Seals and Inscriptions1, Collections in India, Annales Academiae Scientiarum Fennicae, B 239,* Helsinki: Suomalainen Tiedeakatemia.

Kenoyer, J. M. and H. M. L. Miller, 1999, Metal Technologies of the Indus Valley Tradition in Pakistan and Western India, V. C. Piggot (ed.), *The Emergence and Development of Metallurgy*, Philadelphia: University Museum.

Kenoyer, J. M., M. Vidale and K. K. Bhan, 1991, Contemporary Stone Bead Making in Khambhat, India: Patterns of Craft Specialization and Organization of Production as Reflected in the Archaeological Record, *World Archaeology 23 (1) Craft Production and Specialization.*

Kenoyer, J. M., M. Vidale and K. K. Bhan, 1994, Carnelain Bead Production in Khambhat, India: An Ethnoarchaeological Study, Allchin, B. (ed.), *Living Traditions; Studies in the Ethnoarchaeology of South Asia*, New Delhi: Oxford and IBH Publishing Co. Pvt. Ltd.

Khadkikar, A. S., C. Rajshekhar and K. P. N. Kumaran, 2004, Palaeo-geography around the Harappan Port of Lothal, Gujarat, Western India, *Antiquity 78.*

Khatri, P., 1982, *Bowls of Gujarat,* Unpublished M.A. Dissertation, Department of Archaeology and Ancient History, The Maharaja Sayajirao University of Baroda, Vadodara.

Krishnan, K., 1982, *Identification and Determination of the Chemical Composition of the Pigments used in the Decoration of Chalcolithic Period Pottery in Gujarat*, Unpublished M.A. Dissertation, Department of Archaeology and Ancient History, The Maharaja Sayajirao University of Baroda, Vadodara.

Krishnan, K., 1986, *Chemical and Petrological Studies in Ancient Indian Pottery,* Unpublished Ph.D Thesis, Department of Archaeology and Ancient History, The Maharaja Sayajirao University of Baroda, Vadodara.

Krishnan, K., 1992, An Analysis of Decorative Pigments and Slips on Harappan Pottery from Gujarat, *South Asian*

Studies 8.

Krishnan, K., 2002, Survey of Ceramic Analysis with Specific Reference to Pottery, S. Setter and R. Korisetter (eds.), *Indian Archaeology in Retrospect Volume - I Prehistory -Archaeology of South Asia*, New Delhi: Manohar Publishers and distributors.

Krishnan, K. and K. Dimri, 2005, Exploration in the Lilka River-basin in Saurashtra, Gujarat: A Preliminary Report. K. K. Chakravarty and G. L. Badam (eds.), *River Valley Cultures of India*, Bhopal and New Delhi: Indira Gandhi Rashtriya Manav Sangrahalaya and Aryan Books International.

Krishnan, K. and K. T. M. Hegde, 1988, Chemical and Petrographic Studies in Pottery of Harappa Culture in Gujarat, *Journal of the M. S. University of Baroda 1986-87 (Humanities) 35-36 (1).*

Krishnan, K. and V. Rao, 1994, A Study of Clay Paste Preparation by Potters Through Grain Size Analysis, *South Asian Studies 10.*

Kumar, K. S. A., 2016, *Medieval Glazed Ceramics production at Lashkarshah, Khambhat, Gujarat: a typological approach*, Unpublished M.A. Dissertation, Department of Archaeology, University of Kerala, Thiruvananthapuram.

Kumar, K. S. A., 2017, *Typo-Technological Analysis of Medieval Glazed Ceramics from Lashkarshah, Khambhat, Gujarat*, 2017, Unpublished M.Phil. Dissertation, Department of Archaeology, University of Kerala, Thiruvananthapuram.

Kumar, K. S. A., S. V. Rajesh and G. S. Abhayan, 2019, Glazed Ceramics and Indicators of Glazed Ceramic Production from Lashkarshah, Khambhat, Gujarat, Rajesh S. V., G. S. Abhayan, P. Nayar and E. R. Ilahi (eds.), *Human and Heritage: An Archaeological Spectrum of Asiatic Countries (Felicitation to Professor Ajit Kumar)*, Volume – I, New Delhi: New Bharatiya Book Corporation.

Kumar, K. S. S., 1996, *Chemical Characterization of a Few Ceramic Samples from Vagad*, Unpublished M.A. Dissertation, Department of Archaeology and Ancient History, The Maharaja Sayajirao University of Baroda, Vadodara.

Lal, B. B., 1963, Scientific Examination of the Pottery from Rangpur, S. R. Rao (ed.), Excavation at Rangpur and Other Explorations in Gujarat, *Ancient India (Bulletin of the Archaeological Survey of India) 18 and* 19 .

Law II, R. W., 2008, *Inter-Regional Interaction and Urbanism in the Ancient Indus Valley: Geologic Provenience Study of Harappa's Rock and Mineral Assemblage,* Unpublished PhD Thesis, Madison: University of Wisconsin.

Leshnik, L. S., 1968, The Harappan Port at Lothal: Another View, *American Anthropologist 70 (5).*

Majumdar, A., 1994, *Disposal of the Dead During the Chalcolithic Period of Gujarat: A Study of the Harappan Burial Customs,* Unpublished M.A. Dissertation, Department of Archaeology and Ancient History, The Maharaja Sayajirao University of Baroda, Vadodara.

Margabandhu, C., 1981, Early Historic Terracottas from Gujarat: A Study, M. S. N. Rao (ed.), *Madhu – Recent Researches in Indian Archaeology and Art History (Shri M. N. Deshpande Festschrift)*, Delhi: Agam Kala Prakashan.

Mate, M. S., 1985, Harappan Fortifications: A Study, S. B. Deo and M. K. Dhavalikar (eds.), *Studies in Indian Archaeology - Professor H. D. Sankalia Felicitation Volume*, Bombay: Popular Prakashan.

Mehta, R. N., 1968, Excavation at Nagara, *Maharaja Sayajirao University Archaeology Series No. 10*, Department of Archaeology and Ancient History, Vadodara: The Maharaja Sayajirao University of Baroda.

Mehta, R. N., 1978-79, The Excavation at Ahmedabad (Calico Mills), *The Journal of the Maharaja Sayajirao University of Baroda, Vols. 27-28 (1).*

Mehta, R.N., K.N. Momin and D.R. Shah, 1980, Excavation at Kanewal, *Maharaja Sayajirao University Archaeology Series No. 17*, Vadodara: Department of Archaeology and Ancient History, The Maharaja Sayajirao University of Baroda.

Merh, S. S., 1995, *Geology of Gujarat*. Bangalore: Geological Society of India

Mirchandani, R.M., 1980, *Archaeological Survey of Ahmedabad District Upto 1300 AD.*, Unpublished PhD Thesis, Department of Archaeology and Ancient History, The Maharaja Sayajirao University of Baroda, Vadodara.

Misra, V. N., 1965, Book Review: Ancient India (Bulletin of the Archaeological Survey of India) 18 & 19 (1962-63) 1963: *The Eastern Anthropologist 18 (1).*

Momin, K. N., 1974, Chalcolithic Settlements in Bhalbara Taluka, Cambay, Gujarat, *Journal of the M. S. University of Baroda (Humanities) 20 (1) - 21 (1).*

Momin, K. N., 1976a, The Chalcolithic Settlements in Khaira District, Gujarat State, *Journal of the M. S. University of Baroda 22 (1) – 23 (1).*

Momin, K. N., 1976b, Chalcolithic Settlements in Bhalbara Taluka, Cambay, Gujarat, *Archaeological Congress and Seminar 1972,* U. V. Singh. B. N. (eds.), Kurukshetra: Chakravarty University.

Momin, K. N., 1979, *Archaeology of the Kheda District (Gujarat) Upto 1300 AD.*, Unpublished PhD Thesis, Vadodara: Department of Archaeology and Ancient History, The Maharaja Sayajirao University of Baroda.

Momin, K. N., 1984, Village Harappans in Kheda District of Gujarat, B.B. Lal and S. P. Gupta (eds.), *Frontiers of the Indua Civilization,* New Delhi: Books and Books.

Munsell Soil Colour Chart, 1954, Munsell Colour Company, Inc. Baltimore, Maryland.

Panjwani, P. A., 1981, *Comparative Study of the Ceramics of Gujarat (From the Beginning up to 10th C AD),* Unpublished PhD Thesis, Vadodara: Department of Archaeology and Ancient History, The Maharaja Sayajirao University of Baroda.

Panjwani, P. A., 1989, Petrography of Harappan Pottery from Lothal, *Man and Environment XIII.*

Possehl, G. L., 1976, Lothal: A Gateway Settlement of the Harappan Civilization, Kenneth A. R. Kennedy and G. L. Possehl (eds.), *Ecological Backgrounds of South Asian Prehistory*, Ithaca: Cornell University South Asia Programme, Occasional Papers and Theses, No. 4.

Possehl, G.L., 1994, Radiometric Dates for South Asian Archaeology, *An Occasional Publication of the Asia Section*, Philadelphia: University of Pennsylvania Museum of Archaeology and Anthropology.

Possehl, G. L. and K. A. R. Kennedy, 1979, Hunter-Gatherer/Agriculturalist Exchange in Prehistory: An Indian

Example, *Current Anthropology 20 (3).*

Rajesh, S. V., 2011, *A Comprehensive Study of the Regional Chalcolithic Cultures of Gujarat*, Unpublished Ph.D Thesis, Department of Archaeology and Ancient History, The Maharaja Sayajirao University of Baroda, Vadodara.

Rao, S. R., 1956, Excavations at Lothal, *Lalit Kala 3-4.*

Rao, S. R., 1962, Further Excavations at Lothal, *Lalit Kala 11.*

Rao, S. R., 1963, Excavation at Rangpur and Other Explorations in Gujarat, *Ancient India (Bulletin of the Archaeological Survey of India) 18 and 19 .*

Rao, S. R., 1965, Shipping and Maritime Trade of the Indus People, *Expedition 7 (3).*

Rao, S. R., 1973, *Lothal and the Indus Civilization*. Bombay: Asia Publishing House

Rao, S. R., 1979, Lothal: A Harappan Port Town, 1955-62, *Memoirs of Archaeological Survey of India, No. 78. Vol.1,* New Delhi: Archaeological Survey of India.

Rao, S. R., 1985, Lothal: A Harappan Port Town, 1955-62, *Memoirs of Archaeological Survey of India, No. 78. Vol. 2,* New Delhi: Archaeological Survey of India.

Reimer, P.J., M.G.L. Baillib, E. Bard, A. Bayliss, J.W. Beck, P.G. Blackwell, C. Bronk Ramsey, C.E. Buck, G.S. Bun, R.L. Edwards, I. Friedrich, P.M. Grootes, T.P. Guilderson, I. Hajdas, T.J. Heaton, A.G. Hogg, K.A. Hughen, K.F. Kaiser, B. Kromer, F.G. McCormac, S.W. Manning, R.W. Reimer, D.A. Richards, J.R. Southon, S. Talamo, C.S.M. Turney, J. van der Plicht and C.E. Weyhenmeyer, 2009, IntCal09 and Marine09 Radiocarbon Age Calibration Curves, 0-50,000 Years cal BP., *Radiocarbon 51.*

Rogersdotter, E., 2006, Negligible Details? On a Study of Terracotta Miniature Carts from a Harappan Site in Gujarat, *Ancient Asia 1.*

Sankalia, H. D., 1941, *The Archaeology of Gujarat (Including Kathiawar)*, Bombay: Natwarlal and Co.

Sankalia, H.D., 1946, *Investigations into Prehistoric Archaeology of Gujarat*, Baroda: Baroda State Press.

Sonawane, V. H., 1991, The Antiquity of Pulley Shaped Terracotta Ear Studs of Gujarat. C. Margabandhu, K. S. Ramachandran, A. P. Sagar and D. K. Sinha (eds.), *Indian Archaeological Heritage, Shri K. V. Soundara Rajan Felicitation Volume* I, Delhi: Agam Kala Prakashan.

Sonawane, V. H., 2000, Early Farming Communities of Gujarat, India. P. Bellwood, D. Bowdery, D. Bulbeck, D. Baer, V. Shinde, R. Shutler and G. Summerhayes (eds.), Proceedings of the 16th Congress of the Indo- Pacific Prehistory Association, Melaka, 1 to 7 July 1998, *Bulletin of the Indo-Pacicif Prehistoric Association 19 (Indo-Pacific Prehistory the Melaka Papers 3)*, Indo-Pacific Prehistory Association, Canberra: Australian national University.

Sonawane, V. H., 2002, Post-Urban Harappan Culture in Gujarat. S. Setter and R. Korisetter (eds.), *Indian Archaeology in Retrospect Volume II Protohistory -Archaeology of the Harappan Civilization*, New Delhi: Manohar Publishers and distributors.

Sonawane, V. H., 2005, Harappan Sacrificial Fire Altars from Vagad, G. Patel and B. Shelat (eds.), *Rasik Bharati- Prof.*

R. C. Parikh Commemoration Volume, Gandhinagar: Sanskrit Sahitya Academy.

Sonawane, V. H. and Ajithprasad, P., 1994, Harappan Culture and Gujarat, *Man and Environment XIX (1-2).*

Sonawane, V.H. and R.N. Mehta, 1985, Vagad- A Rural Harappan Settlement, *Man and Environment IX.*

Subbarao, B, 1958, The Personality of India- Pre and Proto-Historic Foundation of India and Pakistan, *M. S. University Archaeology Series No. 3,* Vadodara: Maharaja Sayajirao University of Baroda.

Vats, M. S., 1935, Trial Excavations at Rangpur, Limbdi State, Kathiawar, *Annual Report of the Archaeological Survey of India (1934-35)* and *XII-XIV*

Vats, M. S., 1937, Trial Excavations at Rangpur, Limbdi State, Kathiawar, *Annual Report of the Archaeological Survey of India 1934-35.*

Vyas, S., 1998, *A Study of Ancient Towns of Gujarat*, Unpublished Ph.D. Dissertation, Department of Archaeology and Ancient History, Faculty of Arts, The Maharaja Sayajirao University of Baroda, Vadodara.

5

Reconstructing Prehistoric Environments in the Son and Belan Valleys, North-Central India : Retrospect and Prospect

Martin Williams

Introduction

It is worth stating at the outset that any attempts to reconstruct prehistoric environments using alluvial sediments suffer from one huge disadvantage, namely, the innately fragmentary nature of the fluviatile record (Williams 2012a: 2093-2122). Any reconstructions of past environments deduced from discontinuous fluvial sedimentary records will inevitably be incomplete. However, even an incomplete environmental reconstruction is preferable to no reconstruction at all. With this caveat in mind, we can now consider what we have learned from the river deposits preserved in the Son and Belan valleys.

The Son is one of the great rivers of north-central India *(Fig. 1)*. It flows from west to east in a relatively deep and narrow valley. The valley is bounded by a steep sandstone escarpment to the north. This escarpment marks the southern boundary of the deeply dissected uplands of the Kaimur Ranges which are part of the rugged Vindhyan Plateau *(Plate 1)*. To the south the land is lower in elevation and the Son valley is flanked by a series of narrow strike ridges which run roughly parallel to one another. The location of the valley may well be controlled by a major fault system aligned parallel to the modern channel.

The Belan is a much smaller river than the Son. It rises immediately to the north of the Kaimur Ranges and flows west where it joins the Tons *(Fig. 1)*. The Tons flows north and joins the Ganga about 20 km downstream of its confluence with the Yamuna. The historic city of Allahabad (renamed Prayagraj in 2018) is located at the junction of the Ganga and Yamuna and the mythical Sarasvati River, and is the site of the great annual Kumbh Mela pilgrimage.

The ancient city of Kaushambi is located in this region and was excavated under the direction of the late Professor G.R. Sharma, who had earlier worked with Sir Mortimer Wheeler when he was conducting the early excavations at Harappa and Mohenjo Daro.

Exploratory phase

Professor Sharma's interests were not simply confined to historic archaeology. He was eclectic in his approach to archaeology and catholic in his interests. With a team of energetic archaeologist colleagues and brilliant young postgraduates (of whom Jaganath Pal was one), he surveyed, mapped and excavated a large number of prehistoric sites in the Son and Belan valleys during the 1970s. He and his team also identified a number of sandstone rock shelters in the Kaimur Ranges that contained Mesolithic artefacts and wall paintings of hunting scenes and of the contemporary fauna and excavated a series of Mesolithic and younger burials in the Ganga valley (Sharma 1973: 106-110; 1975: 1-20). Based on this work, Professor Sharma proposed that seasonal migrations between alluvial plain and sandstone plateau in Mesolithic times eventually led to more intensive use of wild plants, culminating in the early domestication of plants and animals that ushered in the Neolithic cultural phase which had such a profound effect upon humans and their environment (Sharma et al. 1980: 200).

The sites in the Son and Belan valleys ranged in age from Lower Palaeolithic through to Neolithic and younger. Most of the mapped sites were situated close to the present river channels. They were almost always most clearly exposed in recently eroded bank sections. The sediments exposed in these channel bank sections consisted of fluvial gravels, sands, silts and clays. In the middle Belan valley three gravel units appeared to be very widespread and were identified as the lower, middle and upper gravel units, known, respectively, as Gravel One, Gravel Two and Gravel Three. Lower Palaeolithic artefacts were found within what was considered the lower gravel unit or Gravel One; Middle Palaeolithic artefacts within the postulated middle gravel unit or Gravel Two; and Upper Palaeolithic artefacts within the putative upper gravel unit or Gravel Three. However, reliance on river gravels to determine the age of any prehistoric cultural tradition has many pitfalls, which I discuss in the following section.

Stratigraphic mapping

Professor Sharma invited the distinguished British archaeologist Professor Desmond Clark from the University of California at Berkeley to join his team. This he did for two seasons of work in 1980 and 1982, each three months in duration (Sharma and Clark 1983: 320). Desmond brought with him a small team of graduate students. I had earlier worked as geomorphologist/Quaternary geologist/ soil scientist with Desmond in the Sahara, Nile Valley and Ethiopia and so was also an invited member of the team. Our initial induction into the prehistoric archaeology of the Son and Belan involved a rapid tour of the main sites conducted by Professor Sharma. It soon became clear both to me and to Desmond that the inferred correlation between gravels and prehistoric cultural phases was open to question, for several reasons.

First, any artefacts found within river gravels must, by definition, have been transported and so were not in primary context, however abundant. Any artefacts close to the river channel could be incorporated into the gravel traction load, irrespective of age, so that artefacts within a given bed of gravel could be of quite different ages. All that could be said is that the artefacts within a bed of gravel were either about the same age or, more often, older by an unknown amount. What also became clear to me during later stratigraphic mapping was that there were multiple gravel beds, not just three, and they were generally discontinuous.

There was therefore a need for careful "hand-over-hand" stratigraphic mapping along long continuous stretches of exposed alluvial sections. The method adopted was to map the stratigraphy while following the river-bank sections on foot. Representative sections were then chosen and wherever possible they were exposed in more detail by excavating a step trench from the base to the top of the selected section. For each stratigraphic section examined, I recorded the thickness of each stratigraphic unit, the nature of its contact with adjacent units, its Munsell Chart colour (both wet and dry), soil structure, consistence and hardness, field texture (to within ~5% clay content, for sixteen soil textural classes), sand particle shape and degree of roundness (under x10 magnification), sedimentary structures, carbonate concretions (shape, size and %), and presence of any shells, charcoal or other material. Where appropriate, samples were also collected for luminescence and/or radiocarbon analysis.

Depositional environments were inferred from the sediment texture (i.e., grain size), sedimentary structures and fossil content (e.g., aquatic snail shells). In 1980, working in partnership with Macquarie University Earth Sciences Honours student Keith Royce, I was able to identify and describe four major alluvial formations in the middle Son valley *(Fig. 2)*. From oldest to youngest these were the *Sihawal, Patpara, Baghor and Khetaunhi Formations* respectively (Williams and Royce 1982: 219-233). During later work in the middle Son valley in November-December 2005 with Professor J.N. Pal *(Plate 2)*, we identified an additional Formation (the *Khunteli Formation*) intermediate in age between the Sihawal and the Patpara Formations (Williams *et al.* 2006). We were also able to relate these alluvial formations to concentrations of prehistoric artefacts, some of which were later excavated. Unfortunately, a full analysis of the artefacts collected during the 1982 season and stored in the Department of Archaeology at the University of Allahabad was never completed. However, they were examined by Dr Sacha Jones from the University of Cambridge during her later visits under the initial guidance of Dr J. N. Pal. This study provided a useful springboard for their subsequent joint archaeological work in the middle Son valley (Jones and Pal 2009: 323-341).

The Middle Pleistocene *Sihawal Formation* consists of two stratigraphic units: a lower member comprised of local alluvial fan gravels interspersed with Lower Palaeolithic Acheulian artefacts and a grey silty clay upper member entirely devoid of artefacts. Williams and Royce (1982) interpreted this unit as wind-blown dust or loess on the basis of grain-size, sorting, lack of sedimentary structure and absence of artefacts, although it may have been in part re-worked by overland flow. Some of the artefacts appeared relatively fresh with sharp edges, denoting that they were probably in primary context.

The Upper Pleistocene fluvial sands and gravels of the *Khunteli Formation* also contain Middle Palaeolithic artefacts (including a Levallois flake excavated by Professor J.N. Pal in November 2005) as well as deposits of relatively pure volcanic ash derived from the eruption of Toba volcano in Sumatra 74,000 years ago. The significance of this ash is discussed in sections 4 and 5. Widespread precipitation of calcium carbonate throughout the deposit is consistent with a relatively dry semi-arid climate during or soon after the formation was laid down.

The Upper Pleistocene *Patpara Formation* is a fining-upwards alluvial deposit of gravels, sand and clay with abundant agate, chalcedony and jasper pebbles in the lower gravel members, pointing to a source in the Deccan Traps near the interfluve of the Son River (Williams and Royce 1982: 139-162). The Middle Palaeolithic artefacts within this formation range from highly abraded and transported to retaining sharp edges indicative of a nearby source. Many of the artefacts show signs of heat treatment, which would have made them easier to work. All of the Patpara sediments had undergone extensive weathering and ranged in colour from red to reddish-brown, indicating precipitation of iron under oxidising conditions during a time of wetter than regional climate.

The *Baghor Formation* extends in time from at least 40,000 years ago until the early Holocene and also displays a fining-upwards depositional sequence. It consists of two main depositional units: a coarse-grained Lower Member and a fine-grained Upper Member. The Lower Member consists of cross-bedded and planar-bedded coarse sands *(Plate 3)* and fine gravels and contains abundant transported and carbonate-cemented vertebrate fossils, which were studied by Umesh Chattopadhyaya (Department of Archaeology, University of Allahabad) for his doctoral degree at the University of Cambridge. The Lower Member spans the Last Glacial Maximum (21 ± 2 ka) (Mix et al., 2001) which was a time of weaker summer monsoon and significantly colder and drier climate across peninsular India (Duplessy 1982: 494-498; Williams 1985: 219233). Plant cover was sparse, hillslope erosion more rapid, and sedimentation more active in the Son and Belan valleys. The Upper Member consists of horizontally bedded alluvial clays that accumulated as flood plain deposits during the very late Pleistocene and early Holocene. Deposition of the Upper Member was followed by incision to a depth of about 30-35 m in the middle Son valley. The river terraces exposed along the southern margin of the middle Son valley indicate that this channel incision was intermittent, with phase of stability and local aggradation alternating with phases of vertical incision *(Plate 4)*. The Upper Member contains Mesolithic and early Neolithic artefacts, including the hoofprint of a Sambur deer *(Plate 5)* while the Lower Member contains abraded and transported Upper Palaeolithic artefacts.

It is interesting to note that the Nile has a very similar late Quaternary depositional history to the Son and Belan rivers, for similar hydro-climatic reasons. During the cold dry late Pleistocene, the Nile was transporting sands and gravels and aggrading. With a return to warmer, wetter conditions in its headwaters during the early Holocene, the Nile became a suspension load river, depositing silt and clay across its floodplain. During the last 7-8 ka the Nile has been engaged in incising its channel into its former floodplain (Williams 2019: 405).

The late Holocene clays, silts and sands of the *Khetaunhi Formation* represent a brief interval of fine-grained floodplain sedimentation during a short wetter climatic interval in the late Holocene followed by a return to a more seasonal climate and limited channel incision.

Toba volcanic ash discovery

Perhaps the most important contribution of the 1980 fieldwork season was the chance discovery of volcanic ash close to the Son-Rehi confluence *(Fig. 3)*. It is worth explaining in some detail how it happened, how the ash was identified as having come from the eruption of Toba volcano in Sumatra, Indonesia, some 74,000 years ago, and its significance for Indian prehistoric archaeology. This ash was the first Quaternary volcanic ash ever identified in India. First, the discovery. Here I quote from Williams (2016: 105-6).

> *Our task was to define and map Quaternary sedimentary formations associated with prehistoric stone artefacts ranging in age from Lower Palaeolithic through Middle and Upper Palaeolithic to Mesolithic and Neolithic. In this we thought that we had been reasonably successful until we were confronted with an unusual deposit near the foot of a 35 m high bank section close to the junction of the Son and Rehi rivers. We had seen nothing like it before. I remarked casually to Keith [Royce] that if this had been Ethiopia, I would have called it a volcanic ash or, at least, a diatomaceous ash, but no Quaternary ash had ever been recorded anywhere in India. I decided to sample it at close intervals.*

Discovery of the ash stimulated earth scientists across India to search for other exposures and it eventually became evident that all of peninsular India had been covered in a layer of ash *(Fig. 3)* 10-15 cm thick (Acharyya and Basu 1993: 10-19). Much of the ash was reworked soon after initial deposition by a combination of soil creep, raindrop impact and overland flow to accumulate lower in the landscape in depressions and valley bottoms to form secondary deposits up to several metres thick.

Identifying where the ash came from proved an interesting exercise (see Williams and Clarke, 1995, pp. 287-8 for details). Microscopic analysis by Dr D. A. Adamson at Macquarie University in Sydney confirmed that the 'fine aeolian sands' that we had sampled were indeed composed of sherds of volcanic ash. Detailed particle size analysis by Dr Grant McTainsh at Griffith University, Australia, showed that all the grains were of similar size, with a modal range of 30-50 µm. Strontium isotope analysis by Dr David Whitford (CSIRO Division of Mineralogy, Sydney) of the Son volcanic ash pointed to an origin from the Toba volcanic caldera in Sumatra (Whitford 1975: 1287-1302), later confirmed by Dr C.A. Chesner from Eastern Illinois University, who showed that the Son valley ash came from the youngest of the three major Toba eruptions of the last million years, dated at that time to about 75,000 years ago (75 ka) (Rose and Chesner 1987:913-917; Chesner *et al.* 1991: 200-203). Detailed geochemical analyses have subsequently confirmed that all the volcanic ash then sampled across India belonged to the youngest Toba eruption (Shane *et al.* 1995: 200-204; Westgate 1998:107-112; Pearce *et al.* 2014: 729-734), which has since been precisely dated to 73.88 ± 0.32 ka (Storey *et al.* 2012: 18684-18688).

Significance for prehistoric archaeology

The discovery of the 74 ka Toba ash in many parts of India has important implications for prehistoric archaeology. We noted in section 4 that this discovery prompted geologists across India to search for this ash, which is known as the Youngest Toba Tephra or YTT. It soon became clear that deposits chemically similar to the YTT were widespread across the sub-continent. The YTT ash occurs in three main forms in India. Most commonly, the ash has been reworked and re-deposited in depressions and valley bottoms on a number of occasions since initial deposition. Ages obtained on sediments above these redeposited beds of ash are invariably younger than 74 ka and so cannot be used to study the environmental (including climatic) impact of the initial eruption on India. The second most common occurrence of YTT ash consists of material that has been locally reworked quite soon after the eruption but that has been protected from subsequent erosion. This ash is very pure but much thicker than the initial airfall ash. The third and least common occurrence of the ash consists of a thin band no more than 10-15 cm thick of YTT ash in primary context. These deposits can be used most confidently to determine the possible impact upon prehistoric peoples and ecosystems of the YTT eruption. In addition, the ash that is in primary context can be used as an isochronous marker, enabling prehistoric environments and cultural remains evident before the eruption to be compared with those evident after the eruption. In addition, deposits of relatively pure ash that were transported and deposited soon after the initial airfall can also be used as isochronous stratigraphic marker beds provided due care is taken to establish that they were indeed displaced and buried very soon after the eruption of the YTT (Biswas *et al.* 2013: 14-25).

Toba environmental impact

Marine sediment cores from the Bay of Bengal show that the YTT was about 10-15 cm thick (Ninkovich *et al.* 1978a:1-13; 1978b: 574-577& 722). We can therefore infer that continental India was also covered in 10-15 cm of Toba ash soon after Toba erupted 74,000 years ago. Isotopic analyses of pedogenic carbonate collected from fossil soils above and beneath the YTT along an east to west transect from the Son valley to the Narmada show that in north-central India forest and woodland were widespread before the eruption and were replaced by grassland and open woodland after the eruption (Ambrose *et al.* 2007: 168-668; Williams *et al.* 2009: 295-314). Pollen from a marine sediment core collected from the Bay of Bengal shows drier conditions after the eruption (Williams *et al.* 2009: 295-314). In Greenland dust blown from Asia shows drier conditions in central Asia immediately following the eruption and temperatures fell sharply in Greenland immediately after the eruption (Zielinski *et al.* 1996: 837-840). Isotopic evidence from a precisely dated speleothem from a cave in New Mexico show prolonged dry conditions immediately after the Toba eruption (Polyak *et al.* 2017: 843-846). Cooling was already under way before the Toba eruption. It is likely that the eruption may have accentuated the global climatic cooling, but it did not cause it.

At present, the debate is polarised between those (mainly archaeologists) who claim no impact and those (mainly earth scientists and climate modellers: e.g., Jones et al. 2007; Robock *et al.* 2009) who claim an impact ranging from moderate to severe and lasting from decades to centuries (see Williams, 2012b for details). Historic eruptions like Tambora (1815), Krakatau (1883), Agung (1963) and Pinatubo (1991) were all associated with a global fall in temperature of up to one degree C in the 12 months following the eruption. In the case of Tambora, the 'year without a summer", crops failed, and famine ensued in Europe and North America. The volume of equivalent rock erupted from Tambora amounted to 30-33 cubic km. The others were somewhat less. The volume of equivalent rock erupted from the 74 ka Toba eruption amounted to 2500-3000 cubic km, of which about 600 cubic km were ash. This is two orders of magnitude more than the historic eruptions. The lack of high-resolution dating of the putative environmental impacts has hindered progress (See Williams, 2012b). To progress, we need high resolution dating of different environmental archives (speleothems, ice cores, lake sediments, marine sediment cores, pollen spectra) to establish prevailing conditions in different regions before and after the Toba eruption (Williams 2012c: 87-93).

There is still no consensus. I suspect that the key reason why current ideas about the impact of the Toba eruption remain so polarised is our lack of fine resolution chronology to define the nature of the environment immediately before and after the YTT eruption. A possible recent exception is Polyak *et al.* (2017), who have used fine resolution uranium series dating of a speleothem from New Mexico to show a rapid onset of regional drought synchronous with the onset of Greenland ice core stadial 20 as well as with the onset of the Toba eruption. The drought ended abruptly 1560 years later, at the end of stadial 20. They infer that the Toba eruption acted as a trigger or catalyst for more prolonged and widespread climatic change than the initial brief impact, which seems very credible.

Evidence used to reconstruct the possible impact of the 74 ka Toba eruption includes comparison with historic eruptions (Williams *et al.* 2006: 2619-2631); climate models (Williams *et al.* 2009); molecular biology (Ambrose 1998:623-651; Williams *et al.* 2009: 295-314); prehistoric archaeology (Petraglia *et al.* 2007:114-116; Clarkson *et al.* 2020); ice cores (REF); stable isotope geochemistry (Ambrose *et al.* 2007:114-116; Williams *et al.* 2009: 295-314); pollen analysis (Williams *et al.* 2009: 295-314; Van Der Kaars *et al.* 2012: 45-53); geology and geochemistry (Chesner *et al.* 1991; 200-203;

Acharyya and Basu 1993;10-19; Shane *et al.* 1995: 200-204; Westgate *et al.* 1998: 107-112); geomorphology (Williams and Royce 1982: 139-162; Williams and Clarke, 1995: 282-308;Williams *et al.* 2009: 295-314); and marine sediment cores (Ninkovich *et al.* 1978a: 1-13; 1978b: 574-577; Duplessy 1982: 494-498; Bühring and Sarnthein 2000: 275-278). The genetic evidence that is sometimes proposed in favour of a major impact is still too poorly dated to allow any sensible interpretation over the role of Toba in causing a genetic bottleneck (Ambrose 1998: 623-651; Rampino and Ambrose 2000). Table 1 lists some of the impacts of the Toba eruption.

Current research

Research in the Son and Belan valleys during the past few decades follows several, often overlapping, pathways. One involves a re-appraisal of the alluvial stratigraphy and depositional environments (Williams *et al.* 2006: 2619-2631; Giblin *et al.* 2008: 391-410). The second is a focus on improving the chronology of the alluvial sediments, prehistoric sites and YTT outcrops (Pal et al. 2004 51-62; Williams *et al.* 2006: 2619-2631; Jones 2010: 336-350; Biswas *et al.* 2013: 14-25). The third is aimed at more detailed and more rigorous archaeological excavation and analysis (Clarkson *et al.* 2020). The fourth and in many respects the most innovative is the use of novel geochemical and isotopic techniques to improve our understanding of past climate and prehistoric cultures in this region (Jha *et al.* 2020: 106-121).

Future directions

For archaeologists seeking to study prehistoric artefact assemblages in deposits stratigraphically above and beneath the YTT, it will be imperative to demonstrate beyond any reasonable doubt that the volcanic ash exposed within the excavated archaeological sections is either in primary context or at least has not been extensively reworked (Biswas *et al.* 2013: 14-25). This will require input from geochemists, field geologists/geomorphologists/soil scientists. Unless this can be done, it is unlikely that a simple comparison of archaeological assemblages recovered in primary context from sediments located stratigraphically above and beneath the putative YTT ash will be particularly informative.

A mere demonstration that the artefact assemblages above and beneath the YTT are essentially similar (Clarkson *et al.* 2020) does not tell us much about any possible local or regional environmental changes associated with the 74 ka Toba eruption and YTT deposition across India. All it tells us is that the assemblages remained similar and humans were present at that particular site. They may or may not have experienced some impact.

Independent evidence from many different proxies, buttressed by a fine resolution chronology, is needed to determine whether or not there were changes in environment caused by the eruption. Only then will it be possible to throw further light upon human responses to possible environmental change and so contribute to the broader question of prehistoric human migrations in South Asia

(O'Connell *et al.* 2018: 8482-8490).

Acknowledgements

I owe a great debt of gratitude to the late Professor J. Desmond Clark and the late Professor G.R. Sharma for inviting me to take part in their joint archaeological investigations in the Son and Belan valleys of north-central India during the two field seasons in 1980 and 1982. I also thank my colleagues from the University of Allahabad and the University of California at Berkeley for their friendship and cooperation. Among these was Jaganath N. Pal who also guided us to the Toba volcanic ash outcrop at Khetaunhi in November 2005, where I sampled the ash with Professor Stan Ambrose from the University of Illinois at Champaign-Urbana and Dr Parth Chauhan, now at Indian Institute of Science education and research Mohali, with whom I had worked in 2001 in the Himalayan foothills.

References

Acharyya, S.K. & P.K. Basu, Toba ash on the Indian subcontinent and its implications for correlation of late Pleistocene alluvium, *Quaternary Research,* 40.

Ambrose, S.H., Late Pleistocene human population bottlenecks, volcanic winter, and differentiation of modern humans, *Journal of Human Evolution* 34.

Ambrose, S.H., M.A.J. Williams, U. Chattopadhyaya, J.N. Pal & P. Chauhan, Environmental impact of the 73 ka Toba eruption reflected by paleosol carbonate carbon isotope ratios in central India. INQUA 2007, Abstracts, *Quaternary International* 8.

Biswas, R.H., M.A.J. Williams, Juyal R. N. & A.K. Singhvi, Methodological studies on luminescence dating of volcanic ashes, *Quaternary Geochronology* 17.

Bühring, C. & M. Sarnthein, Toba ash layers in the South China Sea: Evidence of contrasting wind directions during eruption ca, 74ka, *Geology* 28 (3).

Chesner, C.A., W.I. Rose, A. Deino, R. Drake, & J.A. Westgate, Eruptive history of earth's largest Quaternary caldera (Toba, Indonesia) clarified, *Geology* 19.

Clarkson, C. & 15 others, 2020, Human occupation of northern India spans the Toba super-eruption ~74,000 years ago, *Nature Communications* doi.org/10.1038/s41467-020-14668-4.

Duplessy, J.C., Glacial to interglacial contrasts in the northern Indian Ocean, *Nature* 295.

Gibling, M.R., R. Sinha, N.G. Roy, S.K.Tandon, & M. Jain, Quaternary fluvial and eolian deposits on the Belan River, India: paleoclimatic setting of Paleolithic to Neolithic archaeological sites over the past 85, 000 years, *Quaternary Science Reviews* 27.

Jha, D.K., P. Sanyal & A. Philippe, Multi-proxy evidence of Late Quaternary climate and vegetational history of north-central India: Implication for the Paleolithic to Neolithic phases, *Quaternary Science Reviews* 229.

tps://doi.org/10.1038/s41467-020-14668-4

Jones, M. T., R.S.J. Sparks, & P.J. Valdes, The climatic impact of supervolcanic ash blankets, *Climate Dynamics* 29.

Jones, S.C., Palaeoenvironmental response to the <"74 ka Toba ash-fall in the Jurreru and Middle Son valleys in southern and north-central India, *Quaternary Research* 73.

Jones, S. & J.N. Pal, The Palaeolithic of the Middle Son valley, north-central India: Changes in hominin lithic technology and behaviour during the Upper Pleistocene, *J. Anthropological Archaeology* 28.

Mix, A.C., E. Bard, & R. Schneider, Environmental processes of the ice age: land, oceans, glaciers (EPILOG). *Quaternary Science Reviews* 20.

Ninkovich, D., R.S.J. Sparks & M.T. Ledbetter, The exceptional magnitude and intensity of the Toba eruption, Sumatra: an example of the use of deep-sea tephra layers as a geological tool, *Bulletin Volcanologique* 41.

Ninkovich, D., N.J. Shackleton, A.A. Abdel-Monem, J.D. Obradovich, & G. Izett, K–Ar age of the late Pleistocene eruption of Toba, north Sumatra, *Nature* 276.

O'Connell, J.F., J. Allen, M.A.J. Williams, A.N. Williams, C.S.M. Turney, N.A.Spooner, J. Kamminga, G. Brown, & A. Cooper, When did *Homo sapiens* first reach Southeast Asia and Sahul? *Proceedings of the National Academy of Sciences* 115 (34).

Pal, J.N., M.A.J. Williams, M. Jaiswal, & A.K. Singhvi, Infra-Red Stimulated Luminescence ages for prehistoric cultures in the Son and Belan valleys, north central India, *Journal of Interdisciplinary Studies in History and Archaeology, Allahabad* 1 (2).

Pearce, N. J. G., J.A. Westgate, E. Gatti, J.N. Pattan, G. Parthiban & H. Achyuthan, Individual glass shard trace element analyses confirm that all known Toba tephra reported from India is from the 75 ka Youngest Toba eruption, *J. Quaternary Science* 29.

Petraglia, M.,R. Korisettar, N. Boivin, C. Clarkson, P. Ditchfield, S. Jones, J. Koshy, M.M. Lahr, C. Oppenheimer, D. Pyle, R. Roberts, J.C. Schwenniger, L. Arnold, & K. White, Middle Pleistocene assemblages from the Indian subcontinent before and after the Toba super-eruption, *Science* 317.

Polyak, V.J., Y. Asmerom, & M.S. Lachniet, Rapid speleothem "^{13}C change in southwestern North America coincident with Greenland stadial 20 and the Toba super-eruption, *Geology* 45 (9).

Rampino, M.R. & S.H. Ambrose, Volcanic winter in the Garden of Eden: The Toba supereruption and the late Pleistocene human population crash. In *Volcanic Hazards and Disasters in Human Antiquity*, F.W. McCoy & G. Heiken (eds.), *Geological Society of America Special Paper* 345.

Robock, A., Ammann, C.M., Oman, L., Shindell, D., Levis, S. & Stenchikov, G., 2009, Did the Toba volcanic eruption of w74 ka B.P. produce widespread glaciation? Journal of Geophysical Research 114 (D10107), 1e9. doi:10.1029/2008JD011652.

Rose, W. I. & C.A. Chesner, Dispersal of ash in the great Toba eruption, 75 ka, *Geology* 15.

Shane, P., J. Westgate, M. Williams, & R. Korisettar, New geochemical evidence for the Youngest Toba Tuff in India, *Quaternary Research* 44.

Shane, P., J. Westgate, M. Williams, & R. Korisettar, Reply to Comments by S. Mishra and S.N. Rajaguru on 'New Geochemical Evidence for the Youngest Toba Tuff in India'. *Quaternary Research* 46 (3).

Sharma, G.R., *Stone Age in the Vindhyas and The Ganga Valley, Radiocarbon and Indian Archaeology*, D.P. Agrawal & A. Ghosh (eds). TIFR, Bombay.

Sharma, G.R. ,1975, *Seasonal migrations and Mesolithic lake cultures in the Ganga Valley*, K.C. *Chattopadhyaya Memorial Volume*, G.R. Sharma (ed.). Allahabad University, Allahabad.

Sharma, G.R., V.D. Misra, D. Mandal, B.B. Misra, & J.N. Pal, 1980, *Beginnings of Agriculture,* Allahabad: Abinash Prakashan.

Sharma, G.R. & J.D. Clark, 1983, *Palaeoenvironments and Prehistory in the Middle Son Valley, Madhya Pradesh, north central India*, Allahabad: Abinash Prakashan.

Storey, M., R.G., Roberts, & M. Saidin, Astronomically calibrated $^{40}Ar/^{39}Ar$ age for the Toba supereruption and global synchronization of late Quaternary records, *Proceedings of the National Academy of Sciences* 109, (46).

Van der Kaars, S., M.A.J. Williams, F. Bassinot, F. Guichard, E. Moreno, The influence of the 73 ka Toba super-eruption on the ecosystems of northern Sumatra as recorded in marine core BAR94-25, *Quaternary International* 258.

Westgate, J.A., P.A.R. Shane, N.J.G. Pearce, W.T. Perkins, R. Korisettar, C.A. Chesner, M.A.J. Williams & S.K. Acharyya, All Toba tephra occurrences across peninsula India belong to 75 ka eruption, *Quaternary Research* 50.

Whitford, D.J., Strontium isotopic studies of the volcanic rocks of the Sunda Arc, Indonesia, and their petrogenetic implications, *Geochimica et Cosmochimica Acta* 39.

Williams, M.A.J., 1985, Pleistocene aridity in tropical Africa, Australia and Asia, *Environmental Change and Tropical Geomorphology*, I. Douglas & T. Spencer, (eds.) London, Allen & Unwin.

Williams, M.A.J. , 2011, Environmental Change, *Handbook of Geomorphology*, K. Gregory, D. Walling & A. Goudie (eds) London: Sage.

Williams, M., River sediments, *River History*, C. Vita-Finzi (ed.), *Philosophical Transactions of the Royal Society of London, Series A*, 370.

Williams, M., The Toba super-eruption: history of a debate, *Quaternary International* 258.

Williams, M., Did the Toba super-eruption have an enduring effect? Insights from genetics, prehistoric archaeology, pollen analysis, stable isotope geochemistry, geomorphology, ice cores, and climate models, *Quaternary International* 269.

Williams, M., 2019, *The Nile basin: Quaternary Geology, Geomorphology and Prehistoric Environments,* New York: Cambridge University Press 405.

Williams, M.A.J. & M.F. Clarke, Late Quaternary environments in north central India, *Nature* 308.

Williams, M.A.J. & M.F. Clarke, Quaternary geology and prehistoric environments in the Son and Belan Valleys, north-central India, *Geological Society of India Memoir* 32.

Williams, M.A.J. & K. Royce, Quaternary geology of the middle Son valley, north central India: Implications for prehistoric archaeology, *Palaeogeography, Palaeoclimatology, Palaeoecology* 38.

Williams, M.A.J., J.N. Pal, M. Jaiswal, & A.K. Singhvi, River response to Quaternary climatic fluctuations: Evidence from the Son and Belan valleys, north central India, *Quaternary Science Reviews* 25.

Williams, M.A.J., S.H. Ambrose, S.Van der Kaars, U. Chattopadhyaya, J.N. Pal, P.R. Chauhan & C. Ruehlemann, Environmental impact of the 73 ka Toba super-eruption in South Asia, *Palaeogeography, Palaeoclimatology, Palaeoecology* 284.

Williams, M.A.J., S.H. Ambrose, S. Van der Kaars, C. Ruehlemann, U. Chattopadhyaya, J.N. Pal, J & P. Chauhan, Reply to the comment on 'Environmental impact of the 73 ka Toba super-eruption in South Asia' by Martin A. J. Williams, Stanley H. Ambrose, Sander van der Kaars, Carsten Ruehlemann, Umesh Chattopadhyaya, Jagannath Pal, Parth R. Chauhan [*Palaeogeography, Palaeoclimatology, Palaeoecology* 284; *Palaeogeography, Palaeoclimatology, Palaeoecology* 296.

Zielinski, G. A., P.A. Mayewski, L.D. Meeker, S. Whitlow & M.S. Twickler, Potential atmospheric impact of the Toba mega-eruption ~71,000 years ago, *Geophysical Research Letters* 23.

6

Bird Bone Palaeolithic Flutes : Inputs from Archaeology Ethnomusicology and Archaeoacoustics

Fernando Augusto Coimbra

Introduction

Some examples of large bird bones, some of them decorated, found in archaeological excavations in caves with Palaeolithic occupation were initially interpreted in different ways such as tubes for blowing colour pigments, recipients for needles and as musical wind instruments like flutes. According to music archaeologist Graeme Lawson, the well defined finger-holes that appear on them "are capable of playing tuneful music rather than disorganized noise" (Devereux 2001: 134). Furthermore, bird bones like vulture's ulna present excellent dimensional qualities, with a section practically circular, and a regular internal surface, which contribute to a good acoustic performance (Dauvois 2005: 2225-241).

Today, it is generally recognized that bones from large birds like vultures, griffon vultures, eagles and swans were frequently used in the Upper Palaeolithic to produce flutes, such as the examples found in Gravettian, Solutrean and Magdalenian deposits from the cave of Isturitz, in the French Pyrenees (Buisson 1990: 420-433; D'Errico & Lawson 2006: 41-57), and, more recently in the Jura Valley (Germany), in Aurignacian layers from the caves of Geißenklösterle, Hohle Fels and Vogelherd (Münzel et al 2002107-118; Conard *et al.* 2009: 737-740), besides other few Magdalenian examples from the Provinces of Asturias and Cantabria, in Spain (Menéndez and García 1998: 167-177).

During the Upper Palaeolithic there are also some flutes produced in mammoth ivory, but in a general way, regarding Europe, bones such as the ulna of large birds seem to have been preferred, probably due to their acoustic properties. This aspect may be related to the lightness of bird bones when comparing them to thicker bones from other animals, producing this way a better sound in a frame of early musical behaviour (Coimbra 2018a: 13-21).

We do not discuss here the controversial "flute" from Divje Babe, in Slovenia, attributed to Neanderthals, and constituted by two holes in a young bear bone that several authors considered to be the result of a carnivore attack (Cross, 2001; D'Errico & Lawson, 2006) regarding the mentioned bear and by no means of anthropic origin (Nevertheless, the discussion about this possible musical artefact is still open).

Furthermore, being this possible case produced in bear bone, it is out of the aims of the present article, which focus only in flutes made of bird bones.

The present text does not intend to be an inventory of these musical instruments but it is rather an interpretive view based in the contribution of the inputs from archaeology, ethnomusicology and archaeoacoustics in what concerns the so called Palaeolithic bone flutes.

Bird bone palaeolithic flutes

Research carried out so far revealed that the flute made of swan radius, found in 1990 in the cave of Geißenklösterle (Southwestern Germany), constitutes what seems to be the first intentionally built musical artefact (Coimbra 2018a: 13-21). It was initially dated between 37 000 BP and 33 500 BP (Münzel *et al.* 2002: 107-118) but more recent dating attributed to this flute the chronology of 42 000 BP (Higham *et al.* 2012: 664-674). It has several cut-marks near the finger-holes (Fig.1), suggesting that they were previously measured, which leads to the idea "that this aspect of the flute was designed with something in mind: perhaps a pitch standard/scale, or physical practicality, or pedagogy" (Killin 2018: 6).

In 1973, another bird bone flute had been found during excavations at Geißenklösterle, wich is labeled now as Flute 2 and the discovery from 1990 labeled as Flute 1 (Conard *et al.* 2009: 737-740).

Experiments with replicas of these two flutes from Geißenklösterle, allowing playing a wide range of possible tones, demonstrated that they are "fully developed musical instruments" (Conard & Malina 2008: 14), suggesting also that their level of sophistication may indicate "a long history of musical technological production" (Killin, 2018: 6). As a matter of fact, several researchers agree that "musical technology has a much older past, currently (...) hidden from the material record" (idem, ibidem).

Archaeological excavations at the cave of Hohle Fels, in 2008, revealed an Aurignacian flute[1] made of griffon vulture radius, besides other two flutes but made of mammoth ivory (Conard *et al.* 2009: 737-740).

The cave of Isturitz has the largest collection of Palaeolithic bone flutes, totalizing twenty-two different cases, all made from vulture radius, considered most of them as Gravettian, existing however also Aurignacian and Magdalenian examples (Buisson 1990: 420-433). Some of them are decorated with repeated incisions (Dauvois 2005: 225-241), being all kept in the *Musée des Antiquités Nationales*, in Saint Germain-en-Laye, near Paris, France. However, we wonder why the most beautiful examples, with decorations, are not displayed to the public (Fig.2).

As mentioned by Iain Morley (2009: 168-169), this cave "was an important focal point for large groups of people throughout the Upper Palaeolithic" and the flutes discovered in its interior "are particularly significant in appearing to indicate large scale communal musical activity or, at least, musical activity at large scale communal gatherings."

But were these flutes used only for playing music or did they have other functions?

In order to try answering this question the author used the input from Ethnomusicology and from Archaeoacoustics (Sound Archaeology), which are important contributions to analyse this problematic in a deeper way.

Experienced ethnomusicologist Cajsa Lund mentions that still in the 19th century Swedish shepherd used bone flutes, similar to the Palaeolithic examples, playing "sharp, high-pitched signals (...) in order to scare away his worst enemy – the wolf" (Lund 2012: 62). These animals, having an accurate hearing capacity, would certainly run away due to the unpleasant high-pitched sounds produced by the bone flutes (The author, after acquiring a replica of a Palaeolithic bone flute, made the experiment of playing high-pitched sounds in front of his dog, with a similar hearing system of wolves, and the poor animal run away immediately). This suggests that Palaeolithic groups could also have produced similar sounds on their flutes in order to keep away certain predators. Therefore, bone flutes could have had more functions that merely a musical instrument being "considered to be a weapon against real or supernatural enemies" (Lund 2012: 62).

Still in the field of Ethnomusicology, regarding Hunter-Gatherer music, Iain Morley (2006: 103) after analysing cultures such as Native Americans of the Plains, African Pygmies, Australian Aborigines and Eskimo of Alaska (Yupik) and Canada (Inuit) concludes that all those groups "have music which is predominantly vocal, and is accompanied mainly by percussion instruments. The use of melodic instruments is minimal."

This argument makes one questioning the use of bone flutes for playing only music in the Palaeolithic, as mentioned by some authors. Indeed, if modern musicians are able to produce melodies using replica of Palaeolithic bone flutes it is crucial to keep in mind that Prehistoric populations did not have any schools for learning music and applying that knowledge to instruments. As a matter of fact, as musicologist Ian Cross (2001) mentioned, early musical behaviour must have been initially vocally expressed, predating the construction of a musical artefact, most likely by a considerable period. Therefore, Palaeolithic bone flutes must have become musical instruments only after a long period of time, after an initial musical behaviour based on vocalizing and percussion using handclapping and other types of percussion (lithophones) (Palaeolithic lithophones are known in several caves in Europe, where stalagmites and stalactites, sometimes marked with red dots, "ring like a xylophone when struck" (Till 2018: 22) and rhythm (rasps).

In the frame of Archaeoacoustics, the author, together with Physicist Bruno Fazenda (Salford University, UK), in March of 2018 carried out research (Fig.3) inside the Cave of Escoural (Southern Portugal), which has some panels of Palaeolithic rock art and later Neolithic burials. Although the main goal of the fieldwork was to observe in what extend there would be a direct relation between the acoustics in the cave and the location of the rock art figures (These preliminary tests are still unpublished, being necessary another fieldwork inside the cave in order to get further data) the team also made acoustic tests using a replica of a Palaeolithic bone flute and clapping hands. For example, regarding the flute, it was noticed that some areas of the cave environment act as a natural sound amplifier (The tests with the flute and handclapping were recorded in an audiovisual documentary by journalist Raquel Castro, with the aim of being presented in a program about early acoustics in the Portuguese TV, Channel 2). This way, some sounds produced with the flute inside the cave became more "powerful" than those played at open air, what can have been an experience felt also by Palaeolithic people.

Similar experiments with bone flutes had been made before at the cave of Tito Bustillo (Asturias, Spain), where the sound of the flutes was enhanced by the local reverberation (Till *et al.* undated).

Also the cave of Isturitz "was possibly valued for its peculiar acoustics and might have been used for ceremonial gatherings" (Both 2018: 17), mainly because of "a large chamber where sound resonates intensely for seven seconds, longer than in most churches" (Till 2018: 23). With such an intense resonance, the sound of the several flutes found there, played at the same time, despite constituting melodic music or not, must have left a deep impression on the minds of the participants in those gatherings. Furthermore, mind/body experiences accompanied by altered states of consciousness may have happened in these reverberating cave environments. However, this would be a theme for another article bridging Archaeoacoustics and Psychoacoustics.

Final Note

Research in Archaeoacoustics, despite methodologies and aims may vary among different investigators, has been trying to identify intentionality in the use of acoustic spaces or objects. For example, according to Michel Dauvois (2005: 225-241) Palaeolithic bone flutes have a large variety of melodic interpretations. However, regarding this period, it is necessary to distinguish "sound" from "music", which generally requires combined elements such as rhythm, melody and harmony that hardly could be present in an early musical behaviour, despite the concept of music can vary from context to context and from individual to individual (Cross 2001; Coimbra 2018a: 13-21). Nevertheless, several bone flutes played at the same time inside a cave with a minimum of resonance could have become a memorable and pleasant happening in the minds of our ancestors. Furthermore, the gatherings for playing flutes must have functioned as a factor of cohesion among groups of hunter-gatherers, what might have helped to create social harmony (Coimbra 2019b).

The use of sound in ritual context, during the Palaeolithic, can also be analysed through rock art examples (Coimbra, in press), as in the case of the Cave of Trois Frères (Ariège, France), where a human figure with a bison mask seems to be dancing and playing "what appears to be either a nose flute or a mouth bow (a chordophone)" (Garcia Benito 2018: 27; Fig.4), having a Magdalenian chronology of about 13 000 B.C. (Some authors have interpreted this instrument as a nose flute, while others considered it as a musical bow (Diaz-Andreu & Mattioli 2019).

As a conclusion it is necessary to stress that the so called Palaeolithic bone flutes must be considered, first of all, as sound making artefacts. Indeed, as Etienne Safa (2015: 23-46) mentioned, more than musical instruments, these flutes may have had several functions: musical, protective, cynegetic or ritual.

Secondly, the use of bird bones as raw material for Palaeolithic flutes must be understood according to the lightness of these same bones when comparing them to thicker examples of other animals, what can have an important role in acoustic and musical performances. However, musical performances using bone flutes must have happened only after some experience of musical behaviour based on vocalizing and percussion (Coimbra 2018b).

After the Palaeolithic, bird bone flutes continue to be used, as in the Neolithic examples from Jiahu, China (Fig.4), "made from the ulnae of the red-crowned crane" (Zhang *et al.* 1999: 366), having between five and eight holes.

References

Both, A. A., 2018, Music at the Dawn of Humanity, In, *Music and Sounds in Ancient Europe, Contributions from the European Music Archaeology Project.* De Angeli, S.; Both, A. A.; Hagel, S.; Holmes, P.; Jiménez Pasalodos, R.; Lund, C. S. (eds.), *European Music Archaeology Project.*

Buisson, D., 1990, Les flûtes paléolithiques d'Isturitz (Pyrénées-Atlantiques), *Bulletin de la Société Préhistorique Française, 87, n°10-12.* Société Préhistorique Française, Paris.

Coimbra, F. A., 2018a, Archaeology, Archaeoacoustics and Early Musical Behaviour, *Archaeoacoustics III: the Archaeology of Sound*, Florida: Old Temples Study Foundation, Myakka City.

Coimbra, F. A., 2018b, Bird bones as raw material for Palaeolithic flutes: an archaeoacoustic Approach, *Evolução, N. 2.*, Centro Português de Geo-história e Pré-História, Lisboa.

Coimbra F. A., 2019, Sound as a factor of social cohesion among small human groups: some case studies since Prehistory till the present times, Oosterbeek, L.; Caron, L. (eds.), *Resilience and transformation in the territories of low demographic density*, Mação: *ARKEOS, 48*, Instituto Terra e Memória.

Coimbra, F. A., (in press), The contribution of rock art for understanding the origins of music and dancing, *Telestes, I, An International Journal of Archaeomusicology and Archaeology of Sound*, Roma.

Conard, N.& M. Malina, 2008, New evidence for the origins of music from the caves of the Swabian Jura, A.A. Both; R. Eichmann, E. Hickmann & L.C. Koch (Eds.), Challenges and objectives in music archaeology, *Rahden: Studien zur Musikarchaologie VI, Orient-Archaologie 22 Verlag Marie Leidorf*.

Conard, N.; M. Malina; S.C. Münzel, 2009, New Flutes Document the Earliest Musical Tradition in South-Western Germany, *Nature, 460;* doi:10.1038/nature08169 .

Cross, I., 2001, Music, mind and evolution, *Psychology of Music, 29 (1),* London: SAGE Publishing.

Dauvois, M., 2005, Homo musicus palaeolithicus et Paleoacustica, San Sebastian: *MUNIBE, Antropologia-Arkeologia, 57.*

D'Errico, F. & G. Lawson, 2006, The sound paradox: How to assess the acoustic significance of archaeological evidence? *Archaeoacoustics,* C. Scarre & G. Lawson (eds.), Cambridge: McDonald Institute.

Devereux, P., 2001, *Stone Age Soundtracks,* London: Vega.

Díaz-Andreu, M., T. Mattioli, 2019, Rock Art, music and acoustics: a global overview, B. David & I.J. Mcniven (eds.), Oxford: *The Oxford Handbook of the Archaeology and Anthropology of Rock Art,* Oxford University Press.

García, Benito C., 2018, Wind from the Sky, Wind from the Earth, The Earliest Bone Pipes and

Whistles, *Music and Sounds in Ancient Europe, Contributions from the European Music Archaeology Project.* De S. Angeli, A.A. Both, S. Hagel, P. Holmes, R. Jiménez Pasalodos, C.S. Lund (eds.), European Music Archaeology Project.

Higham, T., L. Basell, R. Jacobic, R. Wood,C.B. Ramsey, N.J. Conard, 2012, Ôesting models for the beginnings of the Aurignacian and the advent of figurative art and music: The radiocarbon chronology of Geißenklösterle, *Journal of Human Evolution, 62 (6), Elsevier.*

Killin, A., 2018, The origins of music: Evidence, theory, and prospects. *Music & Science, Vol I,* SAGE; DOI: 10.1177/2059204317751971.

Lund, C. S., 2012, Sound Tools, Symbols or Something Quite Different? On Possible Percussion Instruments from Bronze-Age Sweden " Including Methodological Aspects of Music-Archaeological Research, *Studien zur Musikarchäologie VIII, Orient-Archäologie, 27,* Deutsches Archäologisches Institut, Rahden.

Menéndez, M., E. García, 1998, Instrumentos musicales paleolíticos: la flauta magdaleniense de la Cueva de la Güelga (Asturias), *Espacio, Tiempo y Forma, Serie I, Prehistoria y Arqueología, t.* 11, UNED, Madrid.

Morley, I., 2006, Hunter-gatherer Music and its implications for identifying intentionality, *Archaeoacoustics,* C. Scarre & G. Lawson (eds.), Cambridge: McDonald Institute .

Morley, I., 2009, Ritual and music — parallels and practice, and the Palaeolithic, C. Renfrew & I. Morley (Eds.), *Becoming human: Innovation in prehistoric material and spiritual culture,* Cambridge University Press .

Münzel, S., F. Seeberger, & W. Hein, 2002, The Geissenklösterle flute: discovery, experiments, reconstruction, H. Hickmann, A.D. Kilmer & R. Eichmann (eds.), *Studien zur Musikarchäologie,* Leidorf .

Safa, E., 2015, L'Archéologie du son: transmettre les connaissances et les savoir-faire de la France paléolithique à la

France médiévale, *Polymatheia 1,* Éditions Tourmaline, Vanves .

Till, R., 2018, Sounds and caves. In, *Music and Sounds in Ancient Europe, Contributions from the European Music Archaeology Project*, De S. Angeli, A.A. Both, S. Hagel, P.Holmes, R. Jiménez Pasalodos & C.S Lund (eds.), *European Music Archaeology Project.*

Till, R., S. Wyatt, B. Fazenda, J. Sheaffer, C. Scarre (undated), Initial report on a study in the Cave of Tito Bustillo, Asturias, Spain; https://songsofthecaves.wordpress.com/bibliography/; Accessed on 28 May 2020.

Zhang, J., G. Harbottle, C. Wang & Z.Kong, 1999, Oldest playable musical instruments found at Jiahu early Neolithic site in China, *Nature, 401.*

7

A Study of Prehistoric Tools Collected from Santal Parganas and Deposited at Cultural History Museum, Oslo, Norway by Reverend Paul Olaf Bodding

Soumyajit Das and Ranjana Ray

Introduction

Reverend Paul Olaf Bodding was a Norwegian missionary as well as an eminent linguist, ethnographer and a folklorist. He came to India in 1889 and was stationed in the district of Santal Parganas in Bihar. At present most of Santal Parganas is in the newly formed state of Jharkhand. He stayed at the town of Dumka and at Mahulpahari, a village 25 kms away from the town of Dumka.Bodding got interested in the life and culture of the people among whom he lived and started to collect and analyze material objects of everyday life and those of ritual significance for the Santals. The Ethnographic Museum at University of Oslo was given custodianship of a huge collection of prehistoric and ethnographic objects and manuscripts donated by him between 1901 and 1935. Present paper is on the prehistoric materials, which Bodding collected between the years 1890 to 1934.

Bodding wrote two articles on his collections (1901and 1904), which came out in the Journal of the Asiatic Society. No information is given by him on the site and geological context of the stone tools. He got them from the possession of the Santal tribes. Sometimes he had to purchase them. The Santali people informed him that the artifacts were collected from various places, such as in the fields, while digging or tilling, from the riverbed, from the soil surface, from the forest or from clefts in the rocks, etc. The Santals call these pieces as *'ceterdhiri'*, meaning thunderstones. The Santals believed that the axe shaped stonesfell from the sky when lightning struck the ground. They also believed that such thunder stoneswill protect the house against hazards of lightening. They also believed that the celts had great medicinal properties. Santals used them for treatment of various illnesses and considered them to be very precious. The Santals also used them for ritual purposes. Bodding realized the archaeological importance of the artifacts. He knew that the tools were mostly Neolithic celts.He had deposited most of his collectionsin several lots at the Ethnographic Museum of the University of Oslo, presently known as the Museum of Cultural History.These are carefully stored in the museum ever since. Some artifacts ofBodding collection were presented to Pitt Rivers Museum and to Bihar and Orissa Research Society. Since the Oslo University and the Museum is the custodian of the huge collection of Bodding, the authorities were eager to digitize the collection, so that scholars over the world may have access to the artifacts, at least on the internet. Recently the present authors had the opportunity to study them first hand. And even help selection of some representative types for exhibition in the museum. The paper is on the prehistoric tools in the Bodding collection.

Earlier Studies of the Bodding collection

Four significant publications came out on the collection. The first study was made by P.O. Bodding himself (Bodding 1901: 259-282; 1904). Bodding's papers dealt with the description of some tools as well as comparing them with the finds of other places in India and Southeast Asia. Bodding had conceded in the first paper that he did not go into archaeological perspective of the tools but rather restricted his discussion with the belief system of the Santals of his time associated with the stone implements. He had discussed at length the belief of the Santals in the preventive, protecting and medicinal property of the celts. Cases like easing of difficult pregnancy and subsequent delivery, healing cramps, against boils and carbuncles and for certain pains in the back. The water in which the "thunder bolt" was soaked or water with which the stone was rubbed against a mortar and contained parts of the celt was taken either internally or applied externally. This was considered to have great healing property. Many of the celts were reduced in size due to occasional rubbing. Some of the celts were considered as votive stones or worshipped as *Mahadev* because it had dark rings on it. Bodding found that many of them were smeared with oil and vermillion as a result of worship. He also had noticed that the celts were also used as hones to sharpen country made razors. Bodding did not encounter any other use of the celts. He mentioned that often people would use wedge shaped pieces of hard stones like quartzite to fell small trees. Four plates in the article illustrated the celts (Bodding 1901: 154-157).

Second paper is entitled, "Shoulder headed and other forms of stone implements in the Santal Parganas" (Bodding1904). In it, detailed account of the celts are given from the archaeological point of view. He specifically mentioned that all the collections were from Dumka. He wrote that the collections were similar to the ones that he had reported in his earlier paper excepting for five new forms. He gave brief description of the tools. Some forms were with more curved edges; some with square and parallel sided edges; others were small oblong pieces of stones with notches along one of the long edges, which might have been used as saw to cut wood. Largest of the celts measured 4"x2.5" and smallest one as 2.5"x1.5". There were chips and flakes of flint and chert etc. found from different places. Perforated circular pieces better known as ring stone by the archaeologists were found and Bodding considered them as mace heads. He mentioned four shouldered celts found from Dumka. He had compared his findings with other reported ones in India and Southeast Asia. Bodding had farther made a comparative study of the Santal metal headed axe and adze of the present day with those of the stone made ones but he could not arrive at a conclusion. However, Allchin (1962: 306-330) with his experience of working with Neolithic tools in India could find abrasive marks on the stone celts, which according to him were formed due to hafting of the celts to a shaft, so as to use them as axe, adze or hammers.

Soon after the final installment was sentto Oslo in 1935, Dr. Arne Beng Andersen made an extensive study on these tools for his Ph. D. degree at the University of Oslo. His thesis was not published and hence no information of his study is present in the academia except for a note of his lecture that he gave at the *Congress International des Sciences Anthropologiques et Ethnologiques* in 1938. He mentioned that there were about 3000 prehistoric artifacts, which were mostly Neolithic axes with pointed butts. Other categories included some shoulderedcelts, threePaleolithictools, a few copper artifacts, a clay axe and clay with circular ornamentations. He mentioned three types of manufacturing techniques, namely chipping, grinding and pecking.

The third major study was made by Professor F.R.Allchin of Cambridge University (Allchin1962: 306-330). Allchin studied a total of 2620 stone tools, a part of the collection. Heclassified them into Neolithic and Late Stone Age assemblages. Earlier he had gone through the small collection donated by Bodding to the British Museum. According to him three fourth of this collection were tools and one fourth were waste materials. Allchin had sufficient experience in working with Indian Neolithic implements both surface finds and excavated materials. Allchin found remarkable homogeneity in the implement types and concluded that the collection came from a single well-defined area. He referred to Bodding's letters accompanying the collections. In a letter written in 1902, Bodding referred that those were found within 50 kms. Of Mahulpahari. It is certain that there was no excavation and the collections were surface finds, though some is referred to as coming out of the ground at the time of tilling of the soil. The area of collection as defined by Allchin is in the southern part of Santal Parganas district, lying between the Rivers Bansloi and Ajay, on a long ridge on the southern part of Rajmahal hills. Out of the total collection a small portion consists of pieces of pottery, one copper axe, very similar to those of copper hoard culture of eastern Ganga valley. Allchin also mentioned a letter of Boddingwhere the Reverend mentioned finding of a bronze brooch, iron tools and a brass ring with gold plating. These were found from a grave site near Mahulpahari. Since there is no account of any other particular site for the occurrence of the tools, nothing can be said about the chronology of those materials. It appears that the area may show continuous association of celts from Neolithic up to early historic times.

Allchin classified the collection on the basis of probable function of the tools deposited at the museum in Oslo. It may be mentioned that he has not mentioned whether he had taken up the celts deliberately for analysis because the actual collection at Oslo is almost double the number of tools analysed by Allchin (Ray 2019: 83-104).Allchin's analysis is mainly of celts. On the whole there were celts in the forms of axes, hammers, chisels, shouldered celts and rubbing stones. The axe, adze, hammer and chisel are mostly heads, which were hafted in shafts for working. There are a miscellaneous variety of blades, flakes and chips, which Allchin considered as debitage.

Ranjana Ray, the second author of this paper, visited Cultural History Museumin the year 2018, to study the stone implements. She was there for four days and made an extensive study within such a short time (Ray 2019: 83-104). Ray found that a total of 4,749 stone implements were deposited in the Museum of Culture History, University of Oslo. These were arranged in 16 tubs. The tools were laid in rows, one row on top of the other. Each row was separated by thick spongy papers for protection of the tools against abrasion. All the tools are serially numbered excepting for 53 unnumbered pieces.

Since Allchin had given an exhaustive account of different types of celts with plates and drawings, she had gone through those collections and paid attention to other tools in the collection. It may be mentioned that the stone objects, which Allchin considered as waste material were not so. Those could be elements belonging to earlier cultural phases like Palaeolthic and Mesolithic. In Eastern India, some of the earlier tool types continued to be manufactured and used through Neolithic, Chalcolithic and even during historic times. Occurrence of flake, blade and microliths were found by Professor Jagannath Pal (2009: 263-281) at Jhusi and Hetapatti in Middle Ganga plain. Similar findings were made at Kuanr in Keonjhar, Odhisa (Ray *et al*. 2013: 111-118).

It would be convenient to give a little definition of the different types of celts. A celt is generally considered as a prehistoric stone tool with a beveled cutting edge. According to the nature of the beveling it can farther be divided into axe or adze. A celt is an axe when the beveling of the cutting edge is symmetrical. Usually these are hafted on a shaft with the working edge parallel to the shaft. On the other hand, adze is with an asymmetrical beveling at the working edge and is hafted with the edge at right angle to the shaft. Stone axe, adze and the chisel are heads, which are hafted and used as wood working tools. However, an axe can also be used as a weapon (Ray 2019: 83-104). Allchin (1962: 306-330) classified some celts as hammers. These look the same in general shape as the axe or the adze but has got a thick broad, blunt working edge meant for hammering and not for cutting. These are made on hard rock types by chipping, pecking, grinding and polishing techniques.

Recent study of the Bodding Collection

In order to continue farther with analysis of the collectionthe first author, Soumyajit Daswent to Oslo on a grant from the Museum of Culture History, Oslo, in 2019 and stayed there for 27 days to study those stone artifacts with the help of latest methodologies available at the Museum. This paper is based on the study made on those tools by both the authors.

Methodology followed

Data was collected of the artifactslying at the storage facility of Culture History Museum of University of Oslo. Some representative artifact types were measured along its length, breadth and thickness using digital calipers. All the artifacts were weighed using digital weighing machine. The striking features, if any,of the stone tool were noted. The photographs of all the stone artifacts were taken with high resolution camera from all its sides, namely, dorsal, ventral, laterals, proximal and distal; keeping them on 1mm graph paper one at a time. Measuring scale and Kodak Gray Scale were used while taking the photographs. Most of the artifacts were measured using the photos and the noteworthy features were carefully recorded.The geology laboratory of the Culture History Museum also helped in analysis of the embedded materials in the artefacts, which confirmed that some of the artefacts, especially some celts and the phallic stones were worshipped with oil and vermillion.Stereo zoommicroscope was used for noting the use mark or any other notable features. There were some data available in the database of University of Oslo, whichwere also taken into account. The data was analyzed in Microsoft Excel software.Das had also conducted preliminary field work in Dumka area (Das and Mondal 2019: 97-106) in search of stratigraphic context of Bodding's collections.

Typological analysis

The typological analysis is carefully done by the first author using digital scaling. Soumyajit Das during his stay at Oslo analyzed 3104 stone tools that he found to be present in the storage facility of Culture History Museum, University of Oslo at the time of his visit. The tools are classified on the basis of typology and placed them in categories based on trait complexes (Ghosh 1970: 1-68; Ray 2019: 83-184). Numerical distributions are also given below.

1. Neolithic types: 1962 axes, 256 adzes, 148 chisels, 9 wedges, 202 hammer stones, 15 pestles, 24 whetstones or hones, 6 ring stones and 11 shouldered celts.
2. Flake-Blade types: 28 arrowheads, 10 bolts, 3 choppers (reused), 44 scrapers, 4 Borers, 22 knives, and 1 fluted core.
3. Microlithic types: 3 awls, 12 blades, 6 crystal beads (3 of them tied together with a thread), 5 lunates, 1 micropoint, 2 trapeze, and 3 triangles.
4. Unidentified stone objects: 326
5. Unidentified fossilified object: 1

Below is the general description along with the morpho-metric analysis of the above-mentioned types of tools.The tools are carefully measured and morphological features are noted.

A. **Axes –** Weights range from 2.48g to 2.48kg. Sizes range from 1.6cm to 27.4 in length, 1.4cm to 14.2cm in breadth, 0.4 to 7.7 in thickness. Most of the axes are either triangular (53.06%) or trapezoidal (21.97%). Rest of the shapes include rectangular (8.97%), square (7.34%) and oval (3.36%). 1.88% are irregular in shape. 1544 (78.69%) out of total 1962 pieces of axes are complete and the rest are broken, but the broken pieces could be identified as axes as the cutting or working edge is intact in them. Techniques used for making these axes are varied. The finished axes show different stages of tool making technology. 24.46% of total axes are fully polished. Apart from that, 36.54% of the axes show partly polished surface. Among them, the polished surface is mainly found on dorsal surface, ventral surface and on working edge. 34.1% of the total axes are fully ground. 9 pieces are only flaked and 3 pieces are only pecked. Chipping is found in 11.62% of the total axes. Two axes were made by chipping, pecking, grinding, and polishing. The marks are visible. 79.1% of the axes have straight working edge, and 15.65% have convex working edge. The working edge of 5.15% of axes is broken. Moreover, one axe has pointed working edge, and one has concave working edge. 45% of the axes have V shaped pointed butt end, 22.73% have straight butt end, 10.09% have U shaped butt end, and 7.34% have flat butt end. The butt end of 14.83% of axes is broken. 48.88% of the total axes have straight line of profile, and 39.35% have flattened lateral margin. The rest consists of S shaped and wavy line of profile. 120 pieces are so broken that the line of profile could not be understood. 143 axes have marks pointing to their use in rituals and clear use-wear marks are noted in 423 axes.

B. **Adzes –** Weights range from 8.59g to 658.5g. Size ranges from 2.7cm to 15.1cm in length; 2.3cm to 8.5 in breadth and 0.9cm to 5cm in thickness. Most of the adzes are either trapezoidal (39.45%) or triangular (25.39%) in shape. Others are rectangular (22.26%) andoval (3.9%). 220 (85.94%) out of 256 pieces of adzes are complete and the rest are broken, though they could be identified through their intact working edge and beveling angle.22.26% of the adzes are fully polished, 33.59% are fully ground and two piecesare fully flaked. 38.67% have partly polished surface. 77.73% of the adzes have straight working edge, 16.01% have convex working edge and the working edge of 6.25% of adzes are broken. 28.9% of adzes have V shaped butt end, 37.5% have straight butt end, 16.01% have flat butt end, 8.98% have U shaped butt end, and 8.59% have broken butt ends. 51.17% of adzes have flat lateral sides and 45.32% have straight line of profile. There are 8 adzes with wavy line of profile and one is broken at the lateral margin. 18 adzes have marks on them, which showed their use in ritual and 47 adzes have use-wear marks.

C. **Chisels –** Weights range from 7.72g to 1.27kg. Size ranges from 2.3cm to 22.3cm in length; 1.7cm to 8.3cm in breadth and 0.8cm to 5.2cm in thickness.72.3% of the chisels are rectangular and 22.3% are trapezoidal in shape. Most of the chisels, 121 (81.76%) to be exact, are complete in nature and the rest broken in some parts of the tools.26.35% of chisels are fully polished, 39.86% are fully ground, and one piece is only flaked. One of the chisels is completely worn out and could be identified by its elongated shape. 30.4% have partly polished surface.83.1% of chisels have straight working edge, 11.49% have convex working edge, and 5.4% have broken working edges. The butt end of the chisels is mostly flat (71.62%). Besides, straight (5.47%) and U-shaped butt end (3.12%) are also found. The butt end of 13.51% of chisels is broken. 86.49% of chisels have flat lateral margins, and 10.13% have straight line of profile. There are three chisels having wavy line of profile and two are broken. 22 chisels have been found to have ritual marks on them and 51 chisels have use-wear marks.

D. **Wedges –** Weights range from 70.48g to 2.1kg. Size ranges from 11.15cm to 33.2cm in length; 2.6cm to 7.2cm in breadth and 1.5cm to 5.3cm in thickness. Four shapes of wedges,namel,y triangular, rectangular, trapezoidal and pentagonal are found to exist.Except one piece, all are complete tools. Only one wedge is fully polished. The rest are all fully ground.The narrower end of 6 out of 9 wedges are pointed, 2 are straight and one is broken.The broad end of 5 wedges is flat and two each are U shaped and straight. The lateral sides of four wedges are straight and that of the rest are flat. Two wedges have ritual marks and two wedges have use-wear marks.

E. **Hammer stones –** Weights range from 8.93g to 2.34 kg. Size ranges from 2.5cm to 22.6 cm in length; 2cm to 11.6cm in breadth and 0.8cm to 8.6cm in thickness. These are mostly triangular (50%), rectangular (21.78%), trapezoidal (11.39%), and square (7.42%) in shape. 180 (89.1%) out of 202 hammer stones are complete and the rest are broken.28.22% of the hammer stones are fully polished, 40.1% are fully ground and one piece is fully flaked. 29.7% are partly polished at dorsal surface, ventral surface and working edge. 88.12% of total hammer stones have straight and flattened working edge, 9.40% have convex working edge, one piece has concave working edge and four pieces have broken working edges. 46.03% of the hammer stones have pointed V shaped butt end, 14.85% have U shaped butt end, 17.33% have straight, 14.36% have flat and 7.42% have broken. 62.87% of hammer stones have flat line of profile, and 35.64% of hammer stones have straight line of profile. Three hammer stones each have S shaped, wavy and broken line of profile. Ritual marks and use wear marks have been found on 28 and 57 hammer stones respectively.

F. **Pestles –** Weights range from 21.51g to 4.1kg. Size range from 6.2cm to 30.4cm in length, 1.7cm to 11cm in breadth and 1.4cm to 11.2cm in thickness. 57.14% of them are rectangular in shape, 28.57% are oval and the rest are either trapezoidal or triangular. Except for one pestle, all are complete. 5 pestles are fully polished and the rest fully ground.78.57% of the pestles have broad and flattened working edge.Two pieces have convex working edge and one piece have broken working edge. 46.67% of the pestles have flat butt end and 26.67% have U shaped butt end. In addition, one pointed, one straight and two broken butt ends are present. 9 out of 15 pestles have straight line of profile and the rest have flat. 5 pestles have ritual marks on them and 5 have use-wear marks.

G. **Whetstones** – Weights range from 67.48g to 525.03g. Size range from 5.1cm to 12.1cm in length; 3.3cm to 8.6cm in breadth and 1.5cm to 6.6cm in thickness.37.5% of them are triangular, 20.83% are rectangular, 16.67% are circular and 12.5%are circular. All of the whetstones are complete. Two whetstones are fully polished, 17 whetstones are fully ground and5 whetstones have both polished and ground surfaces on it. 4 whetstones have ritual marks on them. 11 whetstones have use-wear marks on them.

H. **Ringstones** – Weights range from 464.73g to 1.56 kg. Outer diameter of theringstones range from 10.7cm to 18.1cm whereas the inner diameter ranges from 1.8cm to 3cm. 4.6cm to 7.1cm is range for thickness. Out of six ringstones, four are circular, one isrectangularoid, and one is triangularoid. 50% of the ringstones are broken and 50% complete. The entire ringstones are fully ground except one which has around 80% polished surface on both its dorsal and ventral sides. All the ringstones have flat lateral sides.

I. **Shouldered Celts** – Weights range from 34.51g to 273.78g. Size ranges from 4.8cm to 16.8cm in length, 2.8cm to 6.4cm in breadth and 1.1cm to 2.7cm in thickness.Out of 11 shouldered celts, 7 have prominent shoulders and are T- shaped. The rest 4 are rectangular, triangular and trapezoidal each. All of the shouldered celts are complete.Four celts are fully polished, six are fully ground, and one piece is polished with around 30% chipping near its sides and working edge. All of the shouldered celts have straight working edge except for one which is broken around its working edge.All the shouldered celts have flat butt end and flat line of profile. One shouldered celt has ritual marks and three have use-wear marks.

J. **Arrowheads** – Weights range from 0.32g to 160.59g. Size ranges from 1.1cm to 8.3cm in length, 1cm to 6.9cm in breadth, 0.2cm to 4.2cm in thickness. These are mostly triangular (53.57%) in shape. Others are pentagonal (10.71%), oval (7.14%), Leaf shaped (7.14%) etc. 4 arrowheads are found to be irregular in shape. All the arrowheads are complete except for one piece.Only one arrowhead is polished, 8 are ground, 12 are flaked and 3 are partly polished.Except for one piece, all have pointed working edge. 11 arrowheads have flat butt end, 16 have straight butt end and one have U shaped butt end. 19 arrowheads have straight line of profile, 7 have flat line of profile and 2 wavy line of profile. Two arrowheads have use-wear marks on them.

K. **Bolts** – Weights range from 5.38g to 66.5g. Sizes ranges from 1.85cm to 5.1cm in length,

1.7cm to 3.6cm in breadth, 1cm to 3.5cm in thickness. In shape, 40% of the bolts are triangular, 20% are square, 20% are trapezoidal. One piece is rectangular and one is irregular in shape. All of the bolts are complete. All the bolts are flaked. All of them have flat blunted working end. 6 out of 10 bolts have pointed at the butt, 3 have straight edge and one convex butt. Bolts are similar to fluted cores.

L. **Choppers –** Weights range from 58.76g to 250.82g. Size ranges from 5.4cm to 11cm in length; 3.7cm to 6.8cm in breadth, 2.8cm to 3.7cm in thickness. Among three choppers, one is triangular, one is square and one is irregular in shape. All the three choppers are complete. All the choppers are ground with some percentage of flaking, pecking and chipping on them. The choppers are found to be made from different tools maybe after those tools broke or were no longer usable.Two choppers have straight and zigzag working edge whereas one has an irregular cutting edge. 1 chopper has use-wear mark. Choppers are usually considered as type tool of Lower Palaeolithic culture but these continued with some change in manufacturing technique throughout the Stone Age, even up to early historic times.

M. **Scrapers –** Weights range from 1.98g to 254.9g. Size ranges from 2.1cm to 11.6cm in length, 1.5cm to 9.5cm in breadth, 0.6cm to 3.8cm in thickness.Most of the scrapers are irregular (40.90%) in shape. Some have regular shapes like triangular (18.18%), square (13.63%), rectangular (9.09%) and oval (11.36%).61.36% of the scrapers are only flaked. 5 are fully ground, and one is fully pecked. Four pieces have some percentages of polished surfaces in them. All the scrapers have straight working edge, mostly at the sides. 2 scrapers have ritual marks and 1 have use-wear mark.

N. **Borers –** Weights range from 7.76g to 66.41g. Size ranges from 3.3cm to 6cm in length, 3.1cm to 4.2cm in breadth, 0.8cm to 4.7cm in thickness. One is fully ground and one is fully flaked. Two borers are ground with chipping on them, and one of them has around 40% polished surface. All the borers have pointed and extended working end.

O. **Knives –** Weights range from 2.55g to 214.81g. Size ranges from 3.4cm to 11.7cm in length, 1.4cm to 8.4cm in breadth, 0.8cm to 3.9cm in thickness.In shape, 40.90% of the knives are rectangular and 22.72% are triangular. The rest are trapezoidal, oval, square. Only one knife is broken. 72.72% of knives are only flaked. One knife is completely polished, one is fully ground, and one is fully pecked. Two knives are partly polished.All the knives have straight working edge. 77.27% of the knives have flat lateral margin opposite to the working edge. 22.72% have straight margin. Three knives have use-wear marks.

P. **Fluted Core –** Weight is 74.95g, size is 9.3cm in length, 3.6cm in breadth, 3.9cm in thickness. It is irregular in shape. It is cylindrical in shape.

Q. **Awls –** Weights range from 5.67g to 33.72g. Size ranges from 3.3cm to 5.4cm in length, 2cm to 4.4cm in breadth, 0.5cm to 1.9cm in thickness.Three awls are triangular, D shaped and tear drop in shape respectively. Two of them are flaked. One is half ground and half chipped. All the awls have pointed working end and straight butt end.

R. **Blades** – Weights range from 0.49g to 14.04g. Size ranges from 2.1cm to 5.2cm in length, 0.5cm to 2.4cm in breadth, 0.35cm to 1.3cm in thickness. Out of 12 blades, 5 are rectangular, 2 are trapezoidal, 2 leaf shaped, 1 triangular, 1 pentagonal, and 1 D shaped.All the blades have straight working end except one which has a pointed end.

S. **Lunates** – Weights range from 0.45g to 2.3g. Size ranges from 2.5cm to 3.2cm in length, 0.5cm to 1.7cm in breadth, 0.4cm to 0.8cm in thickness. The lunates are roughly semilunar in shape with concave or straight sharp working end and blunted back.

T. **Trapezes** – Weights of the trapezes are 0.45g and 1.25g with maximum length x breadth x thickness of 2x0.8x0.3 cm and 1.9x1.1x0.7cm respectively. The trapezes have straight working edge.

U. **Triangles** – Weights range from 0.88g to 1.73g. Size ranges from 2.15cm to 2.7cm in length, 0.5cm to 1.1cm in breadth, 0.2cm to 0.65cm in thickness. All the three triangles have straight working edge.

V. **Micropoint** – Weight is 0.42g. Its size is 1.3cm in length, 1.1cm in breadth, 0.3cm in thickness. It is triangular in shape. It has pointed working end.

W. **Crystal Beads** – Weights range from 6.22g to 17.97g. Size ranges from 1.9cm to 4.5cm in length, 1.2cm to 2.4cm in breadth, 0.5cm to 1.7cm in thickness. The beads are of different shapes such as diamond shaped, circular, oval and rectangular. Five of the beads are polished and one is ground.

X. **Stone Fragments** – Weights range from 0.68g to 1.21kg. Size ranges from 1.1cm to 18.8cm in length, 1.1cm to 10.3cm in breadth, 0.5cm to 5.8cm in thickness. These fragments are broken pieces of tools. Their shape varies from triangular (35.89%) to rectangular (17.18%) to trapezoidal (7.97%). The rest are D shaped, circular, leaf shaped, pentagonal, square, and U shaped. There are 19.32% of fragments which are irregular in shape.10.12% of the total stone fragments are fully polished, 30.98% are ground, and 9.2% are flaked. 6 fragments are pecked. 39.26% of total stone fragments are partly polished.All the fragments are broken on its working end and hence the type of tool could not be identified. 33 stone fragments show ritual mark and 22 fragments show use-wear marks.

Y. **Fossilized object** – Its weight is 69.91g. Its size is 4.9cm in length, 4.4cm in breadth, and 3.3cm in thickness. It is circular in shape.

Neolithic Cultures of Eastern India

In order to get an idea about the geo-chronological context of Bodding collection, it is essential to understand the Neolithic culture of Eastern India, especially of Santal Parganas. The district is one of the divisions or commissionaires of Jharkhand. All the collection of Bodding came from places around Dumka, the headquater of Santal Parganas.

Good amount of work had been done in eastern India stretching from central highlands to greater Assam (Dani 1960). Large number of Neolithic sites had been discovered in this region. Many of them had been intensively explored and some were systematically excavated. Some of the sites had given radio carbon dates. The first finds of celts in India was reported by H.P. LeMesurier (1861: 81-85). He found them from the temples and sacred places around River Tamsa (or Tonse) in Rewa and Satna districts of Madhya Pradesh. The celts were worshipped as *Mahadev* or Lord Shiva and offered to the temple and placed at some sacred spots by the local people.Subsequently Theobald Jr. (1862: 81-85), V. Ball (1875) and others reported findings of celts from the eastern plateau region. Coggin Brown (1917), in hisfamous catalogue, reported many other unpublished finds, which were donated to the Indian Museum by different individuals.

The famous anthropologist S.C. Roy (1916: 61-77) published a paper on prehistoric stone implements found by him in the Ranchi district. He collected nearly hundred celts and its fragments, a few from the surface and the rest from Munda and Oraon tribes. Similar to the Santals of Bodding's finds the tribals kept them in their house with a belief that they were thunderstones and had curative values. Roy mentioned several contemporary uses of the celts; such as, for treating sicknesses like, headache, difficult urination, rheumatic or other pain in any part of the body, lung disorders, etc. Some considered them as object that prevents lightning, some treated them as object that attracts lightning, some considered them useless and threw them away or gave them to children to play, some reused them as whetstones to sharpen household razors and knives, some worshipped them as Mahadev, and some carried them during journey at night as a protection from ghosts or spirits. Roy hypothesized that the celts collected by Bodding are more highly polished and of varied shapes and hence they belong to a later age than the celts of Ranchi district.However, most of the earlier collections were from secondary sources procured from other people's collections.

Anderson published an article in which he described several Neolithic implements that he found upon exploring the Sanjai river valley (Anderson 1917: 349-362). The older alluvium lying over upper gravel bed and 18′ to 20′ above the river bed was identified as the earliest stratum yielding Neolithic artifacts. This was corroborated by Sen (1950) and other scholars. Dharani Sen (1950) classified the tools from Chakradharpur into seven groups. These were graded from only chipped to fully polished. He also observed eight forms of cutting edge,ten forms of butt endand different forms of sides of the celts. These were surface collections but in the context of stratigraphy.

After this period, several explorations were carried out by different institutions such as, universities, research organizations, State Archaeology departments and Archaeological Survey of

India in different parts of Chotanagpur plateau. A large number of Neolithic sites came to light.Scholars like, D.K. Chakrabarti (1993), R.K. Chattopadhayay (Chattopadhyay *et al.*2013), K.K. Basa (1999) and several others have discovered plenty of Neolithic sites all over Chota Nagpur plateau(Dikshit 2013).

Second authorof this paper, Ranjana Ray had been part of the team that carried out intensive exploration of Sanjai river valley in search for Neolithic sites, under a grant of the Australian National University. She had also taken part in the excavation of Neolithic sites at Barudihand Dugni in Jharkhand (Ghosh *et al.* 1984: 24-28). The 5′5" deposit consisting of Neolithic artifacts at Barudih is divided into two phases, I and II respectively. Phase Iis earlier in date and yielded Neolithic axes, adzes, chisels, and flake-blade tools along with handmade potteries. Phase IIwas later in sequence and yielded Neolithic axes, adzes, chisels, ringstones, both handmade and wheel made potteries, one iron sickle along with some charred rice(Das 1964). The charcoal and charred rice were dated through radiocarbon method, the date came around 1000 B.C.E. (Sen 1969: 17-29). Phase II is considered as Chalco-Neolithic phase (Chakrabarti 1993). Similar phase of Chalco-Neolithic culture was found by Ray (1993) from the site Kuanr in Keonjhar district of Odisha. The site had yielded chipped and ground Neolithic celts, lots of flake and blade tools, microliths, pottery, evidences of wattle and daub structures and brass bangles, rings and other ornaments. The summary of observation from Barudih and other sites in eastern India suggests that Neolithic culture started in the early part of Holocene epoch but the traits of Neolithic such as celts, pottery, and some other stone tools like flakes, blades, microliths, and grinding stones continued throughout the later part of Holocene into historic times (Ray and Mondal 2013:115).Salient features of Neolithic culture of Eastern India was systematically brought out by the exploration and excavations conducted in Middle Ganga Valley by G. R. Sharma, V. D. Misra, J. N. Pal and other scholars from the department of Ancient Indian History, Culture and Archaeology, Universityof Allahabad (Sharma *et al.* 1980; Pal and Gupta 2005: 163-168; Pal 2009: 263-281). Two phases of Neolithic culture; one Neolithic proper and the other Chalco-Neolithic, were identified (Dikshit 2013: vii-xii) in Eastern India. As a result of the extensive archaeological research in Middle Ganga valley and in foothills of the Vindhyan range and at other sites in Eastern India, a number of absolute dates came out.

Chronology of Neolithic-Chalcolithic cultures in Eastern India

Absolute datesfor Neolithic and Chalcolithic culture was found by means of C14 and/or thermo-luminescent methods.Similar to the findings at Barudih andKuanr (Ray 2019: 83-184), Professor J. N. Pal and his colleagues divided the Neolithic culture into two phases, early and late on the basis of absolute dates.The dates from some of the sites in Eastern India are given below (Misra, Pal and Gupta 2013: 233).

The dates are divided region wise, namely, those found from (a) Middle Ganga Plain and those from (b) Vindhyanhills and Plateau regions. Both the regions are important for throwing light on the probable dates of Bodding collection (Ray 2019: 83-104).

(a) Dates from Middle Ganga Plains are as follows:

Jhusi, (8140 ± 220 B.P., 6760 ± 190 B.P. and 7110 ± 170 B.P.; Lahuradeva (5320 ± 90 B.P. and 6290 ± 160 B.P.);

Chirand (1760 ± 150 B.C. and 1680 ± 135 B.C.E).

(b) Dates from Vindhyan and Plateau region are as follows:

Tokwa (ca. 6591 B.C., 5976 B.C. and 4797 B.C.E),

Koldihwa (4530 ± 185 B.C.E, 5440 ± 240 B.C.E and 6570 ± 210 B.C.E,

Mahagara (2265 B.C.E and 1616 B.C.E, 1400 ± 150B.C.E, 1330 ± 120 B.C.E, 1440 ± 100 B.C.E and 1480 ± 110 B.C.E),

Kunjhun (1565-1265 B.C. and 3530-3335 B.C.),;

Barudih from Sanjay valley average of average of 810 _+ 55 B.C.E

GolbaiSasan and Sankarjang suggest duration of 2200 to 700 B.C.E

All of the above mentioned dates place back Neolithic culture to more than c. 7000 B.C.E or to c. 9000 B. P. Evidences show that rice was the cereal cultivated in the area. Both wild (*Oryza rufiprogan*) and domesticated (*Oryza sativa*) varieties of rice are found from excavation of the sites. The Neolithic people were producing both rainy crops and winter crops. Rice was the staple food. Fishing and hunting still continued. Cereals were supplemented by fish and games. Bovids and goat were domesticated by Neolithic people of eastern India (Misra, Pal and Gupta 2013: 230-231).

Conclusion

Bodding's collections are from Santal Pargana and procured from the people belonging to Santal Tribe. Present authors' observation reveals that some of tools such as arrowheads especially bolt type, choppers, knives, scrapers, though belonged to prehistoric period,probably were reused by the Santals after they had collected them. They might also have re-shaped the tools. Since Reverend Bodding spent 44 years with the Santals and his major work was on the tribe, he tried to find the link between the archaeological finds and the Santal ancestry. He was not successful, though he tried to find an answer through social, cultural and linguistic points of view. Present authors have noted that bolt type arrows, called as *tutti* by the Santals are with blunt flat head, made of wood and stone are still used by them. This is commonly used by the tribals in the plateau area to stun the prey without bloodshed.Several of the celts have shown smearing of oil and vermillion or scratch mark on them. Santals have used them either as ritual object or rubbed to get medicine (Bodding 1901). There are some pieces that represent phallic symbols worshipped by contemporary people. There are a number of small celts varying in length from 4cm to 2.5cm.Bodding considered them as reduced due to subsequent rubbing for medicinal purposes and Allchin considered them as toys. On closer examination, they appeared to the present authors to be fine wood working tools. Santals are proficient at wood working and might as well have used them for the same purpose ((Ray 2019: 83-104). Though the Santals of Bodding's time had no memory of the use of the celts, but axe and adze play a vital role in the life the Santals, especially those who live away from the Metropolitan city. Their life cycle rituals, folklores, folk songs revolve around forest. Axe and adze are very important tools for them. Allchin (1962: 306-330) identified evidence of hafting. Soumyjit Das with the help digital appliances identified definite marks of hafting and of use. No doubt these implements were useful to their makers, both in woodwork and agriculture. The stone axes and adzes continued for a long time because firstly, metal was costly and it needed expertise of the smith. Secondly, stones were easily available to the mass, therefore cheap. Linguistics often provide clue to prehistoric puzzles. Hansda, (1980) has given some example in his thesis, entitled, "Differential transformation of culture and language among the Santals" (Unpublished ph. D. Thesis of Calcutta University). Dr. BoroBaski of Bishnubhati, Birbhum, West Bengal, informed us that use of axes and adzes are very common among the Santals. These are with iron heads but resemble the celts excepting for the sockets.For the Santals *Tangoych*is a common term for any kind of axe or adze. The *tangoych* used for scraping wood (adze) is known as *Bosle*or *Tirchhutangoych.* The spade and hoe used for digging the soil is known *Tamni.* The *Tangoych* used for sacrifice of animals is *kappi.* There exists morphological and functional difference between a *Tangoych*(Axe) and *TangoychKappi* (the sacrificial axe). The latter has a wide working edge. This is termed by the archaeologists as splayed axe. This type is found in Bodding's collection of axes. A Santal is always portrayed carrying axe, and bow and arrow. The arrow heads could have been of a pointed or a blunt one. Representations of both types of arrow heads are found in Bodding collection. Bodding wanted to find the link of the prehistoric artifacts to the Santals. The Bodding' s collection no doubt at one time belonged to the ancestors of the people living continuously in the Eastern plateau area.

Acknowledgement

The authors would like to offer their gratitude to Tone Bleie, Professor, Dept. of Sociology, University of Tromsø - the Arctic University; Øivind Fuglerud, Professor of Social Anthropology, Museum of Cultural History, University of Oslo; Ralfs Znotins and FaridehFaramarzi, Senior Executive Officers, Section for Ethnography, Culture History Museum, Oslo, Norway. Special thanks to Dr. Gro Birgit Ween, Head of the Department of Ethnography. University of Oslo for arranging for the grant for Soumyajit Das for the study of Bodding collection.

References

Allchin, F.R., 1962, The Neolithic Stone Industry of the Santal Parganas, *Bulletin of the School of Oriental and African Studies, 25(2).*

Anderson, C.W., 1917, Note on Prehistoric Stone Implements found in the Singbhum District, *Journal of Bihar and Orissa Research Society 3.*

Ball, V., 1867, List of localities in India where ancient stone implements have been discovered, *Proceedings of the Asiatic Society of Bengal.*

Basa, K.K., 1999, Neolithic and Post-Neolithic Cultures of Orissa; An Overview, S. Pradhan (eds.) *Reconstructing Indian History and Culture No.6 Orissa: History, Culture and Archaeology,* New Delhi: D.K. Printworld (P) Ltd.

Bodding, P. O., 1901, Ancient Stone Implements in the Santal Parganas, *Journal of the Asiatic Society of Bengal 56(2).*

Bodding, P. O., 1904, Shoulder-headed and other forms of stone implementsin the Santal Parganas, *Journal of the Asiatic Society of Bengal, LXXIII .*

Brown, C.J., 2013, *Catalogue Raisonné of the Prehistoric Antiquities in the Indian Museum at Calcutta,* London: Forgotten Books (Original work published 1917).

Chakrabarti, Dilip K., 1993, *Archaeology of Eastern India: Chhotanagpur Plateau and West Bengal,* New Delhi: MunshiramManoharlal Pvt. Ltd.

Chattopadhyay, R. K., Paramita Bose, Dipshikha Achary and Kukmkum Bandyopadhyay, 20013, Ground/polished stone tool industries of Eastern India: A reappraisal of sites, contents and contexts, *Neolithid-Chalcolithic cultures of Eastern India,* K. N. Dikshit (ed.), New Delhi: Indian Archaeological Society .

Dani, A.H, 1960, *Prehistory and Protohistory of Eastern India,* Calcutta: Firma Klm Private Ltd.

Das, Ranjana, 1964, *Study on celt typology in the Sanjai Valley, Singhbhum district,* Calcutta University, unpublished M. Sc. Thesis .

Das, Soumyajit and Debasis Kumar Mondal, 2019, A study of findings of prehistoric remains from Dighi area of Dumka in Jharkhand, *Journal of Kolkata Society for Asian Studies, 5 (1).*

Dikshit, K.N.(ed), 2013, *Neolithic-Chalcolithic Cultures of Eastern India,* New Delhi: Indian Archaeological Society.

Ghosh, A. K., 1970, The Palaeolithic Cultures in Singhbhum, *Transactions of the American Philosophical Society, N. S. 60.*

Ghosh, A. K., Ranjana Ray, and P.G. Chatterjee, 1984, Barudih: A Neolithic Site in Bihar, *Bulletin of the Indo-Pacific Prehistory Association 5 .*

Gupta, M. C., J. N. Pal and V.D.Misra, 2008, Beginnings of Agriculture in the Middle Ganga Plan with Special Reference to Recent Excavations at Jhusi, L. Gopal &V.C.Srivastava (eds.), *History of Agriculture in India upto C.*

1200A.D., New Delhi:Concept Publishing Company.

Le Mesurier, H. P., 1861, Letter from H.P. Le Mesurier, Chief Engineer, Jubbulpore Line, E.I.R. *Proceedings of the Asiatic Society.*

Misra, V. D., J. N. Pal and M. C. Gupta, 20013, The Neolithic-Chalcolithic Cultures of the MiddleGanga Plain: Some reflections, *Neolithic-Chalcolithic Cultures of Eastern India,* K. N. Dikshit (ed.), New Delhi: Indian Archaeological Society.

Pal, J. N., 2009, The Early Farming Culture of the Middle Ganga Plain With Special Reference to Jhusi and Hetapatti, *Prâgdhârâ, Journal of the U.P. State Archaeology Department, Lucknow 18.*

Pal, J. N. and M. C. Gupta, 2005, Excavations at Hetapatti: Some Preliminary Observations, *Journal of Interdisciplinary Studies in History and Archaeology 2(1).*

Ray, Ranjana and Debasis Kumar Mondal, 2013, Chalco-neolithic culture of eastern India with a focus on the findings from the site Kuanr, Keonjhar, Orissa, *Neolithic-Chalcolithic Cultures of Eastern India*, K. N. Dikshit (eds.), New Delhi: Indian Archaeological Society.

Ray, Ranjana, 2019, The Stone Implements collected by Rev. P. O. Bodding and deposited at the Ethnology Museum in Oslo between 1901 and 1934, *Journal of the Asiatic Society of Bengal 61(1).*

Roy, S.C., 1916, Note on Some Prehistoric Stone Implements found in the Ranchi District, *Journal of Bihar and Orissa Research Society 2.*

Sarma, G. R., V. D. Misra D. Modal, B. B. Misra and J. N. Pal, 1980, Beginnings *of Agriculture : from hunting and food gathering to domestication of plants and animals : Epi-Palaeolithic to Neolithic : Excavations at Chopani-Mando, Mahadaha, and Mahagara*, Allahabad: AbhinashPrakashan.

Sen. D., 1969, Profile of a Pre Literate Culture in The Sanjai Valley, *Journal of Indian Anthropological Society 4.*

Theobald, W., 1862, Celts found in Bundelkhand, *Proceedings of the Asiatic Society of Bengal*

8

One Cave, Multiple Traces : The Rock Art of the Archaeological Site of Algar da Água, Central Portugal

Alexandra Figueiredo, Fernando Coimbra and Cláudio Monteiro

Introduction: the archaeological site of Algar da Água

Algar da Água is a small cave with about 130 square meters, 20m long and 10m large. It is located in the summit of the mountain of Alvaiázere, in the municipality with the same name, district of Leiria, in the littoral centre of Portugal (Fig.1). It is the largest cave of this region and has several examples of rock art figures produced by different techniques representing also different typologies.

Archaeological research was carried out in this cave from 2017 to 2019, having been excavated part of the main room during the several fieldworks (Figueiredo 2017: 127-140; 2018: 5-16; 2019: 99-111; Figueiredo et al. 2019; 2020). North gallery was not surveyed, due to the presence of a bat colony, protected by environmental laws.

The excavations revealed, after recent layers, several sequential horizons: Medieval, Roman, Iron Age, Late Bronze Age, Early Neolithic and Mesolithic (Figueiredo 2019: 99-111). As a matter of fact, the analyses of the archaeological remains and absolute dating allowed concluding the existence of funerary depositions since Late Mesolithic/Early Neolithic till the Bronze Age (Fig.2). The occupation of the cave continued during Iron Age, a period to where the majority of the rock art seems to belong (Figueiredo *et al.* 2020: 27-45), except for some older cases, as we are going to discuss later.

Near Algar da Água there are more than ten other small caves (Figueiredo *et al.* 2020: 27-45) (but, so far, without the presence of rock art, except for the cave called Buracas da Serra, where a single motif of the type "asterisk" was found, having possibly an astronomical significance and dating possibly from the Iron Age) (Figueiredo *et al.* 2017: 127-140).

Still in the mountain, in *et al* the north area, there is a fortified Bronze Age and Iron Age settlement (Félix, 1999), being Algar da Água located in the interior of the area surrounded by its walls (Fig.1).

The archaeological contexts excavated at Algar da Água (Figueiredo 2017: 41-58; 2018: 5-16 ;

2019: 99-111 ; Figueiredo. 2019; 2020) revealed the presence of disperse and short structured fireplaces, with few materials associated (fauna included) that could be associated to other activities inside the cave, leading our interpretation almost exclusively to a function of lighting the place, which may be related with the need of illumination for elaborating the engravings, since there are no traces of settlement activity in this place during Protohistory.

The Rock Art

The rock art that exists in the walls of Algar da Água can be dated since Late Prehistory till recent times. The recording of the engravings identified 44 panels with different techniques and chronologies: eight panels by filiform incision, one by red painting, three by scraping, five combining incision and abrasion, fourteen combining incisions with a medium and thin groove and, finally, thirteen inscriptions and recent signatures, most of them made with charcoal (Figueiredo *et al.* 2019: 99-111). The archaeological excavations carried out in the cave did not reveal any other figures on the walls after the removal of the more recent soil (Figueiredo 2019: 99-111).

In this text we focus only in the more suggestive figures from Prehistory and Protohistory, which represent less than 15 examples, being the panels presented as a kind of catalogue. The other cases are essentially constituted by dates, names and signatures since the 18th century till the 20th century, except for a possible pre Roman inscription.

Methodologically, the engravings were traced over polyvinyl plastic and recorded by digital photography, by photogrammetry and by spectrophotogrammetry, being the survey carried out during the fieldworks of 2017 and 2018. Posterior laboratory work managed to build tridimensional models of the engraved surfaces, using photogrammetry, in a way of working those models with artificial light and elaborating the virtual tracing of the figures. Thus, an experimental methodology combining three softwares ("Agi Soft Photoscan", "Blender" and "Gimp2") was developed. It consisted in creating a tridimensional model of each panel in order to be later submitted to several kinds and angles of lighting trough Blender software.

Depending on the angle and light intensity it is possible to virtually replicate the results of a section of technical photography, which allows enhancing the engravings. After that treatment, the images were converted into JPEG and several filters of imaging contrast were used, trough Gimp2, in order to increase the figures' grooves and removing the maximum possible of "noise imaging".

It was intended to compare the precision of tracing over polyvinyl plastic and its capacity of getting acute information with the results of digital photography, being observed a fair compatibility of both methods. This double analysis allowed getting a better perception of the engravings, mainly in the case of superimpositions.

Nevertheless, the quality of the digital photos depends on the equipment and on the accuracy of the photographic field registration, in order of reproducing models of high resolution that will contribute for better results. However, since the engravings are located inside a cave, it was necessary to constantly adapt their lighting during the imaging capture, in order to obtain good digital photos, what sometimes is a difficult process.

The use of spectrophotogrammetry was made in a preliminary and experimental way but it revealed a promising potential for future research of rock art in caves.

Panel 1

It shows the presence of an anthropomorphic figure, with a conic head, (possibly a helmet) and arms in an "orant" attitude. In the right side there are some lines that may represent weapons. A central line probably indicates the male sex (Fig.3). This figure was made by incision followed by abrasion. Another anthropomorphic "orant" of a similar chronology can be seen at Rock 1 of Fratel, in the Portuguese Tagus Valley, having a sword on the belt (Gomes, 2001; Coimbra, 2013a: Fig.9), but without any helmet. However, other human figures with the depiction of helmets appear in the rock art of central Portugal, as it happens on Rock 1 of Sesmarias, in the municipality of Oleiros (Coimbra 2013a: 163). Possible chronology: Protohistory. Fig. 3 : A poosible conic helmet

Panel 2

In this cave there is only one painted panel, consisting in four red figures (Fig.4), being the example on the left similar to schematic headless anthropomorphic figures from two Late prehistoric painted rockshelters from Alentejo, in Southern Portugal: the rockshelter of Vale de Junco/Lapa dos Gaivões (Breuil 1917: 1-11) and the rockshelter Pinho Monteiro (Martins 2014: Fig.24), both sites in the municipality of Arronches.

This type of anthropomorphic figures appears also in Central Portugal, with several examples in the area of Fratel, in the Tagus Valley (Gomes 2010: 1643), and with six examples in the rock of Foz do Ribeiro da Enchacana I, municipality of Idanha a Nova (Henriques et al, 2013: Fig.8), but all these cases are made by pecking.

Schematic headless anthropomorphic figures can be seen also in painted rockshelters from Spanish Extremadura, dating from Late Prehistory (Domínguez García et al. 2013: 279-286).

The example from Algar da Água is the more Western case of this type of figures in the Iberian Peninsula. Possible chronology: Late Prehistory.

Panel 5

It has multiple lines made by incision, some with medium grooves and others with thin (filiform) grooves, consisting generally in abstract figures (Fig.5). However, it is possible to identify some motifs such as a circle, parallel and convergent lines and some triangles, which may eventually represent arrow heads as it happens with some figures from the rock art sites of Molelinhos (Cunha 1991: 13) and Pedra Letreira de Góis (Coimbra 2016: 1-12), among others from Central Portugal, such as

Rocks 1, 2 and 3 from Figueiredo (Coimbra & Garcês 2016: 55-65). Possible chronology: Protohistory.

Panel 9

The engravings of this panel were made by incision with some cases of sequent abrasion. The thematic is composed by some parallel and some curved lines, being some of them eventual representations of zoomorphic figures, being the interpretation difficult since the engravings and rather eroded (Fig.6). Possible chronology: Protohistory.

Panel 13

This panel is one of the examples with several superimpositions of figures, since old engravings till recent signatures, which overlap the earlier motifs, constituted by vertical filiform parallel and convergent lines. It was registered by spectrophotogrammetry trough a wave length from 700 to 1000 nanometers, which allowed a better understanding of the overlapping. Possible chronology: Protohistory (filiform engravings) and Contemporary (signatures).

Panel 19

It consists in seven parallel and convergent lines (Fig.7), a motif that is among the more represented figures in the Post-Palaeolithic incised rock art from Southern Europe (Coimbra 2013b: 179-185). This particular case was produced by incision followed by abrasion. Possible chronology: Late Prehistory (?) Protohistory.

Panel 20

It shows several parallel and convergent lines and many indeterminate figures. On the top right of this panel there are some motifs that seem to be organized and are very similar with others from Molelinhos and also from Rock 1 of Figueiredo (Coimbra 2013a: 163), which can constitute Pre-Roman inscriptions. Possible chronology: Protohistory.

Panel 21

The engravings of this panel were made by pecking, consisting in a group of three "chevron" (inverted V) (Fig.8), which is a kind of motif that appears often in Calcolithic pottery of the Iberian Peninsula. Interestingly, one example of such pottery was found a few kilometers south of Algar da Água, in the archaeological site of Castelo da Loureira (Figueiredo et al. 2014b). Possible chronology: Late Prehistory.

Panel 22

The engravings from this panel were made by scraping. They consist in a small circle with a kind of "crescent" in its interior, both surrounded by a larger half circle. Similar figures (however without the crescent), can be seen in the so called Rock of the Signs (Barcelos, Portugal), with a chronology from the end of the III millennium BC/ beginning of the II millennium BC (Coimbra 2004: 37-70). Possible chronology: Late Prehistory.

Panel 29

The engravings of this panel were made by filiform incision, being very thin and difficult to observe. Besides some "angles" and indeterminate lines, the more interesting motif is an "asterisk" (Fig. 10), a figure that appears in other rock art sites from central Portugal (Coimbra & Garcês 2015: 46-77) and that is widespread in Southern Europe (Coimbra 2013a: 163; 2016: 55-65), having sometimes an astronomical significance. Interestingly, this kind of motif appears in Buracas da Serra (Figueiredo et al. 2017: 41-58), the other cave with rock art in the region of Alvaiázere.

Final Statements

So far, *Algar da Água* is the only cave in Portugal with incised Post-Palaeolithic Rock Art. The archaeological contexts excavated during the fieldworks of 2017 to 2019 are an important contribute for better understanding the chronology of this kind of art. Furthermore, the red painted schematic anthropomorphic figure from this cave constitutes the more western example of this type of motif in the Iberian Peninsula.

The proposed chronologies in this text were established through analogy with other rock art sites from Central Portugal, which have more developed studies. As a matter of fact, this research about the rock art from Algar da Água must be considered as preliminary, still existing several considerations that need further development, mainly with the recording of the engravings that sometimes are eroded or have superimpositions by more recent carvings.

However it is possible to recognize that the countless filiform engravings identified inside this cave have some similarities with open air rock art sites with the same kind of art, such as Rocks 1, 2 and 3 from Figueiredo (Coimbra & Garcês 2016: 55-65), Molelinhos (Cunha 1991: 13) and Pedra Letreira de Góis (Coimbra 2016: 55-65), all located in central Portugal as it happens with Algar da Água.

In the same way, the "asterisk" from panel 29 appears, as mentioned before, inside another small cave from the region of Alvaiázere, called Buracas da Serra (Figueiredo et al. 2017: 41-58), which is located less than 1km from Algar da Água.

Considering the number of engravings from this cave it is possible that other examples may exist in the interior of other small cavities from this region, being necessary a closer attention to this subject during future survey. Indeed, the proximity of Algar da Água with the Bronze Age/Iron Age settlement is a landmark that we must stress, being necessary, when possible, to make this connection, for a broader and deeper understanding of the archaeological remains from Alvaiázere.

Furthermore, analyzing the landscape, this cave and another one also located inside the protohistoric wall, would be the best spots for obtaining water. This situation is still visible in the name of the site (Algar da Água means cave of the water) and in the memory of nearby population, which say that, some time ago, it was possible to hear the sound of underground water, maybe in a gallery covered by time or without direct connection with the cave. Water resource would guarantee a certain sustainability of the site that could be, by this same reason, a place of election for ritual devotion and for the several engravings that usually are found on open air outcrops near rivers.

References

Breuil, H. ,1917, La Roche peinte de Valdejunco à la Esperança, près Arronches (Portalegre), *Terra Portuguesa 13,* Lisboa.

Coimbra, F.A., 2004, As gravuras rupestres do concelho de Barcelos (Portugal), Subsídios para o seu estudo, *Anuário Brigantino 27,* Arquivo e Biblioteca Municipais de Betanzos.

Coimbra, F.A., 2013ª, Ruptejo : Arqueologia Rupestre da Bacia do Tejo, Arte Rupestre da Idade do Bronze e da Idade do Ferro na Bacia Hidrográfica do Médio / Alto Tejo Português, Síntese descritiva, Tomar, Ceiphar.

Coimbra, F.A. , 2013b, Common themes and regional identities in European Late Prehistoric filiform rock art, *Art as a Source of History,* XXV Valcamonica Symposium, Centro Camuno di Studi Preistorici, Capo di.

Coimbra, F.A. ,2016, Late Prehistoric incised rock art in southern Europe: a contribution for its typology, COIMBRA, F.A.; SANSONI, U. (eds), *Post-Palaeolithic filiform rock art in Western Europe,* Oxford: Archaeopress.

Coimbra, F. A., S. GARCÊS, 2015, Filiform and "polissoir" rock art between the Tagus and Mondego rivers (Portu-gal): inventory, typology, parallels and chronology, Mailland, F.; Coimbra, F.A, Prestipino, C., (eds) Lits, *Quaderni del Mediterraneo 2,* Milesimo: Istituto Internazionale di Studi Liguri.

Coimbra, F. A., S. Garces, 2016, The rock art from Figueiredo (Sertã, Portugal): typology, parallels and chronology, Coimbra, F.A.; Sansoni, U. (eds), *Post-Palaeolithic filiform rock art in Western Europe,* Oxford: Archaeopress.

Cunha, A. M. L., 1991, *Estação de Arte Rupestre de Molelinhos,* Notícia Preliminar, Tondela: Câmara Municipal de Tondela.

Dominguez garcia, I. M., H. Collado Giraldo, J.J. Garcia Arranz, 2013, Un siglo de investigación para la pintura rupestre esquemática de la provincia de Badajoz, *Evolución de la metodología y nuevas aportaciones,* Martinez Garcia, J., Hernandez Perez, M. S. (eds.), Ayuntamiento de Vélez-Blanco: Arte rupestre esquemático en la Península Ibérica.

Felix, P., 1999, Serra de Alvaiázere: Um povoado fortificado do Bronze final no centro de Portugal, Almada: *Al-madan, 2ª Série 8.*

Figueiredo, A., 2017, Cenários, dinâmicas e rituais na Pré-história recente na região do Nabão, Leiria: *Cadernos de Estudos Leirienses, Vol. 13.*

Figueiredo, A. , 2018, Comportamentos simbólicos e deposições funerárias na Pré-história recente, na região de Alvaiázere, *Actas do Colóquio: Práticas Funerárias e Atitudes perante a Morte na Região Centro da Pré-História ao Presente: Arqueologia, História, Arte e Antropologia*. Maças de Dona Maria, Leiria: Al-Baiaz – Associação de Defesa do Património.

Figueiredo, A. ,2019, O sítio arqueológico Algar da Água (Alvaiázere), Resultados de 2017 a 2019, Monografia Arqueológica dos trabalhos de intervenção realizados no sítio Algar da Água, Alvaiázere, IPT, *LABACPS*, Tomar: Caaportugal e CM Alvaiázere.

Figueiredo, A., F.A. Coimbra, C. Monteiro, N. Ribeiro, 2017, Preliminary analysis of the rock art from Buracas da Serra, Alvaiázere (Portugal), *Cuadernos de Arte Prehistórico 4*.

Figueiredo, A., F. Coimbra, C. Monteiro, A. Tognoli, A. Peixe, D. Santos, 2020, Arte Rupestre do sítio Algar da Água, Alvaiázere: registo preliminar dos levantamentos realizados, *Estéticas de Poder. Expressões plásticas na II Idade do Ferro do Noroeste Peninsular,* Atas do *II Ciclo de Conferências do Monte Padrão,* 2019, Santo Tirso.

Figueiredo, A. C. Monteiro, A.Tognoli, A. Peixe, 2020, *Algar da Água (Alvaiázere): Retrato preliminar da ocupação da Pré-história à Alta Idade Média, Anais Leirienses – Estudos e Documentos*, Atas do Congresso de História e Património da Alta Estremadura e Terras de Sicó, dias 21 e 22 de setembro de 2019, Leiria: org. Al-Baiäz, Associação de Defesa do Património.

Figueiredo, A., C. Monteiro, A. Tognoli, A. Salgado, 2020, *A mina romana da gruta do Bacelinho, Alvaiázere,* Anais Leirienses – Estudos e Documentos, in Atas do Congresso de História e Património da Alta Estremadura e Terras de Sicó, dias 21 e 22 de setembro de 2019, Leiria: org. Al-Baiäz, Associação de Defesa do Património.

Gomes, M. V., 2001, *Arte rupestre do Vale do Tejo (Portugal),* Antropomorfos (estilos, comportamentos, cronologia e interpretações), Semiótica del Arte Rupestre, Academia de Cultura Valenciana/ Diputación Provincial de Valencia.

GOMES, M. V., 2010, *Arte rupestre do Vale do Tejo, Um ciclo artístico-cultural pré e proto-histórico*, Ph.D. dissertation, Faculdade de Ciências Sociais e Humanas, Lisboa : Universidade Nova de.

Henriques, F., J.C. Caninas, M. Chambino, F, R. Henriques, T. Antonio, C. Santos, A. Canha, 2013, Grafismos rupestres em afluentes do rio Tejo no distrito de Castelo Branco, *Açafa, Online, 6*. Associação de Estudos do Alto Tejo, V. V. de Ródão.

Martins, A., 2014, 20 anos de arte rupestre no sudoeste de Portugal: Um percurso com alguma água à mistura, VIII Encontro de Arqueologia do Sudoeste Peninsular, Câmara Municipal de Serpa.

9

Interpreting Rock Art : Understanding Triangles in Odishan Rock Art

Sadasiba Pradhan

Introduction

Rock art is a purposeful modification of rock surface to produce preconceived forms and images. The study of the subject is fascinating as well as challenging: fascinating because it provides an unexpectedly rich, realistic and colourful insight in to cultures of which otherwise we have only skeletal remains or a few bone or stone tools and implements, as everything else has perished since long; and challenging because it is not easy to define them whether they are "art" from the view point of "art for art's sake" or are "imageries" of functional significance from archaeological point of view. Like all other art rock art cannot be viewed and understood in isolation, but has to be intimately linked to the other traits of the culture that was responsible for its creation. However, unlike our contemporary art where art usually serves for aesthetics to adorn and decorate, rock art in ancient times was not simply for its own sake. Rather it was a product of the pervasive cultural fabric of the prehistoric society. Considering rock art as merely art for art sake would be to ignore the cultural insights inherent in such art.

Odisha is one area in India that has carved out a very distinct position in the rock art map of India for its characteristic regional traits not encountered elsewhere in the Sub-continent. One of the regional characteristics is the large assemblage of non-thematic and non-figurative abstract symbols juxtaposed with a few animal forms. These symbols are both geometric and non-geometric and are so bewildering that no definite name or meaning can be given to these forms. They include a host of parallel vertical or horizontal lines or wavy lines within or without a geometric format; criss-cross, zigzags, grids, curvy liners, bisected inverted triangles or inverted triangles with a shallow depression (cupule) at the center resembling vulva; honeycombs, rhomboids, harpoons, denticulate, diamond chains, spirals, concentric circles, series of dots, cupules, palm, foot, paws and so forth. Ninety percent of rock pictures documented in one hundred six rock shelters are non-thematic symbols and motifs.

It appears as if there is an overwhelming richness in the invention of symbols and men's desire for creating such symbols in prehistoric time was inexhaustible. The symbols are so complex and enigmatic in their given context that they keep puzzling the mind of the serious beholder and researcher with an array of questions such as who made it? When was it made? Why was it made? What does it mean? and so forth.

Symbolism is the central theme in all rock art from the upper-Paleolithic caverns of Franco-Cantabrian region to the early historic rock art in India, Africa or America. It existed throughout the long epoch of primeval art and reigned supreme towards the close of the pre-historic period. It appears symbols appeared earlier than other forms of figurative art. They are found in all portable and parietal art of Paleolithic Europe.

There is no standard or universally accepted method for decoding rock art symbols. Nor they are the words, syllables that can be read or even functional sounds that one can hear. Nor are they doodling – without any significance for its creators. The fact that the same designs and compositions and styles occur repeatedly on the rock surface like the prehistoric implements in an archaeological site and sometimes such designs spread over larger regions, no wonder intercontinental, clearly shows that the makers of rock art world over had something specific in mind to communicate.

According to Theodule Ribot (1915: 385 - 87) the golden age of the symbol was in the pre-historic times. Since then, the hostile pressure of rational thought, which reinforced by experience, has overwhelmed it and gained ground steadily. The *raison deter* of the symbol lies in the human urge to express that, which is inherently inexpressible. Leroi Gourhan's statistical research conducted in more than sixty painted caverns in Europe observes that both abstract symbols and naturalistic forms are related to ritual performances for fertility and procreation. S. Giedion making an extensive survey of pre-historic symbolism concluded that fertility and procreation are the chief motifs of primeval symbolism. Man's struggle for survival was never again expressed in such sublimated forms (Giedion 1962: 254). Garrick Mallery, one of the pioneers of rock art research in America argued that rock art is a form of sign language meant to be read and understood by others who knew the meaning of symbols. J.H. Steward argued that the meaning and purpose of the American Indian rock art could be ascertained through careful study of art symbolism of the present Indian groups and a comparison of these with petroglyphic elements. Emmunal Anati, a foremost scholar in rock art research says that human imagination is quite limited. With few exceptions, the same five subjects recurring constantly all over the world: human figures, animal figures, weapons and tools, topographic signs, ideograms and symbols. He further says that a unified system of science, what he calls pictograms and psychograms, appeared with surprising simultaneity in the earliest pre-historic art in Africa, Europe, Asia, Australia and North and South America.

Heizer (1962) making a statistical analysis of rock art of Nevada and eastern California concluded that ninety percent of the petroglyphs may have meaning in association with the taking of game. He held that as the first humans fanned out across the world, they bore with them a primal artistic idiom and only later the regional singularity did appear. He further believes that certain recurrent symbols: the bisected triangle, pair of short parallel lines, sets of wavy lines are indeed found all over the world and they can be interpreted by applying a measure of empathy and taking into account basic human needs and perceptions in an given environment. Frank Buck remarks that rock art is not a form of writing in the sense of expressing the spoken language, but rather a visible manifestation of the desire for early man to communicate some message in a tangible and permanent manner. No item in the archaeologist's history book is quite so enigmatic as the designs, frozen in perpetuity and constantly eluding decipherment.

A careful study reveals that symbols originate from abstraction of natural forms. Abstraction is, basically, separation and isolation of characteristics element through signs from its totality and the part is so abstracted that it in turn gives a sense to the whole from which it is derived. It transforms the subject into an object and changes a natural appearance into an artistic expression. It is the distillation of essential elements from an intangible multiplicity of forms. These symbols are meaningful and forceful expressions to the initiated and are meaningless and doodling to the unenlightened. To some symbols and symbolism is utterly antiquated to which no attention to be paid in these days of High-tech. Other believes that symbolism is the key to understanding the ancient intellectual world. It is something that communicates anything beyond its own superficial exterior. Symbols do not stand for single constant meaning as heart does not stand for love on every culture. They are whole stories and real-life experiences placed in the familiar world of time and space.

In this context the vast reservoir of rock art predominate with various symbols and motifs, both geometric and non-geometric needs to be looked at seriously to understand the cognitive developments with the prehistoric man. Identical symbols do appear all over in a given time whether in Australia or America or Africa or India. Animal and human forms may appear identical in their execution and depiction because of their standardized physiognomy, which is divine, or the law of the creation, but why and how such uniformity also exists in the composition of certain symbols, which is exclusive to human creativity. Is it because the thought process of the mankind in a given time was alike everywhere wherever they roamed? Or since they shared a common level of subsistence economy of hunting-gathering, environment and insecurity of life, their cognitive development was identical irrespective of their area of operation.

It is against this background an attempt is made in this paper to understand the depiction of inverted triangles, which is the hallmark of all representations in the rock art of Odisha. Out of 106 rock art shelters documented in the state 77 (72%) shelters depict 1369 (20%) specimen of triangles (Pradhan 2017: 127- 129). Representative motifs of triangle are noticed at sites like Bhimmandali (Fig.1&2), and Maricha Taila (fig.3) in Sambalpur distict; Rajbahal-Ushakuthi (Fig. 4), Lekhamoda-VI (Fig. 5) and Tongo in Sundargarh district and Pandava Bakhara in Cuttak district. They are all in engraving. Whereas representative triangles in paintings have come from Lekhamoda-X (Fig. 6) in Sundargarh district and Ulap (Fig.7) in Sambalpur district.

Triangle is a polygon with three edges and three vertices and it is one of the simplest shapes in geometry. In rock panels it is represented with its apex pointing downward or in some cases a vertical line beginning at the apex make the triangle bisected or in few other a shallow depression at the the centre which resemble the triangular shape of a women's sacral region. Hence it is universally identified as the female genitalia otherwise also known as yoni or vulva. Similar representation vulva has also been reported recently from Gawilgarh hills in Madhya Pradesh (Sahu 2013-14: 6-15). Vulva in all conceivable shapes and forms have been reported from various sites world over from Europe, Africa, America, Australia and Asia right from the Upper Palaeolithic period (Marshack 1972). Notable sites are La Ferrassie, Abri Castanet, Abri Blanchard, Abri Labattut, Abri Cellier, Le Roc-aux-Sorcerers, Lalinde, Les Combarelles, Pergouset etc. in Europe and the "Wall of One Thousand Vulvas" in Southern Queensland, Australia. These triangular formations are more pronounced in petroglyphs than pictographs.

Different cultures held different views on vulva with a common view that it is the organ primarily responsible for procreation as life giver and hence reverenced as Venus, the primordial mother of the western philosophy or as *Shakti* or the mother goddess of the Hindu Philosophy. Yoni, in Hinduism, is conceptualised as nature's gateway to all births. Hence an inverted triangle representing female genital is a spiritual metaphor and icon in Hinduism for the feminine generative power (*Hutcherson 2003: 8*). It served as a divine symbol from ancient times and may be one of the oldest spiritual icons across many ancient cultures including Hinduism.

In Trantric tradition in which women play an important role the female principle or the yoni is represented by a downward pointing inverted triangle (Rawson 1973). The esoteric significance of triangle is best illustrated in Tantric Sri Yantra or Sri Chakra which is comprised of nine over lapping triangle that creates a total of 43 smalls triangles. Of the nine triangles, four pointing upwards represent the *linga*, the abstract representation of '*Purusha*'. While five of these pointing downwards represent the *yoni*, the abstract representation of *Shakti/Prakrukti*. The interlocking of these nine triangles symbolically represents the union of the masculine and feminine energies for creation of the universe. (Ryan 2006), In later civilizations triangles pointing downwards are traditionally interpreted as water-symbols and pointing upward as fire symbols. Two triangles superimposed form a complete duality, the six-pointed star (hexagram), a symbol found in wide array of cultures around the world. It is traditionally interpreted as the combination of a watery (female, pointing downward) and a fiery (male, pointing upward) triangle, representing together a closed, harmonically ordered duality that ensures procreation. These are the emblematic representations of the" divinity's productive essence" (Zimmer 1990: 138). Though apparently it is no more than a geometrical device, these intricate compositions suffice the whole sense of the Hindu World of myth and Symbol.

The aniconic representation of the mother goddess Shakti is best represented in the famous Kamakshya temple at Guwahati in Assam where the presiding deity in the sanctum is a yoni-shaped fissure in a natural rock with a natural water spring. It is an important *Sakta* Centre of Hinduism because as per the Puranic tradition the Kamakshya *Yoni* is considered as the *Yoni* of the *Sati*, the daughter of Daksha and consort of Siva. Every year with the unset of monsoon, the natural spring turns red because of iron oxides and vermilion anointed by the devotees and priests, which is celebrated as the annual menstruation of the goddess, when the temple is closed for three days during which the Ambubachi fertility *mela* is held. Similar fissures in natural rocks (Fig.8&9) are also worshipped as noticed in Pooja Dunguri, near Rampur in Subarnapur district of Odisha (Pradhan 2017: 101). Similar vulvar formations are also seen in Southern California. In this context the evidences obtained from Bhagor in Son Valley, Madhya Pradesh, offer an important clue (Kenoyer *et al.* 1983). Here, during the excavations, fragments of triangular-shaped natural sandstone with concentric laminations in the form of triangles were found on the slightly raised circular rubble platform. Even today the members of local Koli and Bhaiga tribes worship similar type of colourful natural triangular stones as a symbol of the female principle or Mother Goddess called *'Mai'* in the local language (Sonawane 1997: 13-14). Mention also may be made of the engraved core found from Chandravati (Rajasthan, India), which also supports the symbolic representation of the Mother Goddess (Sonawane 1997: 11). Similar portable yoni motif carved on stone was reported by J. P. Singh Deo (2004: 45-51), which he recovered from Nuapada district in Odisha. Natural formations as well as those that are enhanced or entirely sculpted are considered sources of power and were used in fertility rituals (McGowan 1978). They are part of a universal system of symbols that persist through time and also a worldview shared by traditional cultures, visible signs that humankind has always celebrated birth, life, and regeneration.'

Fertility has been of supreme concern throughout the history of mankind for ensuring prosperity. Concept of fertility can be expressed in many forms (1) the woman herself (2) depiction of Vulva-symbol of generative power of procreation and nourishment (3) depiction of copulation, (4) female puberty ritual etc. Fertility practices varied in different areas, but there has been a widespread consistency in the use of symbolic representation of the human vulva. Vulva motifs may take many forms, while still referring to the same basic concept, for continuation of life and maintenance of human fertility" (Pradhan 2001).

One of the oldest forms of expressing the absolute is the duality of the sex: Father Heaven and Mother Earth, the Chinese Yang and Yin, the Hindu Siva and *Shakti* represented in erotic symbolism of *lingam* and *yoni*, which is enshrined and worshipped in every Siva temple. The figurative representation of these erotic symbolisms is noticed in the image of Ardhanarisvara and Haraparvati

The former is a composite figure with the right half represented by Siva and the left half by Parvati. The division of the deity into male and female is clearly rendered by ornaments as well as sexual characteristics with the right half usually being *Urdhvalinga* and the left half having prominent female breast. On the pedestal are their respective animal vehicles (*vahana*) , the lion of the goddess and Bull of Nandi of a Siva. The supreme fertility idol of bisexuality is the combination of two sexes as a perpetual generation. In the later goddess Parvati the consort of Lord Siva sits on the left lap of Siva with her right arm turned around his shoulder. Siva is sported in *Urdhvalinga* with his left arm going round the waist of Parvati gently touches the left breast. One can feel their intense love filled with divinely ordained emotions. Though they appear to be two, they are fundamentally one like the *Ardhanarisvara.*(Half female and half male God) Similar figurative representation of the mother goddess exhibiting the triangular genetalia is quite often seen in other historical art as well. A class of deity called "Lajja Gauri", "the shameless Women", "the nude squatting Goddess", "the mother goddess", otherwise also referred to as "Sakambari", "Aditi", "Prithivi", is an enigmatic composition in Hinduism. She sits in birth giving position with splayed out legs drawn up and bent at the knees. Various theories have been held by various scholars. Some opine that she is the embodiment of the process of procreation or the life force because the very representation is in the act of giving birth. Others view that she is shamelessly seductive, a pose of sexuality or *Kama*. Sexuality and fertility are correlated, one being complimentary to the other. These objects are portable and usually seen in plaques of terracotta or stone in relief. They are founding Gujurat, Maharashtra, Madhya Pradesh, Karnataka, Andhra Pradesh, Uttar Pradesh and Odisha. It is believed that she is being worshipped by women who have not been able to bear children.

Conclusion

When the female procreative organ is represented in visual art either it is two- dimensional as seen in paintings or engravings in the shape of an inverted triangle or three-dimensional in the form of nude female statuettes. In archaeological context several female figurines carved from soft stones such as lime stone, calcite, steatite or bone or ivory or terracotta have been unearthed right from the Upper Palaeolithic Aurignacian-Gravettian periods down to the Chalcolithic periods. In global context Palaeolithic women statuettes are widely distributed, from France to Southern Russia as far as Siberia. The female statuttees are always uncompromisingly nude. They are some six to eight centimetres high, made of steatite or ivory. The ivory is bigger than the steatites. They all reflect a well-defined canon: the breasts, the balley, the pelvic region and the thighs fall within a circle from which extend the tapering torso and legs". (Gurhan 1967: 121). The lower and the upper portions of the anatomy are treated extremely secondary without any indication of details. What is emphasised is the public triangle, the protruding abdomen and the breasts : the organs responsible for procreation and nourishment. In contrast the head is faceless, arms and feet are absent. Emphasis is given onwomen's divinely gifted power of conceiving, carrying, giving birth and nourishing the new born, which the prehistoric folk might have realized at same point of time and since then started venerating and adoring the woman for her procreative prowess. Willendrof "Venus" found in 1908, a lime stone sculpture of $4^3/8$" height and pigmented red, now housed in Naturhistoriesches Museum, Vienna (Austria) was found from the late Auriguacian stratum (C. 30,000 BP), the most fully plastic of all prehistoric figurines (Giedion 1962: 437). Similarly, the "Venus of Laussel" carved in lime stone discovery in 1911 and dated to the Upper Perigordian period C. 25,000 B.P. (Breuil 1952: 279 - 281; Sandars 1968) has been well explained by N. K. Sandars (1968:30) as the Mother goddess, a venerated concentrated embodiment of woman and in essence of principle of fecundity because the horn represents the fertilizing function of the bull-the procreative elements and the naked women, in symbolic association with the horn of plenty. The gesture of the left hand upon the abdomen is suggestive of a condition of pregnancy. J. P. Duhard (1989: 105-118) interpreted all the Venus figures as symbols of fecundity. These naked images are highly intricate & overloaded with symbolism. All these Venus cannot be taken as prehistoric pinup girls, but were the deities of fecundity of great spiritual significance.

Later on, these figurative forms were replaced by abstract symbols of vulva which is represented by the downward pointing triangle.

References

Anati, E., 1964, *Camonica Valley*, Jonathan Cape, London: Thirty Bedford Square.

Breuil, 1952, *Four Hundred Centries of Cave Art (English Edition) Montignac.*

Brodrick, A.H., 1948, *Prehistoric Painting*, London: Avalon Press Ltd.

Giedion, S., 1962, *The Eternasl Present : The Beginnings of Art, Bollingen Foundations*, New York.

Heizer, Robert F. and Mortine A. Baumhoff, 1962, *Prehistoric Rock Art of Nevada and Eastern California*, Barkeley & Los Angeles: University of California Press.

Hutcherson, Hilda, 2003, *What Your Mother Never Told You about Sex*, Penguin.

Leroi-Gourhan, A., 1965, *Treasures of Prehistoric Art, Abrams*, New York.

Leroi-Gourhan, A., 1968, *The Art of Prehistoric Man in Europe*, London: Thames and Hudson.

Marshack, A., 1972, *The Roots of Civilization: The Cognitive Beginning of Man's First Art, Symbol and Notation*, New York: McGraw Hill.

Pradhan, S., 2001, *Rock Art in Orissa*, New Delhi: Aryan Books International.

Pradhan, S., 2017, *Silent Rock's An Eloquent Testimony, Rock Art Heritage of Odisha*, New Delhi: IGNCA & B.R. Publishing Corporation.

Rawson, P., 1973, *Tantra-The Indian Cult of Ecastasy*, London: Thames and Hudson.

Ryan, J.D, 2006, *Encyclopedia of Hinduism*, Infobase Publishing.

Sahu, Prabash, 2013-14, Petroglyphs in Recently Discovered Rock Shelters of Gawilgarh Hills, *Heritage and Us, Quarterly e-Journal,* Year 2, Issue 4:

Sandors, N. K., 1968, *Prehistoric Art in Europe,* Harmondsworth: Penguin Books Ltd.

Singh Deo, J.P., 1976, *Prehistoric Cave Painting of Jogimath Donger, The Orissa Historical Research Journal,*

Vol.XXII, No.2

Sonawane, V.H., 1984, An important evidence to date rock paintings of Mesolithic period, New Delhi: K.K. Chakravarty (ed.), *Rock Art in India.*

Theodule, Ribot, 1915, La Pensee symbolique, Paris : Revue Philosophique, LXXIV.

Zimmer, Heinrich, 1990, *Myths and Symbols in Indian Art and Civilization,* Joseph Campbell (ed.), Delhi: Motilal Banarasidass Publishers Pvt. Ltd.

10

A Review of Petroglyphs and Pictographs in Siyotcaves Taluq Lakpat, District Kutch, Gujarat

Ajit Kumar, Rajesh S.V and Abhayan G.S

Introduction

Siyot(23^0 46′ 26.12″N; 68^0 52′34.75″E) is located in Lakpat Taluq of Kutch District. Cut into the sandstone hillock at Siyot is a large rock-cut cave temple, (currently damaged)adjoined by some smaller onesin various state of excavation/preservation and some natural ghettos. Due to various factors like weathering, earthquake and human vandalism, today, the cave temple does not commend any great architectural or aestheticmerit. The rock surface of caves and ghettos here has rock-art in the form of Petroglyphs and Pictographs. While Petroglyphs predominate there are also a few Pictographs. This paper discusses the rock-art in the caves, which does not seem to have gained the attention of scholars, the way they merit.

The main cave

The main cave comprises of a sanctum facing east with a circumambulatory passage around fronted by a hall with two pillars (Fig.1). The pillars of the hall possibly emerge out of a pot base (now partly buried) and the shaft seems to bear flutings which are carried right into the capital. The cave possibly had a stone screen wall with a doorway to the north, now broken away. The doorway of the sanctum is flanked by two pilasters with capital and do not have further jambs or decorations. The absence of further moldings or *shakas*,Ganga and Yamuna etc representations on the door frame, seems to indicate that this cave be earlier than the Mahayana *viharas* at Ajanta dating to the Vakataka-Gupta period. Close to the sill of the door frame is a *chandrashila*. *Chandrashila* starts to get associated with flight of steps for the first time in Buddhist caves of Kanheri by around 2nd CE (Nagaraju 1981: 91). Square *chaitya* halls with stupas became a norm in Buddhist caves of western Maharashtra by around late 2nd cent CE. There used to be circumambulatory passage around stupas, but circumambulatory path around the sanctum or cella housing the stupais apparently a later development.

When compared to other Buddhist caves from Gujarat itself, this cave in its square sanctum and pillared hall draws similarity with the Uparkotecaves at Junagadh.The pillars in the hall of the Siyotcaves are quite worn-out and lack the exquisite decorations and grandeur noticed in the pillars at Junagadh, but they do divulge a muffled similarity in the flutings and the treatment of the base. The style of the chaitya arches within the cave at Uparkotappears similar to the façade of Ajanta cave 26, dating to Vakataka king Harisena's period (475-500 CE).The Siyot cave is rather simple in its style compared to Uperkot caves and may be earlier to it. There are opinions that the cave could date to first century CE, however the possibility of its dating to 3rd or 4th centuries CE seems more potential (Mishra & Ray 74). If it is the same as the Buddhist caves mentioned by Xuanzangas locate at the mouth of Indus then it must have been important Buddhist centre around 7th Century CE (https://en.wikipedia.org/wiki/Siyot_Caves).These Buddhist caves at Siyot are located in close proximity with the old port and habitation and must have commended great reverence and patronage from the trading community stationed here for considerable time.

Excavations conducted at Siyot caves by the Department of Archaeology, Government of Gujarat, in 1988-89, yielded clay sealing with engraved Buddha images some bearing inscriptions in late Brahmi and Devanagiri characters. Also discovered were Gadhaiya coins which were vogue as a currency under various dynasties of Gujarat from around 8th to the 13th century. Possibly after the decline of Buddhism the cave came to be occupied by the Shivites around the 12th -13th century CE, the terracotta Nandi image found may indicate this affiliation (IAR 1988-89: 10).

There are two other attempted excavations to the northeast side of the main cave on the same hillock (Figure.2).

Petroglyphs and Pictographs

It is interesting to note that the rock surface of the main and subsidiary caves and some natural caverns at Siyot bear large number of Petroglyphs. The ceiling of the main cave also has some traces of Pictographs in white.

Petroglyphs

Petroglyphs are found on the rock surface of the cave, and on architectural elements like pillars, doorway, and also on the exterior surfaces. In the main cave, on the left wall, while facing the cave, close to the pillar, the whole surface is covered with Petroglyphs. The motifs include two circles connected by median line; circles with a line running into it, a circle with a narrow like object emerging from it (Fig. 3), a possible anthropomorphic figure with arms raised etc. Similar motifs are also noticed on the back-wall of the cave. Among the motifs in the back wall is a palm leaf or herringbone motif and a square internally divided into eight (Fig.4), a pentagon or star etc., (Fig.5). Just above the cell doorway in the back wall are some deep grooved lines similar to tally marks, a trident, English alphabets etc., (Fig.6). The back wall too has similar motifs along with a latticed square. The two pillars of the hallbear abstract motifs like, wavy line, concentric circles, plus-in-circle, tridents, intersecting or triangular formations, bow and arrow etc., (Fig.7 and Fig.8).

On the ceiling before the sanctum are, Petroglyphs of two horse riders to the right, between them is an anthropomorphic figure, a camel (Fig.9), and a circle with tridentattached (Fig.10), a foot print (Fig.11).To the side wall adjoining the sanctum door are trident motifs, circle with dot, plus-in-circle, plus motif, etc. In the side wall of the sanctum is noticed an animal rider and an anthropomorphic figure with curved hands on the top and also an alphabet resembling Hindi or Devnagiri 'ka' to the bottom. In the back wall of the sanctum, is an outlined camel motif (Fig.12).

Pictographs

The ceiling of the cave contains a few white painted Pictographs. Only one of it is quite clear and seems to be a trident or anthropomorphic creation with two dots above and below (Fig.13).There is also apparently a dog and a horse rider among the Pictographic represented on the ceilings.

To the west of the main cave is a ghetto (Fig. 14). On either rock surfaces of this ghetto are Petroglyphs. The largest one is to the right wall surface (Fig.15). It has three concentric rectangles. There are diagonal lines from four corners running into corners of the inner rectangle. Along the top are three conical projections the central one being the largest. Towards the right of it are two tubular creations with conical tops. To the left wall also is a smaller version of the concentric rectangles, with a single conical spire on top (Fig.15 &16). There is also an unidentifiable motif, which could be schematic representation of a vulva (Fig. 17).The rock-surface of the adjoining incomplete excavation to the northeast also bears a large number of Petroglyphs, and some graffiti in English.

Discussions

Trident, circles with cross within, interconnected circles, circles with arrow marking, circles with trident etc., are the most common motifs among the Petroglyphs at Siyot. Needless to say, that they appear to bear a votive and Shivitein character. It is believed that the Siyot cave assumed a Shivite character consequent to its Buddhist abandonment around the 12th -13th centuries CE. Hence, it is quite obvious that the Shivite symbols like the trident in various styles noticedin the Petroglyphs should have been engraved consequent to 12th -13th centuries.The circle with trident noticed on the ceiling, which lacks a strong patina seems to be the latest in the series of tridents.

Tridents and circles have been noticed in a host of rock art sites across India.Trident motifs have been noticed in Pictographsand Petroglyphsof the Marayoor region of Kerala, dating to almost recent times, (as evidenced from an English alphabet) (Kumar & Varman 2019: 169). Some motifs in Siyot cave like circle with trident, dumbbell, horse rider, and anthropomorphic figures do bear similarity with second phase rock-art from Naidupalli, Prakasham dist. dating to historic times (Fig. 18) (Chandramouli 2002: 173; Fig.49-56).

What is the correlation between the motifs like herringbone, concentric circles with dot or hole in the center, the plus-in-circle and vulva with Shivite affiliation of the cave is difficult to understand. The camels depicted may bear a votive character possibly seeking protection or benevolence for theherder's life stock, from the presiding deity of the cave temple. The footprint may represent salvation of some pious soul, like that in Jainism. The pentagon or star is a symbol of cosmic origin and from Gujarat this symbol has been reported earlier from Senetary and Siyotby Saleem (Saleem 2015: 178; Fig. 5& 15)

There are two horse riders with raised hands depicted in the ceiling of the cave. Pictographs of triangular bodied horses astride with humans like the ones at Siyothave been previously reported from Achala rock shelter in Baroda district dating to the historic period (Ajithprasad 2006: 27). They are associated with the Rathvadcommunity and their horse riding god Pithora. Paintings of this god were done in households by Shamans to get rid of malady or for overall good of the family (Biswas 2015: 170-173).It is quite possible that the horse riding person depicted here in this cave isof Ramdeo peer,who is often depicted riding a horse and has a large number of followers in the Kutch region. However, this cult apparently gainedpredominance in Gujarat only consequent to 15thcent.CE. The motif concentric squares with some sort of cupola or conical spire on the top could be representation of temples according to some locals. Similar concentric squares has also been reported from Senetary locality 3 by Saleem (Saleem 2015: 178-183; Fig. 10).

The so called 'tally marks' noticed above the cell doorwayin the main cave are apparently of very recent origin, as evidenced from English alphabets close to it. Very similar 'tally marks'and some plus-in-circle motifs were also noticed in caverns of a sandstone hillock near NaniVirani, Kutch (23^0 39′ 46.12″ N and 68^0 53′ 43.83″ E (Fig.19)

Pictographs in red, though with no similarity to that from Siyot, hitherto unreported, was noticed in a shelterfrom AmiyaJiva gad, near Amiya (23^0 39′ 23.75″N; 68^0 59′ 07.45″ E). As the Pictograph is indistinct it is difficult to read what it denotes (Fig. 20).

Concluding observations

The Petroglyphs noticed in the caves at Siyot seems to show a strong Shivite affinity rather than Buddhist. The motifs like herring bone and pentagon have been noticed in a variety of context and time period. Here, this motif possibly dates only to the historic period as they are noticed in the back wall of the excavated cave. The trident motif seems to have a votive in character. Even today in Marayoor region of Kerala and some parts of southern Tamil Nadu, trident is planted close to megaliths and at times offeredto the temples of villages deities like Karappuswamyas part of thanks giving consequent to reprieve from maladies (Kumar & Varman 2019: 143). The trident motif so copiously found in the Siyot cave were all apparently executed after the cave taking up a Shivite affiliation in the early Medieval period and have continued to modern times. Many scholars deter to postulate the continuation of rock-art into medieval and modern times; however, there is more and more evidences emerging of rock-art continuing into modern times (Kumar 2018: 572).

References

Ajithprasad, P., 2006, The rock-paintings in the Sukhi Valley and their archaeological and social context, in *Kerala Spectrum Aspects of cultural inheritance Dr. K.J. John Felicitation Volume,* Cochin: The Indo-Portuguese Cultural Institue.

Biswas, Ghosh, Urmi, 2015, Rock-painting and Tribal Art in Gujarat: A Case Study in *Rock Art: Recent Researches and New Perspectives* (Festschrift to Padma Shri Dr. Yashodhar Mahthpal), Ajit Kumar (ed.) Delhi: New Bharatiya Book Corporation.

Chandramouli, N., 2002, *Rock Art of South India*, Delhi: Bharatiya Kala Prakashan.

Kumar, Ajit, 2018, A Reappraisal of Pictographs from Pathipara, Marayoor, District Idukki, Kerala, *Heritage Journal of Multidisciplinary Studies in Archaeology*, Trivandrum: Department of Archaeology.

Kumar, Ajit and Raj K. Varman, 2019, *Petroglyphs and Pictographs in Kerala (Rock- Art in Kerala)*, Delhi: New Bharatiya Book Corporation.

Nihildas, N., 2018, *Rock Art and Megaliths Maraiyur, Kerala,* Delhi: B.R. Publishing Corporation.

Saleem, Shaik, 2015, Prehistoric Investigation in Kutch in *Rock Art: Recent Researches and New Perspectives (Festschrift to Padma Shri Dr. Yashodhar Mahthpal)*, Ajit Kumar (ed.), Delhi: New Bharatiya Book Corporation.

11

Nature and Functions of Agricultural Metal Implements (With Special Reference to Post-Harappan Chalcolithic Cultures of Northern India)

J. P. Upadhyaya

The rise and growth of metallurgy and the concomitant progress in the use of metal implements are found to have been a factor leading to far-reaching industrial and economic consequences for the emergence of successive stages in the development of mans material culture. Since much has been written about the metal implements found from Harapan culture which is the first major landmark in the annals in the development in early India, the present paper aims at discussing the agricultural metal implements found from other chalcolithic cultures other than Harappan culture because of the limited scope of the paper. Attempt has been made to make comparative study of these tools and in their morphological and ecological contexts. It includes a varied and rich repertoire of tools and implements bearing on agricultural technology and other relms of technological evolution, a trend that foreshadows on historical scenario of technological evolution.

The area under study in the paper covers roughly the modern administrative boundaries of Punjab, Haryana, Rajasthan, Madhya Pradesh, Maharashtra, Uttar Pradesh, Bihar, Jharkhand, Orissa and West Bengal. It seeks to redefine the metallurgical components of these regions in terms of typology and chronology. In contrast to prevailing notion, here it has been shown that some of the implements eg. Bar axes, could have served the purpose of digging the land. These bar axes may have also been used for digging a pit of small diameter for fixing the wooden logs in the preparation of huts. Taking the various kinds of the utilitarian nature of these axes tribal people may have accepted the bar axes as an attribute of lord Shiva. The socio-economic change ushered in by metallurgical development in protohistoric India underlined here, is called for a long time. This forms a background far changes in the subsequent and later times in the metallurgical framework of protohistoric India.

The methodology adopted here consists of measurement of metal implements into centimetres, millimetres as of length, breadth/width/thickness, diameter and their mutual relationship. Cross section of tools and implements has been drawn up and edge points, tangs thereof has been taken note of as lacking in earlier studies. The statistical analysis of various tools and implements has been attempted to underline the role of tools and implements has been presented for drawing relevant conclusions. On the basis of the study it has been attempted to underline the role of tools and implements in bringing about socio-economic and cultural change during period under study.

Nature and Functions of Agricultural Metal Implements (with Special reference to Post-Harappan Chalcolithic cultures of Northern India)

During the latter half of the third millennium and almost the entire second millennium B.C., many chalcolithic/copper-bronze using cultures developed in different parts of northern India besides, the Harappan culture. Among them mention may be made of the Neolithic-Chalcolithic culture of Kashmir valley represented by such sites as Burzahom and Gufkral, the red ware culture of parts of Punjab, Haryana, Rajasthan and western Uttar Pradesh with probable association of Copper Hoards in the Gangetic doab region, the Pre-NBPW Chalcolithic culture of Bihar represented by the excavations at Pandu Rajar Dhibi. Most of these cultures generally exhibit an insignificant use of copper/bronze, except the red ware culture of western Uttar Pradesh. Copper Hoards, are generally associated with red ware culture.

Red wares of uncertain affinities have been found widely distributed in Punjab, Haryana, parts of Rajasthan and western Uttar Pradesh, the culture complexes of cemetery-H of Harappa, that of Bara, Siswal, Ganeshwar, Jodhpura, Lal Qila, Atranjikhera, Bahadarabad, Hastinapur, Saipai, Ahichchhatra, Bargaon and Ambkheri, etc, and also possibly Sringaverapur may be mentioned in this regard. Though these complexed do not seem to represents exactly the same ceramic tradition, yet they were all red ware, sharing some common characteristic features. The red wares found ayt a large number of sites in the Gangetic doab of Uttar Pradesh have been very often referred to as Ochre Coloured pottery abbreviated as OCP. It is with this complex that an associational relationship of Copper Hoards of the doab is very often suggested.

The Chronology of these red ware complexes poses vexing problem. There is a small series of thermoluminiscence dates from Atranjikhera, Lal Qila, Narsipur and Jhinjhina, which point out to a time bracket of 2650 to 1180 B.C. Nothing can be said about the Chronology of the other red ware complexes. If, however, the above time bracket is accepted as a basis of the argument it may be suggested that these red ware culture complexes emerged almost simultaneously with mature Harappans and seemed to have outlived with their early contemporaries by more than five centuries. The early beginning of the OCP is also confirmed by one radio carbon date from Jodhpura which falls between 2800 and 2700 B.C. (Allchin 1983: 253).

The Ganga-Yamuna doab forms the main area of the copper hoards although several sites also fall outside it. Nearly thirty seven, copper hoards sites were located by B.B. Lal long ago, which were distributed in the modern administrative states of Uttar Pradesh, Madhya Pradesh, Bihar, West Bengal and Orissa (Lal 1951: 20-29). Since then, there has been much addition to the list, which has increased upto eighty six and now includes sites in the state of Haryana, Rajasthan, Uttar Pradesh, Madhya Pradesh, Bihar, Orissa, West Bengal and distant Karnataka and it is noteworthy that the copper ore exploited for manufacturing the hoard objects was probably the Rakha mines of Bihar (Lal 1984: 33). This is in contrast with Harappan source which was probably Khetri mines of Rajasthan (Allchin 1983: 256).

A group of copper objects, usually of massive size and considerable weight, mostly found in the Gangetic doab and Chhotanagpur plateau as chance discoveries without proper excavations, is very often described as Copper Hoard. Numerous copper hoards have come to light so for from two separate cultural, zones, viz, the Gangetic doab, and the hilly and forested tracts of south Bihar and Bengal, with occasional outliers, such as Gungeria, in Balaghat district of Madhya Pradesh, south of Jabalpur. Though the hoards of these two zones differ substantially in respect of typology of objects, yet they seem to sharemany common characteristics (Lal 1951: 20-29). However, it may be noted that the Copper Hoard sites are almost invariably associated with OCP in the first cultural zone, while no such claim can be made in respect of the Copper Hoard of the second zone. This circumstantial association of the Copper Hoards in the doab region prompted B.B. Lal to assign these copper objects of OCP people as for back as 1951 (Lal 1951: 20-29). This hypothesis seems to have gained ground as a result of a series of excavations of OCP sites, such as Bargaon (Deshpande1965-66: 66-67), Atranjikher (Gaur 1983: 450), Lal Qila (Gaur1983: 450) and Saipai (Lal: 46-49). The circumstancial evidence for the association of the Copper Hoards of Gangetic doab with OCP cannot be easily ignored, and most scholars are inclined to accept the hypothesis of B.B. Lal.

Copper Hoard Implements

The objects of hoards generally show a striking similarity. The most common objects are various types of axes, swords, harpoons, a limited number of anthromorphs, rings, etc. There is no evidence of copper being used for vessels in the chalcolithic or Copper Hoard cultures whereas the Harappans were the only people in India who used the metal lavishly for vessels, including a variety of vases (Agrawal 1998: 10). It is noteworthy that the Harappans used for alloying both arsenic and tin; the Copper Hoard culture used exclusively arsenic alloying and the chalcolithic cultures only tin alloying (Agrawal 1998: 11). In west Asia the earliest alloying was done with arsenic only but later on tin takes over almost globally, perhaps the injuries effects of arsenic alloying on the health of the coppersmiths became known and it was given up (Agrawal 1998: 11). The use of arsenic by Copper Hoard culture appears a bit enigmatic, either it is due to the fact that the ores themselves contain significant amount of arsenic or the Copper Hoard's is oldest copper technology in India (Agrawal

1998: 12). The anthromorphs distinguish themselves for their massive size and heavy weight. Various scholars have assigned different functions to them. Following our scheme of classification of metal implements, it appears possible to screen copper tools of these hoards into three broad categories viz; agricultural implements, implements of war and hunt and household implements. However, we intend to discuss only agricultural implements here.

Agricultural Implements

Under this category mention may be made of various types of axes and a possible ploughshare, besides a Khurpi. It is interesting to note that the implements of this category, particularly axes, most commonly occur in a large majority of Copper Hoards. It is generally admitted that axes were being commonly used by agricultural people for forest clearance with a view to preparing fields. The occurrence of good number of axes in copper hoards may point towards the agriculture base economy of the people. Three main types of axes are found; each having sub-types, besides some other types, mostly limited to Chhotanagpur region. These are discussed as follows-

(A) Type

(i) Flat Axe: Viewed in plan, these axes have broad played out edge, sides converging concavely from the blade edge of rounded or rectangular butt end. These are similar to Harappan specimens. In majority, the edges are blunt and rarely sharp. The edge profile is invariably biconvex. The length ranges between 10 to 26 cms. with a mean of 18. Breadth of the blade ranges between 8 to 18 cms. This type of axe is reported from the sites of Haryana, Uttar Pradesh, Rajasthan, Madhya Pradesh, Bihar and distant Karnataka. The forthcoming table records the details of the specimens. In total nearly three hundred specimens of this type have been recorded so far (Lal 1984: 43; Roy 1985: 123).

Type (ii) Shoulders Axe: In plan, shoulders axes sometimes have the lead portion as much as two-third of entire length, these have a kink or setback near the meeting point of the curved edge and the rest of the blade. The edge is in the form of a semicircular spanning from 180 to 230 degrees. Although the edge profile is biconvex, it does not seem to form an effective cutting edge; thus the edge becomes very often dull and smooth, but end is narrower than the edge and is mostly squarish. The two sides are curved inward. These are 18 to 25 cm in length and 14 to 23 in breadth (Lal 1984: 43). These are reported from the sites of Uttar Pradesh, Bihar, Madhya Pradesh, West Bengal, Orissa and it is interesting that they are not found west of Doab (Lal 1984: 43), Nearly one hundred thirty specimens of this kind have been reported so far and are lodged in various museums (Lal 1984: 43).

Type (iii) Splayed Axe: In this new type of axes exclusively known from eastern Chhotanagpur area of Bihar, neither the edge is sharp nor its corners are prominent and the edge is sufficiently splayed out convex. Sides of the blades are flatish and roundish. Crude casting technique is diagnostic. Profile of the edge is planoconvex; 'dimple' impression on convex face of some specimens is also observed. The length ranges from 13.50 to 22.90 cm. Total number of this type reported is ninety one (Yule *et al*: 124).

Type (iv) Narrow Splayed Axe: This type differs from type (iii) on account of its longer length-breadth proportion and less spalyed out convex edge. In plan, these are also superficially similar to type (i), but are smaller and narrower. Sides are slightly concave and converge towards the rounded butt end. In profile, it is planoconvex and rough cast, Length varies from 12.60 to 16.60 cm. Total specimens known are eleven, all derived from Gungeria hoard, Madhya Pradesh, except one which is from Chhotanagpur (Yule *et al*: 126).

Type (v) Irregular Axe: These are irregular and variously shaped specimens and are found simply by molten copper poured on a flat surface. Edges are roughly splayed out convex and broader than the butt end. They vary in length from 9.70 to 11.90 cm. and are relatively thinner. The total examples known number ten, all derived from Chhotanagpur, Bihar.

Type (vi) Bar Axe or long Narrow Axe: Since these specimens are made of long bars of copper, they are given the name 'bar' axes. These are rough cast and have generally semicircular usually blunt but occasionally sharp edges. In plan, the specimens of eastern group are chisel-like, having edges with plano convex or bell-shaped cross section. Sides are generally straight parallel. Bottom side is either concave or convex and some of the specimens show several cuts on observe surface perpendicular to the length (Yule *et al*: 126). These are 35.50 to 58.80 cm long and 4 to 8 cm broad. The total number of the bar axes is eighty five (Yule *et al*: 126-127). They come from the sites of Rajasthan, Uttar Pradesh, Bihar, Madhya Pradesh, Orissa and West Bengal. Chhotanagpur, Bihar, alone has yielded fifty five such axes including many varients (Lal 1984: 127).

These axes (shouldered and flat type) were probably used for cutting wood or hunting animals (Lal 1984: 43). On the basis of the use marks on the edge, Agrawal suggests that the bar axes were used for mining ores (Agrawal1971: 198). But according to Yule, Chhotanagpur specimens were probably not used as implements to all (Yule: 127-128). He opines that firstly because there are really no traces of ancient use-wears and secondly they are too heavy to have served the purpose often attributed to them. Can it be suggested here on basis of the morphology of these axes that these might have been used for digging pits of small diameter for fixing the wooden logs in the preparation of huts? It is probable that these bar-axes may have also been used for digging purposes especially in the preparation of wells and other household purposes. *Rambhas* and *Gahadalas* of iron of the kind are used in northern India even today in the villages as multipurpose implement. Considering the various kinds of the utilitarian nature of these axes, tribal people may have accepted the bar axes as an attributes of Lord Shiva.

Type (vii) Double Axe: These are made by cutting the circular pieces of copper. Three such specimens are known from Bhangarapir, Orissa and five from Parihati, West Bengal (Coggin & Brown1961: 368-387). Two specimens from Bhangarapir have both the edges sharpened, while the third has only one edge sharp. the double axes might have been hafted in the middle for effective cutting, which were perhaps used to clear the forest to preparing fields for farming. Table-1 records the details of the different types of axes.

(B) Khurpi

This is a new tool type of the Copper Hoards (Gupta: 27). It is long, simple copper blade with a broad cutting edge at one end. The opposite end has a small shouldered tenon meant for hafting, probably in a wooden handle. This type of implement is prevelant in northern India even today for removing unwanted grass from the fields and also for making hay to feed the cattles.

(C) Poughshare

Two examples of probable ploughshares, one each from Kulgara (IAR 1971-72: 51; Pl. LXV,B) and Bhaktabundh West Bengal, have been reported. However, their actual function may be a debatable question; we intend to classify them as agricultural implement for ploughing the fields.

Table 1

Sl. No.	Site	Type	Length x Breadth x Thickness (cms)	Cross Section	Nature of Edge	References
1	Bisauli	Bar Axe	29.20x7.20x0.30	Flat	Biconvex cutting edge is sharpened, slightly broader than the butt end	Ancient India No.7 p 23
2	Nandlalpura (Jaipur)	Bar Axe (6)	27.00x8.0x?	Flat	One end splayed out convex sharp, the other narrower sharp. The specimen is totally different from these of Doab ones.	Agrawal, R.C. 1979; More copper finds from Rajasthan, Man and Environment, Vol.III, pp. 91-92.Pl. III

3	Chhotanagpur	Bar Axe	55.086x8.82x1.76	Flat	Splayed out convex sharp cutting edge, tapers towards butt end.	Yule, et al., Man in India, vol. 65, No. 2 p 125
4	Pondi	Flat Axe	18.00x14.00x0.80	Flat	Splayed out convex sharp Cutting edge, flat butt end.	Ancient India, No.7 p.23; No.6
5	Hardi	Flat Axe	17.60x12.00x1.00	Flat	As above	Ibid., p.26, No.4
6	Bithur	Flat Axe	15.20x11.00x0.50	Flat	As above	Ibid., p.26, No.1
7	Bithur	Flat Axe	16.80x10.00x0.70	Flat	As above	Ibid., p.26, No.2
8	Bithur	Flat Axe	15.80x12.00x1.20	Flat	As above	Ibid., p.26, No.3
9	Bithur	Flat Axe	16.8x12.40x0.50	Flat	Slightly splayed out, convex sharp with flat butt ends	Ibid., p.26, No.7
10	Bithur	Flat Axe	9.20x4.80x0.40	Flat	No difference between cutting edge and butt end	Ibid., p.26, No.9
11	Bithur	Flat Axe	8.40x7.20x0.90	Flat	Sharp splayed out convex cutting edge. Butt end flat	Ibid., p.26, No.11
12	Indilapur	Flat Axe	26.80x19.20x0.80	Flat	Splayed out convex cutting edge.	Ibid., p.26, No.30
13	Majhadpur	Flat Axe	18.00x13.20x1.20	Flat	Straight sharp cutting edge, tapers towards butt end	Yule et al., op.cit., p.125
14	Chhotanagpur	Flat Axe	11.87x14.37x1.25	Flat	splayed out convex sharp cutting edge.	Ibid.,
15	Chhotanagpur	Flat Axe	17.64x14.70x1.17	Flat	As above but edge not sharp	Ibid., p.26, No.2
16	Chhotanagpur	Flat Axe	13.52x11.17x1.17	Flat	As above	Ibid.
17	Chhotanagpur	Flat Axe	9.40x6.46x?	Flat	As above	Ibid.
18	Padaliya (Chittor) Rajasthan	Flat Axe	(20-25)x(8.12)x?	Rectangular	Slightly splayed out, convex sharp with flat butt ends	Agrawal, op.cit., Pp.91-92, Pl.I
19	Elena (Jalore) Rajasthan	Flat Axe	17.00x9.00x?	Rectangular	As above	Ibid., Pl.II
20	Dhaka	Shouldered Axe	19.20x15.20x0.80	Flat	Round sharp cutting edge, flat	Ancient India No. 7, p.26
21	Dhaka	Shouldered Axe	17.20x14.80x0.80	Flat	As above	Ibid., No.6, p.26
22	Dhaka	Shouldered Axe	26.20x17.20x0.80	Flat	As above	Ibid., No. 10
23	Dhaka	Shouldered Axe	21.20x16.40x0.90	Flat	As above	Ibid., No. 12
24	Dunria	Shouldered Axe	20.00x17.60x1.20	Flat	Typical Shouldered celt with round cutting edge and round flat, but end round cutting edge, rest as above	Ibid., No. 8
25	Bhaktabundh (Bankura)	Shouldered Axe	22.50x21.50x?	Flat	As No. 23	IAR, 1966-67, p.81; Pl.LXIII A
26	Bhaktabundh (Bankura)	Shouldered Axe	17.50x14.00x?	Flat	As above	Ibid.,
27	Aguibani (Midnapur)	Shouldered Axe	17.50x15.50x?	Flat	As above	IAR, 1966-67, p.81; Pl.LXIII B
28	Aguibani (Midnapur)	Shouldered Axe	11.25x9.25x?	Flat	As above	Ibid.,
29	Chhotanagpur	Shouldered Axe	18.12x15.00x1.25	Flat	As above	Yule et al., op. cit., p.125
30	Chhotanagpur	Shouldered Axe	21.87x18.75x2.18	Flat	As above	Ibid.,
31	Chhotanagpur	Shouldered Axe	18.75x15.62x1.25	Flat	As above	Ibid.,
32	Kulgara (Pulia)	Shouldered Axe	20.00x16.00x?	Flat	As above	IAR 1971-72, P.51; Pl.LXV (A)

Chalcolithic Cultures of Central India and Deccan

Some of the chalcolithic cultures in the form of pocket cultures, usually non-urban, flourished in different parts of India. These cultures yielded very few copper artifacts, although some of them were more or less contemporary or rather late contemporary with the Harappan culture. Excavations at different parts of the country indicate that makers of these cultures were notably inferior in metallurgical know-how in comparison to that of the Harappans. Dhavalikar, however, maintains that the people of the Kayatha culture of central India had mastery on the copper technology, from a notable exception (Dhavalikar 1979: 233). But the quality of copper artifacts of most of the other post Harappan cultures is definitely inferior to those of Harappans. The reason, however, is difficult to ascertain. These cultures are discussed in the following heads.

(i) Kayatha culture

This culture is known after the name of the site Kayatha, located in the district Ujjain, Madhya Pradesh. The available radiocarbon dates suggest a time bracket of circa 2000-1800 B.C. for this culture (Dhawalikar 1979: 230). The only excavated sites of this culture is Kayatha though, Kayatha wares have been explored from about forty other sites (Agrawal 1984: 222). Only two axes, besides a dozen copper bangles and a fragmentary chisel of copper were unearthed by the excavators (Ansari & Dhawalikar 1975: 151, Pl. XXIII, fig.82).

The axes have been cast in moulds (Dhawalikar1979: 232). This practice is not found in the later Chalcolithic cultures of central India and Deccan, where similar artefacts were made just by hammering and heating. The following table records the various parameters of these axes.

Table 2

Sl. No.	Tool type	LengthxBreadth (cms)	Cross Section	Edge Form	Edge Profile
1	Axe	11.50x8.10	Lenticular	Convex sharp, slightly splayed out, tapers towards thicker butt end, sides bevelled forming a ridge, bears three indentation marks.	Biconvex
2	Axe	16.20x9.99	Lenticular	Convex sharp, slightly splayed out, tapers towards thicker butt end, sides bevelled forming a ridge, bears three indentation marks.	Biconvex

(ii) The Ahar culture

The Ahar or Ahad (Sankalia *et al.* 1969) culture, a late contemporary of the Harappan, is known after the key-sites Ahar near modern Udaipur in south-east Rajasthan. It is also known as 'Banas culture' after the distribution pattern of the key-sites of the culture along the banks of the river Banas and its tributaries. The Banas culture is purely copper using culture at Ahar (Allchin & Allchin1968: 183) but it is chalcolithic (Sankalia 1974: 418) at some other Aharian sites. At Gilund (IAR 1959-60: 41; Allchin & Allchin 1968: 184) a few microliths and copper objects are reported from the Aharian phase. A pure Aharian chalcolithic phase has been found at Navdatoli (Sankalia *et al.* 1969: 13-38). Though more than four dozen sites are known of this culture, only three sites viz; Ahar, Gilund and Navdatoli have been excavated so far (Agrawal 1984: 211). The culture may be assigned a date of circa 1800-1300 B.C. (Sankalia *et al.* 1969: 42) which differs only marginally from the time bracket of circa 2000-1400 B.C. (Agrawal 1984: 214) proposed by Agrawal for this culture. All metal objects are of copper. The following table records the details of the axes-

Table 3

Sl. No.	Site	Type	LengthxBreadthx (cms)	Thickness	Cross Section	Edge, Form etc
1	Ahar	Axe	12.50x11.00	0.35	Lenticular	Splayed out, sharp convex, blade tapers towardsbutt end
2	Ahar	Axe	12.50x9.80	0.50	Lenticular	Splayed out, sharp convex, tapers towards butt end
3	Navdatoli	Axe	6.20x12.00	1.00	Lenticular	Not Splayed out, slightly convex sharp, cutting edge broad.

The table shows that the Aharians used a limited number and variety of agriculture implements like axes. Besides some pieces of copper are indicative or the copper working by these people. It is noted that the axes of Ahar are one of the fine pieces in the chalcolithic culture complex of central, south and western India.

(iii) The Malwa culture:

Since this culture is mainly distributed in the Malwa region in central India, it is usually referred to as Malwa culture in literature. The Ahar culture was succeeded by the Malwa culture without any gap at certain sites, though chronogically, the Malwa culture flourished around cira 1600 B.C. and continued upto1300 B.C. This is also supported by available radiocarbon dates (Agrawal1984: 235). Besides the representative site of Navdatoli, which is the site par excellence of the Malwa culture, it also flourished at Nagada (IAR 1955-56: 14) (Ujjain), Maheshwar (Sankalia *et al.* 1958: 209), Eran (IAR 1960-61: 17), (Sagar) and Awra (IAR 1959-60: 24) (Mandasor) in Madhya Pradesh and Inamgaon (Dhawalikar1979: 236) and Daimabad (Dhawalikar 1979: 232) (both in district Ahmednagar) in Maharashtra. Some remains of Malwa culture have also been found at Kayatha (M.P) and Prakash

(Maharashtra). To the best of our knowledge, metal tools belonging to the Malwa culture have been reported only from Navdatoli, Eran and Awra in Madhya Pradesh and Daimabad in Maharashtra. The available details of the some of the axes is given hereunder:

Table 4

Sl. No.	Site	Tool Type	Length x Breadth x Thick ness (CMS)	Cross section	Nature of edge.
1.	Navdatoli	Axe	16.10x11.90x0.80	Rectangular, converging to a point at one end.	Crescentic sharp, concave tapering sides top flat.
2.	Navdatoli	Axe	12.50x9.80x(?)	Rectangular, converging to a point at one end.	Crescentic sharp, concave tapering sides top flat.
3.	Navdatoli	Axe	12.4x10.4x0.8	Rectangular, converging to a Point at both the ends.	Convex sharp, concave tapering sides. Top Convex.
4.	Navdatoli	Axe	15.6x11.6x1.00	Rectangular. Converging to a point at both the ends.	Convex sharp. Concave tapering sides. Top convex.
5.	Navdatoli	Axe	6.2x12.0x1.	Rectangular.	Slightly convex sharp sides straight
6.	Navdatoli	Axe	5.1x3.3x0.8 (Extant)	Rectangular.	Not clear
7.	Awra	Fragment Axe	No details available.		
8	Eran	(Fragmentary)	12.36x9.04x(?)	Rectangular.	Convex sharp.

On the basis of the above table it may be concluded that at least four sites have yielded objects of metal belonging to the Malwa culture. The inhabitants practiced agriculture is indicated by the axes found in the Malwa culture.

(iv) Lustron Red ware culture:

The evidence of the co-existence of the Harappan and a local style of material culture, known as Lustrous Red ware culture has been found at Lothal and Surkotada in the Saurashtra and cutch region of Gujarat State. The Phase II at Lothal which succeeds the mature Harappan phase At the site is characterised by certain new cultural traits in the pottery forms, painting style etc, besides the existing Harappan features" The period has yielded two calibrated radiocarbon dates 2160 and 2140 B.C (Allchin & Allchin 1983: 243) Here it needs to be emphasised that these dates are indicative of the partial withdrawal of colonial impact of the Harappans from the region" the shift of the Harappans resulted in the growth and development of several new aspects of an independent local culture in the region. This phenomenon of local cultural traits was also noticed at some other sites of the region viz: Rangpur. Prabhas Patan (Somnath) and Rojadi (Agrawal 1984; 193) the final stage of the development of this culture also known as Lustrous Red ware culture after its typical pottery type is represented by Phase III at Rangpur and Prabhas Patan and Phase II at Rojadi Unfortunately. The exact chronology of the culture has not yet been asccrtained. It is generally believed that the lustrous red ware culture continued upto circa 1500 B.C." only Prabhas Patan has yielded an axes of copper, details of which are not available.

(V) The Jorwe Culture

Sotiated on the bank of river Pravara, the site Jorwe (district Ahmednagar, Maharashtra) was discovered by S.A. Sali in 1950 and excavated by H.D. Sankalia and S.B. Deo in 1955 .the culture is known afte the first discovered site. Though some times it is also referred to as Jorwe- Nevasa culture. Theculture flourished nearly all over Maharashtra, excepting the coastal region of Konkan (Agrawal 1984: 235) The pravara-Godavari valleys are the cradle of the culture. ,most of the sites fall in the Deccan plateau. The main excavated sites are Lnamagaon (IAR 1968-69: 19;1969-70: 27; 1077-78: 44) Theur (IAR 1969-70: 20) Songaon (Deo 1969:44) and Chandoli (Deo & Ansari 1965) in district Poona; Bahal (IAR 1956-57) in district Jalgain; Prakash (Thapar 1964-65) indistrict Dhulia and Jorwe, Nasik (Sankalia & Deo 1959) and Nevasa (Sankalia *et al.* 1959) in district Ahmednagar (IAR 1971-72: 35). Besides, the evidence for this culture also comes form Sastevadi district Poona and Daimabad (IAR 1975-76: 33; 1976-77: 36) district Ahmednagar.

The Jorwe ware is the Hallmark of this culture, (Sankalia & Deo 1959: 37-86) It comprises a red or range matt surface painted with geometric designs in black. A time bracket of circa 1400-1100 B.C is assigned to this culture on the basis of radiocarbon dates, although its late phase at some sites like Lnamgaon seemed to have continued upto the early historical period. Metal tools are reported from all the excavated sites except Songaon and Prakash. The available details of agrieultural tools are given in the following table.

Table 5

Sl. No.	Slte	Type	Metal	Length/Breadth (CMS)	Thickness /Dlam.	Cross Section	Nature of edge/point,ete.	Remarks	Pd.phsse
1.	Nevasa	Axe	Copper	4.5x6.10	0.20	Flat	Splayed out convex sharp. Profile bieconvex	Splayed out convex sharp. Profile bieconvex	III
2.	Chandol i	Axe	Copper	10.90x6.70	0.15	Flat	Slightly Splayed out convex sharp	Slightly Splayed out convex sharp	III.IV
3.	Jorwe	Axe	Bronze	6.90x7.30(ext.)	1.20	Flat	Slightsly splayed out convex sharp Profile of edge biconvex	Slightsly splayed out convex sharp Profile of edge biconvex	Jorwe unstratifi ed

4.	Jorwe	Axe	Bronze	6.6x7.5(ext)	1.30	Flat	As above	As above	Jorwe unstratified
5.	Jorwe	Axe	Bronze	14.2x7.20	1.30	Flat	Not splayed Straight sharp edges. Profile concavo convex	Not splayed Edge although excavator classifies it as celt.	Jorwe unstratified
6.	Jorwe	Axe	Bronze	12.6x6.60	1.30	Flat	Slightly splayed out convex sharp biconvex profile	Broken in two parts. Thickness uniform.	Jorwe unstratified
7.	Jorwe	Axe	Bronze	14.3x7.80	1.00	Flat	Not splayed straight sharp cutting edge. Profile biconvex.	Thickness & width uniform	Jorwe unstratified
8.	Jorwe	Axe	Bronze	14.4x7.10	0.90	Flat	Slightly splayed, Slightly convex sharp. Profile biconvex	Some part of edge broken.	Jorwe unstratified

Conclusion

Some of the Copper Hoards contain such utilitarian implements like various types ot axes, one Khurpi one suspected ploughshare and one hatehet (parasu) though these hardly form the diagnostic feature of the Copper Hoards, varous types of the axes, flat axes, shouldered axes, bar axes, double exe, etc, form the single largest group of implements; and these are followed by harpoons anthropomorphic figure and sword. The relative frequency of various implements indicates that the authors of this culture were more or less nomadic people having limited means and needs. The presence of very large number of axes indicates that forest clearance was the basic need of the communities. Pastoralism and fishing appears to be two basic feature of their economy. Agriculture if practised must have been in an incipient stage. The presence of bar axes in fairly large number in Chhotanagpur copper Hoards may perhaps be taken as an evidence for agricultural operations as they could have been best used as digging implements and not as axes. Could it be argued here that they have also been used for digging pits for fixing wooden logs while preparing huts? Agrawal however. Suggest that these bar axes were used for mining ores whereas shouldered and flat type of axes ware probably used for cutting wood or hunting animals.

In the chalcolithic culture of central India and Deccan, copper implements, are rather poorly represented. Almost all the sites representing these culture have yielded copper axes. Though their proportion differs from site to site. Their occurrence signifies that forest clearance was an important need of all these communities, particularly.

for preparing fields for cultivation. The available evidence suggests that all of them were peasant communication, also practising domestication of animals and hunting. was also adopted as a supplement to economy by some of these cultures like Malwa and Jorwe culture. To sum up, the chalcolithic cultures of central and Deccan used copper very sparingly and perhaps carried out their day-to-day activities with the help of stone and wooden objects.

References

Agrawal, D.P., 1971, *The Copper Bronze Age in India* .

Agrawal, D.P., 1984, *The Archaeology of India*, Delhi.

Agrawal, D.P. and Rajan Sheshadri, 1998, The *Matalluragical Tradition of the Harappans Archaeometallurgy in India*, V. Tripathi (ed.), Delhi: Sharda Publhishing House.

Ansari, Z.D. and M.K. Dhavalikar, 1975, *Excavations at Kaytha*, Poona .

Allchin, B. and F.R. Allchin, 1968, *The Birth of Indian Civilization*, Britain .

Allchin,1983, *Bridge and Raymond, The Rise of Civilization in India and Pakistan*, Delhi.

Coggin-Brown, J., 1961, Futher relise of Copper age, *JBAORS.*

Deshpande, M.N., *IAR 1965-66.*

Dhavalikar, M.K., 1979, Early Farming cultures of Central India, *Essays in Indian Protohistory*, D.P. Agrawal and D.K. Chakrabarti (eds.), Delhi.

Deo. S.B., Z.D. Ansari 1965, *Chalcolithic Chandoli*, Poona.

Deo, S.B., 1969, *Songaon Excavaions 1965*, Poona.

Gaur,R.C.,1983, *Excavations of Atranjikhera*, Delhi.

Gupta, S.P., A new Tool-type of the Copper Hoard, *Puratattava 11.*

IAR 1955-56;1956-571959-60; 1960-61; IAR 1961-62; 1962-63, 1963-64; 1968-69; 1969-70; 1971-72; 1975-76; 1976-77;1977-78.

Lal, B.B., 1951, Further Copper Hoadrs from Gangetic basin and a review of the problem, *Ancient India 7.*

Lal, B.B., Excavations of Saipali, *Puratattva 5* .

Lal, B.B., The Cooper Hoard culture of Ganga Velley, *Antiquary 46.*

Lal, Makkhan,1984, *Settlement Histoy and Rise of Civilization in Ganga-Yamuna Dab.*

Sankalia, H.D., B. Subbarao and S.B. Deo, 1958, *Excavations at Maheshwar and Navdatoli*, Poona .

Sankalia, H.D.,1959, *From History to Perhistory at Nevasa*, Poona.

Sankalia, H.D and S.B. Deo 1959, *Reports on the Excavations at Nasik and Jorwe1951*, Poona.

Sankalia, H.D., S.B. Deo and Z.D. Ansari, 1969, *Excavations at Ahar*, Poona.

Sankalia, H.D.,1974, *The Prehistory and Protohistory of India and Pakistan*, Poona.

Thapur, B.K., Prakash, 1955, *Ancient India 20&21.*

Yule, P. and Theil-Hosrtamann, Monika, 1985, The Copper Hoard Artefacts in the S.C. Roy Collection, Ranchi: *Man in India Vol 65.*

12

मध्य सोन घाटी से प्राप्त पुरापाषाणिक अश्मीभूत जैविक अवशेषों का विश्लेषण

विनोद यादव

भारत की प्रागैतिहासिक संस्कृतियों के अध्ययन के लिए मध्य सोन घाटी का विशेष महत्व रहा है। सोन नदी भारत की प्राचीनतम नदियों में से एक है, जो मध्य प्रदेश के अमरकण्टक पहाड़ी से निकलकर उत्तर-पश्चिम दिशा में बहती हुई बिहार प्रान्त के पटना के निकट गंगा नदी में मिलती है। यहाँ पर यह उल्लेखनीय है कि सोन नदी के मार्ग में प्रारम्भ से लेकर अब तक कोई विशेष परिवर्तन नहीं हुआ है। सोन घाटी के प्रागैतिहासिक महत्व की ओर येल-कैम्ब्रिज अभियान दल के डी. टेरा (टेरा एण्ड पैटरसन 1939: 313.) तथा उनके बाद ज्वायनर (1963 : 57) ने विद्वानों का ध्यान आकर्षित किया था। आरम्भ में राधाकांत वर्मा (1964: 73.75) तथा निसार अहमद (1984: 4-117) ने ऊपरी सोन घाटी का सर्वेक्षण कार्य किया। कालान्तर में इलाहाबाद विश्वविद्यालय के प्राचीन इतिहास, संस्कृति एवं पुरातत्व विभाग ने जी. आर. शर्मा के निर्देशन में मध्य सोन घाटी का विस्तृत सर्वेक्षण करके प्रातिनूतन कालीन भूतात्विक जमावों की पहचान की।

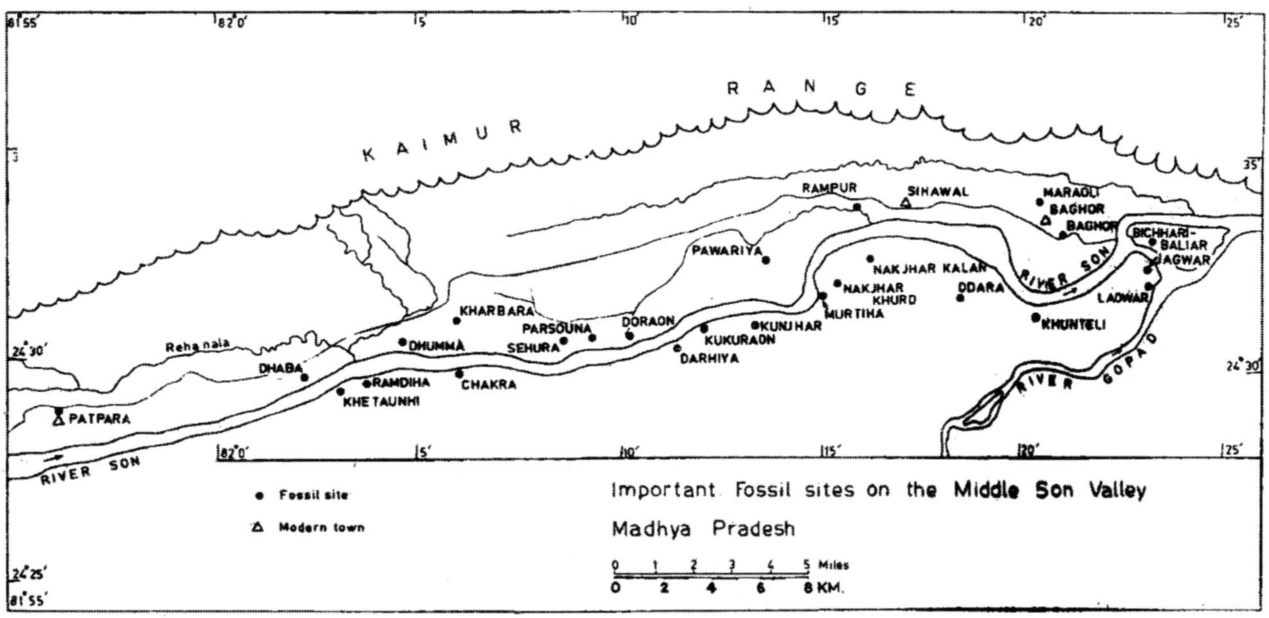

रेखाचित्र 1: मध्य सोन घाटी, जीवाश्म स्थल

इलाहाबाद विश्वविद्यालय के प्राचीन इतिहास, संस्कृति एवं पुरातत्व विभाग द्वारा सन् 1975–78 के बीच मध्य सोन घाटी में किए गए सर्वेक्षण के फलस्वरूप भूतात्विक जमावों से हजारों पशु जीवाश्म मिले हैं। मध्य सोनघाटी से जीवाश्म वितरण प्रक्रिया (Faunal Distribution Patternh) एवं वर्गीकरण (Taxonomic) समूह के आधार पर 1000 तथा कुल लगभग 6000 जीवाश्म एकत्र किए गए हैं। मध्य सोन घाटी में लगभग 14000 वर्ग किलोमीटर क्षेत्र में पुरातात्विक और भूतात्विक सर्वेक्षण किया गया था, जो उत्तर में कैमूर, दक्षिण में सोन तथा गोपद नदी का संगम, पूर्व में बीछी तथा पश्चिम में चुरहट से घिरी है (रेखाचित्र–1)। मध्य सोन घाटी के सर्वेक्षण में सन् 1980–82 ई. में कैलिफोर्निया स्थित वर्कले विश्वविद्यालय के जे. डी. क्लार्क के सहयोगी पुरातत्ववेत्ताओं, नृतत्वशास्त्रियों एवं भूतत्ववेत्ताओं के दल ने भी अपना सहयोग दिया था। आस्ट्रेलिया के मैक्कायर विश्वविद्यालय के मार्टिन विलियम्स तथा उनके सहयोगियों द्वारा मध्य सोन घाटी के भूतात्विक अनुसंधान के परिणाम स्वरुप आधार शिला के ऊपर पाँच भूतात्विक जमाव खेतौंही, बघोर, पटपरा, खुण्टेली तथा सिहावल (ऊपर से नीचे) प्राप्त हुए हैं (विलियम्स एण्ड कीथरॉयस 1983: 9.21)। इनका विवरण तालिका–1 के माध्यम से नीचे प्रस्तुत किया जा रहा है।

तालिका 1: सोन घाटी के भूतात्विक जमाव का विवरण

क्र.	भूतात्विक जमाव	आश्मिक इकाई	संस्कृति	संभावित तिथि	संभावित जलवायु
1	खेतौंही जमाव (10मीटर)	मिट्टी, सिल्ट एवं बालू	मध्यपाषाण, नवपाषाण एवं उच्च पुरापाषाण कालीन संस्कृति	मध्य नूतन काल (10,000 बी.पी.)	आर्द्र (Warm wet)
2	बघोर जमाव (20 मीटर)	सिल्ट, बालू मिट्टी एवं पीली भूरी मिट्टी	मध्य पुरापाषाण से उच्च पुरापाषाण युगीन संस्कृति	अन्त प्रातिनूतन से आरम्भिक नूतन काल (30,000–10,000 बी.पी.)	आर्द से शुष्क (Warm wet to cold dry)
3	पटपरा जमाव (10 मीटर)	ग्रैवेल जमाव एवं लाल मिट्टी	मध्य पुरापाषाण युगीन संस्कृति	उच्च प्राति नूतन काल (100,000–30,000 बी.पी.)	आर्द्र (Dry)
4	खुण्टेली जमाव (10 मीटर)	पीली मिट्टी, ज्वालामुखी राख	मध्य पुरापाषाणयुगीन संस्कृति	मध्यपुरापाषाण काल (100,000–75,000 बी.पी.)	आर्द्र शुष्क
5	सिहावल जमाव	बालू, सिल्ट मिट्टी, ग्रैवेल	निम्न पुरापाषाण युगीन संस्कृति	मध्य से आरम्भिक प्रातिनूतन काल (100,000 बी.पी.)	शुष्क (Dry)

बघोर जमाव दो भागों, नीचे रूक्ष वर्ग एवं ऊपर महीन वर्ग में विभाजित किया गया है। बघोर जमाव का निचला भाग उच्च पुरापाषाणिक संस्कृति से सम्बन्धित है, जिसमें भारी मात्रा में जीवाश्म प्राप्त हुए हैं। ऊपरी भाग में कुछ जीवाश्म पटपरा और बघोर जमाव के संधि स्थल से भी मिले हैं, इसमें जैविक अवशेष अपेक्षाकृत कम प्राप्त हुए हैं।

1. बघोर जमाव के केवल निचले भाग से 40 से अधिक प्रकार के पशुओं के जीवाश्म प्राप्त हुए हैं। इन एकत्र किए गए जीवाश्मों में 5.10% जीवाश्म पटपरा एवं बघोर जमाव के संक्रमण से उपलब्ध हुए हैं। खुण्टेली एवं सिहावल जमाव

से अभी तक कोई जीवाश्म नहीं प्राप्त हुआ है। खेतौंही जमाव से भी कुछ जीवाश्म प्राप्त हुए हैं, लेकिन ये अच्छी दशा में नहीं हैं। इन पशु जीवाश्मों में अधिकांशतः खोपड़ी, जबड़ा, हड्डी, दाँत एवं अन्य अस्थियाँ हैं। इनमें अधिकतर जीवाश्म टूटे हुए हैं (बादाम, मिश्र, पाण्डेय एवं पाल 1989: 41-46)। मध्य सोनघाटी से प्राप्त इन पशु जीवाश्मों में वार्किंग डीयर (मुन्टिआकस मँटजक), हॉग डीयर (एक्सिस पॉर्सिनॅस), ऐन्टिलोप (ऐन्टिलोप सर्वीकप्रा), चीतल (ऐक्सिस-ऐक्सिस), गॅजेल (चिंकारा), नीलगाय, साँभर डीयर, बारहसिंगा आदि प्रमुख हैं, जिनको अन्त प्रातिनूतन काल से नूतनकाल के मध्य रखा गया है। इनके अतिरिक्त बॉस नमडिकस (चित्र-1), इक्वॅस नमडिकस, एलीफॅस नमडिकस (चित्र-2, 3) मध्य से अन्त प्रातिनूतन काल के मध्य रखे जा सकते हैं। इस प्रकार के साक्ष्य प्रायद्वीपीय नदी घाटियों से भी मिले हैं। अधिकांश नदी घाटियों के जीवाश्म अन्त प्रातिनूतन काल से नूतनकाल के मध्य रखे जा सकते हैं।

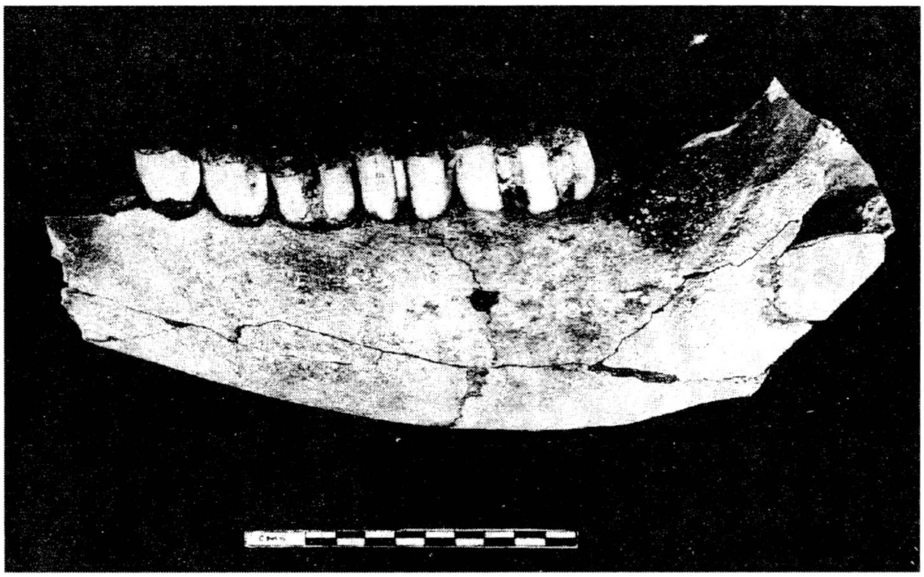

चित्र 1: सोन घाटी से प्राप्त बॉस नमडिकस के निचले जबड़े का जीवाश्म

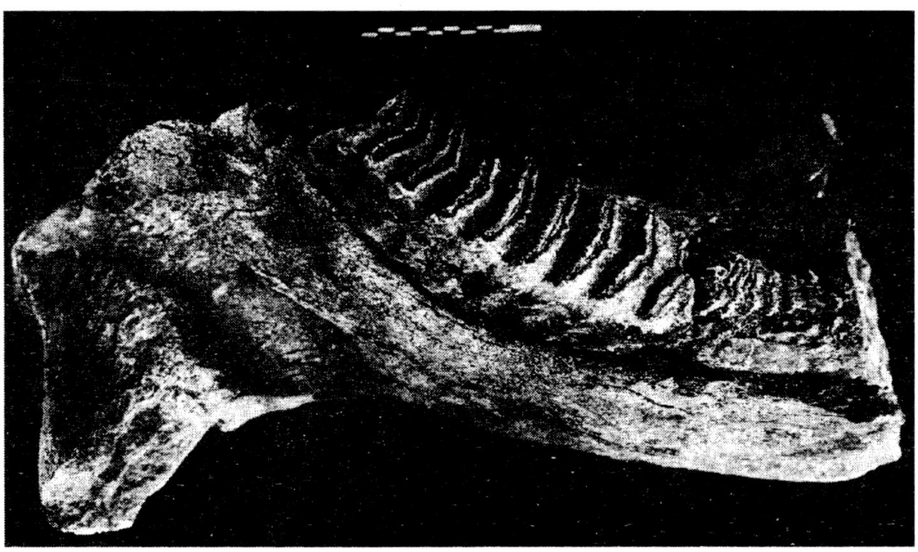

चित्र 2: सोन घाटी से प्राप्त हाथी के निचले जबड़े का जीवाश्म

चित्र 3: सोन घाटी से प्राप्त हाथी का जीवाश्म

मध्य सोनघाटी से प्राप्त जीवाश्मों का विवरण इस प्रकार है (बादाम, मिश्र, पाण्डेय एवं पाल 1989: 43)। बघोर जमाव से प्राप्त पशु जीवाश्मों में बॉस नमडिकस, बॉस, गौर बॅवलस, ऐन्टिलोप, बॉस एलीफॅस, चौसिंहा, चिंकारा, चीतल, साँभर, हिरण, सुस, दरियाई घोड़ा (चित्र-4), गैंडा, इक्वॅस नमडिकस, इक्वॅस एसिनॅस, इलीफॅस, घड़ियाल (चित्र-5, 6), कछुआ, कार्निवोर और कृन्तक (रोडेन्ट्स) प्रमुख हैं (ब्लूमेनसाइन एवं चट्टोपाध्याय 1983: 281-84)।

1. पटपरा और बघोर जमाव के संधि स्थल से बॉस नमडिकस, बॉस गौर, दरियाई घोड़ा, इक्कस, साँभर, चीतल, घड़ियाल इत्यादि के जीवाश्म उपलब्ध हुए हैं।
2. खेतौंही सोन की अन्तिम वेदिका का जमाव है, यहाँ से भी कुछ जीवाश्म मिले हैं।
3. खुण्टेली और सिहावल से कोई भी जीवाश्म प्राप्त नहीं हुआ है।

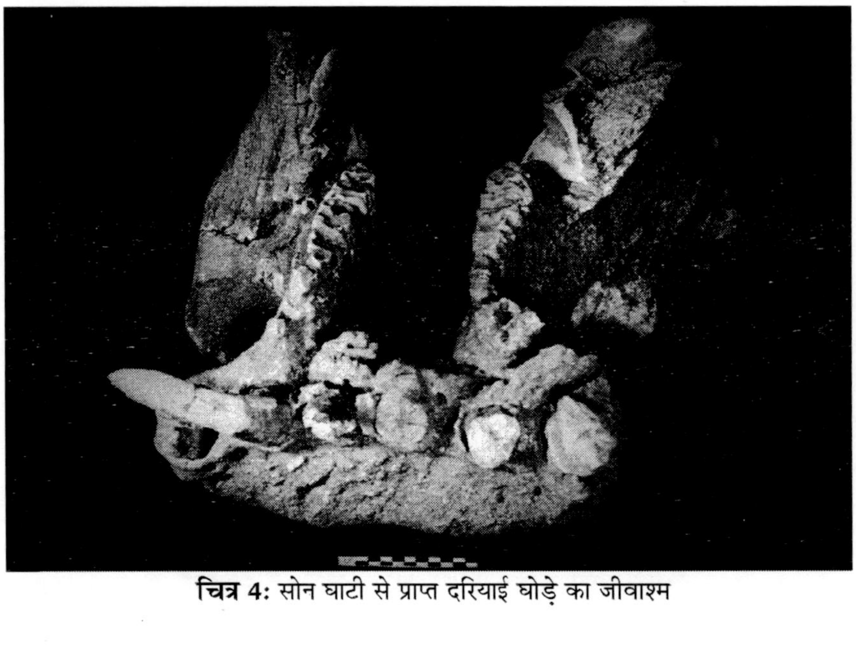

चित्र 4: सोन घाटी से प्राप्त दरियाई घोड़े का जीवाश्म

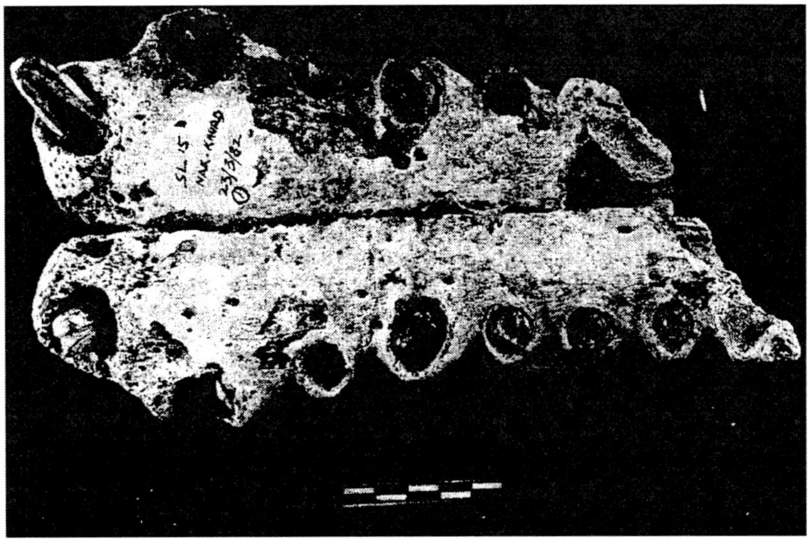

चित्र 5: सोन घाटी से प्राप्त घड़ियाल के ऊपरी जबड़े का जीवाश्म

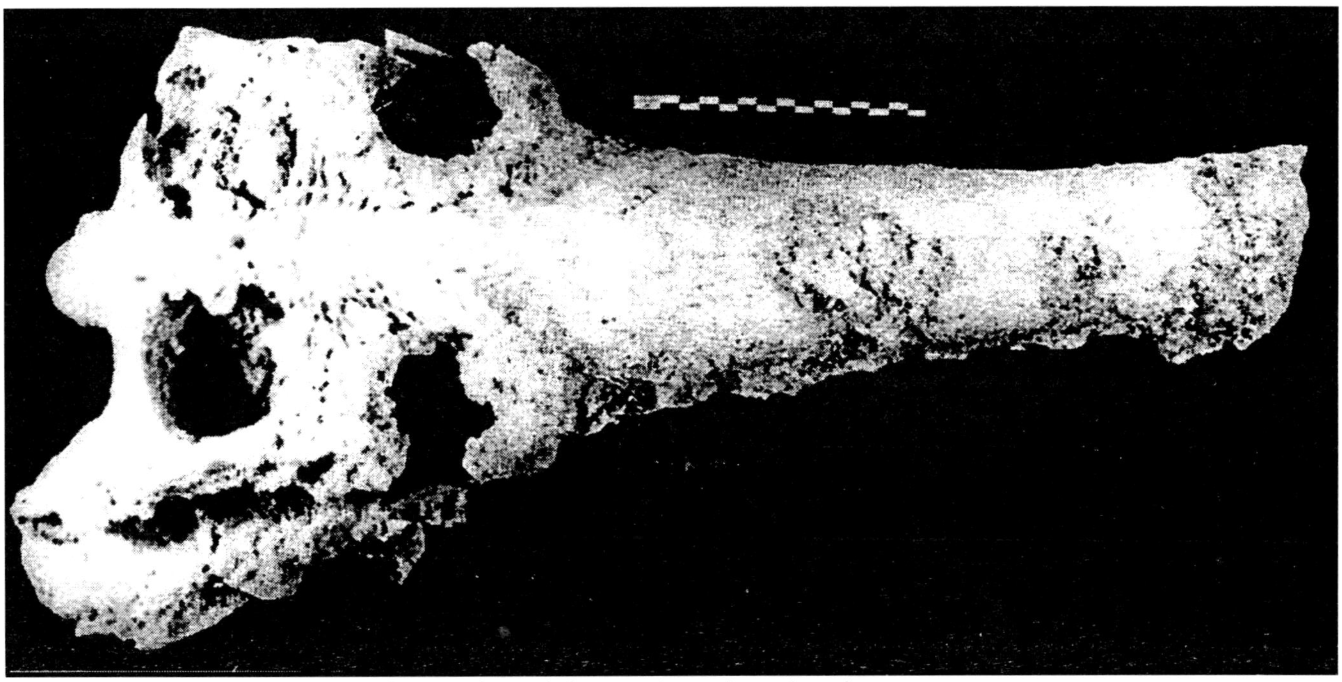

चित्र 6: सोन घाटी से प्राप्त घड़ियाल के ऊपरी जबड़े का पृष्ठभाग

अत: मध्य सोन घाटी से प्राप्त कतिपय जीवाश्मों को विशिष्ट वर्गों में वर्गीकृत किया जा सकता है। हिमालय के शिवालिक क्षेत्र तथा नर्मदा घाटी से भी पशु जीवाश्म मिले हैं। कतिपय जीवाश्म गोदावरी घाटी से तथा कुछ गंगा एवं यमुना के प्राचीन जमावों से प्राप्त हुए हैं। इस प्रकार विन्ध्य क्षेत्र से प्राप्त जीवाश्म उत्तर में हिमालय तथा दक्षिण में नर्मदा से प्राप्त जीवाश्म के खाली स्थान को पूर्ण करते हैं। जीवाश्मों की बहुलता की दृष्टि से सोन घाटी, नर्मदा घाटी से भी अधिक महत्वपूर्ण है (मिश्र 2007: 1-14)।

मध्य सोनघाटी से प्राप्त जीवाश्मों में सम्पूर्ण में से 85% वर्गीकृत किये गये हैं। एकत्र किए गए कुल जीवाश्मों का 88% अभिज्ञेय (Identifiable) है। इनमें 90% जीवाश्म दाँत एवं जबड़े हैं। परन्तु कुछ जीवाश्म अभिज्ञेय नहीं हैं। अभिज्ञेय जीवाश्मों का वर्गीकरण निम्नलिखित प्रकार से किया गया है (ब्लूमेनसाइन एवं चट्टोपाध्याय 1983: 281-84)।

1. आरटियॉडक्टिला

1. बॉस गौरस
2. नीलगाय
3. चिंकारा
4. चौसिंहा
5. सॉभर
6. चीतल
7. सुस (सुअर)
8. हिरण
9. जंगली सुअर।

2. पेरिसडक्टिला

1. इक्वॅस स्पेसीज
2. गैंडा

3. एलीफैन्टिडा

1. एलीफॅस स्पेसीज।

4. कार्निवॅरा (बादाम1979: 250)

1. जंगली बिल्ली
2. लकड़बग्घा जाति (Hyaena)
3. लंगूर
4. भालू।

5. रॉडेन्टिआ

1. गिलहरी
2. जॉबिल (हिरनमूसा)
3. चूहा
4. खरगोश
5. साही।

6. अस्तनधारी (Non-Mammalian)

1. कछुआ
2. घड़ियाल
3. घोंघा (Mollusca)

1. इसी प्रकार बेलन घाटी से प्राप्त पशुओं की हड्डियों के प्रतिशत में 24% हाथी, 64% गाय, 4% बारहसिंगा तथा 8% अन्य पशु हैं। सोन घाटी में गाय और भैंसा 45%, हाथी 5%, घोड़ा 9%, बारहसिंगा 12%, हिरण 6% तथा दरियाई घोड़ा, गैड़ा आदि 2% है (शर्मा 1985: 25)।
2. सोन घाटी के पटपरा से प्राप्त बहुसंख्यक पत्तियों के जीवाश्मों के आधार पर यह कहा जा सकता है कि वर्तमान काल की वनस्पतियों की तुलना में प्रातिनूतन काल में वनस्पतियाँ अधिक सघन थी। इन वनस्पतियों में टुण्ड्रा एवं टैगा प्रकार के पेड़-पौधों की प्रमुखता थी। मध्य सानेघाटी से प्राप्त पत्तियों के जीवाश्मों से पुरापर्यावरण के अध्ययन में विशेष सुविधा मिलती है (वर्मा 1991: 180-83)।

संदर्भ

अहमद, निसार, 1984, *द स्टोन एज कल्चर्स ऑफ द अपर सोन वैली,* मध्य प्रदेश, पीएच.डी. थीसिए, पुणे: दकन कॉलेज

ज्वायनर, एफ. ई., 1963, *इनवायरनमेंट ऑफ अर्ली मैन विद स्पेशल रिफरेंस टू द ट्रापिकल रीजन्स,* बड़ौदा : एम.एस. राव विश्वविद्यालय

डी. टेरा, एच.एण्ड टी.टी. पैटरसन, 1939, *स्टडीज ऑन द आइस एज इन इण्डिया एण्ड एसोसिएटेड ह्यूमन कल्चर्स,* वाशिंगटन : कारनेजी इंस्टीट्यूट, पब्लिकेशन नं. 493

ब्लूमेनसाइन, आर.जे. एवं यू.सी. चट्टोपाध्याय, 1983, ए प्रीलिमिनरी रिपोर्ट ऑन द टर्मिनल प्लाइटोसीन फौना ऑफ द मिडिल सोन वैली, जी.आर. शर्मा एण्ड जे.डी. क्लाक (सं.), *पैलियोएनवायरनमेण्ट्स एण्ड प्रीहिस्ट्री इन द मिडिल सोन वैली,* मध्य प्रदेश, नार्थ सेण्ट्रल इण्डिया, इलाहाबाद : अविनाश प्रकाशन

बादाम, जी.एल. 1979, *प्लाइस्टोसीन फाना ऑफ इण्डिया,* पुणे: दकन कॉलेज पी.जी.आर.आई.

बादाम, जी.एल., वी.डी. मिश्र, जे.एन. पाण्डेय एवं जे.एन. पाल, 1989, ए प्रीलिमिनरी स्टडी ऑफ प्लाइस्टोसीन फॉसिल्स फ्राम द मिडिल सोन वैली, मध्य प्रदेश, *मैन एण्ड एनवायरमेण्ट XIII*

मिश्र, वी.डी., 2007, स्टोन एज कल्चर्स, देयर क्रोनोलॉजी एण्ड विगनिंग ऑफ एग्रीकल्चर इन नार्थ-सेण्ट्रल इण्डिया, *मैन एण्ड एनवायरनमेण्ट, वाल्यूम 32, नं.1*

वर्मा, आर. के., 1964, *स्टोन एज कल्चर्स ऑफ मिर्जापुर,* डी. फिल. थीसिस, इलाहाबाद: विश्वविद्यालय

वर्मा, आर. के., 1991, *रीवा थ्रो द एजेज,* अवधेश प्रताप सिंह विश्वविद्यालय, रीवा: मध्य प्रदेश

वर्मा, आर. के., एस.एन. मिश्रा एण्ड एस. भटनागर, 1994, पैलियोबायोलॉजिकल एक्सप्लारेशन ऑफ आर्कियोलॉजिकल साइट नियर पटपरा इन चुरहट, सीधी (म.प्र.), *आर्ट एण्ड आर्कियोलॉजी ऑफ दि विन्ध्यन रीजन एण्ड आर्यन्स : ए मिथ आर रियलिटी,* आर. के. वर्मा (सं.) रीवा: ए.पी.एस. यूनिवर्सिटी

विलियम्स, मार्टिन एण्ड कीथरॉयस, 1983, एलुवियल हिस्ट्री ऑफ द मिडिल सोन वैली, नार्थ-सेण्ट्रल इण्डिया, *पैलियो इनवायरनमण्ट्स एण्ड प्रीहिस्ट्री इन द मिडिल सोन वैली,* शर्मा जी.आर. एण्ड जे. डी. क्लार्क (सं.), इलाहाबाद: अविनाश प्रकाशन

शर्मा, जी.आर., 1985, *भारतीय संस्कृति: पुरातात्विक आधार,* नई दिल्ली: नेशनल पब्लिसिंग हाउस

13

Excavations at the Early Iron Age Megalithic site of Mahurjhari, Vidarbha (2001-2004); Reinvestigation and All Over Again : A Model Expansion

R.K. Mohanty

Introduction: Vidarbha Megaliths and Place of Mahurjhari

Vidarbha, the north-eastern region of the Maharashtra state comprising of districts viz. Yavatmal, Akola, Amravati, Wardha, Buldhana, Washim, Nagpur, Chandrapur, Bhandara, Gadchiroli and Gondia is abounded with archeological remains starting from the Palaeolithic to the late historical period. The region is rich in mineral resources, fertile landscape inter spaced with low-lying hills and deciduous forest coverage. Besides moderate precipitation in monsoonal seasons, the natural waterbodies and rivers (Wainganga and it's major tributaries, the Wardha, Kanhan, and Painganga and in the northern part it is drained by five small tributaries i.e. Khapra, Sipna, Gadga, Dolar and Purna of the river Tapti) provided a conducive atmosphere for people to occupy this region at different cultural phases. Though Vidarbha was extensively inhabited during Iron Age, the megalithic burial custom and traditions of these people are discovered in many of these districts (Mohanty and Vaidya 2017; Sontakke 2014, Vaidya 2014) There are more than 100 Megalithic sites known from this region (Fig.1). These sites can be broadly classified into three categories looking into the present state of investigations of the Megalithic period. They are, 1) Megalithic Burial sites, 2) Megalithic Burial cum Habitation sites and 3) the habitation or settlement sites where megalithic cultural phase is present but not the burials in the nieghbourhood. The burials found in this region are mostly cairn circles and a few sites have given evidence of menhirs, pit burials, and cist burials (Mohanty and Vaidya 2017, Mohanty et al. 2017). Vidarbha has a few Megalithic habitation-cum-burial sites. They are Takalghatkhapa (Deo 1970), Mahurjhari (Deo 1973) Naikund (Deo and Jamkhedkar 1982), Khairwada (IAR 1981- 82: 51-52) , Bhagimohari (IAR 1982-83: 61-62; 1983-84: 57-58) and Pachkheri (Nath 2001-02). Except for Naikund, all these sites were also occupied during the Early Historic period. However, Mahurjhari was believed to be one of the few Megalithic sites known from Vidarbha, which was reported as early as 1933, to have been occupied only during the Early-historic period.

Though the site was operational for several hundred years during the Megalithic period, the evidence of the Early Iron Age/ Megalithic settlement at Mahurjhari remained enigmatic throughout its previous investigation. The occasional survey of the Early Historic settlement at Mahurjhari had, however, revealed the evidence of a copper plate, seals, Intaglios (Hunter 1933), beads, bricks, pottery and other antiquities of the Satavahana-Gupta / Vakataka period (C. 100 BC to about 500 AD) (Deo 1973a).

Mahurjhari: It's personality

The advent and spread of the Iron Age and associated Megalithism across the Indian Subcontinent and its manifestation in a regional context often vary in many ways. Its beginning, progress and time of spread, nature of expression, the very essence of iron processing methods, manufacturing of implements and further refinement and pattern of use seem not to be uniform across the Indian Subcontinent. One of the visible cultural revelations of the period was Megalithic ritual burials with diverse internal and external architecture using big stones (*Mega-Lithos*). Some of the burial types, though belonged to this cultural phase and appeared in the same burial ground, did not have stone appendages. Sometimes they are represented both in the sepulchral and non-sepulchral ways.

However, the credit of discovering the first Megaliths burials during the recent past is accredited to Babington in Malabar Coast, Kerala (Babington 1923: 324-30). Soon after his findings in India, the investigation in this field attracted several colonial antiquarians, officials and a few scholars coming from different parts of Europe. As some of them were amateur with limited experience and exposure in their own country, they approached the Indian findings in their perceived ideologies (Mohanty and Selva 2002: 313-335).

Keeping this in tempo, the investigation of Megaliths in the Vidarbha region similarly began under the urges of British officials and missionaries who were fascinated about discovering exciting cultural remains of the past in their functioning areas. These amateur and antiquarian colonial administrative officials-cumarchaeologist mostly used these findings in showcasing their intellect by reporting them in journals and often carried them to their native place as souvenir. The scholarship was valued and recognized in European society in accordance with aristocracy at that time (Pearse1869: 207-217). During the nineteenth century, several regions came under the Megalithic map and many sites were explored and some digging of burials also took place (Leshnik 1974, Moorti 1994, Mohanty and Selva 2002, Sundara 1975, 1998, Krishnaswami 1949; Kennedy 1975). From the early part of twentieth century, the scenario changed, explorations and excavations continued persistently revealing some of the most unknown facets of the Indian Megalithism (Mohanty and Selva 2002: 313-335).

Before getting into the Mahurjhari megalithic system, let us observe some of the early works which certainly remains important and probably continued to influence further research in later period in this region. As early as around 1849-50, Rev. Stephen Hislop a missionary functioning at Nagpur made valuable observations from his digging of megaliths at Takalghat, a few miles to the south-west of Nagpur city, in Vidarbha region of Maharashtra (Hislop1857: 671-672; Thakuria *et al.* 2012). Similarly in 1867, Major Pearse, who was employed in the Kamtee cantonment before leaving for England on vacation excavated a megalithic burial at Wurreegaon (about one and half km. from Kamptee, Nagpur district) in July 1867, about 20 km to the north of Nagpur (Pearse 1869: 207-217). He carried the recovered antiquities and presented the findings to the British Museum where it is preserved. His observations and arguments based on cultural findings in relation to the then understanding of the Indian Iron Age and Megalith's understanding were beyond his times. Taking circumstantial evidence available then, he had argued that the date of the beginning of the Iron Age and especially the building of megaliths in India and also at Kamtee should go back to 12thcentury BC.(Pearse 1869: 207-217).

Megalithic remains in Vidarbha formed an ideal region for a cohesive study. It not only has a concentration of more than 100 megalithic sites and many settlements pertaining to Iron Age culture, but it falls in the central zone of the subcontinent bridging Northern and Southern India forming an integral region for assimilation and dispersal of cultural personalities. The occurrence of Iron in the Indian context and the association of Megalithism remains a hot topic as it is debated to have given rise to the second urbanization and emergence of cities later on, besides its origin and diverse affiliation of ethnic groups. To peep into the emerging complexity of the society and to justify such a cultural-political development to accomplish a state of chronological development in many settlements' histories would certainly have helped. This was lacking.

However, an association of megaliths with settlements of this period was probably not keenly observed by the explorers and excavators during those days in India. This could be due to factors like megaliths were impressive, had noticeable visibility and easily recognizable on the landscape, and excavation produced valuable arte facts of cultural value which were more appreciated. They became a prized possession, formed mementos, displayable objects in the museums and rarely used for scientific analysis. The perception still has not drastically changed.

Looking into the Vidarbha region during the 20th century and till recent times, it remained under further investigation time and again not only for understanding Megalithism but for other historical cultural remains. The region, as mentioned above has more than 100 Iron Age Megalithic and numerous Early Historic settlements of which some of them being fortified sites, like Adam and Nagardhan and many more.

Among the explored and excavated sites in Vidarbha, Mahurjhari is one of the well-known Megalithic and Early Historic sites. It has many unique features and remains a very important site to understand the Iron Age Megalithism and subsequent Early Historical period. The site is situated in the District of Nagpur, Maharashtra (21o 14′ N; 79o 30′ E). It was first reported as early as 1933 by G.A.P. Hunter, a colonial antiquarian who wrote mostly on the casual findings from the surface (Hunter 1933: 30-35). The site is not far away from Nagpur city and is located some 18 km. north–east of the city, on the Nagpur–Katol road. The site was further visited by several scholars, but the systematic excavations of burials were undertaken for the first time by Late Prof. S.B. Deo, during the late sixties when he was teaching at the Nagpur University (Deo 1973a). The impressive burial complexes, dispersed in 10 locations (Fig.2), with variable external architecture with an arrangement of huge boulders occasionally with cup-marks dominates the landscape. The excavations have revealed disposal of the dead soon after the death or even twin burials in association with multiple secondary burials sometimes in one and same burial. The amount and placement of grave goods especially iron objects and other offerings are matchless as can be viewed in a regional perspective or even also can be compared in subcontinent specific (Deo 1973a). As the excavation had provided excellent evidence, Deo again took up the site for further excavation when he was back in his *alma mater*, Deccan College during 1978-79 (IAR 1978).

However, before taking up excavations at Mahurjhari, Deo had excavated at the site of Takalghat-Khapa a burial-cum- habitation site (Deo 1970). While the site was discovered by Rev. Hislop way back in the 1850′s, it had remained untouched till then. Now the site is completely destroyed. The site for the first time revealed a rare combination of megalithic sites associated with settlements with verifiable similar cultural remains. In most of the burial sites, this combination could not be found or believed to be absent. The disparity between the burial locations/sites with that of related habitation sites continued as a vexed problem till date in most regions in the sub-continent. Many hypotheses emerged of their absence and rare presence and sites were classified accordingly (Mohanty and Selva 2002: 313-335; Mohanty and Joshi 1996: 157-169).

Prof. Deo going for re-excavating at this site again may not be without reasons. Some of the obvious reasons could be evidence of a good number of skeletal remains, both primary and secondary to answer some ethnic-related problems, varied architecture, impressive artefacts reflecting various utility, and economic diversity unparalleled to any other site anywhere in India then. By this time Deo was already known as a pioneer in Early Iron Age megalithic research in the subcontinent. However, due to some unknown reasons,this season′s excavation report is not available except briefly mention of the same in IAR: 1978-79.

In this scenario, with repeated investigations and excavation, with rich and uncommon antiquity remains, the habitation during the Iron Age alluded at Mahurjhari. We are knowing more about their death rituals, but not much about their lifeways. This was puzzling to Deo and Jamkhedkar of State Archaeology, Maharashtra, who were directing the second excavation at the site during 1978-

79. However, there was a settlement in the middle of the dispersed megalithic burial localities. As part of the research team, I had politely asked Deo during the excavation about the evidence of the Megalithic Iron Age settlement and the nature of evidence of the above-mentioned habitation. Their observation from a small digging of the habitation had revealed that it was purely an Early Historic mound without any trace of Iron Age remains. However, they noticed as was by Hunter (1933: 30-35) that there were lots of beads found on the surface. Though extensive megalithic burials in many sites have been carried out in Vidarbha over the years, it remains a region to answer several questionable observations. There are innumerable pertinent questions that need to be investigated and understood especially looking into various aspects of sociocultural- economic structure and cultural behaviour of the Megalithic people of the region (Mohanty 1993- 94). The most ideal site for such observations could be very well further intensive surface investigation and excavating at Mahurjhari. Looking at the recent developments in archaeological investigations, some of the findings both found from earlier excavations and fresh undertaking needed to be judiciously explained.

When Deo came back again to Mahurjhari (1977-78), he was unsure of a contemporary megalithic settlement at the site. This uncertainty and doubt had emerged probably out of the contemporary understanding that most of these burial builders belonged to a nomadic community. They only came back to an ancestral/ or ritual space for erecting a burial monument in the memory of their near and dear ones. This was also probably looking at multiple secondary skeletal remnants or often in the absence of primary burials in many megaliths excavated.

The explorations and excavations of this phase across the country were not contributing to this vexing problem of megaliths versus settlement in a substantial way. When S.B. Deo and A.P. Jamkhedkar were directing the excavation at Mahurjhari, they were well aware of this problem. Deo's earlier excavation at Takalghat and Khapa had both settlement and burials. There were some sites with burial-cum-settlement, and the one i.e., Mahurjhari supposed to be without it did not create any apprehension. To add to this, Mahurjhari burials were exceptionally rich with grave goods of impressive quality than the other sites excavated in this region and even in comparison to the other parts of the country. Again in a wider perspective, Deo's book on Megalithic problems in south India (Deo 1973b) had proposed the lacunae in the contemporary Megalithic research highlighting some of the necessary objectives, one being settlement versus burial sites. The discouraging problem both from the previous researches and contemporary researchers in this field remained inconclusive. The burial sites outnumbered many times to that of settlement sites. This disparity in research continues in many parts of the country not only in Vidarbha. The recent understanding and socalled paucity of habitation sites in relation to the burial sites across the subcontinent needs more intensive investigations rather than assuming nonexistent. The possibility of many cemeteries being associated with some nearby settlement may not be out of consideration By many scholars, the absence or non-availability of settlements close to the burial sites was not considered then as unusual but normal (Mohanty and Selva 2002: 313-335), the assumption continues till recently (Sundara 2015).

During the 1978-79 season, Deo carried out excavation where presently the Dhamma Naga Vipassana centre has come up. The excavations exposed twelve Megalithic burials in the locality-3 or as later marked as locality "D" close to Nagpur -Delhi railway line. All those burials were chosen looking into their impressive external architectures, larger in size and were situated apart from each other at this location (IAR 1978-79:71). The evidence from this excavation had confirmed that the megalithic burials at Mahurjhari, besides primary and secondary skeleton remains, were associated in general with rich antiquity remains in comparison to those from other sites excavated in Vidarbha and Peninsular India known till then.

While participating in the excavation carried by Deo, the author had visited the Mahurjhari village which is situated on the ancient mound to see if he can find some beads as reported by Hunter (1933) and Deo's Mahurjhari 1970 report. It was a bead treasure hunting site as can be seen from both the reports, so much so it was sold then in Nagpur wayside shops. Before the author could look for beads, the villagers gave him a lot of beads that they had collected post rainy season. So throughout the author's involvement of Megalithic excavations in Vidarbha, it was always hunting his conscience to go back and look for the settlement and do some investigation on beads to see if any correlation with rich burial antiquity and bead remains can be established. After 17 years, he got an opportunity to go back to Mahurjhari for some exploration. A casual surface investigation and a small trial dig were carried out during 1994 at Early Historic Mahurjhari settlement. It revealed plentiful evidence of a large-scale bead-manufacturing centre (Fig. 3 & Fig.4.) The evidence showed that it was operative for several centuries at the site (Mohanty 1999a: 79-89;1999b: 6-8). It had all the stages of bead production including various types of raw material and refuge/wastage.

However, as there were no proper excavations carried out at the this Early Historic habitation mound earlier, surface findings and observations made out of occasional digging for the foundation of modern house constructions, wells and garbage pits did not reveal any evidence to suggest the contemporaneous of the habitation during Megalithic burial builders at the site. As mentioned above, though, the site was explored and excavated several times for its Megalithic burials by eminent scholars in the past, the result of their research did not provide any in-depth insight into various facets of the life ways and settlement aspect of the Early Iron Age people at this site. The recent advancement made in the field of archaeological research has opened up ample avenues to approach the site again with a set of pertinent problems/ questions to tell something more about the people and their cultural behaviour.

The aims for Reinvestigating Mahurjhari 2001 to 2004

The main purpose of reinvestigating and excavating the Early Historic habitation mound was to locate, if possible, the alluding traces of megalithic settlement somewhere in the earlier levels. This was assumed that the ephemeral ancient settlements grew gradually and got covered entirely by later habitation beyond identification unless it could be struck at some right place. Sometimes, rare occasional appearance of some artefacts or in this case ceramics in the way of site formation process show up on the surface. In general presumption, at the beginning of initial settlement, it may not have been big what it manifested after several centuries of occupation and expansion along with the growth of population or new settlers.

Quite often, sites show episodic occupation at different times and again occupying different locations. Looking at the kind of rich diversified craft specialized equipment found during previous excavations, it was not believable that they came from outside and built numerous huge burials, dedicated enormous beautifully manufactured valuable diversified artefacts without having a residence of their own at least at Mahurjhari. Hence, it was hypothesized that a number of small trenches in different parts of the mound may reveal the earlier settlement. The other important aspect was to know more about the nature and antiquity of bead production at the site which was abundantly found having all stages of production, from raw materials to final product. It was also envisaged to document with an intensive surface survey of the Megalithic burials surrounding the site in all the localities along with their various attributes, placement pattern and utilization of the land space and availability of building material in the surrounding landscape to find out for such a purpose. Besides that, it was planned to excavate a cluster of burials irrespective of their size and shape to see if there are any internal relationships to suggest socio-ethnic-cultural and economic relationships. These aspects needed to be investigated to further our understanding to some extent of the inhabitants. It was proposed that the ideal could be to excavate at least one cluster in each locality irrespective of size, volume and shape. It could have helped not only to see their purpose for such an arrangement in the landscape and separating them in different cemeteries belonging to the same site. The emerging evidence could be evaluated by looking into the differentiation between localities and analyzing the artefacts in micro levels to say something about social, cultural, economic and status variability within a settlement.

If at all, this could be achieved, could probably have shown some personality and ideological engagement within the groups and an emergence of very structured diversified complex social organization, and maybe having professional diversity at least within a regional perspective reflected in burial offerings. This could have certainly paved the way in understanding the rapid progress towards state formation and begging or for that matter laying seed for the emergence of regional movement towards second urbanization.

Brief Results of Exploration and Excavations at Mahurjhari - 2001 to 2004: Excavation of Habitation in the Village Mahurjhari

With above objectives in mind, the excavation, exploration and intensive documentation of megalithic burials and looking for Iron Age settlements were carried in three seasons starting from 2001 to 2004. During the first year (2001-2002), the excavation was confined to the early historical mound. The whole purpose of reinvestigating the site as mentioned above was to look for the Early Iron Age remains. The hypothesis, current at that time, was not to always relate megalithic burials with possible links associating them with the settlements. There were divergent views. One view believed that settlements could be associated with the burials. However, most of the scholars proposed the pastoral nomadic way of life with occasional permanent habitation. According to this second view, people return to ancestral place for ritual purposes, one of the rituals could be the disposal of the dead (Mohanty and Selva 2002: 313-335). This settlement versus burial assumption was not different in the case of Vidarbha megaliths. This was because out of the large number of burial sites in Vidarbha, only a couple of sites were recognized to have habitation associated of with the period. However, there were many contemporary settlements without burials in their vicinity. This was not very well understood. At this time, it seems that the research did not focus more on settlement orientation understanding, rather looked for material culture, associated artefacts and deceased related burial placement and internal and external architecture. The focus was especially on large impressive ones with a prospect of a good amount of antiquity retrieval. It is difficult to comprehend why a pertinent aspect of the lifeways related to people and their habitations should not have been continuously attempted where a large number of burials were present. Again it was a case of exception; whereas grave goods in Mahurjhari burial were diverse, numerable and impressive in comparison to the sites already excavated either with megaliths and burial-cum-habitation sites known from the region. The artefacts from previous excavations suggested a complex society with weapons of offence-defence, agricultural tools (Fig.12), valuable personal ornaments in gold and copper, semiprecious stone beads, highly technically developed tools requiring highly skilled craftsmen to use and often requiring constant technological development and innovation for improvement in utilization. Some of the complex products could be the work of master craftsmen or procured from high skilled craftsman of the period, like the copper hilted dagger (Fig.13), copper bells, Copper bowls and decorative lids (Fig.10), copper Lota, and beads. Some of these artefact used bimetals, produced using copper and iron and also used sophisticated technic of forging, riveting and welding.

As Takalghat and Khapa, Naikund, Khaiwada and Bhagimohari had already revealed Iron Age settlements and these excavations had shown identical ceramic assemblages from the burials and habitation, it would be unusual that Mahurjhari did not have one. Hence it was thought proper to do an intensive investigation to look for Iron Age-Megalithic contemporary settlement at Mahurjhari which had alluded to the earlier researches. This seemed to be the most ideal site to look for such evidence at this juncture. Not finding the settlement would have led to either accepting the pastoral-monadic ideology and or finding the settlement would change the concept that non-availability rests on our investigation strategy. If the settlement could be located, this could change the misnomer to a great extent. The obvious place to attempt initially to find the evidence led to the already know early historic mound. Again the location of the mound was so situated, surrounded by Megalithic burial localities in all directions. Looking into the present ecological constructs, this site was the most suitable place to have settlement.

To augment this proposition, the central part of ancient settlement was subjected to intensive surface investigation and further prospective trenching at different locations was done to unearth the probable remains of the earlier period. The mound is spread over an area of about five hectares. These fringe areas were leveled to some extent earlier both for cultivation or for homestead. Some ancient deposit was removed and further ploughing had upturned quite a bit of the upper deposit. The central part was occupied by houses having courtyards, backyards and there were some open spaces on both sides of the village pathway. There was not much scope to excavate in the elevated central part of the mound, where the deposit seems to be more. As our major aim was to locate the earlier levels belonging to the Megalithic period, the excavation was carried out on the flattened cultivated fringe part of the mound to get to the lower levels sooner. Here the deposit was about 1.25 to 1.80 m as visible from diggings for house construction. As substantial deposit had already been removed, it was found suitable to reach lower levels before looking for Iron Age material. In the absence of large-scale horizontal excavation, it was planned to tap available localities in different areas of the mound to have a good representation of cultural material along with possible different activities. Here, the trenches were undertaken. It was aimed also to see the magnitude of variability if any belonging to their place of occurrence along with their contexts.

The excavation was carried out in five trenches located in four cardinal directions in the peripheral zones. The trenches A (East), B (southeast), C (northeast), D (northwest) were located in all four directions of the mound, and trench E was located thirty meters inside the western part of the mound. Trench "A" measuring 2.5 x 2.5 m and trenches B and C measuring 3 x 3 m with a total area of 36.75 sq. m were undertaken initially. The other two trenches (D and E), 3 x 3 m in size, were taken later. The main objective always remained to look for Early Iron Age remains. This was vacant and a suitable place available inside close to the present village. Though all the trenches were dug up to the natural soil level, nowhere could the Early Iron Age settlement generally associated with the typical Black and Red ware of Megalithic culture be located. As noted earlier, the excavation could not be undertaken in the core central part of the mound which was assumed could to have the earlier phase. However, the Early Historic deposit in this mound was confined to layers 1-5. They yielded mostly early historical material except for a few modern materials occasionally coming from the upper levels, up to 10-15 cm below the surface.

Because of small-scale excavations, proper structural remains could not be encountered. However, a large amount of full-sized burnt bricks and brickbats belonging to the Satavahana and Gupta-Vakataka period brick types were found at different levels in the site. In trench B, layer three, the bricks were found arranged in a small platform. A large number of brickbats scattered at different levels in the site suggest that some of the important structures and houses were built with burnt bricks. The pottery assemblage is similar to the early historic pottery reported from this region, especially from Adam (IAR 1988-89: 50-62; 1989- 90: 61-68), Kaundinyapura (Dikshit 1968; Smith 2001) and Pauni (IAR 1993-94:73-77). It was represented by thick and thin variety of Red ware with slip on the upper part or whole, polished micaceous Red ware with small mica flecks, Gray ware, a few pieces of coarse Black and Red ware and a small quantity of pottery with appliqué or stamped floral designs on them similar to the Gupta-Vakatak period ceramics.

During 2002-2003, the excavation was conducted at few other localities at Mahurjhari. In the previous year, the excavations at the site were limited to the Early Historic period and was carried in the fringe areas. The main purpose of locating and augmenting the Early Iron Age-Megalithic phase at the site could not be accomplished last year. This year arrangements were made to excavate in the central part of the mound where it seemed to have good amount of deposit and was the most elevated within the settlement. It was within an enclosed housing complex. The house and the large courtyard belonged to the local landlord (known as Raja Shaheb, belonging to Gond ethnicity), who now lives in Nagpur city. When, the author met him for permission, he gladly agreed and the place was available for excavation. The trench 'F' measuring 5 x 5 m was laid at this place. The excavations of two more small trenches 'G' and H' measuring 2 x 2 m were undertaken in the north and northeastern periphery of the mound for similar purposes searching for Iron Age settlement. Simultaneously, the foremost aim for looking into the Megalith/early Iron Age habitation remains continued in this area.

All trenches including trench "F" in the central part of the mound revealed several floor levels (Fig.5) along with a large number of burnt bricks and brickbats belonging to the Satavahana to Gupta-Vakataka period. There was no change in the pottery assemblage that was reported in the previous year as mentioned above. Besides a large amount of ceramics, other antiquities found in the excavation here were a large number of semiprecious stone beads and pendants, bead polishers and T.C. beads, skin rubber, kohl stick, stopper, shell and glass beads and bangles, lamp with stands, iron nail, iron clamp, iron knife, iron chisel, adze, iron arrowhead, copper rings and blades, T.C. animal figurines and T.C human figurines. A large number of animal bones of sheep-goat and cattle along with varieties of charred grains were recovered from the site. This gives a fair idea of their economic life.

Further, the excavations revealed ample evidence of a flourishing well-established settlement occupied by the Early Historic people for several centuries. The houses of the affluent class of the early historic period were constructed out of burnt bricks, similar in size to that of the Gupta-Vakataka period found at Adam and Pauni. Other people had wattle and daub houses. Besides a large number of utilitarian pottery of coarse and fine varieties, the other antiquities found in the excavation include semiprecious stone beads and pendants, bead polishers and T.C. beads, glass beads, glass bangles, skin rubber, kohl stick, stopper, shell and T.C. bangles, lamp with stands, iron nails, iron clamps, iron knifes, iron chisel, adze, daggers, arrowhead etc. Besides these objects, a few broken pieces of copper objects, T.C. animal figurines, T.C human head of the Gupta-Vakataka period and a plaque of Lajja Gauri on lime stone were found. The Lajja Gauri plaque which was found in layer 5 of trench 'B' of the early historic settlement at the site and can be assigned to the first or second century BC. and This probably belongs to the Satavahana period.

Mahurjhari Bead Evidence

The trench "F" had a deposit of 3.15 m and from the beginning, it had evidence of extensive bead manufacturing. Here also, there was no evidence of Early Iron age settlement remains. While the Early Iron Age remains were not found, the site for the first time revealed to be one of the mass bead production centre from the beginning of the settlement here. The extensive surface survey and a trial trench taken earlier had given sufficient evidence of Mahurjhari being a Primary Lapidary Manufacturing Centre (Mohanty 1999a: 79-89; 1999b: 6-8). The Excavation during 2003-04 season revealed that it is probably the largest semi-precious stone bead and pendant manufacturing centre ever known in an archaeological context in the subcontinent and even in global context till date. The people of Mahurjhari were proficient in lapidary work, a craft specialization that was perhaps not uncommon among the early megalithic builders (C. 800 BC.) of Vidarbha. Though later investigation and excavation in the Iron Age settlement here did not give the kind of profuse bead production seen in the Early historic mound, there was enough evidence to suggest that bead production was already practiced during this period (Vaidya and Mohanty 2015: 400-409). To testify further, there were finished, semi-finished beads and some bead processing debitage were found at different levels while excavating megalithic burials. It was observed by Deo (1973a) as well during our megalithic excavation at the site. This activity with gap continued at Mahurjhari and it flourished to be a major craft production centre during the Early Historic period (C.100 -600 AD.) in this region (Mohanty et al. 2019: 15-28) Looking at the bead manufacturing evidence at the site, the focus now revolved to know more about bead production and the Early Iron Age remains.

However, in due course, the focus also had changed a bit to understand the nature of the evidence of semi-precious stone bead manufacturing activity at different localities. During the process of documenting the bead findings, it was observed that it was not a uniform in all the trenches excavated. The raw material used and the shapes of beads along with their debitage recovered had remarkable variations. It was showing that each area had probably different expertize and specialized craftsmen at the site.

The result of the previous year's excavations had firmly established Mahurjhari being a Primary Bead Manufacturing Centre. However, this season's work provided further evidence on the functional aspect of the production system, such as bead napping and fashioning floors/ platforms with associated materials at different levels, tools such as iron points, semi-finished and finished beads with plenty of debitage found everywhere from the earliest level of this settlement. Most of these platforms had bead polishers, large vessels embedded in the floor probably for storing water required while polishing and often small earthen pots containing ash along with unfinished beads. Some of these pots were probably used further to heat agate beads at different stages of production to achieve the desired colour, especially turning the fashioned agate beads, pendants and cabochons into beautiful red carnelian of various shades. The finished and unfinished beads, lots of charcoal associated with these vessels along with bead polishers found at different levels in trenches F (Fig 5), G and H suggest a large-scale intensive continuous lapidary work from the beginning of the settlement till it was abandoned. Within the site, localities with a preference of use of raw material, the varied standard of workmanship and special functional areas like bead polishing with intact polishers and a good number of broken ones were observed. At different levels, the associated living floors observed with the bead manufacturing platforms, which could have belonged to the craftsmen of the period in that locality.

Though, the excavations in all trenches were carried out till the natural soil level, the evidence for the Early Iron Age-Megalithic settlement could be found in this mound. All the evidence coming from the two seasons excavations in this mound suggested that it was occupied only during the Early Historic period. The antiquity of the settlement here may go back to the beginning of the first–second century BC during which the early Satavahana ruled over the Deccan and continued during or after the Gupta- Vakataka. This Gupta–Vakataka evidence is attested by stamped pottery and box headed seals and intaglios found at the site (Hunter 1933: 30-35)

A survey of semi-precious stones used for making beads at this site was carried out. Huge chunks of agate, chalcedony nodules, big pieces of quartz crystals and blocks of jasper both in red and green were located as outcrops on eroded basaltic low-lying hill formations in the close proximity of the site, around 300 m from megalith locality "A". Again large quartz pieces were noticed coming out from the quarrying site about 150 m from locality "A" and where the locality "H" was located. The burials in locality "H" were all in a good state of preservation and most of them were impressive when we had visited during Deo's second season of excavation (1997-78). Then there were more than fifty megaliths here. By the time of our excavation in 2001-04, most of the burials had gone under quarrying. During a recent visit, it was observed that almost all megaliths have disappeared.

The bead-making craftsmen certainly got varieties of other raw material in large quantity from other sources as can be observed from the amount of west material and refuges found at the site.

Excavation of Megaliths at Mahurjhari

The excavation and exploration during the second season (2002-2003) were not only aimed at looking for Megalithic contemporary settlements but also excavating some burials with a different perspective. Along with the previous year's excavation, an intensive survey of the megaliths was undertaken in all the localities surrounding the Early Historic settlement in all directions. The documentation was aimed at keeping various hypotheses and recent advances made in the archaeological investigations, to see the arrangement of burials in the landscape with their various surface manifestations. One of the aims was to choose and excavate burials closes to each other found in a cluster irrespective of their size, deposit or configuration in a locality or cemetery.

It was on the backdrop of a practice by earlier scholars and investigators, who most of the time looked for an impressive, large burial, probably having a decent amount of deposit to excavate expecting a good evidence of varied cultural remains including extraordinary antiquities. It did suffice to some extent revealing the general economic condition, understanding of their use of implements and probably associated profession. They were more material cultural oriented selective study, and hence the understanding of their economic, profession and status analyzed in micro local level and then looking at regional perspective may remain biased and unfair as things were rapidly changing towards power and public position achievement (Mohanty 2018: 77-94; Moorti 1994). There was much more to know beyond the burial remains towards looking into the all-inclusive lifeways of the then society (Mohanty 1993-94).

As the intensive documentation of the burials was going on, it came to the notice that there are many more burials beyond what was documented earlier by Deo (1973a). Moreover, each locality had numerous clusters of burials of various dimensions separated from each other making their configurations and patterns. To answer some of the questions, a cluster in locality or cemetery A was undertaken for excavation. Here, instead of searching for impressive burials, for the first time, all the adjoining burials starting from smallest to largest were taken for exposing. In the process adjacent burials no. 10 (Fig.6), 3 and 1 were exposed in this locality.

The excavation was carried out in two adjoining megalithic burials, number 10 and 3 in the locality 'A' during 2002-03. These burials formed a part of a cluster, among several burial clusters in this locality. Burial no. 10 contained six partial secondary burials and two primary dead bodies brought soon after death to be buried in a good dugout pit in the central part of the megalith. There was a second burial near the western periphery that seemed to be inserted at a later date.

These extended burials were arranged in supine position lying down on the back; head to the east and feet to the west. The principal and primary burials were performed in the centre of the stone circle, probably brought and placed on a cot (Charpai). On the four corners of the burial, the pit had well-marked potholes in 3 x 6 feet respectively. The dead was placed in a rectangular pit dug into the natural soil. The pit was initially covered with a thick layer of pure black soil, a series of pots and a few iron implements, upon which the extended bodies of the deceased were placed on the cot. Again some of the grave goods were placed along with the dead. It reveals that then the whole pit, the cot was packed with black soil making it completely, both below the cot and above sealing it from all sides. This covered the entire skeleton and the grave goods up and below the cot appearing in segments. This was observed as there were filling layers between the grave goods below, the skeleton remains and the grave goods placed along with the deceased.

Top of which was placed the boulders, pebbles and packed with brown soil. This arrangement and pressure of the stone filling over the years had completely pulverized the skeletons. To this was added the black soil effect which contracts and expands making wide gaps in the association of water and seasonal changes.

Several Black and Red and Micaceous pots probably with cooked food were placed below as well as near the skeleton. The pots below the skeletons when carefully exposed showed some kind of residue attached to the inner part of the pots. They were subjected to lipid analysis and showed that they contained carbohydrates, organic fats and protein probably derived from aquatic sources (Mohanty and Vaidya 2017: 21-25). The burial was provided with a large amount of iron and copper objects. The grave goods include iron implements of offence and defense like knives, spear daggers etc. and craft tools like a variety of chisels, adzes, axes, hoes and personal items like nail-parers, capper bangles, semi-precious stone beads etc.

There was primary burial also in the northern periphery having a single adult skeleton. The second one seems to have been interred at a later date as the placement of the body has disturbed the original architecture of the megalithic monument and the burial pit was not neatly made. It was not placed on the same horizon as the central one and had a few grave goods associated. Burial no. 3 which was closely located almost touching the no. 10 was excavated. This megalith has evidence of five fragmentary partial secondary burials. All these burials accompanied with gave goods of a few pots and some assorted artefacts in no way comparable to megalithic no. 10. The one burial close to the centre, the bones were kept close to a copper bowl. Next to it, there was a beautiful copper decorative tripod found associated with a secondary burial in Megalithic no. 3. This tripod stand which joined at the top had the cast images of three stags, six perching birds and three fishes in it (Fig.7). The fragmentary secondary burials in both the megaliths opened were mostly located in the marginal areas of the eastern half of the stone circle. Again they were concentrated more in the north-east quadrant. It is interesting to note that the internal arrangements and placement of remnants within burials were identical in both the megaliths opened even though they contained several skeletal remains.

The deceased dead were placed in east and west direction, head towards the east. Though in practice, the quadrant method is adopted in exposing the stone circles, while excavating the burial No. 10 a horizontal grid was laid in the landscape surrounding the open space available in the western and southern side. This was intended to see possible ritual activity/remains of any kind left during the burial building. Outside the extended area, beyond the megalith, there was no indication of any stone appendages except green patches of grass unusual from the surrounding. After exposing these open areas, to our surprise, there were several burials of the period that had taken place outside the main megalith circle. They were inconspicuous from their surface indications and there were no significant visible surface markers to locate them except for comparatively green grass and type of vegetation growth on these burials (Mohanty 2005). These simple primary burials were arranged digging a pit, filling with black soil without visible stone appendages. This evidence suggest that organized ritual large megalithic burials were not common rather special. The number of secondary skeleton remains found in some of these megaliths certainly tells a very complex belief system of disposal of the dead here. The fractional skeletal remains deposited in the megaliths might have been retrieved/ salvaged from these normal burials probably to arrange a visible recognizable memorial monument in due course for reverence by the family members/ close relatives.

During the 2003-04 season, excavation at Mahurjhari was carried out in three localities comprising of two megalithic burials, one in locality 'A' close to burial no. 10 and one in locality 'H' and as the excavation continued at the megalithic habitation. During the previous year, a limited excavation in megalithic habitation and two burials in locality 'A', placed adjacent to each other, were carried out. They had provided significant evidence not known earlier. The excavation of megalith 10 here was planned in a different way not keeping the normal tradition of digging in the quadrant method but extending to all directions within the vacant space available surrounding the burial. The author applied the horizontal method taking a larger area keeping the Megalith 10 in between. It was intended to see if any remains during megalith construction or associated ritual process or object could be unearthed outside the adjacent burial architecture. It provided unexpected evidence of normal primary burial in the same orientation in the open space next to the Megaliths (Mohanty 2005). There were two burials each on the western and southern sides without visible stone appendages. The dead were buried soon after the death, as the skeleton looked articulated. The other evidence associated were a few iron implements which were completely pulverized and two/three small boulders in some cases could be noticed close to the skeleton. As the pits were dug into the rocky surface and the dead was placed covered with black soil, which is prone to contraction and expansion depending on the weather, had an impact on the skeletal remains. After careful exposing only the outline of the skeleton could the seen. As the burial pit was not very deep and very close to the surface, the site formation and weathering action of black soil had destroyed the skeletal remains making it difficult to understand any aspect of the deceased - physical feature, age or sex etc. In each case, there were a few black and red and micaceous ware accompanied the deceased. There were two burial pits with skeleton found within the Megalith, one in the centre and one towards the western periphery. The one on the western side close to the periphery of the stone circle seems later introduction; as a pit was dug removing an earlier deposit for reorganizing the dead was observed. The other significant thing was that in the north–east quadrant there were four places close to the peripheral boulder, in each case a few broken secondary bone pieces with one or two pots were placed. An exactly similar observation was made while exposing the closely located burial number 3. Besides the central main burial within the stone circle in a well-organized pit, with usual grave goods of the period, the north-east quadrant had two residual burials of fragments of bones with few similar ceramic vessels found with the main pit burial.

The excavation of burials had given excellent evidence of burial practices, remains of material culture, along with primary skeletal remains and a few secondary skeletal remains in them. These two burials had exhibited a kind of pattern in disposing of the dead in particular architectural background and also in case of placement of secondary burials in the main burial complex. The excavation on the periphery of burial no. 10 in locality 'A' had given evidence of two pit burials, which were not recognizable from the surface indications. This kind of evidence was noticed for the first time when it was thought to excavate the surrounding areas to find out remains of activity during the burial building if any. Hence, it has widened our understanding of megalithic people, who not only buried their dead in the burial monuments but also used to bury them in the cemetery without much elaborate ritual process. This was probably due to some socioeconomic and circumstantial reasoning.

To understand such reoccurrence of primary pit burials in the centre and several secondary burials with a few bones with negligible grave good in the north-east quadrant, burial no. "1", situated a few meters to the south-east of previously excavated no.10 and in the same cluster, was undertaken. It had a different external and internal architecture unlike the previous two. This was a fully secondary burial, where fragments of bones were found in the southeastern and southwestern quadrants in multiple locations, along with a large amount of iron implements consisting of axes, hoes, chisels, spearheads, knives, nailparers, plough-shares, etc. Black and Red, and Micaceous Red ware were found in several clusters at different levels in all the quadrants. The placement of ceramics, implements associated with secondary burials showed that they are not similar in nature. Some of the antiquities were placed at different levels implying that they were placed at different times while burial building was going on. However, like the earlier observations, a few fragments of bones with a few pots were found in the northeastern quadrant. This pattern quite tallies with the one found from burial no. 10

and 3 of the same locality that were excavated last year. This patterning of ritual processes, regarding the placement of the primary burial near the centre and the secondary burial in northeastern part of the burial in this cluster, had some significance probably related to the mortuary behavioural aspect of the members of the same family or group or clan who used this cemetery or at least this cluster.

To find out this kind of evidence in another locality and cluster, it was thought proper to excavate a burial in an untapped locality. Burial no. 28 from locality 'H' was chosen. It was a large burial with a 13-meter diameter having thirty-seven large peripheral boulders, two of which had cup marks. The total deposit of the burial was 45-50 cm, containing black soil and pebbles of different sizes. In the centre of the burial, there was a pit dug into the natural soil and the skeleton was found as laid over a thin layer of black soil with large no. of micaceous and black and red pots, especially kept near the head of the dead. The skeleton was found oriented East-West, with head to the east. This position of the skeleton tally with the evidence from the burials excavated in the last two seasons at the site.

There were a few bone fragments found in the southwestern quadrant along with a cluster of pots and a large number of beads of semi-precious stones and iron objects. An interesting observation was made that the black soil used to cover the skeleton was probably brought from some water source as this kind of fine, silty and black soil is found only in the washed way black soil in water bodies like pools of the locality. The upper black soil with heavy sand particles which covered the major part of the burial was procured from the neighboring fields available within a distance of 500 m from it. The total content of the burial including soil, pebbles and peripheral boulders weighed around 120 tons. Over the years, part of the upper soil cover had eroded as can be seen flowing to the outer side of the megalith. This burial after excavation was lifted to be reconstructed close to its original morphology, in all aspects as was found for open-air display at Indira Gandhi Rashtriya Manav Sangrahalay, Bhopal. Though, we took partial mechanical support to reconstruct the megalith here, the earlier experiment conducted at Bhagimohari suggest at least 200 to 250 man days must have taken along with ritual activity and feastings to construct such a megalith (Mohanty and Walimbe 1993: 93-103).

Excavations in the Iron Age Megalithic settlement

As there was no evidence of the Early Iron Age at this excavated Early Historic mound, a systematic site prospective intensive survey of the landscape was undertaken keeping in mind the changes it might have undergone during several centuries after the Iron Age people abandoned the site. The survey was carried out in a radius of five kilometer keeping in mind the location of cemeteries. Possible suitable parameters required for a settlement were taken into consideration. The topographic map was thoroughly investigatedfor water sources in the past that may have changed. It may have been suitable in the past but not now. The advantageous location and surrounding landscape in the past were speculated. Three/four localities were explored. To our surprise, the Megalithic habitation at Mahurjhari was brought to light some 1.5 km southwest of the present village, which was alluding for the past 70 years. The mound is preserved over an area of about three hectares. A small-scale excavation here revealed that the antiquity of the megalithic settlement will go back to the Neolithic –Chalcolithic phase in Vidarbha i.e., to the later part of the second millennium BC. This finding of the Iron Age settlement after 70 years of research at the site after an intensive and persistent investigation completely changed the perception of not finding or associating settlements of the period with the culture. Soon after finding the settlement, many sites which were not known to have settlement of this period were discovered. It is so much so that the research work carried out by Vaidya in this region showed that there are many more habitation sites of this period than the megalithic burial sites. The only difference is that many of these settlement sites do not or rarely have megalithic burials nearby (Vaidya 2014). Now even in other parts of the country, especially in south India, such settlements are recorded in large numbers recently. The problem still deters, though positive advances have been made recently in this field by Mohanty and Vaidya in the Vidarbha region and Rajan in Tamil Nadu (Mohanty 2005, Vaidya 2014, Rajan 1997, 2013 , Das *et al.* 2013).

During the 2003-2004 season, the megalithic habitation was excavated in a larger (130 sq. m.) area to look for the structural remains of this period and the activity surrounding these structures. Besides this, it was also intended to reach the natural soil level in some areas to confirm the cultural findings revealed from the previous year's excavation. Several floor levels were exposed along with hearths, roasting places, silos, fireplaces, circular and oblong washing platforms made with pebbles resting on clay platforms (Fig.9). As these platforms were used for long time, the soil had a different colour, grey-black and sometimes with broken potsherds and fragments of bones. The house floors were made by ramming the black clay upon which stone chips were laid and then it was covered with a thin layer of brownish earth, sticky fine clay paste probably to even the floor. The other findings from habitation are a large amount of pottery comprising of Black and Red ware, Micaceous red ware, grey ware, and thick red slipped ware. Some sherds of black painted on red ware were also found. The lower levels have given evidence of pottery resembling the late phase of Neolithic tradition from the south along with stone tools (Fig.12). A well-preserved iron battle-axe was found in the late levels. Several etched carnelian beads, terracotta beads, clay tablets, pottery discs, and grounded-flat-circular stones of different weights were found in large numbers.

The excavation has produced ample evidence of megalithic phase activity in Vidarbha. The pottery assemblages are typically the same as has been found at Tekalght-khapa, Naikund, Bhagimohari and Kairwada and also found from the Megalithic burial excavated by Deo in the past and recently by the author. However, the percentage of fine Black and Red ware are much more here, in comparison to the other sites mentioned above. This was probably keeping the economic tradition of rich antiquities recovered from the Megaliths. Here, the habitation deposit is about 2.85 m. The lower layer of 25 to 30 cm contains the late Neolithic- Chalcolithic pottery along with stone tools made out of chert and chalcedony blades. Profuse quantities of animal bones and grains of several species were found during the excavation. The faunal remains retrieved from the Iron Age settlement show a wide range of animals both domesticated and wild along with aquatic sources. The evidence tells that the inhabitants of megalithic Mahurjhari exploited *Bos indicus* (domestic cow), *Bubalus bubalis* (domestic buffalo) *Bos/Bubalus* (cattle/buffalo), *Capra hircus* (goat), *Ovis aries* (sheep), *Canis familiaris* (dog), *Sus domesticus* (pig), *Equus caballus* (horse), *Gallus domesticus* (chicken), *Tetracerus quadricornis* (chowsingha), *Axis axis* (chital), *Antilope cervicapra* (black buck), *Boselaphus tragocamelus* (nilgai), *Sus scrofa* (wild pig), *Lepus nigricollis* (Indian hare), *Herpestes edwardsi* (mongoose), *Varanus* sp. (monitor lizard), and *Rattus rattus* (house rat). A variety of birds, fresh water fish, and many varieties of molluscan shells have also been recorded. In addition, there were bones of carnivorous animals such as of *Canis lupus* (wolf), *Panthera pardus* (leopard), and cat, which probably introduced during the Early historic period (Deshapande Mukharjee , Thomas and Mohanty 2015). The Plant remains from this site remains under investigation. However, the excavations at Bhagimohari and Naikund Iron Age settlements have given conclusive evidence of archaeobotanical remains of both cultivated during Ravi and Kharif seasons as well as collecting edible plant products from natural resources. The grains found suggest double harvesting both during Ravi and Kharif season. The major crops found in the Iron Age settlement are wheat, barley, rice, cotton, pigeon pea (Tur), horse gram, black and green gram and kodo millet as these have been reported from Bhagimohari and other megalithic sites of Vidarbha (Kajale 1989).

Intensive Surface Survey and Documentation of Megaliths at Mahurjhari

During the previous investigation at Mahurjhari by Deo (1970, IAR 1977-78), the recording of some of the megaliths localities had been carried out. The documentation was more towards counting and locating the burials in some of the cemeteries. This certainly provided an idea of different locations and the number of burials within the Mahurjhari environment. Its importance can still be seen as by the time our documentation began a lot of destruction of burials due to new settlement coming up on the way to the village and quarrying had already taken place in the locality "C" and "G", respectively. Looking into the different aspects of Megalithic ritual burial construction, it was thought prudent to freshly document taking all available parameters available on the surface, before they are destroyed. It was also because the site was close to Nagpur city and the city was expanding rapidly. Now, while writing this in 2021, I think we took a wise decision then. Now, the whole area has been modified as in the locality "D" the Dhamma Naga Vipassana centre, the Nagpur ring road passes through the locality "A" "C", "E", and various factories and farms have come up in these areas surrounding the site. While expanding the urban utility area, without considering the heritage of the regions, the unplanned activities have obliterated the evidence. Before proceeding for documentation, a casual land walk was carried out. It was found that the megalithic burial grounds were recorded by Deo numbering them "I to V" and in the process had also combined some cemeteries into one group. Our documentation of burial locations revealed that he has missed out quite a few localities. It was also taken into account to do an intensive surface investigation of the Megalithic burials surrounding the site in all the cemeteries. It was planned not only to locate, number them, but record their various attributes, placement pattern and utilization of the land space and availability of building material in the surrounding landscape. It was intended to look for any special feature like cup marks, the number of stones used, are they all locally available, the visible external arch, nature of filling, associated megaliths with the general configuration within the locality. A specific attempt has been made to see how they are oriented and why they are often seen segregated even in the same cemetery.

After documentation megaliths and their distribution, it was planned to select a cluster to excavate possibly all burials irrespective of their sizes and shapes to see if there are any internal relationships to suggest socio-ethnic-cultural and economic relationships. These aspects need to be investigated to further our understanding to some extent of the inhabitants and their social ideological diversities which necessitated such arrangement if any. It was proposed, the ideal could be to excavate at least a cluster in each locality irrespective of configuration, size, volume and shape. It could help not only to see their purpose for such an arrangement in the landscape and separating them in different cemeteries even belonging to the same site.

The emerging evidence from the excavation of clusters would be valuable in evaluating looking into differentiation emerging between localities by analyzing the artefacts in micro levels to say something about social ideology, traditional differentiation, economic and status variability within a settlement. If at all, this could be achieved, could probably show some assortative group personality and ideological engagement within the groups and an emergence of very structured diversified complex social organization. There could be having professional diversity, family projection at least can be predictable within a cemetery, site or can extend to regional perspective reflected in burial locational arrangement and accompanied offerings at different stages. The stoppage or gradual decline of the megalithic practice could tell the turmoil the society was going through. This kind of evidence is expected from deliberate social functions and activities. If the continuity of settlement through the Iron Age and Early Historic can be observed from the extensively excavated site at Bhagimohari, it shows the material culture especially reflected in ceramics does not show refinement and development. The settlements were getting abandoned and some of the Iron Age agricultural settlements were expanding, becoming populated and showing intense activity. This transformation can very well be noticed in burial customs if this intense cluster digging and analysis is undertaken. As our excavation of a cluster in locality "A" shows, things were changing faster. This has certainly paved the way in the rapid progress towards state formation or for that matter laying seed for the emergence of regional movement towards second urbanization.

This intensive survey of the Megalithic burials in the site has brought to light three more localities of megalith burials with several clusters in them not recorded earlier. The Megaliths were constructed on hills, hill slopes and rocky landscape, and not a single was found on cultivable land. It was certainly deliberate to spare the fertile land for agriculture. All the burial localities were close to the water bodies, either a natural pool or small *Nala* and rivulets. Some of these burial localities were visible to the settlement. In all these cemetery localities, the burials were arranged in clusters. Each cluster has about 5 to 15 burials of different shapes, sizes and has different types of external features observable from the surface deposits. Our intensive investigation documented in total more than 350 burials in all these 10 localities, out of which more than 60 burials have been destroyed recently by the stone quarries. At present, due to the expansion of Nagpur city, construction buildings, factories and the construction of the ring road in the middle of the site has destroyed a large number of burials and has changed the landscape beyond recognition. Conjecturing and prospecting of the landscape surrounding the ancient settlement, the lifeways of the Early Iron Age people lived in such an important site may not be possible to a great extent even with the application of available advanced technology in Archaeology in recent times.

Discussion

The excavations of megaliths all within a cluster in a locality proved to be rewarding in many ways as revealing the burials followed an ideological burial ritual by placing the secondary residual skeletal remains in one particular segment like north-East quadrant, besides normal primary burial in the appropriate central location in a pit. The number of grave goods differs from principal interment to subsidiary ones. Some of the grave offerings accompanied the dead, while some implements were deposited in the process of construction of the burial, often seen not properly oriented put haphazardly. The dead were also buried in simple pit burials with a minimal grave offering of the period. A large number of pots probably had processed food offered to the deceased and also who had passed away long back as the secondary burials suggest. The construction materials were procured from the local basaltic formations and soil from the surrounding. However, the black soil which covered the dead came from a place where the soil was fine, probably collected from a washed-away deposit in a nearby waterbody. The rest of the soil looks to have been brought from the neighbouring field. The cup marks were neatly done with different patterns having most of the time the same depth and dimension. Due to the formation process action of black soil on the skeleton, the remains were never found in good condition, rather broken into pieces. Surrounding the habitation, there were several cemeteries. With limited and selective excavation, it is difficult to precisely say why such activity was practiced though enough space was available at each location. The excavation in the now confirmed Early historic mound where the present village is located was occupied during the early historic period. A few 14C dates available from the middle and upper levels suggest that the site was operative at least from 3rd./4th. C. AD to about 6th. c. AD (Table 2 and Table 3.) (Mohanty *et al.* 2019: 15-28). The ceramic studies from the sites also go well with the time period (Lefrancq *et al.* 2019). The bead manufacturing evidence from Mahurjhari is unparalleled to any manufacturing centre known till date (Mohanty 1999a: 79-89; 1999b: 6-8; Mohanty and Thakuria 2016; Mohanty 2017: 317-346). Though studies have been done, it needs an exclusive analysis to provide far-ranging implication in the then cultural and economic scenario besides it ornamental use.

Then comes the evidence of the megalithic Iron age settlement after 70 years of first exploration and subsequent several seasons of excavations and documentation of burials across the landscape. The excavation not only confirmed the centuries of occupation here but also at lower levels the finding of late chalcolithic ceramics with stone blades. A few 14C dates (Table 1) again available from upper levels reveal that the site was well established with all its activities, like iron working, various craft productions and use, house constructed using wood/bamboo plastered walls with thatched roofs. The amount and variety of carpentry tools found from burials show their expertise in woodworking and probable use in household objects and agricultural tools. The evidence of house floors also shows successive house construction in the same place again and again. Some of the houses provided evidence of silos and hearths and nearby washing platforms (Fig.9). The subsistence evidence recovered tells that they cultivated a large number of grains and pulses and reared cattle, sheep and goat, domestic pigs and horse. The finding of the Megalithic settlement at Mahurjhari changed to a great extent the conception of Megaliths versus habitation of the period.

Acknowledgements

I am especially grateful to Prof. Peter Ucko, Director, Institute of Archaeology, University College London, and The Charles Wallace Trust for providing me a Fellowship to collect relevant data and interact with scholars in UK, for my Megalithic research in Vidarbha. I thank the villagers of Mahurjhari, especially Maushi (Vaishali Chaudhari) and his family for feeding us for all the those years we investigated there. I thank the Indira Gandhi Rashtriya Manav Sangrahalay, Bhopal for fully funding excavation of a megalithic burial, documentation, transport and reconstruction in the campus as open air exhibition. Indi years. I sincerely acknowledge the help and co-operation from my senior colleagues Dr. P.K.Thomas, Dr. S.R.Walimbe and Dr. M.D. Kajale who participated in the excavation for specialist studies. My special thanks are to the Research Scholars of the Department of Archaeology, Deccan College, Sarvashri Dr. Gurudas Shete, Dr.(Ms.) Shete Kailash Pawar, Dr.(

Ms). Shobha, V., Dr. Rizza Abbas, Dr. David Teso and Dr.(Ms.) Utpala Adhav, Dr. Vaishali Velenkar, Dr. Tilok Thakuria, Dr. Veena Mushrif and Mr. Vaman Gavade, Mr. Chandrakant Shendge who all helped and supervised the excavations. I thank Dr. Pankaj Goel for meticulously going through the final draft. I also thank the authorities of Deccan College, Indian Council of Historical Research and Archaeological Survey of India for providing generous financial support for thisproject.

Table 1: List of radiocarbon dates from Early Iron Age Settlement, Mahurjhari, Vidarbha. (*All radiocarbon dates were sent to SUERC or Beta Analytic. Standard pre-treatment methods were used (acid/alkaline washes)

1	Archaeological	Provenance	Material	Lab no.	Radiocarbon Age	.d13C
	MHR_TrA_Ly5 Early Iron Age 1.31 m	Trench A, Layer 5, Depth	Charred pulses (fragments)	Beta-501552	2470 +/- 30 BP	- 23.8 ‰
2	MHR_TrA_NE Early Iron Age Depth 1.76m	Trench A, Locus NE	Charred pulses (fragments)	Beta-501551	2520 +/- 30 BP	- 22.3 ‰
3	MHR_02_15_C Early Historic Period	Dig 15, Trench C, Mesolithic	Triticum sp. (fragments)	SUERC-73796	1626 +/- 29 BP 23.6 ‰	-

Table 2 : Results of AMS Radiocarbon dating analyses of samples from Early History habitation Mahurjhari Trenches C and F

Sample	Trench	Lot	Layer	Probable Date (AD)	OxCal (IntCal 13)
1	C	12	4	870-985	778-790 CE (1.7%), 809-815 CE (0.5%), 826- 841 CE (1.4%), 863-995 CE (91.8%)
2	C	16	5	570-655	566-655 CE (95.4%)
3	F	134	5	18th/19th century	1691-1730 CE (24.3%), 1810-1924 CE (71.1%)
4	F	146	6	17th/18th century	1685-1733 CE (26.3%), 1807-1928 CE (69.1%)
5	F	145	6	17th/18th century	1669-1780 CE (43.1%), 1798-1891 CE (36.8%), 1909-1945 CE (15.5%)
6	F	155	7	340-400	256-299 CE (16.3%), 318-416 CE (79.1%)
7	F	150	7	425-540	426-588 CE (95.4%)
8	F	443	6	575-640	561-651 CE (95.4%)
9	F	124	3	17th/18th century	1664-1707 CE (16.7%), 1719-1826 CE(47.4%), 1832-1884 CE (12.6%), 1914 CE + (18.6%)
10	F	638	6	560-650	566-655 CE (95.4%)

Table 3: Reconstructed chronological sequence for Trench F, based on 14C dates and relative dating

Layer	14C Date(s)	Range
1	_	19th to 20th century
2	_	17th to 18th century
3	1719-1826	17th to 18th century
4	_	Post10th century
5	1810-1924	7th to 10th century?
6	560-650/575-640	6th to 7th century
7	340-400/425-540	4th to 6th century
8	_	Pre 4th century
9	_	Pre 4th century

References

Babington, J., 1823, Description of the Pandoo Coollies in Malabar, *Transactions of the Literary Society of Bombay 3.*

Das, N.N., P.P. Joglekar and R.K. Mohanty, 2013, New Light on the Unresolved Problem of Megalithic Habitation Sites in Kerala, *Artha Journal of Social Sciences, 12 (3).*

Deo, S.B., 1970, *Excavations at Takalghat and Khapa (1968-69),* Nagpur: Nagpur University.

Deo, S.B., 1973a, *Mahurjhari Excavations (1970-72),* Nagpur: Nagpur University.

Deo, S. B., 1973b, *Problem of South Indian megaliths,* Dharwar: Kannada Research Institute, Karnataka University.

Deshpande, Mukherjee, A., P.K. Thomas and R. K. Mohanty, 2015, Faunal Exploitation Patterns during the Iron Age in the Vidarbha Region of Maharashtra with Special Reference to Mahurjhari, in *Megalithic Traditions in India*

Archaeology and Ethnography, Vol.II, K.K. Basa, R.K. Mohanty and S.B. Ota (eds.) Keynote Address, New Delhi : Aryan Books.

Deshpande, P.P. and R.K. Mohanty, 2015, Iron Age and Steeling in Ancient Vidarbha Region of Maharashtra:

Technical Aspects, in *Megalithic Traditions in India: Archaeology and Ethnography,* K.K. Basa, R.K.Mohanty and S.B.Ota (eds.), New Delhi: Aryan Books International, Vol.II.

Dikshit, M.G., 1968, Excavations at Kaundinyapura, Bombay: Director of Archives and Archaeology, Maharashtra State.

Hislop, S., 1857, Letters (Excavations at Takalghat), *Journal of Bombay Branch Royal Asiatic Society 5.*

Hunter, G.A.P., 1933, The Antiquities of Mahurziri, *Sharadashrama Varshik 5.*

IAR: Indian Archaeology- A Review

Kajale, M.D., 1989, Archaeobotanical Investigation on Megalithic Bhagimohari and its Significance for Ancient

Indian Agricultural System, *Man and Environment, XIII.*

Kennedy, K.A.R., 1975, The Physical Anthropology of the Megalithic-Builders of South India and Sri Lanka,

Canberra: Australian National University Press, *Oriental Monograph Series17.*

Krishnaswami, VD., 1949, Megalithic Types of South India, *Ancient India 5.*

Lefrancq, C., Hawkes, J., C.M. Jaseera and Mohanty, R.K., 2019, A Typology of Practice: The Archaeological

Ceramics from Mahurjhari, *Internet Archaeology 52.* https://doi.org/10.11141/ia.52.9

Leshnik, L.S., 1974, *South Indian Megalithic Burials - The Pandukal Complex,* Wiesbaden: Franz Steiner Verlag GmbH.

Mohanty, R.K., 1993-1994, Vidarbha Megalithic: A New Perspective for field Investigations, *Bharti 20 (1-2).*

Mohanty, R.K.,1999 a, Significance of Bead a Manufacturing Centre at Mahurjhari: District *R.K. Mohanty* 153

Nagpur, Maharashtra, *Man and Environment 24 (2)* .

Mohanty, R.K., 1999 b, A Bead Manufacturing Centre at Mahurjhari, Nagpur District,

Maharashtra, *Bead Study Trust Newsletter, London* 33.

Mohanty, R.K., 2017, Antiquity of Stone beads from Deccan, Technology and Antiquity of stone beads in India, Alok Kanungo (ed.), IIT Gandhi Nagar, Gujarat.

Mohanty, R. K., 2018, Early Iron Age Megalithic Culture of Vidarbha, Maharashtra: Implications and Consequences of Economy - A Consideration, in *Socio-Economic Dynamics of Indian Society: A Historical Overview,* A. Tilak, D.H. Jawane, N. Chitnis and R.A. Vaishampayan (eds.), Mumbai: Vivek Group Publication.

Mohanty, R.K, and S.R. Walimbe, 1993, A Demographic Approach to the Vidarbha Megalithic Culture, *Man and Environment, XVIII (2).*

Mohanty, R. K and P.S. Joshi, 1996, The Megalithic Problems of Vidarbha: Retrospect and Prospects, *Spectrum of Indian Culture,* Vol. II, C. Margabandhu and K.S. Ramchandran (eds.), New Delhi: Agam Kala Prakashan .

Mohanty, R.K and V. Selvakumar, 2002, The Archaeology of Megaliths in India: 1947-1997, *Indian Archaeology in Retrospect-Prehistory: Archaeology of South Asia* Vol. 1, S. Settar and Ravi Korisettar (eds.) New Delhi: Manohar Publication.

Mohanty, R.K. and T. Thakuria, 2016, *Indian Beads: History and Technology,* New Delhi: Indus Infinity Foundation, Pentagon Press.

Mohanty, R.K. and S. Vaidya, 2017, An Investigation into the dynamic Synergy between Early Iron Age Settlements and Megalithism in Vidarbha, in *Rethinking the Past: A tribute to Proffessor V.N.Misra,* S. G. Deo, A. Baptista and J. Joglekar (eds.), Indian Society for Prehistoric and Quaternary Studies, Monograph No.7 .

Mohanty, R.K., S. Vaidya, J. S. Kharakwal, V. Sontakke and T. Thakuria, 2017, The Early Iron Age Megalithic Culture of Vidarbha in a Broarder Perspective: A pragmatic Observation, *Shodh Patreeka 68 (1-2).*

Mohanty, R. K., Jason D. Hawkes, Coline Lefrancq and Riza Abbas, 2019, Report on the Dating of the Historical Period Site at Mahurjhari, Vidarbha, *Heritage*: *Journal of Multidisciplinary Studies in Archaeology 7.*

Mohanty, R.K., Jason D. Hawkes, Coline Lefrancq and Riza Abbas, 2019, Report on the Dating of the Historical Period Site at Mahurjhari, Vidarbha, *Heritage: Journal of Multidisciplinary Studies in Archaeology 7.*

Moorti, U.S., 1994, *Megalithic Culture of South India: Socio-Economic Perspectives,* Varanasi: Ganga Kaveri Publishing House .

Pearse, G.G., 1869, On the Excavation of a Large Raised Stone Circle or Barrow near the Village of Wurreegaon, One Mile from the Military Station of Kamptee, Central Province of India, *The Journal of Ethnological Society of London* Vol. 1 (no. iii).

Rajan, K,1997, *Archaeological Gazetteer of Tamil Nadu,* Thanjavur: Manoa Pathipakam.

Rajan, K., 2013, The Iron Age in Tamil Nadu, *Political History and Administration till c. 200 B.C.,* Vol. VI, D. K. Chakravarti and M. Lal (eds.), New Delhi: Aryan Books International.

Sundara, A., 1975, *The Early Chamber Tombs of South India: a Study of the Iron Age Megalithic Monuments of North Karnataka*, New Delhi: University Publishers.

Sundara, A., 1998, *South Indian Megalithic Culture: Some Aspects of the Studies Since Independence,* National Seminar on Fifty Years of Indian Archaeology: Retrospect and Prospect, Allahabad University.

Sundara, A., 2015, The Megalithic Culture in South India: Problems and Prospects. in *Megalithic Traditions in India Archaeology and Ethnography,* Vol.I, K.K. Basa, R.K. Mohanty and S.B. Ota (eds.) Keynote Address, New Delhi: Aryan Books.

Sontakke, V., 2014, *Early Iron Age Archaeology of Upper Wainganga Valley with special reference to Gondia District,* Unpublished Ph. D. Dissertation, Pune: Deccan College Post Graduate and Research Institute.

Vaidya, S., 2014, *Emergence of Complex Societies and Urbanization during the Early Iron Age and Early Historic Period in the Wardha and Nagpur Districts of Vidarbha.* Ph. D. Dissertation, Pune: Deccan College Post Graduate and Research Institute.

Vaidya, S. and R.K. Mohanty, 2015, Antiquity of Bead Manufacturing at Mahurjhari and its relevance in Early Iron Age Megalithic Culture of Virarbha, *Heritage: Journal of Multidisciplinary Studies in Archaeology* 3.

14

Breaking the Stereotypes : Temple Building without Religious Rationale

Sachin Kumar Tiwary

Introduction

Temples are the symbol of god, who seat there as his or her house for the welfares of public. Temple is a spiritual destination as well as landmarks around which ancient arts, community celebrations and economy to flourish. It is the centre for the direct communications to the common public. It is believed that the structure of the temple itself a symbolic representation of a pious god. The description of temple root is well defined in the Vedas and Puranic literatures. Though we don't have well established example of temple before Gupta period, it is believed of several scholars like Prof. V. S. Agrawal that it was prevalent even in Vedic period. But due to its perishable material nature we are not in position to get its archaeological instances.

Do we think that the tradition of constructing temple were only for religious? For the question answer we should think in context and in epigraphs of regional level especially south India. The answer is very much thrilling as the temple were the centre of two importance things *e.i.* :

1. Positive Aspects like: Centre of Education, Religion, Art, Architecture, Nature, Defense, Treasure and at the same time,
2. Negative Aspects like: Education for special class only, Corruption, Dirty Politics, Extortion, An Act of Temple Managers like feudal lords, enjoying the property of the temple and making the poor to work in the fields, Centre for keeping kings black money, Some time centre of Social injustice, Protection of Caste System, Centre of Social Corruption etc.

Educations were allowed only to few privileged classes like kings and priest. As per my personal discussion to Dr. S. Krishnamurthy "Only few privileged could get employment in temple and that too hereditary... Not the common people. See the example of Mayurasarman a Brahmin and founder of Kadamba dynasty. He was denied entry into the *ghatika i.e.* educational institution at Kanchipuram by the Pallava soldiers and Mayurasarma, took to sword to avenge his insult". The present attempt to describe about the different purposes of the temple built.

Descriptions of each point are as follows -

1. Legalizing Kingship and a Political Head

King as the political head, in order to establish his kingship and make an influence over the masses, constructed temples. By stating his divine origin, and initiating temple construction, he relates himself as the embodiment of God on earth. For example the Tamil word, "Kovila" for temple literally means the "House of The King". The temple concept is South India was looked upon in relation with the king, the highest abode of "The King of the Universe" as seen in scriptures or folklores. Being his representative and to set an influential example in the sight of common people. He associated directly or indirectly kingship next to Godliness.

2. Winning Hearts of People-Social Control

By construction of temples, the king portrayed his great faith and reverence towards deities, which were adorned majorly by the folk people. Often despite the king follow a different religion or declares a state religion, he also supports the religion of common brass by giving donations in form of wealth, land etc. and by constructing temples directly or indirectly having a control over the society and the people. As, the king enjoys the support of people, his statesmanship is strengthened and assured.

3. Temple Acting as Centre of all Social Activities

Temples acted as centre of all activities especially in South India. Art, music, dance developed in them. Judiciary and local assemblies, marriage and other Samskara customs were conducted here. Learning and Libraries were important part of them. So in some or the other way, a direct association to or influence over society is created. Hence, ensuring a direct hand of the king over the society.

4. Economical Control

Temples for example Somanath in Gujarat or in South India, acted as a treasure house of wealth with all riches stored in them. All the donations for them were kept in here often acting as banks for common people or niches part of the society, storing wealth with security, giving loans and other banking facilities offered by the temple. Evident too now, people are appointed to count and keep record of this wealth. The *Srenis* played an important role in this procedure. Trade of commerce was also associated to temples, in way such as:

I. Taking loans or depositing wealth by trades,

II. Centers of Kanjeevaram silk in Kanchipuram in addistion to bell-metal and brass and brass-copper metallurgy set to support Brihadeshwar temple in Thanjaur or other temples in the land.

III. The temples equally promoted employment opportunities in various ways- Metal makers, Cloth makers, Garlands, Oil makers, Clearance, Priests, Musician-Dancers etc.

So, directly or indirectly having an importance socio-economic control.

5. Prevention of Revolt

The constructions of temples especially after victory in wars by kings indicate an important political reason. This erection of temples or victory pillars show their political achievements but majority to create a psychological effect on others. By showing his valour, through these media, firstly executes an image of the king among his subjects, which he is very powerful and thus, ensures no public revolt takes place and a powerful influence over the other kingdoms to either be inactive or supportive towards the king.

6. Knowing Geographical Extent of Empire

The erection of temples ensures the region which is under the rule of the king. It will be only in his kingdom or empire or the territory under his rule, he mainly build temples. Like inscriptions mark the boundaries or extent of his territory, in case of Asoka, these temples marks the geographical extend of the kings rule.

7. Showing Political Supremacy

Construction of temples is often carried as mentioned before majority after his victory in wars. By destroying temples of other kings or religion, he marks his authority and set of belief over others. The construction of temples in other kingdoms had shown a political diplomacy making peaceful relations with the neighboring rulers or marking the powerful kings authority or superiority over in other kingdoms. Often modifying temples of other faiths or sects of other kingdoms after victory over the other states, marks a political, psychological authoritarian position of the king in minds of his enemies and common folk.

8. Period of Power, Peace and Diplomacy

The construction of temples marks a period of peace and power. Arts develop only in the period of non-flux and peace. Under the rule of a sovereign king or being himself as sovereign and powerful over others, there exists a period of peace. This peace can only be ensured when the bound aries have been secured efficiently and the diplomacy of the state is superior and efficient enough to suppress weaker states under itself. This shows an important political achievement.

9. Executing Sufficient Resources and Well-administration

It is through sufficient wealth, well-administration and support of common folk, a king can erect up a temple because an efficient management of wealth-administration and its requirement boots up these constructions. The proper-administration and diplomacy makes a peaceful scenario, with the treasure properly filled in without atrocities, to support the execution of the temple. This over choose a political achievement by creating and executing a powerful and well administration and sufficient resources for the state and common folk.

10. Temple-as a Political Message Centre

Brihadeshwara temple inscription for public welfare, and to execute his massages and orders, what the king did for as the welfare of folk, executing his rulers and regulations for people of the state.

11. Showing Power through Iconography and Gigantic Structure

I. Tripurantaka on Brihadeshwara temple on 03 sides symbolically represents the won all 03 directions of other empire.

II. Image of god s a medium to co-relate with kings authority, Chola paintings of Guru and Rajaraj –I discussing about state matters.

III. Chandineshwar temple-Gangaikindacholapuram-Shiva revering 'Chanihera' as Raja Rajeshwara.

IV. Rajarajeshwara-I image at one niche at the outer wall of mandapa,

V. Setting relation to the constructor (Raja Raja-II),

VI. Naming temples on the names of the kings, Queen or the erector of the temple.

VII. Ajanta is also one of the examples of international relation where an African man meeting to Pulkesin-II.

12. Centre for Communication to the Public

Temples as today in south India are the important place where people use to gather for their ritual and other religious activities. That is why many massages of King usually announced there. The temples played an important role for delivering the massages, like todays government News channels.

Conclusion

Above all are showing several positive and negative approaches under the banner of a temple. It was not the temple, it was the ruler and the priest who misused the temple and still one can see in the South Indian temples especially where one cannot enter without paying the money. The person who wants to get *darshan* of the god, they need to pay. The big joke is those who has more money can get *darshan* comfortably and without standing in queue. Many temple of East, West and especially south India were and are the centre for keeping money, jewelry, coins, costly idols etc. There are still several questions for the purpose of temple. Without studying the context base case study one should not come to conclusion about the purpose of temple were only for negative or only for positive. This is just a small attempt to describe about the different purposes of temple construction. The writeup is based on the personal experience of visits to the temple site in all over India, Epigraphs and personal communication with the scholars of respective field.

15

Recently Discovered Megalithic Burials on the Banks of Vena River Nagpur District, Maharashtra

Ankush Dahat

Introduction

The development of human culture is hardly possible without water because water is the main source of survival among all sources. It is not possible to imagine life without water, probably that's why to improve the flow of life, in this direction the primitive culture developed where water easily available (Butzer 1964: 338). The eastern part of Maharashtra is known as Vidarbha. The remains of the culture from Stone Age to historical period are found from the vena river valley which is located in the south direction of Mahadgad hill of Katol Tehsil in Nagpur districtof Vidarbha, Maharashtra(Russell 1908: 6). This paper presented by the author has discovered sites of megalithic culture from his exploration at Wadgaon right bank of Vena River in HingnaTehsil, Nagpur district. Discuss about Nagpur district megalithic burial they are found nearby at 45-50 km areaand the distance between two sites is about 2-3 km (Moorti 1984-85: 57). The discovery of megalithic culture started in Indian subcontinent in 1816 (Mohanty & Walimbe 1993: 93). The first megalithic investigation and excavation done by Babingtonat Malabar (Babington 1823: 324-25; Deo 1973:1).Since then many sites of megalithic culture was discovered and excavated, as a result some questions related to this culture have appeared like , why this burial were erected ? Or was this burial was made for or erected for every person in the society or only for those who were very special(Mohanty & Walimbe 1993: 93). As far as Vidarbha is concern for the discovery of megalithic sits credit goes to major Pearse, Rivett Carnac and Hislop who explore and excavated the megalithic burial at Wadgaon and Takalghat near Nagpur (Sawant 2015: 411-412).

Geographical and Geological condition

Nagpur district is situated in the north east of Maharashtra N 210 08 59, E 790 08 50. The Madhya Pradesh is situated northern side of Nagpur, Bhandara in the east part and Chandrapur in the south and Wardha district in the west side. In Nagpur there are two main rivers, one is the Pench and another is Kanhan river and both rivers are originated from the Satpura mountain (Dahat 2018:19) due to the Deccan plateau in

The background of Megalithic culture of Vidarbha

Every archaeological researcher identifies the Vidarbha for their megalithic culture from the middle of the 19th century the Vidarbha is known for their megalithic culture, mainly from Nagpur district and eastern part of Vidarbha. Wardha-Wainganga valley we have received many megalithic cultural sites. Like other sites of Vidarbha we have found the different types of megalithic culture from this area which include cairn circle, cairn, stone circle, cists burials etc (Dahat 2018:20). The archaeological researcher excavated these burials in large quantity and studied their culture which includes some important burial site Mahurjhari (*IAR*, 1992-93), TakalghatKhapa (*IAR*, 1967-68, Deo 1970:1), Naikund (*IAR* 1979-80), Khairwada (*IAR* 1981-82), Junapani (*IAR* 1961-62), DhamnaLinga (*IAR* 2002- 01), Vyahad (*IAR* 1961-62,Kellellu 2006), Raipur (*IAR* 1989-90, Deglurkar & Lad 1992 : 2) etc.

Description

The present megalithic site is situated on the east side of the village Wadgaon, at the right bank of the Vena River. The site is spread in an area of 8-10 acres. 63 cairn circles were discovered from here, the Megalithic site Raipur and Takalghat Khapa are situated in the north and south of Wadgaon respectively. Both the sites definitely have some connection with the people of megalithic culture located in Wadgaon. Large number of burials means that the settlement of this people must have been around here. But as we know the settlement found here are much lesser than the burials. On this site an attempt to find the habitation of people was tried, but none was found. The stones which have been used to erect this kind of burials must have been obtained from the river, because there was a lot of quarrying activity seen near the riverbed. The documentation of all 63 cairn circles was not possible but some burials have been documented by author which is mentioned below.

Table 1: Geographical Coordinates of the Explored Burials

Sl. No.	N-S	E-W	North	East	Elevation
1	18 M	18 M	20^0 58 05.4	78^0 59 31.0	304 M
2	12M	15 M	20^0 58 06.6	78^0 59 31.0	303 M
3	12.60 M	12.60 M	20^0 58 08.1	78^0 59 32.3	301 M
4	10.30 M	6.90 M	20^0 58 09.6	78^0 59 38.2	298 M
5	7.40 M	6 M	20^0 58 09.5	78^0 59 40.6	291 M
6	6 M	6 M	20^0 58 10.4	78^0 59 49.6	283 M

7	14 M	14 M	20^0 58 14.3	78^0 59 50.4	280 M
8	14 M	11 M	20^0 58 14.3	78^0 59 53.3	282 M
9	12.40 M	13 M	20^0 58 34.3	78^0 00 18.2	285 M
10	14 M	14.20 M	20^0 58 07.7	78^0 59 52.9	274 M

Conclusion

Despite excavation and exploration of Raipur, Takalghat Khapa etc around these sites, this burial site came into light only with the help of this paper and put forth before future researchers and scholars for further study,this isthe main purpose of presenting this article and bringing forward hereto unknown Megalithic Cairn Burial in Nagpur District.

Acknowledgements

The author is extremely thankful to Dr. PriydarshiKhobragade and K. S. Chandrafor valuable suggestions and guidance incorporated in this article and also expresses gratitude to Mr.AmardeepBarsagade and Ms. Ekta Meshram for their sincere help during exploration.

References

Babington, S. 1823. Description of the pandoo coolies in Malabar, Transaction of the Literary society of Bombay vol-3

Butzer, K.W. 1964. Environment and archeology an introduction to Pleistocene, Methuen & co. limited, London

Dahat, A.R. 2018. New findings of megalithic burials in Mohgaon district Chhindwara Madhya Pradesh,*Arnava Vol. VII-1*, ISSN-2320-0103

Dahat, A.R, Dongre.N and Gorle. S, 2019, Discovery of New Megalithic Burials in Gadchiroli District (Vidarbha), Maharashtra Madhya Pradesh, *Arnava Vol. VIII-1*, ISSN-2320-0103

Deo, S.B. 1970. Excavation at Takalghat and Khapa (1968 69), Nagpur: Nagpur University

Deo, S.B. 1973. Problem of south Indian megaliths, Karnataka University, Dharwad

Deglurkar, G.B. and G. Lad, 1992, Megalithic Raipur (1985 1990), Pune: Deccan CollegePostGraduate and Research Institute *Indian Archaeology: A Review*: 1961-62, 1967-68, 1981-82, 1989-90, 1992-93, 2001-02.Archaeological Survey of India, New Delhi

Ismail Kellellu, 2006, Excavation at Vyahad, (paper presented in XXXIV annual Conference of ISPQS), Raipur

Moorti R. 1984-85, Socio economic aspects of megalithic Vidarbha, Puratattva, Bulletin of the Indian archaeological society Vol-15

Mohanty, R.K and Walimbe, S.R, 1993, A Demographic Approach to the Vidarbha Megalithic Culture,*Man and Environment XVIH (2),* Deccan College Pune

Russell, R.V. 1908. Central provinces district gazetteer of Nagpur district, Vol. A, Time Press, Bombay

Sawant R. 2015. Megalithic studies in Nagpur division: contributions of colonial period, Heritage Vol-3, ISSN 2347- 5463

Wadia, D.N. 1944. Geology of India, Macmillan and co. Ltd. London

16

Major Crafts of Harappan Civilization

Jagpal Singh

Introduction

Harappan cherished Beads and ornaments. Their stone and terracotta figurines and also the human figures inscribed intaglio on their seals amply demonstrate how much they enjoyed adorning themselves with headbands, earrings, necklaces, bracelets, bangles and waistbands. Apparently, both men and women wore ornaments, a vital part of which consisted of beads: a large variety of stunning beads.

A majority of Harappan sites have yielded massive quantities of these trinkets. Indian women who follow sanatana Dharma wear black glass beads as an emblem of Suasti in their Mangalsutra. Abundance of beads at nearly all Harappan sites makes one wonder if the tradition of carrying beads as an emblem of Suasti originated within the Harappan Civilization (Possehl 1982: 239-244).

Harappan beads are varied in their shape, size and material. Some are cylindrical, globular, spheroidal, biconical, segmented. Many a time, they are embellished with trefoil or circular designs. Material together with gold, silver, copper, carnelian, agate, chalcedony, steatite, shell and clay were used. The prevalence of these beads in abundance and in many varieties at nearly all Harappan sites clearly shows how much they were appreciated.

Agate

The production and trade of assorted forms of carnelian beads or agate has played a vital role in native and regional economics of the historic and prehistoric periods in South Asia. Presently the town of Khambhat (Cambay) is one among the biggest stone bead operating centres of the globe, and it has been a vital centre for more than 3000 years of documented history. With the help of archaeological analysis, the stone bead trade in western India and Pakistan can be derived back to the cities and villages of the Harappan phase of the Indus tradition (Allchin 1994: 281-286).

(Agate Industry of western India)

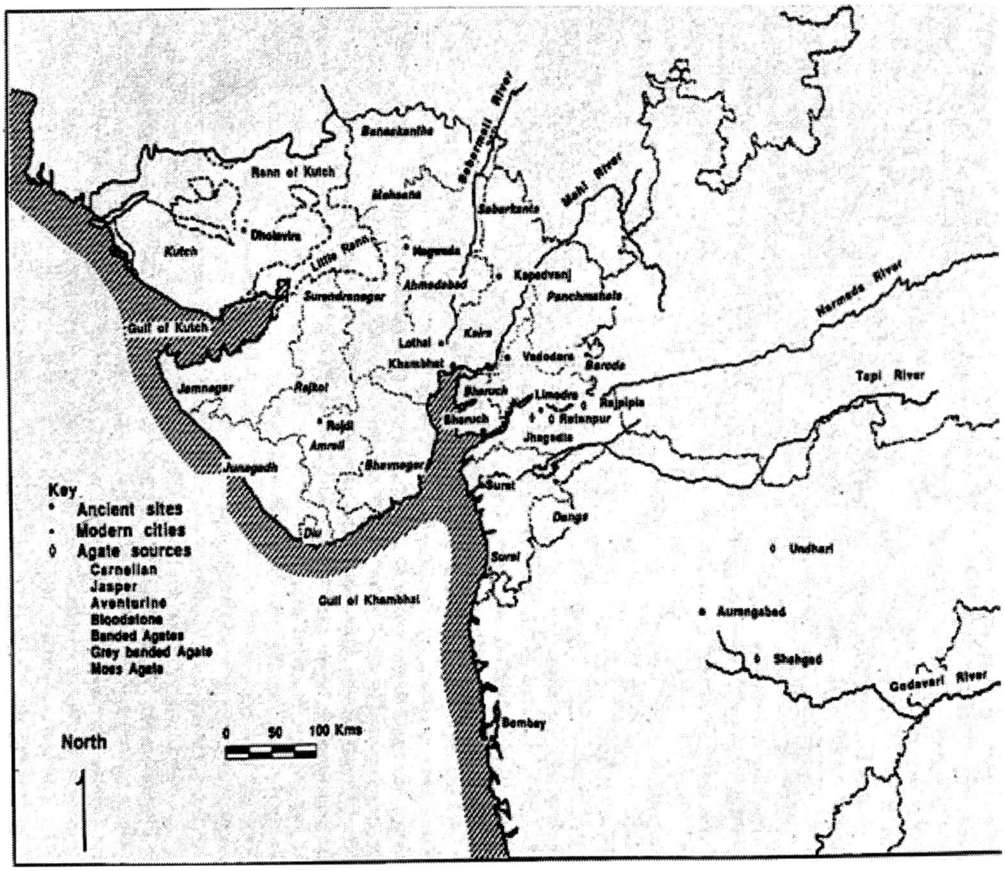

Fig. 1: Map
(Source: Allchin, B.(Eds.) Living Traditions, Oxford & IBH Pub., N. Delhi, 1994, pp.282)

The ethno archaeological study of Khambhat bead making has been an effort to record a wide set of information on this ancient specialized industry before it is utterly remodeled by technological modification and the introduction of contemporary socioeconomic relationships. The general objective of this project has been to document and correlate the dynamic and sophisticated socioeconomic relationships of the bead industry with specific archaeological pattern. In my study I will focus solely on the production of red-orange agate beads, more often stated as carnelian.

Archaeologically discernible patterns are often attributed to the various kinds of workshops and there are distinctive patterns of variation in finished merchandise resulting from tiny and large-scale production. By correlating the archaeological patterning of producing waste and finished objects with different features like architecture and settlement layout it is possible distinguish levels of organization and management of production.

The initial results from this study indicate that an enormous amount of archaeological relevant data may be obtained through systematic ethno archaeological analysis of an ancient craft, like bead making. On the premise of this info it is possible to propose new analysis methods and informative models for the study of prehistoric bead making.

During the last century there has been a proliferation of documentary accounts of the bead industry at Khambhat and also the mining in near regions. one amongst the foremost comprehensive vital historical accounts of the bead industry in Gujarat has been provided by Peter Francis however there are various discrepancies in his description of the region, the prevailing techniques employed in totally different localities, and different aspects of the industry that are crucial to archaeological interpretations.

Several different scholars have reported on their visits to Khambhat or have stated this industry in their studies of bead making at specific archaeological sites, whereas all of these many accounts of the bead industry are vital historical documents, the data on material culture aspects and details of technology are not recorded adequately for archaeological purposes (Allchin 1994: 281-286).

Chert and lazuli

The key sources of brown-grey chert for the Harappan phase were most likely the huge limestone outcrops at Rohri (Central Pakistan). There are, however, sources of similar materials to the south and occasional nodules of equally coloured sherts were found within the rivers flowing out of Baluchistan. The Elaborated studies on cherts and different materials that were used to build flaked stone need to be performed to outline more precisely this vital network.

One amongst the foremost vital varities of artefacts created from grey - brown chert is the cube shaped weights used throughout the Harappan phase that were found distributed far beyond the boundaries of Harappan cultural dominance. These weights were also created with agate and different hard stones, however much less in numbers. This can be explained by the specific gravity of the chert that is totally different from agates, and also by the availability of the raw material. It had been a lot easier to form different sized objects from chert, whose weight distribution was way more than that of agates, and that was also more easily accessible (Wezler 1995: 193-235).

The main supply centres for lapis lazuli could be near the areas of the Chagai Hills in the Southern Baluchistan and within the area of Badakshan, Northern Afghanistan. it is impractical to determine if any of the regions was a primary supply spot; it is a lot probable to say that by the end of the Harappan phase each of the areas were being employed at the same time.

Shell

The shell industry of the Harappan period also reflects the stratification within the trade of raw material and also the movement of finished goods. At Mohenjodaro, Chanhudaro, Harappa,

Nagwada, Rangpur, etc. we see a good variety of objects being primarily created for markets within the sites and also the adjoining sites. One the other hand little rural cities or coastal sites like Allahdino, Balakot, Nageshwar and Gola Dhoro created a limited range of artefacts.

At Balakot, the intensive production of Tivela damaoides bangles seems to have been specifically for native inhabitants. Nageshwar, however, appears to have been specialised centre for the assembly of bangles and ladles and Gola Dhoro for bangles manufactured primarily for the regional and extra - regional markets. In contrasts to specialization technology was quite standardized (Bhan *et al.* 1998: 4141-151).

Steatite Beads

White microbeads were recovered from excavations at Harappa, Chanhudaro, Kalibangan, Lothal, Rojdi and Zekda. However, so far, solely the excavator of Chanhudaro has described them in some detail these beads recovered in the excavation of the Harappan site at Zekda.

(Harappan sites that have yielded Steatite Micro beads).

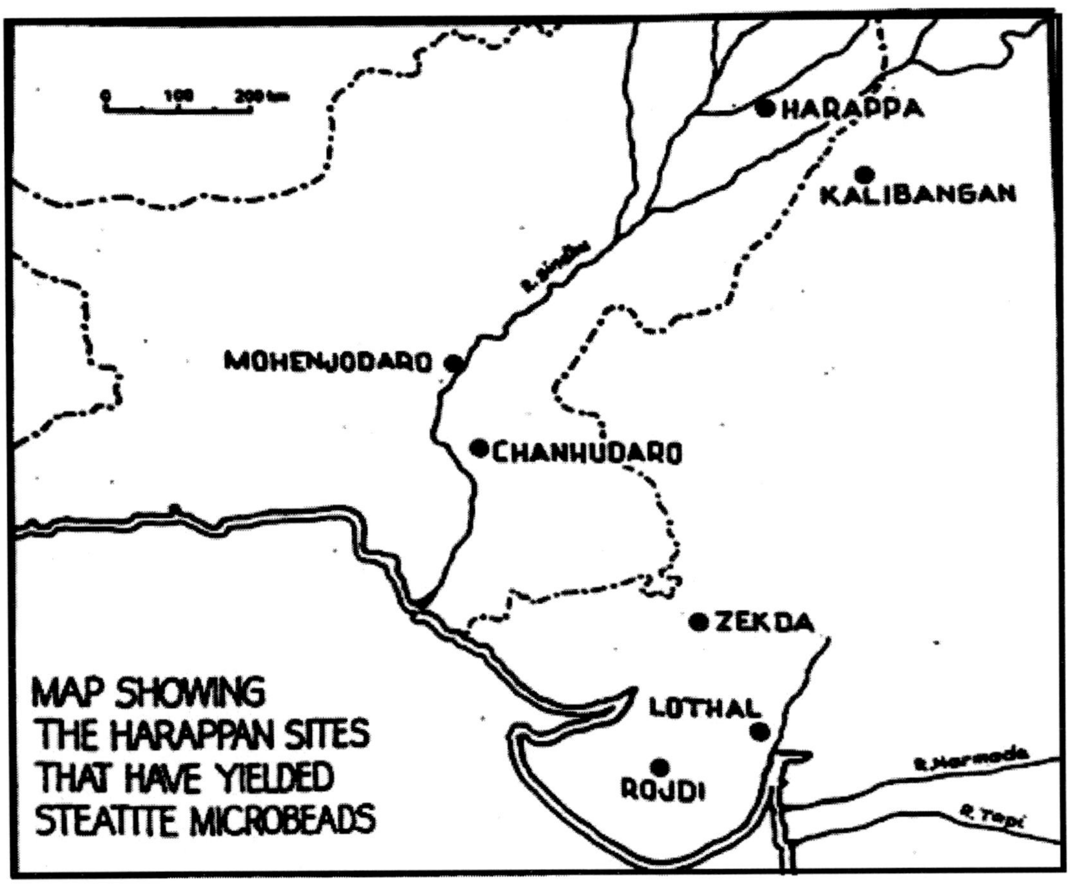

Source: Possehl, G. L., Harappan Civilization, Oxford & IBH Pub., New Delhi, 1982)

Zekda is a very important Harappan site, set in northern part of Gujarat state. Zekda was discovered by Parikh and was excavated by the M.S. University of Baroda, during the field season of 1977 - 78, under the direction of Professor R.N. Mehta.

The excavation disclosed a Harappan habitation of significant period. It yielded several characteristic varieties of Harappan pottery with a number of the distinctive ornamental motifs, perforated vases, terracotta cakes, chert blades, chert cores with crested ridge flaking, fragments of copper objects, together with the sherds of White Painted Black and Red Ware that is often stated as "Ahar Ware." This Harappan settlement is, therefore, one amongst the relatively late Indus settlements, where the material remains of the Harappans unified, without any clear break, into that of the Post - Harappan Culture. Among different vital discoveries made in the excavation of the site aretwo hoards of microbeads (Possehl 1982: 239-244).

The beads were found carefully preserved in two tiny pots. One amongst them was covered with a well - fitting, hollow, cork - like pottery stopper. The other one was carefully placed within another vessel and the outer pot covered with a solid, fitted, baked clay lump. Each of the pots were found buried beneath house floors. They were recovered from layer two of Trench B, cut close to the central part of the mound. The great care with which they preserved the beads at Zekda clearly shows how extremely the Harappan valued them. At Chanhudaro a hoard of white microbeads was also found in a very tiny pot. The Zekda pots so had roughly 34,000 beads (Possehl 1982: 239-244).

References

Allchin, Bridget, 1994, *Living Traditions*, Oxford & IBH Publishing Company Pvt. Ltd., New Delhi.

Bhan, K.K. and J.M. Kenoyer, 1984, Nageshwar: A Mature Harappan site on the Gulf of Kutch, *Journal of the Oriental Institute 34 (1-2).*

Possehl, G.L., 1982, *Harappan civilization: contemporary perspective,* Oxford & IBH Company Pvt. Ltd., New Delhi.

Wezler, Albrecht and Michael Witzel, 1995, (eds.), *Indian Philology and South Asian Studies, Vol.1,* Walter de Gruyter, Berlin, New York.

17

A Review of Pottery Types During the Mahajanapadas

Mohammad Nazrul Bari

Introduction

Pottery was invented to meet man's need to store, transport and barter food, once food production became the norm. In the first instance, a hollow stone or a skull might have served this need. But people might have found the objects available in nature inadequate to meet their requirements. Then by some stroke of chance, it would have struck his inquisitive mind to use clay, which is abundantly available, soft, flexible and easy to handle. Containers of the desired shape and size made out of clay were then sun-dried. But the problem of making these pots waterproof and hard, so that they could be used for cooking food, still remained. Only after a good deal of trial and error, people would have learned the baking of clay pots and making them water tight (Dahiya1986: 36). The earliest fragments of pottery were documented in Mesolithic levels at Bhainsaura in Mirzapur, Kutch in Gujarat and Mangaureki – Bauthi and Mohana in Banda district (Dahiya 1986: 36).

In this paper an attempt has been made to discuss the ceramic industry and the functions of different utensils used by the people. Besides clay, stone, metal, wood, leather and shells (The shell of fruits is normally used by *Sadhus* (hermit) of the present days) of fruits might have also been used for making vessels for daily use. Unfortunately, due to their perishable nature, archaeological evidence is lacking. But their possible use is surmised on the ground that all these are still used in pot making. *Jaina* (Dev 152-53: 33) and *Buddhist* (Mahavagga,vi,14.2) literatures too, provide a list of materials in which all the above mentioned materials are employed in pot making. But only earthen vessels offer us an opportunity for detailed study, the rest is so meagre that no generalization appears possible.

The existence of a ceramic industry is proved from the discovery of pottery pieces from the excavations at different sites. The potteries of the period under research generally include the

Black and Red Ware (BRW), the Black Slipped Ware, Grey Ware, Red Ware and most importantly the NBPW.

Black and Red Ware (BRW)

The Black and Red Ware is pre-NBPW in origin but continues even after the introduction of NBPW as reported from most of the sites in India. Different forms of BRW known to us include such shapes as basins, bowls, dishes, dish on stand in both coarse and fine varieties, the former being numerically better represented than the latter. The coarse ones were fired under low temperature while the finer ones are a result of firing to a high temperature (Kumar 1986:76).

About its place of origin and date, Singh (Sinha 1969: 67) points out that BRW has been found mainly in two contexts, one belonging to the proto-historic period from south-eastern Rajasthan with Ahar as the type-site and the second, in association with the megalithic pottery found in innumerable iron-age graves and urn-fields of south India. But Subbarao (1958: 179), Wheeler (1958: 166-167) and Soundara Rajan have traced its origin to Ahar.

Black Slipped Ware

It has been observed that the smooth surface of the Black Slipped Ware has a basic resemblance with NBPW, minus its gloss(Ghosh 1989: 240). In these ware different types of bowls are the most commonly found type while the dish, followed by the jar, vase and miniature vessels, comes next in order of frequency. Its earliest occurrence has led to the assumption by Ghosh that it represents an experimental stage in the development of the NBPW (Ghosh 1989: 240). At Rajghat, Prahladpur, Kausambi, Sravasti, Hastinapura, Ahichchhatra, Ujjain, Vaisali, Rajgir, Pataliputra, Chirand and Sonpur etc. the Black Slipped Ware has been found in the NBPW levels along with the Black and Red Ware which is occasionally painted (Ghosh 1989: 240).

The Grey Ware and the Red Ware

These two ceramic industries were the most common ones. In Grey Ware the shapes most commonly found are dishes, bowls, lipped bowls, carinated *handis* etc. At Chirand, according to Kumar "the Grey Ware is found in the Neolithic strata and continues in the chalcolithic period" (Kumar 1986: 90).

The increased frequency of Red Ware as compared to other wares suggests that it was the most commonly used ware in all cultural periods at each site. The ware includes the usual types, e.g., basins, vases, dishes, bowls (lipped and plain), *handis*, big jars, pots with decorative spouts, pans and other miniature pots including goblets (Kumar 1986: 90). Deva (Deva & Mishra1969:42) suggests that some miniature pots might have been used as toys for children and others as thimbles. The different shapes might have served different purposes. Basins, vases and *handis* were used for cooking purposes. Red Ware (Deva & Mishra 1969:42) has also been found in fine, medium and coarse fabrics. But, all these wares were not plain. Some have been found with decoration, too. We notice interesting decorations on a large jar at Vaisali (Deva & Mishra 1969:92).These decorations include the taurine symbol, which has been punched deeply, impressed rosettes resembling spoked wheel with pellets and solar designs. Some sherds are also found impressed with *srivatsa*or *purnaghata*motifs on the body and small rosettes on the neck with angling hooks on the shoulder.

Northern Black Polished Ware (NBPW)

This ware, a hallmark of this period, signifies the zenith of technology in the ceramic industry. The NBPW has a very wide distribution. About its geographical distribution Thapar (Thapar 1957:1) writes that it was from "Charsadda near Peshawar and Udegram in Swat in the north, Tilaurakot in the Nepalese 'tarai', PrabhasPatan on the Kathiawar littoral in the west, Ujjain, Maheshwar and Nasik on the trunk route from the Ganga-Yamuna Doab to the Arabian Sea, Ter and Brahma Puri in the Deccan, Kauandanpur and Berachampa in the east."

The shapes (1954-55: 51) in the NBPW are represented by (i) dish with inverted or straight sides, (ii) bowl with inverted, convex, corrugated or tapering sides, (iii) lid with a flat terminal and (iv) the sharply carinated *handis*. Of these, bowls and dishes are the most common types. This ware was made of well-levigated clay and fired to a high temperature under reducing conditions. The uniform firing of NBPW suggests that they were possibly fired in a sagger (Kumar 1986: 85).The ware ranged in different colours like black, steel blue, pinkish, silvery, golden etc. Similar shades are reported from Kausambi, Prahladpur, Hastinapura, Ahichchhatra, Vaisali, Sonpur, Oriup and many other sites of Bihar (Singh 1985: 84). The available shapes and frequency of the NBPW from different excavations shows that this ware had a restricted use, either for eating or, in some cases, storing liquids or some precious material.

But at Rajghat (Ghosh 1989:253) the NBPW accounts for nearly 50% of the total pottery recovered from c 600-200 BCE. This can broadly be divided into two groups, namely monochrome and bichrome. All the monochrome specimens have a fine thin fabric. They are made of well-levigated clay with little tempering material. They are invariably made on a fast wheel and have a strikingly lustrous surface. The core is blackish grey but in some cases reddish. The colour of the surface, of almost 90% pieces in this group is jet-black, brownish black or bluish black. But the other 10% are steel blue, pinkish, silvery, golden, brown, chocolate, violet or deep red.

The bichrome ware is much less frequent though it shares all the features of the monochrome group. The NBPW found in such large numbers suggests that the industry was in a flourishing state. Production was possibly not for local consumption but to exports to other centres. It may also be surmised that besides catering to the local requirement the pottery may also have its trade significance. Since Rajghat is generally identified with ancient Varanasi it may, on the evidence of a *Jataka* (A separate suburban village of potters near Varanasi is shown to exist).Be postulated that the potter's industry here was in a flourishing state. Motichandra citing *DhammapadaAtthakatha* states, "A potter from Varanasi loaded his earthen vessels on a donkey and carried them from city to city to sell them" (Chand 1977: 57).

Archaeologists generally consider pottery as primary cultural material. They study the pottery mainly with a view to identify cultures and establish the chronological sequence of sites. However, except Sankalia,(Sankaliya: 47-52) who in his short article attempts to discuss the functional significance of vessels of the earlier periods along with other objects, no serious attempt in this direction has yet been made.

Another difficulty is that even one pot might have often served more than one function as today. Examples are of the bowls and dishes, which will normally come under the broad classification of vessels used for eating. But during the course of the present study, it has been observed that they might have been used for various purposes, depending upon their size and forms. The bowls could have been used as containers, lid-cum-bowls, and drinking cups. Bowls recovered at Nagara (Mehta 1968: 43) and Kumrahar (Alltekar & Mishra 1959) have the outer surface of their base blackened due to fire, indicating that some of them were even used for cooking purposes. We can broadly classify the different potteries as follows:

(i) Cooking vessels
(ii) Eating vessels
(iii) Drinking vessels or vessels for storing water
(iv) Pots for storage purposes and
(v) Industrial utensils

(i) Cooking Vessels: In this category we can safely put the*handis, karahis*and basins having a lipped spout (Gaur 1983: 310-313). Cooking vessel were generally red, grey and black slipped. Majority of the cooking pots, which were large in size, were made of Red Ware. The percentage distribution of these wares suggests that the most frequent variety was Red Ware. Cooking vessels in this variety were often decorated. The appliqué mode of decoration of the preceding phase, which was very poor in execution, greatly improved during this period. In addition to this, incised decoration was also introduced. These decorations (Singh 1985: 84) on the vessels have been noticed at three places, viz. at the edge of the rim, on the external part of the body, and occasionally on the neck portion, particularly in the case of miniature pots. There are very few examples in which the decoration is noticed below the mid portion of the pot.

(ii) Eating Vessels: This type of vessel comprises dish, bowl, and lipped bowl. The dish can be identified as *thali* for taking daily meals, either in dry or liquid form. They were represented in almost all types and varieties of pottery assemblage of the period. They were of varying sizes and forms. Singh on the basis of diameters of the dishes at Rajghat, divides them into three types, viz., small, medium and large. Of these, the diameter of the first group, according to him ranges from "20.4 mm. to 26.2 mm. with their main concentration being between 20.4 mm. – 25.5 mm" (Singh 1985: 86). All these have flat or flattish bases, which would not require any support when placed on the ground. The specimens belonging to the second and the third varieties "range in diameter from 26.3 mm. to 38.4 mm. But their main concentration is between 30.3 – 37.6 cm. Most of them were *thalis,* to be used by the adults. These were mostly with rounded, straight, convex and straight, tapering sides and usually, flat and flattish bases" (Singh 1985: 86).

The bowls (*katora* or *katori in Hindi*)have been found in fairly good numbers. All these specimens have either incurved, convex, rounded or vertically straight sides. The last one is mainly available from Sarai Mohana (IAR1967-68: 48).

(iii) Drinking Vessels or Vessels for Storing Water: A fragment of a tub (Sinha & Roy 1969: fig.35) and *surahi* (Sinha & Roy 1969: fig.37-40) of red ware reported at Vaisali are the best examples of vessels of this category. Singh (1985: 80) divided the Rajghat vessels of this kind into three types. "(i) stemmed bowl, (ii) bowls used as cups or tumblers, and (iii)*lota* like vessels" and adds, "of these three, first two are made mostly in the slipped variety, while the last is in the ordinary red ware". At Rajghat a large number of *lota* like objects made of dull red ware are reported in the pits of privies. Since these pots are without slip or wash and their fabric is rough, Roy, suggests "it is not unlikely that they were used as *lotas*for carrying water by persons using these pits as privies or latrines" (Roy 1983: 193-194). A *lota*type of miniature vase of red ware is also reported at Vaisali (Sinha & Roy 1969: fig.44).

(iv)Pots for Storage Purposes: Inthis category two types of vessels make their appearance in several excavations: one for the ordinary foodstuff or grain and the other for storing liquid. The vessels of the first type were mostly made of red ware, whereas the vessels used for the latter purpose were mostly produced in black slipped and other slipped ware (Roy 1983: 193-194).

In contemporary literature the word *kumbha* (Singh 1969: 304) is used for the vessel used to store liquid and *kusula* (Vasu 1962: 56) for storing grains. They are of various sizes. Their height, in a majority of cases, could not be determined. As mostly the rim portion is available, their sizes are tentatively gauged on the basis of the diameters of the rim and their thickness. The vessels of the first group were most probably used for storing grains. This can be postulated on the basis of their forms. Most of these have a carinated neck and their body in all cases is rounded. The second group comprises vessels which are pitchers (*ghara*or *matka*in Hindi). Their purpose appears to have been the same as that of the *ghara*of the present day. From Champa, Prasad cites an interesting miniature waterpot (*surahi*) made of NBP ware, which according to him has "thin section, the outer surface of which seems to be polished with silvery colour having bluish tint and finally fish scale design is painted on it in buff-like colour" (Prasad 1987: 114). Such type of pots are not available from the other sites.

The above mentioned vessels, though broken, are found in large quantity from different sites. These vessels, it seems, were used by the people to keep their surplus grains for ready availability in times of need. Besides such storage vessels, granaries also were discovered at Atranjikhera and Mathura (Allchin 1965:112).The granary found at Atranjikhera has three cells, partitioned by walls. Each cell is rectangular in shape, measures 1.75 meters in width and is provided with two openings or doors (Gaur 1983: 249) (Plate No.9).

(v)Industrial Utensils: In this category pots generally used as crucibles are encountered. The pottery of this kind is reported at Kausambi (Sharma 1969:97) and Rajghat (Singh 1985: 88). Two crucibles were also found at Rajghat in this phase. One of them is small and almost intact. Its capacity is given as 46cc. The other one seems to have been of a larger size. Both these specimens show a vitrified and enamelled outer surface. This phenomenon is said to be due to the high temperature to which it may have been subjected. Both have rounded bases and convex sides. Singh suggests that "they were used for melting purposes, which is evidenced by the presence of green rusted bits of metal sticking on the inner walls of the specimens" (Singh 1985: 88).

Each of the above mentioned utensils is reported in excavations. The different shapes and varieties of the ware lead us to suppose that Grey Ware and Red Ware were the common man's pottery. The Black and Red Ware (BRW) and NBPW are available in certain specific types but grey and red wares were of all the shapes required for household chores, namely cooking, storing and eating. The small to medium sized vessels seems to dominate the NBPW at every site. It appears that NBPW vessels had a restricted use, either for eating, or in some cases, for storing only liquids or precious materials like ghee, oil etc. This pottery is so unique and delicate that it is regarded as the prince (Prasad 1987: 96) among the potteries or deluxe ware (Sinha 1969: 146). The value attached to this ware can be judged from the repair done by means of copper wire or pin riveting as reported by the excavators of Rupar, (Sahay:146) Bairat (Sahay: 146), Ujjain(Sahay:146), Sonpur(Sahay:146), Kumrahar(Sahay: 146), Khairadih(Sahay: 146) etc. It appears, therefore, that instead of throwing away these pots they were used or preserved by the people. It is also interesting to note that these repaired vessels are found not only from those places where they might have been imports, but also from Sonpur and Khairadih (Sinha 1969: 85) which have been suggested as centrrs of production. From the above discussion, it is possible to infer that NBPW was a prized commodity of the period and produced largely to cater to the need of the elites in the society.

References

Allchin, F.R., (ed.), 1995, *Archaeology of Early Historic South Asia*, Cambridge.

Altekar, A.S. and Mishra, V., 1959, *Report on Kumrahar Excavation: 1951 – 55*, Patna

Ancient India, Vol. 10 &11.

Chanda, Moti, 1977, *Trade and trade routes in Ancient India*, New Delhi.

Dahiya, Neelima, 1986, *Arts and Crafts in Northern India*, Delhi.

Deo, S.B., 1952-53, Pots and Utensils from Jain literature, *Bulletin of Deccan College Research Institute (BDCRI), Vol. XIV, No.1* .

Deva, Krishna and Mishra, Vijayakanta, 1961, *Vaisali Excavation: 1950*, Vaisali.

Gaur, R.C., 1983, Excavations at Atranjikhera, Delhi.

Ghosh, A. (ed.), 1989, *Encyclopaedia of Indian Archaeology*, New Delhi: Vol.1.

Indian Archaeology: A Review(IAR), 1967 – 68.

Kumar, D., 1986, *Archaeology of Vaisali*, New Delhi.

Mehta, R.N., 1968, *Excavations at Nagara*, Baroda.

Prasad, Ram Chandra, 1987, *Archaeology of Champa and Vikramsila*, Delhi.

Roy, T.N., 1983, *The Ganges Civilization*, New Delhi.

Roy, T.N., 1986, *A Study of Northern Black Polished Ware Culture*, New Delhi.

Sahay, Sachchidanand, Origin and Spread of the Northern black Polished Ware, (ed.) B.P. Sinha, *Potteries in Ancient India.*

Sankalia, H.D., Functional Significance of O.C.P. and P.G.W. shapes and associated objects, *Puratattva 7.*

Sinha, B.P., 1969,(ed.) *Potteries in Ancient India*, Patna.

Sinha, B.P. & Roy, S.R., 1969, *Vaisali Excavations, 1958 – 62*, Patna.

Singh, B.P., 1985, *Life in Ancient Varanasi*, Delhi.

Singh, Shivaji,1969, Vedic Literature on Pottery, Sinha, B.P. (ed.), *Potteries in Ancient India*, Patna.

Sharma, G.R., 1969, The Excavations at Kausambi: 1949 – 50, New Delhi: *Memories of Archaeological Survey of India, No.74.*

Soundra Rajan, K.V., Community movement in pre-historic India, An Archaeological perspective, *Journal of Oriental Institute, Baroda, Vol.II, No.1.*

Subharao, B., 1958, *Personality of India*, Baroda.

Thapar, B.K., *Ancient India, Vol.13* .

Vasu, Srisa Chandra,1962, (edited and translated) *Astadhyayi of Panini*, 2 vols, reprints, IV. 3.

Wheeler, M., 1958, *Early India and Pakistan*, London.

18

A Study of Kollam Coins of Tang Dynasty

Aswani O. K. and Vinuraj B.

Introduction

The coast of Kerala popularly known as Malabar Coast forms a single geographical and ethnical unit with similar customs and social organisation and marks as a separate entity in India. This strip of land has always been a hotspot of maritime trade especially for its geographical prospects and for being the hub of spices. Malabar Coast has been in direct contact with the sea- faring people from the West Asia and East Asiafrom very early periods onwards (Panikkar 1929: 1). Kollamport has a long history when it comes to its maritime intercourse. It was perpetuated by the Venad Chieftains, and they turned it into one of the most important ports of Medieval Kerala. The large volume of foreign trade from here was being handled by Christian, Jews and Muslims. It eventually became the most important transhipment centre for the trade between China and Persian Gulf countries (Kumar *et al.* 2016: 3-7). Kollam is known in ancient records as Colon, Kulam, Ku lin, Gu-lin, and Mahlai (Sarasan 2014: 09). Earliest reference to Kollam is obtained from an account given by Byzantine monk and Alexandrian traveller Cosmos Indicopleustus in his book *TopographiaIndika Christiania* (522 CE). Cosmos refers Kollam as Male and it is quite evident from his description that this city had the earliest evidence of Christian activity in Kerala (Mackenzie 1901:4).

Kollam as Gleaned from Chinese Sources

The maritime connection between India and China grew rapidly during 8th -9th century CE with the emergence of intermediate ports-of-trade in Southeast Asia(Sen 2006: 421-422). Chinese accounts also yield historical information about Kerala, Chinese travellers who have visited India has left their personal observations about this country and Chinese annals also mention of diplomatic embassies and exchanges during trade intercourses between India and China (Nainar 1942: 3). The Indian portsconsolidated their status as vital transhipment centres for goods originating from or destined for the Chinese markets. Kollam was the major port of call between Persia and China, the vessels from the west towards China and back was bounded through Indian peninsular coast, thus Kollamestablished its supreme position as a transhipment centre(Dikshitar 1946: 157-158). Kollam became the chief destination of the Chinese vessels by around 8th-9th centuries CE and retained this preferential position for the next six centuries, till the emergence of Calicut port during 14th-15th CE centuries. The commercial contacts between Kollam and China during this extended period coincide with the reign period of four major dynasties namely Tang (618-907 CE), Song (960-1229 CE) Yuan (1229-1368 CE) and Ming period (1368-1644 CE).

A passage in the text of Pan Kou, an early Chinese writer and historian attests the existence of an active intercourse between China and states of Southern India during the Han Period beginning from Second century BCE (Sastri 1939: 4). The accounts of Chinese historian Ma- Twan- Liu attest the presence of brisk trade between South India and China during 6th Century CE (Dikshitar 1946: 161). Some scholars argue that Chinese pilgrim Hiuen Tsang had visited Kerala in 7th Century CE, even though there are no substantial evidences to prove this (Menon 2007: 33). Chinese traveller Ma Huan mentions that Quilon was known to the Chinese navigators from 7th century CE onwards (Panikkar 1929: 6). According to records of Tang dynasty (618-913 CE), Quilon was their chief settlement and they give it the name of Mahlai (Menon 1964: 74). The mention of settlement indicate that Kollam was not just a trade outpost to the Chinese, but they considered it as a major centre for establishing trade activities in the Indian coast.

The itineraries compiled by Kia Tan, a Chinese geographer between 785 CE and 805 CE dealing with the sea-route from Canton to the Persian Gulf (Hirth and Rockhill 1911: 09-10), mentions that Chinese had trade relations with Kulam (Kollam) on the Malabar Coast (More 2003: 3). Kollam is termed as *Kulam Malay*, and is located on the Southern tip of India and regarded as a major port in the direct sailing route between China and Arab countries (Nakumara 1987: 147-148). Zhou Qufei (1178 CE) in his book *Ling-wai-ta-ta*, states that Kollam had become a busy and well known Entrepot and Chinese traders on the way to Arab countries spent their winter in Kollam and waited for favourable monsoon winds for their onward journey. Zhou gives a brief description of the journey towards Gu-lin (Kollam), it takes a seventy day journey on ship from Song china through Lanli (Sumatra) (Sen 2017: 67) and Chinese who wish to go to the country of Arabs must tranship at Kollam into smaller boats (Hirth and Rockhill 1911: 91). Chau-Ju-Kua (1225 CE), in his book *Chu-fan-chi* gives a detailed description of Ku-Lin (Kollam), Chau-ju-kua says that the port at Kollam had ships sailing from far places to trade here and back, from this inference it is quite clear that Kollam was the principal port of call for the Chinese traders and an important transhipment centre (Hirth and Rockhill 1911: 89-91). Apart from these textual and literary references, Kollam was a frequent spot of several diplomatic missions between China and Kollam.

The Chinese Coins

Coinage began in China when general barter was replaced by the use of certain products or objects to affect an exchange. These products include natural and manmade products like cowries, grain, textiles and tools (Ament 1888: 284). Chinese started by using cowrie shells for money, inscriptions and archaeological evidences points out that cowrie shells were regarded as objects of value in Shang dynasty. This early form of currency continued to be served as money over a long period of time (Thierry 1998: 15). By the end of the Shang dynasty bronze coins appeared which started an era of metal coinage (Sarasan 2014: 17). The first Chinese currency appeared in the shape of spades and knives, these shapes were derived from their common work implements of everyday use. Later round coins replaced spades and knives. These round holed coins were easy to carry. Round holed coins in turn gave way to square holed coins.

Thousands of Chinese coins have been recovered from the Kollam port as a result of dredging activities at the port in the year 2014 and the coin hoard is undoubtedly the largest Chinese coin hoard discovered in India (Kumar *et al.* 2016: 3-7). Several institutions and antiquity collectors were involved in the collection of this accidental find, thus it is difficult to ascertain the total number of coins recovered from the site. The Chinese coins are valuable sources when it comes to the maritime trade. Like Chinese ceramics, Chinese coins are also find in many parts of the world. Generally Chinese coins are composed of an alloy of copper and zinc or copper and lead and are always cast coins, not struck. Initially they were made out of stone moulds, but were replaced by wax moulds during the period of Tang dynasty (Ament 1888: 286). Their commercial tariff was based on the form and general size of the specimens. The intrinsic value of the metal had no role in the circulation of coins. The weight and the various patterns were regulated by the State, and everyone, including guild merchants of private and town communities, subject to these rules was at liberty to issue his own coins, bearing his distinctive symbol (written characters) or name (Lacouperie 1892: 28).

The Kai Yuan Tong Bao Series from Kollam

The Tang dynasty and its early emperors laid the foundation for the modernisation and standardisation of Chinese Currency (Edkins 1901: 5 & Wei 1914: 17). The Kai Yuan Tong Bao series of coins invented by them continued for centuries and changed the course of Chinese currency. The Tang Emperor GaoZu abolished the earlier versions of the currency and began minting the *Tong Bao* series of coins (Liuliang and Hong 2004: 12). *Kai Yuan Tong Bao* is the first edition of the *Tong Bao*series which began its minting from 621 CE and Continued till 907 CE. This particular group of coins were inherited by Qin dynasty coins with an outer circle and inner square and with a standard diameter and weight. Mints were established in several important cities to mint this series and were put under the observation of government executives. Counterfeiting of these coins were made punishable by

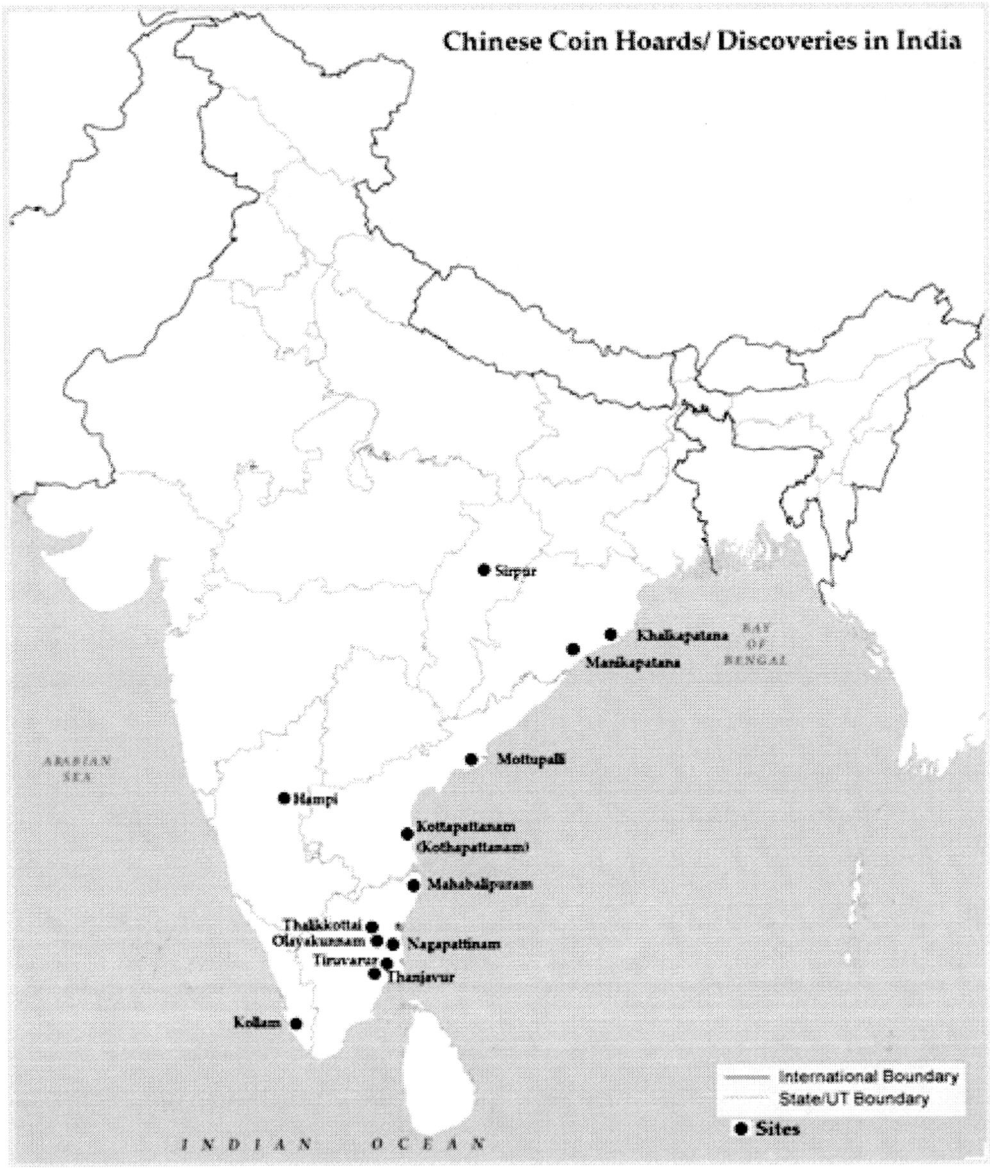

Fig. 1 : Map showing sites of Chinese Coin Hoards and Discoveries in India

confiscation of property and death (Wei 1914: 17). The Coin contained the Inscription Kai Yuan Tong Bao, in the standard character, *Kai* is the top Character, *Yuan* on the bottom, *tong* in right and *bao*in left. The *Kai Yuan* means "an opening of a new era" and *tong bao* means "universal currency" (Johnson 2013: 72).

A total of 1264 Chinese coins, recovered from Kollam were studied and systematically documented and a detailed catalogue has been prepared. Out of the 1264 coins 65 of them are the Kai Yuan Tong Bao series coins (Detailed description of the Coins are included in Annexure). Many coins were eroded and the legends are poorly visible. The coins generally have a standardised diameter range between 22 mm to 24 mm and a metallic weight between 2 gm to 4 gm. The Kai Yuan Tang Bao proves to be the earliest archaeological evidence reported from the site with its time period ranging between beginnings of 7th Century CE to the early decade of 10th Century CE.

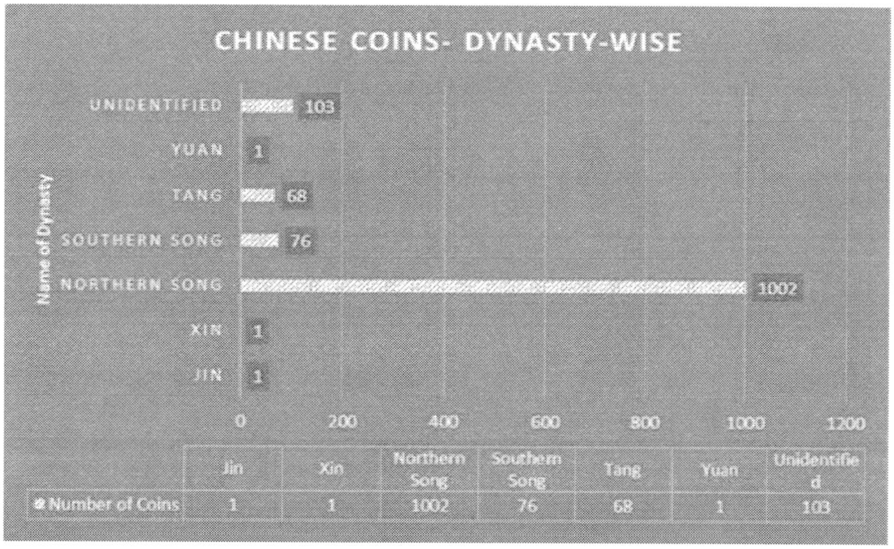

Fig. 2 : Graph showing the dynasty Wise distribution of Chinese Coins from Kollam

Concluding Observations

The Merit of the analysis of Chinese coins particularly in the case of Kollam is that they play as a strong agent for supporting the historical antiquity of the Kollam Port from 7th Century CE onwards. Even though many literary evidences suggest the trade activities bound at Kollam Port from 6th to 7th Century CE onwards, there are no substantiate archaeological and monumental evidences to withstand this claim. This gap is strongly filled by the *Kai Yuan Tong Bao* series of coins issued by the Tang Dynasty. These coins were issued between 618 CE to 907 CE and were found in many sites all over the world, indicating the spread of Chinese trading communities to the far places. The Tang dynasty records claim that Kollam or Mahlai was one of their chief settlement in the Indian Ocean and it is validated through the discovery of the coins of the same dynasty. The Chinese always held a stronghold in the trade activities of the Malabar Coast and the *Kai Yuan Tong Bao* coins testifies an early origin of this bond over trade. But there are no undisputed perspectives between the scholars about whether these coins had any circulation value in the local setting, considering the fact that Chinese were one of the major stakeholders of trade in Kollam, it should be checked that what might have been used in the large volume of trade and would there be an alternative measure used in the trade exchange. However,these disputes do not harm the fact that the historical authenticity and antiquity of the Kollam port is established through the means of the *Kai Yuan Tong Bao* series of Coins of the Tang Dynasty, China.

Table

Coin Number: KLM 01

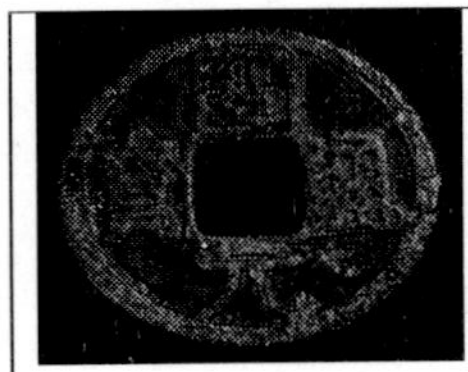

Weight: 4 gm
Diameter: 21.6 mm
Dynasty: Tang
King: Unknown:
Legend:開元通寳
Kai Yuan Tong Bao
Period: 621-927 CE

Coin Number: KLM 02

Weight: 2.88 gm
Diameter: 24.75 mm
Dynasty: Tang
King: Unknown:
Legend:開元通寳
Kai Yuan Tong Bao
Period: 621-927 CE

Coin Number: KLM 03

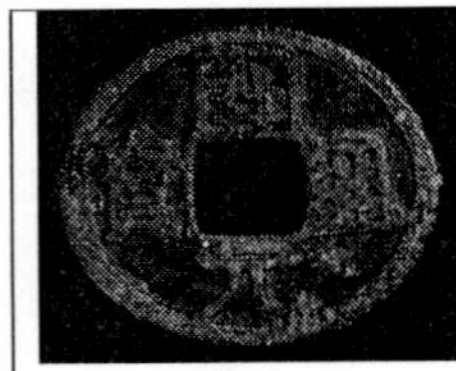

Weight:2.77 gm
Diameter: 24.07 mm
Dynasty: Tang
King: Unknown:
Legend: 開元通寳
Kai Yuan Tong Bao
Period: 621-927 CE

Coin Number: KLM 04

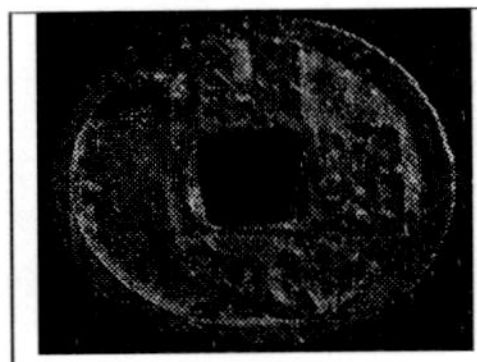

Weight:2.97 gm
Diameter: 23.72 mm
Dynasty: Tang
King: Unknown:
Legend: 開元通寳
Kai Yuan Tong Bao
Period: 621-927 CE

Coin Number: KLM 05

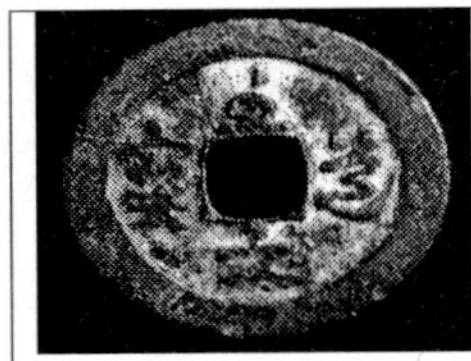

Weight: 2 gm
Diameter: 24.62 mm
Dynasty: Tang
King: Unknown:
Legend: 開元通寳
Kai Yuan Tong Bao
Period: 621-927 CE

Coin Number: KLM 06

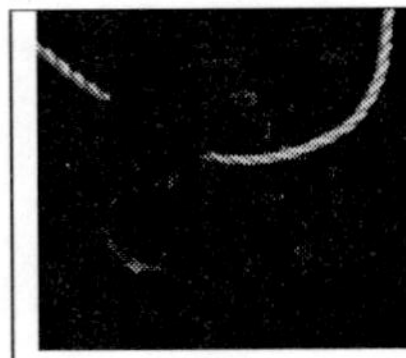

Weight: 4 gm
Diameter: 23.7 mm
Dynasty: Tang
King: Unknown:
Legend: 開元通寳
Kai Yuan Tong Bao
Period: 621-927 CE

Coin Number: KLM 07

Weight: 4 gm
Diameter: 24.7 mm
Dynasty: Tang
King: Unknown:
Legend: 開元通寳
Kai Yuan Tong Bao
Period: 621-927 CE

Coin Number: KLM 08

Weight: 2 gm
Diameter: 24.6 mm
Dynasty: Tang
King: Unknown:
Legend: 開元通寳
Kai Yuan Tong Bao
Period: 621-927 CE

Coin Number: KLM 09

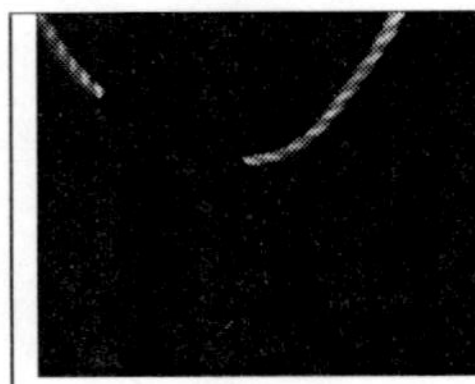

Weight: 2 gm
Diameter: 23.6 mm
Dynasty: Tang
King: Unknown:
Legend: 開元通寳
Kai Yuan Tong Bao
Period: 621-927 CE

Coin Number: KLM 10

Weight: 4 gm
Diameter: 24.6 mm
Dynasty: Tang
King: Unknown:
Legend: 開元通寳
Kai Yuan Tong Bao
Period: 621-927 CE

Coin Number: KLM 11

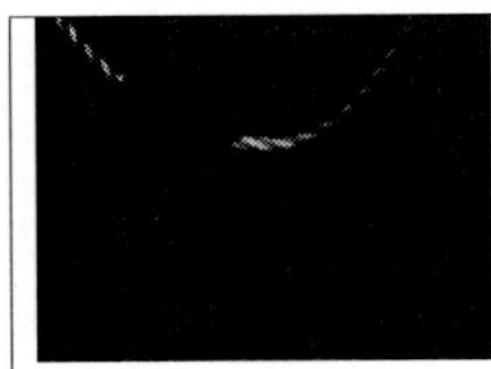

Weight: 2 gm
Diameter: 22.7 mm
Dynasty: Tang
King: Unknown:
Legend: 開元通寳
Kai Yuan Tong Bao
Period: 621-927 CE

Coin Number: KLM 12

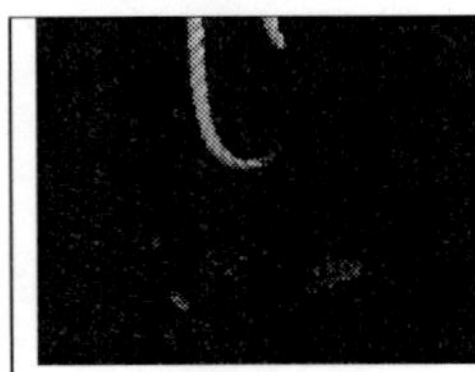

Weight:2 gm
Diameter: 23.5 mm
Dynasty: Tang
King: Unknown:
Legend: 開元通寳
Kai Yuan Tong Bao
Period: 621-927 CE

Coin Number: KLM 13

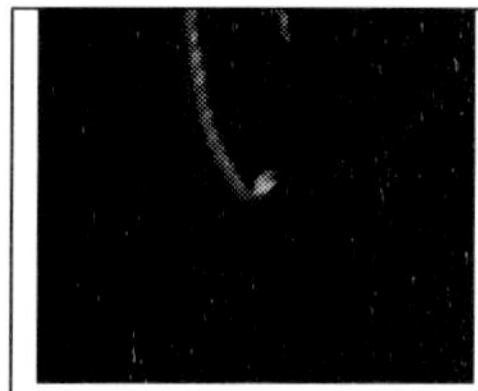

Weight: 2 gm
Diameter: 23. 6 mm
Dynasty: Tang
King: Unknown:
Legend: 開元通寶
Kai Yuan Tong Bao
Period: 621-927 CE

Coin Number: KLM 14

Weight: 2 gm
Diameter: 22.6 mm
Dynasty: Tang
King: Unknown:
Legend: 開元通寶
Kai Yuan Tong Bao
Period: 621-927 CE

Coin Number: KLM 15

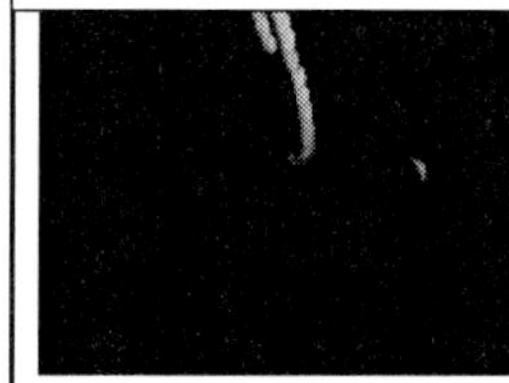

Weight: 2 gm
Diameter:24.7 mm
Dynasty: Tang
King: Unknown:
Legend: 開元通寶
Kai Yuan Tong Bao
Period: 621-927 CE

Coin Number: KLM 16

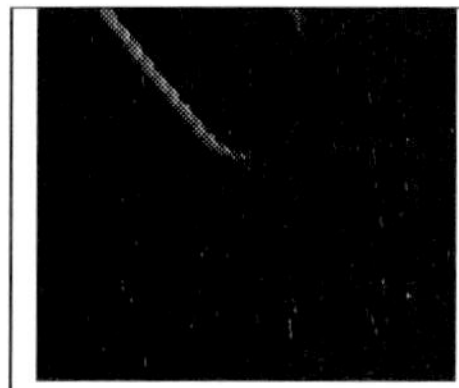

Weight: 3 gm
Diameter: 24.5 mm
Dynasty: Tang
King: Unknown:
Legend: 開元通寶
Kai Yuan Tong Bao
Period: 621-927 CE

Coin Number: KLM 17

Weight: 3 gm
Diameter: 24.6 mm
Dynasty: Tang
King: Unknown:
Legend: 開元通寶
Kai Yuan Tong Bao
Period: 621-927 CE

Coin Number: KLM 18

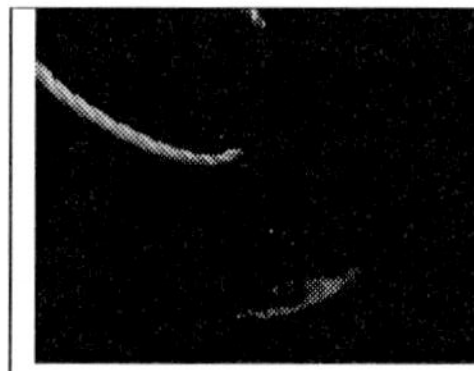

Weight: 3 gm
Diameter: 23.6 mm
Dynasty: Tang
King: Unknown:
Legend: 開元通寶
Kai Yuan Tong Bao
Period: 621-927 CE

Coin Number: KLM 19

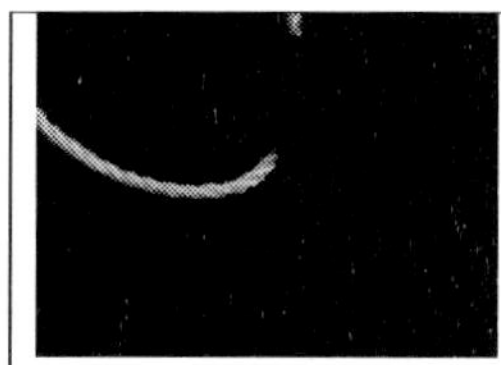

Weight: 3 gm
Diameter: 24.6 mm
Dynasty: Tang
King: Unknown:
Legend: 開元通寶
Kai Yuan Tong Bao
Period: 621-927 CE

Coin Number: KLM 20

Weight: 2 gm
Diameter: 22.6 mm
Dynasty: Tang
King: Unknown:
Legend: 開元通寶
Kai Yuan Tong Bao
Period: 621-927 CE

Coin Number: KLM 21

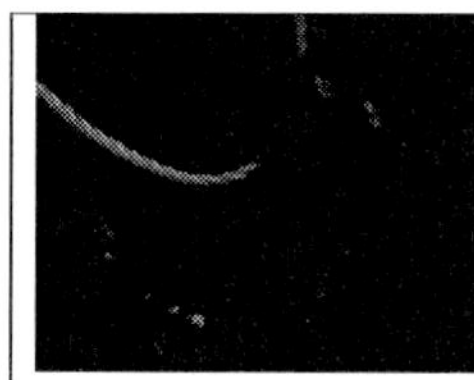

Weight: 2 gm
Diameter: 23.7 mm
Dynasty: Tang
King: Unknown:
Legend: 開元通寶
Kai Yuan Tong Bao
Period: 621-927 CE

Coin Number: KLM 22

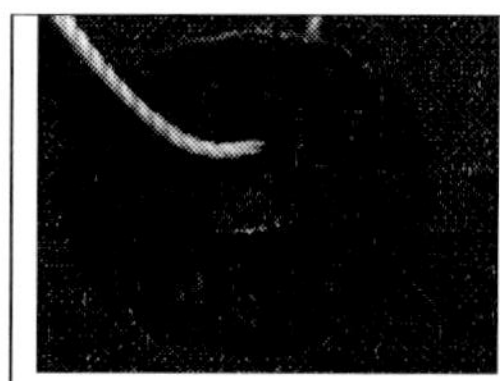

Weight: 2 gm
Diameter: 21.6 mm
Dynasty: Tang
King: Unknown:
Legend: 開元通寶
Kai Yuan Tong Bao
Period: 621-927 CE

Coin Number: KLM 23

Weight: 3 gm
Diameter: 22.7 mm
Dynasty: Tang
King: Unknown:
Legend: 開元通寶
Kai Yuan Tong Bao
Period: 621-927 CE

Coin Number: KLM 24

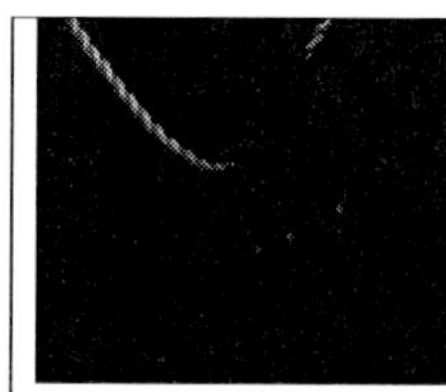

Weight: 3 gm
Diameter: 23.5 gm
Dynasty: Tang
King: Unknown:
Legend: 開元通寶
Kai Yuan Tong Bao
Period: 621-927 CE

Coin Number: KLM 25

Weight: 3 gm
Diameter: 23.6 mm
Dynasty: Tang
King: Unknown:
Legend: 開元通寶
Kai Yuan Tong Bao
Period: 621-927 CE

Coin Number: KLM 26

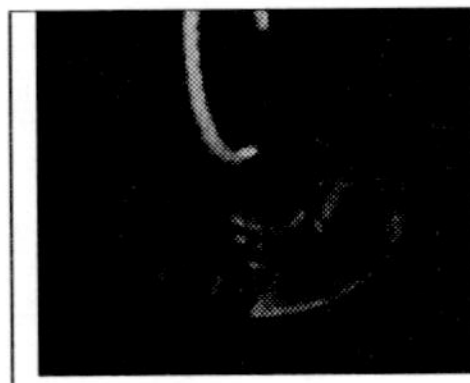

Weight: 3 gm
Diameter: 24.6 mm
Dynasty: Tang
King: Unknown:
Legend: 開元通寶
Kai Yuan Tong Bao
Period: 621-927 CE

Coin Number: KLM 27

Weight: 2 gm
Diameter: 23.5 mm
Dynasty: Tang
King: Unknown:
Legend: 開元通寶
Kai Yuan Tong Bao
Period: 621-927 CE

Coin Number: KLM 28

Weight: 3 gm
Diameter: 24.5 mm
Dynasty: Tang
King: Unknown:
Legend: 開元通寶
Kai Yuan Tong Bao
Period: 621-927 CE

Coin Number: KLM 29

Weight: 2 gm
Diameter: 22.7 mm
Dynasty: Tang
King: Unknown:
Legend: 開元通寶
Kai Yuan Tong Bao
Period: 621-927 CE

Coin Number: KLM 30

Weight: 2 gm
Diameter: 24.7 mm
Dynasty: Tang
King: Unknown:
Legend: 開元通寶
Kai Yuan Tong Bao
Period: 621-927 CE

Coin Number: KLM 31

Weight: 2 gm
Diameter: 24.7 mm
Dynasty: Tang
King: Unknown:
Legend: 開元通寶
Kai Yuan Tong Bao
Period: 621-927 CE

Coin Number: KLM 32

Weight:2 gm
Diameter: 24.7 mm
Dynasty: Tang
King: Unknown:
Legend: 開元通寶
Kai Yuan Tong Bao
Period: 621-927 CE

Coin Number: KLM 33

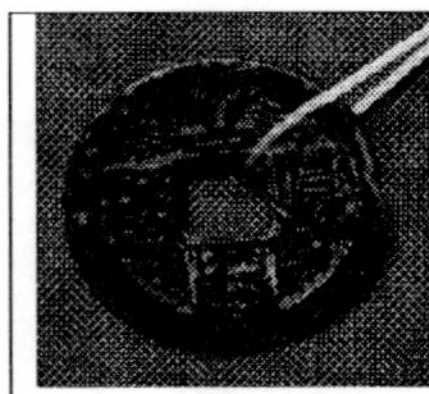

Weight: 2gm
Diameter: 24.7 mm
Dynasty: Tang
King: Unknown:
Legend: 開元通寶
Kai Yuan Tong Bao
Period: 621-927 CE

Coin Number: KLM 34

Weight: 2 gm
Diameter:
Dynasty: Tang
King: Unknown:
Legend: 開元通寶
Kai Yuan Tong Bao
Period: 621-927 CE

Coin Number: KLM 35

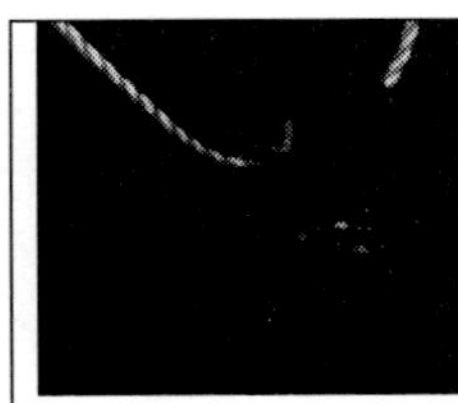

Weight: 2 gm
Diameter: 24.6 mm
Dynasty: Tang
King: Unknown:
Legend: 開元通寶
Kai Yuan Tong Bao
Period: 621-927 CE

Coin Number: KLM 36

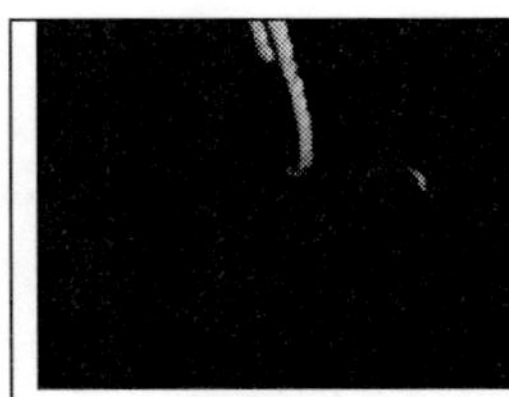

Weight: 2gm
Diameter: 21.6 mm
Dynasty: Tang
King: Unknown:
Legend: 開元通寶
Kai Yuan Tong Bao
Period: 621-927 CE

Coin Number: KLM 37

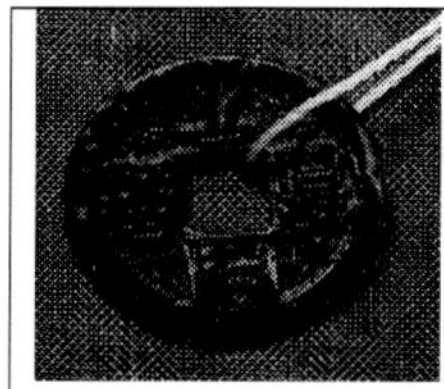

Weight: 4 gm
Diameter: 21.6 mm
Dynasty: Tang
King: Unknown:
Legend: 開元通寶
Kai Yuan Tong Bao
Period: 621-927 CE

Coin Number: KLM 38

Weight: 2 gm
Diameter: 22.6 mm
Dynasty: Tang
King: Unknown:
Legend: 開元通寶
Kai Yuan Tong Bao
Period: 621-927 CE

Coin Number: KLM 39

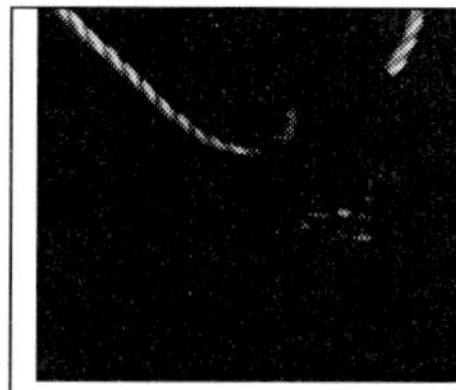

Weight: 2 gm
Diameter: 25.7 mm
Dynasty: Tang
King: Unknown:
Legend: 開元通寶
Kai Yuan Tong Bao
Period: 621-927 CE

Coin Number: KLM 40

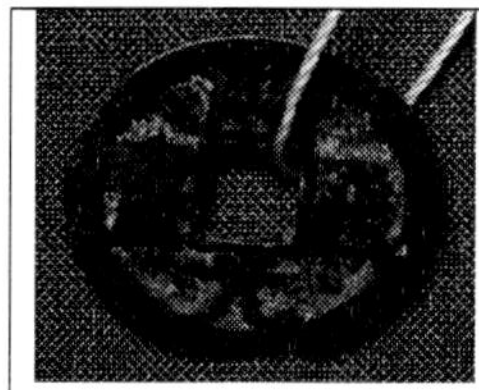

Weight: 2 gm
Diameter: 26.6 mm
Dynasty: Tang
King: Unknown:
Legend: 開元通寶
Kai Yuan Tong Bao
Period: 621-927 CE

Coin Number: KLM 41

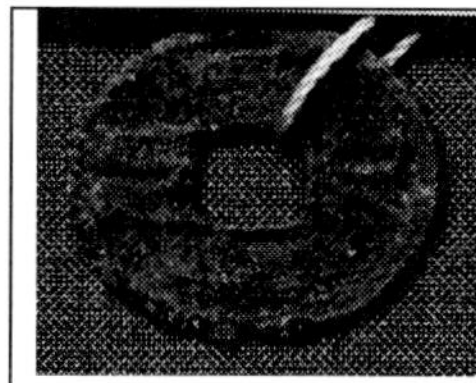

Weight: 2 gm
Diameter: 24.7 mm
Dynasty: Tang
King: Unknown:
Legend: 開元通寶
Kai Yuan Tong Bao
Period: 621-927 CE

Coin Number: KLM 42

Weight: 2 gm
Diameter: 23.6 mm
Dynasty: Tang
King: Unknown:
Legend: 開元通寶
Kai Yuan Tong Bao
Period: 621-927 CE

Coin Number: KLM 43

Weight: 2 gm
Diameter: 23.7 mm
Dynasty: Tang
King: Unknown:
Legend: 開元通寶
Kai Yuan Tong Bao
Period: 621-927 CE

Coin Number: KLM 44

Weight: 2 gm
Diameter: 23.7 mm
Dynasty: Tang
King: Unknown:
Legend: 開元通寶
Kai Yuan Tong Bao
Period: 621-927 CE

Coin Number: KLM 45

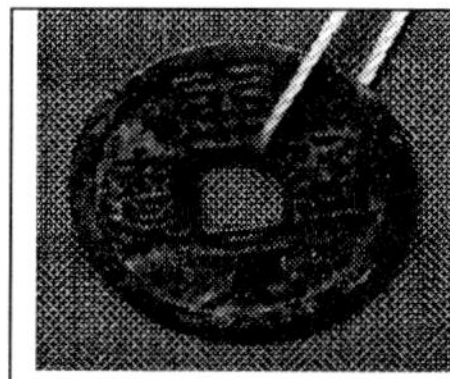

Weight: 4 gm
Diameter: 23.7 mm
Dynasty: Tang
King: Unknown:
Legend: 開元通寶
Kai Yuan Tong Bao
Period: 621-927 CE

Coin Number: KLM 46

Weight: 2 gm
Diameter: 23.7 mm
Dynasty: Tang
King: Unknown:
Legend: 開元通寶
Kai Yuan Tong Bao
Period: 621-927 CE

Coin Number: KLM 47

Weight: 2 gm
Diameter: 24.7 mm
Dynasty: Tang
King: Unknown:
Legend: 開元通寶
Kai Yuan Tong Bao
Period: 621-927 CE

Coin Number: KLM 48

Weight: 2 gm
Diameter: 22.6 mm
Dynasty: Tang
King: Unknown:
Legend: 開元通寶
Kai Yuan Tong Bao
Period: 621-927 CE

Coin Number		Weight	Diameter	Dynasty	King	Legend	Period
Coin Number: KLM 49		Weight: 2 gm	Diameter: 23.7 mm	Dynasty: Tang	King: Unknown:	Legend: 開元通寶 Kai Yuan Tong Bao	Period: 621-927 CE
Coin Number: KLM 50		Weight: 2 gm	Diameter: 23.7 mm	Dynasty: Tang	King: Unknown:	Legend: 開元通寶 Kai Yuan Tong Bao	Period: 621-927 CE
Coin Number: KLM 51		Weight: 2 gm	Diameter: 24.6 mm	Dynasty: Tang	King: Unknown:	Legend: 開元通寶 Kai Yuan Tong Bao	Period: 621-927 CE
Coin Number: KLM 52	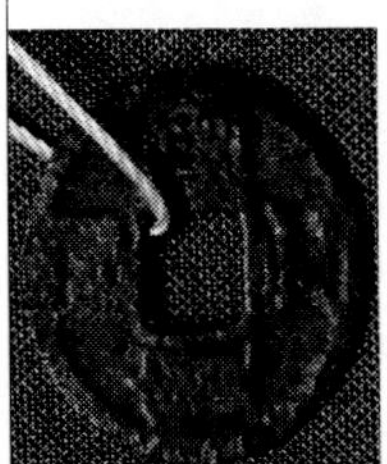	Weight: 2 gm	Diameter:23.7 mm	Dynasty: Tang	King: Unknown:	Legend: 開元通寶 Kai Yuan Tong Bao	Period: 621-927 CE
Coin Number: KLM 53		Weight: 2 gm	Diameter: 22.7 mm	Dynasty: Tang	King: Unknown:	Legend: 開元通寶 Kai Yuan Tong Bao	Period: 621-927 CE
Coin Number: KLM 54		Weight: 2 gm	Diameter: 22.6 mm	Dynasty: Tang	King: Unknown:	Legend: 開元通寶 Kai Yuan Tong Bao	Period: 621-927 CE
Coin Number: KLM 55	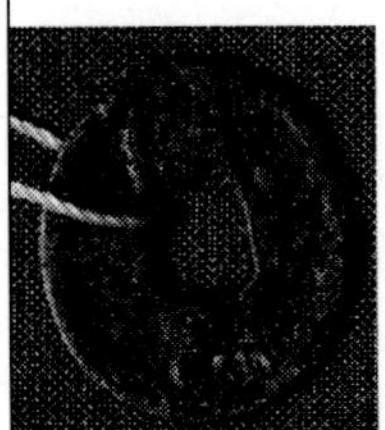	Weight:2 gm	Diameter: 23.7 mm	Dynasty: Tang	King: Unknown:	Legend: 開元通寶 Kai Yuan Tong Bao	Period: 621-927 CE
Coin Number: KLM 56		Weight: 4 gm	Diameter: 21.7 mm	Dynasty:Tang	King: Unknown:	Legend: 開元通寶 Kai Yuan Tong Bao	Period: 621-927 CE
Coin Number: KLM 57		Weight: 2 gm	Diameter: 23.6 mm	Dynasty: Tang	King: Unknown:	Legend: 開元通寶 Kai Yuan Tong Bao	Period: 621-927 CE
Coin Number: KLM 58		Weight: 2 gm	Diameter: 21.6 mm	Dynasty: Tang	King: Unknown:	Legend: 開元通寶 Kai Yuan Tong Bao	Period: 621-927 CE
Coin Number: KLM 59		Weight:2 gm	Diameter: 24.6 mm	Dynasty: Tang	King: Unknown:	Legend: 開元通寶 Kai Yuan Tong Bao	Period: 621-927 CE
Coin Number: KLM 60	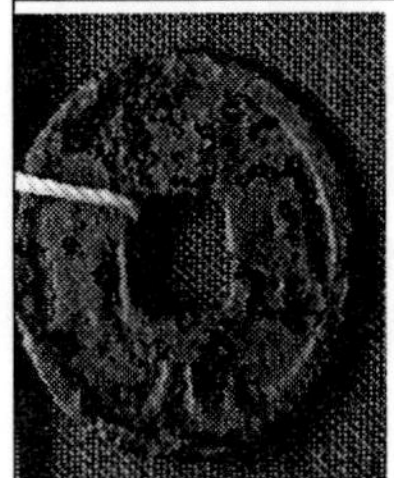	Weight: 2 gm	Diameter: 24.7 mm	Dynasty: Tang	King: Unknown:	Legend: 開元通寶 Kai Yuan Tong Bao	Period: 621-927 CE

Coin Number: KLM 61

Weight: 2 gm
Diameter: 23.7 mm
Dynasty: Tang
King: Unknown:
Legend: 開元通寶
Kai Yuan Tong Bao
Period: 621-927 CE

Coin Number: KLM 62

Weight: 2 gm
Diameter: 22.6 mm
Dynasty: Tang
King: Unknown:
Legend: 開元通寶
Kai Yuan Tong Bao
Period: 621-927 CE

Coin Number: KLM 63

Weight:2 gm
Diameter: 22.7 mm
Dynasty: Tang
King: Unknown:
Legend: 開元通寶
Kai Yuan Tong Bao
Period: 621-927 CE

Coin Number: KLM 64

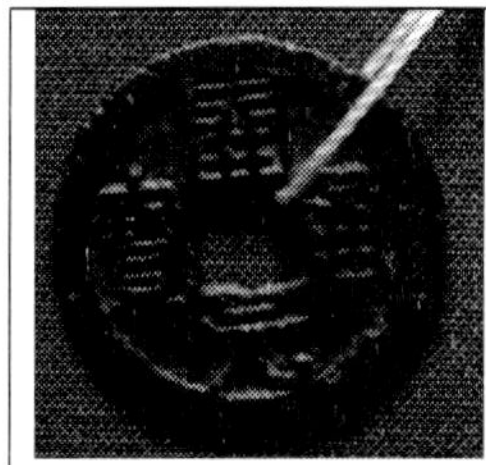

Weight: 2 gm
Diameter: 24.7 mm
Dynasty: Tang
King: Unknown:
Legend: 開元通寶
Kai Yuan Tong Bao
Period: 621-927 CE

Coin Number: KLM 65

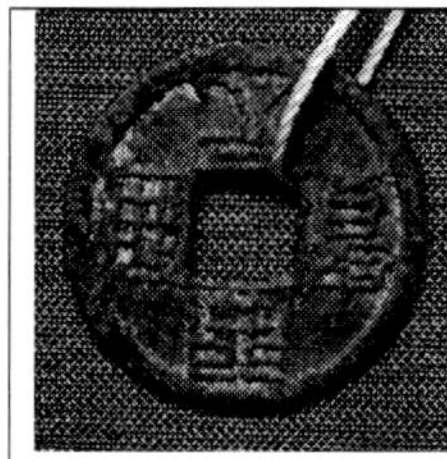

Weight: 2 gm
Diameter: 24.6 mm
Dynasty: Tang
King: Unknown:
Legend: 開元通寶
Kai Yuan Tong Bao
Period: 621-927 CE

References

Ament, W. S., 1888, The Ancient Coinage of China, *The American Journal of Archaeology and of the History of the Fine Arts, Vol. 4, No. 3,* Archaeological Institute of America.

Dikshitar, V.R.R., 1946, *South India and China First (ed),* Madras.

Edkins, J., 1901, *Chinese Currency,* Shanghai: Presbyterian Mission Press.

Hirth, F. and W.W. Rockhill, 1911, *ChauJu-Kua : his work on the Chinese and Arab trade in the twelfth and thirteenth centuries, entitled Chu-fan-chi,* Imperial Academy of Sciences, St. Petersberg.

Johnson, D.A., 2013, *Lost Churches on the Silk Road,* New Sinai Press.

Kumar, A. B, Vinuraj S.V, Rajesh G.S, Abhayan and H. Sasaki, 2016, Allusions and

Artefacts of Chinese Trade from Kollam, South Kerala, India, *Journal of Indian Ocean Archaeology 12.*

Lacouperie, T., 1892, *Catalogue of Chinese Coins,* London: Order of the Trustees.

Liuliang, Y. and Y., Hong, 2004, *Chinese Coins Money in History and Society,* Sanfrancisco: Long River.

Mackenzie, G. T. 1901, *Christianity in Travancore,* Trivandrum: Travancore Government press.

Menon, A.S., 1964, *Kerala District Gazetteers: Quilon,* Thiruvananthapuram: Government Press.

Menon, A. Sreedhara, 2007, *A Survey of Kerala History* (English), Kottayam: D C Books.

Nainar, M.H., 1942, *Arab Geographers Knowledge of South India,* Madras: University of Madras.

Nakumara, H., 1987, *Indian Buddhism A survey with Bibliographical Notes,* New Delhi: Motilal Banarasidass Publishers.

Panikkar, K. M., 1929, *Malabar and the Portuguese: being a history of the relations of*

the Portuguese with Malabar from 1500 to 1663, Bombay: D.B. Taraporevala sons & Company.

Sarasan, B., 2014, *Chinese Cash in Ku Lin Vestiges of Kollam's Maritime History,* Thiruvananthapuram : Akshara Offset.

Sastri, N., 1939, *Foreign Notices of South India,* Madras: University of Madras.

Sen, T., 2006, The Yuan Khanate and India: Cross-Cultural Diplomacy in the Thirteenth and Fourteenth Centuries, *Asia Major, Third Series, Vol. 19, No. 1/2.*

Sen., T., 2017, *India, China and the World, a connected history,* London: Rowman & Littlefield.

Thierry, F., 1998, The Origins and Development of Chinese Coins, O. Bopearachchi and D.P.M. Weerakkody (eds), *Origin Evolution and Circulation of Foreign Coins in the Indian Ocean: 15 62,* New Delhi: Manohar Publication.

Wei, W.P., 1914, *The Currency Problem in China,* New York: Columbia University

19

A Revisiting to the Nemesis of Nālandā Mahavihāra

Ishani Sinha

Introduction

Established by Kumāragupta I of the imperial Gupta dynasty in 5th century CE, Nālandā Mahavihāra (district Nālandā, Bihar state) eventually and deservingly earned the distinction of a celebrated centre of oriental learning during the Gupta and Pāla periods. It shot into prominence for its impressive structured curriculum, faculty of international fame, elaborate and meticulous admission process, organized scholastic-cum-monastic lay out, marvellous art & architecture, strict discipline and many more things. The cause of its end is generally assigned to its being put on fire by Muhammed Bakhtyār Khiljī around 1205 CE. Records put it that the invaders killed the monks, razed down the monastery and set on fire the large libraries of Nālandā namely *Ratnasāgara, Ratnodadhi* and *Ratnarañjaka*.

It is believed that the fire lasted for about six months as there was a huge collection of manuscripts in it. Bakhtyarpur, a place about 40 kms north of Nālandā, is believed to be the camping site of the military general during his exploits in east India (Bihar and Bengal) and owes its name to the ruler. Minhāj-i-Sirāj Jūzjānī, a Persian historian of the 13th century CE has also described in his book *Tabaqāt-i-Nāciri* that Muhammed Bakhtyār Khiljī destroyed a city in western Bihar which they called Bihar and which was found to be a place of study (Raverty 1881:552). Since etymologically Bihar has originated from the sanskrit word *vihāra* which means monastery, it is believed that the reference is of Nālandā Mahavihāra which was a place of study with similar geographical location as described by the historian. Incidentally, the headquarter of Nālandā district, Bihar Sharif, located about 12 kms from the Nālandā ruins is even now popularly abbreviated as Bihar which the historian has referred as name of the destroyed city. Tāranātha, the Tibetan historian of 17th century CE has also stated that the turks conquered the whole of Magadha and destroyed many monasteries, at Nālandā they did much damage and the monks fled abroad (Ghosh 2006:14). There are many post-baked burnt bricks and black soot marks, remnant of fire activity, at the site like in the cells of monastery 1 *(figure 1)* which are cited as testimony of these references.

Nālandā Mahāvihāra

Dharmasvāmin, the venerable Tibetan monk traveller of 13th century CE whose Tibetan name was *Chag-lo-tsa-ba-chos-rje-dpal* has left an eye witness account of the destruction at Nālandā during his visit to the place in 1235-36 CE (Roerich and Altekar 1959: VI). Based upon these references and other historical accounts, it is obvious that Bakhtyār Khiljī had inflicted major injury to the coveted establishment. But it is hard to digest that such a prosperous institution can die under the impact of a single incidence. Therefore it is imperative to look for the other available evidences in this context. Immediately our attention goes to the fact that Nālandā Mahavihāra was subjected to damage, though of limited intensity, by fire earlier also on few occasions but was repaired subsequently.

An inscription on a stone door jamb belonging to the inner gateway was discovered by captain Marshall early in 1864 while excavating the Bālāditya temple at Nālandā. The same inscription was afterwards re-discovered by Broadley in 1871 during excavation of Nālandā temple site 12, also known as Bālāditya temple (Cunningham 1994: 122-23). It is now housed in the Indian Museum, Kolkata (Patil 1963: 333). The inscription consists of 10 short lines and records that Bālāditya, who originally came from Kauśāmbī and was now resident of Tilā

haka, restored the structures (of Nālandā) after a conflagration (*agnidāhoddhāre*) during the 11th regnal year of Mahipāladeva (Misra 1998:203) identified with Mahipāla I. The period of Mahipāla I is variously taken to be 988-1038 CE or 992-1040 CE and therefore the inscription may be ascribed to around 999 or 1003 CE. Thus it is amply clear that a fire had engulfed the temple site 12 before the beginning of last millennium, at least two centuries before devastation caused by Bakhtyār Khiljī.

The extant structures of Nālandā temple site 12 stand in proof of its restoration which is manifest in multiple ways. Most importantly, the restoration phase is marked by the plain character of its exterior, without any pilasters, niches or mouldings so characteristically defining the earlier phase *(fig. 2).* It may imply that the site had somewhat lost its vigour and vibrant attention by the time of its repair at the advent of 11th century CE, most probably due to sliding popularity of buddhism which limited the capacity to invest in terms of finance and the creative ideas of aesthetics. The repair was done with the simple objective of regaining the structural stability. Further, along the edge of the platform of this structure, a parapet wall was raised of which traces are still available on the west, south and north sides *(fig. 3).* Probably this was intended to be a protective compound wall around the shrine which needed a defence against the threats of other relatively more empowered religious streams at the time of restoration. Necessity of structural protection is felt only when the intrinsic strength of a religion is on decline which was actually the case with buddhism as early as about two centuries before the invasion of Bakhtyār Khiljī in the beginning of 13th century CE.

Another significant evidence in this context is an inscription on an image (now lost) found from Shahpur near Bihar Sharif, the current headquarter of Nālandā district. It is dated to the Harsha year 66 which is calibrated to 672-73 CE and belongs to the reign of Adityasena (Ghosh 2006: 11-12). It records that one Śālapaksha, the *Balādhik[ita* (high army officer), installed a stone image, probably of the Sun-god at Nālandā *Mahāgrahāra*. Presence of a tank known as Suraj-kund or Suraj-pokhar at Badgaon near the Nālandā remains may be cited as a substantiation of the reference. By implication it may indicate existence of a brahmanical temple dedicated to the Sun god. Probably temple site 2 of Nālandā Mahavihāra, which is assigned to the same period, that is, 7th century CE, represents the temple in question and thus it may be inferred that *vihāras* and *agrahāras* flourished side by side at Nālandā (Misra 1998: 198-99). It is remarkable that Nālandā temple site 2 faces east as prescribed for a Sun temple. Further, this temple is located at the back of monasteries completely disoriented to the organized general plan lay out of the buddhist structures at Nālandā and contains many brahmanical gods amongst the dado of sculptured panels over the stone plinth. Therefore the assumption of some persons that the word *mahāgrahāra* of the Shahpur inscription probably referred to the *mahavihāra* does not seem to be correct. The two words indicate two different entities related to two different religions, buddhism and brahmanism. In this context it is significant to note that *Pag-sam Jon-Zang*, a Tibetan authority refers to a scuffle between the buddhist and brahmanical mendicants and the latter, being infuriated, propitiated the Sun-god for twelve years, performed a fire sacrifice and threw the living embers and ashes from the sacrificial pit into the buddhist temples which eventually destroyed the great library at Nālandā called *Ratnodadhi* (Patil 1963: 327). But it is difficult to ascertain the authenticity or historicity of this story.

In the structural constructions at Nālandā, wood was used for pillars in the verandah and roofs of monasteries. Also, there are traces of hearths in the verandah of some monasteries and ovens in the open courtyard of some others, clearly indicating that cooking inside the monasteries was a norm. Use of lamps and torches in the night was also very common. Thus accidental fires on some occasions cannot be ruled out which might have caused some damages. Traces of burnt wooden pillars, beams and rafters used in the roofs have been noticed in the excavations which indicate burning activity. Although the excavations frequently mention that the particular monastery was probably destroyed by fire, the probable cause of such fire has never been stated by them. While excavating the site, heaps of ashes and charcoals were unearthed even on the topmost levels after the removal of layers of earth which covers up various sites (Spooner 2002: 20)

While assessing the impact of Bakhtyār Khiljī's invasion around 1205 CE it is pertinent to note that despite the severely devastating attack on it, Nālandā Mahavihāra was neither completely destroyed nor fully deserted by the teachers and students. This is quite clear from the eye witness account of Dharmasvāmin, the Tibetan monk traveller who remained at Nālandā for few months in 1235-36 CE. He has recorded that thousands of monks belonging to the establishment had fled away but MahāpaG

ita Rāhulaśribhadra, continued to reside and declined to flee. He has further recorded that only two vihāras named *Dha-na-ba* and *Ghu-na-ba* were in serviceable condition. There were 70 monk scholars reading under him, being supported by king Buddhasena of Bodh Gaya and a rich lay brahmana disciple named Jayadeva living at Odantapurī or Bihar Sharif (Roerich and Altekar 1959: XX) Tāranātha, another Tibetan monk belonging to 17th century CE, also gives precisely the same information. Dharmasvāmin also describes that the higher and deeper study of grammar was still pursued in the post Khilji period.

Dharmasvāmin further informs that the threat of sudden attack from "turushkas" was always there. The possibility of re-attack was a nightmare for the monks due to severity of invasion by Bakhtyār Khiljī. Persian chronicler Minhāj tells that the onslaught was so severe and thorough that the monks were killed one and all so much so that none was left to explain the contents of books that the victor found at the place (Sankalia 1972: 239). The structures in the precincts were also ruthlessly plundered and the materials were carried away to Odantapurī (now Bihar Sharif located about 12 kms from Nālandā) for building mosques there. Probably for this reason the buddhist monks were scared and reluctant to return back to the monastery after deserting it in the wake of brutal invasion by Bakhtyār Khiljī. However, despite all these odds, restoration work was put in place. The Tibetan authority *Pag-sam-jon-zang* refers that the temples and vihāras were repaired once again by a sage named *Mudita Bhadra* and one *Kukkutasidha*, a minister of some king of Magadha, erected a temple. Thus there is evidence of the external regeneration of the monastic order (Panth 2000: 161)

A review of fire activities at Nālandā as described above indicates that there were several instances of it at different points of time and invariably on all those occasions repair works were undertaken to undo the damage. Indeed the degree of attempted reversal of damage depends upon the nature, degree and intensity of destruction, but most crucial to it is the institutional health at that particular point of time which determines the will and capacity to recover. The damage resulting out of earlier fire activities, like the one in the 7th century CE or the first decade of 11th century CE, was more successfully controlled and undone as it was the flourishing period of buddhism when the religion had the will, energy and capacity to bounce back for survival and sustenance. The robust health of institution in terms of educational parameters also helped. But by the 12th-13th century CE, buddhism had steeply declined which, it can rationally be surmised, made the recovery from Islamic assault much more difficult, rather impossible. The main cause of the end of Nālandā was therefore, the decline of buddhism itself. However, for the loss of such a great institution as Nālandā, mono causal explanation appears to be too simplistic in nature. There were many other reasons for its end which must be taken into account.

Probably as a collateral effect of the decline of buddhism, the number of teachers and students in this educational institution was also going down as the 7th century CE was reaching its end. This is obvious from the accounts of two celebrated Chinese monk pilgrims Xuan Zang (629-649 CE) and Yiching (671-695 CE) who visited Nālandā in the 7th Century CE. Xuan Zang who joined the university in the first half of 7th century CE mentions that "the priests belonging to the convent or strangers residing therein always reach to the number of 10,000 who all study the great vehicle" (Li and Beal 1973: 112). But in the second half of 7th century CE when Yiching visited the university, its strength had markedly fallen down. Yiching describes that "in the Nālandā monastery the number of priests is immense and exceeds three thousand" (Takakusu 1966: 154). This number is based upon Julien's text although some other texts put the figures at 3,500 to 5000. By any consideration, the strength of Nālandā Mahavihāra had gone down from 10,000 to at least 5000 signalling a sharp reduction of more than 50 % in the 7th century CE. The fall in popularity of this institution and the resultant drop in the students' strength might be the consequence of rising intrinsic conflict within buddhism itself and the challenges it faced from the revival of brahmanism. When the Tibetan monk Dharmaswamin visited Nālandā in 1235-36 CE, he noticed that in the monastery lived MahāpaG ita Rāhulaśribhadra, four other paGitas and about 70 other monks (Roerich and Altekar 1959: 90). Although this miniscule number was more the consequence of insecure condition in the aftermath of Bakhtyār Khiljī's attack, it can reasonably be inferred that even before the attack the strength of university must be quite low as buddhism had almost faded away by that time. The fall in number might also be a consequence of declining ease of living for the student monks. We know that Harshavardhana (606-647 CE) had remitted the revenue of about a hundred villages as endowment of the convent and two hundred households in these villages contributed the required amount of rice, butter and milk (Ghosh 2006: 5-6). Therefore the students were relieved of the anxiety to beg for their daily needs and devoted their full energy to study leading to their academic perfection. This privilege, which was concomitant with the popularity of buddhism, was lost later on as the social base of religion eroded. With losing strength of students, a critical parameter for sustenance of an educational establishment, Nālandā Mahavihāra was bound to approach its dusk.

One of the key factors responsible for the rise and sustained prosperity of Nālandā Mahavihāra was the royal patronage received by it. Ever since its establishment in 5th century CE by Kumāragupta I, it was patronized under a succession of powerful rulers of Gupta dynasty. It reached its zenith during the reign of Harshavardhana and continued to flourish in the age of Pālas. As such there was no problem of resources needed by the institution to prosper. But the rise of Pāla dynasty in 8th century CE had a strong bearing on the fate of Nālandā Mahavihāra in at least two major ways. Firstly, the Pāla rulers became instrumental in the establishment of four more monasteries at Odantapurī, Vikramaśilā, Somapura and Jagaddala, all of which developed into great education centres. One of them, Odantapurī, was set up at Bihar Sharif, only about 12 kms away from Nālandā posing a tough regional challenge to it. Another one at Vikramaśilā located in Bhagalpur district of Bihar evolved into a pioneer centre of study for tantric buddhism seriously challenging the status of Nālandā Mahavihāra in terms of faculty, curriculum and international repute. The Tibetan scholar Tāranātha even states that the head of Vikramaśilā monastery had control over Nālandā (Ghosh 2006: 10). The other two at Jagaddala and Somapura Mahavihāra (both in Bangladesh) also developed as competing monasteries. Establishment of these four additional monasteries created a diversion in the resources at command as well as the activities of buddhist scholars. Shared patronage and split attention of the Pāla rulers became instrumental in the losing vitality of institution. Secondly, it so happened that the power centre of the Pālas shifted to further east near Munger or Monghyr in Bihar as known from the epigraphic evidences. The Monghyr copper plate inscription of Devapāla datable to the middle of 9th century CE, and the Bhagalpur copper plate inscription of NārāyaGapāla datable to the beginning of 10th century CE are purportedly the charters issued from the victory camp at Mudgagiri which is identified with the present Munger (Sahai 1983: 75-76 & 80). This accentuated the problem for Nālandā as distance from the imperial power centre, generally speaking, adversely affects control of any institution and contribution to its development.

Observations

The above placed facts, observations and arguments establish beyond doubt that after attaining its peak around 7th - 8th century CE, Nālandā Mahavihāra began to suffer gradual death in sync with the decline of buddhism, reduced level of royal patronage and competing institutional interests. Only the final fatal blow was inflicted on this already dying educational institution by Bakhtyār Khiljī around 1205 after which it could not revive despite limited efforts made for it by the adherents of buddhism.

Acknowledgement: Archaeological Survey of India for photographs.

References

Cunningham, A,1994, *Archaeological Survey of India Reports, Vol. III*, Delhi: Rahul Publishing House.

Ghosh, A, 2006, *Nālandā*, New Delhi: Archaeological Survey of India.

Li, Shaman Hwui & Samuel Beal,1973, *The Life of Hiuen-Tsiang*, Delhi: Academica Asiatica .

Misra, B.N, 1998, *Nālandā, Vol. I*, Delhi: B.R. Publishing corporation .

Panth, R., 2000, Heritage of Nālandā and its continuity (edt.), *Nālandā,* Nava Nālandā Mahavihāra.

Patil, D.R., 1963, *The Antiquarian Remains in Bihar*, Patna: K.P. Jayaswal Research Institute.

Raverty, H.G., 1881, *Tabaqāt-i-Nāɑri*, (tr.), Calcutta: Asiatic society of Bengal,

Roerich, G. & A.S. Altekar, (tr.), 1959, *Biography of Dharmaswamin*, Patna: K.P.Jayaswal Research Institute.

Sankalia, H.D.,1972, *The University of Nālandā*, Delhi: Oriental Publishers.

Spooner, D.B., 2002, *Annual Report of the Archaeological Survey of India 1921-22*, New Delhi: Archaeological Survey of India.

Takakusu, J. (tr.), 1966, *The Buddhist Religion as practised in India and the Malay Archipelago by I-Tsing*, Delhi: Munshiram Manoharlal.

20

सारनाथ : कला एवं स्थापत्य

सुनील कुमार झा

परिचय

सारनाथ 25°, 18' अक्षांश उत्तर तथा 83°, 1' देशान्तर पूर्व में स्थित है (सिंह 18)। यह वाराणसी नगर से उत्तर दिशा में लगभग 10 किलोमीटर की दूरी पर स्थित है। वाराणसी नगर (नेविल : 1) गंगा के बीच किनारे पर अर्द्धचन्द्रकार (मोतीचन्द : 1) आकृति में बसा है। यहां से सारनाथ की दूरी लगभग 10 किलोमीटर व वरूणा नदी से 3 किलोमीटर उत्तर में है। जातक में सारनाथ एवं तक्षशिला की दूरी 120 योजन बताई गई है (भिक्षुधर्म : 12) तथा उरूवेला (बोधगया) से यह दूरी 18 योजन है। सारनाथ तथा उसके आस-पास के क्षेत्र भूमध्य रेखा से दूर होने के कारण यहां की जलवायु समशीतोष्ण है। किसी भी जगह की जलवायु उसकी भौगोलिक स्थित और प्राकृतिक बनावट पर निर्भर होती है (इन्साइक्लोपीडिया ब्रिटानिका 2 : 715)। बुद्ध ने 'धर्मचक्रप्रवर्तन' करते हुये प्रथम वर्षावास सारनाथ के घने जंगलों में ही व्यतीत किया था। 535-485 ई. पूर्व के बीच बुद्ध अनेकों बार विहार करते हुये यहां आये। भगवान बुद्ध का सारनाथ अथवा यों कहिए इसिपतन से संबंध सभी को विदित है। यहां बुद्धत्व प्राप्त करके गौतम बुद्ध इसिपतन की ओर रवाना हुए, क्योंकि उनके साथी पंचबग्गिय भिक्खु उन्हें कठिन तप से निरत होते देख उन्हें छोड़कर इसिपतन चले गये थे (जातक 1, 68)। बुद्ध उरूवेला से इसिपतन की ओर पैदल चलकर आये और रास्ते में उनकी आजीवक उपक से भेंट हुई। पास में पैसा न होने से शायद बुद्ध को गंगा नदी उतरने में अड़चन पड़ी। अनुश्रुति है, कि बिंबिसार ने यह सुनकर तपस्वियों और ब्राह्मणों को नदी पार जाने के भाड़े में छूट कर दी। इसिपतन में पहुंचकर उन्होंने आषाढ़ी पूर्णिमा को धर्मचक्रप्रवर्तन किया और इस तरह *'बहुजन हित बहुजन सुख'* और *'लोकानुकंपा'* का अपूर्व संदेश संसार को दिया। यह कहने में कोई अतिश्योक्ति नहीं, कि बुद्ध के मध्यम-मार्ग का कार्य सारनाथ से ही आरंभ हुआ। बौद्ध साहित्य से पता चलता है कि बुद्ध सारनाथ में कई बार ठहरे। उन्होंने यहां बहुत से सूत्रों का उपदेश दिया और सारनाथ में रहने वाले यश (विनयपिटक 1, 15) एवं उसके मित्रों को यथा विमल, सुबाहु, पुण्णजि, गवांपति जो सब अच्छे घरानों के थे, बौद्ध धर्म में दीक्षित किया। वाराणसी अथवा इसिपतन में ही बुद्ध ने भिक्षुओं को ताड़ के जूते न पहनने का आदेश दिया था (विनयपिटक 1, 18)।

धर्मचक्रप्रवर्तनसूत्र के सिवा बुद्ध ने सारनाथ में निम्नलिखित सूत्रों का पाठ किया-पंचसुत्त, रथकार या पच्चेतनसूत्र, दोपास सुत्त, कटुविजय सुत्त, परायण की मेत्तयपञह पर व्याख्या तथा धम्मदिन्नसुत्त जो धम्मदिन्न नाम के एक प्रसिद्ध नागरिक को उपदेश स्वरूप में दिया गया।

जान पड़ता है, बौद्ध संघ के कुछ प्रधान भिक्षु समय-समय पर इसिपतन में रहा करते थे। इसिपतन में रहते हुये सारिपुत और महाकोट्ठिक के वार्तालापों का कई जगह वर्णन है। एक स्थल पर महाकोट्ठिक और चितहत्थि सारिपुत की बातचीत की चर्चा आयी

है। इसिपतन में छन्न को उसकी कठिनाइयों में सहायता देने के लिए कई भिक्षुओं का आपस में संवाद भी आया है।

धर्मचक्रप्रवर्तनसूत्र के बुद्ध वचन में बुद्ध की महत्ता वर्णित है, जो निश्चय ही बाद में संकलनकर्ताओं द्वारा जोड़ी गई मालूम पड़ती है। सारनाथ में धर्मचक्रप्रवर्तन करने का हेतु यह जान पड़ता है कि यहां पंचवर्गीय भिक्षु थे। पर ऐसा भी हो सकता है कि वाराणसी की उस समय इतनी ख्याति थी कि वहां धर्मचक्रप्रवर्तन करना बुद्ध के नये उपदेश के उपयुक्त था। जो भी हो, बुद्ध उरूवेला से सारनाथ की ओर चल पड़े। बोधगया और सारनाथ के बीच उनकी उपक आजीवक से भेंट हुई। उपक ने बुद्ध की कांति देखकर उनके परिव्रजित होने की बात जान ली। बुद्ध क्रमशः यात्रा करते हुये ऋषिपतन मृगदाव में, जहां पंचवर्गीय भिक्षु थे, वहां पहुंचे। पंचवर्गीय भिक्षुकों ने भगवान को दूर से आते देखा और उन्हें देखते ही आपस में बातचीत करने लगे-आवुसो, साधना भ्रष्ट संचय-कर्मी गौतम आ रहा है। इसे अभिवादन नहीं करना चाहिए, न इसके लिए खड़ा होना चाहिए, न इसका पात्र और चीवर लेना चाहिए। केवल आसन रख देना चाहिए, यदि इच्छा होगी तो बैठेगा। लेकिन, जैसे ही बुद्ध उनके पास आये उनकी सब बातें हवा हो गयीं। एक ने बढ़कर पात्र-चीवर लिया, दूसरे ने आसन बिछाया, तीसरा पैर धोने का पानी लाया और चौथे ने पादपीठ और पाद कठलिका ला रखी। भगवान ने अपने पैर धोये। बातचीत में बुद्ध ने अपने अर्हत्व की बात उनसे कही, परन्तु उन्होंने इसे मानने से इनकार कर दिया। तब भगवान ने उन्हें उपदेश दिया।

भिक्षुओं, दो अतियों की सेवा यथा अनर्थों और कामवासनाओं से लिप्त अति और दुःखमय, आत्मपीड़क अति की जाती है। भिक्षुओं, इन दोनों अतियों में न पड़कर तथागत ने मध्यम मार्ग निकाला है जो परम दृष्टि देने वाला, ज्ञानबोधक, शांतिदायक तथा अभिज्ञा, परिपूर्ण ज्ञान और निर्वाण के लिए है। यह वही आर्य अष्टांगिक मार्ग है, जिसमें सम्यक् दृष्टि, सम्यक् संकल्प, सम्यक् वचन, सम्यक् कर्म, सम्यक् जीवन, सम्यक् जीविका, सम्यक् प्रयत्न, सम्यक् स्मृति और सम्यक् समाधि निहित है। यह है भिक्षुओं, मध्यम मार्ग।

भिक्षुओं, दुःख आर्य-सत्य है। जन्म, जरा और मरण दुःख है, अप्रियों का संयोग और प्रियों का वियोग भी दुःख है। इच्छित वस्तु का न मिलना भी दुःख है, संक्षेप में सर्व भौतिक अभौतिक पदार्थ ही दुःख है। भिक्षुओं दुःख का कारण आर्य सत्य है। फिर से जन्म लेने की आकांक्षा, राग सहित जहां-तहां प्रसन्न होने की प्रवृति जिसे काम, भव और विभव तृष्णायें कहा है, ये सब तृष्णाएं हैं। हे भिक्षुओं, यह दुःख निरोध आर्य सत्य तृष्णा से विरक्त होना है। भिक्षुओं, यह दुःख निरोध-गामिनी-प्रतिपद् आर्य सत्य है, यही आर्य अष्टांगिक मार्ग है।

यह दुःख आर्य-सत्य है और परिज्ञेय है ऐसी मुझे दृष्टि उत्पन्न हुई। यह दुःख समुदय, यह दुःख निरोध और यह दुःख निरोधगामिनी-प्रतिपद् आर्य सत्य है, इसका भी मुझे ज्ञान हुआ।

जिस समय बुद्ध ने इसिपतन में धर्मचक्रप्रवर्तन किया उसके थोड़े ही बाद यश की प्रवज्या हुई। यश वाराणसी के श्रेष्ठि का पुत्र था। उसके पास वैभव की कमी न थी, सब ऋतुओं के योग्य महल थे। रात भर तेल दीपों के प्रकाश में नाच-रंग होता रहता था। एक दिन एकाएक यश की निद्रा खुली तो उसने अपने परिजनों की अस्तव्यस्त अवस्था देखी और यह सब देखकर उसे अत्यन्त घृणा हुई और वह सीधे मृगदाव में बुद्ध के पास पहुंचा। बुद्ध उस समय सवेरे उठकर टहल रहे थे। यश को देखकर वे आसन पर बैठ गये, उसे अपने पास बैठाकर उन्होंने प्रवज्या दी। बाद में यश के माता-पिता भी बुद्ध के उपासक हुए, यश के पिता को बौद्ध धर्म का प्रथम उपासक कहा जाता है। इसके बाद यश के मित्रों ने यथा विमल, सुबाहु, पूर्णजित और गवापति ने प्रवज्या ग्रहण की। फिर क्या था, काशी में प्रवज्या लेने की होड़-सी लग गयी और यश के बहुत से जानपद रही मित्रों ने भी प्रवज्या ग्रहण कर ली। अंत में भगवान बुद्ध ने भिक्षुओं को अपना अमर उपदेश सुनाया, जिसमें आदि से अंत तक कल्याण की भावना टपकती है -

चरथ भिक्खवे चारिकं बहुजनहिताय बहुजन सुखाय
लोकानुकंपाय अत्थाय हिताय सुखाय देवमनुस्मानं।
देसेथ भिक्खवे धम्मं आदि कल्याणं परियोसान कल्याणं
सात्थं सव्यंजनं केवल परिपुण्णं परिसुद्धं ब्रह्मचरियं पकासेथ।

हे भिक्षुओं, जनता के हित के लिए, जनता के सुख के लिए, लोक पर अनुकंपा करने के लिए, देवताओं और मनुष्यों का हित सुख करने के लिए विचार करो। आरंभ में कल्याणकर, मध्य में कल्याणकर, अंत में कल्याणकर धर्म का शब्दों और भावों सहित उपदेश करके सर्वाश में परिपूर्ण, परिशुद्ध ब्रह्मचर्य का प्रकाश करो।

सारनाथ से उद्घोषित बुद्ध का यह अमर उपदेश हजारों भिक्षुओं द्वारा इस देश के कोने-कोने में फैला, साथ ही नदी-नद, समुद्र, पर्वत और भीषण रेगिस्तानों को पार करता हुआ एक ओर जापान से लेकर अफगानिस्तान तक और दूसरी ओर सुवर्णभूमि से लेकर सिंहल तक फैल गया। शताब्दियों बाद बौद्ध धर्म के इस जाज्वल्यमान संदेश के स्थान पर वज्रयान और मंत्रयान के पूजा पाठ ने अपना घर कर लिया, लेकिन सदियों के गहरे अंधेरे को चीरती हुई अब भी बुद्ध की यह अमरवाणी हमें बहुजनहित के लिए आह्वान कर रही है।

सर्वेक्षण एवं उत्खनन

सारनाथ लगभग दो सौ वर्षों से अधिक समय से विद्वानों एवं पुरातत्वविदों के लिए आकर्षण का केन्द्र रहा है। जोनाथन डन्कन ने 1794 ई. में अपने विवरण में बाबू जगत सिंह द्वारा सारनाथ मंदिर के निकट दो मंजूषाओं की प्राप्ति के बारे में लिखा है (डंकन: 350)। जगत सिंह वाराणसी के राजा चेतसिंह के दीवान थे, उन्होंने 1793-94 ई. में इमारती सामग्री की खोज में स्तूप के टीले को खुदवा डाला और उससे प्राप्त प्रस्तरों एवं ईटों से अपने नाम से नगर में एक बाजार बनवाया। स्तूप के अंदर से बलुए पत्थर के गोल बक्से में संगमरमर की बेलनाकार मंजूषा में रखी अस्थियां, स्वर्ण तथा रजत के आभूषण, मोती तथा माणिक्य मिले थे। प्राप्त अस्थि अवशेष आदि को गंगा नदी में विसर्जित कर दिया गया। बाद में कनिंघम ने उस गोलाकार बक्से को खोज निकाला जो स्तूप में छूट गया था, तथा उसे बंगाल एशियाटिक सोसाइटी को भेंट कर दिया। सन् 1815 ई. में कर्नल सी. मैकेंजी सारनाथ में पुरातात्विक उत्खनन प्रारम्भ करने वाले प्रथम व्यक्ति थे (आ. स. रि. 1903-04: 112)। सन् 1835-36 ई. में कनिंघम ने व्यापक उत्खनन कार्य करवाये। सन् 1851-52 ई. में मेजर मार्खम किट्टो द्वारा उत्खनन करवाया गया। किट्टो के असमय मृत्यु से उत्खनन का रिपोर्ट प्रकाशित नहीं हो पायी। कनिंघम द्वारा उत्खनन में जो महत्वपूर्ण तथ्य प्रकाश में आये उसमें धमेख, धर्मराजिका, चौखण्डी स्तूपों के अतिरिक्त महाविहार जो धमेख स्तूप के उत्तर दिशा में स्थित था (आ. स. रि. 1903-04: 112)। धमेख स्तूप का लम्बवत् उत्खनन उन्होंने ऊपर शीर्ष से करवाया था। धर्मराजिका की मोटाई जानने के उद्देश्य से बाहरी दीवारों के चारों ओर भी उत्खनन कराया था। कनिंघम ने चौखण्डी स्तूप का उत्खनन कर यह सिद्ध किया कि यह स्मृति में बनवाया गया स्तूप था तथा इसकी पहचान ह्वेनसांग द्वारा उल्लेखित हरिण उद्यान विहार के दो अथवा तीन ली दक्षिण में स्थित स्तूप से की, जहां पंचवर्गीय भिक्षुओं ने पहले बुद्ध का विरोध किया था, परन्तु समीप आते ही बुद्ध को भरपूर सम्मान दिया (आ. स. रि. भा. 1:103)। सारनाथ के महत्वपूर्ण उत्खननों में एक सन् 1904-05 ई. में एफ. ओ. ऑरटेल द्वारा प्राचीन मृगदान के केन्द्र में उत्खनन किया गया जिसमें मंदिर, सिंह-शीर्ष सहित अशोक-स्तंभ, धर्मचक्रप्रर्वतनमुद्रा में बुद्ध प्रतिमा, कनिष्क के शासनकाल के तीसरे वर्ष में बनी प्रस्तर-छत्र सहित बोधिसत्व प्रतिमा और 476 प्रतिमा खण्ड एवं 41 अभिलेख प्राप्त हुये (ह्वेनसांग की भारत यात्रा : 333-37)। सन् 1907 एवं 1908 ई. में सर जॉन मार्शल ने स्टेन कोनो, डब्लू. एच. निकोलस, दयाराम साहनी एवं बी. बी. चक्रवर्ती के सहयोग से सारनाथ के एक विस्तृत क्षेत्र में उत्खनन कार्य किया। उन्होंने उत्तरवर्ती कुषाणकाल के तीन महाविहारों को उद्घाटित किया। इसके अतिरिक्त उन्होंने मुख्य मंदिर के पूर्व एवं पश्चिम भाग तथा अस्पताल क्षेत्र में भी उत्खनन कार्य किया। सन् 1914-15 ई. में एच. हरग्रीब्स ने मुख्य मंदिर के पूर्वी एवं पश्चिम क्षेत्र में उत्खनन कर गजपृष्ठाकार मंदिर, जो मौर्योतर काल का है, के अतिरिक्त परवर्तीकाल की अन्य संरचनाओं को उद्घाटित किया। सन् 1921-22 ई. में यहां पर दयाराम साहनी द्वारा बड़े स्तर पर उत्खनन कार्य किया गया, जिसके फलस्वरूप धमेख स्तूप एवं मुख्य मंदिर के बीच की संरचनाएं तथा अलंकृत ईटों से निर्मित स्तूप तथा मार्ग प्रकाश में आये।

सारनाथ के महत्वपूर्ण अवशेष

मूलगंधकुटी बिहार : सारनाथ पुरास्थल के लगभग मध्य भाग में धर्मराजिका स्तूप से उत्तर दिशा में मुख्य मंदिर 'मूलगंधकुटी

विहार' अवस्थित है। मंदिर वर्गाकार योजना पर बनी है, जिसकी प्रत्येक तरफ लम्बाई 18.29 मी. है तथा इसका प्रवेश द्वार पूर्व की ओर है। इस मंदिर को ह्वेनसांग ने 61 मी. ऊँचा बताया है (आ. स. रि. 1904-1905 : 30)। इस मंदिर के दीवारों से प्रतीत होता है कि यह मंदिर विशाल एवं भव्य रहा होगा। मंदिर का निर्माण ईटों से किया गया है, इस पर प्लास्टर भी किया गया था। मंदिर निर्माण में आवश्यकतानुसार पाषाण का भी उपयोग किया गया है। इस मंदिर का निर्माण मूलत: गुप्तकाल में किया गया था। इसी मंदिर से सारनाथ की प्रसिद्ध धर्मचक्रप्रर्वतन मुद्रा की बुद्ध प्रतिमा प्राप्त हुई है। इस मंदिर का अनेको बार जिर्णोदार किया गया है जो वर्तमान में इस मंदिर के दीवारों को देखने से ज्ञात होता है।

इस मंदिर निर्माण के पूर्व भी यहां पर मंदिर रहा होगा, क्योंकि बुद्ध के रहने के जगह को ही मूलगंध कुटी विहार कहा जाता है, अत: उनके विश्राम का जगह यही रहा होगा, जो समय के साथ बड़ा एवं वैभवशाली होता गया होगा। (चित्र 2)

धर्मराजिका स्तूप : सारनाथ में चीनी यात्री ह्वेनसांग ने चार बड़े स्तूपों की चर्चा अपने यात्रा विवरण में किया है, जिसमें से तीन ही स्तूप प्राप्त है। यह स्तूप मूलत: मौर्यकालीन है, लेकिन समय-समय पर जीर्णोद्धार के द्वारा इसका विशाल स्वरूप होता गया। यह मौर्यकाल की पालिशयुक्त वेदिका से घिरा उद्देशियक स्तूप है। यह संभवत: अशोक के पूर्व एवं सारनाथ का प्रथम स्तूप हो सकता है। चीनी यात्री ह्वेनसांग ने अपने यात्रा विवरण में इस स्तूप के अतिरिक्त तीन और बड़े स्तूप की चर्चा की है। संभवत: यह स्तूप बुद्ध के निर्माण काल के कुछ समय बाद ही बना हो, इसके अंदर से हरे रंग की मंजूषा (Reliquary) मिली थी। इसमें संभवत: भगवान बुद्ध के अस्थि अवशेष थे (ह्वेनसांग की भारत यात्रा : 333-37)। इस स्तूप से प्राप्त इस मंजूषा पेटी को वरूणा नदी में विसर्जित कर दिया गया। अशोक काल में इस स्तूप का व्यास 13.50 मी. रहा, जिसे बाद में विस्तारित किया जाता रहा। (चित्र 3)

धमेख स्तूप: सर्वप्रथम कनिंघम महोदय द्वारा इस स्तूप में उत्खनन कार्य किया गया। इस स्तूप की स्थापना मूलत: मौर्यकाल में किया गया था, जिसे समय-समय पर विस्तृत किया गया था। धमेख स्तूप ठोस बेलनाकार बुर्ज की भांति है, जिसका व्यास 28.5 मीटर और ऊँचाई 33.58 मी. (नींव समेत 42.20 मीटर) है। इस स्तूप में सामान्यत: पायी जाने वाली आधार पीठ नहीं है। आयाताकार आधार को छोड़कर गोल आकार वाले अण्डभाग की ऊँचाई 11.20 मी. है। प्रस्तर के प्रत्येक स्तर लोहे के शिकंजे से बंधे हैं। इसकी मेधि के ऊपर ईटों की बेलनाकार आकृति है। मेधि की आधी ऊँचाई पर आठ आले बने हैं, जिसमें संभवत: प्रतिमायें स्थापित की गई थीं। इसके ठीक नीचे चौड़ी अलंकृत पाषाण पट्टिका है जिसमें ज्यामितीय एवं पुष्पीय अलंकरणों के साथ पक्षियों एवं मानवीय आकृतियों को सुन्दर ढंग से बनाया गया है। यह अलंकृत पाषाण पट्टिका गुप्त कला कौशल का उत्तम नमूना है। इस स्तूप के कलाकृतियों का अनेक विद्वानों के उल्लेख किया है (फाह्यिान : 75)। (चित्र 4)

चौखण्डी स्तूप: चौखण्डी स्तूप सारनाथ पुरास्थल से दक्षिण दिशा में थोड़ी दूरी पर ईटों द्वारा ऊँचा टीलानुमा बना है। इसके ऊपर अष्ठकोण बुर्जनुमा गृह निर्मित है। इस गृह का निर्माण राजा टोडरमल के पुत्र गोवर्धन ने राजा की आज्ञा से सन् 1583 ई. में बनवाया था (फरगुसन : 46)। यहां पर मुगल शासक हुमायूं एक दिन रूका था। यह स्तूप मूलत: गुप्तकालीन है, क्योंकि उत्खनन में गुप्तकालीन ईटें व अन्य कलाकृत उत्खनन से प्राप्त हुये। कनिंघम ने सन् 1935 ई. में इस स्तूप का भी उत्खनन करवाया था (मजूमदार : 28)। (चित्र 5)

मनौती स्तूप: सारनाथ में अनेकों मनौती स्तूपों को निर्मित किया गया था। मनौती स्तूपों के निर्माण में ईटों एवं प्रस्तरों का उपयोग किया गया है। मनौती स्तूप का निर्माण भक्तों द्वारा मन्नत पूर्ण होने के उपलक्ष्य में बनवाया जाता था। इस स्तूप के निर्माण की शुरूआत संभवत: भगवान के महापरिनिर्वाण के बाद से शुरू हुआ होगा। किन्तु अशोक के शासनकाल और उसके बाद इसे निर्मित करने का चलन बढ़ा होगा। उस समय से लेकर लगभग 12वीं शती ई. तक के मनौती स्तूप सारनाथ में प्राप्त होते है। (चित्र 6)

चैत्य: बौद्ध धर्म में जिस प्रकार स्तूप एवं वृक्ष की पूजा होती थी, उसी प्रकार चैत्य की भी पूजा होने लगी। अश्वलायनगृहसूत्र में इसका विधान मिलता है (अश्वलायन गृहसूत्र 1, 12)। सारनाथ में मुख्य मंदिर के पश्चिम भाग में एक चैत्य की खोज की गयी जो संभवत: मौर्यकालीन है। इस चैत्य का आकार 10.80 मी. लम्बा एवं 8.70 मी. चौड़ा है। इस चैत्य से एक भिक्षा पात्र के अतिरिक्त अन्य अवशेष मिले थे। महावंश से यह भी ज्ञात होता है, कि सम्राट अशोक ने स्तूपों के साथ-साथ विहारों का भी निर्माण

अपने साम्राज्य में किया। संभव है, कि सारनाथ में भी उसने विहारों का निर्माण करवाया हो, परन्तु इसकी पुष्टि प्राप्त साक्ष्य से नहीं होती। सारनाथ के उत्खनन से अभी तक सात विहार प्रकाश में आये हैं। उक्त सभी विहारों में भिक्षु रहते थे। अधिकांश विहारों में चारों ओर भिक्षुओं के रहने के लिए कोठरियां, बीच में आंगन एवं कुआं का निर्माण किया गया है। (चित्र 7)

अशोक स्तम्भः मुख्य मंदिर से पश्चिम में प्रसिद्ध अशोक स्तंभ खण्डित अवस्था में अवस्थित है। मूल स्तंभ अपने जगह पर है, जिसमें ब्राह्मी लिपि में अशोक द्वारा संघ भेद के खिलाफ राजाज्ञा उत्कीर्ण करवाया गया है। उक्त स्तंभ के खण्डित चार खण्ड उसके अगल-बगल में बाद में लगा दिया गया है, जो उत्खनन से प्राप्त हुए थे। इस स्तंभ का सबसे महत्वपूर्ण भाग सिंहशीर्ष था। स्तंभ के सिंह शीर्ष भाग समीप में ही बने संग्रहालय में प्रदर्शित है, यह सिंहशीर्ष गणतन्त्र भारत का राष्ट्रीय प्रतीक है। (चित्र 8, 12)

पुरातत्व संग्रहालय

सारनाथ के पुरातात्विक उत्खनन से प्राप्त अवशेषों को रखने एवं प्रदर्शित करने हेतु सन् 1904 ई. में स्थलीय पुरातात्विक संग्रहालय की योजना बनाई गयी थी। इसका भवन सन् 1910 ई. में तैयार हुआ और जितना अब तक निर्मित है उसे किसी प्राचीन संघाराम के भू-विन्यास का आधा भाग कहा जा सकता है (मणि 2010 : 56-64)। यह संग्रहालय भारतीय पुरातत्व सर्वेक्षण विभाग की पहली पुरास्थलीय संग्रहालय है। भवन के मुख्य कक्ष, चार वीथिकाओं तथा बरामदों में मूर्तियों को व्यवस्थित किया गया है। इस संग्रहालय के पास कुल 6832 पुरावशेष सुरक्षित है। इन में से लगभग 301 पुरावशेषों को संग्रहालय में प्रदर्शित किया गया है। कुछ महत्वपूर्ण अवशेषों का यहां उल्लेख करना समीचीन होगा। (चित्र 9)

मौर्य सम्राट अशोक द्वारा निर्मित स्तंभ का ऊपरी भाग सिंहशीर्ष खण्ड सबसे महत्वपूर्ण अवशेषों में से एक है। यह सिंहशीर्ष भारत का राष्ट्रीय प्रतीक चिन्ह है। मौर्यकला की सबसे प्रसिद्ध यह मूर्ति स्तंभ के ऊपरी भाग पर लगा हुआ था। इस सिंहशीर्ष की ऊँचाई 2.3 मी. है। तथा वास्तविक अवस्था में नीचे से ऊपर की ओर इसके 4 भाग हैं- प्रथम भाग उल्टे कमल की पंखुड़ियों से ढका हुआ घंटाकार कलश, द्वितीय भाग गोलाकार चौकी जिसमें चौबीस तीलियों वाली चार चक्र एवं बुद्ध के जीवन से संबंधित चार पशुओं को भी प्रदर्शित किया गया है। तृतीय भाग उस गोलाकार चौकी पर पीठ से पीठ सटाकर उकड़ूं बैठे तथा चारों दिशाओं में मुंह किये चार सिंह का प्रदर्शन किया गया है, एवं चतुर्थ भाग सबसे ऊपर एक धर्मचक्र था, जिसमें 32 तीलियां बनी रही होंगी उसके केवल चार टुकड़े ही मिले हैं।

स्तंभ के शीर्ष पर चार सिंहों की रचना अत्यन्त स्वाभाविक है, एवं इसमें उत्कृष्ट कोटि की कला झलकती है। नेत्र में बारीक छेद है, जिनमें मणि-रत्नों की बनी हुई पुतलियां स्थापित रही होगी, जो वर्तमान में नहीं है। अण्डाकार चौकी के ऊपर चार दौड़ते पशुओं यथा गज, वृषभ, अश्व, सिंह बीच में चार धर्मचक्र अलंकरण हैं।

संग्रहालय में प्रदर्शित लाल बलुए पत्थर की एक विशाल बोधिसत्व मूर्ति जिसे कनिष्क के राज्यकाल के तीसरे वर्ष में भिक्षु बल ने स्थापित किया, आरंभिक कुषाणकालीन मथुरा कला का अति उत्तम कलाकृति है। इस मूर्ति के पीछे अष्टकोणीय यष्टि के ऊपर छत्र स्थापित था। स्तंभ पर एक अभिलेख है, जिसमें मूर्ति की स्थापना का विवरण अंकित है। इसके अतिरिक्त दो अन्य बोधिसत्व जो कि चुनार के बलुए पत्थर से निर्मित है, मुख्य कक्ष में प्रदर्शित है। (चित्र 10 अ एवं ब)

गुप्तकाल में सारनाथ कला के क्षेत्र में अपने वैभव की पराकाष्ठा पर पहुंच चुका था। गुप्तकालीन कला पर मथुरा के कुषाण कला का स्पष्ट प्रभाव दिखता है, बाद में सारनाथ स्वयं कला केन्द्र के रूप में विकसीत हो गया। सारनाथ में चुनार के बलुए पत्थरों से निर्मित अनेकों कलाकृतियों का उत्कृष्ट नमूना सारनाथ संग्रहालय में प्रदर्शित एवं रखी हुई हैं। गुप्तकालीन कला का सर्वोतम नमूना धर्मचक्रप्रवर्तनमुद्रा में बैठे बुद्ध का है। निश्चित रूप से यह प्रतिमा संसार के कुछ सर्वोकृष्ट प्रतिमाओं में से एक है। (चित्र 11)

सारनाथ संग्रहालय में मौर्यकाल से लेकर लगभग 12वीं शताब्दी ई. तक के अनेक कलाकृतियां संग्रहित एवं प्रदर्शित हैं। भगवान बुद्ध के विभिन्न मुद्राओं में खड़ी व बैठी मूर्तियां तथा जीवन चरित्र की घटनाओं यथा-बोधिसत्व, पद्मपाणि, वज्रपाणि, मैत्रेय, मंजुश्री, सिद्धैकबीर, अवलोकितेश्वर, लोकनाथ, नीलकंठ, हारिति, तारा आदि की मूर्तियां संग्रहालय में संग्रहीत हैं। सारनाथ

संग्रहालय में हिन्दू देवी-देवताओं के भी अनेकों मूर्तियां हैं, जिसमें छोटे देवालय रूपी मंदिर, शिव, पार्वती, विष्णु, लक्ष्मी, नवग्रह, गणेश, सूर्य, कार्तिकेय, अग्नि, भैरव, अर्द्धनारीश्वर, हरिहर, शिवलिंग आदि प्रमुख हैं। शिव के अंधकासुरबद्ध (चित्र 13)का दृष्य वाली मूर्ति यहां की विशिष्ट मूर्तियों में से एक है।

सारनाथ बौद्ध तथा हिन्दू धर्म के अतिरिक्त जैन धर्म का केन्द्र भी रहा है। यहां पर जैन धर्म के भी अवशेष प्राप्त हुये हैं। जैनधर्म के 24 तीर्थंकर में से एक का जन्म स्थल सारनाथ का सिंहपुर ग्राम भी रहा है। इसलिए यहां पर जैन मूर्तियां भी मिली हैं- ध्यानमुद्र में मूर्ति या मूर्ति खण्ड एवं आयागपट्ट इत्यादि मिले हैं।

उपसंहार

अत: हम कह सकते हैं, कि सारनाथ प्राचीन काल से ही ज्ञान एवं सर्वधर्म सम्भाव वाला स्थल रहा है। यहीं से सर्वप्रथम सर्वजन हिताय और सर्वजन सुखाय का उपदेश संसार को प्राप्त हुआ। आज के युग में इस ज्ञान की नितांत आवश्यकता है। पुन: संसार को प्राचीन काल में हुए सारनाथ की धर्मचक्र प्रवर्तन की घटना को ध्यान में रखते हुये शान्ति तथा समृद्धि को आगे बढ़ाना चाहिए।

संदर्भ

सिंह, रामलोचन, *बनारस- ए- स्टडी ऑफ अर्बन ज्योग्राफी।*
नेविल, आर. एच., *बनारस गजेटियर।*
मोतीचन्द, *काशी का इतिहास।*
भिक्षुधर्म, रक्षिम, *सारनाथ का इतिहास।*
इन्साइक्लोपेडिया ब्रिटानिका, भा. 2.
डंकन, जे., *बनारस गजेटियर।*
आ. स. रि., 1903-04, 1904-1905.
ह्वेनसांग की भारत यात्रा।
फाह्यान ।
फरगुसन, जे., *हिस्ट्री ऑफ इण्डियन एण्ड ईस्टर्न आर्किटेक्चर भा. 1 .*
मजूमदार, बी. ए., *गाइड टू सारनाथ।*
मणि, बुद्ध रश्मि, 2010, *सारनाथ- पुरातत्व, कला एवं स्थापत्य,* नई दिल्ली।

21

Sculptural Heritage of Bauridi and Ladhurka in the Purulia district of West Bengal: Some Observations

Shubha Majumder

Introduction

The district of Purulia (23° 42´N-22°43´N and 86° 54´ E- 85° 49´E) encompassing a landmass of about 6259 sq.km in area is an extension of Chhotanagpur Plateau region. This western most district of West Bengal is in fact a cut off part of earlier Manbhum district and is mainly characterized by a hilly western part and an open upland eastern part (Chakrabarti 1993: 116). This district has already yielded a large number of prehistoric stone implements. Its rich prehistoric heritage is easily traceable in the hilly tract of the district mostly covering the upland areas of the west. The sequence of lithic objects recovered so far, tends to show that the region harbours Palaeolithic hunter gatherer who gradually developed their refined surviving strategy in the Mesolithic phase mostly by using microlithic tools (Chakrabarti *et al.* 1983: 131-141; see also Chakrabarti 1993). Though, the presence of hunter gatherer Mesolithic survival tradition is an interesting phenomenon of the Plateau as a whole and the region particularly. What is intriguing is that there is apparently no clear cut evidence demonstrating the existence of Early Village Farming settlement which we generally identified with BRW bearing Proto-historic assemblage, and even the data associated with Early Historic phase in the district is yet to trace to reconstruct the early historic sequence of this region.

However, the early medieval phase was really important of this district and during this period the cultural heritage received special impetus with the arrival of political lineages and religious ideologies during the early medieval period (Chattopadhyay & Acharya 2010: 9-31). The monumental feature of settlement structure especially during the early medieval period is categorically envisaged by the enormous wealth of archaeological relics in form of abandoned temple complexes, architectural members and sculptural remains of this region. In all probability the said database is the best signifier of its early medieval socio-cultural milieu. Interestingly, the impressive array of Jaina sculptures and architectural members from this region verify the fact that the region abounds in Jaina heritage and there were different flourishing Jaina centre at least for a considerable time of the early medieval period. On the other hand Brahmanical religious ideology was simultaneously flow in the then society and we get a huge number of sculptural remains associated with this religious order.

During the course of our explorations in this district we came across a large number of archaeological sites yielding old habitational remains as well as sculptural and architectural fragments (Majumder 2015; Ray, Chattopadhyay & Majumder 2014-15: 205-36; Majumder 2017). Most of the sites are associated with Jaina ideologies which underwent socio-religious transformation under the influence of the Brahmanical mode of appreciation. In the present paper we will discuss the archaeological contexts and iconic details of some Jaina and Brahmanical sculptural specimens from both the sites of Bauridi & Ladhurka. These two sites are archaeologically very potential and we have documented sculptural remains along with architectural remains and also some Hero stones. Most of the earlier works while investigating individual sculptural specimens, a temple or group of temples, have often ignored not only the archaeological context of their findings but also comparative stylistic study with reference to other contemporary Jaina remains found at other sites. Often, while reporting the Jaina images from this district, they have placed them within the early medieval/ medieval time bracket without suggesting the stages of stylistic development.

Sites and their Archaeological Assemblages

A. Bauridi: The present village, Bauridi is a large village and situated under the jurisdiction of the Hura Police Station and is about 3 to 4-------- km from the Ladhurka temple complex, which is another important site in this region and also discuss in the present paper (Majumder 2017). In a recently constructed Siva temple opposite a Primary School of this village we recorded five Jaina icons, of which four are Tirthankara icons and the fifth one is an image of Ambika (Fig. 1). It is evident that the temple has been constructed on a low structural mound which has the scattered ruins of a remarkable ancient temple. The local villagers claim that they frequently find fragmentary Jaina sculptural and architectural remains from different parts of this mound. We also recorded two Siva lingas from the eastern part of this mound. The temple site itself is locally known as Bhairavathan and this village was earlier known as Haralia-dih.

Details of Sculptures

1. The image of Tirthankara Candraprabha is damaged and only the lower portion (below the waist) of the image is extant (Fig. 2). It reveals the Jina standing in stiff kayotsarga posture on a double-petalled lotus seat placed on panca-ratha pedestal. A stylized lotus creeper with scrolled leaves and buds occupies the centre of the pedestal. The centre lower projected portions of the pedestal contain the crescent moon, identifying the cinha of the Jina and the remaining portion decorated with geometrical motifs. Stylized representations of crouching lions occupies the both

the side of decorated lotus creeper. A meal and a female devotee kneeling in namaskara mudra along with ratna – patras heaped with offering are placed on the remaining portions of the pedestal. The Jina is flanked on both sides by stout male cauri-bearers. Unfortunately, the left side cauri-bearer is completely damaged and the face of the right side cauri-bearer is mutilated. The cauri-bearer wear deeply incised loin cloth and elaborate jewellery. They stand on lotus pedestals and their left hands are in katyavalambita posture and the right hands hold a fly-whisk. This is a caubisi type of image. However, the edges of the back stele, on a projected frame, is relieved with twelve – figures of miniature Tirthankaras arranged in three vertical rows of two each on either side of the mula-nayaka. Like the principal image, they also stand in kayotsarga posture on a lotus pedestal and their respective lanchanas are carved at the centre of their thrones. They have a plain oval shaped halo. On the basis of their respective lanchanas the twelve – figures of miniature Tirthankaras are identifiable. Right side of the mula-nayaka the Tirthankaras are Vimalanatha, Anantanatha, Kunthanatha, Aranatha, Naminatha and Neminatha (top to bottom). On the left side the Tirthankaras are Dharmanatha, Santinatha, Mallinatha, Munisuvrata, Parsvanatha and Mahavira. The existing portion of the present image shows that the mula-nayaka bears a svelte figure and the carving of the image is very sophisticated. The arms of the Jina hang down vertically along the stiff torso and the finger tips touch the thigh on either side.

2. Among the three images of Rsabhanatha, comparatively well preserved specimen is made of chlorite stone and measures 88 cm x 47 cm x 15 cm (Fig. 3). Visually, it is quite schematic and rigid and the plastic tendencies are minimal. The Jina is standing in *kayotsarga* posture on a double-petalled lotus placed on a *panca-ratha* pedestal. The bull *lanchana* of the *mula-nayaka,* is neatly carved on the centre of the pedestal and placed between two crouching lions. A male and a female devotee in *namaskara mudra* (folded hands) occupies the both the end of the pedestal. The upper portion of the back stele of the image is completely lost and the face of the Tirthankara is slightly mutilated. The *mula-nayaka* obviously devoid of any worldly attire, has elongated ear-lobes, and most probably wears an elegant *jatajuta.* The *kesa-vallari* of the Jian is falling down the sides of the head and over the shoulders. An almost circular *sirascakra* with leafed edges adorns the head of the saviour. The Jina is flanked on both sides by stout male partially damaged *cauri*-bearers. They wear deeply incised loin cloths and elaborate jewellery and both of them have plain, small oval shaped halos. Obviously, the modulation of surfaces apparent from the drapery and jewellery are restricted to these *parikara* elements. These *cauri*-bearers stand in *dvi-bhanga* pose and holding a fly-whisk in their right hands and left hands are in *katyavalambita* posture. The back throne of the image consists of posts decorated with mouldings and criss-cross scratched pilasters, supporting a horizontal cross-bar with lightly incised square rhizomes at its ends, above which there are triangular foliated plaques. On the projected part of the back

stele there are eight planets (Joytiska-devas) arranged in a vertical row of four on either side of the Jina. Unfortunately, only six planetary deities with bad stage of preservation presently exist. These on the dexter side appear to be Mangal, Brhaspati and Sani; while those on sinister side are Budha, Sukra and Rahu. The image of Surya and Soma are completely lost here. All these figures are seated on high *visvapadmas* (except Rahu) and show individual iconographic features. The figures of the planetary deities are not possible to study with minute iconic details due to their defaced condition except the Sani, Sukra and Rahu. Sani (Saturn) is clearly distinguished by his peculiar sitting pose and the staff with a roundish top. On the left side Sukra is depict just above the Rahu. In this image the defaced planetary deity Sukra seated in *samparyankasana* and his right hand is damaged and left hand is resting over his thigh and holding *kamandalu*. According to the Jaina conical texts Sukra is the ruler of the south- Eastern region and teacher of Demons. None of the Jaina texts refer to the terrific form of un-auspicious planetary deity Rahu who has only been referred to as ruler of south-Western. In the present sculpture the bust portion of the Rahu with his robust like head is visible and his hands are in the *tarpana mudra* same as in the Brahmanical *Navagraha* sculptures. In the present image the organization of space evident from the entire composition is remarkable as well as static. Elaborations in the back-slab are kept to a minimum.

3. The second image of Rsabhanatha (Fig. 4) is measures 86 cm x 60 cm x 18 cm and the head of the *mula-nayaka* along with the upper part of almost rectangular stele is completely missing. The Jina stands on a lotus placed on a *panca-ratha* pedestal having a bull flanked by stylized representations of crouching lions in the central part. The right side corner of the pedestal is occupies by the kneeling donor couple while the other side decorated with a *ratna-patra* heaped with offerings. Though the head of the image is missing however, some hair locks of the Jina is visible. He is attended by two stiff and robust looking *cauri*-bearers, profusely bejeweled, with their left hands in *katyavalambita* posture and the right hands holding *camaras.* They are wearing short almost transparent lower garments and simple ornaments including armlets, wristlets and *ekavali*. The Jina figure is flanked by pillar like structural appendages surmounted by triangular entities. This is a *caubisi* type of image. On the edge of the back-slab, on a projected frame, are miniature figures of twenty-four Tirthankaras (presently only twenty exist) arranged in six vertical rows of two each on the either side of the *mula-nayaka.* Like the principle image they also stand in *kayotsarga* posture with their respective *lanchanas* carved below each on a small lotus throne.

4. The third image of Rsabhanatha (Fig. 5) is very much similar with the earlier image. This is also a damage specimen; only the lower portion (below the abdomen) of the image exists, which is measuring 88 cm x 68 cm x 19 cm. The remaining portion of the edge of the back – slab is relieved with twelve-figures of miniature Jinas arranged in three vertical rows of two each on

either side. Like the principle image they also stand in *kayotsarga* posture with their respective *lanchanas* carved below each on a small lotus throne. The surviving portion of the body of *mula-nayaka* shows his natural body and the arms of the Jina hang down vertically along the torso and the finger tips touch the thigh on either side. In this image the *mula-nayaka* stands in *kayotsarga* posture on a on a double-petalled lotus placed on a *panca-ratha* pedestal. The Jina is flanked on both sides by stout male *cauri*-bearers stands on double-petalled lotus placed on same pedestal. They wear deeply incised loin cloths and elaborate jewellery. Obviously, the modulation of surfaces apparent from the drapery and jewellery are restricted to these *parikara* elements. These *cauri*-bearers stand on lotus pedestals and their left hands are in *katyavalambita* posture and the right hands hold a fly-whisk. The pedestal of the image is of considerable iconographic interest. A stylized lotus creeper with scroll leaves and buds occupies the centre of the pedestal below, under which there is a decorated bull, the identifying *cinha* of the Jina. The bull is flanked by a male and a female devotee kneeling in *namaskara mudra.* Two lions crouching in opposite direction occupies the both the end of the pedestal.

5. Like the other images of this collection the image of Ambika, Yaksi of Tirthankara Neminatha, is also damaged (Fig. 6). In this image only the lower portion (below the abdomen) of the deity is surviving and its measures 77 cm x 57 cm x 17 cm. The bejeweled goddess stands in graceful *abhanga* posture on a double-petalled lotus placed on a *panca-ratha* pedestal. She is holding a frolicking little child, who is her younger son Prabhankara, with her left hand. In her right arm she possibly holding the branch of a mango tree, unfortunately this is broken now. A male attendant, who is her elder son Subhakara, stands in cross leg posture to her right side and holding a *punthi* in his left arm-pit. The goddess wears a diaphanous *sari* fastened by an ornamented girdle and profuse jewellery. Some parts of her long scarf falling on her both side. She wears multi-stranded armlets, *mekhala, ratnopavita,* etc. Left side of the damaged stele of the deity consist a lady *cauri*-bearer. The projected part of the pedestal below reveals a lion, the *vahana* of the Yaksi. The stylized lion is flanked by a male and a female devotee kneeling in *namaskara mudra.* Iconographically the present image of Ambika is more or less similar with the Ambika images from Pakbirra. On the basis of stylistic ground and iconographic features the above discuss Jian images are belongs to c. 10th to 12th century CE.

Except these above mention Jaina images some broken architectural parts are scattered in the nearby area of the modern temple and according to the local villagers they collected these type of structural remains from this mound. These sculptural relics along with the architectural ruins indicate that there must be a huge Jaina temple during the early medieval period. This site needs proper scientific excavation to known the hidden history of this site.

B. Ladhurka: The present village is a well known locality laying on Purulia and Hura road, approximately 20 km. east of the former and 16 km. to west of the later this site is situated on western bank of a tributary of the River Kasai. Ladhurka is well known for a temple complex of Chandeswar clearly indicates its affluent condition as a popular religious site from a very long time suggesting the tradition of uninterrupted continuity of worship. The present temple complex apparently stands on the ruins of an earlier structure. The present site possesses a few sculptural remains and four *insitu* specimens of some memorial stones lying inside the temple complex. The natural occurrences of such Hero stone suggest that this complex was used for memorial purpose. The details of these specimens are given below.

Details of Sculptures

1. Among these four specimens of Hero stone three are similar and representing the *Jhampasingha* type or Warrior type (without horse). The lower portions of these three specimens are buried. The first specimen (Fig. 7) is measuring 95 cm x 50 cm x 25 cm. and is carved in a very crude manner. Probably it depicts the image of a deceased hero in common posture with widened legs. The left hand is shown holding a bow where as arrow is held by the right hand. A broad and heavy weighted rampart lion caps the slab on its top. Modeling and proportion are more or less conspicuous by their absence.
2. The second example (Fig. 8) is measure 70cm x 50cm x 25cm and iconographically is similar with the earlier one. In this specimen the figure of the warrior carved in a low relief and it is only shown up to its waste portion. The hero stands with usual attributes held by both the hands i.e. sword in his left hand and bow in his right hand. This whole part is kept with a giant figure of lion. The figure of lion is very crudely carved.
3. The third one is measuring 67cm x 50cm x 20cm and it is a prototype of the earlier two specimens.
4. The last one among the four specimens is very unique and it represents a *linga* type of specimen. It measure 128cm x 28cm x 28cm. and look like a monolithic miniature form of *rekha deul*. It is *tri-ratha* in plan. The *padapitha* portion of the present specimen is not visible. The *gandi* portion of this specimen has three divisions. The frontal side of the central *paga* of the specimen has a small niche. Inside the niche a small *yoni patta* type of *linga* is neatly carved. The two *kanika pagas* are plain. This miniature temple is crowned by a small *amalaka* and it surmounted by most probably a *kalasa*.

Besides there are some other fragment pieces of hero stones scattered at the site. It is to be noted that the site was earlier a memorial spot which was converted into temple complex dedicated to Chandeswar Siva linga in latter period. In this temple complex we also document some Jaina and Brahmanical stone sculptures (Fig. 9). Among them two are identifiable i.e. image of a Jaina tutelary couple and Surya image. The Jaina tutelary couple image is measure 58cm x 25cm x 23cm and lower portion of the image is presently buried. The couple is seated on a throne in *ardha-paryankasana* posture under a tree on a full blown lotus, placed on a *tri-ratha* pedestal. However, it is very difficult to record the iconographic details of the sculptures because of its abraded condition. The male figure holds a child on his left lap by his left hand and the right hand is in *abhaya-mudra*. He wears a *dhoti* like garment reaching well below his knee, and elaborate jewellery comprising bracelets, armlets, beaded necklace, large circular *kundalas*, and an elegant *ratna-mukuta*. The female figure holds a child in her left lap while her right hand is in *varada-mudra*. The female is attired in a diaphanous lower garment reaching down to her ankles and is bejewelled in the same fashion as the male, except that a short three-crested crown adorns her head. Her hair is arranged in an elegant bun resting on her shoulder. The stylized foliages of a tree shelter the couple and a miniature seated Jina in *dhyana-mudra* is depicted above one of the branches. The *lanchana* of the Jina is not clearly visible. *Vidyadharas* are in their usual position at the top corners of an apsidal stele.

The image of Surya is highly abraded and it measure 60cm x 22cm x 23cm. In this image the god stands in *samapadasthanaka* posture. The lower portion of the image is under soil and the chariot of the god is not visible. His cloth descends down to the knees and a second piece of tight cloth round the waist is profusely ornamented and is further decorated with ornamental hangings. The breast is protected by armor, the outlines of which intertwine to form a knot on the breast. The god wears elaborate necklaces and earrings and an intricately worked-out coronet bedecks his head. He holds two lotuses in his two hands which rise a little above his shoulders. Bearded, pot bellied *Pingala*, stands on the left side of the god holding an indistinct object, which could be a pen and an inkstand. *Dandi*, who is also shown in armor, stands on the right with a sword in his right hand and the left resting on a staff. The two wives of Surya stand respectively on the left and the right sides of the god.

Observations

In the foregoing pages we have analyzed our data to achieve a clearer picture of archaeological sites and their sculptural remains. It is quite clear from the above data that these evidences, ascribable to the Jaina pantheon, are well connected with the growth of Jainism and the spread of Jaina settlements, rituals and their relationship with the sculptural art of the said region. It is quite obvious that such concentration of Jaina heritage is not restricted to these particular sites. There are some other sites/settlements associated with Jaina ideology in an around this region. It is also worth mentioning here that during our survey in this area we documented some Brahmanical sculptural specimens i.e. Surya images etc along with hero-stones. The presence of the Surya image and other Brahmanical images indicates that though Jainism was very much popular in the area, however, Brahmanism was also simultaneously marked its presence in the religious life of the people of the region.

Sculptures briefly described and discussed above are on stylistic and iconographic grounds may be assigned to the period between the eleventh and the twelfth centuries CE. These, including the other stupendous sculptural remains from this district as well as other parts of the *radha* region of Bengal, were products created by the fusion of the art idioms of neighboring areas of the Chhotanagpur plateau region and were laid in an essentially local matrix from which came out this distinct school of a regional tradition. This regional tradition was guided by powerful local ateliers which were not driven necessarily by the ideas of the plastic art exhibited in the mainstream 'Pala-Sena' idiom of expression. However, these local artists became perfectionists in their own way (Majumder 2016: 240).

The present work thus shows that the western sectors of West Bengal deserve more careful archaeological investigation in order to understand the nature and pattern of distribution of early medieval sites/settlements and of locating the regional cultural and artistic identities as well as the nature of their religious character. This type of present study indicates that such micro-regional case studies are expected to throw welcome light on the nature of linkages witnessed by the different religious and ideological orders within a given local tradition, which also help us to reconstruct an overview about the history of the socio-religious character of the region as a whole.

References

Chakrabarti, Dilip K., D.K. Bhattacharya & R.K. Chattopadhyay, 1983, Lithic Industries of Purulia, *Man and Environment,7.*

Chakrabarti, Dilip K, 1993, *Archaeology of Eastern India: Chhotanagpur Plateau and West Bengal,* New Delhi: Munshiram Manoharlal.

Chattopadhyay, R.K. & D. Acharya, 2010, Contexts of Early Mediaeval Remains of Purulia: Researching Ideologies, *Pratnatattva 16.*

Majumder, S., 2015, *Jaina Heritage of Chharra,* New Delhi: Shri Bharatvarshiya Digamber Jain (T.S.) Mahasabha.

Majumder, S., 2016, Recent Explo rations at Balarampur (Purulia district, West Bengal), *Puratattva, 46.*

Majumder, S., 2017, *Jain a Remains of Ancient Bengal: A Study in Archaeology, Art and Iconography,* unpublished PhD thesis submitted to the University of Calcutta

Ray, Swati, R. K. Chattopadhyay & S. Majumder, 2014-15, Exploring the Jaina Sculptural Remains in Ancient Manbhum, *Berliner Indologische Studien* (Reinbek) 22.

22

Religious Heritage from Balasore, Orissa: A Note

Abir Kumar Gorai

Introduction

An exploration was undertaken at Balasore, under Orissa for my research work. The coastal region of Balasore district and its adjoining area forming a transition zone between the coast and the upland are known to have been under consistent occupation in the early historic and early medieval periods from C. Third –Second Century BCE to twelfth – Thirteenth Century CE (Chakrabarti 1993: 67).

Balasore District is very much famous for its glorious history, art and culture. There are many beautiful temples and spots to be seen here at Balasore District. The History of Balasore District is the amalgamation of several cultures and civilizations colonized the region for a couple of years. This place was a part of ancient Kalinga, which later came under the jurisdiction of Toshala or Utkal till the death of Mukunda Deva. The history of Balasore witnessed a quick succession of several dynasties in its bosom's. As far as the history of Balasore District is concerned; there was a constant strife among the different rulers over the entire tract of the District (Hunter 1908: 328).

Religious Heritage

The people of the various religious beliefs residing here, viz. Hindus, Muslims, Sikhs, Christians etc, amply display the cultural genesis of this District. The copper coins collected from Bhograi and the collection of statues of Lord Buddha from places like *Avana, Kupari, Basta* and *Ayodhya* magnifies the existence of Buddhism here. Buddhism is also popular during *"Bhoumakar"*. The statue of Lord *Jaina* at Jaleswar, Balasore and Avana hints about Jainism that is practiced in this District, which was also popular during 10th and 11th centuries.Balasore District is highly famous for its *Saibapitha's*, many temples of Lord Shiva is seen at places throughout the district. The temples of Lord Shiva at Chandaneshwar, Baneshwar, Jhadeshwar, Panchalingeshwar, Bhusandeshwar and Maninageshwar are highly popular. But, here in this article present author mainly concentrate on the findings from Chandaneswar temple and its history.

The present paper is focusingof recent findings in a field investigation at Chandaneswar temple, Balasore as a part of the author's research work. This work is endeavored to a detailed documentation of each and every sculptural and architectural remains at Chandaneswar temple complex (Fig. 1). It seeks, by no means, to minimize the empirical of the merit of their earlier pioneering works; rather an extension of the study so far carried out by the eminent scholars in this region. The focal points of the concentration of the present article is to give an inventory of the hitherto reported and unreported sculptural and architectural remains documented from the temple complex along with their iconographic details.

Chandaneswar Temple is a famous Shiva temple situated in Baleswar, Odisha. It is said to be one of the oldest temples in and around Digha. This temple is quite close to New Digha. It attracts tourists from all places because of its wonderful and ancient architectural structure and design. It is at a distance of 8 kms from New Digha. The Odia New Year Maha Vishuva Sankranti day is very famous festival here around this temple premise, which is locally called *UdaParba, NilParba* after worshipping *Nilkantha Shiva* and *Charakyatra*. A half million people are gathered around this temple on this famous occasion and do fasting of several days to fulfill their wishes. Every year in the month of Chaitra (according to Bengali calendar) i. e. 14th March to 14th April Orissa's famous *Charakmela* or *Chaitra mela* is arranged here and it continues for 13 days. These 13 days means 13 *arghyas*(offering something to God), they do fast for whole day, not even swallowing their spit, last three *arghya* days are known as *Kamina Baha* (marriage of lord Shiva with *Kamina*, daughter of demon *Nila*, Second *arghya*day is Nil *parba*and the first is *Paata Parba*. Some devotees prick their bodies and tongue with iron nails. More than half million people are gathering in this occasion and that is why sometimes it is called second Puri in Orissa.

Three sculptures are kept in the sanctum of this temple, in which two Visnu image and one is Uma- Maheswar. We are well aware of a series of researches on the image worship of Visnu. (Rao 1914: 89), (Vidyavinod 1920: 245), (Banerji 1980: 101-108), (Bhattasali 1929: 77-107) J. N. Banerjea observed : "One of the most important of the *Brahmanical* cults that came into being some centuries before the beginning of Christian era centered round Visnu, but this god was not identical with Vedic Visnu ...In the Epics and Puranic age Visnu is regarded as the most influential member of the later *Brahmanical* triad, Brahma, Visnu and Siva – the Creator, the Preserver and the Destroyer ....Numerous are the iconographic texts which describe the images of Visnu and his various aspects, one of the earliest among them being the five couplets in *Brihatsamhita* (Banerjea 1974: 385-427).

Sridhar from of Visnu is in *samapadasthanaka* posture on a *pancharatha* pedestal adorned with donor couple to the right and figure of Garuda to the left along with floral motifs. Visnuis accompanied by Laksmi with flywhisk in the right hand and a stalk of a lotus in the left hand and Sarasvati carrying a *vina* standing to the left (Fig. 2). Visnu has four arms. Clockwise the attributes in the hands of Visnu are; lower right hand is in *varadamudra* with the palm marked by a lotus and placed on a lotus; upper right holds a *cakra;* upper left holds a *gada* and the lower left hand is broken. Visnu is bejeweled with a *kiritamukata, kundala-s, hara, upavita* and decorated waist band and dhoti with *vanamala.* The back slab of this image is not so decorated. On back slab at shoulder level of the deity a bird like figure is being observed whereas the upper portion of the slab depicts two *vidyadhara-s* with their consorts set against the clouds on the either side of *kirtimukha* (Donaldson 2001: 1-30). This sculpture is dated to 11th century CE and according the decoration, attribution of this image influences of local cultural beliefs may highlighted.

Another Visnu image is found from here. This standing figure of Visnu is quite interesting. Present author have mentioned earlier that may be local belief, their rituals play an important role to create all these figure here and the creator always keep this him or her mind when prepared this type of sculpture (Fig. 3). Here we see that Visnu is standing with two wings like Garuda. The pedestal of this image is also different from any other sculpture, it is decorated as like as snake skin. Attributes in deity's hand are also different. Clockwise lower right hand hold a small *gada* depicted like a *danda;* upper right hand holds a *sankha; cakra* is there in upper left hand and unidentified object (may be lotus bud) hold in lower left hand. Visnu is bejeweled with a *kiritamukata, kundala-s, hara, upavita* and a decorated waist band. The back slab of this image is not so decorated except a temple shape decorated panel is there over the *kiritamukuta* with some floral motifs and two lotus motifs have also seen on either side of panel. The main deity is accompanied by a standing figure and a seating figure may be Laxmi and Sarasvati, but the attribution of these figures and all over this image is not so good. It will clearly see if we look the hand of the main deity.This image is dated back to 11th -12th century CE (Bidyabinod 1991: 22-23).

An image of Uma-Mahesvara (Sharma 1982: 104), is depicted as seated on a lotus pedestal. *Urdhalinga*Siva is seated in *lalitasana*with the right leg dangling down and left leg rest on the pedestal (Fig. 4). The image is not so clear. Siva has four hands; clockwise lower right hand is partly broken; upper right hand holds *trisula,* upper left hand holds a lotus bud and lower left hand also broken. Siva is bejeweled with hara, *kundala-s, nupura-s* decorated waist band and a *jatamukuta.* Devi also seated in *lalitasana,* just opposite pose of Siva. Her left leg of Devi dangling down and right leg rest on the pedestal. Devi has two hands; right hand is on *abhaya*mudra and left is not seen in this image.Uma is adorned with *hara, valaya, kundala-s,* decorated waist band and a *jatamukuta* (Sengupta and Saha 2014: 69).

The above findings related to the Socio-religious perspective though the paper has limited scope for exploring this area. The most fascinating information related to the settlement history of this village and adjoining areas could be viewed in different way. So far as the presence of structural evidence along with our concern (Fig. 5). The settlement suggests its association with the development of both secular and religious sector.According to local people some stories and myth is continuing about this temple and place. Present temple structure was built later, and if we see this temple's structure are there, two parts were built separately. Before that, there was a stone (*Makra* Stone) temple which is totally destroyed which can proves some evidences are available there. Actually this place is very close to sea and surrounded by two rivers, so that it can be possible to think that ancient temple was there. It cannot be wrong if we think that this place maybe was a very important at that time towards business purpose, because this place was easily communicative for the businessman, exchange commodities and other work related to business for its located and this coastal area played a vital role for the maritime trade with foreign countries also. If we see the history of coastal area of Bengal and Orissa then we can find out that the total coastal bend from south Bengal to Orissa played an important role for maritime trade with foreign countries for a long time. The business man, who went to other place for business purpose, they were worshipped here and offering *arghya* to god and after they started their journey, which was a ritual said by a local man and this story is continuing by generation.After that temple was ruined but the myth and stories are continues by generation wise. Now, this modern temple is built and now also millions of people has come and worship the great Siva. Time has changed but the picture remained same, again that local man said.

There are possibilities to prove that before it was a Visnu temple before and *Vaisnava*sect had a strong hold at this place. According to Niharanjan Roy there was a common ritual to establish a Garuda*stambha* or pillar in front of Visnu temple. At the top of the pillar Garuda was placed with *anjalimudra*and this same type of pillar we have seen at Chandaneswar temple **(Plate-VII)** at the entrance where Garuda is placed on a pillar. This type of Garuda pillar is found throughout the Bangladesh. At the time of Narayan Pal, a Garuda pillar is found from Dinajpur also on which the *Badalprasasti* was engraved. The sculptural and architectural representations of the study area convey the religious mode of appreciation of various ideologies. However, one cannot ignore the fact, that ethno-archaeological survey provides sufficient information regarding the contribution of folk elements, and the dominance of folk religious traditions in the functioning of religious establishments, both orthodox and otherwise. One surely faces difficulties in the chronological study of religious expressions and also in determining when the folk elements were actually incorporated in the functioning of temples, installation of deities and in the mechanism related to the rituals of the devotees, besides, the involvement of priest and the patrons. It is quite evident that the local beliefs and practices incorporated the Puranic or orthodox religious elements as well as folk traditions.

Our recorded sculptural and architectural specimens could be tentatively dated between *c.* eighth and twelfth centuries CE on the basis of their stylistic grounds. The iconic forms recorded here have close association with their counter parts reported from other regions of Orissa and Coastal Bengal. It is obvious that during the post-Gupta and specifically in the Pala-Sena period, the spread of Buddhist and Brahmanical settlements in the Bengal, influenced or extended up Orissa and its adjoining region. While summarizing the present database we cannot ignore a development related to a change of religious ideology, i.e., Brahmanical that enveloped the dominance of the earlier one (Banerjea 1985: 385-427). This is clearly apparent in our study area. A reason for this change could be viewed in two perspectives. Firstly, the expansion of Guptas-later-Guptas in Orissa was a prime factor for the shifting to the Brahmanical ideology.

The evolution of Vaisnavism certainly had bearing with the present settlement though it is very difficult for making any permanent statement for the same. The development of post-Gupta phase and the emergence of major-minor settlement in West Bengal could be viewed in terms of the sprayed of *Vaisnism* in the Pre-*Chaitnya* era and on the other hand the presence of the image of Uma- Maheswar certainly had association with the Saivism. Unfortunately the recorded specimens are isolated evidence so far as religious history concern. This brief note is an attempt to highlight both the secular and religious association of this settlement. Finally one may note that the habitational record found in the village demonstrate the growth of this settlement along the coastal line and during the course of time, it became a part of the settlement history of this region.

The above archaeological findings though preliminary explored artifacts provide some scope to explain some aspects of culture, economy and society of the region concerned. It is to be noted that the present paper emphasized the documentation of sculptural remains recorded during exploration. However, we need more data to explain the beginning of the settlement here. The continuity of settlement may not be ignore and during the early mediaeval period received special impetuous possibly due to the political appreciation. The presence of sculptures datable in between 8th century CE to 12th Century CE suggests the development of the religious system and obviously the presence of *Vaishnavism* and *Brahmanism*at that particular place is mentioned here.

Conclusion

The subject focusing on sculptural art carved out of stone recorded in the Bengal – Orissa border area specially Balasore, Jaleswar, Baleswar, Baripada and Sambalpur was never considered as the matter of absorbing interest as routine survey works by several British administrators and oriental scholars of that time enriched our knowledge about the same considerably. Undoubtedly the fabrication of such sculptural specimens was taking into shape from the early mediaeval period onwards. Though all these detailed documentation has never been properly employed as an appropriate tool to understand the actual context of the specimens along with other associated cultural assemblages. This paper essentially explored the contextual aspect of such findings along with socio-religious element involved in the site formation process through the lens of such specimens and their associated archaeological components mainly in form of structural vestiges and habitational remains which contains them. Nevertheless the entire database also brings into one compass certain issues highlighting the historical process which went into the making of early mediaeval society, appropriation of religious ideology with the formation of sub-regional and regional temporal authority and the process of forging of linkages across communities for social integration.

References

Banerjea, J. N., 1974, *Development of Hindu Iconography*, Delhi.

Banerjea, J. N., 1985, *The Development of Hindu Iconography*, New Delhi.

Banerji, R. D., 1980, *Eastern Indian School of Mediaeval Sculpture.*

Bidyabinod, B. B., 1991, *Varieties of the Vishnu image*, Memoirs of the Archaeological Survey of India, Delhi: Swati Publication.

Bhattasali, N. K., 1929, IBBS, Dacca.

Chakrabarti, Dilip. K, 1993, *Archaeology of Eastern India: Chhotanagpur Plateau and West Bengal*, New Delhi.

Donaldson, Thomas E., 2001, *The Iconography of Vaisnava images in Orissa*, Delhi.

Gopinath, Rao, T. A.,1914, *Element of Hindu Iconography*, Madras: Vol.I.

Hunter, W.W., 1908, *Imperial Gazetteers of India*, Vol. VI.

Sengupta, G and Sharmila Saha, 2014, *Vibrant Rock (A Catalogue of Stone Sculptures in the State Archaeological Museum, West Bengal)*, Kolkata.

Sharma, I.K., 1982, *Development of Early Saiva art and Architecture,* New Delhi.

Vidyavinod, B. B., 1920, Varieties of the Visnu Image, *MASI*, No.2, Calcutta.

23

Sun Deity in Central and Western Indian Historical Testimonies of Rājputa Age

Surabhi Srivastava

The adoration of the Sun dated from the earliest times. *Ṛgveda* contains some ten hymns in the honour of *Surya*. He is described as far-seeing, all-seeing and beholding all the good and bad actions of men. He was reckoned among the *Ādityas*, son of *Aditi*. In some passages he is identified with some members of the animate world, whereas in others, he is described as an inanimate object, being called the "Gem of the sky." He measures days, prolongs life, dispels sickness, disease and all creatures depend upon him for life.

The *Purāṇas* give different account of the origin of his birth, and describe him as dark red with three eyes and four arms. He holds red lotus in two hands, with the third he is bestowing blessings and with the fourth, he encourages his worshippers. He sits upon a red lotus and is drawn in his chariot by seven horses or with one horse with seven heads.

In the time of *Upaniṣads* and later writings we find the Sun mentioned as being worshipped daily thrice with offerings of water, flower and sandal. A legend prevailed that Sāmba, a grandson of śri-Kṛṣṇa constructed a temple in honour of the sun-god on the banks of the modern Chenab, and brought a speacial sect of sun-worshippers called *Magas* from outside India. That these *Magi* continued down to the 10th century A.D. as worshippers of the Sun, is borne by the testimony of Varāhmihir, who writes that the installation and worship of the Sun should be entrusted to a certain set of people called the *Magi* and also of Alberuni, who states that the *Magi* existed in India when he visited it. During the Gupta rule the Sun worship prevailed like other sects and many temples seem to have been erected in his honour. Thus exlusive sect of sun-worshippers arose who came to be known as *śauras*.

Sūrya was worshipped during the period under consideration is evident from epigraphs of the dynasties of the regions. Thus the present paper aims to explore the inscriptions of two different dynasties of Central India, viz. the Gurjara-Pratiharas and Parmāras who ruled over the region from

8th-10th Century A.D. and 10th – 12th Century A.D. respectively. The Paramāras often came at wars with the Chaulukyas of the Gujarat region in the west also known as the Solankīs resulting into the often changing boundaries of their kingdoms. Therefore the charters of the Chaulukya rulers have also been taken into consideration along with other archaeological & literary sources to throw a welcome light on the position of Sūrya as a deity in brahmanic religion as well as an independent sect in the given space and time.

Amongst the Gurjara-Pratīhāras Rāmbhadra and Vināyakpāla held *Sūrya* as their tutelary deity. Their records render the following names for Sun-god- *Indrādityadeva* (Epigraphia Indica XIV: 23-28), *Indrarājaditya-deva* (Epigraphia Indica XVI: 182) *Taru Gaditya-deva* (Epigraphia Indica IX: 1-9) *Bhaillasvāmīdeva*(Epigraphia Indica I,177), etc. The image of *Ādityabhammāraka* has been found from Dinajpur district of Bangladesh (Epigraphia Indica XXXVII: 204) on the foot hold of which there is a legend of two lines, tells us that the image of the Sun-god, bearing the epigraph was built by a person named Lokanandin, the son of Gangānandin in the 12 reignal year of Mahendrapāla. Two Copperplates of Mahendrapāla discovered at Ūṇa (Epigraphia Indica IX: 109), (Junagarh, Gujarat) refer to a Sun temple as *TaruGādityadeva,* which stood on the bank of river Kanakvīra. Two grants were made to this temple, a village Jayapura and another a piece of land by the Chaulukya feudatories Balavarmana and Avantivarman II. Similarly the Partabgarh inscription (Epigraphia Indica XXIV: 176) records the existence of several temples at Ghoṇtāvārcikā, where the chief temple belonged to *Indrādityadeva* i.e. the Sun-god, also called the deity of Ghoṇtāvārcikā. Several Sun temples of this period have been brought to light, which include the Sun temples at Umri and village Mankhḍā in Tikamgarh district of Madhya Pradesh while another one exists at Sesai, district Shivapuri, Madhya Pradesh (Srivastava 2008: 174-175).

Bhilsā was the famous seat of sun-worship during the Paramāra dominion. The antiquity of the famous *Bhaillasvāmin* temple of Bhilsā goes back to 878 A.D. (Epigraphia Indica XX: 213) Two Stone inscriptions brought to light from this place testify to its reputation as one starts with *Om namaḥ sūryāya* and the second one is the euology of the sun-god composed by Mahākavichakravartin Paṇḍita Chhittapa, who flourished under the patronage of king Bhojadeva (Epigraphia Indica XXX: 215). In another epigraph Mahākumāra Hariśchandra is said to have made his land-grant in the presence of god *Bhaillasvāmin,* situated on the banks of Vetravatī, i.e. Betwa, at Bhilsā (Epigraphia Indica XXIV: 223).

Bhinmal appears to be another important centre of Sun worship with its renowned Sun-temple *Jagat-Svāmin*. We learn from Bhinmal Stone inscription of ṛṣṇarāja dated v.s. 1117 that a Brāhmāṇa offered a *kalaśa* of gold to this temple at his own expense (.... Śri Jagat-svāmī-devasya deva bhavan- jīrṇoddhā ..... (kā) rāptitaṁ bhavanasyopari svarṇṇa-kalasaṁ brāhameṇa para (mandhā) rmiken jejākén nija-dravyéṇa kāritamiti | |) (Corpus Inscritionum Indicarum VII: 322, Pl 2). In the Jaina inscription of Jagaddeva, the first two verses are devoted to the praise of the god *sūrya*, and it also referes to a temple of *Nimbadityadeva*, constructed by the wife of Lolāraka, the minister of Jagaddeva (Oṁ namaḥ Sūryaya | akālepi rave-rrvvāré nimbi(ba) puṣpodgamairayaṁ | pratyayaṁ purayan bhānurnniratyaya mumāstāṁ (pāssyatāṁ) |......) (Epigraphia Indica XXII: 54-63) At Gyāraspura, near Vidisha, there are ruins of a temple called *Vajramamha*, a figure of the Sun driven by seven horses (Archaeological Survey Report X: 31-34). Queen Lahiṇī is said to have restored a Sun temple at Vamapura i.e. Vasantagarh, during the reign of the Paramāra chief Purṇāpāla (Epigraphia Indica IX: 14). There is a beautiful marble temple dedicated to *Sūrya-narāyaṇa* at Varman (Progress Report Archaeological Survey Western Circle 1916-17: 71-72). A standing image of Sun is enshrined in it. The inclusion of *Sūrya* in the trinity formed *Śiva, Viṣṇu, Brahmā* and *Sūrya* in one body have been found at *Kirāū (PRASWC 1907-08: 41)*. According to G.H.Ojha there was no village in Sirohi state of the period 600-1400 A.D., which did not have a temple or broken image of Sun-god (Ojha 2018: 24). *Sṛṇāramañjarīkathā*, a literary work of the age which throws a welcome light on the socio-religious conditions of the period under study refers to *Sūrya* being worshipped on the *Vijayasaptamī* day for begetting a son (*Śṛṇāramañjarīkathā*: 19) The Chandellas traced their lineage to moon (*Chandrātreya*) (......chandratreyamunérmahīyalīkule...; EI, I: 217.... tasmādjani rajanīvallabhādviśvakāḥ....) (Epigraphia Indica I: 228-229). Their charters do not contain reference to *Sūrya pūja*. But amongst their monuments at Khajuraho, the temple commonly known as *Chitragupta* temple is the only temple at this place dedicated to *Sūrya*, and is, indeed on of the few shrines in all of North India dedicated to the Sun-god (built under the *Chandella* regime). The main image in the sanctum is an impressive sculpture of *Sūrya* standing in a chariot driven by seven horses. Three similar but smaller figures of *Sūrya* are depicted on the lintel of the ornate doorway (Khajuraho: 56-57).

Sun was worshipped in Gujarat from early times the Mandasor Stone inscription of Kumārgupta I is a testimony to it. Burgess in *Architectural Antiquities of Northern Gujarat* speaks of many old sun temple from Gupta to the late medieval period, from Multan to Kutch. Widespread prevalence of this Cult in this land is substantiated by the monumental remains of Modhera Sun temple (Solankī monument) as well as the discovery of numerous stone sculptures of this pantheon during the period under study (Majumdar 1956: 299).

The most important Sun temple at Modhera, built by the Chaulukya ruler Bhima I. The grandeur of the temple described below makes sun-worship a very important cult under the Sokanki rulers.

Modhera is an extensive complex with the main Temple at the centre, surrounded by other structures which were built at different times. These are: a free-standing dancing hall, an ornamental gateway, a large masonry tank, a temple to the northern side of the main temple and some other minor structures.

The imposing main temple is the centre of the whole complex. The east facing temple (9m x 11.5m square), is built of bright yellow sandstone. It has two major parts - a closed hall *(gūḍha maṇḍapa)* in the front and a shrine *(garbhagṛha)* behind, both connected by a narrow passage. The hall and the shrine are square but when placed together on one axis they create a rectangular plan.

Modhera is one of the most evolved temples of western India, i.e. Gujarat and Rajasthan. Although its entire superstructure *(Śikhara)* has been destroyed, it enables us to visualize the fully developed form of a North Indian temple.

Modhera was first described by the British archaeologists James Burgess and Henry Cousens in the early twentieth century. From the presence of the twelve *Ādityas* on the shrine's outer walls and elsewhere, it has always been believed that the temple was dedicated to Sūrya, the Sun god.

In ancient Indian art, the Sun god was sometimes combined with *Śiva* and both were represented together in one image. Therefore, it has recently been pointed out that since at the Modhera temple, the twelve forms of *Śiva's* consort (twelve *Gaurīs)* are given equal importance as the twelve *Ādityas.* The central block on the doorway depicts *Śiva* and there is a prominent image of *Trīpada Bhairava,* it is possible to view the Modhera temple as being dedicated to both *Sūrya* and *Śiva.*

In addition to the main complex comprising the *kuṇḍa, toraṇa, raṅga-maṇḍapa* and the main shrine, there is also a small *Śiva* shrine on the north side of the main temple. It is a rather plain structure without the sculptural wealth of the structures (Modhera 2015).

The *Saraswatî-Purāṇa* refers to another Sun-temple built by Siddharāja by the side of the *Sahsralinga* lake and the shrine was known as *Bhaylāsvāmī.* Here the possibility cannot be ruled out that Siddharāj forcibly carried away a Sun-idol from Malwa to Gujarat for his temple.

We learn from the Gaṇśa inscription dated v.s. 1291(ABORA IIX: 179) that the famous Jaina minister Vāstupāla installed two images of *Ratnadevi* and *Rājadevi,* consorts of *Sūrya.* This deity was even worshipped by the non- Brāhmanical sections of Gujarat like the Jainas. Muralidhar inscription of v.s. 1354 testifies to the existence of a Sun-temple as it contains *maṅgala* verses in praise of Sun and two verses (vv. 20-21) refer to the attainment of *Sūryaloka* by a warrior, so that it is evident that the *praśasti* was composed in connection with the erection of a Sun-temple (Majumdar 1910: 299).

The worship of *Revanta,* described as the son of *Sūrya* in *Purāṇas* was also prevalent both in Central and Western India during early medieval period, e.g. the Vanthali inscription of Śāraṅgadeva's reign open with an invocation to god *Revanta* (Poona Orientalist III: 26).

Temples like *Sūrya-Nārāyaṇa* enshrine the composite figures of Sun and *Viṣṇu.* It has also been propunded that references to *Bāl-Nārayan* and *Roop-Nārāyana* in the charters of the age might have represented the composite aspect of *Viṣṇu* and *Śiva,* A.K. Majumdar opines that it is difficult to accept this theory yet it seems that Dharmādiya, for whom a swing was erected by an officer of Kumārpāla, was a composite figure of sun and *Viṣṇu,* since *Dharma* is known to be one of the Minor incarnations of *Viṣṇu* (Majumdar 1910: 299). In northern Gujarat at Delmal in the compound of *Limboji Mātā* temple there is a shrine dedicated to *Sūrya*, there is enshrined a curious sculpture on which Burgess remarks, "In one figure the four divinities, *Viṣṇu*, *Śiva* and *Brahma* or the *trimurti* (Trinity) - with *Sūrya* and *Brahma* or the *trimurti* (Trinity) - with *Surya*, appear blended; or shall we rather say it represent a *viṣṇava Trimurti*, with *Sūrya-Nārayaṇa* as the Central figure, seated on his *Vāhana* Garua?" (Burgess & Cousens 1975: 88-89).

The above survey of the historical sources in the form of epigraphs, literary works and monuments clearly brings out that Sūrya was a popular deity amongst the common folks of the region during the period under study. He came to occupy an important position not only in Brahmanical pantheon but the followers of other pantheons viz. the Jainas also worshipped this deity. A good number of temples were erected in his honour and images along with his family (supposedly) were also installed by the people.

References

ABORI, IX.

Archaeological Survey Report (Cunningham), X.

Burgess, J and Cousens, H., *The Architectural Antiquities of Northern Gujarat*, Varanasi, 1975.

Corpus Inscriptionum Indicarum, vol. VII.

Epigraphia Indica I, IX, XIV, XX, XXIV, XXX, XXXVII.

Khajuraho, ASI publication, New Delhi.

Majumdar, A.K., *Chaulukyas of Gujarat, Bhartiya Vidya Bhavan,* Bombay, 1956.

Modhera, ASI, New Delhi, 2015.

Ojha, G.H., *Sirohī Rājya kā Itihāsa*, R.G. Group, 2018.

PRASWC, 1907-08.

Progress Report Archaeological Survey Western Circle, 1916-17, *Poona Orientalist, III.*

Srivastava, Surabhi, *Socio-Economic History of The Gurjara-Pratīhāra Times*, New Royal Book Co. Lucknow, 2008. *Śṛṅgāramañjarīkathā.*

24

Unique Lajjā Gaurī Sculpture from Tarsang, Gujarat

V.H. Sonawane

Introduction

The genesis of worship of the Mother Goddess can be traced to the hoary past. The Great Mother, who had been the source of creation, was the earliest deity worshipped in the fertility cult. In wide perspective of time and space, right from the Upper Palaeolithic Period, she has been represented both by non-iconic and iconic forms focussing on divergent traits of her manifestations (Kenoyer *et al.* 1983: 88-94). Out of her several forms, one in which she is shown nude with emphasised pudenda and breasts, has attracted the attention of scholars because of her unusual and somewhat odd-looking way of depiction. Such sculptures showing a highly flexed posture of the nude goddess, with or without head, torso, bearing well developed breasts and leg stretched apart so as to display the pudenda prominently – often exaggerated in size – are now recognized by scholars as the representations of Lajjā Gaurī.

Lajjā Gaurī is one of the cult divinities whose nomenclature and iconography along with its origin and development are yet to be completely understood. She has not formed the subject of a detailed study probably because:

1. She does not occupy an exalted position in the pantheon of Hindu deities unlike other Mother Goddesses and
2. The non-availability of her textual description supported by standardised iconography.

This peculiar form of representation of the goddess began to appear from c. second century B.C. and continued until about twelth/thirteenth centuries A.D. Her stereotyped depictions with little variations are now found scattered in different frequency from various parts of Indian subcontinent. This vast area roughly covers the modern states of Uttar Pradesh, Madhya Pradesh, Chhattisgarh, Rajasthan, Gujarat, Maharashtra, Andhra Pradesh, Odisha, Karnataka, Tamilnadu and Kerala besides

North-West Frontier Province of Pakistan. However, from their distribution pattern, it appears that they were more common in Gujarat, Maharashtra, Andhra Pradesh and Karnataka. This wide distribution clearly reflects on the unbroken continuity in the popularity of the deity representing a concept for quite a few centuries.

Though scholars like Stella Kramrisch (1956: 259-270), H.D. Sankalia (1960: 111-123) and J.N. Tiwari (1971) initiated to study the nature and significance of the image of Lajjā Gaurī some decades ago, none of them could satisfactorily explain the true significance of the nudity aspect of the goddess. She has been variously identified by them as Aditī Uttānpad, Nude Goddess or the Shameless Woman. Later on, this challenging task, to some extent, was handled by R.C. Dhere (1978) and C.R. Bolon (1992) by giving detailed treatment to the subject under review. It is interesting to note that though we termed her as Lajjā Gaurī based on a popular legend, among the rural folks she is known as *Yellammā, Reṇukā, Mātaṅgī, Jogulaṁbā, Nagnakabaṅdha* and so on. A similar image discovered at Garh Seoni in Chhattisgarh state is locally called as *"Dhuṅdhi Rākśasi"* (Srivastava 2002-2003: 37-40). Likewise, a bronze seal discovered recently at Kashmir Smast in Pakistan this goddess is referred to as Acima or Acirma, which appears to be another local name prevalent in the ancient Gandhara during the early centuries of the Christian era (Khan 2002: 83-90). There is not a single text which describes the iconographic features of this goddess. Perhaps the reason lies in the fact that this folk goddess never got a place of honour in the orthodox Hindu Pantheon. For obvious reasons some scholars identified Lajjā Gaurī as *Pṛthvi, Aditī Uttānpad* and *Pārvatī Uttānahasta/Uttānapani* referred in the ancient Sanskrit literature (Kumar 2007: 151-164).

The images of this goddess were generally made of terracotta, kaolin, limestone, schist, slate, sandstone and granite. Their size ranged between 7cms and over life size. These were manufactured in round as well as in high and low relief. A solitary faience pendant from Ter in Maharashtra also bears an effigy of this goddess. Large stone sculptures were most probably installed in temples and other public places including step-wells, whereas the small terracotta and stone plaques were meant for household adoration by the women folk desirous of having children and safe maternity. In Tamilnadu, Kerala and Karnataka the Lajjā Gaurī figurines have been found in association of the Megalithic burials (Mitragotri 1997: 539-543) while at Padri in Gujarat two terracotta figurines representing this goddess were found placed on the oval shaped mud platform, identified by the excavator as the temple of Lajjā Gaurī, belonging to the Kshatrapa period (Shinde 1994: 481-482). The bronze seals reported from Kashmir Smast might have been employed for producing clay sealings, likely used as mementoes, by the pilgrims visiting the Great Cave (Mahâ Guhâ) dedicated to this goddess, locally called as Acima or Acirma (Khan 2002: 86). Apart from these, an interesting depiction of this form of goddess has also found place in Rock Art for the first time at Chintakunta in Andhra Pradesh in the form of rock painting (Neumayer 1993: 206, Fig. 553).

As appears, the image of Lajjā Gaurī did not emerge suddenly in their full-fledged form. It rather evolved slowly in the long course of time span as seen invariably in other forms of mother goddess. From the extant remains, it appears that unbaked clay female figurine without head but having heavy breasts, found carefully buried within the house floor belonging to the Early Jorwe period at Inamgaon was the earliest and can be regarded as the prototype of historic Lajjā Gaurī, identified by the excavators as *Vishira* (Dhavalikar *et al.* 1988: 571-579). For the occurrence of images of Lajjā Gaurī during the historic period, scholars like R.C. Dhere (1978), C. R. Bolon (1992) and Krishna Kumar (2007: 151-164) have suggested respectively three, four and ten developmental phases. These categories may be conceptualised as progressing from a minimally anthropomorphic form towards the completely anthropomorphic goddess. However, these various categories are not strictly adhering to their chronological progression.

Lajjā Gaurī Sculpture from Tarsang

Tarsang (22 56 N, 73 28 E) is a small village situated about 30 km to the north – west of Godhara, the district headquarters of Panchhalals. While working on the Archaeology of Panchmahals in 1971 for my Ph. D. Dissertation, I happen to come across a unique Lajja Gauri plaque as surface collection from one of the habitation mounds at Tarsang (Sonawane 1988: 27-35). This (Figure I) fine – grained grey schist plaque of Lajja Gauri measures about 8.5 x8.5 x 1.5 cms. of which major portion on the lower right corner is broken off. Though the figure has been carved in a low relief, the details are quite visible. The goddess is shown seated as usual in her characteristic manner, as she is known for, keeping legs stretched apart and hands kept upright, resting on the knees raised upwards. Most likely, she holds a flower, probably a lotus in each of her hands. Unlike, the other representations of this deity, she does not seem to be shown nude. There is a suggestion of folds of the lower garment on her left leg. A similar image of a terracotta Mother Goddess, which is also not nude, is found from Shamalaji. She is also shown in a squatting posture keeping legs upright (Shah 1960: 121, pl. 24). The image is decked with simple traditional ornaments such as *ekavali,* multiple armlets and bracelets, long circular Patra – *kundalas* and bejewelled *katimekhala.* The simple halo - like *prabhavali* behind her head adds charm to the whole composition and signifies her divinity.

Unlike others, owing to the inclusion of a stylised *trishula* and the feet *(shripada)* just immediately below, at the upper left corner, this plaque is somewhat unusual in its composition. The damaged figure at the lower left may be that of a devotee if the sculpture follows the regular arrangement of many other representations where this corner is shown with a devotee often in *anjalimudra.* Likewise, just above the broken lower right corner, there is a depiction of a *Shiva Linga* adorned with a *brahmasutra rekha.*

The modelling of the figure under review shows some resemblance in its anatomical features to the other sculptures reported from the same site. Particularly, the prongs of the stylised *trishula,* breasts and the abdominal portion of the goddess described here are reminiscent of the female – half representing Parvati in the composite image of Ardhanarishvara found at Tarsang ascribed to c. sixth cent. A. D. It is worthwhile to note that the sculpture of a *Lajja Gauri* of the same period is reported by Gorakshakar from Gharapuri (Elephanta caves, Mumbai) as a surface find (Gorkshkar 1982: 23).

The present sculpture representing the Lajja Gauri (Fig-1) aspect of the Divine Mother shows quite interesting features. Though her association with Nandi (Bull), Shiva Linga, Ganesha and female devotee occurs sporadically in the sculptures of the early centuries of the Christian era, apparently it became almost a regular feature in the iconography of Lajja Gauri during the sixth and succeeding centuries. In this context, the Lajja Gauri plaque obtaind from Tarsang is quite unique owing to the addition of Trishula, Shripada and Prabhavali (halo) in the composition of the image. Originally, there may have been Nandi and Ganesha also on the now missing lower right portion of the image, just below the Shiva Linga. The association of Nandi, Ganesha, Shiva – Linga and Trishula with Lajja Gauri leaves no doubt regarding her Shaiva affiliation. Thus, in light of the above evidence, she can very well be considered as a manifestation of Shakti aspect of Shive. Secondly, the presence of an attendant or a devotee in her composition clearly suggests that she was worshipped or recognised as a regular goddess. The depiction of Prabhavali also signifies the attainment of divine position by this cult image. In the present state of our knowledge, we have at least fifteen sites in Gujarat from where images of Lalla Gauri have been reported. This number is quite substantial in providing the popularity of this cult image in this province, mainly covering parts of south and central Gujarat, Kutch and Saurashtra peninsula.

Fig. 1 : Lajja Gauri from Tarsang

References

Bolon, C.R., 1992, *Forms of the Goddess Lajjā Gaurī in Indian Art*, Pennsylvannia: The Pennsylvannia State University Press.

Dhavalikar, M.K., H.D. Sankalia and Z.D. Ansari, 1988, *Excavations at Inamgaon*, Vol. I, Part II, Pune: Deccan College Post-Graduate and Research Institute.

Dhere, R.C., 1978, *Lajjāgaurī* (in Marathi), Pune.

Gorkshkar, Sadashiv, 1982, The Parel Mahaveva Reassessed and Two Newly Discovered Images from Parel, *Lalit Kala, No. 20.*

Kenoyer, J.M., J.D. Clark, J.N. Pal and G.R. Sharma, 1983, An upper Palaeolithic Shrine in India, *Antiquity 57.*

Khan, M.N., 2002, Lajja Gauri Seal and Related Antiquities from Kashmir Smast, Gandhara, *South Asian Studies 18.*

Kramrisch, Stella, 1956, An Image of Āditī Uttānapāda, *Artibus Asiae* 19.

Kumar, Krishna, 2007, The Cult of Aditi Uttanapada in Indo-Pak Subcontinent: An Assessment in the Light of New Discoveries, *Pragdhara 17.*

Mitragotri, V.R., 1997, Mother-Goddess of Curdi-Goa and Some Parallels, *Facets of Indian Civilization: Recent Perspectives*, Vol. II J.P. Joshi (ed.), New Delhi: Aryan Books International.

Neumayer, Erwin, 1993, *Lines on Stone: The Prehistoric Rock Art of India*, New Delhi: Manohar.

Sankalia, H.D., 1960, The Nude Goddess or Shameless Woman, Western Asia, India and South Eastern Asia, *Artibus Asiae 23.*

Shah, U. P., 1960, Sculptures from Shamalaji and Roda, *Bulletin of the Baroda Museum and Picture Gallery, Vol. XIII.*

Shinde, Vasant, 1994, The Earliest Temple of Lajjāgaurī? The Recent Evidence from Padri in Gujarat, *East and West, 44 (2-4).*

Sonawane, V.H., 1988, Some Remarkable Sculptures of Lajjā Gaurī from Gujarat, *Lalit Kala 23.*

Srivastava, A.L., 2002-2003, Bhagavati Lajja Gauri, *Kala Vaibhava 12.*

Tiwari, J. N., 1971, *Studies in the Goddess Cult of Northern India*, Ph. D. Thesis submitted to the Australian National University, Canberra.

25

Ancient Srughna: A Brāhmi Lipishala

Vibha Rathod, Deepak Kumar and Jagdish Parshad

Introduction

Situated about 5 kms to the east of Jagadhari in Yamunanagar District of Haryana and surrounded by the Old Yamuna (Western Yamuna canal) by three sides the archaeological remains at Sugh are covered by the modern villages of Dayalgarh, Sugh, and Amadalpur. The site was excavated in 1964 and 1965 by Punjab University under Suraj Bhan. It has also been subjected to explorations a number of times by various researchers. The site has revealed a large number of ceramics, coins, temple remains, metal objects and other finds from different periods but the most interesting findings are the variety of molded as well as handmade human and animal terracotta figurines, majority of which comes from the Sunga-Scytho-Parthian Period. The earliest phase at the site dates back to 500 B.C characterized by the P.G.W. and N.B.P.W. sherds but given the recent excavations and researches on the P.G.W and N.B.P.W culture the chronology given by Prof Suraj Bhan requires a review.

The site of Sugh has been identified by Sir Alexander Cunningham with the ancient Srughna on the basis of the description given by the Chinese traveler Hieun Tsang, who visited the place in the 7th Century A.D. during the reign of Harshavardhan of Pushyabhuti dynasty. Patanjali in his *Mahabhashya* has given detail description of Srughna as a prosperous city. From Mathura there was a direct road to Srughna. It was capital of Srughna Janapada, strategically positioned on the crossing point of Yamuna on the main route from Punjab to the Gangetic plains via Ambala-Saharanpur. He has also described the palaces and other buildings and people of Srughna. From the account of Kashika it appears that Srughna was located on the main route from pataliputra to Takshila. In his accounts Hieun Tsang has referred to various Stupas and 5 monasteries along with numerous other buildings at Sugh, acknowledging the continuing importance of the ancient city culturally as well as commercially even during 7th Century A.D.

Sunga period in Indian history witnessed a proliferation of art that was indigenous and traditional in nature and known for its variety and richness of the themes and Sugh seems to be one of the important centers where this art flourished. The T.C figurines from Sugh belonging to the Sunga period are characterized by elaborate ornamentation, transparent drapery or nude features, confirming to the Sunga art tradition of the Gangetic Valley. An interesting type among these T.C figurines is figurine of a nude boy learning Sunga period Brahmi alphabets on a wooden tablet. This depiction of learning Brahmi script which is the only archaeological evidence of its kind from all over India is significant not only from the palaeographic viewpoint but also from the perspective of ancient Indian education system. This paper deals particularly with these figurines to explore ancient learning system of India and to study these terracotta figurines within that context to infer learning processes and socio-cultural aspects. Although these figurines have been subjected to analysis by scholars earlier, however briefly pondering only over the functional aspects. In contrast the present attempt is on situating these figurines in the context of ancient education system of Sung period.

Ancient Education system

The Sungas played an important role in patronizing indigenous art and culture and it was during this period that Brahmins revived Vedic culture. In ancient India the Gurukuls were the centers of learning where students learned two major fields of education, knowledge of the material world called *vidya* and the knowledge of the spiritual world called *vrata.* In ancient Haryana also as Mahabharata and other texts has discussed that there were Gurukuls of Veda Vyas on the bank of river Sarasvati near Kurukshetra and Jamadgni's on the bank of river Drishadvati near modern Narnaund and various others. Students with different backgrounds from very early age joined these Gurukuls to learn art, mathematics, grammar, philosophy, reading and writing, etc. Patanjali in his *Mahabhashya* has provided that a child should initiate reading and writing after the *Chudakarma Samskara.* Kautilya also referring to the initiation of a child's education has recommended that the *Lipi* (writing) and *Sankhyan* should begin after the *samskara* of *Chudakarma.* During Sunga period the common script was Brahmi and the common languages were Sanskrit and Pali. The development of Sunga Brahmi took place in Brahmin schools and is connected with the revival of literary activities under the Sunga dynasty. In *Mahabhashya* the terms like *Manav, Dandamanav, Brahmchari* and *Chhatra* have been used to denote students. The term *Manav* particularly represents the small children who enter the *shalas* for elementary education. *Dandamanav* were those students who entered Guru's *ashrams* with *danda, mrigcharm* and *kamandalu.*

The Figurines

After the discovery of the terracotta figurine of a nude boy writing Brahmi Alphabets on a *Takhti* (wooden tablet) from Sugh, now housed in National Museum, New Delhi, a number of similar terracotta figurines have been found, some which are with the Gurukul Museum Jhajjar and Prachin Bhartiya

Shodha Parishad, Gurukul, Gautam Nagar, New Delhi.

B.C. Chabra in his paper has suggested that the figurine represent the Lord Krishna as a child at Lipishala in his Teacher Sandipani's hermitage at Avantipura. However given the variety of these figurines found later, emphasizing on the Brahmi alphabets and learning stages of child, it rather appears that the figurines instead represent small students or *Manav* who enter *pathshalas* to receive elementary education at an early age as referred by Patanjali in his *Mahabhashya.* While discussing about the content of the wooden tablet he says that it is a *Barakhadi* but on a close examination one finds that this is not the case and there are four lines of vowels only whereas in a Barakhadi there are vowels and consonants.

Yoganand Shastri has classified these figurines in three classes on the basis of the Brahmi alphabets written on the wooden tablet capturing different stages of learning by small children. However in our analysis we have added fourth class.

First Class

The figurine from National Museum (Fig. 1) comes under this class in which the child is learning by pointing his finger on the Brahmi vowels written in four lines on the wooden tablet. The platform is decorated with floral design and unlike other figurines the inkpot is missing which suggest that the child is in the initial stage of learning alphabets and has not started writing yet. He is wearing *Kataka* on his wrist and *nupur* on his feet. The upper part of his body is damaged. His sitting posture is typical of a child where both of his legs are in lying position.

Second Class

In this class (Fig. 2) it appears that the child is practicing over the already written vowels and consonants. The sitting posture is little different to the figurine of the first class. The right leg of the child is in lying position and with the upright left leg he is holding the wooden tablet. He is wearing *Kanthabhushana* in the neck, *Mekhla* over the waist and *Kundala* in his ears. Unlike the figure from first class there are no *Katak* and *Nupur.* He is also wearing double knot turban over his head, a typical style of the Sunga period

Third Class

There are three figurines representing the next stage in the child's learning. This class can be categorized further in two sub-categories, in the first sub-category represented by two figurines (Fig. 3 & 4) the child is writing vowels and consonants with a stylus in one and a half lines. In the second sub-category represented by only one figurine (Fig. 5) the child is writing vowels and consonants with a stylus in two and a half lines. The plate 3 shows the child sitting in position similar to that of the second class figurines but rather more firmly. He is wearing double knot turban over his head, large *kundala* in his ears and *Malaya* in his neck. He is also wearing *Kataka* and *Nupur*. An inkpot is placed near his feet on the platform which is not decorated. The Fig. 4 shows the child similar to the child shown in Fig. 3 but with a little difference which seems to be because of the different moulds they were made in. In the Fig. 5 the head of the child is damaged, he is wearing *mekhla, Malaya, Nupur,* and *Kataka*. There is toy of elephant shown on the left side of the child and a fruit? placed on the platform.

Fourth class

This class has figurine (Fig. 4) in which the child appears to be in an advanced stage of learning alphabets where he is shown writing *Barakhadi* in a random method called *katama*. The wooden tablet is shown divided in three columns, the first and third columns are already written and now he is writing in the middle column. The figurine is mostly damaged but a fruit? is shown on the right side of the child. The child is also wearing *mekhla* and *Malaya* which are more decorated than the other figurines.

Summary

The Sunga period witnessed the revival of the art particularly the terracotta art that is known for the themes that generally reflect folk traditions. The *Mahabhashya* of Patanjali is a source of immense value as it provides us to visualize and corroborate the archaeological data of this period into the information provided in it as our analyses of the Terracotta figurines have shown regarding the education system during the Sunga period. Sugh was a city that was significant culturally as well as commercially as recorded in the Patanjali's *Mahabhashya*. Even as late as 7th Century A.D. Hieun Tsang in his *Su Yu Ki* records that there were 5 monasteries at Sugh. All of these facts suggest that Sugh must have been an important education center. The fact that the recording of children learning Brahmi script in these figurines apprehends detailed, stage wise learning processes, and also that the terracotta art generally capture the folk traditions further substantiate the argument that Sugh was an ancient education center during Sunga period.

References

Singh UV, 1974, Terracottas from Sugh, *Journal of Haryana Studies*, vol. VI, Nos 1-2, Kurukshetra University.

Bhan, Suraj, 1977, Report of Excavation at Sugh (1964 and 1965), *Journal of Haryana Studies*, vol. IX, Nos 1-2, Kurukshetra University.

Swami Omanand Sarswati and Virjanand Devkarni have collected number of antiquities from the sites which are now housed in Gurukul Museum Jhajjar (Haryana).

PGW researches.

Cunningham,A., 1871. *The Ancient Geography of India*. London: Trubner and Co.

Agnihotri Prabhu Dayal, 2001, *Patanjalikalin Bharat*, Patna: Bihar Rashtrabhasha Parishad.

Kashika, a *Bhashya* of Panini's *Ashtadhyayi* composed by Vamana and Jayaditya

Handa Devendra, 2010, Terracottas from Sugh, Haryana, *Kala: the Journal of Indian Art History Congress*, vol. VI.

Virjanand Devkarni, 2009, *Prachina Tamrapatra evm Shilalekha,* Jhajjar: Haryana Prantiya Puratattva Sangrahalaya.

Chabra BC, 1970, Sugh Terracotta with Brahmi Barakhadi, *National Museum Bulletin,* vol. 2, No 2, New Delhi.

Shastri Yoganand, 1999, *Prāchin Bharat main Yaudheya Ganarajya*, New Delhi: Prachin Bharatiya Itihaas Shodha Parishad.

26

Intricacies of the Idea of Karma in Buddhism (With special Reference to *Milindapañha)*

Renu Shukla

Theory of karma and its ethical consequences has been a common belief of all the religions originated in India though with certainn difference and diversity in their opinions. The doctrine is unique with regard to the acceptance of the superiority of an individual (human action) over his destiny or god as it says that man is the master of what he receives in his present life and future existences by performing good or bad deeds. Since his own deeds are responsible for his pleasant or painful experiences so every one should do as much good as possible. Thus doctrine of karma not only raises the status of an individual by assigning him power to change his destiny but also restrict his deeds by putting some checks and balances in order to ensure the formation of a better harmonious society of individuals.

In its simplest form the law of Karma means that all actions, good or bad, produce their effect in the life of the individual who acts (Chatterjee 1960: 74). It is accepted in Buddhism as one of the central ideas. According to it our own suffering is due to our former sin, in this or a previous life, just as one's well-being is due to one's former goodness. The doctrine of karma (action) denotes both the original moral act and its power for subsequent reward or punishment. It perceives past, present and future life of a being in a sequence and continuity associated with each other through the karma which transmigrates from one to another being without the existence of a permanent entity (soul). The doctrine seems to be simple in concept but is actually complicated in its implications. The present paper focuses on such intricacies regarding the theory of karma in Buddhism in the light of a non canonical Buddhist text the *Milindapañha*. The book *Milindapañha* was written in the transitional phase of Buddhism when new trends were emerging in beliefs and practices of the followers of the faith. The *Milindapañha* held a high regard, and a very different approach to the doctrine under consideration according to which human actions are held responsible for the cycle of rebirth and death. In Buddhist view the doctrine is universally applicable and no one can escape from it even the

Buddha (In many Jataka tales in his previous birth Buddha has been projected as a person of lower status or animal existence) or Gods (Majjhimnikaya 1960-64: 132) are not immune to rebirth in a status according to their past karmas. Buddha clearly states about the impact of the good or bad *kamma* passing on to the next life and resulting in good course (*sugati*) or bad course (*duggati*) respectively (Majjhimnikaya 1960-64: 178-179). Kamma is considered as a causal factor also with respect to certain differences between individuals. According to *Milindapañha* all men are not alike because of the actions, they have done in the past' (…*kammānam nānākarṇena manussā na sabbe samkā*) ((Majjhimnikaya 1960-64: 52) '..some are short and some long lived, some sickly and some healthy, some ugly and some beautiful, some without influence and some of great *power*, some poor and some wealthy, some low born and some high born, some stupid and some wise'(Majjhimnikaya 1960-64: 52) because it is the *kamma* that divides them up into low and high and the like divisions (Milindapañha IV.1.8: 103). In general it is propounded in Buddhism that beings are the inheritors of their own *kamma* but in *Milindapañha* it is said that all pains do not have their origin in *kamma* (Milindapañha IV.1.8: 103). Nāgasena states 'There are eight causes by which sufferings arise, by which many beings suffer pain,...Superabundance of wind, and of bile, and of phlegm, the union of these humours, variations in the temperature, the avoiding of the dissimilarities, external agency, and *kamma* (Milindapañha IV.1.8: 103). So what arises as the fruit of Kamma is much (*Imehi kho Mahārāj Athahi Karṇhi Puthusatta vedanā vedayanti. Tatha ye te puggalā satte Kammam Vibādhantī ti Vadeyyum te ime satta satta kāraṇam michhā ti*) less than that which arises from other causes (even in *Samyutta* and *Aṅguttara Nikāyas* seven causes of suffering in addition to the effect of Kamma are listed see *Samyutta Nikāya*, IV.230-231; *Aṅguttara Nikāya* II.87-88; III.131;V.110) (Milindapañha IV.1.8: 103). Here the interpretation in matter relating to cause differs from that of the general notion regarding the theory. In the same book while answering a question of king Milinda regarding the bodily pains from (Milindapañha IV.1.8: 104). Which Buddha has suffered Nāgasena says that '...although the Blessed One never suffered pain which was the result of his own *kamma*, or brought about the avoidance of dissimilarity, yet he suffered pain from each of the other six causes (Milindapañha XXXV). The role of present *kamma* as a decisive factor for future suffering or happiness has been minimized and sometimes denied in the instances of *Milindapañha*. In a reference question was asked by Milinda that if Buddha's injury by Devadatta's rock splinter is neither attributed to his past *kamma* nor it can be explained in terms of the standard non-karmic causes then what other explanation can be given for its origin. Nâgasena's answer to this question is quite interesting. He answers that 'so also was it irrespective of any act done by him that splinter of rock fell upon his foot' (Milindapañha XXXV).Thus according to Nāgasena at least in certain specific instances suffering may arise as a result of chance which means he has given up strict adherence to the universal applicability of *kamma* and made it clear that the actions done by Buddha do not bear any fruit. Buddhists do not believe in a permanent soul which transmigrates so the question arises that without transmigration how is rebirth possible? (Milindapañha XXXV). Nāgasena says that what is reborn is name-and-form and this name-and-form is the result of the previous *kamma*. One, who is born, neither remains the same nor does he become another (Milindapañha III.5.8: 58) to make it more clear Nāgasena gives an illustration. 'It is like milk, which when once taken from the cow, turns, after a lapse of time, first to curd, and then from curd to butter, and then from butter to ghee. Now it would not be right to say that the milk was the same thing as the curd, or the butter or the ghee?" (Milindapañha II.2.2: 32). The question is how an act can bear fruit, how a man can be heir to his own deeds, if the individual is defined as a constantly changing series of aggregates. Buddhist view on this issue is that the act itself is held to exist in all times, past present and future. If the result of the actions performed by a man influence and shape his present life where do they live, where are they stored? To the question Nāgasena replies that they can not be said to exist at a particular place unless their results become manifest. The deeds done by one name and form follow it like a shadow (Milindapañha III.5.8: 58). Early Buddhist teachings characterize *puñña* (merit) as a medium of exchange in the religious life of the householders, which can be used to buy heaven, good, rebirth and happiness. According to a reference from *Mahāvagga* when Buddha formally allows the acceptance of householder-given robes (*gahapaticīvara*) by renunciants, the people are overjoyed by saying, 'now we will give gifts, we will make merit (*Te cha manussā hammhā ahesum udaggā. –'Idāni kho mayam dānāni dssām puññāni karissām, yato bhagvatā bhikhhūnam gahapaticīvaram anuññātam ti'. Mahāvaggapāli*) (Maxmuller: 195). The early Buddhist concept of merit as a medium of exchange for worldly pleasures and better rebirth has developed further in later period. In the process of evolution the idea of transfer of merit (McDermott 2002: 44) came and it has been accepted that merit can be used not only for the spiritual advancement towards *nibbāna* of the doer only but also to alleviate the sufferings of others (Gombrich1971: 204). The *Milindapañha* refers to the transfer of merit to the dead. Milinda wants to know the possibility of ascribing to departed ancestors gifts given in this world. His curiosity is do they obtain any benefit as a result? (Milindapañha V.3.4: 210) Nāgasena's answer is that some of the departed can obtain benefit through having charitable acts ascribing to them. However, there are others who can receive no benefit regardless of what is done in their names (McDermott 2002: 109-110). In holding that the aspiration of merit can be effective in some cases, he has been influenced by the popular folk belief in transfer of merit so-called. But making a technical distinction of the notion he has transcended the folk level of the belief. It is something different from common kammic notion, which stresses, individual responsibility for individual actions, urging renunciants and non-renunciants alike to think of themselves as islands and as refuges unto themselves: be 'an island unto yourself, a refuge unto yourself, 'taking no one else as a refuge' for you (Woodward 2003: 37). In one other instance also Milindapañha seems to follow the idea of transfer of merit. Nāgasena speaks not only of the ascription of charitable acts to others, but also the possibility of sharing (saṁvibhajāti) good deeds with others- "whosoever in this world gives gifts, and lives in righteousness, and keeps uposatha, he becomes joyful, gladdened, cheerful, happy, becomes filled with a sweet sense of trust and bliss, and bliss ruling in his heart his goodness grows still more and more abundantly (*Idh, Mahārāj, yo Kochi danam deti silam samādiyati, uposath kammam karoti, so hattho pahattho hasito pamudito passanamānaso vedajato hoti. Tassa aparāparam pīti uppajjati pītimanass bhiyyo bhiyyo Kusalam pavadhati*) (MilindapañhaV.3.4. 211)... If even through a hundred years, a man was to keep on transferring to others (the merit of) any good he had done, the more he gave it away the more would his goodness grow and he would still be able to share it with whomsoever he would" (*Kuslam bhiyyo bhiyyo pavdhati. Vassasate pi che Mahārāj, puriso Katam Kusalam Aāvajjeyya, āvajjite āvajjite bhiyyo Kusalam Pavadhati, tassa tam Kusalam sakka hoti yathichhkehi sadhim saṁvibhajitum*) (Milindapañha V.3.4: 211). By transferring good in this way one is tapping a never-ending source of merit. Thus Nâgasena holds that a surplus of merit *(Kusala)* can be shared with others. It means that the benefit of merit obtained by one individual by performing good deeds can be enjoyed by some other individual who might or might not be apt for it. This goes against the general concept of karma and rebirth theory. The theory of merit sharing gives rise to another very interesting question- can the demerit accruing from bloody deeds, etc. also be shared with those who had no actual part in the deed? (Milindapañha V.3.4: 210). Nāgasena's answer is 'No' to this question 'an evil deed can not be shared with one who has not done, consented to it' (Milindapañha XXXVI). The statement of *Milindapañha* is the first unique and explicit statement of its kind in the literature that a man can not assign his demerits to another. Milinda raises one more question 'Why so'? (Milindapañha XXXVI). Nâgasena explains 'Vice, O king, is a mean thing, virtue is great and grand. By its meanness vice affects only the doer, but virtue by its grandeur overspreads the whole world, God and men (Milindapañha XXXVI). For if a man does good he becomes blissful because bliss rules his heart, his goodness develops still further. In contrast an evil doer comes to feel remorse; as a result evil deed does not prosper (Milindapañha III.7.7: 68).

A great dilemma occurs in the text regarding the theory is that what is the explanation for those doings which are not been done consciously. Milinda puts this question before Nâgasena- 'Whose, is the greater demerit- he who sins consciously, or he who sins inadvertently? (Milindapañha III.3.7: 68). Nâgasena's answer is interesting and some what unexpected -'He who sins inadvertently has the greater demerit (Milindapañha III.3.7: 68). This view of Nāgasena seems inconsistent with Buddhist view of considering *kamma* as cetanā (intentional impulse etc.) He gives an illustration in support of this statement to clarify his point. If one man were to seize hold intentionally of a fiery mass of metal glowing with heat, and another were to seize hold of it unintentionally, ...The one who did not know what he was doing, would be more burnt (Milindapañha III.3.7: 68). Here Nāgasena seems to be very much in support of the very Buddhist notion that action taken apart from knowledge of the true nature of things is not only without merit but produces more severe results. In the *Kathāvatthu* also there is a brief discussion regarding the claim "That the five cardinal crimes even if unintentionally committed, involve retribution immediately after death" (Jonathan 2007: 260). In another context too Nāgasena maintains the ideology by saying ' whosoever deprives a living being of life without knowing that he does so, he accumulates very serious demerit (Milindapañha IV.2.6:119). Nāgasena's view that serious demerit accrues to him who unknowingly does an evil deed seems to be quite different from the canonical view. Nāgasena appears to represent the view that the actual physical act is of greater ethical significance than is the thought, motive or intention behind it.

In *Milindapañha* Milinda puts before Nâgasena two complex problems connected with the theory of *kamma*. One is regarding Vessantara who gave his wife and children to a Brahman, thereby causing the children great anguish. He asks-'he, who gives gifts in such a way as to bring forth fruit in happiness, does it lead to rebirth in states of bliss?' (Milindapañha V.3.1: 197) Nāgasena's answer is- 'yes' (Milindapañha IV.2.6: 197). The question arises how come an act of charity which makes others suffer could result in happiness and heavenly rebirth. Nāgasena's explanation to this problem is that we can not accuse Vessantara for his act of charity because giving away his wife and children shows that he has relinquished all desire for personal pleasure. His wife agreed to it because she knew the greatness of his meritorious act but children could not understand it because of their tender age (Milindapañha V.3.1: 196) so the suffering of his children is derived from their own ignorance, rather than from any misdeed of their father. Thus Nāgasena very intelligently and lucidly explained that men are heirs of their own *kamma* and do not suffer because of the actions of others. The other problem Milinda puts before Nagasena regarding the theory of *kamma* is- why meritoriousness of certain acts happen to result in suffering? Why the meal given by Cunda the smith resulted in Buddha's illness, (Milindapañha IV.2.7: 119) which leads to his death? Why Buddha's preaching of Dhamma resulted in the suffering of monks? (Milindapañha IV.3.2: 123)Nāgasena answers that Buddha became ill only because of pre-existing weakness in his own body. This weakness must not suppose to be the result of any bad *kamma* accumulated by the Buddha. According to Nāgasena, in this case, the illness and affliction due to it was a physical matter. But it was not so in case of the affliction of the monks. Nāgasena says the blood which came from the mouth of sixty monks when they heard Buddha's discourse was a result of the pre-existing weakness of the afflicted monks, which was a fruit of their past *kamma*. So 'what happened to them was not the Tathāgata's doing, but their own' (Milindapañha IV.3.2: 123).Thus according to Nāgasena in both the cases the adverse result of meritorious acts originated from different causes which makes it clear that not every relationship which appears to be causal is properly classified as so being. In an illustration in *Milindapañha* Nagasena describes that kamma is the price (*Kammamūlam gahetvāna, āpaṇam upagachhakulīntā Ārammaṇam kiṇitvan, tato muchhatha muttiya ti*) (Milindapañha V.4.1: 236) to purchase things from the blessed one's city of righteousness (*...satipathanvīthiyam evarūpa āpaṇā pasāritā hoti. Seyyathidam puffapaṇam falāpaṇam agadāpaṇam osadhāpaṇam amatāpaṇam ratanāpaṇam sabbāpaṇam ti*) (Milindapañha V.4.1: 235) where all manner of merchandise like Long life, good health, beauty, rebirth in heaven, high birth, Nirvana are available for sale (*Āayu arogatā vaṅñam saggam uchchhakulīntā Asaṁkhata cha amatam, atthi sabbāpaṇe jine Appena bahukenāpi Kammamūlen gayahati kiṇitva saddhamūlena samiddha hotha, bhikhavo ti*) (Milindapañha V.4.1: 241). All these blessings can be obtained whether smaller or bigger by exchanging the good kamma in the same amount. It has been asserted by the scholars that the Theravada Buddhism is actually two distinct religions– (i) the "*kammatic*" which leads to better rebirth (ii) the "*nibbānic*" leading to escape from rebirth. The techniques, goals, and quality of life within these two 'religions' are seen as radically distinct (King 1964: 168; Aronson 1979: 28), with householders being associated with the former and monks, the latter. According to Winston King, *kammatic* techniques involve the cultivation of moral dispositions such as love, compassion, and sympathetic joy as well as practicing good deeds (King 1964: 150-161, 166). These activities, "the fighting of the battles of right and wrong," are performed for the sake of pleasurable future rebirth (King 1964: 168). On the other hand both King and Spiro, see meditation as the *nibbānic* technique leading to withdrawal from the world of good and evil (Spiro 1972: 41-48). But the reference in *Milindapanha* does not support the suggested polarization. Rather, it is clear that the karmic activity is the stepping stone to nirvānic realization. The *Milindapañha* has categorized the worldly gaining and *Nibbāna* in the same category as all these blessings can be obtained whether smaller or bigger by exchanging the good *kamma* in the same amount. Since *nibbāna* is the highest attainable bliss so the highest *kamma* price is said to be necessary for its purchase. In another instance vows of righteousness and the Uposatha observance considered to be of relatively great merit and could be paid to purchase the blessings in Buddha's bazaar. In such instances *Milindapañha* goes off in directions unacceptable from strict theravadin Buddhist ideology. Some other references regarding *thūpa* veneration or considering honour paid to the relics of the Buddha of great value are in deep contrast with the notion of karmic retribution which believes in morals and not in rituals.

The various instances regarding the theory of karma and rebirth found in *Milindapañha* are good examples of the complexities of this theory. On one hand it has been explained in accordance with the established view that a good and evil doer attain happiness and misery on account of his deeds but on the other hand it presented some unique ideas with a different approach towards the doctrine. There are enough of instances to understand the intricacies of the idea of the karmic retribution and an attempt to clarify dilemmas regarding the theory.

References

Aronson, Harvey B., 1979, The relationship of the Karmic to Nirvanic, *Theravada Buddhism in the Journal of Religious Ethics VII,1. Aṅguttara Nikāya,* II.

Chatterjee, Satish Chandra,1960, *Fundamentals of Hinduism,* Calcutta.

Gombrich, Richard F.,1971, *Merit Transference' in Sinhalese Buddhism: A Case Study of the Interaction Between Doctrine and Practice, History of Religions, II.2.*

Jonathan, A. Silk, 2007,*Good and Evil in Indian Buddhism: The five Sins of immediate retribution, Journal of Indian Philosophy, XXXV,1,* Phyllis Granoff (ed.), U.S.A.

King, Winston,1960, *In the hope of Nibbana,* La Salle: Open Court.

Maxmuller, F., (ed.), *Vinaya Texts, SBE, XVII,* T.W. Rhys Davids (tr.)

McDermott, James Paul, 2002, *Development in the early Buddhist concept of Kamma,* New Delhi.

Milindapañha, II, III, IV,V, SBE, XXXV,XXXVI, T.W. Rhys Davids (tr.) .

Samyutta Nikāya, IV .

Spiro, Melford, 1972, *Buddhism and Society,* New York.

Trenckner, V. and R. Chalmers (eds.),1960, *Majjhima Nikāya, II,III,* London: PTS.

Woodward, F.L., 2003, *The Book of Kindred Sayings,* Rhys Davids (tr.), Delhi.

State of Religion Under the Candella Dynasty

Vishwanath Verma

Introduction

The political history of Northern India, after the death of the great Harsha, is very complex and difficult to follow, a tale of several kingdoms continually at war, of the fall of considerable empires, and of the the rise of vassal states to independence and greatness. With the decline of the mighty Pratihara dynasty of kanauj, early in the tenth century, India's history becomes even more complicated, as the states which emerge from the ruins of the Pratiharas increase in power, and begin to fight one with another.

The Candellas were one of the most important dynasties of Northern India between the decline of the Pratiharas and the establishment of Moslem rule in India. Practically nothing was known of the dynasty until the publication of Cunningham's Archaeological Survey reports, (Volumes 2, X and XXI).The value and Importance of these reports and the contribution of Cunningham can be measured by the fact that even today no study of the period is possible without the help of his reports, and many of the conclusions made by Cunningham, from the limited material available to him, still stand today. On the basis of these Reports and other inscriptions, Smith wrote a scholarly article on the Candellas in 1908, in Volume XXXVII of the Indian Antiquary.

Religion

The Candellas were devout worshippers of Siva and Vishnu. The majority of the inscriptions begin with an invocation of either of the two gods and most of the temples of Khajuraho are dedicated to them. In the inscriptions Siva is variously worshipped as Mahadeva, Vishwanath, Mahesvara, Kedara and Vrisabha. An image of Nandi, one of the two chief attendants of Siva, and an image of a bull, the Vahana of Siva, have been found at Khajuraho (ASI Reports II: 423). The Copper Plates of the dynasty refer to Siva as one who holds the moon (From whom the Candellas claimed descent) on his head. The biggest temple of Khajuraho is dedicated to Siva and is nowadays known as the Kandariya Mahadeva temple. A large number of Siva lingams have also been found in Khajuraho.

1. Vishnu is also often mentioned in the inscriptions, and many images of him have been found in the Candella dynasty. The Caturbhuja temple of Vishnu is one of the best known temples of Khajuraho (Chaturbhuja is futher epithet of Vishnu).The Narasimha, 'The Man- Lion incarnation', the Varahavatara, 'the Boar incarnation,' and the Vamanavatara, ' the Dwarf incarnation,' were the most popular forms in which Vishnu was worshipped in the Candellas dynasty. He also mentionedas the destroyer of enemies and as Vasudeva, a title generally at this time applied to his most famous incarnation, Krishna.

The allegorical Sanskrit drama, Prabodha-Chandrodaya of Krishna Misra tries to show the greatness of the Advaita system of philosophy, and it propagates devotion to Vishnu (Vishnubhakti) as the only true religion. The reader of Probodha-Chandrodaya may be inclined to think that Vaisnavism and Saivism were two distinectly separate religious doctrines in Candella dynasty. But this is far from the truth. In the inscriptions, Vishnu and Siva are often mentioned with the same respect and devotion and there are inscriptions which begin with the invocation of Siva and later praise both Siva and Vishnu (Epigraphia Indica I: 327). A temple of Khajuraho was dedicated both to Siva and Vishnu (Indian Antiquary XXXII: 132), and images of one god have been often been found in the other's temples.

Other gods frequently mentioned in the inscriptions, or to whom temples have been dedicated, or whose images have been found, are- Parvati,Ganesha, Lakshmi, Sarasvati, Surya. Indra, Chandra....etc (Indian Antiquary XXXII: 132). The consecration of images in temples (devata pratista) was recommended in the Puranas as a work of great religious merit, and especial emphasis was put on the consecration of the images of Vishnu and Siva, and of the Sivalingam. The Candella king followed thispractice and inscriptions of the ministers and other important dignitaries record the erection of images and temples (Epigraphia Indica I, 211).[6] " abandoning of the body" in sacred water after attaining a very old age, as was done by Dhanga and Kirtivarman's minister Ananta, was one of the religious customs prevalent in the dynasty(Epigraphia Indica I: 206).

The granting of lands to Brahmanas was regarded as the highest act of religious merit in Ancient India. Ancient law writers say that, whatever sin a man may commit when in straightened circumstances, he is purified therefrom by making a gift of only as much land as would be covered by the hide of cow. One sacred test say that "gifts of gold, cows and land save even the wicked." The Candella Copper Plates show that the Candella kings granted land in strict accordance with the rites prescribed in the sacred literature. Yajanavalkya states that apart from the daily duty of making gifts, gifts must be made on special occasions and if so made are more meritorious than the gifts made daily. The Candella inscriptions often mention the kings making gifts of gold, cows, corn, umbrellas, etc to Brahmanas, but all the Copper Plates discovered show that the grants were made on auspicious days. One of the two land grants of Devaverman was issued on the occasion of the anniversary of his mother's death (Epigraphia Indica I: 206). The purpose of the land grant was to acquire religious merit not only for the donor but also for his parents and the Candella Grants also mention this. Before donating land the king had to go through religious ceremonies; the verse recording these ceremonies usually run as follows- "The king had bathed according to the rule in the water of a sacred tirtha, had satisfied gods, men and manes, had worshipped, after an adoration of the Sun, the lord of the movable and immovable, the divine husband of Bhavani, and had offered an oblation in fire." The gift was completed by the donor's pouring out of water, purified by the Kusa grass, on the hands of the done and the letter's expressing hus acceptance by uttering the word Svasti (Dixit 1951).

According to the ancient law writers, the donor of land enjoys bliss in heaven for sixty thousand years and he who destroys or resumes the gift or who abets its destruction dwells in hell for the same period. The Candella Copper Plates also record that the grant is not to be taken away or to be resumed and ask future kings to protect it. Of the fifteen Candella Copper Plates found, only one is a confirmation of a grant made by a former king (Epigraphia IV: 266-247). This indicates that land grants were generally respected by later kings, and no confirmation was necessary at the beginning of a new regin.

Epigraphic evidence indicates that different schools of philosophy, such as Sankhya, Nyaya, Mahabhasya, etc, were well-known to the learned people of the dynasty. But the Moslem invasion and the existence of various doctrines antagonistic to the fundamental ideals of the Vedas fostered the growth of a sense of unity among the followers of the different philosophies. This is clearly stated in the Probodha-Chandrodaya which says "when a commonenemy attacks the sastras, which though decended from the same source, are at mutual variance, they form an auspicious coalescence; and thus notwithstanding the internal disagreement of the sastras, which proceed from the Vedas, they all unite in defending the Vedas , and in repelling the materialists.

Buddhism and Jainism were also prevalent in the Candella kingdom, and many magnificent Jain and Buddhist temples are still in existence in Khajuraho. Statues of Buddha and the Buddhist goddess Tara have been found and references to Shantinath, Sambhanath, Adinath and Prashvanath, the Jain Trithankaras are found in some Jain Inscriptions. As in allotherparts of India, Buddhism was on the decline in the Chandella dynasty, and a reference to this is found in the Probodha-Chandrodaya. After the successof Viveka over Mahamoha, it is said that the Saugatas fled into Sindhu, Gandhara,

Magadha, Andhra, Huna, Vanga, kalinga and country of the Mlecchas. The heretics, the Digambaras and the Kapalikas fled to Pancala, Malva, Abhira andto the sea coast. The place names are of little importance, but the passage itself indicates the predominance of Brahminism over other religions at that time.

As a staunch Vaisnavste, Krishna Misra had great hatred and contempt for any other religion, and this is often reflected in various passages of his drama. In one place Shanti (peace), seeing a Digambara Jain, says to her sister Karuna (Mercy), " He is Digambara Siddhanta, sent by the great king Mahamoha, who by all means ought to be kept at a distance, and we should turn our backs to avoid the sight of him." The hatred for Buddhism is expressed when a Buddhist Bhiksu says, " How excellent is the religion of the Saugatas, which grants both sensual enjoyments and eternal felicity; it permits us to inhabit elegant houses and to possess women obedient to our wills; it removes the restriction as to the time of eating; it allows us to recline on soft beds and to pass the shining moonlight nights in amours with young damsels." Besides condemning these two religious, Krishna Misra attempts to show the contempt of the Jainas and Buddhas for each other.

The picture of the religious life of the state, as painted by Krishna Misra, is not only coloured by his fanatic zeal for Vaisnavism, but is entirely misleading. Far from a relation of mutual hatred and jealousy, one of the most outstanding features of the Chandellas was their wonderful spirit of religious toleration. Dr Beni Prasad says that "as a rule, Hindu monarchs, evenburning enthusiasts like Ashoka, tolerated all creeds, preached toleration and even went to the extent of patronising sects other than their own"(Prasad 1928: 505-506). Epigraphic and other evidence shows that the Chandellas carried out a similar religious policy. There are many Jain and Buddhist temple in Khajuraho which were built side by side with the Brahmanical temples. Commenting on the striking similarity in the magnificence, architecture, and designs of the temples of the different religious, Fergusson says, " It looks as if all had been built by one prince, and by some arrangement that neither sect should surpass or be jealous of the other" (Fergusson 1910: 49) Even when granting villages to the Brahmanas, the Chandella kings scrupulously safeguarded the interest of the land belonging to temples or shrines of other religions.

Conclusion

The Khajuraho Jain temple inscription records a number of giftsmade by one Pahilla, "who was held in honour by Dhanga and was a devotee of the lord of the Jinas". The inscription also mentions one Vasavacandra who is described as the Maharajaguru. Dhanga's respect for Pahilla (apparcently a Jain) and the indicated presence of the Royal priest at the time of a gift made bya Jain are very significant, and thisfurther points to the privilege and protection enjoyed by the people of other sects in the Chandella dynasty.

References

Archaeological Survey Reports of India, vol. II.

Archaeological Survey Reports of India, 1935-36.

Dikshit, R.N., 1951, Land grants of the Chandellas, *Journal of the Utter Pradesh Historical Society.*

Epigraphia Indica, vol. I& IV.

Fergusson, J., 1910, *History of Indian and Eastern Architecture, vol. I & II,* London.

Indian Antiquary, vol. XXXVII .

Prasad, Beni, 1928, *The State in Ancient India,* Allahabad.

28

सहारिया जनजातिः सामाजिक एवं सांस्कृतिक विशेषताएं

मृदुला खुराना

परिचय

बुंदेलखण्ड के ललितपुर जनपद (उत्तर प्रदेश) तथा दतिया जनपद (मध्य प्रदेश) में निवास करने वाली सहारिया जनजाति जो कि भारत की सबसे पिछड़ी आदिम जनजाति है, भारत की ही मूल निवासी है। इन्हें देश के अलग-अलग भू-भागों में अलग-अलग नाम से जाना जाता है। जैसे- सवारा, सोरा, सओरा आदि। माना जाता है कि इन्हीं शब्दों से सहारिया की उत्पत्ति हुई है। बुंदेलखण्ड में इन्हें रावत के नाम से भी पुकारा जाता है, जो कि एक संस्कृत शब्द राजदूत और राजपुत्र से लिया गया है।

सहारिया लोग प्रकृति के बहुत करीब होते हैं, क्योंकि उनका बसाव, उनकी आवश्यकताएँ, सभी प्रकृति से पूरी होती है। ये गंभीर, मासूम, नरम तथा शर्मीले स्वभाव के होते हैं, तथा एकान्त में रहना पसंद करते हैं। इनकी प्रमुख सामाजिक तथा सांस्कृतिक विशेषतायें निम्न हैं -

सहारिया शब्द की उत्पत्ति

सहारिय शब्द की उत्पत्ति अरबी शब्द के 'शेर' से हुई है। जिसका तात्पर्य जंगल से होता है। ऐसा माना जाता है कि मुस्लिम शासकों ने इन्हें जंगल में निवास करने के कारण सहारिया नाम दिया। दरअसल सहारिया शब्द की उत्पत्ति दो स्वतंत्र शब्दों सा-हारिया (सा से साथी) तथा (हरिया से शेर) से मिलकर हुई है। जिसका अर्थ 'शेर का साथ' है (Mandal 1999: 4)। इससे स्पष्ट होता है कि सहारिया मूलतः आदिम जाति के समूह से थे। सहारिया अपनी उत्पत्ति भीलों से भी मानते हैं, तथा अपने को भील ठाकुर हैं। कर्नल टॉड (Bhil 1969:14-15) ने भी सहारियों को भीलों का ही एक परिवार माना है। ये कोलरियन समुदाय की जनजाति है जो प्रोट्रो आस्ट्रोलायड समूह की है (Tiwari 1984)।

उत्पत्ति संबंधी मान्यतायें

बुंदेलखण्ड क्षेत्र में निवास करने वाली सहारिया जनजाति वहाँ की कुल जनसंख्या का 0.21 प्रतिशत है। अपनी उत्पत्ति एवं वंशजों से संबंधित इतिहास के सम्बन्ध में कोई तथ्यात्मक ज्ञान नहीं है, फिर भी पारंपरिक रूप से ये अपनी उत्पत्ति रामायण काल में शबरी से करते हैं। पौराणिक किंवदन्ती के अनुसार कहा जाता है कि ब्रह्मा जब सृष्टि की रचना करने में व्यस्थ थे, तब उन्होंने एक स्थान का निर्माण किया, जहाँ सभी मनुष्यों को बैठना था, सबसे पहले उन्होंने एक सहारिया को बिठाया जो कि मन्दबुद्धि का तथा मूर्ख था। उसके बाद एक-एक करके सभी लोग आते गये और उस सहारिया को खिसका कर बैठते गये, सहारिया खिसकता-खिसकता उस स्थान के कोने में पहुँच चुका था और ब्रह्मा जी उस सहारिया की नाकाबलियत पर नाराज हुए। ये कहानी संकेत करती

है कि सहारिया भारत के मूल निवासी थे, परन्तु बाहर के आक्रमणकारियों ने उन पर आक्रमण कर उन्हें जंगलों में रहने पर मजबूर कर दिया।

एक अन्य मान्यता है कि सहारिया की उत्पत्ति, हिन्दू धर्म में भगवान शिव के एक भक्त बैजू से हुई है।

धर्म तथा धार्मिक देवता

सामान्य रूप से बुंदेलखण्ड की सहारिया जनजाति हिन्दू धर्म के रीति-रिवाजों में आस्था रखती है तथा हिन्दू धर्म में मान्य सभी देवताओं को मानती है, परन्तु उनके नाम या उनके रूप को वे पृथक दृष्टि से देखते हैं। सहारिया जनजाति द्वारा मान्य देवी देवताओं के नाम निम्न हैं-

1. तेजा जी
2. ठाकुर बाबा
3. दुर्गा माता
4. हनुमान
5. लालबाई
6. बीजासन
7. प्रेत माता
8. भैरव बाबा

बलि प्रथा

देवी-देवताओं को प्रसन्न करने हेतु पशु-पक्षियों की बलि देने की प्रथा प्राचीन काल से चली आ रही है। सभ्य एवं विकसित समाजों में अब यह प्रथा बन्द हो चुकी है, जिसका मुख्य कारण इनमें ज्ञान एवं शिक्षा का प्रसार है। वर्तमान समय में जनजातियों में इस प्रथा का प्रचलन है। समान्य रूप से मुर्गा-मुर्गी, सुअर तथा बकरा आदि की बलि दी जाती है।

धार्मिक तीज त्योहार

बुंदेलखण्ड क्षेत्र की सहारिया जनजाति हिन्दू धर्म में विश्वास रखती है तथा वे सभी त्योहारों को उत्साहपूर्वक मनाते हैं। तीज त्योहार किसी भी समाज की सामाजिकता, सामूहिकता एवं सहकारिता की भावना सुदृढ़ करते हुए उनमें परस्पर निर्भरता में वृद्धि करते हैं। इनके द्वारा मनाये जाने वाले प्रमुख धार्मिक त्योहार निम्नलिखित हैं।

1. रामनवमी
2. होली
3. दीपावली
4. दशहरा
5. शिवरात्री
6. नागपंचमी
7. मकर संक्राति आदि।

भाषा

बुंदेलखण्ड क्षेत्र में मुख्य रूप से बोली जाने वाली भाषा हिन्दी है, जिसकी बोली में स्थान और दूरी के साथ अन्तर आ जाता है। पूर्वी चम्बल क्षेत्र में बुंदेलखण्डी तथा उसके दक्षिणी भाग में मालवी सहारिया लोग बोलते हैं। बुंदेलखण्ड के ललितपुर में बसे सहारिया आम तौर पर बुंदेलखण्डी तथा हिन्दी बोलते हैं, वहीं दतिया जनपद में सहारिया समुदाय में हिन्दी के अलावा मालवी भाषा का भी प्रयोग होता है। कुछ सहारिया परिवार जो आज भी जंगल तथा विंध्याचल की पहाड़ी क्षेत्रों में रहते हैं उनकी स्वयं की भाषा सहारिया है। आम बोलचाल में एक कहावत है कि हर 10 कोस (30 कि.मी.) में भाषा या बोली बदल जाती है। हालांकि, ये परिवर्तन सिर्फ बोलने में ही होता है। आमतौर पर ये लिखने में देवनागरी लिपि का ही प्रयोग करते हैं (Thakur & Thakur 1994)। जब से सहारिया जनजाति के लोग गाँवों में निवास करने लगे हैं तब से इनकी बोली, भाषा व रहन-सहन क्षेत्रीय लोगों से मेल खाती है। अतः हम कह सकते हैं कि इस क्षेत्र के सहारियाओं की भाषा के अनुरूप खड़ी हिन्दी तथा बुंदेलखण्डी है।

विवाह संस्कार

विवाह एक महत्वपूर्ण सामाजिक संस्कार है। सभ्यता के अभ्युदय के साथ ही विवाह संस्कार अपने अस्तित्व में आया। विवाह एक सामाजिक समझौता भी है। वैसे स्त्री-पुरूष के यौन संबंधो को सुपरिभाषित एवं नियमित करने वाले सामाजिक संस्कार का ही परिवर्तित रूप 'विवाह' हैं भारत की जनजातियों में आठ प्रकार की विवाह पद्धतियाँ प्रचलन में हैं-

1. परीक्षा विवाह
2. क्रय विवाह
3. अपहरण विवाह
4. परीक्ष्य विवाह
5. सेवा विवाह
6. पलायन विवाह
7. विनिमय विवाह
8. प्रक्षित्व विवाह

बुंदेलखण्ड के ललितपुर तथा दतिया जनपद में पायी जाने वाली सहारिया जनजाति में सामान्य रूप से उपरोक्त विवाह पद्धतियों में से किसी का पूर्ण रूप से अनुसरण नहीं किया जाता है। चूंकि ये सभ्य समाज से काफी घुल-मिल गये हैं। अतः इनकी प्राचीन विवाह पद्धति बदल गयी है। उसे क्रय विवाह की श्रेणी में रखा जा सकता है पर वरपक्ष औपचारिक रूप से वधू मूल्य नहीं देता है।

विवाह पद्धति

सहारियाओं की संस्कृति काफी पारदर्शी है। विवाह हिन्दू रीति-रिवाजों से होता है। यह बहुत साधारण तरीके से होता है, जो कि स्थानीय व्यक्ति करवाता है, जिसे 'मारही' कहते हैं। इसे ब्राह्मण धर्मगुरू द्वारा नहीं करवाया जाता है। (Mandal 1999: 19)। विवाह में साथी की सहमति जरूरी होती है। विवाह का दिन व तारीख परिवार के पुरुष मुखिया द्वारा अन्य पुरुष सदस्यों की सहमति से तय की जाती है। इनमें 'पत्नी लेना' और 'पत्नी देना' के बीच में कोई अन्तर नहीं होता है। ठीक उसी प्रकार 'बराती' व 'घराती' में कोई दबाव एवं तनाव नजर नहीं आता है। विवाह में खाना परोसा जाता है और वह जैसा भी होता है सहारिया उसे बिना नाराजगी के स्वीकार करता है। ये एक ही वंश बिरादरी या गोत्र में विवाह नहीं करते हैं।

विवाह की आयु

सहारिया समुदाय में बाल विवाह का प्रचलन है, विवाह के समय लड़की की उम्र 12-15 वर्ष होती है, तथा लड़के की उम्र 15-18 वर्ष होती है। (Chauhan 1999: 169) बुंदेलखण्ड के ललितपुर तथा दतिया जनपद में सर्वेक्षण से यह तथ्य सामने आया है। 15-16 वर्ष की आयु तक लड़की माँ भी बन जाती है तथा उसी पर घर की सारी जिम्मेदारी आ जाती है। नीचे दी गयी सारणी 6.1 में सर्वेक्षित गाँवों के सहारिया परिवारों में विवाह की आयु को दर्शाया गया है।

सहारिया जनजाति में तलाक तथा पुनर्विवाह का भी प्रचलन है, जिसे 'नैट' कहते हैं। महिलाओं पर कोई दबाव नहीं होता है। वे विधवा होने पर भी सामान्य महिलाओं की तरह कपड़े पहनती हैं तथा पुनविवाह कर सकती हैं। ललितपुर जनपद के सर्वेक्षित गाँव रमपुरा में जहाँ पर लगभग 40 प्रतिशत महिलायें विधवा हैं, कुछ को छोड़ लगभग सभी ने दूसरा विवाह कर लिया है। इस प्रकार महिलाओं को दूसरे की पूर्ण आजादी है।

सारणी 1: सर्वेक्षित सहारिया परिवारों में प्रथम विवाह की आयु

क्र.सं.	आयु वितरण	पुरुष प्रतिशत	स्त्री प्रतिशत
1	5-8	X	8
2	9-12	20	29
3	13-16	68	12
4	17 से ऊपर	12	9
	योग	**100**	**100**

उपरोक्त सारणी से स्पष्ट होता है कि ललितपुर तथा दतिया जनपद की सहारिया जनजाति में आज भी बाल विवाह का प्रचलन है। आज भी 80 प्रतिशत पुरुषों तथा 91 प्रतिशत महिलाओं का विवाह बाल उम्र में ही हो जाता है। केवल 9-12 प्रतिशत स्त्री पुरुष हैं, जिनका विवाह सही उम्र में होता है, यहां यही दर्शाया है कि इन जनजातियों में आधुनिकता तथा शिक्षा का प्रसार हो रहा है। अत: हम कह सकते हैं कि इन जनजातियों में अभी शिक्षा के प्रचार तथा प्रसार के माध्यम से जागरूकता लाने की आवश्यकता है। जैसे-जैसे इनमें शिक्षा का प्रसार होगा, विवाह की आयु में बढ़ोत्तरी होगी।

नातेदारी व्यवस्था

जनजातियों के विशेष संदर्भ में एक पुरुष और एक स्त्री के समाज स्वीकृत तरीके से विवाह बंधन में बंध जाने के पश्चात पति-पत्नी की स्थिति प्राप्त हो जाती है। इसके साथ ही दोनों पक्षों में अन्य सदस्य भी होते हैं, जिनसे ये सदस्य विभिन्न रूप से जुड़ जाते है। इन्हीं संबंधों को नातेदारी कहा जाता है। ये संबंध दो रूप में स्थापित होते हैं-

1. खून का रिश्ता
2. सामाजिक संबंध

इस प्रकार से स्थापित संबंधों के आधार पर नातेदारी के तीन स्तर होते हैं।

सारणी 2: सहारिया जनजाति में नातेदारी व्यवस्था

क्र.सं.	प्रथम कोटि	द्वितीय कोटि	तृतीय कोटि
1	माता	नाना, नानी, बुआ, दादा, दादी	मामी, माँ के चाचा, चाची
2	पिता	चाचा, ताऊ, बुआ, दादा, दादी	चाची, फुफा
3	पति	जेठ, देवर, ननद, सास-ससुर, साला, साली	जेठानी, देवरानी, नन्दोई, सरहज, पत्नी के मामा, चाचा
5	पुत्र	पुत्रवधु, नाती, भतीजे, भतीजे	पुत्र के साले, साली
6	पुत्री	दामाद, पौत्र, प्रपौत्र	पुत्री के सास-ससुर
7	सगे भाई	भाई भवह	भाई के भाई, उनके माता-पिता
8	सगी बहनें	जीजा, बहनोई, भांजा, भांजी	बहिन जेठ, देवर आदि

बुंदेलखण्ड की सहारिया जनजाति में नातेदारी एवं उनके संबंधों का क्षेत्र अन्य हिन्दू जातियों की भांति ही है। सामान्य रूप से प्रथम कोटि के सम्बधों में लगाव बहुत अधिक होता है। द्वितीय कोटि में पहुँचते-पहुँचते यह कम हो जाता है। इसका कारण यह है कि द्वितीय कोटि और तृतीय कोटि के सदस्यों की संख्या अधिक होने लगती है। अत: आत्मीयता कम होने लगती है।

वैसे भी, आज के आधुनिक समाज में रिश्तेदारी को बहुत आगे तक नहीं देखा जाता, परन्तु आदिवासियों में यह पीढ़ी तक देखा जाता है। यह इतना अधिक विस्तृत हो जाता है, कि वे अपने कुल के आदिकाल को ढूंढ़ते-ढूंढ़ते किसी काल्पनिक पूर्वज को अपने वंश का प्रवर्तक मानते हैं। इसी आदि पुरुष का वंश प्रवर्तक की खोज का परिणाम गोत्र चिन्ह है। प्रत्येक आदिवासी समुदाय अनेक गोत्रों में बंटा होता है और प्रत्येक गोत्र समूह अपना एक ही पूर्वज मानता है, उनमें अन्य गोत्रों की तुलना में अधिक निकट संबंध पाया जाता है। सहारिया, गोत्र की खोज विवाह एवं अन्य धार्मिक क्रियाकलापों के दौरान करते हैं।

संस्कार

जन्म, विवाह एवं मृत्यु मानव जीवन के तीन महत्वपूर्ण संस्कार माने जाते हैं। प्रत्येक समुदाय में अपने ढंग से इन संस्कारों पर विशिष्ट कार्य कर्मकाण्ड या धार्मिक अनुष्ठान किये जाते हैं। ऐसा कहा जाता है कि *''जन्माते जायते शुद्र: संस्कारे डिज उच्चते''* अर्थात्

जन्म लेते समय सभी व्यक्ति शूद्र या निम्नस्तर का होता है और निश्चित संस्कारों के पश्चात वह उच्च स्थिति को प्राप्त करता है।

बुंदेलखण्ड के ललितपुर तथा दतिया जनपद के सहारिया जनजाति के लोग सैकड़ो वर्षों से हिन्दू रीति-रिवाजों तथा धर्मिक मान्यताओं से प्रभावित हैं, इसलिए वे हिन्दुओं के सभी संस्कारों को मान्यता देते हैं। विवाह संस्कार का वर्णन जैसा पहले वर्णित है, के पश्चात जन्म-मृत्यु संस्कार का वर्णन भी आवश्यक है।

जन्म संस्कार

ललितपुर तथा दतिया जनपद में सहारिया जनजाति समुदाय के लोगों में बच्चा पैदा होने पर निम्न जन्म संस्कार होते हैं-

1. छठी : यह जन्म से छठे दिन मनायी जाती है। छठी के दिन नवजात शिशु एवं माँ को स्नान कराकर स्वच्छ कपड़े पहनाये जाते हैं। सगे-सम्बन्धियों एवं बिरादरी के लोगों का भोजन एवं आव-भगत की जाती है।

2. अन्नप्राशन संस्कार : यह पांच माह बाद मनाया जाता है। इस दिन प्रथम बार बच्चे को अन्न खिलाया जाता है। बरही एवं पासनी संस्कार गरीब परिवारों में आर्थिक स्थिति खराब होने के कारण सामान्य रूप से ही आर्थिक स्थिति के आधार पर ही किये जाते हैं। बच्चे का नामकरण घर के बुजुर्ग द्वारा किया जाता है। जनजातीय बच्चे का नाम अक्सर देवी-देवता के नाम पर रखा जाता था। परन्तु अब आधुनिक नाम भी रखे जाते हैं।

3. मुण्डन : हिन्दुओं के समान जनजातियों में भी मुण्डन संस्कार का महत्व है, वे बच्चों का मुण्डन अक्सर पहले या तीसरे वर्ष करवाते हैं। ये बच्चों का मुण्डन किसी नदी के किनारे या फिर मंदिर में करवाते हैं।

4. मृत्यु संस्कार : हिन्दुओं की भांति सहारियों में भी शव दाह संस्कार किया जाता है। दाह संस्कार के पश्चात् 10 दिन तक शोक मनाया जाता है। दसवें दिन घर की साफ-सफाई कराई जाती है। दसवें दिन परिवार के पुरुष सदस्य नदी-नाले या तालाब के किनारे मुण्डन कराने के बाद स्नान आदि करते हैं।

5. तेरहीं संस्कार : मृत्यु के तेरहवें दिन मृत्यु भोज दिया जाता है। उस दिन मृतक आत्मा की शांति के लिए यथाशक्ति भोजन कराया जाता है। बरसी भी मनायी जाती है। कुछ लोग क्वार माह में पितृपक्ष के समय श्राद्ध भी करते हैं। इसे ब्राम्हण द्वारा सम्पन्न कराया जाता है। जो पूजन कराते हैं पर भोजन नहीं करते, क्योंकि इन्हें अछूत समझते हैं। अब खान-पान भी विचारणीय नहीं रहा है।

पोषाक एवं वेषभूषा

प्राचीन काल से ही आदिवासी बहुत कम कपड़े प्रयोग में लाते हैं। परन्तु उन कपड़ों में भी उनकी वेषभूषा और रंग-पसंदगी बहुत चित्तकर्षक लगती है। विकास के साथ-साथ संभवत: कपड़ों का उपयोग भी बढ़ा है। अन्यथा पहले उनके यहाँ कपड़ों की कोई भूमिका नहीं होती थी। आज भी कई जंगली जनजातियाँ हैं, जो निर्वस्त्र रहती हैं या सिर्फ पत्तों का प्रयोग करते हैं।

बुंदेलखण्ड में सहारिया जनजाति समुदाय में कोई विशेष वस्त्र नहीं पहन जाता है। वे काफी साधारण कपड़े पहनते हैं। पुरुष लोग अधिकतर धोती तथा 'सलूका' (शर्ट) पहनते हैं और सर में साफा (Turban) बांधते हैं। चप्पल बहुत कम पहनते हैं।

महिलायें रंग-बिरंगे कपड़े तथा जेवर पहनती हैं परन्तु अधिकतर सहारिया महिलायें बुंदेलखण्ड में घाघरा की जगह साड़ी पहनती हैं (Chauhan 1999: 168)। आमतौर पर महिलायें पहले सिर्फ साड़ी पहनती थीं जो उनके ऊपर के हिस्से तथा घुटनों से थोड़ा नीचे तक रहती थी। स्तन का आधार हिस्सा दिखता रहता था। परन्तु समय और सभ्यता के साथ उन्होंने ब्लाऊज पहनना प्रारंभ कर दिया है, जो शरीर को अच्छी तरह ढककर रखता है। विधवा भी सामान्य महिलाओं की तरह ही कपड़े पहनती हैं।

शादी के कपड़े अलग होते हैं। पुरूष लोगों का विवाह में साफा पहनना अनिवार्य होता है जो उनके रिवाज में आता है। जब कोई आदमी शादी के लिए जाता है तो साफा जरूर पहनता है। ये उसके रूतबे को बढ़ाता है। साफे का रंग सफेद या पीला होता है। महिलायें पीले रंग की साड़ी या घाघरा पहनती हैं।

बच्चे जो 5 वर्ष से कम होते हैं आमतौर पर बिना कपड़ों के होते हैं, जो लड़के थोड़ा बड़े हो जाते है वे लंगोट पहनते हैं। लड़कियाँ घाघरा पहनती हैं तथा ऊपर ब्लाउज या सलूका (शर्ट) पहनती हैं।

सहारिया महिलायें आभूषण की शौकीन होती हैं पर गरीब होने की वजह से चाँदी, ताँबा, एल्यूमिनियम, कांसा तथा कांच के जेवर पहनती हैं। अधिकतर महिलायें काँच की चूड़ी पहनती हैं तथा बाँहों में मोटा चूड़ा, पैरों में बिछिया, तथा नाक में कील पहनती हैं। अधिकतर सहारिया महिलायें गुदना गुदवाती हैं तथा हाथों और पैरों में मेंहदी लगवाती हैं। समय के साथ बदलाव का असर बुंदेलखण्ड के सहारिया परिवार में भी नजर आता है। नये जमाने के युवा पैंट-शर्ट पहनते हैं तथा लड़कियाँ सलवार कुर्ता व महिलायें साड़ी पहनती हैं।

परिवार का स्तर तथा आपसी संबंध

सहारिया जनजाति में परिवारों का स्तर एकांकी है। विवाह के पश्चात पुरुष अपने तथा अपनी पत्नी के लिए अलग झोपड़ी बनाता है। पत्नी संयुक्त परिवार में नहीं रहना चाहती है, जिससे कि उसे बहुत सारे बंधनों का सामना न करना पड़े। पति-पत्नी द्वारा अपने लिए बनायी गयी नयी झोपड़ी को 'टपरा' कहते हैं (Chauhan1999: 169)। जो कि पति के अपने भाई बन्धुओं के नजदीक ही होती है, जिससे कि जरूरत पड़ने पर एक-दूसरे का साथ दे सकें।

ललितपुर तथा दतिया जनपद में सर्वेक्षित सहारिया परिवारों में साक्षात्कार के समय अधिकतर परिवारों में सदस्यों की संख्या 7 से 12 तक पायी गयी है। सर्वेक्षण से यह भी ज्ञात हुआ है कि एक सहारिया परिवार में पति-पत्नी तथा उसके बच्चे शामिल होते हैं एवं माता-पिता अपने बच्चों को सम्पत्ति के रूप में देखते हैं तथा बच्चा एक तरह से आर्थिक उत्पादन की इकाई माना जाता है, जो परिवार के भरण पोषण हेतु अल्प आयु से ही सहायक हो जाता है। सारणी 6.3 में ललितपुर तथा दतिया जनपद में सहारिया जनजातीय परिवार के सदस्य संख्या पर प्रकाश डाला गया है।

सारणी 3: ललितपुर तथा दतिया जनपद में सहारिया परिवार में सदस्य संख्या

क्र0सं0	सर्वेक्षित गांव	परिवार संख्या	सदस्य संख्या			
			1–3	**4–6**	**7–9**	**10Above**
1	श्रमपुरा	20	0	6	12	2
2	छपरठ	25	1	8	15	1
3	जाखलौन	30	2	10	18	0
4	ज्मालपुर	30	4	12	14	0
5	कालापहाड़	30	2	12	16	0
6	बनपुर	20	2	8	9	1
7	सौराई	30	4	18	8	0
8	गोराघाट	25	5	10	10	0
9	सुनारी	30	7	12	10	1
10	तिलैठा	20	2	10	8	0
	योग	**60**	**9**	**06**	**20**	

उपरोक्त सारणी से स्पष्ट होता है, कि ललितपुर तथा दतिया जनपद की सहारिया जनजाति तथा दतिया जनपद की सर्वेक्षित सहारिया जनजाति में परिवार के सदस्यों की संख्या सामान्यतः अधिक होती है एवं अधिकतर परिवारों के सदस्यों की संख्या 7-9 होती हैं, जिसमें पति-पत्नी के अलावा 5-7 बच्चे होते हैं। बहुत से परिवारों में 4-6 सदस्य संख्या भी है अर्थात् पति-पत्नी के अलावा 2-4 बच्चे, ऐसे परिवारों का प्रतिशत भी काफी अधिक है। परिवार में सदस्यों की संख्या भी साक्षरता के निम्न स्तर को दर्शाती है।

सामान्यतः सहारिया बहुत ही साधारण, शान्ति पंसद तथा बच्चों से प्यार करने वाले शान्त लोग होते हैं। पति-पत्नी के बीच का सम्बन्ध महत्वपूर्ण होता है। कहा जाता है कि यदि सहारिया पुरुषों के पर्याप्त धन हो तो वे जाकर एक और विवाह कर लें। जैसा कि स्थानीय किसान करता है, कि धन होने पर एक नया कुआँ खुदवा लेता है। यह पत्नी धन तथा बहुपत्नी प्रथा को दर्शाता है।

कार्य सहभागिता

सहारिया परिवारों में कार्य का बंटवारा लिंग के आधार पर बिल्कुल भी नहीं है। पति घर के कार्यों में पत्नी की पूरी मदद करता है तथा बाहर के कार्यों को भी संभालता है। जैसे- मजदूरी करता है, खदानों में काम करता है, इत्यादि। इसके बावजूद महिलाओं पर कार्य का बोझ अधिक होता है, महिलायें बहुत मेहनती होती हैं तथा पुरुष की तुलना में अधिक मजदूरी करती हैं। इसके साथ ही उनकी मुख्य जिम्मेदारी घर संभालना, साफ-सफाई करना, घर सजाना, बच्चों को पालना, खाना बनाना तथा इसके साथ ही साथ ईंधन की व्यवस्था करना एवं लकड़ी काटकर लाना, पानी भरकर लाना आदि-आदि हैं। इस प्रकार महिलाओं पर कार्य का भार बहुत अधिक होता है। छोटी बच्चियाँ अक्सर अपनी माँ का हाथ बटाती हैं एवं मुख्य रूप से छोटे बच्चों को संभालती हैं। विवाह-समारोहों तथा त्योहारों में महिलायें सबका हाथ बंटाती हैं एवं मुख्य रूप से घर की साफ-सुफाई, सजावट, खाना पकाना आदि कार्यों में सहयोग करती हैं। इस प्रकार घर के कार्यों में स्त्री पुरूष तथा बच्चों सभी की पूर्ण सहभागिता होती है।

भोजन पेय एवं पोषकता

सहारिया लोगों का मुख्य भोजन गेहूँ तथा ज्वार की रोटी है। ये चावल केवल त्योहारों, उत्सवों एवं समारोहों में खाते हैं। खाने की श्रेणी तथा मात्रा इनकी आर्थिक स्थिति पर निर्भर करती है तथा इनके दिन के भोजन की मात्रा या खुराक मौसमी दिनचर्या से निर्धारित होती है।

साधारणतः जब ये खेतों में कठिन परिश्रम करते हैं, तब ये दिन में तीन बार भोजन लेते हैं- सुबह, दोपहर तथा रात। इनके भोजन में रोटी, थोड़ी दाल व रसेदार सब्जी होती है, परन्तु बरसात के मौसम में जब इनके पास काम नहीं होता है, तब इन्हें दो वक्त का खाना जुटाना भी मुश्किल होता है। ऐसे में ये महुआ, बेर तथा अन्य वन्य उत्पादों से अपनी भूख मिटाते हैं। जुलाई से सितम्बर के माह में काम न होने से सिर्फ एक दिन में एक वक्त ही खाना खाते हैं।

सहारिया मांसाहारी भी होते हैं पर वे केवल विवाह समारोहों में या किसी खास मौकों पर ही मांसाहारी भोजन खाते हैं। वे बकरे, सुअर तथा हिरन का मांस खाते हैं, जो बहुत साधारण तरीके से तेल नमक एवं मिर्च से बना होता है। कभी-कभी छोटे-छोटे जानवरों को भूनकर भी खाते हैं। फिर भी, उनका दैनिक भोजन शाकाहारी है।

सहारिया परिवार गर्मियों में फल, फूल, जड़ी बूटियाँ तथा अन्य उपयोगी चीजों को जंगल से इकट्ठा करते हैं तथा बड़ी मात्रा में उनका उपभोग भी करते हैं। इनमें आम, अचार, जामुन, तेंदू, बेल तथा बेर प्रमुख हैं। वे दालें भी प्रयोग करते हैं, जिनमें चना, मटर, तथा फलियाँ प्रमुख हैं।

रोटी के अलावा ये गेंद के आकार में बाटी भी बनाते हैं जो एक सप्ताह तक सुरक्षित रखी जा सकती है। गेहूँ तथा ज्वार को ये पहले अपने घरों में ही चक्की के सहारे पीसते थे, पर अब ये मशीनी चक्की में भी पिसवाने लगे हैं। उत्सव-समारोहों में ये पूड़ी, सब्जी व लड्डू भी लेते हैं। त्योहारों का मुख्य भोजन चावल ही होता है।

सहारिया जनजाति के लोग बीड़ी, चिलम, गाँजा तथा सिगरेट भी पीते हैं। शराब पीने के वे बहुत आदी होते हैं, जिसे वे गर्मियों में महुआ के फल को इकट्ठा कर के बनाते हैं। उनके सभी उत्सवों, त्योहारों में शराब पीना आम प्रचलन में है। इस प्रकार बुंदेलखण्ड

के सहारिया क्षेत्र में केवल कम लोग ही ऐसे हैं जिन्हें बीड़ी, तम्बाकू या शराब तीनों में से एक की भी लत नहीं है। सहारिया लोग पीढ़ी दर पीढ़ी नशे से जुड़ रहे हैं। इसलिए इनकी आर्थिक स्थिति बहुत कमजोर है। एक सहारिया महिला सुबह जाकर 15–20 रूपये की लकड़ी काट लाती है। उसे बेचकर शराब की थैली अपने पति के लिए ले आती है और 5–6 रूपये आटा, मसाला इत्यादि पर खर्च करती हैं।

इस प्रकार सहारिया पुरुषों कि व्यक्तिगत बुराईयों के कारण शारीरिक कुपोषण की शिकार महिला और बच्चे अधिक होते हैं जो निम्न परिणामों से परिलक्षित होता है।

1. 5 वर्ष से कम उम्र के बच्चे कुपोषण के शिकार हैं। उनके हाथ और पैर पतले-पतले तथा पेट बड़ा होता है।
2. पोषक भोजन न मिलने के कारण अधिकतर महिलायें ऐनीमिया की शिकार होती हैं।
3. सहारिया परिवारों में मातृ मृत्युदर तथा शिशु मृत्यु दर अधिक है।
4. नशे की लत के कारण अधिकतर पुरुष क्षय रोग के शिकार हैं।

व्यक्तिगत सफाई

सहारिया बहुत अधिक साफ सफाई पसंद नहीं होते हैं। लंबे बाल रखते हैं, दाढ़ी भी रोज नहीं बनाते, न ही नियमित स्नान करते हैं तथा न ही रोज धुले वस्त्र पहनते हैं, क्योंकि पानी की समस्या होती है। ये समस्या गर्मियों में और भी विकट रूप धारण कर लेती है। एक बाल्टी पानी के लिए उन्हें बहुत दूर तक जाना पड़ता है। बच्चे भी नियमित स्नान नहीं करते हैं तथा शौंच जाने के बाद हाथ धोने के लिए मिट्टी का इस्तेमाल करते हैं।

बुंदेलखण्ड में सहारिया बाहुल्य क्षेत्रों में अनेक सरकारी नीतियों तथा कार्यक्रमों के तहत जगह-जगह हैंडपंप लगवाए गए हैं, जिससे सहारियाओं को पानी की समस्या से बहुत हद तक छुटकारा मिला है, जिसका प्रभाव उनके स्वयं की साफ सफाई व स्वच्छता पर पड़ा है। आमतौर पर अब काफी लोग नियमित रूप से स्नान करते हैं तथा धुले कपड़े पहनते हैं। नहाने और कपड़े धोने में साबुन का इस्तेमाल करते हैं। उनके इस सकारात्मक बदलाव में काफी हद तक सरकारी व गैर सरकारी संस्थाओं की प्रमुख भूमिका है।

स्वास्थ्य एवं उससे संबंधित समस्यायें

स्वास्थ्य के दृष्टिकोण से सहारिया जनजाति का स्तर काफी निराशाजनक तथा कमजोर है। ये समाज लंबे समय से कुपोषण, क्षय रोग, मुख्य रूप से मलेरिया, फाइलेरिया, कुष्ठ तथा कुछ संक्रामक बीमारियों से प्रभावित हैं। इनके खराब स्वास्थ्य तथा उससे जुड़ी समस्याओं के लिए निम्न कारण उत्तरदायी हैं-

1. बुंदेलखण्ड के ललितपुर जनपद में अधिकतर सहारिया जनसंख्या अपने रोजगार तथा रोजी रोटी के लिए पत्थर की खदानों में काम करते हैं, जिससे लगातार पत्थरों से निकलने वाली धूल उनके फेफड़ों को नुकसान पहुँचाती है और वे क्षय रोग जैसी बीमारी से ग्रसित हो जाते हैं जो स्वच्छता की कमी व लापरवाही से और भी अधिक फैलती है। ये बीमारी अधिकतर पुरुषों को होती है जिससे कि सामान्यतया सहारिया पुरुषों की 35-40 वर्ष की आयु तक मृत्यु हो जाती है।

गाँव रमपुरा जो कि ललितपुरा जनपद में है को अगर हम विधवाओं का गाँव कहें तो कुछ गलत नहीं होगा। गाँव में सर्वेक्षण के दौरान दो-चार बुजुर्गों को छोड़ कोई भी पुरुष 40 वर्ष की आयु से अधिक का नहीं पाया गया, जो पुरुष थे, वे सभी क्षय रोग जैसी गंभीर बीमारी से ग्रसित थे।

सरकारी प्रयासों से डाट्स सेंटर तो बना दिये गये हैं पर (उस गाँव के मरीजों के अनुसार) वास्तविकता यही है कि उनके पास इन दुर्गम स्थानों में कोई भी उन्हें क्षय रोग की दवा देने नहीं आता है। उन्हें स्वयं दूसरे गाँवों में सेंटर से 400 रूपये देने पर दवा मिलती है। कल्याण, रधुबीर, अजन, हन्नू, गज्जू, बोरा ये कुछ उन पुरुषों के नाम हैं जो क्षय रोग की बीमारी से ग्रसित पाये गये।

2. सहारिया जनजाति में बच्चों में कुपोषण की समस्या बहुत लम्बे समय से चली आ रही है तथा अभी भी लगातार जारी है। आर्थिक स्थिति कमजोर होने से इन्हें दो वक्त का भोजन जुटाना भी मुश्किल होता है। जिससे ये अपने बच्चों को संपूर्ण पोषित भोजन

नहीं उपलब्ध करा पाते हैं, जिसके कारण उनमें कुपोषण तथा स्वास्थ्य संबंधी अनेक विकृतियाँ आ जाती हैं। जैसे 5 वर्ष से कम उम्र के बच्चों के हाथ पैर पतले-पतले होते हैं तथा पेट बहुत बड़ा होता है। सहारिया जनजाति के लगभग 40 प्रतिषत बच्चों की 5 वर्ष की उम्र से पहले ही मृत्यु हो जाती है।

3. सहारिया जनजाति में महिलाओं के स्वास्थ्य की स्थिति भी चिंताजनक है। उसका प्रथम कारण उनका बाल विवाह होना, समय से पहले माँ बन जाना तथा गर्भावस्था के दौरान आवश्यक पोषक आहार न मिलना है। जिससे महिलायें भी कुपोषण की शिकार हो जाती हैं, उनमें एनीमिया से शरीर कमजोर हो जाता है। गर्भावस्था के दौरान उनके भोजन का उचित ध्यान नहीं रखा जाता, वो सिर्फ मौसमी सब्जियाँ जो स्थानीय स्तर पर उपलब्ध होती हैं खाकर ही काम चलाती हैं। ऐसा स्वास्थ्य सेवाओं की अनुपलब्धता तथा अत्याधिक गरीबी के कारण होता है। बुंदेलखण्ड के दतिया तथा ललितपुर जनपदों को सहारिया जनजाति में मातृजाति में मातृ मृत्यु दर तथा शिशु मृत्यु दर अधिक होने के यही कारण हैं।

4. सहारिया जनजाति में अंधविश्वास, झाड़-फूंक, टोना-टोटका एवं जड़ी-बूटियों से इलाज आज भी प्रचलन में है। उसका कारण दूसरी दवायें व इलाज इतना महंगा है कि धनाभाव के कारण ये परम्परागत इलाज पर ही निर्भर करते हैं। सरकारी स्वास्थ्य सुविधाओं का बेहद आभाव है, सरकार द्वारा संचालित स्वास्थ्य संबंधी कार्यक्रम एवं स्वास्थ्य सुविधायें आज भी इन दूरस्थ क्षेत्रों में अप्रभाव ही हैं। सहारिया लोग आज भी तेजाजी को पूजते हैं। उनका विश्वास है कि वो उन्हें सर्पदंश से बचाकर उनकी जिंदगी की रक्षा करेंगे। कई बार अधिक बढ़ा देते हैं एवं ऐसे में उन्हें दूसरी दवाओं से बचाना भी मुश्किल हो जाता है।

इस प्रकार सहारिया समाज आज भी स्वास्थ्य सुविधाओं के अभाव में अनेकों गंभीर बीमारियों से ग्रस्त हैं, जो उनके अधिक मृत्यु दर का कारण है।

अधिवास

साधारणतः सहारिया जनजाति के लोग मुख्य गांव से दूर एकान्त में गांवों के छोर पे बसे होते हैं। ये समूह में रहते हैं एवं उनके बसाव क्षेत्र को सहराना कहते हैं, यह समान्यतः घरों का समूह होता है।

सहारियाओं के आवास हमें इतिहास के प्रारम्भ की याद दिलाते हैं, उनके घर बड़े-बड़े पत्थरों से बने होते हैं तथा घर की छत पतली पत्थर की छत्तियों जिन्हें पतोर कहते हैं, से बनी होती है। कुछ गांवों मिट्टी तथा बांस का प्रयोग भी घर बनाने में किया गया है। तथा सामान्यतः सीमेंट का प्रयोग दुर्लभ है। शासकीय सहयोग से बनाये गये भवनों में ही सीमेंट का प्रयोग पाया गया है।

ललितपुर जनपद के सर्वेक्षित गांव रमपुरा में सहारियाओं के लिए सरकारी कालोनियों का निर्माण किया गया है पर वे मकान भी जानवरों को रखने के लिए बने दरबों के समान हैं। वह मात्र 5 फीट ऊँचे बड़े-बड़े पत्थरों से बने हैं। छतों में छत्तियाँ (पतोर) डाली गयी हैं, कोई भी खिड़की या रोशनदान नहीं है। वे लम्बे-लम्बे कमरों की तरह है जिनमें बंद करने के लिए कोई दरवाजा नहीं है। अक्सर, बरसात में उनके अंदर पानी भर जाता है तथा कीड़े-मकोड़े, साँप आदि आ जाते हैं।

साक्षात्कार के दौरान सहारिया लोगों ने बताया कि दिन में अक्सर वे पेड़ के नीचे दिन गुजारते हैं, क्योंकि उनके घर बहुत गर्म व घुटन भरे होते हैं। ये दर्शाता है कि सरकारी योजनाओं का क्रियान्वयन कितना लचर, अव्यवस्थित तथा अनिच्छा से किया गया है।

ललितपुर जनपद के मेहरौनी ब्लाक के एक अन्य गाँव छपरट में सहारिया जनजाति के लोगों के लिए बेहतर सरकारी आवासों का निर्माण किया गया है, जो ईंट तथा सीमेंट से बनाये गये हैं तथा छतों को छत्तियों से पक्का बनाया गया है, परन्तु ये इस जनजाति का दुर्भाग्य है कि अधिकतर मामलों में वे गरीबी के चलते अपने मकानों की छतों की छत्तियाँ निकाल कर बेच देते हैं तथा उसकी जगह सस्ते खपरैल की छत डाल लेते हैं।

जनजातीय क्षेत्र में विद्यमान सामाजिक बुराइयाँ

1. बालश्रमः सहारिया जनजातीय समाज में बालश्रम एक सामाजिक बुराई के रूप में स्थापित है जो कि पीढ़ी दर पीढ़ी प्रचलित है।

जिसे बंधुओं मजदूरी का स्वरूप माना जा सकता है। यहाँ बालिका मजदूरों की स्थिति तो और भी अधिक दयनीय है। बालिकायें 8-9 वर्ष की आयु में ही छोटे-मोटे काम करना शुरू कर देती हैं, जबकि बालक 10-11 वर्ष की आयु में काम करना शुरू कर देते हैं। इस दौरान तेंदूपत्ता इकट्ठा करना, लकड़ी इकट्ठी करना, चरवाहे के रूप में गाय, भैंस व बकरी चराना इनके प्रमुख कार्य होते हैं, जो आयु बढ़ने के साथ-साथ खेतों पर कठिन परिश्रम के कार्यों में परिवर्तित हो जाते हैं। सर्वेक्षण के नतीजों से विश्लेषित होता है कि स्थायी व अस्थायी दोनों प्रकार के कार्य स्वरूपों में अशिक्षित बालक व बालिका बाल-श्रमिकों की संख्या अधिकतम है, जो बालश्रम के अशिक्षा के साथ प्रत्यक्ष संबंध को दर्शाती है।

2. बाल विवाह : सहारिया जनजाति में आज भी बाल विवाह प्रचलित है। भारत सरकार द्वार निर्धारित वैवाहिक आयु बालक व बालिका के लिए क्रमश: 21 व 18 वर्ष निर्धारित की गयी है। परन्तु सहारिया क्षेत्रों में सरकारी अधिनियमों की सरेआम धज्जियाँ प्रशासन की उपस्थिति से उड़ती देखी जा सकती है। जहाँ 12-15 वर्ष की आयु में बालिका का विवाह कर दिया जाता है। बाल विवाह यहाँ एक संस्थागत सामाजिक बुराई के रूप में उपस्थित है।

3. शराब पीना: सहारिया पीढ़ी दर पीढ़ी नशा से जुड़े रहे हैं, जिससे इनकी आर्थिक स्थिति बहुत कमजोर है। सहारिया जनजाति के महिला-पुरुष शाम को घर पर ताड़ी पीकर ही रह जाते हैं। यह तथ्य जनजातिय क्षेत्रों में सामाजिक विकास की अवधारणा पर प्रश्नचिन्ह लगा देता है।

सहारिया जनजातीय क्षेत्रों में विद्यमान समाजिक विभेदीकरण

सहारिया जनजातीय क्षेत्रों में सामाजिक विभेदीकरण व्यापक रूप से उपस्थित है –

1. जहाँ एक ओर बाल मनोरंजन क्षेत्र में वीडियो गेम्स ने विकास का आयाम स्थापित किया है वहीं सहारिया बालक व बालिका इन समस्त मनोरंजनों के साधनों से अनभिज्ञ जंगल में लकड़ी काटना, गाया चराना, तेंदूपत्ता इकट्ठा करना जैसी आर्थिक आवश्यकताओं की पूर्ति कर रहे हैं। यह तथ्य जनजातीय क्षेत्रों में विकास की अवधारणा पर प्रश्नचिन्ह लगा देता है।

2. जहाँ भारत में महिला शिक्षा को भी शैक्षिक अभियानों का एक महत्वपूर्ण घटक माना जाता है। सहारिया जनजाति की महिला साक्षरता का प्रतिशत शायद समस्त भारत के न्यूनतम स्तर पर है, जो कि जनजातीय विभेदीकरण के साथ-साथ लिंग भेदीय स्वरूप को प्रदर्षित करता है।

3. विकास के आयामों में जहाँ शहरी आदमी सितारा होटलों में लजीज खाना खाता है। वहीं सहारिया जनजाति के लोगों को गेहूँ और बाजरा की रोटी भी दिन में एक बार मुश्किल से नसीब होती है। कई बार तो ये सांवा (सहवा) घास की रोटी से ही गुजारा करते हैं।

अत: हम कह सकते हैं कि आधुनिकीकरण व वैश्वीकरण की प्रक्रियाओं ने जनजातीय विकास की अवधारणा को न केवल विस्तार दिया है, बल्कि विवादास्पद भी बनाया है। जहाँ एक तरफ विकास ने मानव जीवन में गुणात्मक बदलाव किये हैं, वहीं इनसे लोगों के बीच दूरियाँ भी बढ़ाई हैं।

आधुनिकता का प्रभाव

आधुनिकता हमारे व्यवहार आचार-विचार को प्रभावित कर रही है। आधुनिकता से हमारी संस्कृति, हमारी भाषा, हमारे रहन सहन का ढंग और हमारे संस्कार प्रभावित हो रहे हैं। जनजातीय समाज जो आज से कुछ दशक पूर्व विकसित समाज से दूर भागने का प्रयास करता था, आज विकसित समाज के प्रभाव में आकर उसके पीछे-पीछे भाग रहा है और इस अन्धी भाग-दौड़ में वह कहीं-कहीं अपने पुराने रीति-रिवाजों और संस्कारों में परिवर्तन करने से भी नहीं रहता। आज जो पढ़ा-लिखा सहारिया है, उसने या तो अपनी कुरीतियों को छोड़ दिया है या उनके प्रति उसका मोहभंग हो गया है। ऐसा सहारियाओं में शिक्षा के प्रसार के कारण हो रहा है, जिसमें गैर सरकारी संस्थाओं की भूमिका उल्लेखनीय है।

1. सामाजिक परिवर्तन

परिवर्तन प्रकृति का शाश्वत नियम है। अतः प्रत्येक समाज में सामाजिक परिवर्तन कम या ज्यादा पाया जाता है। समय या स्थान कोई भी या परिवर्तन प्रागैतिहासिक काल से चला आ रहा है सामाजिक परिवर्तन समाज और संस्कृति की अनिवार्य विशेषता है। परिवर्तन जटिल तथा सतत् चलने वाली प्रक्रिया है। परिवर्तन का सामान्य अर्थ है कि किसी वस्तु में दो समयों में दिखाई देने वाला अन्तर ही परिवर्तन है। यह एक सार्वभौमिक प्रक्रिया है, जो सभी कालखण्डों एवं स्थानों में घटित होती रहती है। परिवर्तन के कारण किसी वस्तु अथवा व्यवस्था के समस्त ढाँचे में परिवर्तन आ सकता है या उसका कोई एक पक्ष ही परिवर्तित हो सकता है। यह किसी भी दशा में हो सकता है। परिवर्तन स्वतः भी हो सकता है और योजनाबद्ध रूप से भी लाया जा सकता है।

'इंटरनेशनल एनसाईक्लोपीडिया ऑफ सोशल सांईसेज' के अनुसार ढाँचे या लोगों के पारस्परिक व्यवहार में आये महत्वपूर्ण बदलाव को ही सामाजिक परिवर्तन कहते हैं। बदलाव किसी समाज के मानदण्ड़ों, जीवन मूल्यों, सांस्कृतिक उपादानों और प्रतीकों में भी आ सकता है। मैकाइवर और पेज ने इसे परिभाषित करते हुए कहा है कि ''समाजशास्त्री होने के नाते हमारी विषेष रूचि प्रत्यक्ष रूप से सामाजिक सम्बन्धों में है, केवल इन सामाजिक़ सम्बन्धों में होने वाले परिवर्तनों को ही सामाजिक परिवर्तन कहते हैं।''

समाजिक परिवर्तन के कारण

समाजिक परिवर्तन एक व्यापक धारणा है, जिसके अन्तर्गत समाज में अमूल-चूल परिवर्तन से लेकर फैषन में होने वाले अति सामान्य परिवर्तन तक शामिल हैं। सामाजिक परिवर्तन एक घटना है। प्रत्येक घटना के पीछे कुछ कारक होते हैं। सामाजिक व्यवस्था में हमेशा कुछ न कुछ परिवर्तन होते रहते हैं, जिसके पीछे या तो कोई आंदोलन कारक हो या मशीनीकरण या जनसंख्या का बढ़ना या घटना अथवा फिर सरकार द्वारा लगाया गया कानून भी परिवर्तनशीलता का कारण हो सकता है। सामाजिक परिवर्तन से संबंधित निम्नलिखित कारक हैं, जिनकी वजह से समाज में परिवर्तन होता है।

1. प्रौद्योगिकीकरण

आधुनिक समय में यांत्रिक उपादान किस सीमा तक हमारे सामाजिक अथवा वैयक्तिक जीवन को प्रभावित कर रहे हैं, यह कहने की जरूरत नहीं है। दूरदर्शन, कम्प्यूटर, यातायात एवं संचार के साधन, प्रतिदिन के उपयोग में आने वाले सामान आदि हमारी मशीनी युग की देन हैं।

2. जैविक अथवा जनसंख्यात्मक कारक

जैविकीय कारक का सम्बन्ध समाज की जनसंख्या तथा उसके गुणात्मक पहलू से है, जो समाज और उसकी प्रक्रियाओं को प्रभावित करते हैं। इनमें कुल आबादी, जन्म दर, मृत्यु दर, आयु समूह, स्त्री-पुरुष का अनुपात आदि प्रमुख हैं।

उपरोक्त परिवर्तनों का निम्नलिखित उप-शीर्षकों के अन्तर्गत वर्णन किया जा सकता है।

(अ) सामाजिक संरचना

यद्यपि आरंभिक जनजातीय परिवार मूल रूप से पितृवंश (पितृसत्तात्मक) आधारित रहा है, तथा इसमें गोत्र दृढ़ता पूर्वक अपनाया जाता था। फलतः जनजातीय समाज इकाई के रूप में उभर कर आया, जिसका प्रत्यक्ष प्रभाव आज भी इनके संयुक्त परिवार प्रथा तथा इनके सामाजिक-आर्थिक क्रियाकलापों का निर्धारण उनके लिंग तथा आयु पर आधारित रहा है। आधुनिक जनजातीय समाज में अब तीव्रतर परिवर्तन देखने को मिल रहा है उपर्युक्त परिवर्तन को निम्नलिखित उपशीर्षकों के अंतर्गत प्रस्तुत किया जा सकता है।

(ब) गोत्र : गोत्र व्यवस्था आदिवासी समाज की विषिष्ट पहचान है। आज भी इसको सहजता से अपनाया जाता है, परन्तु

आधुनिकता की चकाचौंध ने कुछ सहारिया परिवार को विमुख किया है। पहले एक ही गोत्र में शादी होती थी, परन्तु पढ़े-लिखे आधुनिक युवक प्रेम-विवाह तथा कानून विवाह के लिये इसे अनिवार्य नहीं मानते है; किन्तु परम्परागत जनजातीय समाज में आज भी इसे विषिष्ट पहचान के रूप में व्यक्त किया जाता है।

परिवार व्यवस्था

प्रारम्भिक जनजातीय समाज में संयुक्त परिवार प्रथा का प्रचलन रहा है, जिसमें लगभग तीन पीढ़ी एक साथ जीवन-यापन करते थे तथा परिवार का मुखिया घर का बुजुर्ग पुरुष हुआ करता था। गृह कार्य उनकी स्त्रियों को करना पड़ता था। इस प्रकार परिवार के मुखिया पर उनके भरण-पोषण तथा सामाजिक सुरक्षा का दायित्व रहता था। वर्तमान में संयुक्त परिवार का स्थान एकल परिवार ने ले लिया है। अत: आधुनिक जीवन पद्धति, जो वर्तमान जनजातीय समाज के रूप में विकसित है, को नि:संकोच, जनजातीय युवकों द्वारा अपनाया जा रहा है। सहारिया जनजातियों में इस प्रकार के परिवारों का उदाहरण देखने को मिलता है।

धार्मिक मान्यतायें

सहारियाओं में धार्मिक कट्टरता खत्म हो रही है। आज उनके यहाँ भी सत्यनारायण की कथा सुनी जाती है। ऐसा उनमें हिन्दू धर्म के प्रभाव में आने और उच्च वर्ग के लोगों द्वारा अपने में आत्मसात करने की प्रवृत्ति के कारण हुआ हैं। ये बनारस तथा इलाहाबाद तीर्थयात्रा पर भी जाते हैं। नरबलि तथा पशुबलि भी समाप्त हो गयी है। अब सिर्फ सुपारी काटकर बलि चढ़ा देते हैं।

विवाह पद्धति

अध्ययन क्षेत्र की सर्वेक्षित सहारिया जनजाति की विवाह पद्धति में भी परिवर्तन आया है। विवाह को अब वे काफी जोश व उत्साह से करते हैं। क्रय विवाह की प्रथा समाप्त हो रही है। शिक्षा के प्रभाव के कारण विवाह की आयु में भी परिवर्तन दृष्टिगोचर होता है। पहले सहारियाओं में 10-12 वर्ष हो गया है। आज लड़के, लड़कियाँ, पढ़ाई कर रहे है। सर्वेक्षण के आधार पर यह स्पष्ट होता है कि सर्वेक्षित ग्राम रमपुरा की अपेक्षा जमालपुर में सहारिया जनजाति पर शिक्षा एवं आधुनिकता का प्रभाव अधिक पड़ा है।

स्थानीय स्वशासन में जनजातीय सहभागिता

स्थानीय स्वशासन में जनजातीय सहभागिता उनकी समस्याओं को दूर करने का एक कारगर माध्यम है, जितनी अधिक सहभागिता होगी सफलता उतने अधिक अनुपात में होगी। सहारिया समाज की महिलाओं की पंचायती शासन में सहभागिता बहुत अधिक सीमित है। केवल आपात स्थित में ही (उनके विचार तथा इच्छाओं को जानने के लिए) उन्हें पचायत में बुलाया जाता है।

यहाँ तक कि महिला पंचायत सदस्यों की उपस्थिति को उनके परिवार के 3 पुरुष सदस्यों द्वारा ही प्रस्तुत किया जाता है। महिलाओं को पंचायत के निर्णय को मानने की बाध्यता होती है। सहारिया जनजातीय समाज में महिलाओं के कार्यों को घरेलू कार्य, जंगल से लकड़ी लाना, खाना पकाना, बच्चे पालना तथा अधिकतर घरेलू कार्यों में व्यस्त रहना आदि निर्धारित किया गया है। साक्षात्कार के दौरान यह स्पष्ट हुआ है कि केवल 25 (महिलाओं तथा 75) पुरूषों की स्थानीय स्वषासन में भागीदारी है। जनजातीय समाज की मीटिंगों के दौरान ये सामने आया है, कि वे अपने कर्यों को निबटाने के लिए प्रतिबद्ध हैं।

राजनैतिक जागरुकता एवं सहभागिता

आदिवासियों में शिक्षा के प्रचार-प्रसार के माध्यमों से अनेक विकास आयामों की अपेक्षा की गयी है। हो सकता है, कि जनजातीय विकास के प्रथम चरण में ये अपेक्षाएँ संदर्भहीन-सी लगें, क्योंकि उन्हें पहले कुछ सामान्य अवरोधों को पार करने के लिए सक्षम बनाना होगा। प्रारंभिक दौर में शिक्षा न केवल जीवन मे गुणात्मक सुधार के लिए आवश्यक निवेश है वरन् नई विषम परिस्थितियों का सामना करने तथा उसको समझाकर सफलता पूर्वक आगे बढ़ने के लिए एक आवश्यक अस्त्र एवं रक्षा कवच है।

बुंदेलखण्ड के सहारिया जनजातीय क्षेत्र में विकास की प्रक्रिया जनजातीय समाज के एक तरफ छोड़ती हुई अग्रसर हो रही है

तथा वह उनकी नयी चुनौतियों से असम्बद्ध है। अधिकांश सहारिया इस तीव्र परिवर्तन का लाभ उठाने के लिए तैयार नहीं हैं, जबकि भील जनजातीय समुदाय इनकी तुलना में काफी आगे बढ़ चुके हैं।

ललितपुर तथा दतिया जनपद की जनजातियाँ जागरूकता में अभी भी पिछड़ी हुई है, क्योंकि इस समुदाय के अधिकतर सदस्य श्रमिक तथा मजदूर वर्ग के हैं। इसलिए ये अपने मालिकों, (जहाँ काम करते हैं) के राजनैतिक विचारों से प्रभावित होते रहते हैं।

ललितपुर तथा दतिया जनपद की सर्वेक्षित जनजातीय परिवारों में राजनैतिक जागरूकता सारणी 4 से स्पष्ट है।

सारणी 4: जनजातियों में राजनैतिक जागरूकता

क्र.सं.	**विवरण संख्या**	**प्रतिशत**
1	सरपंच	85
2	वर्तमान क्षेत्रीय विधायक	55
3	भूतपूर्व क्षेत्रीय विधायक	35
4	वर्तमान क्षेत्रीय सांसद	37
5	भूतपूर्व क्षेत्रीय सांसद	22

तालिका 4 से स्पष्ट है, कि 85 प्रतिशत उत्तरदाता अपने सरपंच को जानते एवं पहचानते हैं। मात्र 15 प्रतिशत उत्तरदाता संतोषजनक उत्तर नहीं दे सके। इसी प्रकार 55 प्रतिशत उत्तरदाता अपने विधायक का नाम जानते हैं। जबकि भूतपूर्व विधायक को सिर्फ 35 प्रतिशत लोग ही जानते हैं। वर्तमान संसद सदस्य को 37 प्रतिशत उत्तरदाता जानते हैं। यहाँ यह स्पष्ट कर देना आवश्यक है कि ये जनजातीय लोग सांसद और विधायक में अंतर स्पष्ट नहीं कर पाते–राजनीतिक पार्टियों की पसन्द–नापसन्द में विभेद इनकी समझ से परे है।

शिक्षा के माध्यम से राष्ट्रीय नेताओं की जानकारी अपने आप हो जाती है। यदि शिक्षा के साथ राजनैतिक चेतना का भी विकास हो जाय तो व्यक्ति इन राष्ट्रीय नेताओं से भावनात्मक रूप से जुड़ सकता है। शिक्षा न हो तथा केवल राजनैतिक चेतना ही हो, तो भी व्यक्ति कम से कम राष्ट्रीय नेताओं के नाम अवष्य जान जाता है।

राजनैतिक सहभागिता

आज कुछ वर्षों से राजनैतिक सक्रियता में बहुत वृद्धि हुई है। लोग राजनीति को समझें या न समझ राजनीतिक अधिकारों का ज्ञान हो या न हो, लेकिन वे राजनैतिक बातों में बहस जरूर कर लेते हैं। ललितपुर जनपद की राजनैतिक पृष्ठभूमि में जातीय तत्व बहुत प्रभावी हैं। ऐसे में जनजातीय समाज के नेता अपनी अलग पहचान नहीं बना से हैं एवं न ही किसी राजनैतिक दल से जुड़े हैं। लेखक ने इस अध्ययन के द्वारा यह जानने का प्रयास किया है कि जनजातियों के सदस्यों में राजनैतिक सहभागिता किस तरह की है। इस प्रकार हम देखते हैं कि सिर्फ11 प्रतिशत उत्तरदाता यह बताते हैं कि वे सक्रिय रूप से भाग लेते हैं। वे प्रचार में जाते हैं, और चुनाव के समय सक्रिय रहते हैं। शेष 89 प्रतिशत उत्तरदाता अपने श्रम सम्बन्धी कार्यों में व्यस्त रहते हैं और उसमें से कुछ सिर्फ वोट देने चले जाते हैं। मतदान पूर्णतः स्थानीय प्रभावशाली व्यक्तियों के कहने पर करते हैं।

सारणी 5: ललितपुर तथा जनपद में सहारिया जनजाति में राजनैतिक सहभागिता

क्र.सं.	**कथन**	**संख्या**	**प्रतिशत**
1	राजनीति में सक्रिय भाग लेते हैं	33	11
2	सक्रिय भाग नहीं लेते हैं	267	89
3	मतदान करते हैं	120	40

4	मतदान नहीं करते	180	60
5	उम्मीदवार के रूप में चुनाव लड़ा है	18	6
6	पंचायत चुनाव में	...	...

जनजातियों में 40 प्रतिशत उत्तरदाताओं ने बताया कि वे वोट देते तो हैं किन्तु 60 प्रतिशत वोट देने नहीं जाते हैं। इन 40 प्रतिशत लोगों में जरूरी नहीं कि सभी चुनावों में मतदान करने जायें, वे पंचायत के चुनाव में ही विशेष रूप से वोट देने जाते हैं। क्षेत्रीय राजनीति में कोई विशिष्ट नेता ललितपुर एवं दतिया जनपद के जनजातीय समूह का नहीं है और उत्तरदाताओं में सिर्फ 6 लोग ही पंचायत का चुनाव लड़े हैं। यद्यपि चुनावों में उनकी सहभागिता अभी कम है, परन्तु आकांक्षाएं बहुत ऊँची हैं और वे धीरे-धीरे राजनीति में भी सक्रिय हो रहे हैं।

आज का मानव एक ऐसा प्राणी है, जिसके जीवन में राजनीति एक महत्वपूर्ण अंग बन चुकी है। प्रत्येक व्यक्ति की भाषा, बोल-चाल, रहन-सहन आदि समस्त क्रियाओं में, किसी न किसी रूप में राजनीति की स्पष्ट झलक देखने को मिलती है, लेकिन सहारियों में इसका लेसमात्र में भी प्रभाव नहीं पड़ा है। चयनित अध्ययन क्षेत्र के सहारियों के राजनीतिक स्तर का अवलोकन करने से स्पष्ट हो जाता है कि इस भू-भाग में सहारियों की संख्या के अनुपात में इनकी राजनीतिक सहभागिता नगण्य है। सहारियों के राजनीतिक रूप से पिछड़ होने के मुख्य कारणों में शिक्षा का अभाव तो है ही, साथ ही निष्क्रिय एवं चेतनाशूल्य सहारिया रोजी-रोटी की तलाश में अपना अधिक समय व्यतीत करते हैं। सहारिया राजनीतिक गतिविधियों में किसी प्रकार की रुचि नहीं रखते हैं क्योंकि उत्तर प्रदेश एवं मध्य प्रदेश की सरकारें इनके प्रति कोई रुचि नहीं लेती हैं।

दोनों ही प्रान्तों में निवास करने वाली सहारिया जनजाति के लोग अपनी इच्छानुसार राजनीति के प्रभाव से दूर रहना अच्छा मानते हैं। फिर भी क्षेत्र के प्रभावशाली उच्च वर्गीय व्यक्तियों के द्वारा इनको राजनीतिक दलों की ओर चुनाव होने के समय प्रेरित कर लिया जाता है। सहारिया बाहुल्य गाँवों में इनको राजनीतिक सदस्यता ग्रहण करा दी जाती है। महीनों व्यतीत होने के बावजूद इन्हें कोई जानकारी नहीं हो पाती है। चुनाव के समय सरल स्वभाव सहारियों को पार्टी की सदस्यता या अन्य कोई लालच देकर इच्छानुसार मतदान करा लिया जाता है।

क्षेत्रीय सर्वेक्षण के समय जब लेखक द्वारा राजनीति के सम्बन्ध में जानकारी ली गई तो सहारिया किसी बड़े दल का नाम तक नहीं बता सके। सहारियों के पारिवारिक एवं सामूहिक संगठन तो हैं, लेकिन सहारियों की समस्याओं एवं उनके विकास में ऐसे संगठनों की कोई भूमिका नहीं है। इनके द्वारा यह बताया गया कि क्षेत्रीय नेताओं से छोटी-बड़ी समस्याओं को लेकर मिलने जाया जाता है, तो वे मिलते ही नहीं हैं। अधिकांश सहारिया यातायात एवं संचार की सुविधाओं के अतिरिक्त धन को मुख्य कारण मानते हैं। उनकी मान्यता है, कि धनाभाव के कारण राजनीति में भाग नहीं लिया जा सकता है।

स्माज में न्यून आवश्यकता इस बात की है, कि दोनों प्रान्तों के राजनीतिक दल अपने संविधान में संशोधन कर सहारिया जनजाति के लिए एक-दो सीट आरक्षित करना सुनिश्चित करें। इसके साथ ही साथ, राजनीतिक जनचेतना चलाकर सहारियों को राजनीति में आने हेतु प्रोत्साहित करें। अन्यथा, सहारियों की आने वाली पीढ़ी भी राजनीतिक चेतनाशूल्य रहकर बद से बदतर सामाजिक जीवन बिताने हेतु बाध्य होगी।

References

Bhil, R.S., 1969, Preliminary appraisal of Saharia tribe, *Tribal Bulletin, Vol. VI.*

Biswas, R.K., 2006, *Demographic study of primitive tribe: a comparative framework,* New Delhi: Saa Publication.

Chauhan, Abha, 1999, Gender dimension of social interaction's among the sahariya tribe of Madhya Pradesh, R.

Indira (ed.), *Gender and society in India, Vol. 2,* New Dehli: Rural and Tribal Studies.

Mandal, Debarata,1999, *Social structure and cultural change in the Saharia tribe,* New Delhi: M.D. Publications.

Mandal, Debarata,1999, *Social structure and cultural change in the Saharia triabe,* New Delhi: M.D. Publications.

Meena, Kanta, 2010, *Sahariya Janjati ke vikas ka samajshastriya sandarbha, Vol. 57 (11),* Kurukshetra.

Tiwari, D.N., 1984, *Primitive tribe of Madhya Pradesh,* New Delhi: Ministry of Home Affaire, Tribal Development Division.

Thakur, D. and D.N. Thakur, ed.,1994, *Trible in Central India, Vol. 1,* New Delhi.

Tod, J., 1977, *Travels in Western India: 24th Report of the commissions for S.C. and S.T. (1975-76) and (1976-77),* London: Allen & Company.

Sinha, V.C. and Sinha Pushpa, 2009, Principals of Demography, Noida: Mayur Paper Backs.

29

Did Maya Civilization Established by Maya Danava of Ramayana or Mahabharata : A Hyperbole or Hypothetical Truth

K.C. Srivastava and Shashi Bala Srivastava

This controversial Maya Civilization developed in an area extremely differentiated environment, within an area defined by the extent of known archaeological sites and the present (or ethnohistoric) distribution of Maya- speaking peoples. This corresponds to south-eastern Maxico including the entire Yucatan Peninsula, Guatemala, Belize and the western portion of Honduras and El Salvador.

There is reference of Maya Danava in Ramayana as well as in Mahabharata also. In Ramayana he is father of Mandodari who is the wife of mighty king Ravana. Here Maya Danava is not only identified as a Father-in-Law of Ravana but as an architect of Asur community.

The next reference comes in Mahabharata when Hasitnapur King Dhritarasìtra gave Khandavana to Yudhisthirato make his kingdom. Arjun visited the place physically to see its condition with Sri Krishna to plan for starting the work. He, when reached the place, saw the barren land with full of forest he went in depression and saw the Krishna with helpless eyes. Krishna immediately understood the mental position of Arjun, he said that nothing to worry, make your own effort and creat a new way to solve the problem of this hard gotten land and do not sit idle. Put the fire arrow on your bow and get rid of from the forest. Arjun did the same and set the forest on fire. Amidst the forest conflagration a person with fear on his face emerged before Arjun and Sri Krishna with folded hands to rescue him and his family from this catastrophe. In lieu of this he will do for what they have come here because he is an architect and his name is Maya, architect of Asur.

These two references motivated me to know more about them. Whether these identical names (Maya Danava and Maya civilization) are only by chance or it has some solid roots. Through this paper I am trying to bring something solid for this hypothesis.

Now before investigating properly on the relations we must put a birds eye view on the Maya civilization which was established by the so called Mayasura, an architect.

Firstly it is Maya civilization and not Maya. It is very strange that when we speak in Hindi we speak Maya (see the references in Ramayana and Mahabharata) but when we speak in English it becomes Maya. For example when we take the name of Lord Rama in Hindi we say Rama but when we speak in English this becomes Lord Rama. Why it is so, is riddle for me.

Maya Civilization which is also known as Mesoamerican Civilization was established by the so called Mayasura. This civilization developed in an area that encompasses Southeastern Maxico all of Guatemala and Belize and the western portions of Hondurous and El Salvador. This region consists of Northern lowlands covering the Yucatan Peninsula and the highlands of the Sirra Modre, running from the Maxican state of Cheapas across southern Guatemala and onwards into El Salvadore and the southern lowlands of the Pacific littoral plain.

The period of Maya civilization can be dated back to 1500 BCE. They were well known to the agricultural products for their livelihood. The first Maya city developed around 750 BCE and by 500 BCE these city possessed monumental architecture, including temple with elaborate stucco (Coe 2011:91).

Maya people believed in a super natural realm inhabited by an array of powerful deities who needed to be placated with ceremonial offerings and ritual practices (Sharer and Traxler 2006:91). At the core of Maya religiouspractice was the worship of deceased ancestors, who would intercede for their living descendants in dealing with the natural realm (Bruce and Demarest:176). Chilan who was the oracular priests has a very strong hold on the society. Chilan, to facilitate the ruling party, codified the religious cult to justify their right to rule. In the late practices this process culminated in the institution of the divine King, the K'uhul ajaw, endowed with ultimate political and religious power (Sharer and Traxler 2006:91).

Maya people worshipped feathered serpent dieties. By the post classic period the Feathered Serpent had spread to both Yucatan Peninsula and the Guatemalan high lands. Feathered deity was named as Kukulkkan. There are Temples for this Feathered Serpent deity. In Maya civilization kingship was patrilineal and power normally passed to the eldest son.

Maya civilization had a lengthy and complicated mythical origin story that is recorded by the K'che. Maya (based in Guatemala) in the Popol Vuh, the "Book of Counsel" wrote Coe in his book. According to the stories, the forefather gods Tepeu and Q'ukumatz brought forth the Earth from a Watery Void and endowed it with animals and plants (Coe 2011:91). Though other opinions are also there yet this opinion is widely accepted for the origin of Maya Civilization. Regarding identity and migration of Maya people as who were they and from where they have come or are they indigenous. These questions are also not far from controversy.

The relation of both the civilizations are covered with ambiguity can be made thin ,if not put off, by the deep study in terms of similarity. Recent studies suggest a link between Indus Valley and the

Maya people focusing on the calendar of two advanced civilizations. The Indus people fallowed the calendar based on the movement of Jupitar, while Maya people fallowed the Venus. In Hindu mythology Jupitar (Brihaspati) is the mentor of Devata and Venus (Shukra) is of Asura. The traditional aphorism of Hindus state that Asura lived in the opposite side of the Devata and if we see geographically Maxico is exactly opposite in longitude. Here the words Deavta and Asura do not mean good and bad but they simply refer to two different communities with different life styles as energy patterns in different parts of the world are different (Jarus:69).

It has been confirmed that the principles of guidelines on which the Maya structure are made is the same as prescribed in the Vastu Sìastra of India. Remains of the residential layouts of the Maya structures are identical to those found in the Indus Valley Civilization. As in Maya building, Indus people have been using lime mortar for all their stone and brick buildings. This can be seen in the Monumental creation in Mahabalipuram and famed stone Temple of Tanjavur in Tamilnadu. The other surfaces of temple in Indian civilization and Maya civilization were plastered and embellished with lime mortar (Miller:11).

The step pyramid design of Maya temple strickingly similar to the Hindu-Javanese-Sukuh-Temple or the Prasad Thom Pyramid in Angkor Combodia, home to the world's largest Hindu Temple complex.

The most amazing thing which proves the Indian impact on Maya civilization is the engravement of elephant motif in the Maya art specially in the earlier work of Maya people from Copan in Honduras, even though the elephant never existed in that area.

The Board game known as Patoli was widely played by Maya people in Mesoamerica including the Toltecs and Aztecs. It is the similar with the game of Pachisi which has been very popular in India from Vedic period till today. Similarities include the Board cruciform shape, the sequence of moves and the cosmic associations of the pieces and the moves.

There is a mystical story, with regional variation, for rescuing the earth. As explained in Maya mythology that their Almighty god Tepeu with his assistant Q'ukumatz rescued the Earth from a watery void and endowed it with animals ,men, and plants. The Bore incarnation of Visnu has done the same work. He rescued the Earth from the clutches of demon Hiranyaksha living in the nether world (Willey and Sabloff 1977:21-40).

In Hindu mythology serpents are given the status of demigods and they are worshipped by the common people. During the adoration period Hindu people embellished their house with snake figurines. Maya people also worship the serpents but their serpents are feathered (it is a regional variation) and treat them as their demigods. This similarity propounds the relation of both civilizations.

It is very surprising to note that the trend of disappearance of both the civilization Maya and Indus keeping in view the geographical distance for most of the archaeologist and prehistorians. It is just like a twins who reacts as in the same way against any objects though they might not be living in the same place. Is it telepathy working on both the civilizations being identical in name?

For the long many years a number of theories have been proposed to account for this collaps, but still historian are seeking harmony in diversity. The foremost hurdle in detailing of the Harappan civilization is its undeciphered inscription. Historian are wandering in dark. So is the case of Maya civilization. What a coincidence. It must be borne in the mind that, unlike, the demise of civilizations known from its historical record the Maya like Harappan society represents an example of collapse identified solely from archaeological evidence. While historical records of the Maya civilization are being recognized as the result of recent advances in the decipherment of hieroglysphic texts, these sources far are mute as to the events surrounding the collapse.

Now firstly, let us dwell on the theories propounded by historians for the demise of Maya civilization from the available sources.

Establishing the theory of Mayan demise, it is said that the natural disaster was also the culprit of its downfall. The Maya low lands are frequently visited by Carrebbean hurricanes. A major storm of this kind could easily destroy agricultural production over a wide area which was the life line for Maya people. Same theory, with some differences has been propounded by some historians in case of Indus civilization with other probabilities.

The developmental character of each human society is different and unique from others, the understanding process that result in cultural change are often similar. Example of similar process invite examination and comparision to thereby increase our understanding of the past. In this way an examination of the demise of the classic period of Maya civilization may offer useful insights for scholars concerned with the fate of Hrappan civilization. That is, the analysis of the archaeological evidence from the Indus Valley will undoubted reveal examples of factors analogous to those that have been identified as important in the cultural process of the ancient Maya. This could lead to the formation and listing of specific hyper thesis using the Harappan data.

For example economic factors ass shifts in ancient trade routes might have played a major role in changes within Harappan society, just as they did among the ancient Maya.

Of course, it may be advantageous to apply the hypothesis based upon factors identified in the Indus Valley to the ancient Maya. It is said by some scholars that the changes in the flood plain environment forced the Harappan people to vacate the place to save their lives. The second group of historians establish the principles that arid , which prolonged to hundred to two hundred years was the reason for the mobility of Harappan people. But there is no consensus on the principle. Maya people were also affected by the sudden shift in river channels due to flood . though on a smaller scale, had the similar consequences, because, Maya centers were situated in alluvial valleys.

The term "collapse" does not suits to a group of historians. They are of the opinion that slowly by steadly both the civilizations were disappeared due to many factors as envisaged by the historians who are still seeking the harmony in diversity on the theory of their disappearance.

The meticulous study of bothcivilizations give, implicitly and explicitly, strength to the opinion thatsomehow both are related. But we cannot put aside these resemblances by saying that it is a perchance. At present there is no authentic proof for this hypothetical relations but future no body knows.

To early scholars, however, the question of why the Maya and Indus Valley failed were often not as important as the question of origins. Where did they come from? And of course, the question was initially answered by recourse to migration from a host of known civilizations in the old world.

Before closing the article with future hope, I must draw the attention of historians on a image , partly mutilated, found from CIUDAD DE Museum Maxico (curtsey by Dr. Brijesh Rawat, Lucknow). By appearance it is a Jain image. By common sense it is not possible to carry such a heavy image from India to Maxico. Hence, it must be carved by the local artisan under the supervision of Jain monk. It proves two things- one the Maya civilization was any how partly under the influence of Jainism, and secondly, the identical name Maya (Maya of Mahabharat and Ramayan) is not perchance but it has some solid background which is still a subject of research. Now I am leaving this question to the learned scholars. The devolution of both the civilizations have left cluster of unanswered questionsfor the historians who are still struggling to bring a cohesive opinion. Now I put this paper before the scholars for their valuable suggestions, additions, and alterations.

References

Coe, Michael, 2011, Maya Civilization, Thames and Hudson.

Demarest, Bruce A., A kingdom Life.

Sharer, Robert J. and Lox P. Traxler, 2006, The Ancient Maya, Stanford University Press,

Jarus, Owen, The Maya History, Culture and Religion.

Miller, M. E. and K.A. Taube, The gods and Symbols of Ancient Maxico and the Maya, Themes and Hudson, N.Y.

Miller, M.E., After the Fall.

Willey and Sabloff, 1977.

30

Cultural Preservation of the Sanctuary of Machu Picchu (Peru) from the Sustainable Heritage Management Point of View

Brijesh Rawat

Introduction

The ideas and initiatives of cultural heritage conservation are not mutually exclusivewith the consumption of their developmental potentials. Alternatively, both of them should be seen as complementaryas long as they provide a sustainable heritage management that includes a proper analysis of the situationand proactive participation of stakeholders that share community values .

The pandemic bring to us an opportunity to strength the policies that aim to connect with the community and empower them in order to preserve cultural heritage. Furthermore, pointed out that when community create connections through interactions, they can support the sustainability of archeological heritage and also, highlights that digital technology management has positively influence in archeology to the building of social networks too.

It is important to mention that an archeological site needs a particular organization and data that can only be obtained from local people although there is a foreigner advisor expert in heritage,because it is too hard to truly understand the sociopolitical background and would require a prolonged exposure (Winter). However, even considering the international differences in management, countries still follow a standardized framework to assure quality, where they share the importance of community identification to connect with their heritage, dynamics and methodologies to raise their abilities and active participation to introduce cultural heritage management into sustainable development.

Peru has one of the richest and best well-preserved archaeological heritages in the whole world and their importance lies on historical value getting past customs and traditions, cultural value for the collective identification of the citizens and economic value as a source for financial income and generating economic activities and employment through tourism (Fig. 4).

Machu Picchu, one of the Seven Wonders in the World represents an art masterpiece with an invaluable archaeological, cultural and natural figure worldwide and considered the most amazing urban creation and most important legacy of the Inca Empire and standing out for their abundant variety of flora and fauna with 24 ecosystems among Andean and Amazonian.

Protocols in Machu Picchu

The following lines will describe the guideline for biosafety (Sernanp) for the pandemic and the attention of touristic activities which establishes prevention and sanitary control measures to prevent, reduce and contain the risks of transmission and/or propagation of COVID-19 for the staff of the Main Office of the Machu Picchu Historic Sanctuary of the National Service of Natural Protected Areas and the Machu Picchu National Archaeological Park of the Decentralized Direction for Culture of Cusco of the Ministry of Culture, including tour guides and support staff, locals from the District of Machu Picchu in Cuzco and tourists both from Cuzco and other parts of Peru and the world.

Protection of people

The employees and visitants should respect the social distancing protocols that are going to be monitored by the staff. After the entry control, each visitant group will start the tour with a time difference longer than 5 minutes keeping at least 20 meters of distance (Fig. 1).

Just as (ICOM) confirm, it is important to define a maximum number of permitted visitors and the distance between them to finally inform the audience about it.

Take body temperature is compulsory at the entry and exit, then if the result is higher than 37.5°C or other suspicious symptoms appear, must be written in the "Observations' Notebook". Nevertheless, if the result is higher than 38°C the entry is not allowed and would be directed to isolation and notified to the designated authorities.

The (Chilean Ministry of Culture Art and Heritage) advocate to carry out a temperature check and complete a survey in which a checking of symptoms is done before admission in order to verify if the person is COVID-19 positive, if they have symptoms such as fever or cough, or if they have had contact with someone COVID-19 positive (Fig. 2).

Admission capacity

Limit capacity of 40% representing a maximum occupancy of 897 visitants per day(El Peruano, *Machu Picchu Reabre Hoy Con Un Aforo Máximo de 897 Personas Por Día*) and specifically in the Red de Caminos Inka in the Historic Sanctuary of Machu Picchu the capacity is 120 visitants per day. The admittance of groups is distributed in visitants, guides and support staff and each group should have one tourist guide, one support staff and a maximum of six tourists.

The (Spanish Ministry of Culture and Sport) emphasize that the site should have a visitation capacity study, both maximum and sectionalized for each visitation area. It is recommended that guided tours be implemented as a rule, with small groups and the use of PPE.

Cleaning and Disinfection

For the cleaning and disinfection tasks, it must be identified floors, walls, baseboards, windows, ceilings, sinks, doors, toilets, footpaths, signals, handrails, desks, computer keyboards, door handles, among others, where tourism activities are conducted and thus, require regular cleaning and disinfection. As well as tools as phones and radio communication equipment. Therefore, a list will be made of the environments, surfaces and implements identified with their cleaning and disinfection weekly timetables.

To perform disinfection operations in the areas surrounding archaeological monuments, diluted hydroalcoholic solutions, in other words, alcohol dissolved in water, will be used in a controlled application. On the contrary, it is strictly prohibited to apply the solution directly on the pre-Hispanic architecture, and it should only be applied in transit areas, allowing the solution to be sprayed uniformly at a safe distance that does not imply direct contact with the exposed pre-Hispanic architecture (Fig. 3).

(ICOM) consider necessary to ensure that devices such as headsets, audio guides, among others, that require physical manipulation, should be systematically disinfected after each use.

The (Canadian Conservation Institute) suggests methods that allow controlled application of the cleaning solutions and disinfectants, which of course, should have been approved by authorities before. Nevertheless, the CCIpropose isolation as a preferable option rather than disinfection procedures which can damage our heritage acknowledging some studies where the virus deactivate naturally in surfaces recognizing a better way to deal with the contamination of archaeological spaces and pieces (Fig. 4).

Virtual Tours

Through the website designed by the Peruvian Ministry of Culture, it is possible to take a virtual tour of the Manuel Chávez Ballón Site Museum and learn about the history and mysteries of the Inca ruins of Machu Picchu and its archaeological findings since its discovery in 1911 showing info graphics, panels, maps, videos and about 250 pieces of ceramics, lithic objects, metals, bone rests and other items found in the archaeological excavations carried out in the Inca city, as well as in the Inca Trail and surrounding areas (Fig. 5).

Furthermore, there are many websites where you can live the experience of a visit with the help of virtual reality (VR) including full-screen 360-degree images and a virtual guide providing a voiceover with insightful information of the history, architecture and culturalvalue. Among the most popular are (Airpano.com; YouVisit.com; From Cusco.com).

The (Spanish Ministry of Culture and Sport) also recommendthat it is preferred to promote the utilization of the new online technologies to minimize risks, specially operations that do not guarantee social distancing (Fig. 6).

Conclusion

The Inca citadel of Machu Picchu was the first peruvian destination to receive the Safe Travels seal on October 13, 2020. This international recognition was the milestone for the reactivation of tourism in the country, which is one of the most important economic activities with a high impact on Peru's economy and GDP. In 2019, it generated 1.5 million jobs but due to COVID-19 the year ended with 600,000 active jobs although the good management practices discussed previously estimate a 25% growth by the end of the current year 2021providing opportunities to the residents who needed them most. This results impact positively in the communities giving tools to the for a proper heritage conservation reaching a social and economic sustainabilitywhile supporting their resilienceinspiring, empowering and uniting them.

In addition, the (Distrital Municipality of Machu Picchu) announce the launching of Machu Picchu Brandon July 7, 2021 whose main objective is to generate economic dynamism through the promotion of archaeological and natural tourist attractions of the district. The extraordinary heritage management during the previous months of the launch made this great step possible, that not only boosts the economy of the communities, but also allows their active participation to be agents of cultural preservation, internalizing and valuing their richness and sharing it throughout the world.

Acknowledgement

Shri Nirmal Kumar Jain Sethi, President, Shri Bharatvarshiya Dighambara Jain Mahasabha, New Delhi, who has attained eternal bliss, tried to spread and propagate the Jain religion not only in India but in the world also till his death. His method of spreading and propagating the religion was universal. For the said work Shri Sethi used to organize conferences/symposiums and hold religious discussions with the famous scholars of Archaeology and Culture. In this uninterrupted progress he visited Vietnam, Sri Lanka, Myanmar, Cambodia, Greece, Ethiopia, Peru etc., and organized various international Seminars. A Conference was Organized in January 2020 at Lima the capital of Peru. I was also fortunate enough to attend this seminar along with other scholars. Two days prior the Conference, we had an opportunity of visiting for the educational tour of the two earliest civilizations of the world namely The Caral Civilisation and the Machu Picchu Civilization. March 2020 witnessed lockdown due to Covid -19. The idea of writing an article on the cultural preservation of Machu Picchu came to my mind. But due to the lack of research material, I fully utilized the materials available on the internet and prepared the said paper. Hence, I heartily acknowledge Sethiji (Babuji), with whose effort and blessings this work would have been impossible.

Bibliography

Airpano.com. *Machu Picchu — the Ancient City of the Inca Empire*, 2021, https://www.airpano.com/360photo/Machu-Picchu-Peru/.

Andina. *Asómbrate Con Los Hallazgos En Machu Picchu Con Una Visita Virtual Al Museo Chávez Ballón*, 2020, https://andina.pe/agencia/noticia-asombrate-los-hallazgos-machu-picchu-una-visita-virtual-al-museo-chavez-ballon-795595.aspx.

Canadian Conservation Institute, *Caring for Heritage Collections During the COVID-19 Pandemic*, 2020, https://www.canada.ca/en/conservation-institute/services/conservation-preservation-publications/canadian-conservation-institute-notes/caring-heritage-collections-covid19.html#v2.

Chilean Ministry of Culture Art and Heritage. *Patrimonio Cultural y COVID-19. Recomendaciones Durante La Pandemia INTRODUCCIÓN*. https://www.cncr.gob.cl/611/articles-95450_archivo_01.pdf. Accessed 18 July 2021.

Dirección Desconcentrada de Cultura. *Ministerio de Cultura Realiza Limpieza de Seis Wakas En Cusco*. 2020, https://www.culturacusco.gob.pe/noticia/imagen/ministerio-de-cultura-realiza-limpieza-de-seis-wakas-en-cusco.

Distrital Municipality of Machu Picchu. *Promoverá La Economía de Las Comunidades*. 2021, https://www.munimachupicchu.gob.pe/index.php/news/12-turismo-y-desarrollo-economico/65-promovera-la-economia-de-las-comunidades.

El Peruano, *Machu Picchu Reabre Hoy Con Un Aforo Máximo de 897 Personas Por Día*. https://elperuano.pe/noticia/116177-machu-picchu-reabre-hoy-con-un-aforo-maximo-de-897-personas-por-dia. Accessed 12 July 2021.

García-Ceballos, Silvia, et al. "Educommunication and Archaeological Heritage in Italy and Spain: An Analysis of Institutions' Use of Twitter, Sustainability, and Citizen Participation." *Sustainability (Switzerland)*, vol. 13, no. 4, 2021, pp. 1–25, doi:10.3390/su13041602.

García Antón, Ricardo, Cultural Heritage and Sustainable Taxation – Empowering Communities in the COVID-19 Times, *Revista de Estudios Jurídicos y Criminológicos*, no. 2, 2020, pp. 123–44, doi:10.25267/rejucrim.2020.i2.06.

Hribar, Mateja Šmid, et al, Sustainable Heritage Management: Social, Economic and Other Potentials of Culture in Local Development, *Procedia - Social and Behavioral Sciences*, vol. 188, Elsevier B.V., 2015, pp. 103–10, doi:10.1016/j.sbspro.2015.03.344.

ICOM. *Prepararse Para La Reapertura: Garantizar La Seguridad Del Público y Del Personal*. 12 May 2020, https://icom.museum/es/news/prepararse-para-la-reapertura-garantizar-la-seguridad-del-publico-y-del-personal.

Landorf, Chris, A Framework for Sustainable Heritage Management: A Study of UK Industrial Heritage Sites, *International Journal of Heritage Studies*, vol. 15, no. 6, 2009, pp. 494–510, doi:10.1080/13527250903210795.

Li, Ji, et al, Community Participation in Cultural Heritage Management: A Systematic Literature Review Comparing Chinese and International Practices, *Cities*, vol. 96, no. September 2019, 2020, doi:10.1016/j.cities.2019.102476.

PeruRail, Cómo Se Han Adaptado Los Trenes de PeruRail y El Equipo de Servicio a Bordo Para Viajar a Machu Picchu En La Nueva Coyuntura Post Covid19?, *2020*, Dec., https://www.perurail.com/es/blog/como-se-han-adaptado-los-trenes-de-perurail-y-el-equipo-de-servicio-a-bordo-para-viajar-a-machu-picchu-en-la-nueva-coyuntura-post-covid19/.

Peruvian Ministry of Culture. *Manuel Chávez Ballón Site Museum.* https://visitavirtual.cultura.pe/recorridos/MSMCB/museo-sitio-manuel-chavez-ballon/index.html.

Shady Solís, Ruth, El Patrimonio Arqueológico Y Su Importancia En El Desarrollo Del Perú, *Arqueología y Sociedad,* vol. 0, no. 14, 2017, pp. 11–18.

Spanish Ministry of Culture and Sport. *PAUTAS PARA LA GESTIÓN, CONSERVACIÓN Y DISFRUTE PÚBLICO DEL PATRIMONIO CULTURAL EN LA DESESCALADA DE LA CRISIS SANITARIA (COVID-19).* 2020, https://ipce.culturaydeporte.gob.es/dam/jcr:39bc357b-dcf2-4bd4-9ce6-eda384872c99/documento-gesti-n-patrimonio-cultural-covid-19.pdf.

Winter, Tim, Beyond Eurocentrism? Heritage Conservation and the Politics of Difference, *International Journal of Heritage Studies,* vol. 20, no. 2, 2014, pp. 123–37, doi:10.1080/13527258.2012.736403.

Fig. 1/3: Ancient habitation site in farmland (unploughed) at Pamulapadu.

Fig. 1/4: Unslipped red ware of early historical period from ancient site at Pamulapadu.

Fig. 1/5: Cattle teeth and other bone pieces from ancient site at Pamulapadu.

Fig.1/7: Nandi-Naga stone pillar from the old Siva temple at Pamulapadu showing Nandi figure at the top and Old Telugu inscription on one side.

Fig.1/6: Fragmentary palette-like stone object with a central depression probably used for grinding condiments and medicinal plant material and much used polished axe of dolerite.

Fig.1/8: Nandi-Naga stone pillar showing hooded serpent on one side with Old Telugu inscription from the old Siva temple at Pamulapadu.

Fig. 1/9: Old Telugu inscriptions No. 98 on the Nandi-Naga stone pillar from the old Siva temple at Pamulapadu (after Ramayya Pantulu 1986).

Fig. 3/2: General view of the Rupen River

Fig. 3/5: Buddhist Monastic complex from Vadnagar Excavation (Courtesy: Y.S. Rawat)

Fig. 3/6: General view of the site Virta

Fig. 3/7: Potsherds and Bricks are scattered over the Modhera Villlage

Fig. 3/8: Broken Torana part from Modhera village

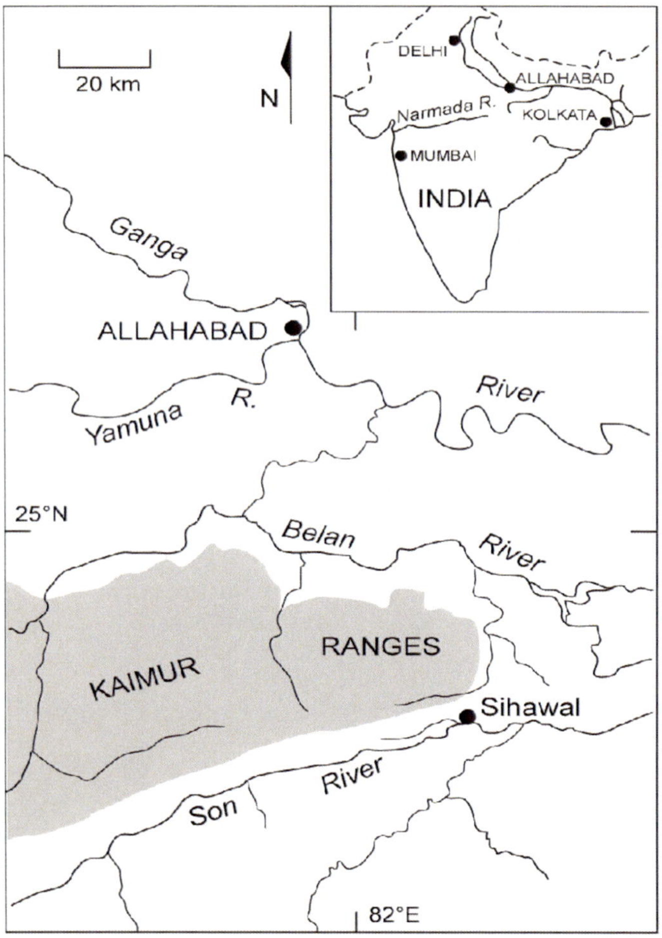

Fig. 5/1: Location map showing the Son and Belan valleys in north-central India. Note that Allahabad has recently been renamed Prayagraj. (Modified from Williams and Clarke, 1984, Fig. 1 and Williams, 2011, Fig. 13.1).

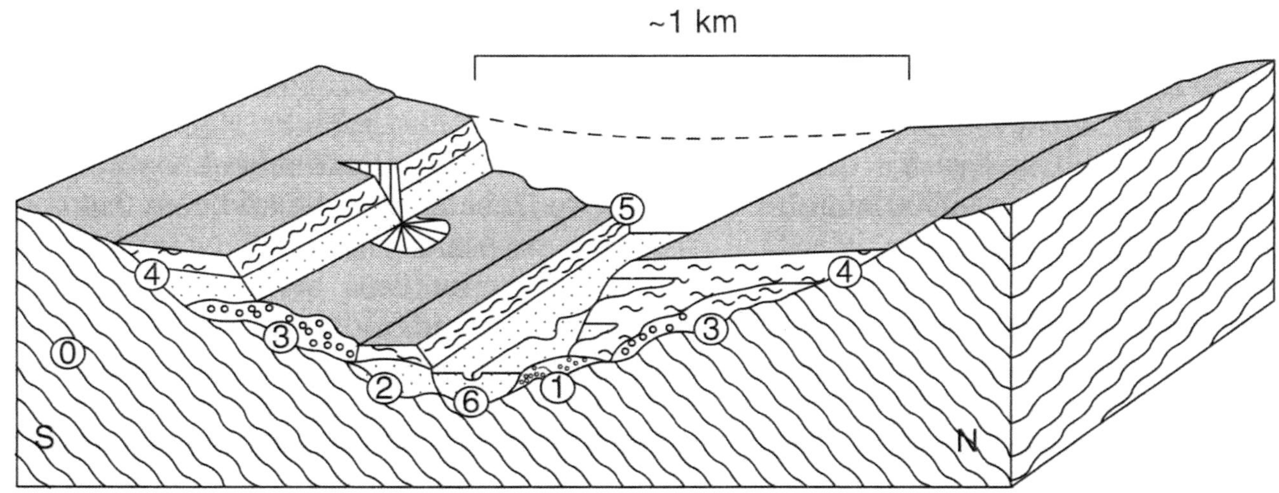

Fig. 5/2: Block diagram showing the five major alluvial formations investigated in the middle Son valley. 0. Lower Proterozoic metasedimentary rocks.1. Middle Pleistocene gravels and clays of the *Sihawal Formation.* 2. Upper Pleistocene sands and gravels of the *Khunteli Formation.* 3. Upper Pleistocene gravels, sands and clays of the *Patpara Formation.* 4. Terminal Pleistocene sands and clays of the *Baghor Formation.* 5. Late Holocene clays, silts and sands of the *Khetaunhi Formation.* 6. Present-day channel sands and point-bars of the River Son. (Modified from Williams et al., 2006, Fig. 3 and Williams, 2011, Fig. 30.2)

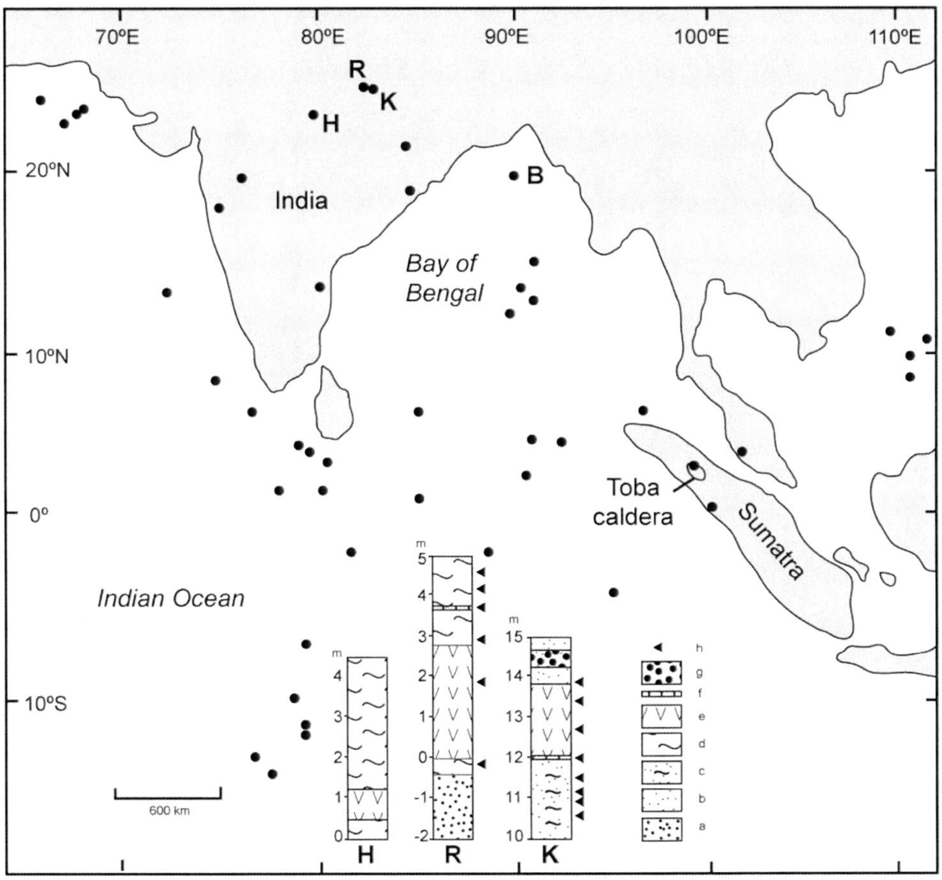

Fig. 5/3 : Distribution of volcanic ash from the 74 ka Toba super-eruption showing location of marine sediment cores and sections sampled in India. The black dots represent Toba tephra occurrences on land and in marine sediment cores. R is the site of the first Toba ash discovery by Williams and Royce in February 1980 at the Son-Rehi confluence. B is marine core S0188-342KL in the Bay of Bengal; K is Khunteli; R is Rehi; H is Hirapur. Key to stratigraphic sections in India: a is coarse sand; b is medium/fine sand; c is silt loam/ sandy loam/interstratified sand and loam; d is clay; e is Toba volcanic ash; f is massive carbonate; g is gravel; h is sampled pedogenic carbonate horizon. (After Williams et al., 2009, Fig. 1 and Williams, 2011, Fig. 30.3).

Fig. 5/4 : The Kaimur Ranges immediately north of the middle Son valley, north-central India. The lowland clay plain is located on the surface of the early Holocene Upper Member of the *Baghor Formation* (see Fig. 2 and section 3). (Photo: Martin Williams)

Fig. 5/5 : Crossing the Son, 26 November, 2005. Third from the left is Professor J.N. Pal; fourth from left, Professor S.N. Ambrose; fifth from left, Dr Parth Chauhan. The remaining four passengers are from the Department of Archaeology, University of Allahabad. We were on our way to sample the Khunteli Formation (see Fig. 2 and section 3) on the right bank of the Son. (Photo: Martin Williams)

Fig. 5/6 : Cross-bedded coarse sands of the Lower Member of the Upper Pleistocene *Baghor Formation* (see Fig. 2 and section 3), middle Son valley, north-central India. (Photo: Martin Williams)

Fig. 5/7 : River terraces along the southern edge of the middle Son valley, north central India. (Photo: Martin Williams)

Fig. 5/8 : Early Holocene Hoofprint of a Sambur deer exposed during excavation of the Upper Member of the Baghor Formation in 1982. (Photo by, and courtesy of, the late Professor Desmond Clark)

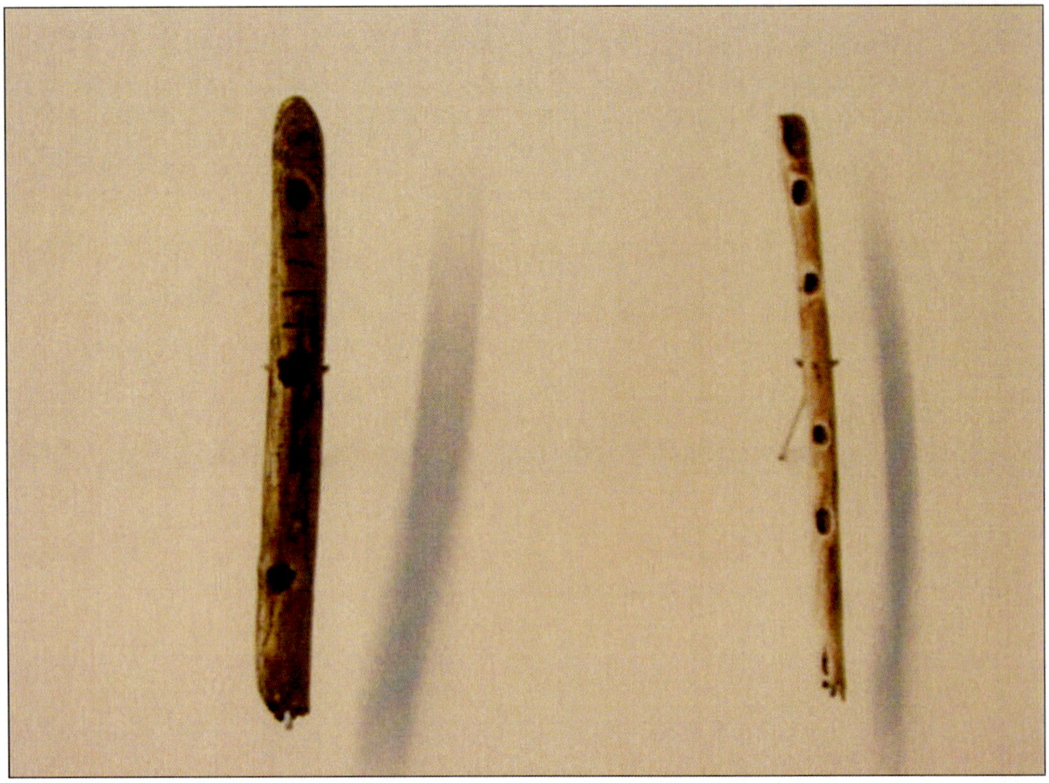

Fig. 6/1 : Flute 1 from Geißenklösterle (left) and flute from Hohle Fels (right), Replicas from the Museum of Human Evolution (Burgos, Spain)

Fig. 6/2 : Fragment of flute from Isturritz, together with other Palaeolithic sound producing objects

Fig. 6/3 : The author playing a bone flute replica inside the same cave

Fig. 6/4 : Neolithic flutes from Jiahu
(After Zhang et al. 1999)

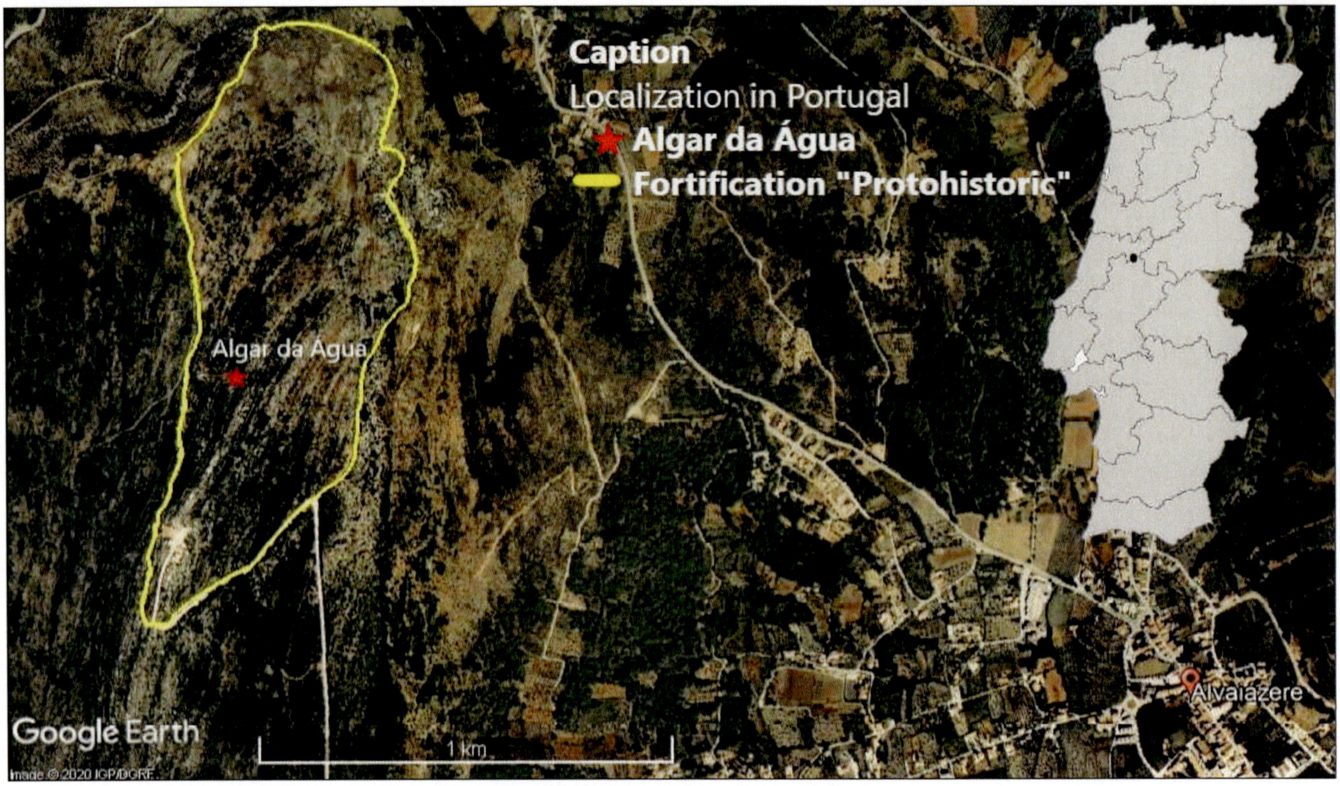

Fig. 8/1 : Localization of Algar da Água

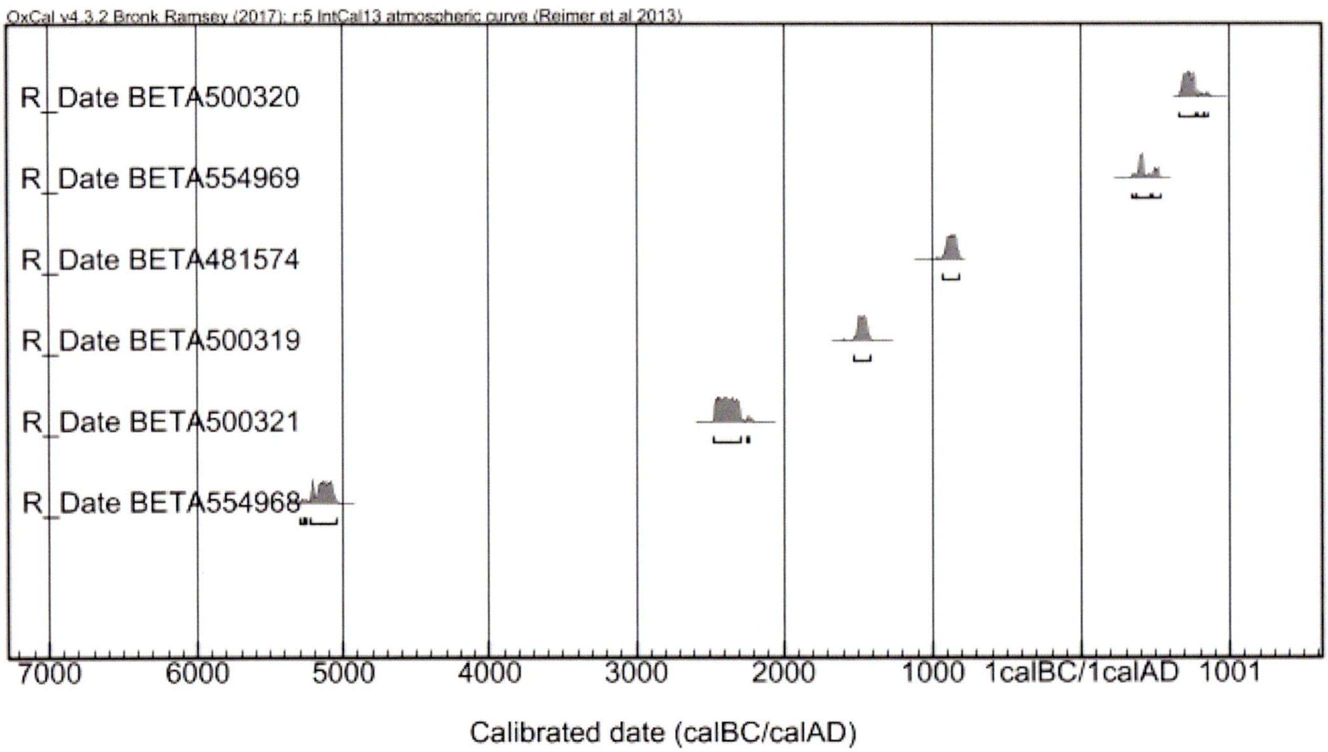

Fig. 8/2 : Chronologies of archaeological materials from Algar da Água

Fig. 8/3 : Anthropomorphic figure with a possible conic helmet

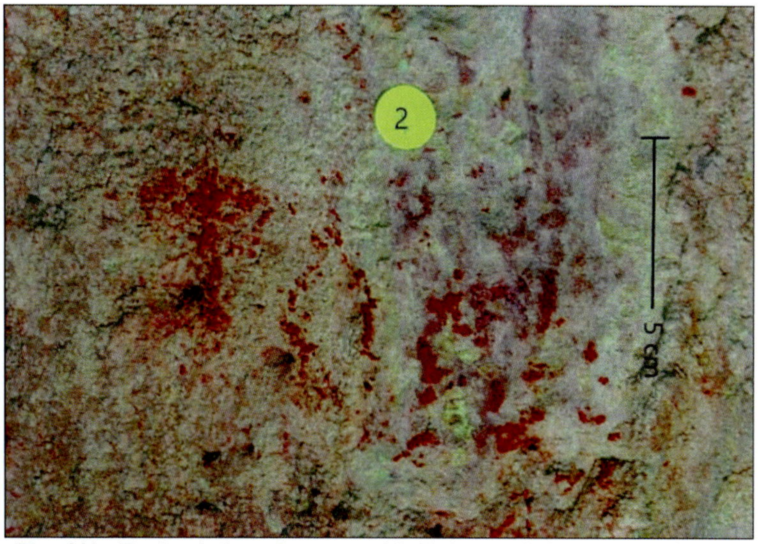

Fig. 8/4 : Red paintings from panel 2. Enhanced photo with DStretch

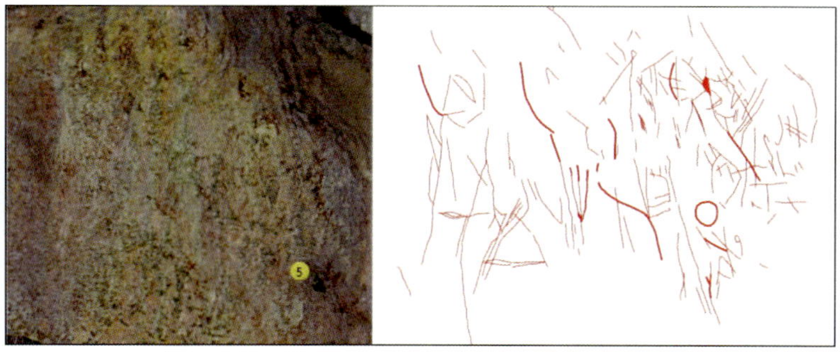

Fig. 8/5 : Engravings from panel 5. Photo and drawing

Fig. 8/6 : Panel 9. Photo and drawing

Fig. 9/1: Bhimmandali

Fig. 9/5: Rajbahal - Ushakuthi

Fig. 9/3: Maricha Taila

Fig. 9/2: Bhimmandali

Fig. 9/4: Rajbahal - Ushakuthi

Fig. 9/6 : Rajbahal - Ushakuthi

Fig. 9/7: Ulap

Fig. 9/8: Pooja Dunguri

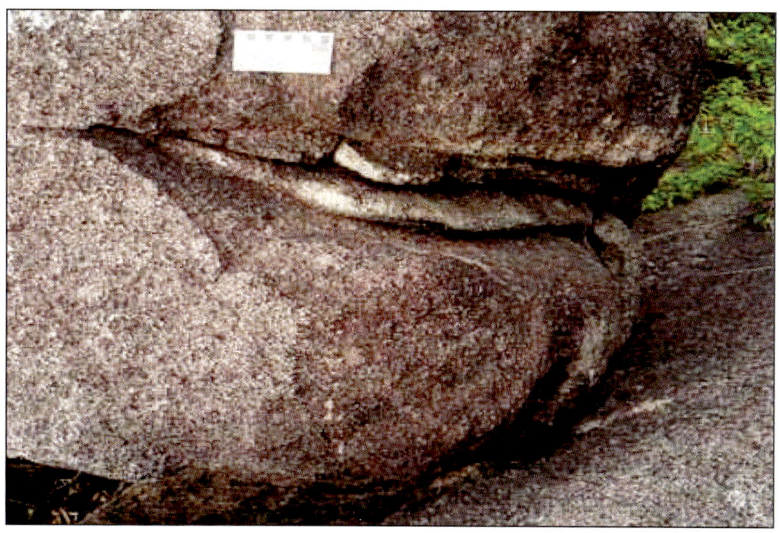

Fig. 9/9: Pooja Dunguri

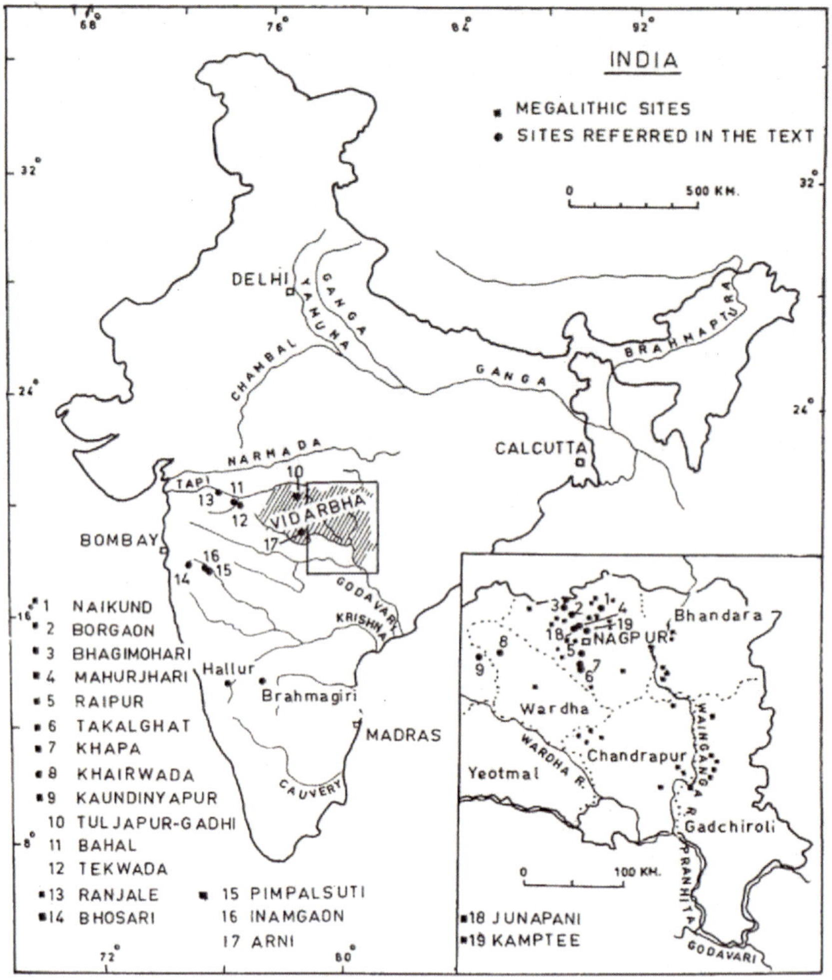

Fig13/1: Map of Important Megalithic sites in Vidarbha

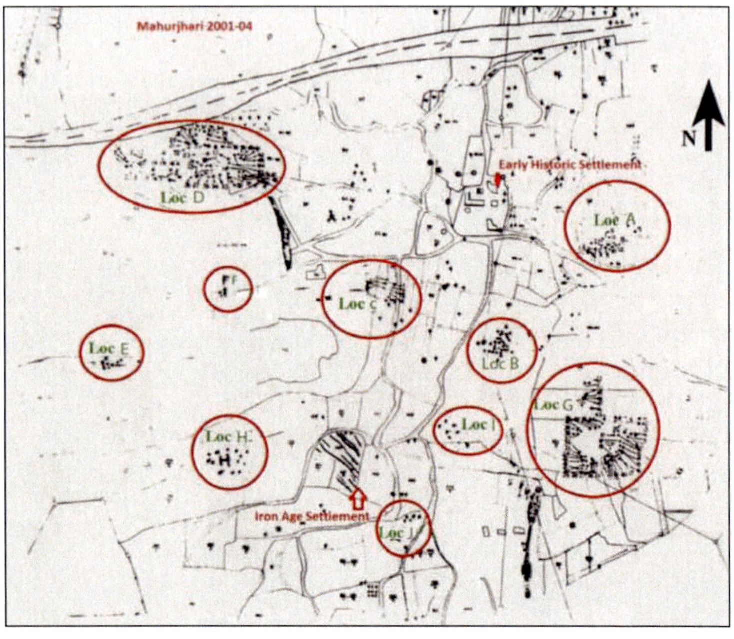

Fig13/2: Distribution of Cemeteries - A to J- at Mahurjhari

Fig.13/3: Nature of Bead and Bead debitage scatter on the surface at Mahurjhari

Fig.13/4: Nature of Un-finished bead, Mahurjhari

Fig.13/5: Trench F Mahurjhari, bead polisher and manufacturing activity from the beginning of the Early Historic settlement.

Fig.13/6: Excavation of Megalithic 10. and periphery, Locality -A. Mahurjhari

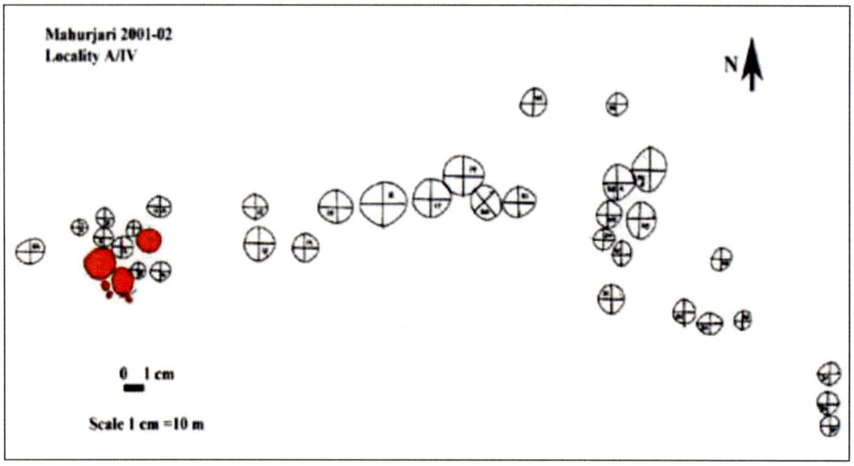

Fig13/7: Mahurjhari.Locality.
A- location of excavation burial in a cluster.

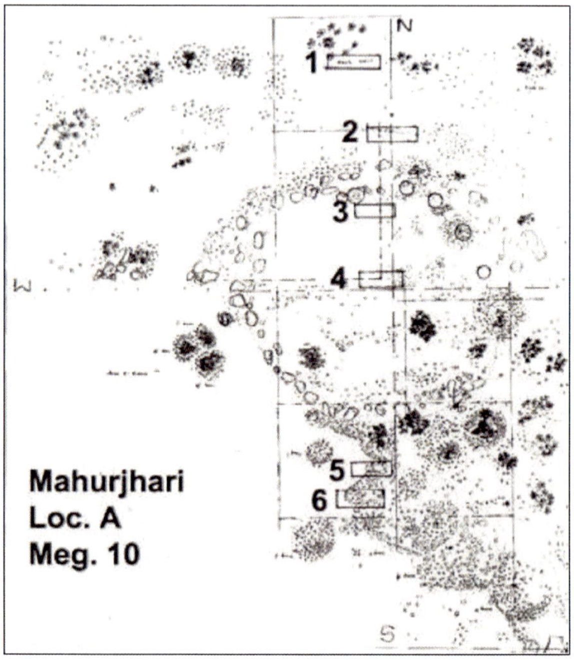

Fig13/8: Excavation of Burial No. 10
& periphery at Mahurjhari

Fig.13/9: Copper tripod from Megalith No.3, Locality. A. Mahurjhari

Fig.13/10: Copper bowl and lid with decorative finials, Mahurjhari

Fig.13/11: Functional remains within a Iron Age house floor at Mahurjhari

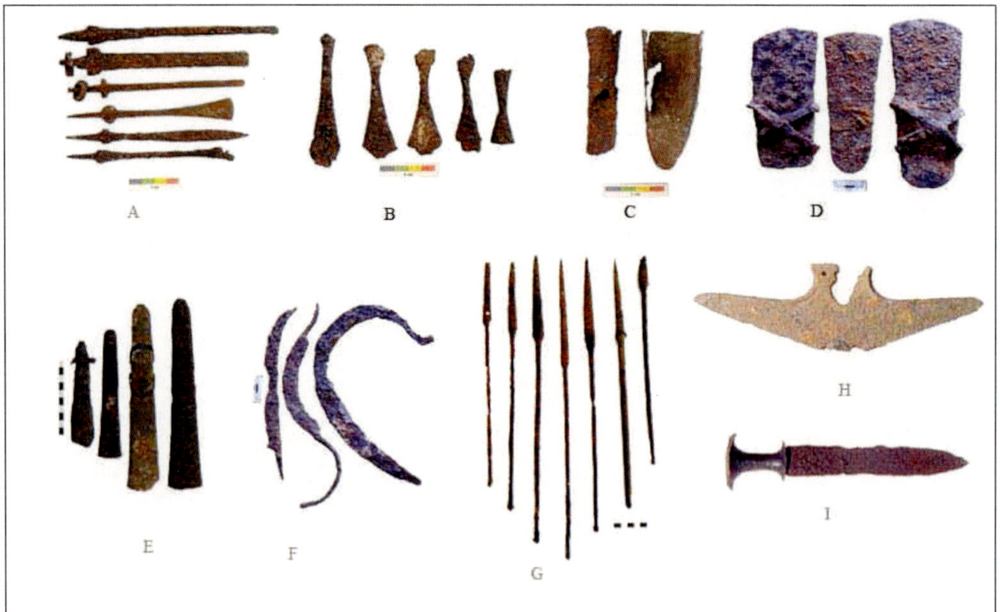

A. Chisels, B. Adzes, C. Hoes D. Axes, E. Ploughshare, F. Sickels, G. Spike, H. Battle Axe, I. Dragger with copper hilt

Fig.13/12: Types of Iron tools from Mahurjhari Megaliths of Vidarbha, Maharashtra

Fig.13/13: Dagger, use of multiple technologies

Fig.13/15: Stone blades from early levels at Iron Age Settlement.Mahurjhari

Fig.13/17: Reconstructed megalith at IGRMS.

Fig.15/3: Google Map of the Burials

Fig.15/4: General View of the Cairn Burial

Fig.15/5: General View of the Burial Farther Side

Fig.15/6: Probable Quarry site for Cairn Burials

Fig.15/7: Cairn Circle

Fig.15/8: Cairn Circle seen along with boulders above

Fig.20/1: उत्खनित पुरास्थल

चित्र 20/2: मूल गंध कुटी विहार

चित्र 20/3: धर्मराजिका स्तूप

चित्र 20/4: धमेख स्तूप

चित्र 20/5: चौखण्डी स्तूप

चित्र 20/6:
मनौती स्तूप

चित्र 20/7: चैत्य

चित्र 20/8: अशोक स्तम्भ

चित्र 20/9: पुरातत्व संग्रहालय

चित्र 20/10: मथुरा एवं सारनाथ में निर्मित बोधिसत्व मूर्तियां

चित्र 20/11: धर्मचक्रप्रवर्तन मुद्रा

चित्र **20/12:** अशोक स्तम्भ

Fig.21/1: Jaina icons from Bauridi

चित्र **20/13:** अंधकासुर वध

Fig.21/2: Image of Tirthankara Candraprabha, from Bauridi

Fig.21/3: Image of Tirthankara Rsabhanatha, from Bauridi

Fig.21/4: Image of Tirthankara Rsabhanatha, from Bauridi

Fig.21/5: Image of Tirthankara Rsabhanatha, from Bauridi

Fig.21/6: Image of Yaksi Ambika, from Bauridi

Fig.21/7: Warrior type Hero-stone from Ladhurka

Fig.21/8: Monolithic miniature form of *rekha deul* type of Hero-stone with *linga* depiction from Ladhurka

Fig.21/9: Jaina tutelary couple and Surya image from Ladhurka

Fig.22/1: A complete view of Chandaneswar Temple

Fig.22/2: Image of Visnu found from the sanctum of Chandaneswar Temple

Fig.22/3: Image of another Visnu sculpture found from same place

Fig.22/4: Image of Uma-Maheswar from Chandaneswar Temple

Fig.22/5: Garuda Stambha or Pillar

Fig.25/1: A nude child learning vowels (From National Museum, New Delhi)

Fig.25/2: A child practicing vowels and consonants (From Prachina Bharatiya Itihaas Shodha Parishad, Gurukul Gautamnagar, New Delhi)

Fig.25/3&4: The nude children writing vowels and consonants
(From Gurukul Museum Jhajjar, Haryana)

Fig.25/5: A nude child writing vowels and consonants (From Gurukul Museum Jhajjar, Haryana) and Plate 6: A nude child writing barakhari in randomly (Prachina Bharatiya Itihaas Shodha Parishad, Gurukul Gautamnagar, New Delhi)

Fig.30/1: El Peruano, Groups of people walking through the Inca Trail keeping their distance

Fig.30/2: El Comercio, Support staff taking body temperature at the entry

Fig.30/3: Peru Rail, Sanitary protocols on the trains in Machu Picchu

Fig.30/4: Dirección Desconcentrada de Cultura de Cuzco, Ministry of Culture carried out a sanitization of six pre-Hispanic temples

Fig.30/5: Peruvian Ministry of Culture, Virtual Tour of Manuel Chávez Ballón Site Museum

Fig.30/6: YouVisit.com, Virtual Tour of Machu Picchu